Understanding Contemporary Society:
Theories of the Present

UNDERSTANDING CONTEMPORARY SOCIETY: THEORIES OF THE PRESENT

edited by

Gary Browning,
Abigail Halcli
and
Frank Webster

SAGE Publications

London · Thousand Oaks · New Delhi

Contents

Preface

The origins of this book lie in a series of seminars, *Theories of the Present*, started at Oxford Brookes University during 1995. The seminars were developed to bring together colleagues and students from a wide range of areas: Planning, Languages, Politics, Economics, Sociology, History.

Nick Hewlett played a big role in establishing these seminars and we wish to acknowledge his part in the project as a whole.

Notes on contributors

Sarah Ansari was appointed Lecturer in Modern Middle Eastern and World History in the History Department, Royal Holloway College, University of London in 1993. She undertook a first degree in History at London University 1979–82, thereafter completing an MA in Area Studies (South Asia) at the School of Oriental and African Studies, University of London 1982–83, and a PhD at Royal Holloway College 1983–87. She was a British Academy Postdoctoral Research Fellow 1988–91. Her major research interests are the history of Muslim South Asia, in particular the province of Sind, nowadays in Pakistan, partition-related migration in South Asia, and broader trends relating to gender in the Muslim world. Her publications include *Sufi Saints and State Power: the Pirs of Sind, 1843–1947* (CUP, 1992) and articles contributed to journals such as *South Asia*.

Barrie Axford is Principal Lecturer in Politics at Oxford Brookes University. He has held posts at Stanford University and at the University of Southampton, and been Visiting Professor at the University of Genoa. Publications include *The Global System: Economics, Politics and Culture* (Polity, 1995), *Politics: An Introduction* (joint author) (Routledge, 1997), *Unity and Diversity in the New Europe* (joint editor) (Peter Lang AG, 1999) and *Democratization and Democracy* (joint author) (Routledge, forthcoming 2000).

Michèle Barrett has been Professor of Sociology at City University. She is currently a Professor at Queen Mary and Westfield College, University of London. Educated at the universities of Durham and Sussex, she is the author of numerous books, including: *Women's Oppression Today* (Verso, 1980), *Destabilising Theory: Contemporary Feminist Debates*, with Anne Phillips (Polity, 1992), *The Politics of Truth: From Marx to Foucault* (Polity, 1992) and

Imagination in Theory: Essays on Writing and Culture (Polity, 1998). She is a past President of the British Sociological Association.

Ted Benton is Professor of Sociology at the University of Essex. He is author of numerous publications on social philosophy, history of biology and, in recent years, ecological issues. Recent publications include *Natural Relations: Ecology, Animal Rights and Social Justice* (Verso, 1993), *Social Theory and the Global Environment* (edited with M. Redclift, Routledge, 1994) and *The Greening of Marxism* (edited, Guilford, 1996). He is a member of the Red-Green Study Group and the newly formed Green Left coalition.

Tim Blackman is Professor of Sociology and Social Policy and Deputy Head of the School of Social Sciences and Law at Oxford Brookes University. He undertook his first degree in Geography at the University of Durham from 1976 to 1979, following which he worked in Belfast as a community worker. He returned to Durham to undertake a PhD in the Department of Sociology and Social Policy. He has taught at the University of Ulster and the University of Newcastle, and was Head of Research at Newcastle City Council from 1990 to 1995. His major research interests are in social and urban policy. He has published articles in journals such as *Sociology*, *Journal of Social Policy* and *Policy and Politics* and his books include *Planning Belfast* (Avebury, 1991) and *Urban Policy in Practice* (Routledge, 1996).

Carl Boggs is Professor of Social Sciences at National University in Los Angeles. He received a PhD in political science at the University of California, Berkeley in 1970. He is the author of two books on the political thought of Antonio Gramsci, *The Impasse of European Communism* (Westview, 1982), *Social Movements and Political Power* (Temple University, 1985), *Intellectuals and the Crisis of Modernity* (SUNY, 1993) and *The Socialist Tradition* (Routledge, 1995). His most recent book is *The Eclipse of Politics* (Guilford, forthcoming).

Harriet Bradley studied Sociology at Leicester University and gained her PhD at Durham. She is currently Senior Lecturer in Sociology at Bristol University, which she joined in 1994, having formerly taught at the universities of Durham and Sunderland. She has research interests in gender, women's employment and industrial relations, and she has written extensively on social inequality. Her publications include *Men's Work, Women's Work* (Polity, 1989), *Fractured Identities* (Polity, 1997) and *Gender and Power in the Workplace* (Macmillan, 1999).

Gary Browning was appointed Professor of Politics at Oxford Brookes University in 1997. He undertook a first degree in History and Politics at Reading University 1971–74, thereafter completing an MSc and a PhD at the

London School of Economics and a further MSc at the University of South-ampton. He has taught at Reading University and the City of London Poly-technic as well as at Oxford Brookes University. His major research interests are in political philosophy and the history of political thought. He has pub-lished articles in journals such as *Political Studies* and *History of Political Thought*, and is co-editor of the journal of the Political Studies Association of the UK, *Politics*. His books include *Plato and Hegel: Two Modes of Philosophis-ing* (Garland, 1991), *Hegel's Phenomenology of Spirit: A Reappraisal* (ed.) (Kluwer, 1997), *Politics: An Introduction* (co-author) (Routledge, 1997), *Hegel and the History of Political Philosophy* (Macmillan, 1999) and *Lyotard and the End of Grand Narratives* (UWP, 2000).

Terrell Carver is Professor of Political Theory at the University of Bristol. He has written extensively on Marx and Engels, including *Engels* in the Oxford 'Past Masters' series and Marx for the Cambridge 'Companions to Philoso-phy'. He is author of *Marx and Engels: The Intellectual Relationship*, *Friedrich Engels: His Life and Thought* and a new study, *The Postmodern Marx*. He has recently completed new translations in *Marx: Later Political Writings* for the Cambridge 'Texts in the History of Political Thought', and three of his own books have been translated into Japanese.

Stephen Crook was appointed Foundation Professor of Sociology at James Cook University (JCU), Australia in 1998. He completed a BA in Philosophy at the University of York in 1973 and a DPhil in Sociology from the same university in 1984. Before moving to JCU he had worked for twelve years at the University of Tasmania and before that at The College of St Mark and St John, Plymouth. He is the author of *Modernist Radicalism and its Aftermath* (Routledge, 1991), co-author of *Postmodernization: Change in Advanced Society* (Sage, 1992) and editor of *Adorno: The Stars Down to Earth* (Routledge, 1994). He has recently published papers on environmentalism in Australia, the cultural riskiness of biotechnology and the concept of 'everyday life'. His current research interests are focused on regimes of risk management, human–animal relations and ways of analysing socio-technical networks.

Avigail Eisenberg is an Associate Professor of Political Science at the Uni-versity of British Columbia where she has been teaching and writing since 1990. She received her PhD in 1991 from Queen's University in Kingston, Ontario, Canada. Her main areas of interest are political theory and Cana-dian politics and jurisprudence. She has published several articles on the subject of cultural relations and group rights in Canadian and international journals. In 1995, she published a critical examination of pluralism entitled *Reconstructing Political Pluralism* (State University of New York Press, 1995). Her most recent book is a co-edited collection of essays entitled *Painting the Maple: Race, Gender and the Construction of Canada* (University of British Co-lumbia Press, 1998).

Elizabeth Frazer is an Official Fellow and Tutor in Politics, New College, Oxford and Lecturer in Politics, Faculty of Social Studies, University of Oxford. Her major research interests are political theory and political sociology. She is the author of *Problems of Communitarian Politics: Unity and Conflict* (Oxford University Press, 1999), and with Nicola Lacey, of *The Politics of Community: A Feminist Critique of the Liberal Communitarian Debate* (Harvester Press, 1993).

Abigail Halcli is a Senior Lecturer in Sociology at Oxford Brookes University. She received her PhD from the Ohio State University, USA. Her research interests are in the areas of social movements, political sociology and gender. Recent publications include 'AIDS, Anger and Activism: ACT UP as a Social Movement Organization' in *Waves of Protest: Social Movements Since the Sixties* (Rowman and Littlefield, 1999) (edited by Jo Freeman and Victoria Johnson). She has also published research on foundation funding of American social movement organizations and on the gendered experiences of female politicians.

Nick Hewlett is Reader and Chair of the Centre for European Research at Oxford Brookes University. He has studied at the Universities of Sussex, Essex and Paris and has taught at South Bank Polytechnic as well as Oxford Brookes University. His major research interests are French politics since the Second World War, the theory and practice of democracy, and the relationship between intellectuals and politics. His books include *Modern French Politics: Analysing Conflict and Consensus since 1945* (Polity, 1998), *Contemporary France* (Longman, 1994 and 1999) (with Jill Forbes and François Nectoux), and *Currents in Contemporary French Intellectual Life* (Macmillan, 1999) (edited with Christopher Flood).

Kimberly Hutchings is Senior Lecturer in Political Theory at Edinburgh University. She is the author of *Kant, Critique and Politics* (Routledge, 1996) and has published work on contemporary continental and feminist philosophy as well as international relations theory. Her recent work includes *Cosmopolitan Citizenship*, (co-edited with Roland Danrouther, Macmillan, 1999) and *International Theory: Re-thinking Ethics in a Global Era* (Sage, forthcoming 1999).

Andrew Kilmister was educated at the Universities of Bristol and Oxford. He has taught Economics at Oxford Brookes University, in the School of Business, since 1987. His main teaching interests are in European economics, financial economics and the Far Eastern economies, especially Japan. He has published articles and chapters on Eastern European transition, socialist models of development, and the British motor industry. He is a member of the editorial board of *Labour Focus on Eastern Europe*.

Krishan Kumar is Professor of Sociology at the University of Virginia, USA. He was previously Professor of Social and Political Thought at the

University of Kent at Canterbury. He was educated at Cambridge University and the London School of Economics. He has been a BBC Talks Producer, a Visiting Scholar at Harvard University, and a Visiting Professor at the Universities of Colorado, Bergen and the Central European University, Prague. Among his publications are *Prophecy and Progress: The Sociology of Industrial and Post-Industrial Society* (Penguin, 1978), *Utopia and Anti-Utopia in Modern Times* (Blackwell, 1987), *The Rise of Modern Society* (Blackwell, 1988), *Utopianism* (Open University Press, 1991) and *From Post-Industrial to Post-Modern Society* (Blackwell, 1995). He is currently working on a study of English national identity and the rise of English nationalism.

Murray Low is a lecturer in Geography at the University of Reading. He was educated at Cambridge University, The New School of Social Research, New York and the Ohio State University. His publications include 'Representation Unbound: Globalization and Democracy' in Kevin Cox (ed.) *Spaces of Globalization* (Guilford Press, 1997) and 'Their Masters' Voice: Communitarianism, Civic Order and Political Representation' in *Environment and Planning A* (1999). He is currently writing about issues of political representation and urban government.

David Lyon is Professor of Sociology at Queen's University in Kingston, Ontario, Canada. He has taught or had visiting appointments at Bradford and Ilkley College (University of Bradford), Calvin College, Michigan, the École des Hautes Études en Sciences Sociales, Paris, The University of Leeds, and Regent College, Vancouver. His main research and teaching interests are in the social aspects of communication and information technologies; religion and culture; historical sociology; and social theory. He is author of a number of books, translated into twelve languages, including *The Information Society: Issues and Illusions* (Polity, 1988), *The Electronic Eye: The Rise of Surveillance Society* (Polity/Minnesota, 1994), *Postmodernity* (Open University Press/Minnesota, 1994, 2nd revised and expanded edition, 1999), and *Jesus in Disneyland: Religion in Postmodern Times* (Polity Press, forthcoming).

Richard Maxwell received his BA (1982) at the University of California at San Diego and his MA and PhD (1990) from the University of Wisconsin at Madison. He has taught at Northwestern University and is currently Associate Professor of Media Studies at Queens College of the City University of New York. He is the author of *The Spectacle of Democracy: Spanish Television, Nationalism, and Political Transition* (University of Minnesota Press, 1995).

Mary Maynard joined the Department of Social Policy and Social Work at the University of York, UK, in 1996 and was appointed Professor in 1997. She was previously a lecturer in the Department of Sociology at the University of York and was Director of the Centre for Women's Studies there from 1984 to 1996. Her major research interests are in women's studies, social and feminist theory, research methodology, ethnicity, and later life. She has published articles in all of these areas. Her most recent books include *New Frontiers in Women's Studies: Knowledge, Identity and Nationalism* (co-editor) (Taylor and Francis, 1996) and *Science and the Construction of Women* (editor) (UCL Press, 1997). She is currently working on a book on feminist research and methodology.

Vincent Mosco was educated at Georgetown (BA, History, 1970) and Harvard (PhD, Sociology, 1975). He has taught at universities in the USA and Canada and has been Professor of Communication at Carleton University since 1989. He is author of several books including *Pushbutton Fantasies* (Ablex, 1982), *The Pay-Per Society* (Garamond, 1989) and *The Political Economy of Communication* (Sage, 1996).

Kaarle Nordenstreng is Professor of Journalism and Mass Communication at the University of Tampere in Finland. He studied psychology and linguistics at the University of Helsinki, where he completed a PhD in 1969. His books include *The Mass Media Declaration of UNESCO* (Ablex, 1984), *Beyond Sovereignty: International Communication in the 1990s*, edited with Herbert Schiller (Ablex, 1993) and *Towards Equity in Global Communication: MacBride Update*, edited with Richard Vincent and Michael Traber (Hampton, 1998). In addition to international communication his major research interests include social theories of the media and the ethics of journalism.

Christopher Norris took his BA and PhD degrees from the University of London (1970 and 1975) and is now a Distinguished Research Professor in Philosophy at Cardiff University. He has been Visiting Professor at Berkeley (1986) and at the City University of New York (1988). He has published more than twenty books to date, among them volumes on literary theory, deconstruction, postmodernism, philosophical semantics, philosophy of science, ethics and musicology. At present he is writing mainly about the logic of deconstruction and also about philosophical issues in the interpretation of quantum mechanics.

David Pepper is Professor of Geography at Oxford Brookes University, and formerly worked with the Soil Survey of England and Wales. He has edited books on nuclear power and geographical issues of war and peace, and has written *Communes and the Green Vision* (Green Print, 1991), *Eco-Socialism: From Deep Ecology to Social Justice* (Routledge, 1993) and *Modern Environmentalism: An Introduction* (Routledge, 1996). His current interests include radical approaches to sustainable development.

Ken Plummer is Professor of Sociology at the University of Essex. His main books are *Sexual Stigma: An Interactionist Account* (Routledge, 1975), *Documents of Life* (Allen and Unwin, 1983) and *Telling Sexual Stories* (Routledge,

1995). He has co-authored (with John Macionis) *Sociology: A Global Introduction* (Prentice-Hall, 1998). He has also edited various collections and written numerous articles on sexuality, life stories, symbolic interactionism and lesbian and gay studies. He is the editor of the new journal *Sexualities*.

Don Robotham is a Professor of Anthropology at the Graduate Center, the City University of New York. Previously he was Pro Vice Chancellor and Dean of the School for Graduate Studies and Research at the University of the West Indies. He did his first degree at the University of the West Indies in Sociology and his PhD in Anthropology at the University of Chicago. In 1996 he gave the annual Distinguished Lecture at the Spring Meeting of the American Ethnological Society on 'Transnationalism in the Caribbean: Formal and Informal' (*American Ethnologist*, May 1998). He has published also on 'Postcolonialities: the rise of new modernities' (*International Social Science Journal*, September 1997). His current interests are theories of multiple modernities, development and social theory.

Saskia Sassen is Professor of Sociology, The University of Chicago. Her most recent books are *Globalization and its Discontents* (New Press, 1998) and *Losing Control? Sovereignty in an Age of Globalization* (Columbia University Press, 1996). Several translations of her book *The Global City* are appearing, among them French (Descartes, 1996), Italian (UTET, 1997) and Spanish (EUDEBA, 1999). She is currently completing a project on 'Cities and their Crossborder Networks', sponsored and to be published by the United Nations University Press.

John Scott studied sociology at Kingston College of Technology and the London School of Economics. He has taught at Strathclyde University and Leicester University, where he was Professor of Sociology. Since 1994 he has been Professor of Sociology at the University of Essex, and he is Adjunct Professor at the University of Bergen, Norway. He is the author of books on social stratification and power, business organization, research methods, and sociological theory. His most recent publications include *Stratification and Power* (Polity Press, 1996), *Corporate Business and Capitalist Classes* (Oxford University Press, 1997) and, with James Fulcher, *Sociology* (Oxford University Press, 1999).

Chris Shilling is Professor of Sociology, University of Portsmouth, where he has lectured since 1995. Previously, he taught at the University of Southampton and at Oxford Polytechnic. He is author of several books, including *The Body and Social Theory* (Sage/TCS, 1993), currently being translated into Chinese and Korean, and, with Philip A. Mellor, *Re-forming the Body: Religion, Community and Modernity* (Sage/TCS, 1997), currently being translated into Chinese, and is presently working on a third volume on the embodiment of sociology and social theory. He is an associate editor of *Body*

& *Society*, and has published widely on classical and contemporary sociological theory in such journals as *Sociological Review*, *Sociology*, *British Journal of Sociology*, and *Social Compass*.

Susan Stephenson teaches Political Theory at the University of Edinburgh. She studied philosophy at the University of Exeter before moving to the University of Southampton where she completed an MSc in Politics and Culture and a doctoral thesis in Political Theory. Her main research interests are in contemporary political theory and she is particularly interested in the relationship between politics and the creative imagination. She is currently writing a book on narrative, identity and political theory.

Frank Webster was educated at Durham University (BA, 1972; MA, 1974) and the LSE (PhD, 1978). He has taught at universities in London, California and at Oxford Brookes. He is Professor of Sociology in the Department of Cultural Studies and Sociology at the University of Birmingham which he joined in 1999. He is author of many articles and books, including *The New Photography: Responsibility in Visual Communication* (Calder, 1980), *Information Technology: A Luddite Analysis* (with Kevin Robins) (Ablex, 1986), *The Technical Fix: Computers, Industry and Education* (with Kevin Robins) (Macmillan, 1989), *Theories of the Information Society* (Routledge, 1995) and, edited with Anthony Smith, *The Postmodern University?* (Open University Press, 1997). His most recent book is *Times of the Technoculture: From the Information Society to the Virtual Life* (with Kevin Robins) (Routledge, 1999).

Chapter 1

Theory, theorists and themes: a user's guide to understanding the present

Gary Browning, Abigail Halcli and Frank Webster

Consider the student of Social Sciences and the Humanities in higher education today. He or she will most likely be signed up to study a named discipline such as History, English or Anthropology. A good number will be combining a couple of disciplines, perhaps majoring in one while taking a few modules in another. And there will be still others who decide to study at undergraduate level a subsector of a particular discipline such as Economic History or Cultural Geography. Nevertheless, these are qualifications to what remains a general truth: the overwhelming majority of students today will be registered for a degree programme with a disciplinary title of one sort or another. As such, they might anticipate an induction into their chosen subject's traditions, key figures and central theoretical approaches. This appears eminently reasonable. After all, when one opts to study a given discipline that is precisely what one would anticipate – at the outset introductory courses which establish the foundations (the most distinguished thinkers, the defining concepts and the lineages of the discipline), then, once these are mastered, perhaps some engagement with controversies at the cutting edge of research in the field.

Disturbingly, especially for the new student, things are nowhere near so straightforward. On the contrary, what he or she will encounter are disciplines without clearly identifiable boundaries and subject areas with disconcertingly 'fuzzy' borders. Hence the student of Geography will find him or herself having to engage with texts from Anthropology, the English Literature student with Philosophy texts, and the Sociologist with works of History. If this were simply a matter of one's chosen discipline including pertinent contributions from outside then we might relax, happy to participate in cross-disciplinary activities which take place at the hinterlands of one's core areas. Some might even welcome this as a return to the more ambitious and integrative thinking that preceded the specialized disciplines that developed during the twentieth century.

What is more perplexing nowadays is that there scarcely appears to be an 'inside' (or core) to one's discipline. What we get beneath the title of, say, Sociology is a choice of materials by which a particular version of the discipline is constructed – which means, of course, that it is pretty hard to argue that there is a discipline of Sociology upon which all practitioners might agree. Instead of *roots* of a discipline, there are *routes* by which academics have arrived at their partial versions of the discipline. *Here* quantitative matter may predominate, *there* ethnographic approaches, elsewhere a strong emphasis on historical and comparative perspectives, still elsewhere there is a focus on policy analysis. Indeed, what is striking is that, casting an eye around departments, there is such a diversity of degree courses sheltered beneath the umbrella title 'Sociology'.

Much the same goes for areas such as Geography, Politics and Anthropology. Degree titles notwithstanding, the subject-matters vary enormously and freely draw on other areas. The discipline of Politics, for instance, has always been eclectic in drawing upon a variety of styles and modes of thinking. But today this diversity is intensified as game theorists and quantitative analysts line up with historians of politics and a wide variety of theorists, some of whom look to the classical past whereas others maintain a subversive post-modernism.

Matters are made still more perplexing by the arrival of new areas that demand a hearing and themselves borrow unabashedly from, and equally contribute to, the older subject areas. Today we have what might be called fields such as Cultural Studies, Information Studies, Gender Studies, Management, and Media Analysis each of which engages promiscuously with both Social Sciences and the Humanities, and this has had radical consequences for the content and conception of established disciplines. For instance, one might consider in this respect the influence on the thinking of Political Science in the 1980s of Stuart Hall's earlier analyses of changes in popular culture. Hall and his colleagues had argued that, in the late 1970s, a 'crisis of legitimacy' was dramatized within popular culture (and mass media especially), around the theme of 'law and order', in ways which connected apparently disparate issues such as black youth, urban decay, trade unions and football hooliganism. The team elaborated these concerns in their study, *Policing the Crisis*,[1] into a claim that the character of politics, and the State itself, were changing in ways that could be gauged from examination of the 'common-sense', everyday thinking that was being displayed in stories told about crime and misbehaviour, and in the language used to consider these matters. Much of this research involved analysis of the mass media, though Hall and colleagues were able to demonstrate that this concern was not restricted to the media, since it drew in all manner of people from politics, industry, police, social services and education. Moreover, the shifts traced by Stuart Hall suggested the possibility of the emergence of a political movement which might capture widespread public support were it able to harness popular cultural concern. Such a movement, Hall argued *before the 1979 election*, was visible in what he called 'Thatcherism' and the 'authoritarian populism' to which it gave voice.[2] After her election in 1979 Mrs Thatcher developed much further just this 'hegemonic' project for over a decade in office. Justifiably, Political Science found it unavoidable that this account should be included inside its professional debates, though the contribution had come from a quite separate area. This account of Thatcherism is by no means a singular case of new fields intruding into established disciplines. For example, one might ponder the influence that analyses, many from the then embryonic area of Cultural Studies, of youth cultures, of gender relations, and of the relations between deviance and media, had on Sociology degree courses during the 1980s, and continue to have to this day.

Partly in response to this erosion of boundaries throughout the Social Sciences and Humanities, we have simultaneously seen the permeation of a generalised 'social theory' (though what it amounts to is far from agreed) into each and every field. At once we witness theory invading formerly theoretically underdeveloped areas such as English Literature and History, and at the same time we see the development of a broad and eclectic body of knowledge that draws on anything of interest, whether it be from philosophy, linguistics, semiology or psychoanalysis. All of this presents the novitiate student with formidable challenges. If one cannot clearly identify one's discipline, if the major thought is highly variable, and if 'social theory' presents itself as coming from pretty well everywhere while applicable anywhere, then just how is one to cope?

This book is designed to help. It might well serve as a text for a general course in contemporary social thought and analysis, of the sort offered by a range of Social Science and Humanities degrees, though it could as readily act as a reference point for students taking a more specialist topic. But putting the use of this book aside for the moment, it is important from the outset to recognize that the fluidity of disciplinary boundaries and contributions is not just a matter of an abstract and unworldly theory. If that were so, then the easy and tempting option – to ignore theory altogether – readily presents itself. On the surface, it does seem eminently reasonable for students to argue that since theory is now so sceptical and self-critical of its own foundations, then it might as well be ignored. The problem with this is that one cannot just opt out of theory and get on with the substance of the discipline. One of the positive aspects of recent decades has been acknowledgement that theory cannot be ignored by denying its presence (that denial is just another form of [naïve] theorizing). However, still more important than this is that the 'real world' itself manifests a similar degree of uncertainty and fluidity to that experienced in the area of theory.

3

We are increasingly able to appreciate the lack of fixity of arrangements in the world today. The collapse of communism in and around 1989 was probably the most dramatic of events which underlined the changeability of the world. Scarcely anyone, even specialists in Political Science, accurately predicted the break-up of the Soviet Union, the reunification of Germany, and the abandonment of communism by a raft of once allied countries such as Poland and Czechoslovakia. But there are many other examples of this changeability of life in the world today. For instance, there is widespread recognition nowadays that nature is no longer a fixed reference point, a foundational boundary for all human activity. This is evident whether we look at deserts which bloom thanks to human ingenuity with water supplies (as well as with horticultural science and chemical engineering), or at the extraordinary interventions in human reproduction over recent decades (such as test-tube babies, spare part surgery and cloning). Consider too the transformations in occupations that have followed deindustrialization (a rapid fall in manual occupations such as those found in factories, shipyards and coal mines) and the expansion of service sector jobs (that are largely white-collar and informational activities). This has been accompanied by feminization of the workforce, especially since the 1960s, and associated challenges to deep-seated presumptions about masculinity and femininity, family organization and behaviour, and even what constitutes 'real' work.

Not surprisingly, appreciation of this changeability of the world has had important intellectual consequences that undermine old certainties about the social world. For example, the one-time confidence that social stratification might best be understood in terms of males' positions in an occupational hierarchy divided, most profoundly, by whether one was a manual or non-manual worker, has taken a battering in view of recent real-world changes. Age, gender, ethnicity and 'race' have come to be regarded as major and irreducible features of stratification today. Similarly, the collapse of the Soviet Union, and the accompanying triumph of market practices, has understandably blunted the critique of thinkers who long felt that the only alternative to capitalism was collectivism (even if it was hoped that it would be a more democratic form than 'actually existing socialism'). At the same time, the continued instability of politics since 1989 (the reassertion of nationalism, religious fundamentalism, globalization and attendant economic unpredictability), as well as deep concerns about environmental damage (Chernobyl, acid rain, contamination of foods, global warming, overpopulation) ensure that any claims that a triumphant capitalism can create a new certainty are readily challenged. Again, the extraordinary development of human control over nature has profoundly undermined those who would argue that there are natural constraints – over appearance, reproduction, sexuality and so forth.

The upshot of all such developments is ferment in the way we think about the world and how the world is actually arranged. Established approaches to understanding the world have been undermined by empirical developments as well as by intellectual critique. For instance, the hold of class analysis has been challenged by the feminist movement. And the large-scale migration of peoples, communication of information and images, and the rapid movement of materials around the globe have combined to bring into question relatively fixed notions of culture, to introduce doubts about cultural heritage and identity, and to raise unsettling questions about how best to think about culture. Elsewhere, the assurances that motivated the development of Anthropology have been undermined by processes of decolonization that have gone in tandem with increased integration and interpenetration of places. This profound and paradoxical development has found expression in 'post-colonial' forms of thought and concern with the 'hybridity' of life today.

Amidst this change and dislocation it is often difficult nowadays to identify dominant theoretical traditions in fiercely contested intellectual realms. There can, for instance, no longer be unchallenged recourse to the safety of familiar frames – such one-time orthodoxies of introductory courses as Weber's paradigm contrasted with that of Durkheim's functionalism are today deeply problematical (and there will be, in addition, fierce debate about just how these thinkers are to be interpreted by today's commentators), so much so that these 'dead white European males' are read – if read at all – in deeply sceptical ways, while alternative intellectual forebears and their ideas are discovered and resurrected, be it William Du Bois (putting race on the agenda a century ago), Harriet Martineau (feminism), or Charlotte Perkins Gilman (feminism plus concern for the environment).

Moreover, there is now no straightforward way in which debates can be characterized as being concerned with, say, relations of production, social classes or the State. Things appear to have changed so much, and seem to continue to change at such a disconcerting rate, what with the explosive growth of media, leisure, consumption, changing employment conditions, travel and so forth, that it seems impossible to fix analysis and explanation in any stable set of terms. At every level, from the intimacy of the body and sexual relationships, to issues such as stratification, substantive developments lead to the redundancy of once accepted concepts and new terms are required to give insight into fast-changing trends. Even on the grand scale established ways of thought have come to be assaulted. Thus in development studies the once comfortable, if conflicting, alternatives of modernization theory and Marxism seem no longer applicable since both share a Western concept of development, even if radically disagreeing about how it might best be arranged. The 'reorientation' of development in recent decades towards Asia – spearheaded by Japan and the other 'Tiger Economies', but awesomely backed by the transformations taking place in China (home of one-fifth of the world's population) – has profoundly challenged the Eurocentric vision of world history shared by radicals and conservatives alike. This is a challenge at once substantive – how can we imagine the West as the centre of the world with Japan the second most powerful economy and China on course to take over the number one slot inside the twenty-first century – and also theoretical since this very reorientation poses critical questions about the primacy of Western thinkers over the last several hundred years. In this light it is perhaps not surprising that a major contemporary thinker, André Gunder Frank, has, in the twilight of his career, re-examined the historical record (and his own influential theoretical contributions to 'development' studies where he has long argued that the West had indeed been a central and pernicious influence on the rest of the world). Frank has now concluded that Europe and the USA are, in the long term, but a 'blip' on history, while Asia has been the centre of the world from time immemorial but for a couple of centuries. If this should be so, then scholars will need to re-examine *all* presuppositions underlying concepts like 'industrialism', 'science' and the 'Enlightenment' itself, and thinkers such as Karl Marx and Max Weber need to be seen as distinctly parochial.[3]

In many discussions of the current situation the disputed and slippery terms of post-modernity and post-modernism are applied. These are problematical concepts, subject to much ambiguity and qualification which, paradoxically, makes these terms simultaneously appealing and unattractive. At once they may invoke conceptions about the sort of world in which we now find ourselves, one which is in constant flux, is astonishingly malleable, and unpredictable; and, at the same time, they may suggest an abandonment – resigned or enthusiastic – of epistemological surety, of the view that, however complicated things might be, the world is knowable and that this knowledge might be agreed upon by dispassionate observers. The attraction of invoking post-modernism and post-modernity lies in their impact on all disciplines and their value in highlighting the distinctiveness of the contemporary situation, this both substantively and conceptually. To be post-modern involves highlighting the present in terms of its fluidity, while often also accepting the elusive, perspectival nature of theoretical accounts of reality. These aspects of post-modernism, its insight as well as its tensions, are reflected in virtually all the chapters of this book. At the same time, however, many of the theories and themes discussed here show an affinity with post-modern discourse without either subscribing to a view of the present as fundamentally different from a pre-postmodern past or embracing post-modernism's out-and-out perspectivism. Moreover, some of the contributions, notably Norris's chapter on post-modernism, argue for a realist position in pointed contrast to post-modern perspectivalism.

This book has been produced in response to the uncertainty and fluidity in contemporary social thought and social reality. Our contributors have been invited to write on a wide and eclectic range of programmes with the needs of university students in mind. Think, we urged, of the undergraduate student, perhaps studying English Literature, Media Studies or Geography, who is assailed by diverse theorists from here, there and everywhere, while simultaneously affected by substantive trends – by the development of the Internet and associated electronic communication, by new social movements such as animal rights activists and ecowarriors, by murderous ethnic divisions within what were once thought advanced nations, by breathtaking technological interventions in human reproduction and performance, by a collapse of tenure in the realms of employment – which themselves subvert and throw awry established ways of thought. Accordingly, we have sought from our authors, in short chapters, lucid yet wide-ranging accounts of major conceptions and developments, in which the tasks of clarification and critique are highlighted. To provide, in brief, a user's guide to a rough and ready, untamed yet fertile, terrain.

But let us be clear about one very important thing: we, and our authors, have not sought in this book to replace the uncertainties of our times and the turmoils of social theory with arguments that resolve all this upheaval with definitive statements. Such an ambition would be out of keeping with the spirit of our times – it may even be that the one supreme piece of postmodern wisdom is that there can be no assured analyses or definitive answers – nor, indeed, would it accord with the characteristically accelerated pace of change that seems set to continue. So, while readers will be able to find guidance and direction in the articles in *Understanding Contemporary Society: Theories of the Present*, they will not be provided with a route map towards any Celestial City where surety and certainty may be found.

Furthermore, it is consonant with this outlook that we have not instructed our contributors to try to produce encyclopaedic, or even dictionary-type, pieces. Each author does review a given topic, of course, but they have been encouraged not to hold back on their own – often sharply critical – slant on the subject. A world in turmoil is bound to be controversial. So too is it with the authors in this book, and readers should be aware from the outset that each is engaged in the controversies of the day.

THEORIES AND THEMES

In the following pages we provide a sketch of the contents of *Understanding Contemporary Society: Theories of the Present* so that users might more easily pick their way through the text. We have divided this volume into two parts – theories and themes – largely on pragmatic grounds. It should be said that this separation reflects a difference of emphasis rather than anything else since, from what has been said already in this introduction, it is obvious that there is a close, even indivisible, relationship between modes of thought and substantive trends, and that we are becoming ever more self-conscious of this interpenetration. Environmental concerns, for instance, have had a remarkable effect on everyday life and political consciousness, as well as on social theory. This has resulted in the reconsideration of what was once thought of as the main choice in analysis, that between Marxist, Durkheimian and Weberian explanations of the social world. Today it is not at all unusual to read arguments that this 'holy trinity', far from opposing one another, actually shared a technocentric approach towards nature, and that, as such, all three were trapped inside a world-view that blinded them to alternatives. This myopic technocentrism is now taken to be something which has led to the reckless control of nature, to disregard of ecological balances and biodiversity, and to the subordination of animals and habitat to the selfish and short-term demands of the human species. An outcome has been that the substantive development of environmental movements and their concerns has penetrated a great deal of theory – about the character of change, about the relationships between humans and other species, about the connections between the social and the natural . . . . A similar interconnectedness between theory and themes is evident between the emergence of feminist theory, the participation of women in labour markets, feminist political agitation, as well as increased control over their bodies and social thinking. In addition, the subsequent fragmentation of feminism into many feminisms and corresponding divisions of feminist social theory, has often been commented on. So when we divide the book into separate parts, this should not be taken to be a sharp split. To the contrary, theory and themes interpolate, and readers should use the book accordingly.

We have in addition subgrouped contributions within these two broad categories into associated areas, an exercise which involves again some pragmatic judgement, though one which also, we believe, makes sense intellectually and will help the reader find his or her way.

THEORIES

The present as post

The five chapters gathered together under 'The present as post' reflect, as the subtitle suggests, the widespread perception that we are living at a time of deep change, in practice as well as in thought. The end of the millennium is upon us, and with it has come a feeling that we are entering a time of 'endism', a period marked by the proliferation of the 'posts'. In recent years we have each encountered assertions that we are entering a period of post-capitalism, post-industrialism, post-socialism, above all perhaps of post-modernism and post-modernity.

However, none of the contributors here are content to endorse, at least without serious qualification, the 'post' agendas. Thus each of the authors in this section engages with the 'posts' – whether with post-modernism itself, post-feminism, post-history, post-Marxism or post-colonialism – duly setting out the particular arguments that they encounter. But each reviewer, in turn, casts a sceptical, and often sharply critical, eye on the more enthusiastic of the 'post' adherents.

Few are more suspicious than Christopher Norris (Chapter 2), in an account of post-modernism which is at once rigorously philosophical and witheringly political, and where post-modern theorists are attacked for their misunderstandings of philosophers such as Kant as well as for their political timidity. Norris contests the way in which post-modern theorists, apparently beguiled by the wide variety of social forms nowadays and by their constant changeability, then take a non-realist position *vis-à-vis* theory itself. To Norris such a collapse into relativism is a retrograde step for theory, abrogating philosophical responsibility as well as political effectiveness.

Next Michèle Barrett examines post-feminism (Chapter 3), acknowledging both its substantive manifestations in 'girl power' and its current appeal to theorists. Barrett concedes a good deal of post-feminism's attraction, for instance in the ways in which self-assured displays by feisty *and* sexy young women can disturb conventional images of feminism (dowdy, embittered, even self-pitying); and Barrett also admits that post-feminism's accenting of differences among women might challenge old-fashioned feminism's ostensible essentialism. Yet Barrett holds back on embracing wholeheartedly post-feminism, unconvinced that it can obliterate problems – of nature, of inequality – that older forms of feminism contested.

Krishan Kumar (Chapter 4) addresses the issue of post-history, the widespread sense of 'living at the end' which infuses a great deal of contemporary writing. In his chapter Kumar is centrally concerned with the very prospect of understanding an age and how (and whether) it is moving in a given direction. In this exercise Kumar examines, with some sympathy, motivations underpinning Francis Fukuyama's influential, but much maligned, argument that the 'end of history' has arrived with liberal capitalism's global triumph and communism's collapse. In Kumar's view this thesis may be faulted on several grounds, but to its credit it does at least acknowledge and address the significance of large-scale historical events in shaping lives, something which also justifies the project of theorizing what might be termed the directionality of change itself.

In Chapter 5 Terrell Carver scrutinizes Marxism in these post-modern times. Some might have thought that all residues of Marxism should have disappeared, so out of fashion has become its intellectual ambition to offer an all-encompassing theory of social development, and so devastating has been the impact of the demise of political regimes that operated in its name. However, interestingly, Carver contends that post-Marxism has led to an opening up of Marxist perspectives in the context of the loss of the former claimed certainties that have followed the fall of Marxism in Eastern Europe. In this way, shibboleths such as the conviction that Marxism is a theory of economic determinism may be safely jettisoned and, as a result, more plural and productive readings of Marx consonant with his voluminous and rich writings are possible.

The final chapter in this section on post-colonialism (Chapter 6) comes from an author from the West Indies, Don Robotham. Most writing on this issue comes at it from a literary and cultural angle, emphasizing terms such as 'hybridity' and 'otherness'. Robotham, however, locates post-colonial theory in a less orthodox but more fruitful framework of changing international relations. He sees post-colonialism as a response to disturbed notions of identity in the wake of developing countries achieving independence from their former colonial rulers. In this process a concern to uproot connections with Western models of modernity resulted in an intoxicating abandonment of Western reason itself. Robotham will have no truck with this, criticizing its development as a backward-looking response (reason ought not to be dismissed as merely a Western trick), and as one which underappreciates the significance of, and opportunities within, a globalized world.

Explanation and understanding

Our next four chapters are among the most determinedly theoretical contributions to this book, and for this reason we present them under the broad umbrella title of 'Explanation and understanding'. None, however, are insensitive to real-world developments, and none leave the substantive realm very far behind, no matter how systematic their theoretical enterprise becomes.

Ted Benton (Chapter 7), whose critical, if appreciative, review of the currently influential theories of reflexive modernization takes to task the seminal work in this area of Anthony Giddens and Ulrich Beck. Reflexive modernization theory is at the heart of contemporary 'Third Way' politics (and Giddens himself is about as close to the British Prime Minister Tony Blair's project as one can imagine such a scholar getting), so one ought not to be surprised that Benton's account ranges far beyond any narrow theoretical debate. In Benton's view advocates of reflexive modernization suggest that the 'late modern' world evidences a number of features which call for new political responses. Accordingly, Benton reviews Giddens's and Beck's central tenets (globalization, heightened reflexivity, detraditionalism, pervasive risk, and so on) and their corollaries of 'identity' concerns and 'lifestyle' politics (old-style collectivist approaches allegedly being out of step with today's self-conscious citizens who will not find acceptable such 'traditional' appeals to loyalty as supporting one's class, trade union or country). Benton is willing to acknowledge some insights and even strengths of reflexive modernization theory, though he objects to much of its revived language of 'modernity'. Still more critically, Benton reminds us of the continued salience of older-fashioned matters such as capitalist interests and class inequalities.

Susan Stephenson (Chapter 8) suggests that narrative has a special contribution to make to social theory because of its compatibility with lived experience. Narratives – stories, if you will – are seen as particularly attractive, given disillusionment with a good deal of contemporary theory which is excessively abstract. For Stephenson, narratives are able to capture the specificity of actual, changing identities as they are lived out in substantive historical contexts. Because of this they are an important counter to so much theory which is dry and deracinated, thereby absenting flesh and blood, thinking and feeling, human beings. She concentrates on tracing the impact that the narrative turn has exerted upon philosophy, political science and literature.

One of the currently more influential approaches in the social sciences is rational choice theory, a perspective which has gained ground especially in sociological circles with ambitions to combine methodological individualism and empirical generalization. John Scott (Chapter 9) revisits rational choice theory, a theory with a lineage traceable to both the German idealism of Max Weber and the interest-based orientation of Chicago economics. Scott sets out to assess rational choice theory's claim to offer a clear account of how individuals are to be understood as choosing and acting during particular courses of action. In Scott's view rational choice theory is seriously flawed, particularly in its scientific pretensions and in its inability to allow for the influence of wider factors than the individual's calculations in conducting social relationships.

Tim Blackman (Chapter 10) provides a much needed review of the attractive but off-puttingly difficult complexity theory. This is presently little understood (if frequently cited), though many dimly perceive it to have some resonance with post-modernism's suspicion of linear and straightforward cause/effect accounts of change. Writing sympathetically, and also from the position of a social policy analyst who is drawn to developing usable and predictive research that can account for abrupt and unexpected change, Blackman outlines the character and potential of complexity theory, noting its possible contribution to research which needs to account for highly complicated and non-repeatable social and economic conditions.

Reconceiving the political

Any attempt to engage with the connections of theory and society nowadays must quickly come across questions of politics. This is unavoidable since political matters, broadly conceived, are ever present when societies undergo change and when people think hard about the sources and significance of such changes.

The concepts of liberty and democracy are absolutely central to modern political thought and practice, and they are also at the storm-centre of much rethinking that has taken place over recent years. Contemporary liberalism is seen by Gary Browning (Chapter 11) as a success story of the late twentieth century. Its practical viability is registered in the ubiquity of capitalism, with which it is closely associated, and also in its success in allowing a plurality of projects and different values to be pursued in society. Yet, at the same time, this very plurality within modern liberalism and in the advanced societies means, paradoxically, that it is difficult to establish a universal case for liberalism itself. Liberalism, having celebrated the variety of forms of life and their incommensurability, is somewhat confounded when it endeavours to present a universal argument for its own existence. Browning teases at this conundrum in his article, particularly as developed in the formulations of leading liberal theorist John Rawls.

Nick Hewlett (Chapter 12) addresses the cognate issue of democracy. He distinguishes the different forms of democracy that are feasible – namely, liberal, representative and direct – while also emphasizing that particular historical circumstances decisively shape any form of democracy that may be adopted in a specific time and place. In this regard, Hewlett recognizes that it is liberal democracy that is currently ascendant, given the advance of market systems and the demise of communism. None the less, Hewlett sees weight in the critique of contemporary forms of democracy undertaken by Pierre Bourdieu, work which, argues Hewlett, points to the continued relevance of direct democracy as propounded by Marx.

Elizabeth Frazer's concerns (Chapter 13) might be regarded as a critique of the abstraction and atomism that can accompany liberal democratic theory. She addresses the phenomenon of communitarianism, a theory as well as a political movement which has enjoyed a resurgence of late, noticeably in societies that have had a strong commitment to liberal tenets of possessive individualism. In her discussion Frazer makes clear that communitarian politics have arisen out of dissatisfaction with theories of society which privilege individuals as autonomous units. Communitarianism insists that the social, in the sense of collective commitment in values and practices, remains an important phenomenon, which cannot be reduced to the sum of individual choices. Frazer sees communitarian politics as being inspired by the idea of promoting togetherness and mutual trust by fostering such values, but she also highlights the ambiguities and uncertainties involved in the notion of community itself.

This chapter is followed by Kimberly Hutchings's (Chapter 14) engagement with new thinking in international relations. She is concerned here with understanding how recent thought on international relations has moved away from previous approaches which presumed real interests or liberal values of states, towards acknowledgement of the enormous complexities of international circumstances. Post-modern, normative, critical and feminist theorists are seen here to be offering more adequate responses to change in the international arena in so far as their theorizing allows appreciation of the full diversity of international actors and the variety of their concerns.

It is appropriate that the final chapter in this section should consider utopias and dystopias, considerations rarely far away from politics.

Stephen Crook (Chapter 15) offers a wide-ranging review of such thought, contrasting, for instance, the Marxist critique of utopian thinking with the abstract and unrealistic character of the utopianism of the likes of Fourier and Owen. Crook notes that the entire project of imagining a distinct and ideal future society, even such as expressed in Anthony Giddens's modest 'utopian realism', is nowadays questionable in the light of the interplay between the divergent theoretical imaginations and highly differentiated realities in the contemporary world. In this post-modern era, according to Crook, the dispersion of separate groups, each maintaining an alternative vision of its reality, forecloses the possibility of imagining any single future for society.

THEMES

It is when we turn to Part II of this work that we become especially aware of the two-way relationships between theoretical understanding and practical developments. While it is clear that real-world phenomena have posed challenges to established theory, we ought not to underestimate the consequences of thought itself for substantive life. Theory gives shape to the diversity and chaos of change, helps make sense of the resultant upheaval and shifts in direction, and can contribute to the very changes themselves.

Characterizing the present

There can be few areas where this is more evident than where thinkers endeavour to capture the character of the fast-changing present. Hence our section, 'Characterizing the present', manifests a high degree of awareness of the intimate ties joining theory and real-world events. David Lyon's Chapter 16 on post-modernity underscores this point. Drawing on the insightful writing of Britain's leading sociologist of post-modernity, Zygmunt Bauman, Lyon highlights the fluidity and uncertainty in today's world. These are observable features of the contemporary situation and they are mirrored in post-modern theories, yet they are also phenomena which are made comprehensible by theory itself (and this theory in turn influences responses to this 'post-modern' world). Lyon observes several important changes, especially a 'cultural turn' expressed in an explosive growth of media and consumer activity, which he regards as central to the spread of post-modernity. Theory, suggests Lyon, might lead us seriously to consider whether these changes, taken together, might appropriately be regarded as constituting a new social system.

Barrie Axford (Chapter 17) tackles the subject of globalization. This issue is frequently presented as simply a *fait accompli* by politicians and business leaders and, in this, starkly illustrative of the mobilizing power of theoretical terms. Axford himself considers globalization as being both a process shaping the contemporary world and as a theory arising out of the need to explain this phenomenon. In this chapter he defends what might be thought of as a 'strong' reading of globalization as a systemic force, in this way interpreting it as a process which exemplifies the properties of a theoretical system.

Restructuring is the prime concern of Andrew Kilmister (Chapter 18). It has been a palpable feature over recent decades, scarcely out of the news, with politicians constantly urging their publics to prepare for necessary adjustments in established practices and business people insisting that new ways of operating are crucial for future prosperity. Any serious attempt to characterize the present must surely treat restructuring with great seriousness. Kilmister, writing from a background in economics while acutely sensitive to the social and political dimensions of economic behaviour, examines two major (if rarely considered side-by-side) accounts of capitalist restructuring. The first sees the realm of work being transformed to ensure a heightened flexibility of production; the second is concerned with financial reorganization whereby high levels of company debt are allowed and financed by 'junk bonds'. Both are grand, generalized, accounts, which, argues Kilmister, need to be scaled down in the face of critical scrutiny and empirical evidence, though there can be little doubt that they have exercised influence in policy-making circles, and continue to do so.

Our final chapter (Chapter 19) under 'Characterizing the present' comes from the well-known urbanist Saskia Sassen. Its subject is cities in the global economy. It is commonplace to observe that modern life is increasingly urban (today about half of all the world's people are town or city dwellers, and the move away from the countryside continues to accelerate). But Sassen takes us far beyond this point. Locating the city in the context of the world economy, she identifies the strategic importance of 'global' cities, such as London, Tokyo and New York, where top-level management and control operations may be found. This concentration of activities in global cities is promoted by economic and social integration of the world, by the infrastructural support of information and communications technologies, and is assisted by the self-conscious conceptualization of these processes. Global cities have not simply emerged from their own inner volition, nor have they developed by some organic force: they have been made by the actions and decisions – underlain by theorizations – of a range of business and political leaders. And, yet, Sassen also highlights how substantive developments may not turn out exactly as the theorists of the information age imagine. In a world in which the constraints of space are being overcome by virtuoso technologies that lead to distance being, in principle, no object to business organization or political intercourse, the growth of world cities stands, paradoxically, as a physical reminder of the continued importance of space.

Culture, media and intellectuals

The next set of chapters is concerned with a series of associated issues which have imposed themselves on contemporary society and our ways of thought. The enormous expansion of culture – whether defined in terms of music and writing, or as the heightened presence of other cultures, or as the continuing increases in consumption (which stimulates fashion, cuisines and 'style' in general), or as an expansion of leisure pursuits, or as the spread of tourism – has had marked effects on the way we live and how we think about ourselves and our times. The massively expanded role of media in all of our lives is, of course, an integral part of this cultural escalation, and it is usually the first thing that comes to mind when one mentions the growth of culture. Its significance is clear at a moment's thought about the pervasive spread of television in its several forms, of personal computers, of video, or even of the Internet.

Unavoidably, such developments as these impinge on theory and society since they are at once manifest developments and, at the same time, they pose profound questions for and about intellectuals. If we define these latter broadly as those who reflect most determinedly about circumstances, then not only might we anticipate them giving concentrated attention to culture and media (which very many do), but we might also consider how culture and media nowadays impose themselves on the activities, and even conceptions, of intellectuals today.

Richard Maxwell (Chapter 20) concerns himself with cultural studies, a field that has given particular attention and impetus to cultural, media and intellectual activities. Maxwell provides a valuable history of cultural studies, tracing its roots to the UK during the 1960s and 1970s, during a time of vigorous anti-racist and anti-imperialist campaigning and the flourishing of feminism. Since then the field has reached out far across the world, to influence a great many spheres of thought. However, Maxwell avoids a celebratory tone, discerning also a waning of the radicalism and political thrust of cultural studies under the influence of marketization, academic incorporation and conservative ideology.

Carl Boggs (Chapter 21) addresses head-on the subject of intellectuals in the world today. Presenting a historical overview, Boggs elaborates on the division in modern society between technocratic and oppositional (critical) intellectuals. He then considers how, in the present era, conditions encourage the growth of fragmented, disparate and localised intellectuals who are found in situations as varied as newspapers, think tanks and the environmental movements, but whose significance has been reduced by the very circumstances of fragmentation and instability encountered in these post-modern times.

Frank Webster, in Chapter 22, pays attention to an important institutional context of intellectual activity, higher education. In this sphere there has been an especially rapid expansion in the UK over recent years (mass higher education is now the norm in advanced societies, by which is meant participation rates of about 30 per cent of the age group), but there has also been a host of associated changes such as reduced funding, new types of learners, and partnerships with outside agencies. Among the major changes in higher education has been a shift in the role of university intellectuals and, indeed, in the knowledges developed by the university – increasingly the call is for 'utility', with courses, research and employment justified on grounds of 'performativity' (rather than, say, understanding and insight). Such trends have led some to conceive of a 'post-modern university' which is congruent with a wider demand for 'flexibility', adaptability to change, increased differentiation and more concern for consumption. These developments, it is suggested, are so extensive as to cast doubt on there being any remaining features of the old-style university. Instead what we have are highly differentiated – and in this sense post-modern – and versatile institutions. Webster outlines this case for the post-modern university, and concedes much of its empirical salience, yet he remains sceptical of the profundity of change.

Two separate chapters pay attention to one of the most striking dimensions of contemporary society – the growth of mass communication and, most recently, the Web. The distinguished Finnish scholar, Kaarle Nordenstreng (Chapter 23), reviews the emergence of mass communication over the past four centuries, its enormous significance for all of us in the contemporary world and its major distinguishing features. Nordenstreng recognizes that the development of the media, in its conveying and channelling of information, raises important questions about the relationship between the media and notions of freedom and democracy that cannot be settled either by owners or by professionals working within the media since their perspectives are shaped by their roles.

Vincent Mosco (Chapter 24) complements this general account with a close and critical review of what is frequently seen as the leading edge of technological innovation, the Web (or the 'information superhighway', the Internet, 'cyberspace', and so on). To many commentators the Internet is synonymous with post-modernity itself, since this mind-boggling complex network society, capable of instantaneous interconnection of millions of dispersed individuals who may organize, disorganize and rearrange relationships on the Web, readily evokes the notion of a shifting, transient and malleable post-modernity. Mosco soberly contrasts the Web's mythologized theoretical potential for extending democratic relations and human communities with its historical development out of military control and the commercial imperative, forces which have exercised an enormous influence on its growth as well as on other developments in communications.

Pluralism and identity

It will be evident from earlier sections of this introduction that differentiation and variation are central themes of contemporary social life as well as of intellectual activity. A post-modern ethos hones in on these to declare the present to be characterized by its differences, by the manifest pluralism of peoples and places. Many commentators, drawn by this ethos, pay close attention to cultural pluralism and to associated issues of identity in a tumultuous globalized era. Frequently in such writing it is evident that pluralism and difference are presumed nowadays to be found at unprecedentedly high levels and to connote a positive value. In this section of *Understanding Contemporary Society: Theories of the Present* we have gathered together three wide-ranging contributions to discussion of these related issues of pluralism and identity.

Murray Low (Chapter 25) discusses nationalism in relation to the development of modern territorial states and legitimacy. Theories of nationalism have often disconnected it too readily from other forms of identity politics. Nationalism is at its most unsettling when we consider how far it derives its force from its relationships with other concepts many find more benign, such as community. Even if nationalism is becoming obsolete (which seems doubtful), its characteristic ways of framing community, identity and history deserve consideration within more open and relational frameworks for understanding political identities and legitimacy.

Sarah Ansari (Chapter 26) sees the themes of differentiation and complexity as central to Islam. In contrast to popular Western images of Islam as monolithic in its sheer contrast to the West, Ansari points to Islam's inner complexity, which allows it to respond dynamically to the forces of modernity. Islam is capable of a range of responses to the modern world that encourage a differentiated religion and culture. Ansari notes that postmodernist theory might open up the space for debate within Islam about its identity in the next century.

Avigail Eisenberg (Chapter 27) focuses directly on the interplay between political power, contested identities and culture. More recent theories of cultural pluralism, according to Eisenberg, are concerned with the distribution of power on a cultural basis. Such power can be dispersed between or accumulated by groups or individuals and is located in a variety of cultural sites. Advocates of the redistribution of cultural power are seen as appealing to considerations of stability and norms of equality and promise-keeping. But Eisenberg warns that in promoting cultural pluralism the role of the State is increased and the goal of equality is not easily achieved by the simple recognition of cultural difference.

Intimate relations

Three chapters are included here which address questions of the intimate realm. Thinking about intimacy has become crucial for recent social theory as well as for the alleged emergence of post-modern society. Few matters can involve more intimacy than families and households, so it is right that

Mary Maynard (Chapter 28) should chart recent changes in these areas, and that she considers how they have altered ways in which Western families have been conceptualized. On a subject which arouses a great deal of controversy and opinion, Maynard is strikingly judicious in her review of how feminist and post-structuralist concepts have responded to and promoted an increased flexibility and plurality of family and household arrangements. Maynard also interprets such changes in very different ways from those who urge a return to a (mythic) former age of the 'stable family'.

Chris Shilling (Chapter 29), in a bold and sweeping account, examines the historical neglect of the body in most social theory, while he urges an analysis which makes embodiment central to consideration of the world today. In this endeavour Shilling acknowledges the contribution of post-modern theorists, notably those drawn to social constructivism in their opposition to 'naturalistic' accounts. While acknowledging the importance of the body in social theory and recognizing the impact of theoretical insight upon practice, he recommends that we use embodiment as a means of reorienting social theory to deal with issues such as poverty and environmental decay in the twenty-first century.

Ken Plummer (Chapter 30) addresses directly intimate choices, emphasizing the plurality of its forms in a contemporary world that he argues is simultaneously traditional, modern and post-modern. This is a world in which many (though not all) individuals have choices about family forms, reproduction, sexualities and genders. This pluralization of intimacy is taken by Plummer as promoting theoretical and political debate to which he contributes by favouring a dialogic, democratic discourse in which to discuss issues of gender and intimate choices.

Trends and movements

Our final chapters address large-scale trends and movements, ones which, if already prominent, promise to increase in significance in the near future. David Pepper (Chapter 31) takes environmentalism as a phenomenon on the move. As a practical concern as well as a contributor to theoretical work, environmentalism has already made a mark, but Pepper's account refines and elaborates its contribution in the light of even more recent developments, notably environmentalism's encounter with post-modernism. This chapter notes the wide-ranging and eclectic character of the environmental movement which has long been shaped by radical and reformist theories and diverse political perspectives. A result is that environmentalism has long had an ambiguous relationship to questions of modernity and post-modernity: environmentalism has often looked backwards while simultaneously peering into the future; and it has often aligned itself with recognizably traditional political forces while being willing to embrace out-and-out post-modern positions. The post-modern celebration of difference and variety permeates environmentalist thinking in terms of the movement's hostility to dominant notions of economic progress and centralization. Yet environmentalism's concern to articulate a political project determined by a comprehensive theory links it to classic modern theories of society.

Abigail Halcli's examination (Chapter 32) of social movements has an obvious resonance with Pepper's subject, since so many new social movements have emerged from, and gathered around, environmental issues (animal rights, anti-nuclear campaigns, fair trade, etc.). However, Halcli considers social movements in the even wider context of struggles for cultural recognition that are such a prominent feature of the contemporary scene. She notes how, since the 1970s, many writers have focused on the 'new social movements', seen as organizing primarily around cultural issues of identity and quality of life. Her chapter highlights how changing perceptions of social movements' activities and activists have been reflected in social movement theory. For example, the civil rights and liberation movements of the 1960s led to a rejection of earlier perspectives which tended to view them as spontaneous and often irrational responses to structural or cultural breakdown. Current trends in social movement theory suggest that identities, belief systems, political opportunity structures and cycles of contention are all essential to a more adequate understanding of the wide variety of contemporary movements.

Finally, Harriet Bradley presents a chapter (Chapter 33) entitled 'Social inequalities: coming to terms with complexity'. She recognizes how the theorization as well as much of the substance of inequality has been transformed in recent decades. She also acknowledges the limitations of old-style class analysis, notably its reductionism and blindness to gender, race, ethnic and age dimensions of social inequality. Bradley places an emphasis on the complexities of inequality today, the recognition of which has emerged with new styles of theorizing such as post-modernism. Evoking contemporary concerns such as identity and hybridity to underline the variabilities of inequality, Bradley reviews the complicated terrain of post-modern stratification while remaining acutely aware of blunt economic divisions which persist (and indeed have worsened) in recent decades.

HOW TO USE THIS BOOK

This book has been designed to help students find their way through the complexities of contemporary social theory. There are over thirty chapters that cover a lot of ground in showing how theory and society are currently being understood. Of course, it does not cover all possible themes and theories, and everyone will be able to think of significant absences. None the less, the large number of topics covered in this book goes a good way towards providing students with a map of the state of theorizing about society. A map of the present, however, cannot disguise its essentially con-tested nature. This sense of contestation is evidenced in all the chapters that review differing ways in which the various topics are currently understood. Indeed, in some of the chapters authors are critical of the theories and standpoints they review. All chapters, however, are concerned to provide a readable and engaging guide to the domains of theory and society that they review. Moreover, all of the chapters raise points which are relevant to a range of disciplines and ways of understanding the present. Students will find it worth while to check out what the book has to offer by making use of the various devices, described below, that are designed to promote its utility as a general reference to theory and society in the present.

The chapters are presented in a way which aims to do justice to the complexity of the thinking involved in their domains while maximizing readability. Each has an introductory section which highlights key features of the area being discussed. The chapters are also summarized by the provi-sion of several bullet points at the end of each chapter which set out their key points. Students wanting to get a sense of the state of play of society and theory today can review each of these sets of bullet points and get a con-densed reading of contemporary social thought. They can follow up this general understanding by focusing on the individual chapters themselves. Subheadings are used throughout the text to enable readers to get a sense of the direction of the argument of each of the chapters.

Students are presented with a listing and discussion of a small number of key further readings for each of the subject areas covered in the chapters. Students who read the book for quick access to high-level discussion of specific themes and theories which are puzzling them can turn to the back of the book, where subject and author index indicate where key terms and names in contemporary social theory are listed.

Above all, the book is meant to be *used* by students. It is designed as a flexible tool serving a variety of interests, and it reflects the way in which much of the social world examined in the book is no longer seen in rigid, unidimensional terms. How students use the book will depend very much upon their purposes and priorities. For instance, students coming to terms with feminist thought will be guided through a highly differentiated and conflict-riven area by the survey of post-feminist thinking provided by Michèle Barrett (Chapter 3). Other readers may approach the book from a more empirical angle, concerned perhaps with the state of universities to-day, and such students will find helpful the chapter on higher education (Chapter 22). Readers will understand theory and society in a variety of ways, just as the authors of these chapters see the social world from a range of perspectives.

We are living at a time during which this interpenetration of theory and society appears to be especially intensive, as well as being conducted at a high level of self-consciousness. There can be no definitive resolution or conclusion to this interplay, but readers are invited to participate in an informed way by reading the following chapters. They might then build upon this by reflecting on how this might find an application in other areas.

Students would benefit, using this book, if they were to keep an alert eye out for developments about which they might theorize and which themselves might pose challenges to theory – for instance, developments in genetic engineering, the future of welfare, ageing, famine, childhood, militarism, and so forth. Likewise, students might expect theoretical innovations to influence social practices. Such examples highlight the need for them to interrogate all the theory they encounter. In doing so they will become better analysts of the contemporary world as well as more adept at handling social theory.

NOTES

1 Stuart Hall, Chas Critcher, Tony Jefferson, John Clarke and Brian Roberts (1978) *Policing the Crisis: Mugging, the State, and Law and Order*. Basingstoke: Macmillan.
2 Stuart Hall (1979) 'The Great Moving Right Show', *Marxism Today*, January, pp. 14–20.
3 André Gunder Frank (1998) *Re-Orient: Global Economy in the Asian Age*. Berkeley, CA: University of California Press.

Part 1

Theories

Chapter 2

Post-modernism: a guide for the perplexed

Christopher Norris

WHAT IS POST-MODERNISM?

We cannot begin to define 'post-modernism' until we have some reasonably clear working notion of what 'modernism' means, though this term is itself used in so many senses and contexts that it eludes any clear cut definition. Literary critics and theorists have a fairly good idea of what they mean by modernism: it is a movement that began in the early twentieth century, more specifically after the First World War (Nicholls, 1995). It applies to certain fictional and poetic techniques, stylistic devices, modes of writing, experimental procedures, the use of spatial form, stream-of-consciousness, the predominance of metaphor, striking juxtapositions of image and style as in *The Waste Land* (Eliot, 1922), techniques of multiple narrative consciousness, the unreliable narrator, all kinds of highly self-conscious, sophisticated literary experimentation. Music critics also have a good working notion of what they mean by musical modernism. Broadly speaking it would include the atonal, serial or twelve-note music of Schoenberg and his disciples; middle-period (neo-classical) Stravinsky and other such gestures of revolt against nineteenth-century Romanticism; more complex or challenging techniques of development, formal structure, harmonic progression, etc.; in other words, as Ezra Pound famously said, the desire to 'make it new' at all costs and throw off the dead weight of inherited tradition. So to this extent music historians and literary critics have a reasonable grasp of what is meant by 'modernism' in their own areas of interest.

However, if you look at how philosophers and intellectual historians use that term, then you will find a very different range of meanings and

25

associations. Depending on your chosen historical perspective you could trace modernism back to the seventeenth century and Descartes' attempt to provide a new foundation for philosophy in his famous declaration 'cogito ergo sum' ('I think, therefore I am'), conceived as an absolute, indubitable ground of knowledge (Descartes, 1986). Thus the one thing of which we could be certain is that the human mind (or thinking substance) must exist in and through the act of thought. And from this point – so Descartes believed – one could start to relay the conceptual groundwork of an objectively existent (mind-independent) world whose reality had been threatened by the demon of sceptical doubt. Then again, moving on some 150 years, one might prefer to date the emergence of 'true' philosophical modernism with Kant and his hugely ambitious attempt to provide a transcendentally justified account of the various human faculties, that is to say, cognitive understanding, practical reason, aesthetic judgement, and reason in its 'pure' or speculative modes (Kant, 1964, 1975, 1978). Indeed it can be argued that all the great philosophical debates since then – debates about truth, knowledge, interpretation, the status of the human or social *vis-à-vis* the natural sciences – have their origin in Kant. From this standpoint modernism is best described as an attempt to establish the scope and limits of the various distinct yet interrelated faculties of reason, knowledge and judgement. For many philosophers this would be a defining moment of modernity, the philosophic discourse of modernity, a discourse that has continued right down to the present day.

One of the most notable and resourceful defenders of that tradition is the German philosopher Jürgen Habermas (1972; 1987). Habermas does not entirely endorse Kant's 'foundationalist' way of treating these issues and instead seeks to give them a more pragmatic, discursive or linguistic turn. Thus Habermas talks about the 'ideal speech-situation' as a kind of implicit understanding or regulative idea that is built into all our communicative acts, our social life-forms and structures of political representation (Habermas, 1984–87). Nevertheless, in his writing there is still a strong commitment to Kantian or Enlightenment values, to what he calls 'the unfinished project of modernity'. Habermas thinks it vital to conserve that critical impulse because the only way we can work towards a more just, equitable, truly democratic society is by keeping our sights fixed upon the possibility of achieving an enlightened consensus, in Kant's phrase a 'sensus communis'. This is *not* just common sense under a fancy Latin name, it is not just a kind of *de facto*, pragmatic agreement on certain matters. Rather, it is the idea of agreement arrived at through an enlightened, democratic, participant debate on issues of shared concern for humanity. Whence Habermas's firmly held belief that we can indeed communicate across cultural differences, or divergences of moral viewpoint, or conflicting ideas of social and political good; moreover, that despite those differences we can at least hope to achieve a broad consensus on the main points of principle. It is a deeply Kantian viewpoint: enlightened, critical, progressive, aimed towards extending the 'public sphere' of participant debate as far and as wide as possible.

Thus we need to keep in mind this distinction between, on the one hand, the cultural-aesthetic modernist movement which emerged at a certain time, the early twentieth century, and was characterized by certain innovations of a chiefly formal and stylistic kind, and, on the other hand, the philosophic discourse of modernity which goes further back and which involves much larger claims. Now, I think we can draw some related distinctions between various uses of the term 'post-modernism'. There is a sense of the term in which it figures as a broad, rather fuzzy, ill-defined, cultural phenomenon. This is post-modernism as described by a culture-critic like Fredric Jameson (1991) who sees signs of it everywhere and who mostly – not always – likes what he sees. Jameson speaks as a Marxist, but a Marxist with distinctly post-modernist leanings. In his view there is no point criticizing, or rejecting, or deploring post-modernism, as if one had some choice in the matter or as if one could simply opt out of it. Jameson views post-modernism as a defining aspect of the way we live now: it affects our lifestyles, our styles of dress, the way we listen to music, the way we watch television, respond to advertising. It is the element we inhabit, the sea we swim in, the very air we breath. It affects and pervades so many aspects of our life that it would be futile for us to declare ourselves 'against post-modernism'. Jameson thinks that basically all we can do is to say that there are some bits we can like and some bits we do not like so much, or maybe not at all. Thus he quite likes the architecture and some of the music, is not so keen on a lot of the fiction that gets itself called 'post-modernist', but in the end concedes that these are matters of taste or individual predilection. After all, the whole notion of aesthetic judgement as appealing to shared (intersubjective or transindividual) criteria is itself just the sort of Kantian argument that post-modernism purports to have left far behind.

A MATTER OF TASTE?

Clearly there is a measure of truth in all this. If you happen to enjoy post-modernist fiction, then I could not hope to persuade you otherwise, and indeed would not want to since I disagree with Jameson in finding it (for the most part) witty, inventive and intellectually rewarding. I might try a bit harder to change your mind if you profess to enjoy 'post-modern' music, or the sorts of music that often get described that way: for instance, the music of minimalist composers such as Philip Glass, Steve Reich, Michael Nyman, and the 'holy minimalists' Aarvo Part and John Tavener. Perhaps I would not really hope to dissuade you or to spoil your enjoyment by coming up with good reasons to think it bad music! On the other hand, I *would* want to say that the argument does not stop there. One can go beyond saying 'I like it' or 'I don't like it', one can remark that much of this music is mind-numbingly repetitive, that it offers no aural or intellectual challenge, requires no effort of structural grasp or ability to follow a complex pattern of harmonic, tonal or rhythmic development. In other words, it does not do what music ought to do, that is, provoke and stimulate the listener by putting up a certain resistance to facile or automated habits of response. Still, I am getting on my high horse here and had better not tax your patience any further. At any rate, as I have said, Jameson has a point when he adopts his take-it-or-leave-it line on the varieties of post-modern cultural taste. For eventually such arguments must have an end and give way to statements of individual preference, even if that stage comes later than Jameson thinks and allows for some worthwhile discussion along the way.

However, this is not the aspect of post-modernism I want to write about at any length here. There is another aspect, besides the broadly cultural-aesthetic, which I think is more open to criticism. This is 'philosophical' post-modernism and it extends into ethics and politics, as well as into other areas like epistemology and philosophy of language. The position is set out by Jean-François Lyotard whose book *The Postmodern Condition* (1984) has been perhaps the single most widely read text on this topic. Lyotard argues that the philosophic discourse of modernity must henceforth be viewed as historically redundant since it has long been overtaken by so many social, political and cultural developments. Once upon a time, it was possible to believe in all those splendid Enlightenment values: truth, progress, universal justice, perpetual peace, the Kantian 'sensus communis', and so forth. Perhaps one could even believe, like Kant, that all the diverse human cultures were destined to transcend their conflicts of interest and achieve some sort of federal world-state – the United Nations as an Idea of Reason, if you like. Such was at any rate the 'grand narrative' of Enlightenment thinking as Lyotard reads it. This narrative of course took different forms and emphasized different details of the picture from one thinker to the next. There was the Kantian grand narrative of reason, democracy, the universal 'kingdom of ends' as an ethical and socio-political ideal. After that came Hegel's dialectical conception of history as moving ever onwards and up through successive stages of conflict and resolution to the stage where *Geist* attained Absolute Knowledge and could thus write the book-to-end-all-books that was Hegel's *Phenomenology of Spirit* (1988). Hegel is actually a better example than Kant of the kind of grand-narrative (or 'metanarrative') thinking that Lyotard hopes we have now left behind with the passage to our present 'post-modern condition'. A metanarrative is a story that wants to be *more* than just a story, that is to say, one which claims to have achieved an omniscient standpoint above and beyond all the other stories that people have told so far. There is also a Marxist metanarrative (or was until recently, Lyotard would say) which seeks to out-Hegel Hegel by inverting his idealist dialectic and introducing such ideas as economic determination 'in the last instance', 'forces and relations of production', the base/superstructure metaphor, and class conflict as the driving force in history. Again, this argument is manifestly constructed on grand-narrative lines, since again it involves the teleological aim towards an endpoint – after the short-term 'dictatorship of the proletariat' – at which all conflicts of class interest will at length be transcended or resolved.

Nevertheless, Lyotard says, we have to let go of these consoling illusions. We can no longer believe in the values that once characterized the Enlightenment project because, quite simply, we cannot ignore all the contrary evidence to date. That is, we have now been witness to so many wars, pogroms, bloody revolutions, counter-revolutions, post-revolutionary terrors, resurgences of ethnic conflict, etc., that the old metanarratives (along with all their values of truth, progress and universal justice) cannot be sustained unless through ignorance or sheer bad faith. We have seen the suppression of 'workers' democracy', of 'socialism with a human face', and of every attempt to carry such principles into practice. We have seen what happened in East Germany (1953), in Hungary (1956) and in Czechoslovakia (1968); also what occurred in the Soviet Union during seven decades of (nominally) communist rule. In other words, there are too many melancholy instances of failed revolutionary hopes for us to believe any longer in those old grand narratives – whether Kantian, Hegelian or Marxist – that placed their faith in the power of reason to extrapolate reliably from past to future events. So we should now abandon that faith, Lyotard thinks, and instead take the tolerant post-modern view that there exist any number of 'first-order natural pragmatic narratives', each of them having a right to express its own distinctive values, belief system or criteria for what should count as a 'truthful' or 'valid' statement (see Lyotard, 1988). Moreover, we now have to recognize – as the one remaining principle of justice in a post-modern epoch – that these narratives are strictly incommensurable, that we can (or should) never presume to judge between them on grounds of justice and truth. For we are sure to commit an ethical wrong if we apply one set of criteria (i.e., our own) in order to criticize the practices or beliefs of others, or in order to adjudicate the quarrel between parties who may not (either or both of them) accept our terms of reference. We have to accept the 'post-modern condition', that is, the fact (as Lyotard sees it) that we nowadays need to make sense of our lives in a context of multiple, open-ended, ever proliferating narratives and language games. We tell many stories about ourselves, about history, philosophy, the human and the natural sciences, and of course about politics and the various lessons to be drawn from past political events. But the chief lesson, Lyotard says, is that we have to respect the narrative *differend* and not make the error – the typical 'Enlightenment' error – of believing any one such story to possess superior truth-telling warrant.

Now, I take it that this is what 'post-modernism' means in the more definite (philosophically articulated) sense of that term. At any rate it is useful, as a kind of preliminary ground-clearing exercise, to distinguish this from the other sense of the term which applies to such a range of otherwise disparate social and cultural phenomena that it becomes just a vague, all-purpose descriptor for 'the way we live now' (though see Chapter 16). Up to a point I would agree with Jameson when he argues that one cannot reject or deplore post-modernism in this latter sense because, quite simply, there is too much of it around; it affects too many aspects of our lives. However, one can, I think, mount a strong case against the kind of thinking to be found in Lyotard and others of a similar (doctrinal-post-modernist) persuasion. One can argue that it is philosophically confused, that it carries some dubious ethical and socio-political implications, and moreover that it gives a very partial (at times a demonstrably false or distorted) account of so-called 'Enlightenment' thought.

MODERNITY REVISITED

Such is the case that I shall argue here, having tried to establish some basic (albeit much disputed) terms of reference. There are three main aspects of post-modernism, and they have to do with epistemology, ethics and aesthetics. These areas of concern were also, of course, very important for Kant, as likewise for the critical tradition in philosophy that has continued from Kant to present-day thinkers like Habermas and Karl-Otto Apel (1985). Epistemology has to do with knowledge, with the scope, that is to say, the powers and the limits of humanly attainable knowledge. This is the realm of cognitive understanding and its rule is that intuitions – sensuous or phenomenal intuitions – must be brought under adequate concepts. 'Intuitions without concepts are blind; concepts without intuitions are empty' (Kant, 1964: 112). It is a question of what we can know or what we can legitimately claim to know. For Kant there were certain kinds of knowledge that were just unattainable: knowledge concerning such matters as freedom of will, the immortality of the soul, or the existence of God, along with certain speculative questions about cosmology, time and the origins of the universe. He thought that if understanding tried to get a hold on these things, then it would overreach itself, it would run into paradoxes, contradictions and antinomies. So in the First *Critique*, the *Critique of Pure Reason*, Kant (1964) is trying to define the proper scope of understanding (or epistemology) in both senses of the word 'define': to specify precisely what it *can* achieve and also to delimit its sphere of operation. Thus if we wish to achieve scientific knowledge, or if we want to understand those objects and events that make up the furniture of our everyday world, then it is the rule in such cases that intuitions be brought under an adequate or corresponding concept. Of course, this is a 'rule' in the constitutive sense that it defines the precondition for possessing such knowledge, and not in the other (regulative) sense of a 'rule' that normally or standardly applies, but which we might just choose to ignore on certain occasions. So what Kant is setting out in the First *Critique* is a theory of knowledge that also involves a strict delimitation of its scope or proper remit.

For there are regions of enquiry where, if we try to achieve such knowledge, then we straight away run into all sorts of problem. If we seek to *understand* the nature of the soul or of divine providence or certain issues in speculative cosmology ('Is the universe finite or infinite?' 'Did time have a beginning?', and so forth), then we strain understanding to a point where it creates insoluble antinomies. Here we possess neither adequate (determinate) concepts nor primordial intuitions of space or time that could possibly serve to ground such knowledge. Kant has a striking metaphor at this point, one of his few really vivid and suggestive metaphors. Imagine a dove that thinks to itself: if only I could soar to a greater altitude where the air is much thinner then my wings would encounter much less resistance and who knows how fast and how high I could climb? But of course, at the limit, those wings would be flapping in a void and hence quite incapable of providing lift or forward motion. What Kant therefore tries to do in the First *Critique* is demonstrate the sorts of illusion that arise when reason (pure or speculative reason) mistakenly proposes to give itself the rule that intuitions must be brought under adequate concepts. Such thinking is perfectly legitimate – indeed, cannot be dispensed with – when it comes to questions of ultimate import for the conduct of our lives in the ethical, political or religious spheres. We can indeed think about God, about the soul, about free will, immortality and other such matters; also – when concerned with the prospects for human moral and political advancement – about ideas of progress, democracy, justice or enlightened social reform. However, these are Ideas of Reason for which there exists no cognitive or factual evidence and which therefore cannot be grounded in the union of concepts with sensuous intuitions. In other words, they involve speculative uses of Reason that go far beyond the limits of cognitive understanding. So for Kant it is a matter of some urgency to establish those limits and thus to draw a line between the spheres of understanding and speculative reason.

In the Second *Critique*, the *Critique of Practical Reason*, Kant (1975) is concerned chiefly with ethical issues and such questions as: how ought we to behave? in accordance with what kinds of guiding maxim or generalized principles of conduct? and how can we apply such universal rules to the various specific situations and complicated issues of choice that we often confront in our everyday lives as moral agents? I shall have more to say about Kantian ethics in relation to the reading of Kant proposed by Lyotard and other post-modernist thinkers. Just now, what I wish to emphasize is the problematic gap that opens up between, on the one hand, those high-level maxims (subject to the ultimate categorical imperative: act always on that maxim such that you could consistently will it to be adopted by everyone in a like situation) and, on the other hand, the detailed practicalities of real-world moral conduct. For it is a problem often noted by Kant's critics – those who reject his universalizing approach to ethical issues – that the maxims do not provide very much useful guidance when one has to choose between different (maybe conflicting) ethical priorities, or where no such rule seems to fit the case. In other words there is a gap between rule and application, universal and particular, moral judgement as derived from abstract pre-scriptions and moral judgement as it is actually brought to bear in cases that are often more complex and difficult than anything allowed for on the strong universalist view. Among Kant's critics in this regard are the commu-nitarian thinkers who urge that we should drop all that high-level talk of rules, maxims or categorical imperatives, and recognize that it is only within certain contexts – cultures, traditions, communal life-forms, language games, shared social practices, and so forth – that moral judgements make any kind of sense (see, for instance, Sandel, 1982; Walzer, 1983; Williams, 1985). Moreover, there is an obvious connection here with Lyotard's call for an end to metanarratives and for a 'post-modern' ethics whose watchword would be: let us multiply language games as far as possible and accept no restriction on the range and variety of first-order, natural, pragmatic narra-tives (Lyotard, 1984).

In Lyotard's case this goes along with a marked shift of emphasis to the Third *Critique*, the *Critique of Judgement*, where Kant (1978) is concerned mainly with issues of aesthetics, though in a sense of that term much broader than its normal present-day usage. For Kant, the aesthetic had to do not only with our response to works of art, our appreciation and evaluation of works of art. It also involved a whole range of issues that included, crucially, the linking-up between sensuous intuitions and concepts, a topic which Kant had first broached in the section entitled 'Transcendental Aesthetic' in the First *Critique* but had left somewhat obscure and under-explained. As we have seen, it is a condition of all understanding that intuitions be 'brought under' adequate concepts in the act of cognitive grasp. But the question remains: by what faculty or power of judgement do we manage to achieve this remarkable though everyday feat? After all, an intui-tion, a sensuous intuition, the phenomenal experience I can have of (say) this table in front of me is a very different thing from my concept of a table. In order to understand what a table is – and perceive this object as a table – I have to bring together my concept of a table and my sensuous intuition of it. But there is a real problem for Kant in negotiating this passage, in explaining just how it is that the two distinct orders of perceptual and conceptual judgement can possibly be bridged or reconciled. This is the point at which *imagination* comes in, and imagination, for Kant in the First *Critique,* is a very obscure thing, a 'blind but indispensable function of the soul, without which we should have no knowledge whatsoever but of which we are scarcely conscious' (Kant, 1964: 112). Kant usually strives for precision in defining his terms, but on this point he becomes notably obscure and even, at times, somewhat shuffling and evasive. Anyway the issue is one that is held over for further, more elaborate treatment in the Third *Critique*. There Kant will take up the question of judgement – aesthetic judgement in the broad sense of that term – in so far as it plays a vital intermediary role in the passage from intuitions to concepts.

As we have seen, there is a similar problem in the Second *Critique* concerning the gap between ethical maxims and imperatives (which aspire to an order of universality remote from everyday experience) and what goes on in particular contexts of ethically motivated conduct and choice. How is it, one may ask, that we are supposed to bridge that seemingly unbridgeable gap? How should we negotiate the Kantian gulf between high-level precepts ('act always on that maxim . . . ', etc.) and the various everyday though complex moral predicaments in which we may find ourselves? Again, this requires an exercise of judgement, of *imaginative* judgement in so far as it cannot be merely a matter of linking up maxims with cases on a one-to-one correspondence principle (see especially O'Neill, 1989). In other words, there is always something more involved than a straightforward matching of precepts with practice, just as there is always something more to the act of bringing intuitions under concepts. In each case that 'something more' has to do with the exercise of judgement and the human capacity to seek out possible ways of deploying our faculties that are not laid down in advance or, so speak, algorithmically derivable from fixed procedures and guidelines.

So there are crucial issues of epistemology and ethics that Kant raises in the first two *Critiques* and which he takes up again for more detailed treatment in the *Critique of Judgement*. As I have said, the Third *Critique* is about aesthetics, but not narrowly, not just about issues concerning art or our appreciation of artworks. It is about judgement in a far more general sense: how is it that we can form judgements of nature, how it is that we achieve a knowledge of natural objects, processes and events, given that these are not known to us directly but always via our various faculties of sensuous intuition, conceptual understanding, and 'imagination' as the synthesizing power that makes all this possible? So the Third *Critique*, where Kant discusses aesthetics, is in fact much wider, more ambitious, a cornerstone of his entire critical philosophy. He is trying to explain how it is that the human mind understands nature, not only under its aesthetic (contemplative) aspect, but also as regards the very possibility of other, scientifically or cognitively oriented modes of knowledge. Then again, Kant resumes certain themes from the Second *Critique*, those having to do with the exercise of practical reason as belonging to a 'suprasensible' realm where it is no longer the rule that intuitions should be brought under adequate concepts. For aesthetic judgements are *indeterminate* (or 'reflective') in the sense that they are always open-ended with respect to the various possible particulars, or items of experience, that may fall within their compass. And conversely, those particulars are not so much in quest of an 'adequate' concept as apt, through their very uniqueness and singularity, to evoke novel modes of judgement that apply to one instance and perhaps to no other.

So aesthetics – in Kant's philosophy – is the place where all sorts of problems are raised and receive not so much a definitive solution as a far-reachingly suggestive and speculative treatment. It is also in the *Critique of Judgement* that his discussion broadens out to encompass aspects of nature – the beautiful and the sublime – that involve some particularly complex orders of aesthetic and reflective response. That is to say, the 'aesthetic' is no longer chiefly defined (as per the First *Critique*) in terms of a relationship – albeit obscure or 'buried in the depths of the soul' – between sensuous intuitions and concepts. Rather, it is conceived in teleological terms, that is to say, as reflecting a certain purposiveness in nature which is intelligible to us in virtue of the kindred teleology that guides our faculties and the relations between them when we respond to nature under its aesthetic (whether beautiful or sublime) aspect. In the case of the beautiful this involves a state of harmonious adjustment between *imagination* and *understanding*, such that we enjoy a 'free play' of the faculties as they seek for some indeterminate (reflective) mode of judgement that would do justice to some given particular. In the case of the sublime, matters are more complex since here it is a question of our coming up against awesome, overwhelming or terrifying kinds of experience or, again, of our trying to entertain ideas (like that of infinity or the mathematical sublime) to which no intuition or concept is remotely adequate. Yet even here there is a positive moment, so to speak, when the mind overcomes its initial state of abjection and acknowledges that there must be something in its own nature – its 'suprasensible' nature – that allows thought to transcend the conditions of perceptual or phenomenal experience. What makes this possible, in the case of the sublime, is a complex interplay between *imagination* and *reason*, such that we attain to an elevated sense of all that lies beyond the sensory domain, including (most importantly for Kant) the dictates of moral conscience. Where the beautiful assures us of a harmonious relationship or interplay between the faculties, as likewise between mind and nature, the sublime takes effect rather by disrupting that harmony, forcing us up against the limits of adequate (sensuous or conceptual) representation. Yet we can still take pleasure in the sublime, albeit a pleasure very different – more complex and ambivalent – than that offered by the beautiful. We can do so, Kant argues, precisely because the sublime points towards a realm transcending the limits of phenomenal or cognitive grasp. Thus nature presents aspects which we can somehow comprehend, although it is very obscure to us, very hard to explain just how we comprehend them.

POST-MODERNISM AND POLITICS

The general point I am making here is that some large issues hang on our interpretation of Kant's doctrine of the faculties. That is to say, it is not just a matter of 'academic' debate, or of mainstream versus post-modernist readings of this or that passage in Kant. Rather, what we make of those passages – and their place within the overall 'architectonic' of Kant's critical philosophy – has a bearing on issues far beyond that specialized domain. Kant was, for his time, a very progressive thinker, a great advocate of progressive social and political values. Of course one needs to qualify this claim in certain respects. After all, Kant was writing at a time (and in a place) when liberal thought could go only so far, when revolutionary views were better expressed under cover of a mildly reformist rhetoric, and when Kant was himself – in his later years – often subject to tight conditions of censorship by church and state. I should also acknowledge – since the point has been made with considerable force by recent scholars – that Kant held some pretty repugnant views on issues of racial, ethnic and gender difference in relation to intellectual powers (see Eze, 1997a, 1997b). Nevertheless, I think that one can draw a distinction – an eminently Kantian distinction, no doubt – between, on the one hand, these expressions of illiberal sentiment and, on the other hand, the social bearing of Kant's critical philosophy. He raises extremely important questions which thereafter became central to the whole tradition of critical-emancipatory thought. He also argues a strong case for the close relationship – indeed one of mutual dependence – between the values of Enlightenment critique and the interests of social, political and humanitarian progress.

I think those values are open to us still, and I think that the current fashionable anti-Enlightenment rhetoric, such as we find in Lyotard, is both ethically disastrous and politically retrograde. But of course it is not enough to put the case in these terms. I am not just saying that I think post-modernism is a bad thing, ethically and politically, but also that it is based on very dubious philosophical arguments. Let me offer some evidence in support of this claim, since otherwise maybe you will think it just as sweeping and facile as the sorts of claim I am rejecting. Epistemologically speaking, post-modernism works out as a deep-laid scepticism about the possibility of knowledge and truth, the possibility of a constructive, co-operative enterprise aimed towards truth at the end of enquiry. This scepticism takes various forms: in Lyotard's case it takes the form of an emphasis on diverse, incommensurable 'language games', that is to say, the argument that there have always been narrative 'differends' in the sense that these issue from conflicting ideologies, disparate projects, rival conceptions of truth, justice, progress, and so forth. Lyotard would say that we are never in a position to judge between them, because if we try to adjudicate the issue and to say one is right and the other wrong, or that both are wrong, or if we impose our own interpretation, we are thereby suppressing the narrative differend and inflicting an injury on one or on both parties. So, for Lyotard, the sole remaining principle of justice, as I have said, is to maximize the range of admissible narratives and strive so far as possible not to adjudicate between them. This is why Lyotard calls himself 'a Kantian of the Third *Critique*', more specifically, an advocate of the Kantian sublime as that which brings us up most sharply against the incommensurability of values, and which thereby imposes a salutary check on our rush to judgement in any given case.

Now, on the face of it, this seems a good liberal prescription. It is obviously good to lend a willing ear to as many as possible of the various narratives (arguments, truth-claims, beliefs etc.) that make up the ongoing cultural dialogue. Just as clearly it is dogmatic and doctrinaire to reject other (from our point of view) false, partial or prejudiced beliefs just because they happen not to fall square with our own way of thinking. So, in a sense, in a very basic sense, there is a good liberal-pluralist principle behind Lyotard's thinking. We should always be tolerant, we should not force our views on other people, and therefore we should be ready to acknowledge that ours is not the only possible viewpoint. All the same there are problems when one tries to follow this programme through to its ultimate post-modernist conclusion. What are we to say, for instance, when confronted with Holocaust deniers who claim either that the Holocaust never happened or that reports of it were greatly exaggerated? Or even when confronted with the 'moderate' version of this argument which says that we should not treat the Holocaust as something uniquely appalling and barbaric because there have been other comparable atrocities past and present? Are we simply to say, with Lyotard, that there is no deciding the issue here since the parties to this particular dispute are applying utterly disparate criteria of truth and historical accountability?

Lyotard comes very close to adopting that line when he writes about the French Holocaust-denier Robert Faurisson (Lyotard, 1988). Thus we may wish to say that Faurisson is lying, that he is suppressing evidence, that he has a deeply repugnant ideological agenda, and that this is his motive for denying that the Holocaust occurred. Nevertheless, Lyotard says, we should be wrong or at least ill-advised to adopt that position in response to Faurisson's claims. For Faurisson is working with different criteria, he is simply not beholden to the historian's usual standards of truth, accuracy, factual warrant, and so forth; nor does he subscribe to anything like the liberal consensus-view of what constitutes a decent, responsible approach to such matters. In other words, there is a radical incommensurability – a full-scale narrative 'differend' – between Faurisson's strong-revisionist claims and the kinds of factual and ethical objection voiced by his various opponents. Again, we may say that Faurisson makes his revisionist case by adopting a wholly inappropriate criterion and then using this to rewrite history in accordance with his own ideological agenda. But if we take this line, Lyotard thinks, then we are falling straight into Faurisson's trap. For he can turn around and accuse us – his high-toned liberal critics – of ignoring or suppressing the narrative 'differend' and thus placing him (Faurisson) in the victim's role.

It seems to me that Lyotard's argument amounts to a wholesale collapse of moral and intellectual nerve. Of course there are different historical narratives, of course historians have different approaches and, very often, widely divergent ideological perspectives. Nevertheless, there is such a thing as historical truth; not Truth with a capital T, not some kind of ultimate, transcendent, all-encompassing Truth, but the sorts of truth that historians find out through patient research, through careful sifting of the evidence, through criticism of source-texts, archival scholarship, and so forth. This debate very often gets skewed because sceptics – post-modernists especially – tend to suppose that anyone who talks about truth must be upholding capital-T truth, a discourse that is repressive, monological, authoritarian, bent upon suppressing the narrative differend. All the same there are standards, principles, validity conditions, ways of treating, interpreting, criticizing, comparing and contrasting the evidence which, if consistently applied, will give the historian a fair claim to be dealing in matters of truth. It is this claim that we have to abandon if we endorse Lyotard's deeply sceptical post-modernist idea that historical 'truth' is indeed nothing more than a product of the various conflicting narratives, language games or 'phrase-genres' that map out the ideological field.

POST-MODERNISM AND HISTORY

Such ideas find support from numerous quarters of present-day 'advanced' thinking in the social and human sciences. Thus, for instance, similar conclusions are drawn by post-modern historiographers such as Hayden White, those who argue – on the basis of notions derived from post-structuralist literary theory – that historical discourse is best viewed as a narrative or rhetorical construct (White, 1978; 1988). Now, of course, these theorists are right up to a point. There is always a narrative dimension to historical writing, at least to any history that does something more than simply list dates and events in a chronicle-like fashion. Once it passes beyond that stage history-writing becomes a narrative: it involves a certain way of plotting or ordering historical events, and that ordering will surely involve a certain interpretive or ideological slant. Moreover, as White observes, there are many features in common between historical and fictive discourse, among them generic conventions (tragedy, comedy, romance, satire) and the famous four master-tropes (metaphor, metonymy, synecdoche, irony) which can be shown to characterize different sorts of historical writing. All these points are well taken and worth consideration by positivist historians, if indeed there are any of the latter still around. However, very often they are pushed much further than this, to the stage where it is claimed that historical truth is *entirely a product* of those various discourses, narratives, modes of rhetorical emplotment, and so forth.

Roland Barthes's essay 'The Discourse of History' was among the first to advance this idea that realism is just a discursive effect, the product of certain culture-specific (mainly nineteenth-century) codes, conventions or narrative devices (Barthes, 1986a; 1986b). It is this line of argument that White picks up and elaborates into a full-scale poetics of historical narrative. But it is not so far from the strain of anti-realism that has emerged as a distinctive trend within present-day analytic (or post-analytic) philosophy. This is the argument – to put it very briefly – that there are not and cannot be 'verification-transcendent' truths, i.e. truths that exist quite apart from our current best knowledge or beliefs, or independently of whether we possess some method or means of finding them out. Here also – in the work of philosophers such as Michael Dummett – there is the notion that history cannot be 'objective' in the sense of involving an object-domain, a realm of actions and events which occurred in the past and are therefore unaffected by whatever we now happen to believe concerning them (Dummett, 1978; also Wright, 1987). Rather, we can make no sense of the idea that there might be truths for which we possessed no evidence, no means of verification, or adequate proof-procedure. In this respect statements concerning the past are on a par with mathematical truth-claims and theories or hypotheses in the physical sciences. For 'truth' we should do better to substitute the notion of 'warranted assertability', since this makes it clear that nothing could count as a *real* entity, an *actual* past event or a *valid* mathematical theorem except in so far as we can bear it out by applying the relevant methods of proof or verification.

In mathematics (where the case looks most plausible) this means rejecting the Platonist view according to which there exist abstract entities – numbers, sets, classes, logical entailment-relations, etc. – that are somehow objectively *there* to be discovered, quite apart from whether we have yet devised (or could ever devise) an adequate decision-procedure. On the contrary, Dummett argues: such items 'exist' solely by virtue of our knowing some rule, some appropriate method of proof for arriving at definite (decidable) results in any given case. Where we possess no such method – as, for instance, with certain speculative theorems in pure mathematics – then the logical Principle of Bivalence fails. That is to say, these theorems are neither true nor false, nor even (as the realist would have it) 'true-or-false' in some ultimate, objective sense that may lie beyond our capacities for deciding the issue. For if the meaning of a sentence, a theorem or a statement is given by its truth-conditions, and if those conditions are themselves fixed by what counts as an adequate proof-procedure, then clearly there is no appeal open to a realm of objective truth-values that would stand quite apart from our current best methods of verification.

Dummett's chief sources for this argument are Wittgenstein's (1958) contextualist doctrine of meaning-as-use and Frege's (1952) dictum that 'sense determines reference'. On this latter view, properly referring expressions are those by which we pick out various items (objects, events, persons, numbers, etc.) in virtue of our knowing just what those expressions mean, their range of senses, semantic attributes, contexts of usage, criteria for correct application, and so forth. Whence Dummett's anti-realist position: that truth-talk is redundant, indeed nonsensical with respect to any item for which we possess no such definite criteria. Now at this point the realist will most likely reply: no, Dummett has got it wrong; if there is one thing we know for sure it is that there are many things we *do not* know for sure, matters whose truth is quite independent of our existing state of knowledge (or ignorance), things that we might perhaps find out in the long run, or again perhaps not, depending on whether they are ultimately knowable to creatures with our particular sorts of cognitive or intellectual aptitude. Of course there is the standard sceptical meta-induction (or 'argument from ignorance') which holds that since we have turned out in the past to be wrong about so many things – scientific truth-claims included – therefore it is a pretty safe bet that we are wrong about most of what we claim to know now. However, the realist will then come back and observe (1) that we are able to *recognize* and *explain* at least some of those past errors; (2) that the sceptic is willy-nilly invoking criteria of truth and falsehood, among them the long-range criterion of progress or truth at the end of enquiry; and (3) that the argument from ignorance can thus be turned around and used to support the realist's case for our knowledge of the growth of knowledge. What it shows is not so much the non-existence of truths beyond our (past or present) best powers of understanding but, on the contrary, the fact that there will always (now and in the future) be matters as to which we can form no judgement but whose truth-value is wholly unaffected thereby. After all, as the realist may further wish to remark, the physical universe – together with its laws of nature – existed long before there were human beings around to observe it and will very likely continue to exist long after those beings have departed.

FACT AND FICTION

Now I do not want to suggest that Dummett's case for anti-realism is just another version of those other (e.g. post-structuralist, post-modernist or 'strong-textualist') doctrines that I have been discussing so far. It is argued with a far greater degree of logical precision and also – especially where truth-claims about the past are concerned – with a much keener sense of the *ethical* dilemmas that arise in this context. (As one who has played a prominent role in campaigns against racial prejudice and violence Dummett is unlikely to treat these matters to the kind of facile paradox-mongering that typifies much post-modernist writing.) My point is, rather, that anti-realist arguments have a currency – and also a range of conceptual resources – well beyond the sphere of present-day fashionable notions in literary or cultural theory. Where Dummett worries (justifiably so) about their extension to issues of historical understanding, no such anxieties seem to afflict the purveyors of current post-modernist wisdom (see, for instance, Jenkins, 1997). Yet it is here that the counter-argument needs stating with maximum clarity and force. For there is a great difference – one that is often blurred in the writing of theorists like Hayden White – between saying that history is narrative and saying that history is fiction. Narrative and fiction are not the same thing, although they are often (of course) aspects or attributes of one and the same text. In the etymological sense 'fiction' means something that is made or constructed. In that sense, yes, history is fictive. But it is *not* fictive in the more familiar and widespread modern sense of being imaginary, having no reference to real-world characters and events, or being *made up* as distinct from constructed out of various sources, documentary records, eyewitness accounts, and so forth. I think that Hayden White and other post-modern historiographers tend to confuse these two things. There are differences between fictive narrative and historical narrative, different constraints in writing history, constraints having to do with matters of causality, agency, chronology, temporality, narrative sequence, a whole range of criteria which distinguish history from fiction.

Of course this is not to deny the existence of what might be called 'post-modern' hybrid or cross-over genres. That is to say, there is a certain kind of historical writing practised by people like Simon Schama, for instance, which exploits fictional techniques such as flashbacks, anticipations, proleptic devices or forms of multiple narrative consciousnesses. When Hayden White reproaches historians for being so 'conservative' and behind the times – when he wonders why they haven't caught up with Joyce and the modernists let alone with post-modern writers such as Barth or Vonnegut or Calvino – then one can see why it is felt as a challenge. Historians like Schama want to accept that challenge and produce something more adventurous than the standard modes of historical discourse: something that mixes in fictive techniques and tries to liven things up. After all, Roland Barthes was making this point many years ago – that historians were still turning out texts ('classic bourgeois-realist' texts) that traded on all the old narrative conventions and might just as well have been written before Proust came along. So you can see why some historians have become very keen – maybe a bit too keen – to cast off this irksome image of themselves as old-fashioned realists ('positivists' is the usual bugbear term) who have not yet learned to play by the new rules of the game.

Nevertheless, even in Schama's work – and I am thinking chiefly of his recent book *Dead Certainties*, whose punning title catches the drift very well – even here there is a marked difference between the passages of well-researched, solid, historical investigation and the other sections which are more inventive, where he is trying to get inside the characters' minds, or sometimes filling in background detail for which there is no evidence (Schama, 1991). And I think it is the case that most readers are quite aware when he crosses the line between history and fiction, or those parts of his narrative that claim factual-historical warrant and those that are making no such claim. On the other hand there are novels – or texts standardly classified as novels – which incorporate large chunks of often quite detailed and well-researched history, 'real-life' characters, socio-documentary material, and so forth. Linda Hutcheon (1989) has coined a useful term for such texts – 'historiographic metafictions' – though they are often lumped together with other sorts of writing under the not so useful term 'post-modernist'. Take, for instance, Kurt Vonnegut's *Slaughter-House Five*, which contains, among other things, a graphic description of the fire-bombing of Dresden, an event that Vonnegut knew quite a bit about, having actually been there at the time and (remarkably) having survived to tell the tale. Other episodes in the novel take place on a planet called Tralfamadore and involve all sorts of surreal or fantastic contrivance such as telepathy, teletransportation and time-warps. In other words, it is an excellent example of the hybrid genre that Hutcheon is referring to. But again we are aware of the cross-over points, the points at which certain generic constraints (those applying to the narrative reconstruction of historical events) give way to other, recognizably fictive or non-truth-evaluable modes of writing. Most readers are quite good at telling the difference, even in cases like *Slaughter-House Five* – or, to take some other well-known examples, Thomas Pynchon's *V* or E.L. Doctorow's *Ragtime* – where novelists have gone out of their way to complicate (if not erase) the boundary-line between fact and fiction.

So we are not, as many post-modernists would have it, now moving into a phase of cultural development where it is no longer possible to make such distinctions, or where 'reality' has given way to what Jean Baudrillard calls the 'precession of the simulacrum', that is to say, the stage at which every-thing becomes an effect of hyperinduced media simulation. (See Baudrillard, 1989; 1990.) Most readers are still capable of distinguishing between fact and fiction, or between historical and fictional narrative discourse, even if some post-modernists appear to have lost that basic ability. One problem is perhaps that they are working with a theory of language and representation which takes Saussurian linguistics (or its own very partial and dogmatic reading of Saussure) as a licence for wholesale pronouncements of the sort: 'everything is constructed in (or by) language', 'there is nothing outside the text', 'narrative realism is a bourgeois illusion', and suchlike (Saussure, 1974). If you start out from that sort of doctrinaire anti-realist stance then most likely you will not have anything very helpful to say when it comes to the more subtle generic distinctions. Some theorists have recognized this problem and have looked elsewhere – for instance, to developments in modal or 'possible-worlds' logic – as a means of explaining just what is involved in the kinds of intuitive adjustment we make when reading various types of texts, whether fictive, historical, mixed-genre, or whatever (Pavel, 1986; Ronen, 1994). Thus it is a matter of epistemic access, of the degree to which such narrative 'worlds' are accessible from (or compatible with) the world that we actually inhabit along with all its objects, events, past history, laws of nature, space–time coordinates, etc. In which case the different nar-rative genres can be ranked on a scale that extends, roughly speaking, from documentary realism at the one end (where any departures from this-world correspondence will most likely be categorized as errors with regard to matters of contingent fact) to fantasy fiction at the other end (where even laws of nature and space–time frameworks may be subject to controlled variation at the author's whim).

This approach seems to me much better – more 'philosophical', if you like, but also more sensitive to important distinctions in narrative theory and historiography – than anything available from post-structuralism or its current post-modernist spin-off doctrines. At any rate there is good reason to reject any argument (such as Baudrillard's) which would treat those distinctions as so many figments of a 'discourse' still nostalgically attached to superannuated notions of truth, reality and critical reason. Terry Eagleton seems much nearer the mark – in his book *The Illusions of Postmodernism* (1996) – when he excoriates the bad faith of intellectuals who raise their own evasion of social and ethical responsibility into a high point of fashionable doctrine.

SUMMARY

- Problems of definition: what is meant by 'modernism' in various contexts (philosophy, literature, music, the visual arts) and in what sense precisely can 'post-modernism' be seen as a reaction against modernist ideas and values?
- 'What is Enlightenment?' Post-modernism as a challenge to the 'philosophic discourse of modernity' or the project of Enlightenment critical thought descending from Kant and nowadays defended by Jürgen Habermas and other (mainly German) philosophers and social theorists.
- The assault on truth. Should we accept the post-modernist argument that 'truth' is a dispensable (indeed undesirable since authoritarian) concept? Or again, that there exist as many versions of truth as there exist different language games, discourses, paradigms, 'first-order natural pragmatic narratives' (Lyotard), etc.? And should we not be worried when post-modern historiographers routinely deny that there is any valid distinction to be drawn between historical (supposedly truth-seeking) and fictive forms of narrative discourse?
- Aesthetics and politics. Post-modernism is here viewed as an 'aestheticization' of ethics, politics and history. This is shown to derive very often from a prevalent post-modernist misreading of Kant, one that lays maximum stress on the Kantian sublime as a highly paradoxical *topos* and hence as a kind of deconstructive lever whereby to problematize his entire critical project. However its proponents – Lyotard among them – appear not to reckon with some of its more intellectually disabling and ethico-politically dubious or retrograde consequences.
- Anti-realism. Post-modernism is just one (albeit extreme) version of the currently widespread movement of retreat from realist positions in epistemology, philosophy of science, ethics, historiography and the sociology of knowledge. By way of counter-argument this chapter puts the

case for a critical realism that holds out against the resultant slide into forms of sceptical and cultural-relativist thinking.

- We should not take post-modernists too seriously when they make these large and unwarranted claims upon the shape and limits of our freedom. On the other hand this need not prevent us from acknowledging much that is of genuine interest and value in the various fields of cultural production – literature especially – where post-modernist ideas (however vaguely defined) have left their imprint.

FURTHER READING

Connor, Steven (1989) *Postmodernist Culture: An Introduction to Theories of the Contemporary*. Oxford: Blackwell. Intelligent, perceptive and independent-minded: sypathetic to many of the writers and theorists under review but resists the more seductive blandishments of post-modern fashion. Raises urbanity to a high point of principle but still manages to provoke and stimulate. Recommended for readers whose main interest is in the literary and cultural-aesthetic aspects of post-modernism.

Docherty, Thomas (ed.) (1993) *Postmodernism: A Reader*. Hemel Hempstead: Harvester-Wheatsheaf. Good collection of essays representing a wide range of interests, viewpoints and critical takes on the so-called 'post-modern condition'. Not exactly even-handed – the advocates far outnumber the critics – but does give a hearing to dissident voices.

Eagleton, Terry (1996) *The Illusions of Postmodernism*. Oxford: Blackwell. Witty, irreverent and (often) hard-hitting survey of post-modernist thought by leading British Marxist literary critic. Required reading (perhaps under plain cover) for students on courses in cultural theory where the options are often 'Post-modernism 1' and 'Post-modernism 2'.

Harvey, David (1989) *The Condition of Postmodernity: An Enquiry into the Origins of Social Change*. Oxford: Blackwell. Excellent on the historical and socio-political dimensions of post-modernity. Informative, detailed and carefully argued: stands in marked contrast to the sweeping pronouncements of other, more fashionable writers. Should be read as an antidote to Baudrillard or in order to gain some grasp of the important issues that are simply suppressed or elided in much post-modernist theorizing.

Jameson, Fredric (1991) *Postmodernism, or, the Cultural Logic of Late Capitalism*. London: Verso. Wide-ranging and immensely well informed; critical of much post-modernist thinking (as might be expected of a writer with Jameson's strong Marxist credentials) though more sympathetic than

Eagleton towards some of its aesthetic (especially architectural) and wider cultural manifestations. Probably the best single-volume survey for those prepared to follow up on Jameson's numerous pointers to further reading in the field.

Lyotard, Jean-François (1984) *The Postmodern Condition: A Report on Knowledge*, trans. Geoff Bennington and Brian Massumi. Manchester: Manchester University Press. The best-known statement of post-modernist ideas about truth, knowledge, language, politics, history, art, and a good many topics besides. Contains an extended polemical postscript attacking Habermas's idea of politics as aimed towards a state of enlightened consensus and urging instead that we should seek to maximize 'dissensus' or the widest range of conflicting views on issues of ethical or political concern.

Norris, Christopher (1994) *The Truth About Postmodernism*. Oxford: Blackwell. Collection of predominantly critical essays devoted to various aspects of post-modernist thought. Includes chapters on Foucault, on revisionist (mostly right-wing) historiography, on the ethical liabilities of cultural relativism, and on the misreadings of Kant current among certain post-modernist thinkers. Heavy going in places (to be honest) but I hope worth reading for those with an interest in the more philosophical aspects of post-modernism.

REFERENCES

Apel, Karl-Otto (1985) *Understanding and Explanation: A Transcendental-Pragmatic Perspective*, trans. Georgia Warnke. Cambridge, MA: M.I.T. Press.

Barthes, Roland (1986a) 'The Discourse of History', in *The Rustle of Language*, trans. Richard Howard. Oxford: Blackwell, pp. 127–40.

Barthes, Roland (1986b) 'The Reality Effect', in *The Rustle of Language*, trans. Richard Howard. Oxford: Blackwell, pp. 141–8.

Baudrillard, Jean (1989) *Selected Writings*, ed. Mark Poster. Cambridge: Polity Press.

Baudrillard, Jean (1990) *Revenge of the Crystal: A Baudrillard Reader*. London: Pluto Press.

Descartes, René (1986) *Meditations on First Philosophy*, trans. J. Cottingham. Cambridge: Cambridge University Press.

Dummett, Michael (1978) *Truth and Other Enigmas*. London: Duckworth.

Eagleton, Terry (1996) *The Illusions of Postmodernism*. Oxford: Blackwell.

Eliot, T.S. (1922) *The Waste Land and Other Poems*. London: Faber.

Eze, Emmanuel Chukwudi (ed.) (1997a) *Race and the Enlightenment: A Reader*. Oxford: Blackwell.

Eze, Emmanuel Chukwudi (ed.) (1997b) *Postcolonial African Philosophy: A Reader*. Oxford: Blackwell.

Frege, Gottlob (1952) 'On Sense and Reference', in Peter Geach and Max Black (eds), *Translations from the Philosophical Writings of Gottlob Frege*. Oxford: Blackwell, pp. 56–78.

Habermas, Jürgen (1972) *Knowledge and Human Interests*, trans. Jeremy Shapiro. London: Heinemann.

Habermas, Jürgen (1984–87) *Theory of Communicative Action*, 2 vols. Boston: Beacon Press.

Habermas, Jürgen (1987) *The Philosophical Discourse of Modernity: Twelve Lectures*, trans. Frederick Lawrence. Cambridge: Polity Press.

Hegel, G.W.F. (1910) *The Phenomenology of Mind*, trans. J.B. Baillie. London: Sonnenschein.

Hegel, G.W.F. (1988) *Phenomenology of Spirit*, trans. Parvis Emad and Kenneth Maly. Bloomington: Indiana University Press.

Hutcheon, Linda (1989) *The Politics of Postmodernism*. London: Routledge.

Jameson, Fredric (1991) *Postmodernism, or, the Cultural Logic of Late Capitalism*. London: Verso.

Jenkins, Keith (ed.) (1997) *The Postmodern History Reader*. London: Routledge.

Kant, Immanuel (1964) *Critique of Pure Reason*, trans. Norman Kemp Smith. London: Macmillan.

Kant, Immanuel (1975) *Critique of Practical Reason*, trans. Lewis White Beck. Indianapolis: Bobbs-Merrill.

Kant, Immanuel (1978) *Critique of Judgement*, trans. J.C. Meredith. Oxford: Oxford University Press.

Lyotard, Jean-François (1984) *The Postmodern Condition: A Report on Knowledge*, trans. Geoff Bennington and Brian Massumi. Manchester: Manchester University Press.

Lyotard, Jean-François (1988) *The Differend: Phrases in Dispute*, trans. Georges van den Abbeele. Manchester: Manchester University Press.

Nicholls, Peter (1995) *Modernisms: A Literary Guide*. London: Macmillan.

O'Neill, Onora (1989) *Constructions of Reason: Explorations of Kant's Practical Philosophy*. Cambridge: Cambridge University Press.

Pavel, Thomas (1986) *Fictional Worlds*. Harvard, MA: Harvard University Press.

Ronen, Ruth A. (1994) *Possible Worlds in Literary Theory*. Cambridge: Cambridge University Press.

Sandel, Michael (1982) *Liberalism and the Limits of Justice*. Cambridge: Cambridge University Press.

Saussure, Ferdinand de (1974) *Course in General Linguistics*. London: Fontana.

Schama, Simon (1991) *Dead Certainties (Unwarranted Speculations)*. Harmondsworth: Penguin/Granta.

Walzer, Michael (1983) *Spheres of Justice*. Oxford: Blackwell.

White, Hayden (1978) *Tropics of Discourse*. Baltimore: Johns Hopkins University Press.

White, Hayden (1988) *The Content of the Form*. Baltimore: Johns Hopkins University Press.

Williams, Bernard (1985) *Ethics and the Limits of Philosophy*. London: Fontana.

Wittgenstein, Ludwig (1958) *Philosophical Investigations*, ed. G.E.M. Anscombe. Oxford: Blackwell.

Wright, Crispin (1987) *Realism, Meaning and Truth*. Oxford: Blackwell.

Chapter 3

Post-feminism

Michèle Barrett

'Post-feminism' is a meretricious category, yet some of the controversies that it signals are interesting ones. At the outset, I want to suggest that the term 'post-feminism' has two major connotations:

1 A popular feeling that a drearily militant feminist politics has been succeeded by a new phenomenon – we can shorthand it as 'girl power' – which puts the femininity back into women's sense of identity and aspiration.
2 Academic developments that have transformed feminist theory through the incorporation of ideas from post-structuralist theory. These ideas cut away so much of the conceptual ground on which feminist theory previously rested, that – to some – they justify the use of the term 'post-feminist'.

It is useful to keep the popular and the academic meanings of post-feminism separate.

GIRL POWER: FEMINISM AND FEMININITY IN POPULAR CULTURE

'Girl power' is much discussed in the media. Girls are doing better at school, girls are sassy, girls are not frightened, girls are confident, girls are even violent. Girls, now, are the beneficiaries of the battles that feminists once fought: they take for granted their equality with boys – even superiority over boys.

Some of the ingredients of this change are spelt out in a feature in the nation's pulse, the *Daily Mail*. This one comes from the 'femail' section of *The Mail on Sunday* (7 June 1998), under the headline 'Clever Girls'. This feature is rather mocking towards fallen Minister of State Harriet Harman – who not only managed to alienate feminists by her policy against single mothers, but also made the old-fashioned mistake of trying to appear dumber than she really is. In the classic study by Mirra Komarovsky (1946), young women admitted to playing dumb in order to attract boys. They lowered their school grades when reporting them to boys, they made deliberate spelling mistakes in their love letters, they pretended to be more stupid than they were – in order not to threaten the boys they were dating. In doing the same sort of thing, Harriet Harman has attracted the scorn of post-feminists as well as the disapproval of feminists.

These post-feminists are into what is called 'grey matter chic'. They want to disprove the theory that clever women must have appalling looks, and that good-lookers are thick. They want to be glamorous, sexually attractive to men and very brainy. The article features a large photograph of Sharon Stone in a low-cut dress, who is presented as the epitome of this trend. *The Mail on Sunday* comments that 'Ms Stone's IQ, a thundering 165, is one of the three things that men admire her for'. The article gives many examples of women whose dual ambition is to both sexy and brainy – models who belong to Mensa, film stars who would prefer to be doing Shakespeare, fashion editors who read philosophy in their spare time.

The Mail on Sunday credits Naomi Wolf, the paradoxically glamorous author of a critical book about *The Beauty Myth* (1990), as well as the egregious character Camille Paglia, for encouraging this trend. In truth, it is a much larger phenomenon, and one where 'post-feminism' sometimes appears under the heading of 'the new feminism'. This is the title of a recent book by Natasha Walter, who aims to rescue a proper feminist concern with equality and power from the unfortunate connotations of political correctness, socialist politics, poor dress sense and worse make-up. Walter goes about this by taking up the case of Mrs Thatcher as an icon for the new feminism – the 'great unsung heroine of British feminism' – who managed to 'normalize female success' (1998: 175). The response to Walter's book was interesting. Although many feminists were critical, some embraced this new philosophy – notably Elaine Showalter (1998) in a prominent review in *The Guardian*. Although Walter's book puts forward some objectives – mainly about economic equality and political power – that feminists of the 1970s political movement would agree with, many of her arguments are framed as a direct attack on the political values and style of that movement. Whether we call it 'post-feminism' or 'the new feminism', there is a readily identifiable current of thought that can be sharply differentiated from the feminism of the earlier period.

This post-feminism is, above all, about reinstating femininity. This is partly, but not exclusively, about heterosexuality. It is more importantly about a feminine presentation of self. Walter, for instance, thinks the lesbianism of 1970s feminism was dreadful, but that glamorous lipstick-lesbianism is fine. Mrs Thatcher's feminine hair-dos are also admired. The package is one in which post-feminism represents the successful combination of traditional feminine good looks with a new exercise of women's power. This is 'girl power' applied to grown women. The corporate executive is stunningly dressed, the financial expert gorgeous. What is desired is both the economic and social success of women in breaking through the glass ceiling and the retention of the classic tropes of femininity.

One interesting cultural representation of this 'post-feminist' woman is to be found in the latest Star Trek series, *Voyager*. Set in the twenty-fourth century, it has at last proved possible to explore in depth a woman in the role of starship captain. The characterization of Captain Kathryn Janeway is fascinating from a 'post-feminist' perspective. Genevieve Bujold parted company with the show after one day's filming, as she lacked 'authority'. She was replaced by a more experienced American television actress, Kate Mulgrew, who reportedly took command of the bridge immediately. Many episodes feature Janeway's extraordinary powers of leadership. Though her crew are in a dire situation (in a distant quadrant of the galaxy, seventy years travel from Earth), they support her loyally. Her leadership is very tough, and the crew have to obey. Her tactical decisions are often courageous to the point of dangerous: she takes very high-risk decisions. That her strategies always succeed is attributable to the fact that as well as being in command of the ship, she is also a distinguished scientist and technical expert. She is often portrayed in situations where violence is the only option – and when this is so, the iconography may involve her being stripped down to a singlet with a menacing phaser rifle in hand. Janeway has to take all the difficult decisions on Voyager, including moral ones about who shall live and who shall die. In the Star Trek universe, there is no one that Janeway is more like than the legendary Captain Kirk – like him, she bends the rules constantly, takes enormous risks, and always wins. In comparison, the other two captains on offer are relatively cautious.

If all this is interesting in terms of gender politics, what is even more surprising is the treatment of Janeway in relation to femininity. It might be thought that the only way this character could function would be as an honorary man – yet this is precisely what she refuses. From day one, Janeway rejects the Starfleet convention of addressing the captain as 'Sir'. Much importance is attached to her long fair hair, which functions to register the insistent combination of captain and woman. For most of three seasons, her hair is up in a businesslike fashion in normal work circumstances, but it comes down in battle and on social occasions. The limited shots of her private self include a classically feminine repertoire of pink peignoirs and frilly frocks. In one episode she is even pictured naked in a bath full of bubbles in the classic mode. The delivery of the part is clearly indebted to a study of Kathryn Hepburn – Janeway raises her eyes, sighs, weeps and comforts in the most typical registers of Hollywood femininity.

The presentation of Janeway is post-feminist in the extreme. The image is that of a woman who has sacrificed not one iota of her femininity in the accomplishment of her job as, effectively, a military strategist and leader. This figure can only be read through an understanding that women's advancement need not be at the expense of compassion, emotional literacy and a very feminine conception of self. This, of course, is easier to do in the imaginative world of the twenty-fourth century. Nevertheless, it is significant that this definition of woman is being elaborated now, in the context of media interest in girl power and post-feminism.

FEMINISM: THE EQUALITY–DIFFERENCE DEBATE

It is worth briefly locating the development of this popular strand of 'post-feminism' in an account of feminist politics. It is, undoubtedly, a reaction to the feminist political movement of the 1970s, now seen as attempting to obliterate the difference between men and women in its serious pursuit of the goals of equality. One way in which this can be thought of is through the older debate between two underlying philosophies of feminism. The first, the 'equality' model, argued that there were no significant differences between men and women – other than those created in a sexist society – and that the task of feminism was to bring about a social and economic order in which that underlying equality was realized. The second model argued, by contrast, that women – on account of their role in reproduction – were different from men and that social arrangements should ensure that they were different rather than unequal.

In some ways, one can read the history of feminism as a long-running debate around these two positions. The implications of the two arguments are very apparent on questions of social policy, and there has been considerable debate about this. One interpretation of the present situation, which Anne Phillips and I discussed in the book *Destabilizing Theory* (Barrett and Phillips, 1992), would be to say that the feminist movement of the 1970s – often referred to as 'second wave' feminism to distinguish it from the early pioneers – was a particularly strong statement of the 'equality' position. The demands of that movement included equality for women in every sphere, giving no quarter to women's particular situation as mothers or in any other way. As Anne Phillips and I suggested, the model was very much a sociological one; the criticisms of that movement, and subsequent theoretical developments, tended to be more attuned to questions of subjectivity and identity – and more sympathetic to the exploration of 'difference'.

'Difference' is a key concept for understanding these shifts over time. The militant mobilization of an awareness of difference did – without exaggeration – bring about the demise of the 1970s feminist movement. This was partly an awareness of difference as it operated in the varying experiences of women from different backgrounds. Racism was the most important of these, with many black women arguing that the feminist movement spoke from a white experience that was taken – illegitimately – to be universal. Differences of social class, age and sexual choice were important too. So differences between women – differences of experience and social location – became seen as more critical. Second, it was argued that the feminist movement's insistence on equality had understated fundamental differences between women and men. Whether understood as biological or psychological in nature, such differences were there and were important. As attention turned to issues of identity, and to the continuing distinct forms of femininity and masculinity in play, the focus on difference was strengthened. Increased attention to these forms of experiential diversity developed at the same time as an interest in the concept of 'difference' in contemporary social theory and philosophy (Barrett, 1987). 'Difference' is a key term in post-structuralist theory (particularly the work of Derrida and Lacan), and it is to this area of theoretical debate that I now want to turn.

POST-STRUCTURALIST THEORY AND POST-FEMINISM

A number of chapters of this book are about something prefixed by the term 'post' – post-modernism, post-Marxism, post-colonialism and so on. That prefix, and that hyphen, can be read with two different emphases: either to mean that we are now decisively *beyond* the substantive noun, or that we have come *from* it. Much of the controversy – of which there is plenty – about the proliferation of the 'post-' terminology comes from this ambiguity. Those who think it is sacriligious to claim that we could ever go beyond feminism find the terminology in itself offensive. Yet it is important to recognize that this new terminology houses a recognition of where we have come from in a particular debate: it is necessary to hold on to *both* inferences.

I want to look briefly at some of the elements that are in play in the wide-ranging theoretical debate that underlies the concept of 'post-feminism'. In sketching these out, it is obvious that some simplification is necessary. Many of the arguments put forward by post-structuralist theorists are implicitly or explicitly critical of the traditional assumptions of social theory, so it is important to be clear what the basic issues at stake are. The most widely acknowledged sources of what are known as post-structuralist ideas are the writings of Derrida, Lacan and Foucault, and these are often regarded as 'difficult' texts to read. These writings, themselves complicated in their implications, have now been reworked by a number of feminist theorists into a set of debates that are yet further removed from conventional social and political wisdom. The category of 'post-feminism' is intended to signal the distance that these theoretical positions take from what was previously understood as the ground rules of feminist understanding. I shall summarize these under the following headings: the self, the social, the political, history, the text, knowledge, and the West.

Post-feminism draws on a reconceptualization of the *self*, subjectivity and identity. It is argued that social theory assumed the existence and validity of the so-called 'Cartesian ego' – the centred, rational, self-aware individual who was able to plan and to act, whose identity was essentially unaltered in the course of their life. This 'centred' self has been displaced by a new understanding of the self, which emphasizes two points. First, that this conception of the self was in practice a rendering of the experience of men: it did not describe the selves of women, or indeed of those of other social groups marginalized in the class and colonial orders of power. Second, this conception of self was too static and too 'essentialist', in its attribution of permanence to the self. It is now argued that identities can change dramatically over the course of a lifetime, that our sense of 'who we are' can alter considerably. In this new model, the self is 'decentred', and understood through a Lacanian lens of 'misrecognition', which emphasizes the unstable nature of the self. A good account of the implications of this approach is given in Jane Flax's book, *Thinking Fragments* (1990). Cindy Sherman's photographs, which conjure up an extraordinary range of images of women – as housewife, as vamp, as homeless and so on – are striking for the fact that they are all self-portraits. They work by drawing our attention to the fact that one person can be made to appear to be so many different people, thus inviting us to see ourselves as a variety of different people.

A second ingredient of post-feminism is a critical reconceptualization of the nature of the *social*. Modernity, far from being a neutral description of industrial societies, is seen as a historical and philosophical category that elevates certain qualities, such as rationalism, at the expense of others. The problem here is that sociology, the academic discipline that attempts to understand modern society, is itself born of this moment and fully signed-up to its values. Zygmunt Bauman has done more than anyone to explain the complicity of sociology in this modern rationalism, and the loss of ethical purchase that this has given rise to (Bauman, 1997). From a feminist point of view, there is the paradox that a theory and politics that aimed to put women's interests first is the product of a more general world-view that was insidiously masculine in its orientation and assumptions. Considerable debate has taken place as to whether feminists are better off criticizing and rearranging modern social theory, or opting for a 'post-modernist' perspective. Susan Hekman's *Gender and Knowledge* (Hekman, 1990) offers a good treatment of this issue, as do Nancy Fraser and Linda Nicholson in their much-reprinted paper 'Social Criticism without

Philosophy: An Encounter between Feminism and Postmodernism' (Fraser and Nicholson, 1990).

The third element of the post-feminist perspective concerns *politics*. Feminism is one of the emancipatory projects that emerged in the modern world. It is a form of egalitarianism that can be compared with the sweeping movements towards democracy, civil rights, anti-slavery and socialism. As such, post-modernist theorists regard it as a 'metanarrative' – a grand story we tell ourselves. This term was made popular through the appropriation of the work of J.F. Lyotard, whose book *The Postmodern Condition* (Lyotard, 1984) has been widely discussed. Post-modern theory can be read as highly critical of the grandiosity of these sweeping emancipatory projects, of which feminism is undoubtedly one. It opts instead for the smaller, more local, more realizable aim. The critique of 'grand narratives' has tuned into the backlash against socialism that has accompanied the fall of the Soviet system and the discrediting of an 'official' version of Marxism. Nevertheless, there is much contention about this when applied to other emancipatory movements such as feminism – are we willing to abandon the great dreams of equality?

Post-structuralist thought offers a different conception of *history* from the one in which such sweeping models are found. Here Foucault's criticisms of 'linear' and teleological approaches to history are relevant. Foucault argued that historiography had been dominated by the attempt to provide a 'total' history, one which tried to reconstitute the overall form and nature of a society, tying everything into an explanatory, causal model. Foucault recommended a different approach: to search for such regularities as might exist in a context of dispersion, to look for the emergence of new phenomena, and to allow for the operation of chance rather than causality (see Barrett, 1991; Rabinow, 1986). Foucault's own histories are subject to much discussion – although they make fascinating reading, they are frequently accused by historians of inaccuracy: that he was simply unable to get his facts right. Neverthless, his understanding of history as about 'how' things happen, rather than a postulate about 'why' they did, has been enormously influential.

Fifth, post-structuralist theory has brought, notably through the work of Jacques Derrida, a reconceptualization of the *text*. It is important to resist the disciplinary squabbles over this – which have literary critics and other textual analysts locked in mortal combat with sociologists and economists and others who think 'social reality' is being given short shrift – and look at this issue more carefully. Derrida challenged the assumption that language is simply a vehicle for the expression of truth, arguing that one cannot summarize or translate a text – that it has its own integrity and existence, and is different from another text. The implication of the Derridan argument is not that nothing exists other than texts, as various expostulating critics claim, but it is more interesting. It is that there is no rigid and impermeable boundary around 'literature' or 'fiction' on the one hand, and our 'knowledge' on the other. All writing is done by means of a text, academic writing included. This can be unsettling, for example in the now well-known studies of the literary devices used by anthropologists and sociologists to make their constructions of reality appear to be descriptions of reality. They use writing strategies to persuade us of the authority of their work (Atkinson, 1990; Barrett, 1998; Clifford and Marcus, 1986). Sociology has found this line of argument particularly troubling – it does not like to think that its classics are literary classics rather than nuggets of pure unadorned truth. What is at stake here is significant. Post-structuralist emphasis on the textual form of theory leads to a 'performative' style of writing. If you like, how something is said is part of what is being said. Post-feminist academic writing certainly shares this orientation towards performativity in the text.

Underlying these debates about the status of the text – and the status of theory – are philosophical disagreements about the nature of *knowledge*, or epistemology. A recent textbook on 'post-feminisms' sees this phenemenon emerging from the meeting of feminism and what are called 'anti-foundationalist' trends of thought. In some ways the notion of an 'anti-foundationalist' position can be said to encapsulate many of the elements I have already sketched out. We cannot assume the stable self, the rational society, the progress of history, the safe separation of fact from fiction – these are all in question. This is not to deny the existence of physical or social reality, it is to problematize our access to understanding it; it is to appreciate that our knowledge is only available through the medium of language as well as thought.

Finally, and drawing together many of these themes, there is the question of the '*Western*' provenance of the modern social theory that academic feminism has been based on. Stuart Hall's widely cited work on 'the West and the Rest' gives the most accessible account of the ways in which modern Western society was not only born in the moment of colonialism but was actually constituted through that colonial encounter (Hall, 1992). The society at the heart of modern feminism is not neutral in regard to colonialism, it is fundamentally created through it. This casts a different light on disagreements between feminists over the issues of race, an argument where many black feminists have accused white feminists of presenting as universal a specifically white political agenda. This, perhaps even more than some of the theoretical developments I have mentioned, gives what might be called 'post-feminism' a political bite. As an exemplar we could look at the work of Gayatri Chakravorty Spivak (translator of Derrida's *Of Grammatology*, Indian citizen, American academic), who uses her ability to move between 'the West and the Rest' to pose troubling questions for complacent Western feminists (Spivak 1993, 1999). Spivak's questions are double trouble for Western feminism as they both challenge their theoretical assumptions from a deconstructive perspective, and challenge their political agendas from an international perspective. Spivak is the productive side of the rather vexed category of post-feminist.

More popular than Spivak, however, is the work of another exemplar of post-feminist theory, Judith Butler. Butler's work has swept to the most extraordinary prominence in a short space of time, and underwrites the fashion for 'queer theory' now *de rigeur* in American cultural and literary studies. Butler takes a shot at the distinction between sex as a biological category and gender as a social category – a distinction on which much feminist sociology was based. Butler argues, in her first major book *Gender Trouble* (1990), that gender is a performance; in the sequel *Bodies that Matter* (1993) she extends the argument to biological sex difference too. The argument is radically deconstructive of our assumptions about biology, claiming that men and women as 'biological' categories are not given but are the product of a 'heterosexual matrix' in which the supposed bedrock of biological difference is reiterated, performed and constructed. Butler's work draws on aspects of Lacanian psychoanalysis and on aspects of Foucault's critique of sexual essentialism, and weaves them into a cultural analysis. It is, perhaps, easy to see why it has proved so popular in a context in which 'queer theory' seeks to transcend the fixity of sexual identity and sexual choice. It is a philosophical position from which performance, play, fluidity and choice can take off.

I want to illustrate this with another character from Star Trek, to highlight the difference between popular post-feminism (power without losing your femininity) and the more rigorous positions current in some academic post-feminism. The Butler position is illustrated not by the decisive yet feminine leadership of Captain Janeway in Star Trek: *Voyager*, but by the figure of Jadzia Dax in Star Trek: *Deep Space Nine*. Jadzia Dax is a symbiotic life form, being a humanoid female who is 'host' to a symbiont – Dax. The symbiont has been implanted in various hosts, over many lifetimes. Some of the hosts have been male, including Jadzia's immediate predecessor, who was known to people who are still alive. Jadzia carries all Dax's memories, including those of all previous hosts. This gives us a human-looking female (an attractive heterosexual woman) with a significant male aspect to her memory and identity, a situation that is played on a great deal. In one much discussed episode ('Rejoined') Jadzia meets the wife of one of Dax's previous hosts – and they fall in love again. This device allows Star Trek to screen a passionate kiss between two women, much against the grain of their usual practice. The figure of Jadzia Dax is the perfect emblem of the 'queer theory' variant of post-feminism – she not only makes choices, she has no unisexual biological foundations to constrain her.

Some may think that this is all going too far, and indeed I do myself. It is, perhaps, one thing to problematize the boundary of the biological and the social, yet it is considerably more rash to obliterate biology altogether. At least, the figure of Jadzia Dax is an imaginative construction in a fictional world not limited by human biology. In so far as some variants of post-feminism are grounded in a rejection of human biology, the jury is still out on whether they are guilty of wishful thinking.

SUMMARY

- Post-feminism has two meanings:
  - a popular sentiment that women can have power without losing their femininity – a response to the perceived lack of femininity in feminism
  - academic thinking that has developed post-structuralist ideas to the extent that its distance from feminist theory as previously understood needs to be marked by a new name.
- Academic post-feminism incorporates a critique of previous assumptions about the self, the social, the political, history, the text, knowledge, and 'the West'.
- Post-feminist work has a productive side, in challenging theoretical assumptions of rational modernity and in challenging the parochial vision of Western feminism.
- The most popular variant of post-feminism in the academy in the USA is 'queer theory', about which reservations may be expressed.

FURTHER READING

Faludi, Susan (1992) *Backlash: The Undeclared War against Women*. London: Vintage. Describes the 'backlash' against the feminist movement of the 1970s.

Moi, Toril (1988) 'Feminism, Postmodernism and Style', *Cultural Critique* (9) Spring. An early discussion of 'Atlantic post-feminism'.

Osborne, Peter (1998) (ed.) *A Critical Sense: Interviews with Intellectuals*. London: Routledge. Contains very useful clear interviews with Judith Butler and Gayatri Chakravorty Spivak.

Barrett, Michèle (1991) *The Politics of Truth: From Marx to Foucault*. Cambridge: Polity. Discusses the general themes of post-structuralism and anti-foundationalism; Chapter 5 relates them more specifically to feminist issues. See also Barrett and Phillips, 1992.

REFERENCES

Atkinson, Paul (1990) *The Ethnographic Imagination: Textual Constructions of Reality*. London: Routledge.
Barrett, Michèle (1987) 'The Concept of Difference'. *Feminist Review*, **26**.

Barrett, Michèle (1991) *The Politics of Truth: From Marx to Foucault.* Cambridge: Polity.

Barrett, Michèle (1998) *Imagination in Theory: Essays on Writing and Culture.* Cambridge: Polity.

Barrett, Michèle and Phillips, Anne (1992) *Destabilizing Theory: Contemporary Feminist Debates.* Cambridge: Polity.

Bauman, Zygmunt (1997) *Postmodernity and Its Discontents.* Cambridge: Polity.

Butler, Judith (1990) *Gender Trouble: Feminism and the Subversion of Identity.* London: Routledge.

Butler, Judith (1993) *Bodies that Matter: On the Discursive Limits of 'Sex'.* London: Routledge.

Clifford, James and Marcus, George E. (eds) (1986) *Writing and Culture: The Poetics and Politics of Ethnography.* Berkeley, CA: University of California Press.

Flax, Jane (1990) *Thinking Fragments: Psychoanalysis, Feminism and Postmodernism in the Contemporary West.* Berkeley, CA: University of California Press.

Fraser, Nancy and Nicholson, Linda (1990) 'Social Criticism without Philosophy: An Encounter between Feminism and Postmodernism', in Nancy Fraser and Linda Nicholson (eds), *Feminism/Postmodernism.* London: Routledge.

Hall, Stuart (1992) 'The West and the Rest', in Hall, Stuart and Gieben, Bram (eds), *Formations of Modernity.* Cambridge: Polity/Open University Press.

Hekman, Susan (1990) *Gender and Knowledge: Elements of a Postmodern Feminism* Cambridge: Polity.

Komarovsky, Mirra (1946) 'Cultural Contradictions and Sex Roles', *American Journal of Sociology*, **52**.

Lyotard, Jean-François (1984) *The Postmodern Condition: A Report on Knowledge.* Minneapolis: University of Minnesota Press.

Rabinow, Paul (ed.) (1986) *The Foucault Reader.* London: Peregrine.

Showalter, Elaine (1998) 'Femme de siecle', *The Guardian*, 15 January.

Spivak, Gayatri Chakravorty (1993) *Outside in the Teaching Machine.* London: Routledge.

Spivak, Gayatri Chakravorty (1999) *Toward a Critique of Post-Colonial Reason.* Cambridge, MA: Harvard University Press.

Walter, Natasha (1998) *The New Feminism.* London: Little, Brown.

Wolf, Naomi (1990) *The Beauty Myth.* London: Chatto and Windus.

Chapter 4

Post-history: living at the end

Krishan Kumar

SITUATING OURSELVES IN TIME

The predicament of social theory today is obvious in the number of 'post' labels and theories around at the end of our century: post-industrialism, post-modernity, post-Fordism, post-tradition, post-history. These suggest a fundamental uncertainty about both our present condition and what the future holds in store. They agree only in the view that things are not what they used to be; that in some crucial sense we are living in a different world from the one we have been accustomed to analysing in the terms inherited from classical social theory. The prefix 'post' points us beyond; but to what is unclear. Hence the radically varying attitudes of hope and pessimism towards the future that we encounter today.

The classical theorists – Marx, Weber, Durkheim – also of course wrote in the midst of a rapidly changing world. But, rightly or wrongly, they felt able to seize with some confidence on the emerging principles of their time, whether class, bureaucracy or the division of labour. This allowed them to make some striking predictions about the future – again the correctness of these is immaterial. It is this confidence that seems to elude us. We seem to feel ourselves suspended in a transitional state where the only certainty is the lack of certainty. We are clear that what we once took for granted – 'modernity', 'history' – are no more, or are at least on the way out. And we can give elaborate accounts of what those things were, and why they do not and cannot persist. We know, in other words, where we are coming from. What our 'post' labels proclaim is our inability to discern the principles of any new emerging order. Hence, again, the popularity of the concept of 'disorder' to describe – or to fail to describe – the world of the coming century.

All theories of the 'post' variety proclaim in their very names a concern with time. Our own times are situated as coming after ('post') certain periods in which particular forms of society or particular ways of thinking predominated. Where the theories differ is in their view of the status of the present period. For some, such as Daniel Bell with his theory of the post-industrial society, or the Marxists who have developed the idea of post-Fordism, the present is clearly transitional towards a new age and a new or radically reorganized society. In that sense, our main problem is that we cannot yet be certain about the precise form the new society will take, although we can suggest some of the principal ingredients that may go into its making (the information technology revolution, new methods of work and organization, a global economy, etc.) (see Kumar, 1995a).

At the other extreme are theories which wish to abolish time altogether. Post-modernists see the present as the moment when we have come to realize that our concepts of time and history are illusory. There is only timeless time. The ancients, and primitive society generally, recognized this with their concepts of immemorial tradition, or a divinely preordained order, or the endlessly recurring cycles of nature. But their understanding was, as it were, 'innocent', unreflecting. We have had to live through the modern period to arrive at a conscious understanding of the meaningless-ness of the flow of historical time. In particular we have had to recognize the deceptive nature of the quintessentially modern sequence, 'past', 'present' and 'future'. Theorists of post-modernity talk freely about the 'pre-post-modern', and make statements such as 'a work [of art] can become modern only if it is first postmodern', and that 'we are all a little Victorian, Modern, and Post-modern, at once' (Kumar, 1995a: 110, 143–44). This insouciant jumbling of times, periods and period-styles is typical of the post-modern attitude to historical time. Essentially post-modernity inhabits a timeless or 'depthless' present, a present in which the 'past' as well as the 'future' are both fictions, material for literary pastiche and playful fantasy (Jameson, 1992: 16–25, 307–11).

There is a third variety of 'post' theory. In this the present is not eternal, as in post-modern theory, nor a transition to a new age, as in much post-industrial theory; instead it marks a definite end, an end to some determinate epoch or some long-term process of evolution or development. In some ver-sions it appears as an end to 'history', conceived as a story with a particular style and significance. In all these accounts what is envisaged is not, as in post-modern theory, an end to time itself, an obliteration or transcendence of time; rather time or history moves into a new key, one in which they have different rhythms and express new possibilities. The end marks a new beginning; but, as with all varieties of 'post' theorizing, what is begun is defined by what it is not, rather than what it is or might be. Theories of the end do not annul the future; but they have a characteristically murky view of it.

Theories of post-industrialism, post-Fordism and even post-modernity can be and often are formulated in the terms of classic social theory, even as they declare the obsolescence of much of the framework and many of the assumptions of such theory. Thus one frequently sees references to Saint-Simon on science and scientists, Marx on capitalism, Weber and Simmel on the city, Tocqueville and Tönnies on community and individuality, Durkheim on religion. Sometimes the references are merely ritual, but in most cases they bear witness to the fact that many contemporary theories still draw their inspiration from classic social theory and seek mainly to discard nineteenth-century or 'modernist' assumptions.

Theories of the end generally hail from a rather different provenance. They tend to be in the tradition of the great philosophies of history – such as those of Joachim of Fiore, Oswald Spengler and Arnold Toynbee – some of which stretch back to biblical times. More immediately they connect up with the writing of 'global history', itself a rediscovery and renewal of the study of the comparative history of civilizations. Much of this springs from the insistently global cast of thought of such theories, a rejection not simply of the nation-state postulate of most modern social theory but also of its ethno-centric, Western, bias. Theories of the end speculate about the fate of humanity as a whole; they acknowledge, as perhaps never before, the interconnection and interdependence of the societies that make up the global system.

THE END OF HISTORY?

Social theory, at least in the West, can almost be said to have begun with theories of the end. In so far as reflection on the biblical story was the ground of large-scale theorizing about the human prospect (Löwith, 1949), the historical pattern laid out in the Old and New Testaments directed all attention to the culminating episode of human history. Whether in the coming of the Jewish Messiah, or the return of the risen Christ to rule with his saints on earth for a thousand years, the biblical account looks forward to the end of human history in the strict sense and the beginning of a new dispensation under God's direct guidance. For the whole of the period since the establishment of Christianity, right up to our own times, apocalyptic and millenarian currents have continued to inspire theories and movements which have been premised on a revolutionary rupture between ordinary, historical time and a new order in which 'time shall be no more' – no more, at least, as it has been ordinarily experienced hitherto (see, e.g., Boyer, 1992). Hegel's philosophy of history, for instance, and the even more influential schema that it inspired in Marxism, are essentially of this kind.

Theories of the end – 'endism' – not surprisingly are alive and well as we approach the end not just of a century but of a millennium. The precise 'millennial' or *fin de siècle* aspect of this can be questioned, though it is difficult not to accept that the customary 'sense of an ending' that Christian societies have attached to the ends of centuries and millennia has had some effect in stimulating these theories (Gould, 1997; Kermode, 1968; 1995). But in any case there are other causes enough to give rise to a heightened expectation of some rupture, some break in the continuity of evolution. There is the worldwide resurgence of nationalism, and of religious fundamentalism, forces which Western societies at least had felt had abated in this century. There is the arrival of an incontrovertibly global economy, propelled by an accelerating revolution in information technology that is transforming societies and cultures and undermining many of the landmarks of national societies. There is a continuing sense of an ecological crisis, compounded now by the fear of new epidemics such as AIDS. Above all there has been the collapse of communism on a world scale, sparking announcements that the world had now entered on a new era of history – or, what might amount to the same thing, that there had been an 'end of history'.

In his comparative study of civilizations, Arnold Toynbee notes a striking feature in their development. As they reach a state of disintegration, in a final rally they throw up a 'universal state', one of whose features is to proclaim that history has come to an end, that civilization has reached such a peak of perfection that there is no need or room for further change. Civilization achieves a kind of stasis. The state or empire is proclaimed to be eternal, its rule the summit of blessings to mankind. Only in retrospect is this seen to be a cruel delusion. At the time citizens of a universal state are blinded by 'the mirage of immortality'. They are prone to regard it, 'not as a night's shelter in the wilderness, but as the Promised Land, the goal of human endeavours.' Such was the case with the Roman, the Byzantine, the Arab, the Ottoman and the Chinese empires (Toynbee, 1963: 7). Elsewhere Toynbee considers the similar case of Western civilization on the eve of its collapse. He puts himself in the place of the middle-class English at the end of the nineteenth century, secure in their industrial and naval supremacy, and in control of a fifth of the world's land mass and a quarter of its population. 'As they saw it, history, for them, was over. And they had every reason to congratulate themselves on the permanent state of felicity which this ending of history had conferred on them.' It took the carnage of the First World War, and the crash of European empires, to destroy this *'fin de siècle* middle-class English hallucination'* (Toynbee, 1948: 17–18).

In the summer of 1989 an American political scientist, Francis Fukuyama, startled the word with the announcement of another 'end of history'. But Fukuyama was a follower of Hegel not Toynbee, that is, he took a view of history as progress. He evoked no prospect of decadence or disintegration. Quite the opposite. Observing the waning of the Cold War, and the decline of socialist and communist ideologies even in those societies formally committed to them, Fukuyama projected a triumphant Western civilization whose principles now held undisputed sway the world over. The contest of ideologies, the substance of 'history' as Hegel understood it, was over. The West had won and history was now at an end.

> What we may be witnessing is not just the end of the Cold War, or the passing of a particular period of postwar history, but the end of history as such: that is, the end point of mankind's ideological evolution and the universalization of Western liberal democracy as the final form of human government (Fukuyama, 1989: 4; see also Fukuyama, 1992: 42).

In the controversy that followed this arresting pronouncement, as well as in the book that he later wrote to substantiate his argument, Fukuyama was at pains to dispel the misrepresentations of his position that were common among those who seem not to have got beyond the title of his original article. He was not saying that there would be no more history in the conventional sense of history as a sequence of *events*. A great deal would continue to happen in the world: efforts to eradicate poverty and inequality, attempts to deal with the gathering ecological crisis, ethnic and national conflicts, perhaps even large-scale war. His point was simply that none of these would involve basic ideological struggles. They would in effect mostly be attempts to realize in practice what the principles of liberal democracy stated as universal ideals. The end of history had strictly to do with the end, as he saw it, of the fundamental opposition of ideologies and world-views that had characterized the history of the world hitherto, and that had achieved a particularly intense and bloody coda in the two hundred years that followed the French Revolution. This was history *à la* Hegel, history understood as the war of differing 'first principles' governing social and political organization. The end of history therefore meant not the end of 'worldly events' but rather that 'there would be no further progress in the development of underlying principles and institutions' (Fukuyama, 1992: xii). This was because 'all of the really big questions' had now been settled. The world had agreed that what the West had accomplished over many centuries of struggle – the establishment of liberal democracy and free markets – was the best possible system for mankind; all that remained – history as 'events' – was for those societies that had not yet reached that goal to strive to arrive there.

THE END OF COMMUNISM AND THE END OF IDEOLOGY

Fukuyama's original article was published at a time – in mid-1989 – when the socialist societies of Eastern Europe were in a state of manifest disintegration but had not yet finally collapsed. But Gorbachev's *glasnost* ('openness') was in full flood, and *perestroika* ('restructuring') was the proclaimed goal from the very top of the Soviet hierarchy. The anti-communist revolutions of 1989 and the break-up of the Soviet Union in 1991 were therefore continuations of a process well in being at the time Fukuyama wrote, and can be regarded as the essential context both of his argument and of its appeal in subsequent years. As Perry Anderson wrote, in one of the few serious scholarly discussions of Fukuyama's thesis, 'what the end of history means, above all, is the end of socialism.'

> The enormous change in the world that gives its central force to Fukuyama's case has been the collapse of the USSR and its *glacis* in Eastern Europe. Without this global turning point, the other parts of his story – restoration of democracy in Latin America, export growth in East Asia, breakdown of apartheid in South Africa – would remain scattered episodes. If the end of history has arrived, it is essentially because the socialist experience is over. Much of the intuitive appeal of Fukuyama's argument comes, indeed, from the sense that we are witnessing across what was once the Soviet bloc a gigantic historical upheaval that for the first time in history seems to bear no new principle within it, but rather to move as in a vast dream where events are already familiar before they happen (Anderson, 1992: 351–2, 358).

It is noticeable that even those who disputed Fukuyama's version of the end of history – especially what they saw as an offensive Western triumphalism – nevertheless thought that 1989–91 marked an end of some fundamental kind, some historic break that went beyond merely the fall of certain regimes. Thus Eric Hobsbawm, while questioning whether the fall of the Soviet Union equals the death of socialism, still observes that

> the end of the Cold War proved to be not the end of an international conflict, but the end of an era; not only for the East, but for the entire world. There are historic moments which may be recognized, even by contemporaries, as marking the end of an age. The years around 1990 clearly were such a secular turning-point (Hobsbawm, 1995: 256; see also 497–99).

But the end of an era in what sense, if not the end of competing ideologies and systems? Like many others on the erstwhile Left, Hobsbawm is at the end forced to admit that the collapse of the Soviet Union throws into doubt not simply other non-Soviet varieties of socialism but even the 'mixed economy' and welfare state of the post-war kind, and indeed 'all the programmatic ideologies born of the Age of Revolution and the nineteenth century' (Hobsbawm, 1995: 565). That he includes in his comprehensive list of casualties the 'utopia' of the pure *laissez-faire* economy, as tried in post-communist Eastern Europe, only heightens the predicament. For while this may pour cold water on Western triumphalism, it leaves us with a world of no ideologies whatsoever. In practice this seems to mean, as Hobsbawm has to concede, that we continue to live in 'a world captured, uprooted and transformed by the titanic economic and techno-scientific process of the development of capitalism' (Hobsbawm, 1995: 584). In other words, capitalism rules, whether or not we accept its ideological legitimation. As so often in the past, the absence of ideologies merely conceals the dominance of one system, which by its very power can substitute itself for ideology in any formal sense.

Hobsbawm's melancholy vision recalls an earlier, more robust, statement of the 'end of ideology', and suggests a correspondence between current 'end of history' theories and earlier versions that made similar claims. Lutz Niethammer has shown that the idea of post-history was first systematically developed by the Comtean positivist philosopher Antoine Augustin Cournot, writing at the time of the French Second Empire. For Cournot post-history marked the end of a transitional period of turbulence and the emergence of a new civilization whose hallmark was 'order with progress'. The new scientific civilization of the West was post-historical because it had overcome fundamental contradictions and conflicts; its remaining problems were mainly technical and administrative. Cournot looked forward to 'a condition where history is reduced to an official gazette recording regulations, statistical data, the accession of heads of state and the appointment of officials, which therefore ceases to be history in the customary sense of the word' (in Niethammer, 1994: 17).

Picking up Cournot's passing reference to the 'beehive' organization of society in post-history, a later generation revived the idea of post-history but replaced its positivistic optimism with a bleak, romantic pessimism. This was the mood characteristic of a group of mainly German and French thinkers – Martin Heidegger, Carl Schmitt, Ernst Jünger, Hendrik de Man, Alexandre Kojève, Bertrand de Jouvenel, Arnold Gehlen – who in the period of the 1930s to the 1960s elaborated a view of contemporary society in which the main feature was an emphasis on mechanical routine and cultural meaninglessness. Cournot had been right in his prediction of a post-historic scientific civilization, but blind or indifferent to its cultural consequences. As Niethammer summarizes the view of this group: 'The picture that looms for theorists of posthistory is of a mortal life lived without any seriousness or struggle, in the regulated boredom of a perpetual reproduction of modernity on a world scale. The problematic of posthistory is not the end of the world but the end of meaning' (Niethammer, 1994: 3).

What is interesting here is not simply the foreshadowing of contemporary theories of post-history – for not just Hobsbawm but Fukuyama and Baudrillard fear the possible boredom and lack of challenge facing the 'last men' in the 'universal homogeneous state' (Fukuyama, 1992: 300–12; Baudrillard, 1994: 109; and cf. Toynbee, 1963: 48). Equally striking is the resonance with the 'end of ideology' theories of the 1950s and 1960s – the theories associated with the writings of Daniel Bell, Seymour Martin Lipset, Edward Shils, Raymond Aron, and others (see, e.g., Lipset, 1981: 524–65). These differed in their optimistic outlook, and in incorporating a Cournot-like positivist confidence in the ability of science and technology to handle all remaining social problems. And they envisaged a convergence of systems, a mutual borrowing of East and West, rather than, as strikes contemporary post-history theorists, the worldwide victory of Western ideology. But they were in fundamental agreement with post-history theorists past and present that, as Arnold Gehlen put it, 'the history of ideas has been suspended', that ideological conflict had been exhausted and that 'humanity has to settle down into the present broad surroundings' (in Niethammer, 1994: 11; see also 146–7).

This correspondence of thought suggests that the singularity of present-day post-history theorists is not so much that they announce the end of ideological conflict as that they claim that one ideology and one system, that of the contemporary West, has achieved unsurpassed – and unsurpassable – dominance. Such a historical consummation was predicted often enough in former times; what is new is the idea that this has actually happened in our own times, at the end of the twentieth century. What warrant might there be for such a belief?

The clash of civilizations?

For Fukuyama the end of communism was the central feature of the end of history. For others it marked the opening of a new chapter of history. Communism was, after all, a Western invention. Marx was a German who settled in England and whose doctrines, based largely on Western European experience, were adopted and adapted by radicals in a variety of countries, several of them non-Western. But communists of all hues had supped at the West's table. The conflict between capitalism and communism – the 'Cold War' – could fairly be taken as a quarrel within the Western family. Liberals could debate with communists because all eventually shared the same modern ideals, derived in the main from the eighteenth-century American and French Revolutions.

Hence the triumph – if such it was – of liberal democracy and capitalism over communism and the command economy could be seen simply as the victory of one modern Western ideology over another. It did not necessarily represent a worldwide victory, a conversion of the entire world to the principles of liberalism, democracy and free markets. For some observers the defeat of communism indeed merely heralded and expressed a much deeper set of fractures in world society. It might reflect a more profound rejection of the West. In a sharp riposte to Fukuyama the American political scientist Samuel Huntington objected strongly to the view that with the fall of communism, Western-style liberal democracy was now the only acceptable path for the world. This argument, he said,

> is rooted in the Cold War perspective that the only alternative to communism is liberal democracy and that the demise of the first produces the universality of the second. Obviously, however, there are many forms of authoritarianism, nationalism, corporatism, and market communism (as in China) that are alive and well in

today's world. More significantly, there are all the religious alternatives that lie outside the world of secular ideologies. In the modern world, religion is a central, perhaps *the* central, force that motivates and mobilizes people. It is sheer hubris to think that because Soviet communism has collapsed, the West has won the world for all time and that Muslims, Chinese, Indians, and others are going to rush to embrace Western liberalism as the only alternative. The Cold War division of humanity is over. The more fundamental divisions of humanity in terms of ethnicity, religions, and civilizations remain and spawn new conflicts (Huntington, 1997: 66–7; see also Huntington, 1993).

For Huntington, Fukuyama has fallen into the typical Western way of thinking of Western civilization as 'universal civilization', and of modern civilization as Western civilization. Western values and institutions are seen as models for the rest of the world to imitate. But 'what is universalism to the West is imperialism to the rest' (Huntington, 1997: 184). Non-Western societies increasingly reject Western notions of democracy, human rights and the 'world community'. They are rediscovering and refurbishing their own indigenous cultures and traditions, especially those founded on the principal world religions. The new 'fault lines' in the world are not economic or political but 'civilizational', and the coming conflicts will reflect a 'clash of civilizations'. The Gulf War and the war in Bosnia have already shown this; Islam is currently the West's greatest antagonist, as it is of other civilizations; but looming up is what will probably be the greatest civilizational conflict of all, that between the West and China (Huntington, 1997: 207–45).

In one aspect, Huntington played Toynbee against Hegel (as well as Fukuyama). Toynbee had argued that civilizations throw up a 'universal state' and announce 'the end of history' just as they are beginning their terminal decline. The universal state gives these civilizations an extended, palsied lease of life, just as Hellenistic civilization lived on not just through the Roman but also the Byzantine and even, bizarrely, the 'Holy Roman' empires. What Fukuyama, following Hegel, sees as the 'universal homogeneous' state thrown up by the West, the state to incorporate all mankind, Huntington reads as the evidence of the West's incipient decline (Huntington, 1997: 301–8; cf. Baudrillard, 1994: 104). Like Rome or China, the end may take a long time to come, but the writing is on the wall.

Huntington evidently does not think that history has come to an end, at least as Hegelians such as Fukuyama see it. One phase of the world order, the Cold War phase, has ended; but a new one is beginning, one in which the word 'disorder' may be more appropriate than order, since what Huntington envisages is a multi-polar, multi-civilizational world in which the interaction of the parts is producing a volatile and highly unpredictable system, quite unlike the relative orderliness of the bipolar world of yesterday (see also Jowitt, 1992).

Nevertheless, this is some sort of an end, and some sort of a new beginning. In that sense Huntington's account chimes in with those many others that, at the end of the century, are announcing a new departure in world history. It also in some ways fits in better with the character of the tradition of thought to which it belongs. Fukuyama and those who think like him see endings without new beginnings. Their accounts are tinged with a certain melancholy at the prospect that there will be nothing new under the sun. All has been seen, all accomplished. 'In the post-historical period there will be neither art nor philosophy, just the perpetual caretaking of the museum of human history' (Fukuyama, 1989: 18; see also Fukuyama 1992: 328–39).

But apocalyptic thought, the ground of all 'end of history' theories, has always joined to its vision of an end the idea of a new beginning (see Kermode, 1995: 258; Kumar, 1995b: 205). Traditionally of course this has been expressed in the tones of the utmost confidence. Apocalyptic thinkers typically look forward to a glowing future, 'a new heaven and a new earth'. But perhaps optimism or pessimism about the future is not the essential thing. What matters is that there will be a future, and that it will be radically different from the present. In that sense Huntington's forebodings are less important than his conviction that something new has happened in the world, and that it will never be the same again. This reflects the true apocalyptic temper.

Jihad v. McWorld

The sense that we are at the beginning of something new is even more marked in those accounts that see the world of the future as riven by diametrically opposed yet interdependent trends. The novelty here is not simply the 'new world disorder', but the spectre of a Manichean struggle taking place between absolutely antithetical principles. We are in the domain simultaneously of both Fukuyama and Huntington. Where Fukuyama sees global consensus, and Huntington a multiplicity of emerging conflicts, based on a multiplicity of civilizational values, these theorists are more struck by what seems a war between global, homogenizing forces and diversifying and discordant local and regional developments. Thus Benjamin Barber (1992; 1996) sees a titanic conflict ahead between 'McWorld' – the global civilization of Western commerce and consumerism – and 'Jihad' – the opposing and fragmenting tendencies of revived religious, ethnic and national passions. In a similar vein, Manuel Castells (1996–98) has painted an elaborate canvas of the emerging age in which the principal feature is a stand-off between the forces of the 'net' – the homogenizing tendencies of the new global 'informational capitalism' – and those of the 'self' – the efforts of ethnic and national communities, subordinate social groups, regions and localities to assert a sense of identity in the face of the forces of the net. In an even more dramatic account Robert Kaplan (1994; 1997) has warned of a 'coming anarchy', a world in which small pockets of 'post-industrial' affluence and security will be besieged by great swathes of poverty, pollution, over-population and ethnic violence. 'We are,' says

Kaplan, 'entering a bifurcated world. Part of the globe is inhabited by Hegel's and Fukuyama's Last Man, healthy, well-fed, and pampered by technology. The other, larger, part is inhabited by Hobbes's First Man, condemned to a life that is poor, nasty, brutish, and short' (Kaplan 1994: 60; see also Brezezinski, 1993; Moynihan, 1993; Tiryakian, 1994: 135).

The common element in these accounts is their duality: homogenization and diversity, globalization and localization, integration and fragmentation, anonymity and identity, order and anarchy, 'local Ayatollah or Coca-Cola' (Regis Debray). Moreover, all thinkers share the view that these dual developments are intimately related, that they feed off each other or are indeed merely two faces of the same phenomenon. Thus Barber warns that we should not think of the forces of 'Jihad' as 'a throwback to premodern times'; they are rather the product of 'cosmopolitan capitalism'. They are in that sense intensely modern, modernity struggling against and contradicting itself.

> Jihad stands not so much in stark opposition as in subtle counterpoint to McWorld and is itself a dialectical response to modernity whose features both reflect and reinforce the modern world's virtues and vices – Jihad *via* McWorld rather than Jihad *versus* McWorld. The forces of Jihad are not only remembered and retrieved by the enemies of McWorld but imagined and contrived by its friends and proponents. Jihad is not only McWorld's adversary, it is its child (Barber, 1996: 157).

This is not the place to adjudicate between these competing visions of the future. One might suspect, as many of these thinkers themselves do, that all are right (and all are wrong) to some extent. They deal, after all, with many of the same trends – the end of the Cold War, the globalization of the economy, the information technology revolution, the rediscovery of place, the resurgence of ethnic, national and religious conflict. Their differences have mainly to do with emphasis and, perhaps, personal temperament.

What unites them at an even more profound level is their concern with time and history. This is a form of theorizing that has revived the tradition of large-scale speculation on historical change. Marxism may be out as a guide to the future, but Marx's concern with the historical development of humanity as a whole seems more appealing than ever before. Hegel, we have seen, is thriving in a number of guises. So too are Toynbee and Spengler, and coming along are revivals of Eric Voegelin and perhaps neglected figures such as Pitirim Sorokin. The work of Fernand Braudel, Paul Kennedy and others has already shown the force and relevance of 'global history'; historical sociology too now has a considerable achievement to its credit, after decades of neglect (for instance Mann, 1986; Skocpol, 1978). What has been lacking, and what seems now to be reviving at the end of our century, is the grand tradition of the philosophy of history.

Fittingly part of that revival is taking the form of a concern with endings and new beginnings. The philosophy of history, at least in the West, has its origins in the apocalyptic and millenarian tradition of Judaeo-Christianity. This was a tradition that always recognized ruptures as well as continuities, novelty as well as the recurrence of past patterns. There was always the danger that thinkers magnified the significance of the changes taking place in their own lifetime. Every age was an age of 'transition' (Kermode, 1995: 255). This allowed later ages to be wise after the event. No doubt some of our thinkers will also suffer the 'condescension of posterity'. But no thinking person at the present time can possibly doubt the momentousness of the changes taking place before our eyes. If, in the event, our thinkers turn out to be wrong in their ultimate assessments, they will be in good company. Certainly no one can doubt the value of such thinking today, nor fail to be impressed by those who have the courage to attempt it.

SUMMARY

- Theories of post-history mark a revival of the philosophy of history in the style of Spengler and Toynbee.
- They are partly connected to the collapse of communism as an ideology.
- In Francis Fukuyama's account, history has culminated in the worldwide triumph of liberal capitalist society.
- Samuel Huntington by contrast sees a 'clash of civilizations' as the principal feature of the future.
- Others such as Benjamin Barber and Manuel Castells foresee a struggle between the homogenizing forces of global capitalism and local and particularistic responses in the form of new nationalist, ethnic and religious movements.
- Whatever their shortcomings, theories of post-history are to be welcomed for their renewed concern with large-scale historical change.

FURTHER READING

Anderson, Perry (1994) *The Ends of History*. London: Verso. A revised and extended version of an earlier essay dealing with Francis Fukuyama's thesis (see 'References'). Considers in addition other *fin de siècle* speculations, such as those of Jacques Derrida.

Baudrillard, Jean (1994) *The Illusion of the End*. Cambridge: Polity. A sparkling and at times outrageous series of reflections on the theme of the end of history and end of the millennium.

Bull, Malcolm (ed.) (1995) *Apocalypse Theory and the Ends of the World*. Oxford: Blackwell. A wide-ranging and accessible collection of essays dealing with apocalyptic, millenarian and utopian thought, past and present.

Burns, Timothy (ed.) (1994) *After History? Francis Fukuyama and his Critics*. New York: Rowman and Littlefield. Thirteen critics debate Fukuyama's argument that democracy and capitalism have triumphed over totalitarianism and socialism. Includes a response by Fukuyama.

Kumar, Krishan (1995) *From Post-Industrial to Post-Modern Society: New Theories of the Contemporary World*. Oxford: Blackwell. In addition to post-industrial, post-Fordist and post-modern theories, considers 'end of history' arguments at the end of the millennium.

Kumar, Krishan and Bann, Stephen (eds) (1993) *Utopias and the Millennium*. London: Reaktion Books. An interdisciplinary collection concerned with utopian and millenarian thought. Includes essays dealing with the 'end of history' and the impact of the changes in Eastern Europe.

Niethammer, Lutz (1994) *Posthistoire: Has History Come to an End*? London: Verso. Considers views of the 'end of history' before Fukuyama and other *fin de siècle* thinkers. Interesting for its treatment of French and German thought on the subject.

REFERENCES

Anderson, Perry (1992) 'The Ends of History', in his *A Zone of Engagement*. London and New York: Verso, pp. 279–375.

Barber, Benjamin R. (1992) 'Jihad vs. McWorld', *Atlantic Monthly*, **269**: 53–63.

Barber, Benjamin R. (1996) *Jihad vs. McWorld*. New York: Ballantine Books.

Baudrillard, Jean (1994) *The Illusion of the End*, trans. Chris Turner. Cambridge: Polity Press.

Boyer, Paul (1992) *When Time Shall Be No More: Prophecy Belief in Modern American Culture*. Cambridge, MA: Harvard University Press.

Brezezinski, Zbigniew (1993) *Out of Control: Global Turmoil on the Eve of the Twenty-First Century*. New York: Scribner.

Bull, Malcolm (ed.) (1995) *Apocalypse Theory and the Ends of the World*. Oxford, and Cambridge, MA: Blackwell.

Castells, Manuel (1996–98) *The Information Age: Economy, Society and Culture*, 3 vols. Vol. I, *The Rise of the Network Society*, Vol. II, *The Power of Identity*, Vol. III, *End of Millennium*. Cambridge, MA. and Oxford: Blackwell.

Fukuyama, Francis (1989) 'The End of History?', *The National Interest*, **16**: 3–18.

Fukuyama, Francis (1992) *The End of History and the Last Man*. Harmondsworth: Penguin Books.

Gould, Stephen Jay (1997) *Questioning the Millennium: A Rationalist's Guide to a Precisely Arbitrary Countdown*. New York: Harmony Books.

Hobsbawm, Eric (1995) *Age of Extremes: The Short Twentieth Century 1914–1991*. London: Abacus.

Huntington, Samuel (1993) 'The Clash of Civilizations?', *Foreign Affairs*, **72**: 22–49.

Huntington, Samuel (1997) *The Clash of Civilizations and the Remaking of World Order*. New York: Touchstone.

Jameson, Fredric (1992) *Postmodernism, or the Cultural Logic of Late Capitalism*. London: Verso.

Jowitt, Ken (1992) *New World Disorder: The Leninist Extinction*. Berkeley, CA: University of California Press.

Kaplan, Robert D. (1994) 'The Coming Anarchy', *Atlantic Monthly*, **273**: 44–76.

Kaplan, Robert D. (1997) *The Ends of the Earth*. London: Macmilllan.

Kermode, Frank (1968) *The Sense of An Ending: Studies in the Theory of Fiction*. London: Oxford University Press.

Kermode, Frank (1995) 'Waiting for the End', in M. Bull (ed.), *Apocalypse Theory and the Ends of the World*. Oxford, and Cambridge, MA, pp. 250–63.

Kumar, Krishan (1995a) *From Post-Industrial to Post-Modern Society: New Theories of the Contemporary World*. Oxford, and Cambridge, MA: Blackwell.

Kumar, Krishan (1995b) 'Apocalypse, Millennium and Utopia Today', in M. Bull (ed.), *Apocalypse Theory and the Ends of the World*. Oxford, and Cambridge, MA, pp. 200–24.

Lipset, S.M. (1981) *Political Man: The Social Bases of Politics*, expanded edn. Baltimore, MD: The Johns Hopkins University Press.

Löwith, Karl (1949) *Meaning in History*. Chicago: University of Chicago Press.

Mann, Michael (1986) *The Sources of Social Power*. Cambridge: Cambridge University Press.

Moynihan, Daniel Patrick (1993) *Pandaemonium: Ethnicity in International Politics*. Oxford: Oxford University Press.

Niethammer, Lutz (1994) *Posthistoire: Has History Come to an End*? trans. Patrick Camiller. London and New York: Verso.

Skocpol, Theda (1978) *States and Social Revolutions*. Cambridge: Cambridge University Press.

Tiryakian, Edward A. (1994) 'The New Worlds and Sociology: An Overview', *International Sociology*, **9**(2): 131–48.

Toynbee, Arnold (1948) *Civilization on Trial*. London: Oxford University Press.

Toynbee, Arnold (1963) *A Study of History*. Vol. 7a, *Universal States*. London: Oxford University Press.

Chapter 5

Post-Marxism

Terrell Carver

By the mid-twentieth century it was something of a truism to say 'we are all Marxists now'. Perhaps the first step in getting from there to the post-Marxism of the present is to explore how this could possibly have been so. To do this I will look from mid-century back towards Marx's own career during the early part of the preceding 100 years, and then I will move from an apparent mid-twentieth century consensus about Marx and Marxism into the fragmentation that characterizes the post-Marxist present. The trajectory from Marx to post-Marxism is not one that proceeds from singularity and simplicity to plurality and complexity. I shall be suggesting that plurality and complexity characterize Marx and his world, as well as ours, and that mid-century singularity and simplicity have become something of an excluded middle.

MID-CENTURY CERTAINTIES

When we were 'all Marxists now', what did this remark signify about 'Marxism'? For Western intellectuals Marx was then a classic thinker and Marxism a political doctrine and social science. While communist political movements may or may not have strayed from this, that was a question separate from the intellectual appropriation of the man and his system undertaken in 'the West'. Indeed the Cold War politics that separated 'the East' from 'the West' ensured that this had to be so. Eastern (i.e. Soviet or Chinese or other partisan) Marxism was not intellectually respected nor respectable in the democratic West, and Western Marxists worked at their subject in ways that were generally within the limits of tolerance that their national security agencies would allow. There were, of course, some spectacular attempts to condemn Marxism and Marx in the West by linking them to the geo-politics and national liberations carried on in their name. The most notable was Karl Popper's *The Open Society and its Enemies* (1966, first published 1945), though Marx and Marxism were by no means the only objects of his ire. My point here is that at mid-century Western intellectuals could tell you what Marxism was, and how Marx made it, with a good deal of scholarly certainty and academic impartiality.

From this mid-century point of view Marxism was by definition a system. While a system of ideas, some of them said to be difficult to grasp and accessible only to the highly attuned, it was also said to embody a 'unity of theory and practice'. It was presumed to be all-encompassing as a science or 'theory' of society, covering history and pre-history, and extending up to the present and predicting the future, or at least sketching a future that could or would be realized. That future was 'communism', the unity of theory and practice implied revolution, and Marxism was therefore a movement as well as an intellectual system. In the West, however, the vicissitudes of 'the movement' were considered, at least in intellectual terms, separable from any political party or actual turn of events. The extent to which Marxism was, or could be, put into practice, became itself a theoretical question, to be discussed and answered in theoretical terms.

The extent to which Marxism reached beyond human society and history to cover 'nature' and 'thought' was keenly debated. For some, Marxism itself was not a science or philosophy as such. Rather Marxism was a system which explained science and philosophy, divided true science from false-hood and bad philosophy from good, and also provided the overall outline of the struggles of human history as well as the inevitable model for their resolution. For others, Marxism was firmly located in the historical and social worlds, and its extension to other realms was not really an issue. Whichever way this was debated, it was clear that Marxism had certain tenets that distinguished it from other systems (or from any inferior, un-systematic thinking), and that these tenets could be stated, utilized and developed in intellectual terms in at least some, if not all, fields of knowledge.

Of course, no one individual nor any one 'school' was in charge of Marxism, and as with all such intellectual currents, participants often seemed to spend more time vituperatively criticizing each other than in employing the eponymous outlook. None the less it was common knowledge what the basic tenets of Marxism were, and it was around those tenets that the most intense debates took place, precisely because there was widespread agreement as to what they were, at a certain level, and why agreement on them was an important thing to achieve. These fundamentals of Marxism included the 'materialist interpretation of history', a distinctive 'dialectical method', and a common point of inspiration, if not an adjudicatory truth, in the 'works of Marx'.

The 'works of Marx' were taken to include the works of his friend, some-time co-author, popularizer and literary executor, Friedrich (or Frederick) Engels, certainly for the major items of theory. Indeed it was hard to separate the two on this, as Engels had introduced, reviewed, expounded and defended words that were indubitably Marx's during the period when Marx was alive and therefore presumably in a position to disagree. While there were variations in which of the two was preferred on which issue, and whether or to what extent the two could be distinguished anyway, there was no doubt that somewhere between the two lay all the texts and ideas required to lay out what Marxism was, initially at least, and therefore to indicate the limits within which any embellishments or additions could be said to be consistent with the founding ideas.

Among these works were a number of particularly notable, even canonical, texts: *The Communist Manifesto* (by Marx and Engels), 'Preface' to *A Contribution to the Critique of Political Economy* (by Marx), *Anti-Dühring* and *Socialism Utopian and Scientific* (both by Engels). For those interested in intellectual subtleties and hence controversial areas there were many other works, perhaps most notably Marx's *Capital* (a three-volume critique of political economy), and Engels's *The Origin of the Family, Private Property and the State*, his *Ludwig Feuerbach and the End of Classical German Philosophy* and also his published manuscripts on the *Dialectics of Nature*. Beyond that there were short, enigmatic works (such as Marx's *Theses on Feuerbach*), polemical works that were still of interest (such as Marx and Engels's manuscripts published as *The German Ideology*), and many works termed 'historical' (though the subjects were sometimes political situations contemporary with the time of writing), such as Marx's *The Eighteenth Brumaire of Louis Bonaparte*, *The Class Struggles in France* and *The Civil War in France*, and Engels's *The Peasant War in Germany* and *Revolution and Counter-Revolution in Germany* (for a time misattributed to Marx). Over and above works of this kind, there were also major personal letters, usually to third parties, detailing the 'outlook' (see for example their *Collected Works*).

Engels was instrumental in claiming for Marx a 'method', and he was certainly cognisant of the fact that this insulated Marx's substantive statements, to a useful extent, from refutation or redundancy. Moreover specifying the method as such was itself an abstruse problem, indeed a major one for those interested in the system. Hence the 'problem of method' was not a defect but a challenge, and there were a set of riddling remarks that had to figure in any account. The first of these concerned the relationship between Marx's method and a similar (but significantly different) method attributed to G.W.F. Hegel. This move, of course, pushed the problem of specifying Marx's method back a stage, deep in the daunting texts of one of the world's most difficult philosophers. Attempts by Engels and Marx to explain this method in relation to Hegel relied on a confusing realm of mixed metaphor.

Engels wrote that in Hegel's dialectic 'the real relation was inverted and stood on its head', while Marx wrote that his method was 'opposite' to Hegel's, because with Hegel 'the dialectic is standing on its head . . . [and] must be turned right side up again'. In so doing Marx promised that he would discover 'the rational kernel in the mystical shell', much as Engels had earlier praised Marx for 'extracting from the Hegelian logic the kernel which comprises Hegel's real discoveries' (quoted and discussed in Carver, 1981: 55).

Although neither writer ever explained these extraordinary metaphors clearly, numerous commentators were more than willing to try, particularly in so far as doing so required them to take a view on matters such as philosophical idealism and materialism, and precisely how Marx's presumed materialism could negate and yet appropriate the achievements that they – along with Marx and Engels themselves – readily attributed to Hegel. Engels ventured a contrasting simplicity with his three laws of dialectics, which were only posthumously published in list form: the law of the transformation of quality into quantity and vice versa; the law of the interpenetration of opposites; and the law of the negation of the negation (Carver, 1983: 130). While seldom repudiated as tenets of Marxism, these abstract formulations excited far less interest than the exegesis required to explicate the biographical and substantive relationships between Marx and Hegel in more extensive terms. At the outer edge of credulity lay the even more formulaic 'thesis–antithesis–synthesis' account of dialectical method, which had been attributed to Hegel by a very minor commentator, and was sometimes reflected on to Marx. For Marxism 'method' was a hugely complex and exciting question, and the answer could never be simple.

The 'materialist interpretation of history' was the most important tenet of all, and more than anything else the distinguishing factor between what could be said to be Marxist and what was necessarily something else. However, it was unclear not just in terms of what it was, but what sort of thing it was. Was it a way of writing history that was intentionally and politically persuasive? Or was it an empirically testable proposition akin to those in science? Was it sufficiently well stated and illustrated by Marx and Engels? Or was it in need of reconstruction and defence? Was it fully and classically stated by Marx in the 'Preface' to *A Contribution to the Critique of Political Economy*? Or was it necessarily supplemented by, yet coincident with, the rather similar remarks in *The Communist Manifesto* or *The German Ideology*?

However these questions were answered, it was obvious where to start, as Marx explained his 'guiding thread' as a view involving social production, and also social relations 'that are indispensable and independent of [the individual] will'. These are 'relations of production which correspond to a definite stage of development of their material productive forces'. The 'sum total,' Marx says, 'of these relations of production constitutes the economic structure of society'. This is 'the real foundation, on which rises a legal and political superstructure'. To that superstructure there 'correspond definite forms of social consciousness'. Summing up, he writes that the 'mode of production of material life conditions the social, political, and intellectual life process in general', as a positive statement. Negatively he remarks that 'it is not the consciousness of men that determines their being, but, on the contrary, their social being that determines their consciousness'. Turning from that static analysis, he moves to a dynamic one, claiming that 'at a certain stage of their development, the material productive forces of society come in conflict with the existing relations of production'. Apparently explaining this, he writes 'or – what is but a legal expression for the same thing – with the property relations within which they have been at work'. Re-employing his base/superstructure distinction, he writes that 'from forms of development of productive forces these relations turn into their fetters [and] then begins an epoch of social revolution', and so 'with the change in the economic foundations the entire immense superstructure is more or less rapidly transformed'. Finally he draws a line between looking at this process 'with the precision of natural science' and the contrasting 'ideological forms' – 'legal, political, religious, aesthetic, or philosophic' – through which 'men become conscious of this conflict and fight it out' (quoted and discussed in Carver, 1982: 22, 41).

It should be apparent from the above paragraph that there is hardly any way of saying what the 'materialist interpretation of history' is without quoting extensively from Marx's notable and presumably definitive statement of it, much as Engels did when he began his career of introducing, explicating and defending this to the world. Crucially what made Marxism 'go' at mid-twentieth century was a reverence for, yet contentious interest in, these defining paragraphs. There were problems of interpretation within the text, and difficulties of interpretation between that text and others by Marx and Engels, that arguably defined what Western Marxism was all about. How could one define or understand the base/superstructure distinction? the forces/relations of production distinction? the ideology/science distinction? the being/consciousness distinction? What was a 'mode of production'? a 'fetter' on 'development'? a 'social revolution'? What exactly did this say about the past? the present? the future? How much determinism was there in 'determines'? What was 'the precision of natural science' within a social science? And how did all this fit with the equally bold but substantially shorter claim in *The Communist Manifesto* that 'all history is the history of class struggles'?

Marxism at mid-twentieth century was not, however, solely an area of debate. Substantively the truism 'we are all Marxists now' argues a claim that economic life is central, if not actually causative or determining, over most collective aspects of life in society and over many of the individual aspects of life from which a collectivity arises. Central to this view is the claim that economic activity has progressed through historical stages (even from pre-historical ones) to capitalist society, a peculiarly productive yet crisis-prone modern form. Corresponding to this economic formation is a political one suited to it, and developing more or less in tandem with it – liberal democracy. Further progress in human civilization is defined as co-incident with the extension and development of these economic forces and political forms. In so far as any reasonable form of social analysis and any workable form of politics had necessarily to focus on 'social issues' in economic terms – as opposed to terms that were purely moral or religious, or racialist or nationalist – then we could all be Marxists now.

So far this formulation is neutral with respect to an evaluation of capitalism and liberal democracy, that is, are they stages on the way to a revolutionary transformation into something necessarily different, even opposite, or are they stages in an evolutionary process of pragmatic change, never negating past achievements? Both sides could be certain that class politics had been important in the nineteenth century. But by the mid-twentieth century Western Marxism had sidelined the view that working-class power, let alone working-class rule, was really a reflection of, and spur to, further economic development in technological and sociological terms. Of course many who called themselves Marxists repudiated as 'revisionist' or non-Marxist any departures from the project of proletarian revolution, and the intellectual framework within which it was said to be inevitable. However, it became more and more difficult for them to sustain the view that other economic theorizations of social life had no basis in argument, or in Marx.

POST-MARXIST FRAGMENTATION

By mid-twentieth century there were already a number of modernized Marxes and heavily modified Marxisms. For those pursuing these lines of thought, the question as to whether they, or their 'orthodox' critics, were the real heirs and rightful guardians of tradition was not particularly important. What was important was the inevitably selective and eclectic business of working out an economic interpretation of social life. Marxist economists, notably Ronald Meek, Ernest Mandel, Joan Robinson, Piero Sraffa and Michio Morishima, tackled 'marginalist' critics who dismissed *Capital* as nonsense, feeling free to rewrite and revise what they took Marx to be saying about the way that capitalism works, and how it is developing globally (see Eatwell, Milgate and Newman 1990). Building on their own critiques of contemporary economics, they have revitalized Marx, and indeed the whole tradition of political economy within which he wrote his critique, as an alternative to the 'mainstream', meeting it to some extent on its own grounds, rather than rejecting it outright as a merely 'ideological' reflection of capitalist society and the interests of its privileged classes.

Mainstream economics and its rigorous and parsimonious methodologies have a life of their own. As game theory and rational choice theory, these ideas were imported into analytical work on social activities that did not themselves involve money, or at least were not conventionally explained as interactions amongst self-interested agents. As these methodologies moved into sociology and political science, and as questions about these methodologies became current in philosophical analysis and in philosophy of social science, so Marx and Marxism became legitimate and interesting targets for updating in this way. In particular a concept that is arguably peculiarly and successfully Marxian – exploitation – began to occupy the attention of theorists interested in models of strategic interaction. They linked these to a claim that convincing explanations of social phenomena must be rooted in presumptions about individuals. What they aimed to expunge from Marx as an outdated methodology was anything to do with the Hegelian dialectic or philosophical holism. Praising Marx for his juxtaposition of labour and capital, they deplored his historical and political speculations. Working from what could be modelled about the contractual exchanges between those who own technical factors of production and those who do not, they claimed to be able to generate exploitation as a social fact in terms that any economist would have to accept. Most famously John Roemer, Jon Elster and Erik Olin Wright have pursued and defended these lines of enquiry (see Carver and Thomas, 1995).

Closely allied to this view are the analytical Marxists, though quite how closely and convincingly this outlook fits together with game theory and rational choice theory is open to debate. The link is said in a positive sense to be 'rigour', and in a negative sense to be the rejection, again, of the Hegelian heritage. Rather than focusing on exploitation in capitalist society by revising Marx's 'economics', analytical Marxists have returned instead to 'the materialist interpretation of history', refining, revising and reconstructing its terms not merely in the light of twentieth-century economic development but in the light of twentieth-century philosophical work, historical investigations and political outturns. G.A. Cohen published what he termed a rigorous reconstruction of the theory of history in Marx and foundational to Marxism, and in subsequent defences of this work itself Cohen's positive outlook on Marx turned into a refutation of the theory altogether. While Cohen's work was avowedly theoretical, though supported with empirical materials, others in these circles took versions of Cohen's work into the field, as it were, to investigate the transition, or non-transition, of various societies from feudalism to capitalism. Arguing that they were building on investigations undertaken by Marx, but utilizing the wealth of materials and insights generated since his time, Robert Brenner and William H. Shaw have pursued these lines of investigation. Adam Przeworski comes close to bridging the interests and methodologies of the rational-choice and analytical schools in his theorizations of class-based party politics in capitalist-market societies (see Mayer, 1994).

As should now be clear there is considerable recognition of, and enthusiasm for, the assumptions and techniques of 'mainstream' or 'capitalist' economics within the fragmentations so far traced. However, one should be wary of leaping from here to the 'New Right' or 'Thatcherism', suggesting that this way of updating Marx is itself coincident with either market-driven deregulation or supply-side management of capitalist economies. Moreover both the 'New Right' and 'Thatcherism' have revealed substantive tenets well away from purely economistic assumptions about maximizing utilities in exchange and much more like moralistic programmes to defend 'family values' or nationalistic ones rooted in 'kith and kin'. Marx and Marxism were always notoriously derided for a refusal to confront ethical issues – Steven Lukes (1985) and R.G. Peffer (1990) contributed notably on this issue – and for an inability to deal convincingly with nationalistic politics (though Erica Benner [1995] has set out to revise this view). None the less if Marx and Marxism were generally said to have gaps in these important areas, they cannot also be criticized for being too closely linked, somehow, with those with substantive views, one way or the other.

Or to put the matter the other way, linking Marx and Marxism persuasively to a religious outlook, like liberation theology, can be done, but it takes a lot of theoretical work to reinterpret both the self-evident atheism in Marx and Marxism with a conception of 'God' and 'redemption' that draws these concepts into a wholly social and conventionally historical frame of reference. Perhaps rather similarly there are Marxist-feminist readings of Engels that explicate his claim that women were the first exploited class, and that the production and reproduction of human life were both equally involved in the outlook on social production and societal evolution developed by himself and Marx, the latter's silences and weaknesses to the contrary (Hartmann, 1981; Hearn, 1987). Linking Marx and Marxism to an economically driven but causally relaxed narrative history, one that prioritized class politics and global capital, was a highly productive and considerably simpler strategy, not least because Marx and Engels had practised it themselves. E.P. Thompson (1963), Eric Hobsbawm (1968) and Perry Anderson (1974) published classics of Marxist historiography at mid-century, as did Raymond Williams (1963) in cultural studies, exploring the political economy of both high art and popular culture within specific relations of production.

POST-MODERN UNCERTAINTIES

At mid-century we could say we were 'all Marxists now' only because disagreements and debates were contained within an assumption that certainty was possible. The post-modern penchant for disturbance, decentring and dissolution unsurprisingly disrupted this. While post-modernists may have blenched at many of the supposedly defining features of Marxism – systematicity, reductionism, privileging – the wide-ranging character of Marxist investigations certainly interested them. Social consciousness in all its forms, every kind of intellectual and cultural life, historical narrative and utopian imaginary – these are things that could be found in profusion in and around the Marxist heritage.

It may seem odd to draw the Frankfurt School and subsequent 'critical theorists' in under this heading, as their tone was hardly one of uncertainty and decentredness, at least until very recently. Rather I am going to emphasize instead their involvement with what might be termed superstructural investigations and explanations, as opposed to the focus on economic foundations that characterizes the fragmentations traced above. Evidently the economic determinism said to be inherent in the base/superstructure model had not worked out as the twentieth century progressed. Technological developments and enhancements of capitalist productivity had not produced crises that issued in revolutionary class politics, or at least not to the extent that they were successful just where they should have been – in the advanced, industrial West. It followed that a strategy, whether a practical one or an explanatory one, that presumed this was due for adjustment. One way of doing this was to broaden the phenomena under serious consideration to include the very 'superstructural' ones that Marx had seemingly dismissed as merely 'ideological'. Perhaps these cultural constructs were more efficacious and interesting in ways that Marx had not taken up, and perhaps intellectual methodologies developed since his time could usefully be added on. Fields of endeavour as apparently remote from economics as aesthetics and its philosophy, and psychoanalysis and its practice, were absorbed into a post-revolutionary outlook that valued insight and understanding, without an apparatus of preconceptions concerning a scientific materialism and an excessively programmatic class politics. Theodor Adorno, Max Horkheimer, Herbert Marcuse and Eric Fromm were notable pioneers in these areas (see Jay, 1973).

In a more engaged and politically focused way Antonio Gramsci pursued a somewhat similar line, laboriously exploring the heritage of ideas and institutions that had, in his view, made the radicalization of the working class so difficult and so apparently unsuccessful. His concepts of hegemony and civil society, and generally open-ended and historical approach to Marxist analysis, did not merely revise Marx as he had been read, but helped to create a new Marx to be found later in familiar and unfamiliar works. In that way the certainties about Marx and Marxism began to unravel further. Once Gramsci was into the mainstream of Western Marxism (which did not really happen until the late 1960s), fragmentation had not simply produced hybrid Marxisms but a number of new Marxes, thus dispelling any idea that 'the man himself' was a reliable guide to what could be known about him for certain (see Martin, 1998).

Perhaps the last notable attempt to reimpose certainty on to Marxism and Marx took place in the structuralist writings of Louis Althusser and his colleague Étienne Balibar. This required drastic surgery on Marx, locating an 'epistemological break' between his Hegelian pre-scientific writings and his post-Hegelian science, in order to make the determinism of the materialist theory of history work by banishing a 'humanistic' conception of the individual subject. What remained were economic structures and ideological state apparatuses, linked in a structure of over-determination rather than mechanical causation. This outlook had an evident attraction in undercutting a liberal individualism that took little notice of class constraint, but had the distinct disadvantage of exhuming positivist notions of science and Engels's infamous 'determination in the last instance'. Post-structuralists had little difficulty in exploding both.

Being somewhat uncertain about economic determinism had a lineage of some respectability well within the Marxist tradition. Being explicitly uncertain about the existence or significance of social class was quite another matter. Following the 'linguistic turn' in philosophy, and post-modern 'constructionist' epistemologies, Ernesto Laclau and Chantal Mouffe (1985) caused consternation by dissolving any notion of the base/superstructure distinction. They did this when they argued that the existence of class interests in society could not be assumed as foundational for and prior to the existence of class as an economic and political phenomenon. In their view class, as with any other social construction of 'identity', was itself discursively formed only as and when people instantiated the activities that define it. Historically it had been very important but philosophically and methodologically it was merely contingent. Rather than duck any normative issues in politics by appealing to 'history' in some developmental and supposedly self-validating guise, Laclau and Mouffe also openly endorsed a 'radical democracy', attempting to decouple democratic institutions on a liberal model from a sometimes disguised or unexamined dependency of liberal thought on the presuppositions of 'economic man'. Calling for an extension of democratic practice throughout society, they linked Marxism to 'new social movements', whose demands for recognition in 'identity politics' had not been wholeheartedly welcomed by either traditional liberals or Marxists. Laclau and Mouffe thus revivified Marx's critique of 'bourgeois democracy' as hypocritical and exclusionary, e.g. to women, sexual, ethnic/racial and other minorities, while dispensing with the certainty that class politics would resolve the difficulties.

Around mid-century philosophy took a 'linguistic turn'. Once the social world is dissolved into language, then linguistic philosophies are all we have. Rather than expressing meanings that are already 'there' in the world, language is said to create meanings, and discursive activities to produce truth. When certainty fragmented, so did power, and Michel Foucault's reconceptualization of power as minutely efficacious, even though dispersed and small-scale, has been taken up within a Marxist framework of concerns. This has resulted in a reconceptualization of the 'economic' as a set of metaphors imbued with the power through which lives are lived, and Marxism as an informative set of tropes that might perhaps be useful in politics.

Guy de Bord's *Society of the Spectacle* (1983) is a parody of Marx's *Theses on Feuerbach* that quotes and parodies Ludwig Feuerbach, the writer Marx praised for bringing a 'heaven' of philosophical critique down to an 'earth' of 'material' interests. De Bord's 'situationist' work suggests that capitalism has entered a phase in which commodified images account for more economic activity than commodified goods, tracing out an apparently unbreakable circle in which corporate interests create needs and desires which constitute the identities of those who must work to consume them. Building on this, the reconceptualization of the modern capitalist economy by Jean Baudrillard (1988) as a circuit of 'signs' (rather than things) and simulacra ('copies without originals') draws playfully on Marx's own terminology and parodies his own style of satirical critique. However, Baudrillard's verbal fireworks concerning the hyper-realities that capitalism now allegedly produces have not convinced many post-Marxists that the more familiarly economic conceptualizations of politics are all that outmoded.

There are also more overtly traditional conceptualizations of these issues, notably Scott Lash and John Urry (1994) and Fredric Jameson (1991), arguing that this kind of theory bears out the view that as the economy changes, so does an ideological superstructure of 'theory'. From their perspective, this is the kind of outlook you get as the world economy moves, unevenly and lurchingly, away from material goods and into services and information. A whirl of 'signs' and a service economy, on their analysis, is rather more characteristic of an image of only a small section of the global economy and hardly characteristic at all of the economic activities and constraints that structure most people's lives. Jacques Derrida (1994) falls somewhere in between these two approaches, reading Marx politically in his texts but excising him as an authorial presence. In his writings Derrida uses the 'textual surface' of tropes and metaphors in Marx to undermine the mechanistic Marxism of which so many were certain at mid-century, and to validate the political promise of change that he sees as a recoverable post-Marxism.

SUMMARY

Rereading Marx in a post-modern way deconstructs the certainty that mid-twentieth-century writers thought was in Marxism because Marx had put it there. Marx himself now looks plural, fragmented, indeterminate and discursively constructed by 'us', his widely differing readers (see for example Carver, 1998). It no longer makes much sense to say 'we are all Marxists now', though I hope I have explained what this once meant. Rather it might make some sense now to say that Marxism has made the economy an inescapably political subject, and that readers make their Marxes in different and unpredictable ways.

- By mid-twentieth century Marxism made the economy, particularly the capitalist one, central to social science and foundational for explanation.
- It was widely assumed with certainty that this represented an intellectual achievement separable in principle from political concerns.
- Since then Marxism as an intellectual outlook has increasingly fragmented into updated and hybrid forms.
- The post-modern perspective removes familiar certainties not just about Marxism and Marx, but about what social activities are, and hence about 'the economy' and 'social class'.
- It is possible to reread Marx productively in this light, as there are certain affinities with post-modernism to be found in his texts that mid-century Marxists were not in a position to see.

FURTHER READING

Benton, Ted (1984) *The Rise and Fall of Structural Marxism: Althusser and his Influence*. London: Macmillan. Overview and evaluation of a major turning point.

Carver, Terrell and Thomas, Paul (eds) (1995) *Rational Choice Marxism*. Basingstoke: Macmillan. Founding articles and major debates in a convenient collection.

Eatwell, John, Milgate, Murray and Newman, Peter (1990) *Marxian Economics*. London: Macmillan. Definitive survey account.

Jay, Martin (1973) *The Dialectical Imagination: A History of the Frankfurt School and Institute for Social Research 1923–1950*. London: Heineman Educational. Challenging history of this intellectual movement.

Lichtheim, George (1968) *Marxism: An Historical and Critical Study*, 2nd edn. London: Routledge and Kegan Paul. Still an excellent survey of lives, ideas, issues.

Martin, James (1998) *Gramsci's Political Analysis: An Introduction*. Basingstoke: Macmillan. Excellent coverage of basic concepts.

Marx, Karl and Engels, Frederick (1975–) *Collected Works*. London: Lawrence and Wishart. Largely complete in approximately fifty volumes. Traditional English translations and many newly translated works. There are also numerous editions of *Selected Works* and shorter collections.

Mayer, Tom (1994) *Analytical Marxism*. Thousand Oaks, CA: Sage. Useful survey of the field.

REFERENCES

Anderson, Perry (1974) *Lineages of the Absolutist State*. London: New Left Books.

Baudrillard, Jean (1988) *Selected Writings*, ed. Mark Poster. Cambridge: Polity.

Benner, Erica (1995) *Really Existing Nationalisms: A Post-Communist View from Marx and Engels*. Oxford: Oxford University Press.

Bord, Guy de (1983) *Society of the Spectacle*. Detroit, MI: Black and Red.

Carver, Terrell (1981) *Engels*. Oxford: Oxford University Press.

Carver, Terrell (1982) *Marx's Social Theory*. Oxford: Oxford University Press.

Carver, Terrell (1983) *Marx and Engels: The Intellectual Relationship*. Brighton: Wheatsheaf.

Carver, Terrell (1998) *The Postmodern Marx*. Manchester: Manchester University Press.

Carver, Terrell and Thomas, Paul (eds) (1995) *Rational Choice Marxism*. Basingstoke: Macmillan.

Derrida, Jacques (1994) *Specters of Marx: The State of the Debt, the Work of Mourning, and the New International*, trans. Peggy Kamuf. London: Routledge.

Eatwell, John, Milgate, Murray and Newman, Peter (1990) *Marxian Economics*. London: Macmillan.

Hartmann, Heidi (1981) *Women and Revolution: A Discussion of the Unhappy Marriage of Marxism and Feminism*, ed. Lydia Sargent. London: Pluto.

Hearn, Jeff (1987) *The Gender of Oppression: Men, Masculinity, and the Critique of Marxism*. Brighton: Wheatsheaf.

Hobsbawm, Eric (1968) *Industry and Empire: An Economic History of Britain since 1750*. Harmondsworth: Penguin.

Jameson, Fredric (1991) *Postmodernism, or the Cultural Logic of Late Capitalism*. London: Verso.

Jay, Martin (1973) *The Dialectical Imagination: A History of the Frankfurt School and Institute for Social Research 1923–1950*. London: Heinemann Educational.

Laclau, Ernesto and Mouffe, Chantal (1985) *Hegemony and Socialist Strategy: Towards a Radical Democratic Politics*, trans. Winston Moore and Paul Cammack. London: Verso.

Lash, Scott and Urry, John (1994) *Economies of Signs and Space*. London: Sage.

Lukes, Steven (1985). *Marxism and Morality*. Oxford: Oxford University Press.

Martin, James (1998) *Gramsci's Political Analysis: An Introduction*. Basingstoke: Macmillan.

Mayer, Tom (1994) *Analytical Marxism*. Thousand Oaks, CA: Sage.

Peffer, R.G. (1990) *Marxism, Morality and Social Justice*. Princeton, NJ: Princeton University Press.

Popper, Karl (1966) *The Open Society and its Enemies, vol. 2: The High Tide of Prophecy: Hegel, Marx and the Aftermath*, rev. edn. London: Routledge and Kegan Paul.

Thompson, E.P. (1963) *The Making of the English Working Class*. London: Gollancz.

Williams, Raymond (1963) *Culture and Society 1780–1950*. Harmondsworth: Penguin.

Chapter 6

Post-colonialism and beyond

Don Robotham

INTRODUCTION

Theories of the post-colonial in the sense in which the term is used today arose in the late 1980s and early 1990s, under the strong (but not exclusive) influence of a group of Indian intellectuals, often working in major universities outside of India (Bhabha, 1994; Chatterjee, 1986; Prakash, 1990, 1995). Unlike many other theoretical constructs, this one therefore has the distinction of not only being elaborated for the developing world but of being largely the theoretical product of developing country intellectuals themselves, albeit largely from a single part of the developing world and usually 'travelling' in the West.

Post-colonial theory sought to capture the peculiar situation of the developing world at this juncture – a period of dramatic political changes in the world order which led to the collapse of many of the 'eternal truths' of social theory and political ideology, especially on the Left. But even more dramatic economic and political changes have continued to take place in the world, since the late 1980s and early 1990s when post-colonialism as a concept gained currency. There is the apparent triumph not simply of capitalism but of a particular version – the Anglo-American model of capitalism. There is the seemingly unending Asian crisis, causing commentators to be even more extreme in their dismissal of an 'Asian Way' than they were in their embrace of it. There is the chronic crisis in Russia and the seeming inability of the economic or political regime to stabilize. There is the British attempt, under the influence of Blair, to find a so-called 'Third Way', beyond Left and Right (Giddens, 1994a). In India itself there is the rise to power of

Hindu nationalism with its notions of what and what is not authentically Indian.

These recent developments (and more will surely follow) make it more difficult than ever to find the firm theoretical ground from which these changes can be understood. Theories of society and concepts which seemed to reign supreme yesterday collapse in the face of new turns in the global marketplace and new political stirrings. The flux is nowhere more complex than in the so-called developing world, by and for whom the concept of the post-colonial originated and where the challenges of poverty, debt, inequality, drugs, corruption, political and social despair make it even more imperative that these forces be clearly understood.

Yet the conceptual apparatus of contemporary social sciences seems woefully unequal to the challenges set by life itself. Whether it be the notions of 'post-coloniality' or the ideas of 'reflexive modernity' or of 'network society' – a persistent feeling of inadequacy prevails. These bodies of ideas do not seem to be able to grasp the rapidly changing realities of the contemporary world nor to convincingly offer a guide to policies which hold any hope of adequately addressing some of the more glaring human and social problems of today. As will be argued below, our conceptual apparatus too seems to have fallen victim to the powerful and unpredictable forces of social change which are abroad in the world and which loosely, notwithstanding the cliché, are captured by the term 'globalization'.

Nevertheless, even if it has been overtaken by events, the concept 'post-colonial' is an important one since to some extent and at one time, it captured some of the central dilemmas which the countries of the developing world faced. This chapter therefore sets out to elucidate this concept by way of a critique in the hope that by so doing one may get a clearer sense of what indeed is the condition of the developing world today and the difficulties involved in comprehending this condition theoretically.

THE HISTORY

In analysing any theory it is useful to attempt to locate it in the period in which it arose, without implying that the concept 'reflects' the period. From this point of view it may be useful to divide the recent history of the developing world into three phases: the period of decolonization which is the period following the gaining of political independence; the post-colonial period proper, which broadly speaking I define as referring to that later period after decolonization in which disillusionment set in with the failure to achieve the promises of the nationalist movements for independence; and, finally, the present period of globalization.

This post-colonial period proper, as defined above, reached a climax in the late 1980s and early 1990s with the rise of the Asian Tigers, the consequent differentiation of the developing world into a number of levels of development; and the collapse of socialism and, with this, the collapse of the notion that there were alternative (socialist) paths to economic development which the developing countries could take. On the other hand, the present period (globalization) is characterized, at the international level, by the crisis of the Asian development model and the triumph of American capitalism. At the domestic level it is characterized by the prevalence of the export-led development model and a more or less neo-liberal macroeconomic policy framework. The most recent example of the triumph of this approach is Brazil under the leadership of Fernando Henrique Cardoso. This government has strengthened the role of market relations internally and implemented one of the largest privatization programmes in the world. It has emphasized the opening up of the country to foreign investment and the maintenance of the convertibility of the local currency and low levels of domestic inflation.

These developments have led to the reinvigoration of orthodox modernization theory. This approach generally held that there was one best way to modernity and that all societies which sought to modernize would have to converge on this single rationalistic market model. However, it is sometimes forgotten that older modernization theory was also quite differentiated. For example, Max Weber – frequently regarded as an important founding father – explicitly rejected the idea that modernization culminated in democracy and repeatedly insisted that there was no necessary relationship between modernization and liberal democracy (Mommsen, 1989: 36).

As with all attempts at periodization, objections may be raised to this one. A substantive concern is the one articulated by Ahmad in which he criticizes the concept of post-colonialism for attempting to include countries which never had a colonial past in the sense of Africa, India and the Caribbean (Ahmad, 1995). How, for example, does Latin America, with its nineteenth-century independence experience, fit into this scheme (Klor de Alva, 1995)? For that matter, how do South Korea and Taiwan fit, with their very different histories of colonialism and conquest? What of Turkey, Iran and the Middle East? It is clear that the periods suggested above, as indeed is the case with the entire concept of post-colonialism, derive from the specific experience of countries that formed part of the old colonial empires of England, France and The Netherlands. Despite this weakness the terms presented above may stand as a useful way in which to understand the overall character of each period, even for countries with a radically different historical background and unique specifics.

DECOLONIZATION AND POST-COLONIALISM

The term post-colonial first gained prominence in the literature in connection with analyses of the role of the state in developing countries during the period of decolonization – the first period. Here the work of Hamza Alavi on Pakistan and Bangladesh was particularly important as generally were analyses of the role of the state in Southeast Asia and Africa (Alavi, 1972; Gough and Sharma, 1973; Saul, 1979). This was during a period when revolutionary social changes in the developing world seemed possible and ideas about a socialist and/or 'non-capitalist' path of development were hotly debated.

What was at issue in these debates was the class character of the leadership of the state in developing countries at that time. It was this class character with its attendant set of class interests which was held to be the explanation of the economic and political directions which these states did or did not pursue (or were or were not capable of pursuing) and the presence or absence of a revolutionary potential in these states. These debates proceeded in a more or less neo-Marxist theoretical framework (Marxism-Leninism, Trotskyism, Maoism, dependency or world systems theory) and were a continuation of much older debates from the time of the Russian Revolution as to how socialism could be built in societies with a low level of industrialization and a weak working class and socialist movement.

In this world before the Asian Tigers had emerged, it was regarded as axiomatic on the Left that no society could develop by taking a capitalist path in a world divided between imperialism and 'real existing socialism' (the Soviet Union and the other countries of the then existing socialist system). Development – let alone development which transformed the economy and improved the standard of living of the people – necessitated the taking of a socialist, or at the minimum, a non-capitalist road. The critical question thus became: how could societies dominated by peasantries or with very weak industrial proletariats and no bourgeoisie of any substance, take such a path?

Equally, where this process was stagnating, with the growth of corrupt 'over-developed' states such as Ghana in the late and post-Nkrumah years, this was clearly yet another expression of post-colonialism. This state, with its dubious class basis, subject as it was to the machinations and narrow self-centredness of the *petite bourgeoisie* necessarily retarded social development. Clearly these debates, now seemingly so arcane, were closely related to some of the most fundamental issues of the day, such as Maoism, the role of the peasantry, the Cultural Revolution and, it has to be said, the massacres of Pol Pot.

The conclusion was drawn by some that a political vanguard could overcome these deeply rooted difficulties and 'speed up' social and economic development if it was ruthless enough (Castells, 1998: 65). The idea also gained ground in this group that this ruthlessness was justified by a 'higher historical morality' – that is by the ends which it purported to be seeking. Hence the fanaticism of Mao Tse-Tung in the Chinese Cultural Revolution and of Pol Pot in Cambodia in embarking on the 'social cleansing' of the professional intelligentsia who were perceived as corrupting and inhibiting the process of social development. This led to the death of millions of people in both countries.

87

Against the concepts of modernization theory, which prevailed in the immediate period after constitutional independence, neo-Marxist approaches posed the more radical agenda of a state-led process of development. In place of the gradualist rationality proposed by the Right it proffered a revolutionary rationality of the Left. Culturally speaking, these two opposing theories conceived of the process of modernity in not too dissimilar ways. The issue was one of overcoming cultural backwardness and institutionalizing the universalizing practices of rationalistic modernity. In general, the superiority of one or the other paradigms of modernity was not in serious debate. What was at stake was which social classes would exercise this rationality and whose economic, social and political interests would prevail. Indeed, Marxism and revolutionary socialism forcefully rejected any tendency to deny its Western roots and claimed that it, not modernization theory, was the true standard-bearer of a world historical universalistic rationality.

In fact the basic claim of Marxism was that capitalism, which, in a previous era, had been the vehicle for rationality against feudal backwardness, was today constrained from being true even to the limited rationality which it once embodied by narrow class interests and the need to contain the struggles of the proletariat. Only socialism, freed of any narrow sectional interests, would have no interest in restricting rationality as well as the need to apply rationality to its fullest, purest extent. Cuba under Fidel Castro – in contrast to the other developing societies in Africa and Asia – with its uncompromising abolition of private property in the means of production, its rapid development of high-quality public education and an excellent health care system – was viewed by many as the very model of the consistent application of socialist rationality.

POST-COLONIALISM PROPER

The basis for the entire debate about post-colonialism was the growing sense that the nationalist movements were in crisis and chronically failing to live up to the expectations of the people, especially in the delivery of social and economic improvements. Thus the *angst* which is unique to this post-colonial phase proper was a result not simply of the collapse of socialism at the global level. In fact it had deep domestic roots in the internal decay of the social forces which led the nationalist movements, and in a number of cases this decay preceded the collapse of socialism by several years. This decline into corruption was, for example, apparent in Ghana as early as 1965 and in India certainly by the late 1970s.

Another critical element was the rise of the newly industrializing countries of Asia, which were coming to prominence precisely at the time when the failures of the nationalist movements were intensifying. As the

successes of these countries in industrializing and modernizing their economies while reducing social inequalities became clear, even more serious
doubts began to arise about the character and possibilities of the post-
colonial national movements. But the third and decisive factor was the collapse of the Soviet Union and the socialist countries of Eastern Europe,
climaxing in the failed *coup* against Gorbachev in 1991. Given the extent to
which development theory had become neo-Marxist, this collapse necessarily created a profound crisis for political, social and cultural theory,
whether in the developed or developing worlds. It was in the context of the
crisis created by these three factors – local and global – that the new concepts
of post-colonialism and post-coloniality emerged.

In this connection, the work of Chatterjee is important because it constituted a kind of transition from the post-colonialism of the decolonization
period, to the post-colonialism of the late 1980s and early 1990s – post-
colonialism proper. Chatterjee's work *Nationalist Thought and the Colonial
World* described itself as 'a study of the ideological history of the
postcolonial state' (Chatterjee, 1986: 49). It focused primarily on the familiar
issue of the class character of the Indian post-colonial state, much in the
spirit of the discussions initiated by Alavi. He discussed at length the character of the classes which constituted the Indian nationalist movement, focusing in particular on the contradictions in the relationship between the élite
groups (represented by Nehru), who eventually came to control the state,
and the peasantry whose natural leader was Gandhi.

He defended the need for such a state to have adopted a reformist strategy
because 'a bourgeoisie aspiring for hegemony in a new national political
order cannot hope to launch a "war of movement" (or "manoeuvre") in the
traditional sense, i.e. a frontal assault on the State' (Chatterjee, 1986: 45). But
he identified the essential failure of the Indian post-colonial state as the
failure 'to fully appropriate the life of the nation to its own' (Chatterjee, 1986:
162). In effect, Chatterjee argued, the post-colonial state became co-opted by
capital – 'striving to keep the contradictions and the people in perpetual
suspension' – and thereby failed to pursue the interests of the peasant
masses who supported it, to their final conclusion. It was not Indian enough.

But what makes Chatterjee's work transitional is that he foreshadowed in
this work what later became the central argument of the post-colonial
school, for he went on to identify the failure of the nationalist movement in
India as essentially an *ideological* failure. He, in turn, attributed this ideological failure to their adherence to a rationalistic discourse which, he claimed,
alienated them from the discourse of the masses of people and locked them
into the concepts of an alien Western culture. This was unlike Gandhi who
remained resolutely of the masses and instinctively saw and thought
through the eyes and mind of the peasantry.

This Western scientific rationality, he argued, was inextricably joined to
capital and 'nowhere in the world had nationalism qua nationalism
challenged the legitimacy of the marriage between Reason and capital'

89

(Chatterjee, 1986: 168). Thus the issue was posed not as a matter of over-coming the limited (bourgeois?) rationality of Indian nationalism with a rationalism of the masses drawn from 'the life of the nation'. This became impossible because 'the life of the nation' (Indian village culture) was pre-sented as fundamentally non-rational – inherently impervious to rationality. The issue for the committed intellectual thus became that of the 'epistemic privilege' enjoyed by rationalism as a whole – the unquestioned assumption of the nationalist intellectuals themselves that the ideology of the national movement had to be based on rationalistic principles rather than on the indigenous outlooks of village India. The root problem for those wishing to renew the nationalist movement therefore was no longer a matter of the necessity to critique rationality but of the necessity to abandon it, *tout court*.

It is this line of reasoning (not pursued at this point by Chatterjee) – that the nationalist movement in the developing world was failing due to a fundamental epistemological defect in its ideology – that became the central argument of post-colonialism in its second phase. The argument went fur-ther to explain that what this defect consisted of was the adherence by nationalism to the rationalistic outlook, methodologies and teleologies of the Western Enlightenment tradition. The key to renewing the nationalist move-ment in this period, therefore, was to renew nationalist ideology. And the only way to renew nationalist ideology, the argument continued, was by escaping altogether from the iron cage of rationalistic thinking, whether this be ideologies of the Left (Marxism) or of the Right (modernization theory) and to immerse oneself in indigenous outlooks.

In Asia, it was perhaps in India that this process of the dissolution of the ideals and policies of the traditional nationalist party – the Congress Party – reached its peak. And it was also among Indian intellectuals in this period that the term post-colonial in its new meaning was most elaborated and gained currency. Here the writings of Spivak and Bhabha and the Subaltern Group have been critical but the works of Prakash have also been influential (Bhabha, 1994; Dirlik, 1994; Guha, 1989; Prakash, 1990, 1995; Spivak, 1993).

In this new usage of the term 'post-colonial' the 'post' no longer simply means 'after', as it did in the writings of Alavi or the early Chatterjee. Here the meaning is more one of 'post' in the sense of 'beyond'. And the idea of this second, more post-modern, notion of being beyond colonialism is not at all that we are in a state temporally after colonialism. In fact, in a certain sense the opposite point was being made. This was a philosophical 'beyond', not a temporal one.

The propositions now put forward were epistemological not sociological ones. Indeed, according to this view, the developing countries were seeking to do the impossible – to overcome colonialism by embracing an even more profound 'Westernism'. They were forever trapped within the thought pat-terns of the West, because the very concepts used by the decolonizing nationalist movement to oppose the West – nationhood, democracy, citizen-ship, revolution, socialism – were concepts of the West and were, in Spivak's well-known phrases, 'coded within the legacy of imperialism', and with 'no historically adequate referent' in the very developing societies themselves (Spivak, 1993: 281). Ironically, at that very moment when the nationalist or revolutionary from the developing world thought he was at his most radical was precisely the moment when he was being most Western!

The entire nationalist project, the very notion itself of a nation, of Western origin, framed within the intellectual narratives of the West, derived its legitimacy from this narrative and was only superficially grafted unto the societies and cultures of the developing world. Hence the nationalism of the developing world was necessarily false, grounded in another culture and, for that very reason, doomed to issue forth in limited and distorted forms. The intellectual in the developing world, therefore, continued to operate within the confines of Western traditions – the very traditions that had colonized him or her. All, whether of the Left or Right, were in this philosophical sense 'travellers' in the West, unless, of course, one wished to fish in the murky waters of chauvinistic fundamentalism.

This criticism by such intellectuals of the West therefore was necessarily a critique *from within*, conducted necessarily from a posture of a 'deconstructive philosophical position' rather than radically from without, for there was no 'without' in that sense, as some intellectuals hitherto had imagined (Spivak, 1993). Ultimately it was a self-criticism, albeit made by intellectuals who had been 'thrown' into the West and were *in*, but not *of* it. This 'hybridity', as Bhabha described it, and the inability to escape Westernization even at the moment of deepest critique lay at the heart of the post-colonial dilemma.

Thus was the existential dilemma of this second post-colonialism constituted. In this later post-colonial period, both colonialism and anti-colonialism were declared to be equally deceptive narratives of epistemic power, alienating and ensnaring shibboleths designed by various élites to entrap the unwary. In such a scenario, post-coloniality was not a state of affairs such as may have been designated by a term such as post-colonialism. Rather it represented the superseding of all such 'states of affairs' by an 'epistemic' reality.

The term post-colonial now took on a meaning different from that which it had in an earlier period, although one can see the continuities with Chatterjee's earlier writings. The emphasis now was on a situation which was full of shattered illusions, on contradictions which seemed incapable of resolution and which led to despair. It referred not just to features of the state as in the earlier formulation but to a condition afflicting society as a whole. At issue now were not notions of classes mobilizing around their class interests to pursue certain rationalistic political and economic goals. Rather we were now faced with an existential state in which there was little room for rational political action.

Neither the rationality of modernization theory nor the rationality of class struggle had relevance any more. These societies seem unable to achieve much on either the capitalist or the socialist road. It was this entire atmosphere of the overwhelming internal decay of a historic movement which is captured so powerfully in the novels of Salman Rushdie, especially in the merciless exposures of 'progressive India' in *Midnight's Children* (Rushdie, 1981) and *The Moor's Last Sigh* (Rushdie, 1995).

The writers of this school sensed the shallowness of the slogans of the religious Right, although some of the arguments of the Hindu nationalists around 'inauthenticity' necessarily resonated (Ahmad, 1995). At the same time they rejected the ideological concepts derived from Marxism because they perceived them correctly as deeply rooted in Western history and culture. They were not as confident as Ahmad in asserting that 'the historically adequate referent for Indian nationhood exists in India in the shape of the history of the national movement itself' (Ahmad, 1995: 4). They regarded such a view as perhaps typical of the uncritical slogans of the Third World Left which often bear little relationship to the unpleasant realities of life in the developing world. They would perhaps argue that as long as one adheres to such views then the failures of the nationalist movement in the postcolonial period were incomprehensible and the possibility of a genuine renewal an unlikely prospect.

Yet this philosophical post-colonialism could only attempt to resolve the dilemma in which it had placed itself by breaking out of the framework of Western rationalism altogether. Logically, it had little alternative but to adopt the Nietzschean stance of what I have elsewhere called 'extreme postmodernism' and to seek for a newer, 'higher' mode of comprehension, in the 'deconstructive' mode (Robotham, 1997). The problem was that these so-called non-rationalistic modes of comprehension too were profoundly Western, deeply rooted, in particular, in the German romantic tradition of the nineteenth century, with Nietzsche and Wagner as its standard-bearers. But in the past, such banners have led in directions far more dangerous than those of Hindu religious chauvinism, providing some of the ideological rallying points against democracy in Europe which later facilitated the rise of Nazism.

GLOBALIZATION: BEYOND POST-COLONIALISM

What one may call, therefore, 'philosophical post-colonialism' ends in a dead end, unless one wishes to journey down the solipsistic, non-rationalistic road. Was it indeed the case that it was the overly rationalistic character of the ideologies of the developing world which was the source of our downfall? On the face of it this seems a thesis most difficult to sustain. Was it also the case that rationalism was so irredeemably tainted with Western ethnocentrism that it could not be a source of ideas which liberated persons of other cultures? One would have to be stamped with an indelibly nationalistic outlook to accept such a proposition. For has not rationalism always had to fight for its very right to exist within Western culture itself? Was it not most recently locked in a life and death struggle against Nazism? And is this struggle not one which has to be fought anew almost daily, be it in the former Yugoslavia, in eastern Germany, France, Chile or Rwanda? Was rationalism really as 'Western' in this indiscriminately totalizing sense, as the post-colonial writers assumed? And was it indeed the case that 'the life of the nation' in the developing world was as non-rationalistic as the intellectuals assumed?

Yet there are even more important issues: these debates have been superseded by more recent events. The crisis in Asia and the apparent triumph of the Anglo-American model of capitalism, the force of the global financial markets and the revolution in knowledge and information systems is rapidly creating an entirely new situation for the countries of both the developing and developed worlds. This is a world which has little or nothing to do with colonialism and on which concepts such as post-colonialism which look to the past have little light to shed. Indeed, some may argue that it is this endless fascination with an examination of the past among the intelligentsia of the developing world which is the source of our failure to come to grips with a world which did not hesitate to change radically while our debates raged. If this view is correct it is not our rationalism but our irrationalism which is the source of our difficulties.

For one thing, a unique feature of the present situation is that all countries in this new order – developed and developing – are subject, to varying degrees for sure and in differing aspects, to the same global marketplace pressures. All countries – from Mexico to Japan – win or lose ground according to the verdict of the international money markets. Post-colonialist theory does not even begin to have an approach to analysing this behemoth. Asian crises notwithstanding, it is more or less clear that individuals, companies and countries (developed or developing) all possess an agency now which can break out of the old structures of power, especially due to the possibilities opened up by information technology. Again, post-colonial theory does not offer us the slightest possibility of theorizing knowledge systems and networks. To do so one must turn to the ideas developed by Beck, 1994; Castells, 1996; Giddens, 1994a, 1994b).

It would be way beyond the scope of this chapter to enter into a lengthy exposition of these theories, which, in any event, are dealt with by other chapters in this book. Suffice it to say that it is in these concepts of 'reflexive modernity' and of 'network society' that I believe a greater prospect is to be found for theories of society and culture which capture the challenges faced by developing societies today. This is not to say that these theories are unproblematic and that they have at last found the solutions to the theoretical and practical issues of the day.

However, there is no doubt in my mind that both these theories are correct to highlight the new opportunities for agency ('reflexivity') which spring from the immense access to modern knowledge which education and information systems have brought. At the same time, it seems to me that these theories are mistaken in their minimization of the new structures of power which have accompanied this knowledge revolution, and the unprecedented monopolies, in the culture industries, biotechnology, software and hardware, and in business and government generally which have arisen. Instead of simply the growth of agency, we seem to have the paradox of the growth *both* of structure *and* agency, in an intensely contradictory interaction.

But these are other issues, critical as they may be to understanding the conditions of developing and, indeed, of all countries. The problematic before us was a different one: the elucidation of the concept of post-colonialism which, hopefully, can now be grasped as the product of another time and space.

SUMMARY

- We are living in a period of especially rapid economic and social change which makes it difficult to theorize modern society.
- The concept of the 'post-colonial' has been superseded by these events.
- The idea developed in two phases. An earlier period in the 1970s was more concerned with the process of decolonization. The main arguments of this phase focus on the issue of the class character of the state in the newly independent countries.
- The later phase of what I call 'post-colonialism proper' is more concerned with epistemological than with sociological issues. The focus is on a critique of the main ideas of anti-colonial thought as derived from a Western tradition which is depicted as rationalistic and alien to the indigenous cultural traditions of the developing world.
- Since the indigenous cultures of the developing world are presented by these writers as non-rationalistic, the adoption of the Western rationalistic tradition by nationalist movements is the chief obstacle to the development of a truly national ideology.
- The critique of rationalism by these authors as 'Western' is one-sided and does not take account of the deep opposition to rationality within Western culture itself. There are different expressions of rationality and there are no good grounds for believing that rationality is the bane of the developing world. Nor is the presentation of indigenous cultures as impervious to rationality acceptable.
- In any event, the debate about post-colonialism has been superseded by the radical changes taking place in the world today. Concepts such as 'reflexive modernity' and 'network society', while tending to minimize the power of structures in the world today, are more useful. This is because they try to theorize contemporary social and economic forces such as the international money markets and the information technology revolution. This differs from the concept of post-colonialism which tends to be harking back to the past.

FURTHER READING

Alavi, Hamza (1972) 'The State in Postcolonial Societies: Pakistan and Bangladesh', *New Left Review*, **74**, July–August. The original article, written from a neo-Marxist point of view, which began the post-colonial debate about the class character of the leadership of the state in developing societies.

Bhabha, Homi (1994) *The Location of Culture*. London and New York: Routledge. Along with the work of Spivak, the central work of what I have called post-colonialism proper. Its main theme is the critique of the homogenous totalizing view of cultures as self-generating organic wholes, uncontaminated by outside influences. Homi argues strongly for privileging the perspective of persons drawn from 'in-between spaces' and for the strengths of 'hybridity' and mixture.

Castells, Manuel (1996) *The Information Age: Economy, Society and Culture, Volume I: The Rise of the Network Society*. Oxford: Blackwell. The first volume of the magnum opus which theorizes the specifics of the currently evolving global society. The argument is that a new 'mode of development' has developed today, derived from information systems and the real time operation of international money markets. The implication is that this 'network society' creates new opportunities for development for all societies.

Chatterjee, Partha (1986) *Nationalist Thought and the Colonial World: A Derivative Discourse.* Minneapolis: University of Minnesota Press. This is the pivotal transitional work in which the process by which the later post-colonial thinking emerged from the old is clearly revealed.

Giddens, Anthony (1994) *Beyond Left and Right: The Future of Radical Politics*. Cambridge: Polity Press. The critical work theorizing the emergence of the 'Third Way'. Now very important to the Blair project in the UK. The key argument put forward is that we are now in a stage of 'reflexive modernity' by which is meant a phase in which (scientific) knowledge is so widely in use that it has weakened the old structures of power and capital. The emphasis is on the new possibilities for agency which arise from this development.

Spivak, Gayatri (1993) *Outside in the Teaching Machine*. London: Routledge. The work which, more than any other, makes the arguments for and captures the philosophical mood of post-colonialism. The emphasis is on the predicament of the post-colonial intellectual who is necessarily in the West but not of it.

REFERENCES

Ahmad, Aijaz (1995) 'The Politics of Literary Postcoloniality', *Race and Class* **36**(3): 1–20.
Alavi, Hamza (1972) 'The State in Postcolonial Societies: Pakistan and Bangladesh', *New Left Review*, **74**, July–August, pp. 59–81.

Beck, Ulrich (1994) 'The Reinvention of Politics: Towards a Theory of Reflexive Modernization', in Scott Lash (ed.), *Reflexive Modernization: Politics, Tradition and Aesthetics in the Modern Social Order*. Cambridge: Polity Press.

Bhabha, Homi (1994) *The Location of Culture*. London: Routledge.

Castells, Manuel (1996) *The Rise of the Network Society: The Information Age: Economy, Society and Culture, Volume I*. Oxford: Blackwell.

Castells, Manuel. (1998) *End of the Millenium: The Information Age: Economy, Society and Culture, Volume III*. Oxford: Blackwell.

Chatterjee, Partha (1986) *Nationalist Thought and the Colonial World: A Derivative Discourse*. Minneapolis: University of Minnesota Press.

Dirlik, Arif (1994) *After the Revolution: Waking to Global Capitalism*. Hanover, NH: University Press of New England.

Giddens, Anthony (1994a) *Beyond Left and Right: The Future of Radical Politics*. Cambridge: Polity Press.

Giddens, Anthony (1994b) 'Living in a Post-Traditional Society', in Scott Lash (ed.), *Reflexive Modernization: Politics, Tradition and Aesthetics in the Modern Social Order*. Cambridge: Polity Press.

Gough, Kathleen and Sharma, Hari P. (eds) (1973) *Imperialism and South Asia*. New York: Monthly Review Press.

Guha, Ranajit (ed.) (1989) *Subaltern Studies VI*, Delhi: Oxford University Press.

Klor de Alva, J. Jorge (1995) 'The Postcolonialism of the (Latin) American Experience: A Reconsideration of "Colonialism", "Postcolonialism" and "Mestizaje"', in Gyan Prakash (ed.) *After Colonialism: Imperial Histories and Postcolonial Displacements*. Princeton, NJ: Princeton University Press.

Mommsen, Wolfgang J. (1989) *The Political and Social Theory of Max Weber*. Cambridge: Polity Press.

Prakash, Gyan (1990) 'Writing Post-Orientalist Histories of the Third World: Perspectives from Indian Historiography', *Comparative Studies in Society and History*, **32**(3): 383–408.

Prakash, Gyan (ed.) (1995) *After Colonialism: Imperial Histories and Postcolonial Displacements*. Princeton, NJ: Princeton University Press.

Robotham, Don. (1977) 'Postcolonialities: The Challenge of New Modernities.' *International Social Science Journal* 153: 357–371.

Rushdie, Salman (1981) *Midnight's Children*. London: Cape.

Rushdie, Salman (1995) *The Moor's Last Sigh*. New York: Pantheon Books.

Saul, John (1979) *The State and Revolution in East Africa*. New York: Monthly Review Press.

Spivak, Gayatri (1993) *Outside in the Teaching Machine*. London: Routledge.

Chapter 7

Reflexive modernization

Ted Benton

Social theorists are prone to see world-historical significance in the key events of their own lifetimes. In our time, the theorists of 'post-modernity' are the most obvious examples of this. There are others, however, who acknowledge the importance of many of the changes described by the post-modernists, but see them as symptoms of transformations within 'modernity', rather than as marking the emergence of a wholly new historical epoch. These theorists have advanced the idea of 'reflexive modernization' to characterize this new phase of 'modernity'. The best-known advocates of this notion of reflexive modernization are Ulrich Beck (born 1944) and Anthony Giddens (born 1938).

According to these theorists, the major sources of social and political identity and conflict which characterized earlier phases of 'modernity' are in process of being displaced as a result of the advance of modernity itself. In the view of these writers and those influenced by them, these changes make established political ideologies and divisions obsolete, and Giddens in particular is noted for his advocacy of a 'third way' in contemporary politics, beyond the old opposition between Left and Right. In their view, the process of radicalization of modernity itself, and the 'sub-politics' of new social movements holds out the prospect of a democratized and sustainable 'new' modernity. In particular, these writers have taken from Green social and political movements an awareness of the significance of ecological destruction and large-scale hazards in transforming the moral and political, as well as the physical landscape.

While I have some sympathy with the value-perspective of these writers, and indeed, for their project of fully incorporating the socio-ecological dimension into social theorizing, I shall be arguing that the analytical concepts they use to explain the rise of ecological politics are deeply flawed, and that this has important implications for their view of the future of radical politics. Perhaps the key difference between the position I shall be advocating and the 'reflexive modernization' school lies in the rival frameworks of ideas through which they locate the present historical period. For the advocates of reflexive modernization, history is understood as a sequence of stages, from traditional, or pre-modern, society through 'simple' to 'reflexive' modernity. Modernity is characterized in terms of a list of characteristic institutional forms or 'dimensions', none of which is assigned overall causal priority. My own, contrasting, view is one which attempts to grasp the qualitatively different ways in which different societies, at different historical periods, socially organize their interchange with nature. These patterns of social relationship to nature have two inseparable aspects. They are, at one and the same time, both the way people act together upon nature to meet their needs, and relations of power, through which dominant groups control this process and acquire the surplus wealth created by it. This theoretical approach is derived from Marx's concept of modes of production, but it gives more emphasis than Marx did to modes of production as ways of interacting with nature, and it is not committed (as Marx sometimes seemed to be) to any notion of necessary relations of succession from one mode to another in the course of historical 'development': on the view I am advocating there are no such relations of necessity, and history is understood as an open-ended process in which contingency plays a very large part in such transformations as do occur.

Another contrast with some (mis)interpretations of Marx is the rejection of economic determinism. My approach is an attempt to avoid both the view that the economy determines everything, and the opposite view that societies are made up of a number of different structures or practices which are all autonomous with respect to each other. On the view I am advocating against reflexive modernization, economic life (taken to include our ecological relationships to the rest of nature) does have a predominating role in shaping the other institutional forms (of the State, legal system, forms of communication, patterns of thought and desire, and so on) with which it coexists. On this view, given the pre-eminence of capitalist economic relations, the globalizing processes of capital accumulation currently have explanatory priority, but because these processes occur unevenly in both space and time, it is not possible to justify any *single* characterization of 'modernity'. Different forms of capitalist economic organization, different forms of combination of capitalist with non-capitalist economic forms, and different modes of combination of economic, cultural and political institutions persist in different parts of the world. If this is accepted, the term 'modernity' and its cognates such as 'reflexive modernization' can only be either sociologically empty ways of referring to the 'present', or an ethnocentric imposition of a certain idealized view of specifically western developments onto the rest of the world.

But this construct of western 'modernity' itself is highly questionable, as is the associated division of 'modernity' into 'simple' and 'reflexive' phases or stages. For Giddens, simple modernity (the West since the Enlightenment) is characterized by four 'institutional dimensions' (Giddens, 1991: ch. 2): political/administrative power (typically representative democracy); an economic order overwhelmingly capitalist in form, with the now defunct communist regimes as a temporary variant; a relation to nature defined by modern science and industrial technology; and a state monopoly on the legitimate use of violence. The conservative, liberal and socialist traditions in politics are clearly, Giddens thinks, connected to this phase of modernization, but are now exhausted as a consequence of processes occurring over the last forty to fifty years (Giddens, 1994). These processes are summarized by Giddens as 'globalization', 'detraditionalization' and 'social reflexivity'. Giddens resists an economic account of globalization, and focuses on the implications of new communications technologies and mass transportation. Partly because of the cultural cosmopolitanism which flows from globalization, traditions which have persisted into or become established during simple modernization can no longer be 'legitimated in the traditional way': they have to justify themselves in the face of alternatives. This implies that individuals no longer have their lives set out for them by the contingencies of their birth, but are constantly faced with choices about how to live: whether to have children, how to dress, what to believe in and so on. The establishment of identity, in other words, increasingly becomes a life project of 'reflexive' subjects.

The newly emergent conditions of reflexive modernization, according to Giddens, render the inherited political traditions obsolete. Traditional forms of class identity are dissolved; changes in the labour market and in gender relations and family forms render the institutions of the welfare state unsustainable and inappropriate; globalization and reflexivity in lifestyle choice and consumption render centralized forms of economic control unworkable; while the established parties and political institutions lose their legitimacy. However, this is not the end of politics – not even of radical politics. Drawing on a schematic account of the new social movements as forms of resistance to each of the institutional dimensions of modernity, Giddens postulates the emergence of a radical 'generative' or 'life' politics beyond the old polarities of Left and Right.

In response to the political/administrative system, there are social movements aiming at the radicalization of democracy, and against surveillance and authoritarianism. Reflexive modernization also involves democratization of personal life, in which relationships between lovers, friends, parents and children and so on are no longer governed by traditional assumptions and expectations. In the sphere of capitalist economic relations, polarization and fragmentation continue to characterize reflexively modernizing societies, but the supposed demise of class politics and of centralized economic control leads Giddens to suggest (rather vaguely) that these problems may be corrected by a 'post-scarcity' order which owes as much to ecology and conservatism as it does to socialism. In the dimension of science and industrial technology, the project of simple modernity to control the forces of nature has generated a new order of risk – 'manufactured' risk – to which the Green movement has responded with a utopian desire for a return to authentic nature. In the dimension of institutional violence, the peace movement points to a growing role for dialogic forms of conflict-resolution in a post-traditional, reflexive world.

The German sociologist, Ulrich Beck, has a great deal in common with Giddens's way of thinking, but has a more highly developed approach to the ecological dimension of reflexive modernization. In his view, the processes of detraditionalization, globalization and reflexivity are leading to the emergence of a new stage of modernity which deserves the title 'Risk Society' (Beck, 1992). Risk and uncertainty increasingly pervade all dimensions of personal and social life: increased rates of divorce and family breakdown, uncertainty and vulnerability in the labour market, and most centrally, for Beck, uncertainty in the face of the hazards generated by new, large-scale industrial technologies and by advances in scientific knowledge.

Beck shares with Giddens a historical periodization of risks and hazards. In pre-modern times, risks, in the shape of disease epidemics, floods, famine and so on, were experienced as having an external source, in nature. Simple modernization, with the development of industrial technology, displaced 'external' risks in favour of self-created or 'manufactured' risks – by-products of industrialization itself. Beck's view, however, is that reflexive modernization ushers in a new order of manufactured risk with profound cultural and political implications. The 'semi-autonomous' development of science and technology unleashed under simple modernization has through its own dynamic yielded new large-scale technologies in the nuclear, chemical and genetics industries which pose qualitatively new hazards, and put modernity itself at risk. What Beck has to say can be summarized under seven main features:

1 New hazards are unlimited in time and space, with global self-annihilation now an ultimate and dreadful possibility.
2 They are socially unlimited in scope – potentially everyone is at risk.
3 They may be minimized, but not eliminated, so that risk has to be measured in terms of probabilities. An improbable event can still happen.
4 They are irreversible.
5 They have diverse sources, so that traditional methods of assigning responsibility do not work. Beck calls this 'organized non-liability'.
6 They are on such a scale, or may be literally incalculable in ways which exceed the capacities of state or private organizations to provide insurance against them or compensation.

7 They may be only identified and measured by scientific means. Consequently contested knowledge claims and growing public scepticism about science itself are important aspects of the 'reflexivity' of the risk society.

The pervasiveness of risk, and especially of the new order of hazards generated by large-scale technologies, leads Beck, like Giddens, to postulate a political watershed in association with reflexive modernization. In Beck's work, two clusters of themes are prominent. The first is the supposed demise of class conflict over the distribution of goods. Beck takes class conflict between capital and labour to be characteristic of simple modernization, but it is in process of being displaced both by a new agenda of political issues and by new patterns of coalition and cleavage. Both Giddens and Beck agree that severe material inequalities continue to exist through reflexive modernization, but for them, globalization, detraditionalization and reflexivity erode traditional forms of class consciousness and identity, so that class relations are increasingly individualized and conditions for collective class action disappear. In this respect Giddens and Beck are in line with a welter of recent announcements of the 'death of class' (see Lee and Turner, 1996). Beck's own gloss on this thesis includes the claim that the political agenda is undergoing a shift from conflict over the (class) distribution of goods to conflict over the (non-class) distribution of 'bads' (the environmental costs of continuing industrial and technical development). The new patterns of conflict characteristic of the risk society will involve conjunctural, shifting patterns of coalition and division defined by the incidence of these costs. So, we can expect workers and managements in environmentally polluting industries, for example, to be in alliance with one another against those in industries such as, say, fisheries or tourism, which suffer from pollution. Finally, there is the implication that the new order of environmental hazards constitutes the basis for a potentially universal interest in environmental regulation, since the relatively wealthy and powerful can no longer avoid these hazards, in the way they could escape the risks associated with earlier industrial technologies.

The second cluster of themes marking a suggested qualitative break with the politics of the past is also centrally connected with environmental hazards. Here, however, it is not so much a matter of differential class incidence, as of the challenge these hazards pose to the steering capacity of modern states, and so to political legitimacy. In essence, Beck's argument is that under simple modernization, legitimacy was achieved through the progressive development of a welfare/security state, in which either public or private institutions provided guarantees against risk in the various dimensions of life – public health care provision, pensions, unemployment and sick pay, welfare benefits and so on. Reflexive modernization, characterized by changed gender relations, family breakdown, flexible labour markets and, above all, hazards of unprecedented scale and incalculability, exposes the growing inadequacy of the welfare/security system to deliver what it has promised. In his more recent writings (e.g., Beck, 1995), Beck has cautiously introduced the notion of a 'sub-politics' which might emerge in response to this situation, pressing for more democratic participation in decisions currently taken by hierarchies of technocrats and top business executives.

It seems to me that the theorists of environmental politics in the light of reflexive modernization successfully allude to significant changes in contemporary societies. Their characterizations of these changes are often imaginative and persuasive. However, in what remains of this chapter, I shall try to show that in several key respects, their claims are empirically mistaken and/or theoretically defective. An alternative, ecologically informed socialist analysis, I shall argue, is more adequate to the explanatory task at hand, and points to quite different political possibilities.

CLASS, POLITICS AND THE ENVIRONMENT

The weight of historical and sociological evidence suggests that the proclaimed 'death of class' is premature. It is arguable that this thesis gains what plausibility it has from an exaggeration of the role of class in the politics of earlier historical periods. Social classes have always been internally differentiated and stratified, and in all industrial capitalist societies there have always been substantial proportions of the population which could not be readily assigned to the two-class model of capital and labour. Moreover, class orientations in politics are always mediated by specific local or regional cultural resources, traditions and historical cleavages, and party-structures and strategies, while ethnic, gender, religious and other sources of social identification may either confirm or cut across class allegiance. All of this is familiar stuff, and there is no reason to suppose it is any more salient now than it was, say, a century ago, at the height of the women's suffrage struggle and the nationalistic appeals of the colonial powers.

It seems likely that the death of class is being proclaimed as an over-reaction to the much more geographically and historically localized demise of the 'neo-corporatist' form of class politics which characterized many of the industrial capitalist countries during the thirty years or so following the Second World War. Changes there have certainly been, but the evidence points against the claims of individualization and class dealignment in politics. Studies of voting behaviour in the UK, for example, show reduced support for the Labour Party between 1979 and 1992, but no significant lessening of the links between class position and voting behaviour in general. The decline of Labour during that period seems to have been linked to a decline in its popularity across the social classes, high levels of working-class abstention, and, possibly most important, a decline in those occupational groups which formed the main social basis of Labour's traditional support (see, for example, Westergaard and Goldthorpe in Lee and Turner, 1996). In the case of the UK, substantial deindustrialization and public sector reorganization during the Thatcher years reduced the size of Labour's 'traditional' working-class base. Two prolonged recessions, combined with both legislative and directly repressive attacks on trade union powers further weakened organized labour as a popular social movement. However, the trade union movement in the UK, while considerably reduced, still has some seven million members. Instead of class dealignment, recent changes are better understood in terms of a combination of class *re*alignment along with shifts in the occupational and class structure.

This is a situation which certainly presents major strategic problems for the Left, but it is not new. At earlier stages in capitalist industrialization, and in the interwar period in particular, organized industrial workers have generally been in a minority, and the Left has been able to exert such influence as it has through broadly based coalitions with other classes and social forces. In those industrial sectors where management regimes and individualized terms and conditions make traditional forms of collective action difficult or impossible, and among many routine non-manual and technical employees, there is evidence of widespread stress, anxiety, insecurity and unhappiness at work. Finally, there is a large residual population with at best a marginal position in the labour market, and dependent upon ever-diminishing and humiliating welfare support. The potential social basis for a broad coalition of the Left clearly does exist, and we have to look for other explanations of the widespread abandonment of class politics by former parties of the Left, such as the British Labour Party.

This takes us on to the place of environmental politics, as a key part of the supposed shift of the content of the political agenda away from questions of distributive justice and public provision of welfare and security. Perhaps the most influential advocacy here has been Inglehart's (1977) identification of 'post-materialist' values, such as environmental quality, as increasingly important as societies and particular groups within them become more affluent. This suggests a growing autonomy of political issues from material interests, and is coherent with notions of reflexivity and detraditionalization. In the case of Beck, environmental issues are treated as concerned with distribution – but of 'bads' rather than 'goods'. Giddens, in contrast, detaches environmental issues altogether from questions of distribution by treating the environmental movement as a response to industrial and technological development.

Against the view of environmental politics as part of a 'post-materialist' agenda, it may be argued that concern about the most basic conditions for survival itself, about the poisoning of food and water supplies, about the danger of industrial accidents, about the unpredictable alteration of global climates and so on, could hardly be more 'materialist'. Moreover, there are many empirical studies which demonstrate the processes through which ecological disruption and degradation impact most devastatingly on the poorest and least powerful communities, both within each country, and globally. This takes us to Beck's claim that the pattern of distribution of bads implies a qualitative break from the politics of the distribution of goods. In part, again, Beck offers a misleading picture of the past. Many thousands of socialist activists in their local communities and in their trade unions have been concerned with environmental health provision, with campaigning against air and water pollution, and with health and safety standards in the workplace. Engels's study of the *Condition of the Working Class in England* (1845) was, after all, a pioneering work of environmental socialism. Socialist analysis has always emphasized the parallelism between lack of 'goods' and a plentiful supply of 'bads' endemic to capitalism.

However, what is indeed new is the intensity and the wider resonance across society of current concerns about ecological destruction. This phenomenon, far from providing grounds for abandoning socialist ideas, offers real potential for broadening their appeal, and that of the Left more generally. However, there is nothing automatic in this. Environmental concern is increasingly differentiated in its expressions, and clear links can be seen between different definitions and policy agendas, on the one hand, and the interests of social groups and classes, on the other. In other words, the content and direction of the contemporary phase of environmental politics can increasingly be seen as an emergent arena of class conflict – but one which transforms and extends our understanding of class as it does so. Both Beck and Giddens counterpose the politics of the environment to those of class. My argument is that class politics has always, and quite centrally, at 'grass roots' level especially, been about environmental questions, and that the new agenda of environmental politics both extends and is intelligibly continuous with that longer history.

However, there is also something which transcends class politics in the new agenda of environmental politics. Beck's identification of a new order of risk does start to capture this, but his optimistic expectation of a recognized universal interest in addressing these hazards is hard to sustain. Knowledge communities are increasingly aligned with interest groups in ways which make the identification and measurement of hazards permanently contested, and rival interests are affected in different ways by different policy prescriptions. Arguably the risks of 'simple' modernization retain more continuing salience than Beck acknowledges, while the new large-scale risks are more contentious in ways which broadly follow class cleavages than he is prepared to allow. However, awareness of the new order of risk, including the potential jeopardization of all life on earth, has, arguably, played a part in a widespread cultural shift in recent decades. A deepening anxiety and moral horror at the scale of ecological destruction is now quite widespread. Social movements which mobilize on this basis have undergone dramatic increases in membership and mobilizing capacity since the 1960s. They and their constituency represent a further possible element in a new coalition of the Left, one binding together both social movements organized on the basis of class interest and ones deriving from a range of moral concerns. Again, in terms of strategy, if not of cultural content, there is no qualitative break between such a project of Green–Left alignment and the past history of coalitions of the Left.

CAPITALISM OR MODERNITY?

In their understandable anxiety to avoid economically reductionist accounts of the relationship between capitalism and other fields of social life, the reflexive modernists are reluctant to assign any causal significance to the economy beyond its own boundaries. We are left with a typology of institutional 'dimensions' of 'modernity', but with no attempt to characterize the *relationships* between them, nor the processes through which they are continuously reproduced as 'dimensions' of a whole society. In the absence of such theorizing, the reader is left with the impression that each dimension is to be understood as an autonomous causal order in its own right. The same applies to the social movements which, in Giddens's account, arise as forms of resistance to each institutional dimension. Though he recognizes the anomalous character of the women's movement as transcending his institutional divisions, he continues to see, for example, the environmental and labour movements as sequestered from each other as forms of resistance to different institutional dimensions.

However, it is important to make a distinction between the general theoretical *question* of the causal links between, say, capitalism and the institutions of the State, on the one hand, and an economically reductionist *answer* to that theoretical question, on the other. For example, we can recognize that state institutions in a society such as Britain will be limited in their capacity to alter unsustainable agricultural regimes, or reduce carbon dioxide emissions for reasons which have to do with the economic power of capital. In some respects this follows from extensive 'colonization' of some ministries by organized agribusiness or road transport interests, and in other respects from the dependence of state economic policy itself on the profitability of the relevant industrial sectors. To point to such interconnections is not to be committed to economic determinism but, rather, to suggest that it is implausible to assume *a priori* that each institutional dimension can be understood independently of its structural ties with the others. So, while Giddens and Beck rightly acknowledge that capitalist development continues to generate material inequalities (in fact, the evidence is of increasing polarization of wealth and power as a result of economic globalization and deregulation), they give accounts of their favoured 'life-' and 'sub-' politics in ways which seem largely innocent of the wider consequences of these material inequalities. The persistence of widespread poverty and social exclusion must necessarily affect the prospects for thoroughgoing democratization of social and political life, for generalized access to social movement activity, and for the leverage of social movements with respect to technocratic and corporate power.

Again, both Beck and Giddens treat the development of science and technology as autonomous processes. In the case of Giddens this is assigned to a distinct institutional 'dimension' separate from capitalist economic relations. In Beck's work a parallel sequestration is achieved by his identification of science and technology as expressions of an abstractly defined 'instrumental reason', the legacy of the European Enlightenment, and characterizing the distinctively modern relationship to nature. The upshot for both writers is a portrayal of ecological crisis and large-scale hazards as consequences of a secular process of scientific and technical development, endemic to a definite stage of 'modernization', and subject to resistance on the part of single-issue environmental movements. These latter are then somewhat condescendingly criticized for their utopian and retrogressive desire to return to an 'authentic' nature (which, apparently, no longer exists: 'Today, now that it no longer exists, nature is being rediscovered, pampered. The ecology movement has fallen prey to a naturalistic misapprehension of itself . . . ' Beck, 1995: 65).

So what is wrong with this? The current concern over the probability of transmission of bovine brain disease to humans in the form of New Variant Creutzfeldt Jakob Disease (CJD) may provide us with an example. Superficially, the case seems to conform to Beck's characterization of the new large-scale hazards. The topic is subject to heated and unresolved scientific controversy, and since the situation is unprecedented, the extent of the risk is literally incalculable. Given the pervasiveness of beef derivatives in the processing of many other foods, medicines and other products, and the global character of contemporary food distribution, the incidence of risk transcends spatial and social boundaries. 'Organized non-liability' is also evident in the impossibility of tracing the source of infection in any particular case of the new form of CJD. However, if we follow the actual course of the politics of bovine spongeform encephalopathy (BSE)/CJD we find something rather different from the emergence of a universal interest. In the UK, the issue shifted from a problem of public health to one of protection of the interests of the UK beef industry in the space of one day (a shift with which the British media complied almost unanimously). The response of the European Union provided an occasion for large sections of the press, and the Eurosceptic wing of the Consevative Party, to define the issue as one in which one's patriotic duty was to eat beef in defiance of malevolent German attempts to damage the British livestock industry. The Labour opposition of the time confined itself to uttering concern about job losses in the beef industry, and demanding a still tougher line with Europe.

All of this illustrates the extent to which there can be no 'reading off' of perceptions of risk and responsibility from some supposedly 'objective' measure. Competing interests and discursive frames offer widely differing and conflicting 'codes' for making sense of the episode. But there are other problems in such approaches as Beck's. For one thing, the hazard was not generated by a technological advance, but rather by changes in animal feed regimes which were adopted in the pursuit of profit, together with changes in standards of feed processing which were made possible by the commitment of the Conservative government to a neo-liberal philosophy of deregulation. The situation was one in which a hazard already foreseen (by the 1979 Royal Commission on Environmental Pollution) was engendered by a cost-cutting non-use of available technology, not one resulting from the implementation of a hazardous new technology. This suggests that the focus on scientific and technological innovation, as such, as primary causes of environmental hazards is much too narrow. Any adequate analysis of the BSE episode would have to recognize it as an outcome of economic, political and cultural processes interacting with one another. It would include the representation of farming interests in the Ministry of Agriculture, Fisheries and Food (MAFF), the dual role of MAFF in relation to both food production and safety, the political ideology of the then Conservative government, the role of the media, and the relation between government regulation and technical advisory bodies.

Power relations which operate between and across the 'institutional dimensions', specific institutional structures, and identifiable sources of pressure and political decision all played their part in the genesis of this particular hazard. The effect of the reflexive modernizers' abstract separation of institutional domains, together with their view of the new order of industrial hazards as endemic to a phase of development of 'modernity', then, is to undermine the possibility of the sort of complex empirical analysis which would be needed to gain social scientific insight into problems like BSE. Moreover, and quite counter to the intentions of Beck, the notion of 'reflexive modernization' leads us to see such episodes as this as just more examples of an 'inexorable' advance of 'modernity', of an impersonal process of technological development making our lives more risky – the issues are depoliticized, and 'organized non-liability' is implicitly endorsed. Giddens's metaphor of a 'juggernaut' out of control is similar in its political implications.

More generally, where technological innovation *is* implicated in the genesis of ecological hazards, as in such cases as nuclear power and biotechnology, the reflexive modernizers' tendency to represent scientific and technical innnovation as occurring in their own, autonomous institutional 'dimension' cuts them off from important insights available from work in the sociology of science and technology. Ever since the work of the late T.S. Kuhn, in the early 1960s, sociologists have been studying the ways in which social processes within the 'scientific community', external interests and wider cultural resources can all affect not just the rate of scientific innovation, but also its very content and direction. This is not to argue that scientifically authenticated knowledge-claims are mere cultural or discursive constructs arbitrarily related to their external referents. It remains possible to acknowledge the place of evidence and scientific reasoning in the shaping of scientific research agendas and knowledge-claims, while still insisting that extraneous social and cultural influences also play a significant part. Similar considerations apply to technological innovation. The reflexive modernizers' segregation of the political/administrative, economic, scientific/ technical and military institutional complexes from one another rules out the kind of integrated analysis which is required. In the area of biotechnology, as in many other fields of scientific research, there have been two notable trends in recent decades. One is that overall investment in scientific and technical research has shifted dramatically away from the public sector and is now concentrated in the R&D departments of the big corporations. The second is that publically funded scientific research is now subjected to criteria of evaluation which give high priority to anticipated commercial use (Webster, 1991; Wheale and McNally, 1988). Under such circumstances, to represent scientific and technical innovation as if it were an autonomous process, a mere correlate of a certain phase of 'modernity', is little short of ideological mystification. The subordination of science in key sectors to the competitive priorities of private capital is all but complete.

CAPITALISM, SOCIALISM AND ENVIRONMENTAL MOVEMENTS

Two consequences follow for our interpretation of the Green and environmental movements. One is that they cannot be confined to the role of resistors to new industrial technologies, in abstraction from the capitalist relations under which those technologies are developed and implemented. In so far as new technologies generate environmental hazards, ecological disruption and damage to people's quality of life, they do so as complex, culturally mediated outcomes of state policies, the product and marketing strategies of capitalist firms, and patterns of class power. Oppositional social movements are both diverse and fluid. Empirically we can observe complex and changing interpretative resources evolving within the social movements, and emergent patterns of differentiation and realignment. Indeed, the formation of the Green Parties in many European countries involved coalitions between previously quite diverse groupings of socialists, anarchists, civic activists, peace movement and feminist campaigners and so on.

The second consequence is that a sociologically informed understanding of processes of scientific and technical innovation renders imaginable a qualitatively different institutionalization of science and technology. Opposition to current directions of scientific and technical change need not take the form of a backward-looking, nostalgic desire for reversion to an earlier stage along a single-line developmental process, as Giddens and Beck represent it. On the contrary, an ecologically informed socialist perspective emphasizes the extent to which the direction of change in science and technology is currently shaped by the requirements of capital accumulation and state strategies in relation to military priorities, surveillance, control over labour processes, and product innovation. On such a perspective, it is not required that we oppose either scientific innovation or technological invention as such. The key questions become, instead, how to detach research from its current embedding within the institutional nexus of capital and the State in such a way as to open up priorities in funding to a wider public debate, and to democratize decisions about the development and deployment of new technologies. Of course, both Beck and Giddens also favour opening up these areas of decision-making to democratic accountability. However, their treatment of science and technology as autonomous *vis-à-vis* capital and the political/administrative system sidesteps difficult questions about the intensity of likely resistance on the part of both capital and the State to any such project, and the immense power vested in these institutional complexes. Only very powerful and broadly based coalitions of social movements could have any hope of making headway with these ideas.

There is a third respect in which trying to understand ecological problems as outcomes of the interaction of technical, economic, political and cultural processes has implications for how we think about environmental politics. To see what these implications are, some more has to be said about the connections between specifically capitalist forms of economic organization and ecological degradation. The dominant forms of economic calculation under capitalism are abstract and monetary, subordinating to their logic substantive considerations about the management of the people, places and materials involved in actual processes of production and distribution. This feature renders capital accumulation particularly liable to unforeseen and unintended consequences at this substantive level – notably taking the form of environmental dislocations of one kind or another. Considerations such as these have led the ecological Marxist James O'Connor (1996) to postulate a 'second contradiction' of capitalism, to complement the 'first contradiction' as identified by Marx (that between capital and labour). This second contradiction is between the 'forces' (including technologies) of production and the 'conditions' of production (including human-provided infrastructures and social institutions as well as ecological conditions). In short, capitalism tends to undermine its own ecological (and other) conditions of existence. It follows that if these conditions are to be sustained or reconstituted, non-economic agencies (for O'Connor, the State) have to intervene. In O'Connor's view, then, the labour and the environmental movements are both forms of social movement response to basic structural contradictions of capitalism. They may constitute alternative or parallel routes to a socialist transformation.

If O'Connor's analysis is right, it suggests that there should be an affinity between radical environmentalism and the labour movement, such that they should appear natural allies. If this were the case, then the sort of coalition outlined above between the labour movement and other social movements, including radical environmentalists, ought to be readily attainable. However, there are serious obstacles in the way of such a coalition. It remains an open question whether existing patterns of *ad hoc* coalition and dialogue between Greens, labour movement activists, feminists, animal rights campaigners, roads protesters and so on will generate a more organically integrated and coherent new social force on the Green Left.

SUMMARY

- The theorists of 'reflexive modernization' offer insightful and persuasive descriptions of important aspects of contemporary social experience.
- However, an ecologically informed socialist approach which analyses ecological hazards as outcomes of complex interactions between cultural, economic, technical and political processes in modern capitalist societies has more explanatory power than the concept of reflexive modernization.
- This alternative emphasizes the role of capital accumulation on a world scale together with the cultural, political and military strategies which sustain it, in generating ecological degradation and hazards which bear down more especially on the poor and the socially excluded.
- Economic polarization, together with the social distribution of ecological hazards, make it likely that class divisions will continue to shape social identities and political cleavages for the forseeable future.
- Far from rendering socialist criticism of capitalism outdated, the intrinsic links between capitalism and escalating environmental damage add a new and deeper dimension to that criticism.

ACKNOWLEDGEMENT

This chapter is a revised version of an earlier article which appeared in M. Jacobs (ed.) (1997) *Greening the Millenium*. Oxford: Political Quarterly/Blackwell. Research for both pieces was supported by an ERSC Research Fellowship, no. H52427505494.

FURTHER READING

Capitalism, Nature, Socialism. Published by Guilford Press, New York. A quarterly journal, which includes empirical articles on environmental issues and social movements in all parts of the world, alongside theoretical debate on 'red/green' issues and political commentary.

Rowell, A. (1996) *Green Backlash*. London and New York: Routledge. A thoroughly researched analysis of the global backlash by nation-states, multinational corporations and the political Right against the environmental movement.

Goldblatt, D. (1996) *Social Theory and the Environment*. Cambridge: Polity. An important critical assessment of the achievements of Giddens, Gorz, Habermas and Beck in addressing environmental issues in modern social theory.

Lash, S., Szerszynski, B. and Wynne, B. (eds) (1996) *Risk, Environment and Modernity*. London: Sage. A valuable collection, explaining the diversity of cultural considerations of risk.

REFERENCES

Beck, U. (1992) *The Risk Society*. London: Sage.
Beck, U. (1995) *Ecological Politics in an Age of Risk*. Cambridge: Polity.
O'Connor, J. (1996) in T. Benton (ed.) *The Greening of Marxism*. New York: Guilford.
Giddens, A. (1991) *The Consequences of Modernity*. Cambridge: Polity.
Giddens, A. (1994) *Beyond Left and Right: The Future of Radical Politics*. Cambridge: Polity.
Inglehart, R. (1977) *The Silent Revolution*. Princeton, NJ: Princeton University Press.
Lee, D.J. and Turner, B.S. (eds) (1996) *Conflicts about Class*. London and New York: Longman.
Webster, A. (1991) *Science, Technology and Society*. Basingstoke: Macmillan.
Wheale, P. and McNally, R. (1988) *Genetic Engineering: Catastrophe or Cornucopia?* Hemel Hempstead: Harvester Wheatsheaf.

Chapter 8

Narrative

Susan Stephenson

No philosophy, no analysis, no aphorism, be it ever so profound, can compare in intensity and richness of meaning with a properly narrated story (Arendt, 1973: 29).

INTRODUCTION

When we turn our attention to story-telling or narrative two important aspects of human existence come into focus. The first is that we are beings who are conscious of our existence through time. Our understanding of the present cannot therefore be separated from our recollections of the past and our aspirations for the future. The second is that we are involved in an ongoing process of *making* sense of our experience. To understand the meaning of human actions is to place them in the context of the ongoing lives of particular human beings. Both individually and collectively, we organize experience through the construction of narratives.

Those theorists who take a narrative approach to disciplines such as psychology, sociology, theology, politics or law are seeking to give due attention to the specificity of human experience. They are often highly critical of theoretical approaches which seek a viewpoint outside of particular historical and cultural contexts. Narratives are always told from a perspective situated in time and space. Stories, as opposed to metaphysical realities or abstract models, are of our world. They disclose the variety and complexity of human experience.

The aim of this chapter is to explore the significance of narrative for our understanding of the present. A discussion of narrative, as we shall see, not only takes us to the heart of recent debates about the nature and scope of social and political theory but also raises crucial questions about identity which are central to current political debate. Although the focus of this chapter is primarily on social and political theory, we shall also briefly consider the potential relevance of literary texts for social and political thought. Finally, we shall examine some of the problems that arise from the turn towards narrative. We can begin by examining why theorists across a diverse range of disciplines have recently been giving narrative so much attention.

WHY NARRATIVE?

Debates about the nature and value of narrative are not limited to the field of literary theory. In his foreword to a compendium of papers, *On Narrative*, W.J.T. Mitchell writes that the collection is intended to 'carry thinking about the problem of narrative well beyond the province of the "aesthetic" . . . to explore the role of narrative in social and psychological formations, particularly in structures of value and cognition' (Mitchell, 1981: vii). A more recent collection of papers, *Narrative in Culture*, brings together theorists from disciplines as diverse as psychology, economics, law, physics, biology, philosophy, politics and sociology. Introducing the collection, Christopher Nash writes: 'What has made it possible to conceive of a book like this one is that the preoccupation with discourse – the forms of our utterances and their functions and effects – is no longer the private province of specialists in literature and language (as if it ever should have been)' (Nash, 1990: xi).

D.N. McCloskey's contribution to that volume, 'Storytelling in Economics', contrasts stories with models. The model in economics is expressed as a mathematical formula. The proof of the formula can be shown by retracing the mathematical steps taken to reach it. But the formula can also be unpacked as a story. The story answers the question 'why?' which is not merely a request for an elaboration of the mathematical steps. When the economist asks for the story behind the model his request is 'an appeal for a lower level of abstraction, closer to the episodes of human life' (McCloskey, 1990: 15).

Narrative explanation is often contrasted with 'nomological' explanation. Nomological explanations involve seeing particular events as instances of general laws which always hold regardless of the time and place of their occurrence. This is the kind of explanation sought in the natural sciences. Narrative explanations insist on preserving the particularity of events and place greater emphasis on temporality and context. The nomological ideal has produced such a high level of success in natural science in terms of explanation and prediction that it might seem reasonable for social and political theorists to emulate this ideal. However, persons cannot be studied merely as natural objects. To be a person is to have intentions and to move purposively in the world. Social and political theory must operate therefore not only in the realm of nature, but also in the human realm of meaning. Human actions cannot be understood simply in terms of general laws because general laws cannot tell us anything about the meaning that the actions have for the actor. Unlike causal explanations, narratives link a sequence of events by showing how they relate to particular human ends and purposes. Some thinkers have therefore argued that there is a fundamental difference between natural science with its timeless laws and the social sciences which seek to explain events that occur in a specific time and place.

When theorists adopt a narrative approach to their discipline, they are searching for an approach which enables them to pay attention to the specificity of lived human experience. For example, narrative theologians such as Stanley Hauerwas, Stephen Crites and John Navone stress the lived experience of Christian faith rather than formal arguments for the existence of God. Individual life stories unfold within a framework of meaning exemplified in the story of the life of Christ and within the ongoing history of the Christian church. H. Richard Niebuhr writes:

> The preaching of the early Christian church was not an argument for the existence of God nor an admonition to follow the dictates of some common human conscience, unhistorical and super-social in character. It was primarily a simple recital of the great events connected with the historical appearance of Jesus Christ and a confession of what had happened to the community of disciples (Niebuhr, 1989: 21).

Narratives organize human experience in such a way that it is rendered significant. They provide a connective thread between one state of affairs and another such that they are given a continuity in the consciousness of the story-teller and the listener. We can describe narratives, then, as complex organizational schema which situate agents and organize events in a temporal sequence. The capacity to gather together and organize past experience into meaningful stories provides us with an identity – a sense of existing through time and of acting purposively in the world.

NARRATIVE AND THEORY

> Abstract philosophy cannot impose a theoretical model of a system on a political community. The best system is always the one that takes into account the particular circumstances in which the citizens of a country live (Laforest, 1993: xiv).

Within recent social and political thought, the concept of narrative is used by a wide range of theorists including Alasdair MacIntyre, Charles Taylor, Michael Walzer, Martha Nussbaum, Carol Gilligan, Richard Rorty and Jean-François Lyotard. While these thinkers diverge quite widely in both the substance and the style of their work, they are nevertheless united in their rejection of abstract forms of theorizing which appeal to an ideal model and neglect the lived experience of political agents. It will be helpful here to look at particular examples, so I shall briefly consider first the arguments that MacIntyre advances for treating political theory as a historical task, and second the use Gilligan makes of narrative in her critique of mainstream theories of moral development.

In *After Virtue*, MacIntyre (1985) argues that if we accept the starting points of analytical liberal theorists such as Robert Nozick or John Rawls we should agree with their conclusions, for their accounts are internally coherent. The problem is that neither theorist can show why we should accept their starting points to begin with. According to Nozick the preservation of individual liberty should be the starting point for thinking about justice. The state should be minimal and social and economic inequality accepted as an unavoidable consequence of protecting freedom. Rawls, in contrast, makes fairness the starting point for his theory of justice and therefore sanctions the redistribution of goods from the better to the worst off by the state.

MacIntyre argues that the dispute between these two positions cannot be settled by appealing to abstract reason. We have to think about the kinds of values and beliefs that are embedded within particular communities:

> This is partly because what it is to live the good life concretely varies from circumstance to circumstance . . . I inherit from the past of my family, my city, my tribe, my nation, a variety of debts, inheritances, rightful expectations and obligations. These constitute the given of my life, my moral starting point. This is in part what gives my life its moral particularity (MacIntyre, 1985: 220).

MacIntyre goes on to argue that contemporary liberal theory fails to capture this moral particularity. But how is such moral particularity captured in MacIntyre's work? Here he turns to the concept of narrative. To characterize a person's behaviour and intentions involves seeing them in a setting and knowing something about their beliefs. In doing this we are constructing a narrative history. We can only understand the meaning of an individual's behaviour or utterances by placing them within the context of that individual's ongoing life-story. Similarly, we can only understand the meaning of political concepts such as rights, justice, freedom and so on by placing them within the context of the ongoing social and political life of a community. The project of a social science detached from a study of beliefs and settings is, according to MacIntyre, doomed to failure. Human experience is narrative in form and human beings are, in their actions and practices, story-telling animals.

Reflection on the nature and scope of social and political theory has become central to recent debates not only because of the vexed question of whether the search for universal foundations is viable, but also because theories that claim to be universal often mask inbuilt bias or prejudice. Feminist theorists have provided particularly useful insights in their challenges to the claimed universality of mainstream theory. Carol Gilligan's work in moral psychology provides a good example here.

Gilligan opens her study *In a Different Voice* with the following statement: 'My interest lies in the interaction of experience and thought, in different voices and the dialogues to which they give rise, in the way we listen to ourselves and to others, in the stories we tell about our lives' (Gilligan, 1982: 2). She claims that developmental theory in psychology is not value neutral but contains a masculine bias. Whereas masculinity is defined through separation – moving from the realm of the family into the formal relations of civil society – femininity is defined in terms of ongoing relationships of care and responsibility. Moral maturity is defined in terms of the ability to individuate oneself, make rule-governed judgements and display organizational skills and competence. Measurements of moral development, such as the scale developed by Lawrence Kohlberg, take male behaviour as the norm.

In her interviews with women, Gilligan detects a 'different voice' which speaks not in terms of abstract moral principles and individual rights but in terms of sustaining particular relationships. She thus identifies two distinct moral perspectives which she designates the 'ethic of justice' and the 'ethic of care'. Both these perspectives, Gilligan argues, are important because they both speak truths – one about the role of separation in defining and empowering the self; the other about the ongoing process of attachment that creates and sustains the human community (Gilligan, 1982: 155).

Gilligan's work in the field of developmental psychology has given rise to a rich debate within political theory about the nature of justice and its relation to care. Liberal theorists, on the whole, work with a highly idealized view of a rational autonomous agent and with highly abstract principles of justice. Gilligan's work shows that the self is situated in a web of relationships with others and that this makes moral reasoning complex and often messy. We may have conflicting obligations to others or our obligations to others may be in conflict with our own needs or interests. Appealing to a hierarchy of abstract principles does not seem to offer an adequate way of dealing with such situations of moral complexity. Through attending to the life-stories of particular individuals, Gilligan is able to pose a challenge to the dominant model of moral development which emphasizes the gendered nature of identity and which pays greater attention to the contexts within which our beliefs and values are formed.

One important effect, then, of work by communitarian and feminist thinkers who draw our attention to narrative is to make us consider where the social or political theorist is situated. If there is no 'view from nowhere' then we need to be more reflective about our own world-views – to see that the theories we construct reflect the history, culture and traditions of the society within which we live. In fact, to speak of 'our' history, 'our' culture or 'our' tradition is already to take too much for granted.

NARRATIVE AND IDENTITY

Many thinkers have drawn attention to the importance of narration in securing identity. In her book *Being in Time* Genevieve Lloyd argues: 'There is not a stable self perceiving a changing world, but a self which is itself shifting and unstable. However, its capacity for reflection saves it from complete disintegration into the fragments out of which its patterns are formed' (Lloyd, 1993: 9). In other words, our sense of self is achieved through our capacity to conceive of our own lives as a unity and this in turn is a result of our capacity to tell the story of our lives. This view is shared by Anthony Paul Kerby who argues that 'the self is given content, is delineated and embodied, primarily in narrative constructions or stories' (Kerby, 1991: 1). The appropriate question to ask about the self is not *what* but *who* the self is. The answer to this question is given through story-telling. This view of the self has important implications for social and political theorists concerned with the concept of identity.

Charles Taylor is one theorist who emphasizes the importance of language and particularly of narrative in thinking about identity. Taylor argues that what is distinctive about human beings is that we are purposive beings. The shape of our lives is therefore a question for us. We do not only have needs and wants but we also seek meaning. We exist within what Taylor calls moral space – a dimension of questions about what kind of life we should lead. We are also beings who exist over time. We therefore have a sense of becoming and changing and of possibility. Our sense of self – of *who* we are – is articulated through narrative. As language users we are situated within 'webs of interlocution' which shape the possible range of identities we can form and the possible ways of making sense of events. Our sense of our own identity is therefore intimately related to the culture and history into which we are born:

> My self-definition . . . finds its original sense in the interchange of speakers. I define who I am by defining where I speak from, in the family tree, in social space, in the geography of social statuses and functions, in my moral and spiritual orientations to the ones I love, and also crucially in the space of moral and spiritual orientation within which my most important defining relations are lived out (Taylor, 1989: 35).

One way in which individuals strive to make sense of their lives is to try to relate their own story to a broader cultural or historical narrative, whether it be Christianity or the coming revolution or the retrieval or continuance of a national culture. The capacity to narrate our personal experience gives us a sense of individual identity but in so far as we are able to relate that experience to a broader narrative, we can also share an identity with others. This has important political consequences since those who cannot identify with the dominant narrative are likely to feel alienated and excluded.

Focusing on the relation between narrative and identity raises important questions about recognition which are often overlooked in political theory. Identity is formed and sustained within a community and it is therefore formed and sustained partly by the recognition of others. Drawing on Taylor's work, Anthony Appiah argues that each person's individual identity includes a collective dimension such as gender, race or sexual orientation. Such collective identities provide 'scripts' that people use in shaping their life plans or telling their life-stories. But these scripts are often written by those who have most power and the scripts offered in the past to women or blacks or homosexuals have often been very negative so that individuals within these groups have not been granted the recognition and respect accorded to other citizens (Appiah, 1994).

Linking identity to narrative therefore draws attention to the construction and representation of identity. This in turn leads on to questions of how individuals achieve recognition and how different groups within society are perceived. Theorists such as Taylor and Appiah are concerned with opening up space for different voices to be heard within the political realm so that the concepts and practices that shape our identity are not simply a reflection of the interests of one class, gender or race but are a result of deliberation between different groups.

THEORY AND LITERATURE

In the introduction to their collection *Literature and the Political Imagination*, John Horton and Andrea Baumeister point out that 'The very birth of the Western philosophical tradition was marked by Plato's desire to banish the poets from the world of the *Republic*' (Horton and Baumeister, 1996: 9). While many contemporary political philosophers also regard literature as philosophically irrelevant or even harmful and confusing, the recent growth of interest in the concept of narrative on the part of political theorists has encouraged a re-examination of the links between theory and imaginative literature. Many theorists who reject foundationalist approaches to political theory also draw attention to the role of art and literature in enlarging our understanding.

David Parker argues that 'literature, working from concretely imagined, context-embedded situations, tends to work by the exploratory interrelating of conflicting moral perspectives' (Parker, 1994: 58). Maureen Whitebrook agrees that:

Literature has a special capacity for illustrating and illuminating 'lived reality'. It can help restore to political thought a more adequately complex view of human nature: to complicate. It can, for example, be especially effective at exploring the realistic complexity of conflicts between the individual and the polis (Whitebrook, 1995: 2).

Literature can provide us with rich descriptions of particular contexts which might be more useful than abstract theory in our reflections on questions of justice, equality, legitimacy and so on.

Martha Nussbaum turns to literature for exactly this reason. Her approach to moral and political thought draws on classical sources. Nussbaum offers what she calls a 'thick, vague conception' of the shape of human life. She terms her conception 'thick' to contrast it with the 'thin' conceptions of the good at work in more abstract political theory. She does not rely on one feature of human life, such as autonomy or pain, but rather seeks to identify all the features which we can take as general, including mortality, the body, sociability, separateness, cognitive capability and so on. Yet her list is 'vague' because it is not definitive. It can be added to as we learn more and the details of each category can be filled out in a variety of ways according to local and personal conceptions (Nussbaum, 1992).

Nussbaum, then, attempts to mediate between universal claims about the essential features of human existence and the particular ways in which these features are brought into sharper definition. It is in pursuit of detail that she appeals to literary narrative. The Aristotelian approach to ethics, which Nussbaum favours, asks the broad and inclusive question 'How should a human being live?' This question does not have a single answer and it is in pursuit of an awareness of the variety of possible answers that Nussbaum turns to literature:

Thus if the enterprise of moral philosophy is understood as we have understood it, as a pursuit of truth in all its forms, requiring a deep and sympathetic investigation of all major ethical alternatives and the comparison of each with our active sense of life, then moral philosophy requires . . . literary texts and the experience of loving and attentive novel-reading, for its own completion (Nussbaum, 1990: 26–27).

In *Contingency, Irony, and Solidarity*, Richard Rorty explains why he thinks it is that forms of narrative have replaced forms of theory as the principle vehicles of moral change and progress. Rorty describes himself as a liberal – someone who thinks that cruelty is the worst thing we do, and an ironist – someone who knows that their deeply held beliefs and values cannot be given foundations. Rorty maintains that the liberal hope which guides social and political action is the hope that we can diminish the amount of human suffering in the world. Cruelty can only be diminished by an extension of solidarity. The process of coming to see other human beings as 'one of us' is a matter of detailed description of what others are like.

> This process of coming to see other human beings as 'one of us' rather than as 'them' is a matter of detailed description of what unfamiliar people are like and of redescription of what we ourselves are like. This is a task not for theory but for genres such as ethnography, the journalist's report, the comic book, the docudrama, and, especially, the novel. That recognition would be part of a general turn against theory and toward narrative (Rorty, 1989: xvi).

Novels such as Orwell's *1984,* or Nabokov's *Lolita,* Rorty argues, may help us to become less cruel by helping us to see the effects of social practices and institutions on individuals or to see how individual idiosyncrasies affect others.

The relation between theory and literature is not straightforward and there are large areas of disagreement among those theorists who agree that literature may bring something important to our considerations of the social and political world. Martha Nussbaum and Richard Rorty exemplify two possible approaches. It could be argued, however, that both thinkers have a somewhat rosy view of literary texts and their power to affect political life. Reading novels and engaging in thought experiments is not sufficient to bring about political change. Nevertheless, recent developments in political theory and literary theory have emphasized the continuities between different kinds of narrative discourse. Historians, biographers and novelists are all engaged in an active process of making sense of experience. Literary theorists such as Terry Eagleton have pointed out that texts cannot be divorced from the wider social relations between writers and readers or from the social purposes and conditions in which they are embedded (Eagleton, 1983). Thus the concern with narrative evident in so many disciplines may well lead to a more fruitful exchange among those working within the humanities and social sciences.

THE LIMITS OF THE 'NARRATIVE TURN'

The thinkers we have been considering agree that our beliefs, values and actions can only be understood in a narrative context. They also agree that political and social theory must draw on ways of seeing which are embedded within the ongoing life of particular communities. We have seen that this raises interesting questions about the nature and scope of social and political theory and the perspective of the theorist. Once we acknowledge that the theorist is situated in a particular historical context, questions about the authority and authorship of social and political theory arise.

Some theorists have argued that the kind of account offered by MacIntyre and Taylor which sees identity, beliefs and values as embedded within a particular community is inherently conservative. From what standpoint can the *status quo* be challenged? Feminists such as Anne

Phillips have pointed out that oppressed groups have often asserted their claims to equality in the name of an abstract and universal conception of humanity (Phillips, 1993).

Michael Walzer offers a response to these concerns by suggesting that while we have to start from the moral beliefs and values of the community we are born into, we can nevertheless challenge existing norms. Walzer sees social criticism not as the discovery of moral truths or as the invention of a new morality, but rather as offering new interpretations of existing beliefs and values:

> We become critics naturally, as it were, by elaborating on existing moralities and telling stories about a society more just than, though never entirely different from, our own . . . The truth is that there is no guarantee, any more than there is a guarantor. Nor is there a society, waiting to be discovered or invented, that would not require our critical stories (Walzer, 1987: 65–6).

Walzer seems satisfied, then, that a narrative approach can be a critical approach to understanding the present. The French post-modernist thinker Jean-François Lyotard is not so convinced that this is the case.

Lyotard acknowledges that narrative can play a decisive role in the construction of stable identities but, precisely because narratives order and confer meaning on events in relation to particular ends, they can prevent us from thinking more critically and seeing things from other perspectives. Lyotard's particular targets are what he terms 'grand narratives' or 'metanarratives' which seek to tell an overarching story of human history and progress. Such metanarratives, Lyotard argues, have been invoked by totalitarian regimes which insist that citizens reproduce the grand narrative even when it bears no relation to their lived experience. The Marxist metanarrative of emancipation invoked by communist leaders was finally undermined, according to Lyotard, by thousands of little stories of individual suffering. In some of Lyotard's work, he seems to suggest that resistance to metanarratives can come from a proliferation of more local and personal stories. In his later work, however, he seems to be antithetical to the narrative genre altogether. Communities 'banded around their names and their narratives' tend to exclude those who are not members from ethical consideration (Lyotard, 1988: 181).

The post-modern condition, as Lyotard describes it, is one in which society becomes ever more complex (Lyotard, 1984). In place of a single community there are now a multiplicity of communities orientated towards different ends. These ends often conflict and we must seek to recognize such conflicts if we are to achieve justice. Narratives tend to mask conflict because, as a genre, story-telling seeks an end; a resolution.

Yet Lyotard does think that it is possible to work towards greater justice. In *The Differend*, Lyotard describes a *differend* as an occasion on which a person who wishes to voice a wrong realizes 'through the pain that

121

accompanies silence' that the language they are using cannot express the wrong that has been done (Lyotard, 1988: 13). Lyotard's own project therefore relies on narrative in order to bring to light the occurrence of *differends* and to defend his account of justice. The answer to the question 'why should we be just?' is given narratively. It consists in showing through narrative description how the imposition of a discourse can result in silence and pain for those who cannot express their experience in that language. As Dwight Furrow points out in his discussion of Lyotard's work, ethics may employ narrative for the purpose of demonstrating the limitations of a particular position (Furrow, 1995). Lyotard's doubts about narrative are important, however, because they draw attention to the need to continually question the stories we tell.

CONCLUSION

The turn to narrative is a turn away from the search for universal foundations or timeless truths towards a historical understanding of how our identity has been shaped. When this turn is taken, questions in social and political theory become questions about the course of our common life and the understandings we already share. The task of the theorist, on this view, is an ongoing process of critical reflection on the past which has shaped us and an imaginative exploration of the limits of our present understanding in the name of a future yet to take shape.

SUMMARY

- Narratives are complex cognitive schemes which organize individual human actions and events into a coherent whole.
- In contrast to abstract theories or models, narratives are constructed from a particular point in time and space.
- Both individual and cultural identity require narrative.
- A narrative approach to social and political theory emphasizes the historical and cultural context of human beliefs and values.
- Defenders of a narrative approach argue that literary narrative has an important role to play in social and political thought.

FURTHER READING

Mitchell, W.J.T. (ed.) (1980) *On Narrative*. Chicago and London: University of Chicago Press. This is an excellent interdisciplinary collection of essays including contributions by Hayden White, Jacques Derrida, Frank Kermode, Nelson Goodman and Paul Ricoeur. The collection as a whole provides a way into the most fundamental debates about the nature and value of narrative as a means of representing and making sense of the world.

Hinchman, Lewis P. and Hinchman, Sandra K. (eds) (1997) *Memory, Identity, Community. The Idea of Narrative in the Human Sciences.* New York: SUNY Press. This recent collection of papers brings together fifteen seminal papers from a range of writers including Alasdair MacIntyre, Stephen Crites, David Carr and Gertrude Himmelfarb. It includes papers from many disciplines such as history, psychology, law, philosophy, political science, sociology and anthropology, and thus provides an extremely useful interdisciplinary collection of work. The editors also offer a very clear overview of the reasons for the current interest in narrative in the human sciences and the central issues and problems that the study of narrative occasions.

Polkinghorne, Donald E. (1988) *Narrative Knowing and the Human Sciences.* New York: SUNY Press. This is probably the single most useful introduction to debates on the nature and value of narrative. Polkinghorne provides an accessible overview of the issues and a more detailed review of the role of narrative within the disciplines of history, literature and psychology. He also considers the ways in which a narrative approach may be used in empirical research.

Lloyd, Genevieve (1993) *Being in Time: Selves and Narrators in Philosophy and Literature.* London: Routledge. Lloyd's book examines how the unity of the self over time is achieved through the construction of narratives. She demonstrates that the question of how human beings deal with being in time has been a recurring question in the history of Western philosophy. Her book also examines the relationship between philosophical writing and literature.

Furrow, Dwight (1995) *Against Theory: Continental and Analytical Challenges in Moral Philosophy.* London: Routledge. Furrow provides an excellent introduction to current debates about the nature and scope of theory. The focus of his discussion is moral theory but the arguments can also be applied to political theory. He offers critical interpretations of Nussbaum, Rorty, MacIntyre and Lyotard among others thus bringing together thinkers within the continental and analytical traditions.

Horton, John and Baumeister, Andrea T. (eds) (1996) *Literature and the Political Imagination.* London: Routledge. This collection incorporates a diverse and interesting collection of essays which demonstrate how productive the interchange between political theory and literature can be. Theorists discussed include Rorty, Taylor, MacIntyre and Nussbaum. Novelists include

123

Swift, Dickens and Orwell. The contributions range from a discussion of nationalism to a consideration of feminist utopian fiction.

REFERENCES

Appiah, K. Anthony (1994) 'Identity, Authenticity, Survival: Multicultural Societies and Social Reproduction' in Amy Gutman (ed.) *Multiculturalism: Examining the Politics of Recognition*. Princeton, NJ: Princeton University Press.

Arendt, Hannah (1973) *Men In Dark Times*. Harmondsworth: Penguin.

Eagleton, Terry (1983) *Literary Theory: An Introduction*. Oxford: Blackwell.

Furrow, Dwight (1995) *Against Theory: Continental and Analytical Challenges in Moral Philosophy*. London: Routledge.

Gilligan, Carol (1982) *In a Different Voice: Psychological Theory and Women's Development*. Cambridge, MA and London: Harvard University Press.

Horton, John and Baumeister, Andrea T. (eds) (1996) *Literature and the Political Imagination*. London: Routledge.

Kerby, Anthony Paul (1991) *Narrative and the Self*. Bloomington and Indianapolis: Indiana University Press.

Laforest, Guy (1993) 'Introduction', in C. Taylor, *Reconciling the Solitudes: Essays on Canadian Federalism and Nationalism*. Montreal: McGill-Queen's University Press.

Lloyd, Genevieve (1993) *Being in Time: Selves and Narrators in Philosophy and Literature*. London: Routledge.

Lyotard, Jean-François (1984) *The Postmodern Condition: A Report on Knowledge*. Manchester: Manchester University Press.

Lyotard, Jean-François (1988) *The Differend: Phrases in Dispute*. Manchester: Manchester University Press.

MacIntyre, Alasdair (1985) *After Virtue*. London: Duckworth.

McCloskey, D.N. (1990) 'Storytelling in Economics', in C. Nash (ed.) *Narrative in Culture. The Uses of Storytelling in the Sciences, Philosophy and Literature*. London: Routledge, pp. 5–22.

Mitchell, W.J.T. (ed.) (1981) *On Narrative*. Chicago: University of Chicago Press.

Nash, Christopher (ed.) (1990) *Narrative in Culture: The Uses of Storytelling in the Sciences, Philosophy and Literature*. London: Routledge.

Niebuhr, H. Richard (1989) 'The Story of Our Life', in S. Hauerwas and L. Gregory Jones (eds) *Why Narrative*? London: Eerdmans.

Nussbaum, Martha (1990) *Love's Knowledge*. Oxford: Oxford University Press.

Nussbaum, Martha (1992) 'Human Functioning and Social Justice: In Defence of Aristotelian Essentialism', *Political Theory*, **20**(2): 202–46.

Parker, David (1994) *Ethics, Theory and the Novel*. Cambridge: Cambridge University Press.

Phillips, Anne (1993) *Democracy and Difference*. Cambridge: Polity Press.

Polkinghorne, Donald E. (1988) *Narrative Knowing and the Human Sciences*. New York: SUNY Press.

Rorty, Richard (1989) *Contingency, Irony, and Solidarity*. Cambridge: Cambridge University Press.

Taylor, Charles (1989) *Sources of the Self: The Making of the Modern Identity*. Cambridge: Cambridge University Press.

Walzer, Michael (1987) *Interpretation and Social Criticism*. Cambridge, MA and London: Harvard University Press.

Whitebrook, Maureen (1995) *Real Toads in Imaginary Gardens: Narrative Accounts of Liberalism*. Maryland and London: Rowman and Littlefield.

Chapter 9

Rational choice theory

John Scott

It has long appeared to many people that economics is the most successful of the social sciences. It has assumed that people are motivated by money and by the possibility of making a profit, and this has allowed it to construct formal, and often predictive, models of human behaviour. This apparent success has led many other social scientists to cast envious eyes in its direction. They have thought that if they could only follow the methods of economics they could achieve similar successes in their own studies. These sociologists and political scientists have tried to build theories around the idea that all action is fundamentally 'rational' in character and that people calculate the likely costs and benefits of any action before deciding what to do. This approach to theory is known as *rational choice theory*, and its application to social interaction takes the form of *exchange theory*.[1]

The fact that people act rationally has, of course, been recognized by many sociologists, but they have seen rational actions alongside other forms of action, seeing human action as involving both rational and non-rational elements. Such views of action recognize traditional or habitual action, emotional or affectual action, and various forms of value-oriented action alongside the purely rational types of action. Weber (1920), for example, built an influential typology of action around just such concepts. His ideas were taken up by Talcott Parsons (1937) and became a part of the sociological mainstream. In a similar way, the social anthropologists Bronislaw Malinowski (1922) and Marcel Mauss (1925) looked at how social exchange was embedded in structures of reciprocity and social obligation. What distinguishes rational choice theory from these other forms of theory is that it denies the existence of any kind of action other than the purely rational and calculative. All social action, it is argued, can be seen as rationally motivated, as instrumental action, however much it may appear to be irrational or non-rational.

A pioneering figure in establishing rational choice theory in sociology was George Homans (1961), who set out a basic framework of exchange theory, which he grounded in assumptions drawn from behaviourist psychology. While these psychological assumptions have been rejected by many later writers, Homans's formulation of exchange theory remains the basis of all subsequent discussion. During the 1960s and 1970s, Blau (1964), Coleman (1973) and Cook (1977) extended and enlarged his framework, and they helped to develop more formal, mathematical models of rational action (see also Coleman 1990).

Rational choice theorists have become increasingly mathematical in orientation, converging more closely with trends in microeconomics. Indeed, some economists have attempted to colonize areas occupied by other social scientists. This trend towards formal, mathematical models of rational action was apparent in such diverse areas as theories of voting and coalition formation in political science (Downs, 1957) and explanations of ethnic minority relations (Hechter, 1987) and, in a less rigorously mathematical form, social mobility and class reproduction. Economists such as Becker (1976, 1981) set out theories of crime and marriage. A particularly striking trend of recent years has been the work of those Marxists who have seen rational choice theory as the basis of a Marxist theory of class and exploitation (Elster, 1983, 1986; Roemer, 1988).

RATIONALITY AND SOCIAL EXCHANGE

Basic to all forms of rational choice theory is the assumption that complex social phenomena can be explained in terms of the elementary individual actions of which they are composed. This standpoint, called methodological individualism, holds that: 'The elementary unit of social life is the individual human action. To explain social institutions and social change is to show how they arise as the result of the action and interaction of individuals' (Elster, 1989: 13).

Where economic theories have been concerned with the ways in which the production, distribution and consumption of goods and services is organized through money and the market mechanism, rational choice theorists have argued that the same general principles can be used to understand interactions in which such resources as time, information, approval and prestige are involved.

In rational choice theories, individuals are seen as motivated by the wants or goals that express their 'preferences'. They act within specific, given constraints and on the basis of the information that they have about the conditions under which they are acting. At its simplest, the relationship between preferences and constraints can be seen in the purely *technical* terms of the relationship of a means to an end. As it is not possible for individuals to achieve all of the various things that they want, they must also make choices in relation to both their goals and the means for attaining these goals. Rational choice theories hold that individuals must anticipate the outcomes of alternative courses of action and calculate that which will be best for them. Rational individuals choose the alternative that is likely to give them the greatest satisfaction (Heath, 1976: 3).

The methodological individualism of rational choice theorists leads them to start out from the actions of individuals and to see all other social phenomena as reducible to these individual actions. For Homans, however, it was also necessary to see individual actions as reducible to these conditioned psychological responses (see also Emerson, 1972a, 1972b). This position was justified on the grounds that the principles of rational choice and social exchange were simply expressions of the basic principles of behavioural psychology. While many other rational choice theorists have rejected this claim – and Homans himself came to see it as inessential – it is worth looking, briefly, at the argument.[2]

A PSYCHOLOGICAL BASIS?

The idea of 'rational action' has generally been taken to imply a conscious social actor engaging in deliberate calculative strategies. Homans argued that human behaviour, like all animal behaviour, is not free but determined. It is shaped by the rewards and punishments that are encountered. People do those things that lead to rewards and they avoid whatever they are punished for. Reinforcement through rewards and punishments – technically termed 'conditioning' – is the determining factor in human behaviour. This behaviour can, therefore, be studied in purely external and objective terms; there is no need to invoke any internal mental states. People learn from their past experiences, and that is all we need to know in order to explain their behaviour.

The inspiration behind Homans's psychology was the behaviourism of B.F. Skinner, developed from studies of pigeons. Food is the basic goal sought by animals, and Skinner held that animal behaviour could be shaped by the giving or withholding of food. Food is a reward that reinforces particular tendencies of behaviour. Humans, however, are motivated by a much wider range of goals. While pigeons will do almost anything for grain, humans are more likely to seek approval, recognition, love or, of course, money. Human consciousness and intelligence enters the picture only in so far as it makes possible these symbolic rewards. Homans did not see this as involving any fundamental difference in the way that their behaviour is to be explained. The character of the rewards and punishments may differ, but the mechanisms involved are the same.

In social interaction, individuals are involved in mutual reinforcement. Each participant's behaviour rewards or punishes the other, and their joint behaviour develops through this 'exchange' of rewarding and punishing behaviours. While any behaviour can, in principle, reinforce the behaviour of another, Homans held that *approval* is the most fundamental human goal. Approval is a 'generalized reinforcer' that can reinforce a wide variety of specialized activities. Because of its generalized character, Homans saw approval as directly parallel to money. Both money and approval are general means of exchange in social interaction, one in economic exchange and the other in social exchange.

Not all rational choice theorists have relied on behavioural psychology in this way. Indeed, many remain quite deliberately agnostic about the ultimate determinants of human action. Following the example of many economists, they have seen their task simply as the construction of logically coherent, predictive theories of human action. Individuals, they argue, act *as if* they were fully rational and, therefore, rationality can be taken as an unproblematic starting point. There is no need to dig any deeper into individual psychology: whatever psychology may say about motivation does not affect the fact that social relations and exchange processes can be understood as if all individuals were purely rational actors. This argument is tenable only if a rather extreme positivist view of knowledge is adopted, and most realists would expect to find some attention given to the psychological basis of motivation and, therefore, to attempts to test out the adequacy of particular psychological assumptions. While these epistemological issues point beyond my present concerns (see Delanty, 1997), they should be borne in mind in the following discussion.

SOCIAL INTERACTION AS SOCIAL EXCHANGE

Following the economic model, then, rational choice theorists see social interaction as a process of social exchange. Economic action involves an exchange of goods and services; social interaction involves the exchange of approval and certain other valued behaviours. In order to emphasize the parallels with economic action, rewards and punishments in social exchange have generally been termed rewards and costs, with action being motivated by the pursuit of a 'profitable' balance of rewards over costs. The various things that a person might do – his or her opportunities – vary in their costs, but they also vary in their rewards. In many cases, there will be a combination of monetary and non-monetary rewards and costs.

The rewards received from goods purchased from a shop, for example, might include the intrinsic satisfactions that can be gained from their consumption and the social approval that is gained from their status display. Stealing a car, on the other hand, might be rewarding because of the pleasures derived from joy-riding and the recognition accorded by fellow car thieves. These same activities, however, also involve costs. Items can be purchased from a shop only by giving up some of the money that a person possesses, and car theft involves penalties, such as imprisonment and social disapproval that will be incurred if the thief is apprehended and convicted.

The strength of a reinforcement is measured by its quantity and its value. For example, the more banknotes that a person receives, and the higher their denomination, the more of a reward they are likely to be. The quantity and value of social approval, on the other hand, is less easily measured, though it may sometimes have a monetary equivalent. Social exchange theories, however, regard this as a purely technical problem that exists only because we have not yet developed adequate methods for measuring it.

For many rational choice theorists it is not even a technical problem, as it can be handled in exactly the same way as the intangible satisfactions that people gain from the objects that they buy or sell with money. The value of a reward, they argue, is the 'utility' that it has for a person. While this subjective utility can vary greatly from one person to another, it is possible to construct preference curves that measure the *relative* utility of one object against another and, therefore, the likelihood that people will try to obtain them. In general, the utility of someone's behaviour is seen in terms of such things as the amount of their time that it takes up and the frequency with which they are able to do it.

Rational choice theorists also recognize that the *threat* of punishment or the *promise* of a reward may motivate people just as much as the punishment or reward itself. The threat of punishment, for example, may call forth appropriate behaviour from those who wish to avoid the punishment. This assumption allowed Homans to recognize the motivating role of threats and inducements in the conditioning of human behaviour.

This can be illustrated by the case where one work colleague helps another to complete a difficult task. Someone who helps another and, in consequence, receives their approval, is likely to help them and others in future circumstances where he or she expects this to meet with approval. Conversely, the more often that approval has been given to those who help, the more often are people likely to help others; and the more oriented a person is to approval-seeking, the more likely he or she is to offer help. However, the more often that a helper has been approved by others, the less likely is she or he to find this approval to be so highly rewarding in the future. Such relationships will also involve an exchange of punishments as well as an exchange of rewards. For example, a person who has been punished for an activity in the past is likely to avoid doing it wherever he or she believes that they are likely to be punished again.

The profit that a person gains in interaction is measured by the rewards received minus the costs incurred. Homans argued that 'no exchange continues unless both parties are making a profit' (Homans, 1961: 61). What this means is that unless each participant finds it profitable, the interaction will not continue. The person who experiences a 'loss' finds the interaction more costly than rewarding and so will have an incentive to withdraw. A sustained social relationship, therefore, rests upon a balance of mutual profitability. Participants in social interaction engage in a calculus of rewards and costs and the interaction will continue in a stable form only if all participants are making a profit. Those who experience a loss will withdraw and will seek out alternative interactions where they are more likely to earn a profit.

Exchange relations are also power relations, as the resources that people bring to their social relations are rarely equal. The outcome of any particular exchange, therefore, will depend upon the relative power of the participants. This bargaining power varies with the dependence of each participant on the exchange relationship, and this dependence varies, in turn, with the extent to which there are alternatives available to them (Emerson, 1962; Heath, 1976: 24). If people are able to obtain a particular goal only through one specific social relationship, then they are highly dependent on that relationship and so will have little power to influence the 'price' that they have to pay. This reflects the fact that a monopoly supplier is able to use its market power to command a high price from its customers. Social exchange systems, like economic markets, range from this monopoly situation through various forms of oligopoly and imperfect competition, to the fully competitive. In recent work, Emerson's colleagues have analysed the generation of power in extensive networks of exchange relationships (Cook *et al.*, 1983).

PROBLEMS IN RATIONAL CHOICE AND SOCIAL EXCHANGE

Three interlinked problems have bedevilled attempts to depict theories of rational action as general theories of social action. These are the problems of collective action, of social norms, and of social structure. Critics have argued that a proper solution to these problems shows the need to go beyond, or even to abandon, the theory.

The problem of collective action is that of how it is possible to explain the co-operation of individuals in groups, associations and other forms of joint action. If individuals calculate the personal profit to be made from each course of action, why should they ever choose to do something that will benefit others more than themselves? The problem of social norms is the related question of why people seem to accept and to follow norms of behaviour that lead them to act in altruistic ways or to feel a sense of obligation that overrides their self-interest. This and the problem of collective action comprise what Parsons (1937) called the Hobbesian problem of order: if actions are self-interested, how is social life possible?

The problem of social structure is that of how it is possible for an individualistic theory to explain and take proper account of the existence of larger structures. In particular, it is the question of whether there are social structures that cannot be reduced to the actions of particular individuals and that, therefore, have to be explained in different terms. This problem is raised for all individualistic theories, but it takes a particular form in relation to rational choice theories.

I will discuss each of these three problems in turn, looking at the answers proposed by rational choice theorists and assessing the adequacy of their arguments.

THE PROBLEM OF COLLECTIVE ACTION

Rational choice theorists have incorporated collective action into their theories by requiring that the actions of groups and organizations be reducible to statements about the actions of individuals. Trade unions, political parties, business enterprises and other organizations may, then, all figure as actors in rational choice theories. Whenever it is possible to demonstrate the existence of a decision-making apparatus through which individual intentions are aggregated and an agreed policy formulated, it is legitimate to speak of collective actors (Cook, O'Brien and Kollock, 1990; Hindess, 1988).

The problem that these theories face, however, is that of showing how such organizations come to be formed in the first place. It is possible to show that rational individuals would join organizations that are likely to bring them benefits that outweigh the costs of membership and involvement, but why should individuals join or support organizations that provide benefits that they will gain even if they do not join the organization? Why, for example, should someone join a trade union if they will receive any negotiated wage increases in any case? Why will they join a professional association that works on behalf of all members of the profession, regardless of whether they are members of the association? This is the problem of the so-called 'free rider'. Rational actors have no individual incentive to support collective action. They will calculate that the costs of membership are high and that their participation can have no significant effect on the organization's bargaining power, and so they will conclude that they have nothing to gain from membership. Each potential member of a trade union, for example, will judge that as the sheer size of its membership gives it the necessary bargaining power, one extra member will make no difference. This leads to a paradox: if each potential member makes this same calculation, as rational choice theory expects them to do, then *no one* would ever join the union. The union would have little or no bargaining power, and so no one will receive any negotiated pay rises or improved conditions of work.[3]

The fact that people *do* join organizations and *do* become active in them must mean that there is something missing from the simple rational action model. Olson (1965) has suggested that collective action is sustained through what he calls 'selective incentives'. Unions might attract members, for example, if they can ensure that only their members will benefit from what they are able to negotiate. Selective incentives alter the rewards and costs in such a way as to make support for collective action profitable. Union membership is a rational choice for individuals if a 'closed shop' can be enforced, if pay rises are restricted to union members, or if unions can offer advantageous insurance or legal advice to their members. Hechter (1987) has generalized this point into the claim that associations are formed if it is possible for them to monopolize a resource and to exclude non-members. The fundamental problem remains, however. Organizations and associations that do *not* act in this way still do manage to attract members and, often, to thrive.

THE PROBLEM OF NORMS AND OBLIGATION

The related question is that of why individuals should ever feel any sense of obligation or wish to act in altruistic ways. Why, that is, should individuals obey norms that lead them to act in non-self-interested ways? Individuals pay taxes or join trade unions, for example, because they feel that they are under an obligation to do so or because they have some kind of moral or ideological commitment to the organization. Rational choice theorists tend to respond that norms are simply arbitrary preferences. Individuals may be socialized into all sorts of value commitments and will then act rationally in relation to these, whatever they may be. If people want to help others and get a sense of satisfaction from doing so, then giving help is an act of rational self-interest.

Other rational choice theorists find a solution in the existence of reciprocity. They argue that where social exchanges are recurrent, rather than episodic, it is possible for co-operation to emerge as a rational strategy. People rapidly learn that co-operation leads to mutual advantage, even if it does not produce the maximum outcome for any one participant. They learn, that is to say, that co-operation, rather than pure self-interest, is the optimum strategy. Ridley (1996: ch. 3) has argued that this must be seen as an instinctive response, as a genetically programmed innate predisposition for co-operation and reciprocity. The question remains, however, whether such an instinct exists and, if it does, whether it is powerful enough to generate the wide range of co-operative and altruistic behaviour found in human societies.

Equally important, it is not at all clear that rational choice theory can explain why co-operative and altruistic behaviour is so often sensed as a normative matter, as a matter of obligation and commitment. Durkheim (1893) argued that all rational economic actions occur within an institutional framework of norms that cannot itself be explained as the result of rational action alone. The norms of fair exchange and reciprocity, for example, cannot be explained in terms of specific contractual acts of exchange.

This was, I have already suggested, the core of the Parsonian critique of the Hobbesian account of social order. Parsons (1937) held that self-interested rational actors cannot generate a stable social order on an economic (or coercive, political) basis. For Parsons, social order could be explained only through the recognition that there is a normative, non-rational element in individual contracts.

Blau (1964) attempted to counter the problem by suggesting that people are willing to incur costs and imbalances in their exchange relations when they are formed into long chains of actions. In these circumstances – which are normal in all societies – they anticipate that any loss can be traded in for a counterbalancing profit at some time in the future. People anticipate a long-term reciprocity that is in everybody's interest and so becomes accepted as a norm. However, this solution assumes that individuals will trust each other, and the whole point of Parsons' argument is that rational individuals have no incentive to build this trust in the first place. The framework of norms and commitments that sustain such trust relations cannot themselves be explained through rational action processes.

Coleman tried to overcome this problem by seeing the emergence of trust in social interaction as a rational response to attempts to build coalitions, but the work of Cook and Emerson (1978) has recognized that the existence of trust cannot be seen in purely rational terms. They show that the norms of trust and justice that individuals use in their actions have a moral force that runs counter to purely rational considerations. The sense of obligation is real and can be felt very strongly.

Elster, among rational choice theorists, has accepted this conclusion. He argues that norms are not 'outcome-oriented' but are internalized and so acquire a compulsive character that cannot be explained in purely rational terms (Elster, 1989: 119). Norms operate, he holds, through shame and guilt, rather than through rewards and punishment.[4] As far as the explanation of norms is concerned, rational choice theory has nothing to offer. Rational choice and normative commitment, he argues, are complementary processes in the formation of social action.

The assumption of instrumental rationality, then, cannot give a complete explanation of social order. A full account must incorporate an awareness of the part that is played by social norms and emotional commitments alongside the exercise of rational choice. This dependence of rational choice theory on assumptions from very different theoretical traditions was recognized by Heath (1976) in his review. While rational considerations may explain why particular individuals introduce and enforce social norms, they cannot explain how these norms come to be internalized:

The rational choice approach can only explain what people *do*. It can explain why people might institute a norm and might then enforce it, but it cannot explain why they should change their values – for this is what internalisation amounts to. Values . . . must always remain a 'given' in the rational choice approach and to explain how they change we should have to introduce additional psychological mechanisms that have nothing to do with rationality (Heath, 1976: 64).

THE PROBLEM OF SOCIAL STRUCTURE

The methodological individualism adopted by rational choice theorists holds that all statements about social phenomena are reducible to statements about individual action. Explanation of social facts in terms of other social facts is, at best, a shorthand summary of the more detailed individual-level processes that produce them. Homans held that there are no independent and autonomous social structures: 'If you look long enough for the secret of society you will find it in plain sight: the secret of society is that it was made by men [*sic.*], and there is nothing in society but what men put there' (Homans, 1961: 385).

Homans claimed that his analysis of the 'elementary social behaviour' of face-to-face interaction comprised the 'subinstitutional' level of social analysis on which all large-scale social institutions depend. The greater complexity of the institutional level simply reflects the more indirect nature of many exchange relations and the greater use of such generalized reinforcers as money and social approval. The employee of a business enterprise, for example, exchanges work time for a wage that is received from a clerk in the salary department and not from a direct supervisor or from the owner of the firm. Instead of a direct exchange between the worker and the person for whom the work is undertaken, there is an indirect exchange that involves one or more intermediaries.

Those features of social life that are conventionally called 'social structures' are, for rational choice theorists, simply chains of interconnected individual actions. They are the 'patterns' that result from individual actions. It is because many of these chains can be quite extensive that social life can appear to have a life of its own. Cook, O'Brien and Kollock (1990) have recently drawn on arguments from social network analysis to suggest that social structures can be understood as chains of interconnection that form extensive exchange networks through which resources flow.[5]

The most successful attempts to explain the distinctive structural features of social life have seen them as the *unintended consequences* of individual action. It is the compounding of unintended consequences that produces social phenomena that individuals may be only partially aware of and that they experience as constraints. The classic example of this is the operation of market relations, as seen in economic theory. Through the operations of the competitive market, it is argued, the supply and the demand for commodities is matched without the need for central planning and co-ordination. The matching of supply and demand is the unplanned and unanticipated consequence of many hundreds of separate individual actions. It must be said, however, that rational choice theorists do tend to deny any autonomy or constraining power for social structures. This claim is not inherent in rational choice theory but in the methodological individualism that, for most of its advocates, is adopted as a philosophical underpinning. In this respect, rational choice theory faces similar difficulties to most other social theories that have focused on action to the exclusion of social structure.

SUMMARY

In this chapter I have argued that:

- Rational choice theory adopts a methodological individualist position and attempts to explain all social phenomena in terms of the rational calculations made by self-interested individuals.
- Rational choice theory sees social interaction as social exchange modelled on economic action. People are motivated by the rewards and costs of actions and by the profits that they can make.
- Some rational choice theorists have seen rationality as a result of psychological conditioning. Others have adopted the position that it is simply necessary to assume that individuals act *as if* they were completely rational.
- The problem of collective action poses great difficulties for rational choice theory, which cannot explain why individuals join many kinds of groups and associations.
- The problem of social norms, the other aspect of the Hobbesian problem of order, also poses difficulties. Rational choice theories cannot explain the origins of social norms, especially those of altruism, reciprocity and trust.
- The problem of social structure is a feature of methodological individualism, rather than rational choice theory *per se*, but it creates difficulties for the theories considered. Solutions to this problem have been in terms of the unintended consequences of individual action.

NOTES

1 This chapter draws, in part, on Chapter 3 in Scott (1995).
2 Ekeh (1974: 111–19) questions the links between behavioural psychology and classical economics. He argues that they were not equated with one another but

independently guided Homans's work. The incompatibilities between them produced contradictions in his work.
3 Coleman's work showed that rational choice theories could explain the formation of voting coalitions *within* organizations, as individuals exchange support for one another, but he did not extend this to the formation of organizations or to citizen support for public goods. See Coleman (1990).
4 See also the argument of Barnes (1992) on this point.
5 The framework of social network analysis, which does not depend on the adoption of rational choice theory, is discussed in Scott (1991).

FURTHER READING

Coleman, James (1990) *Foundations of Social Theory*. Cambridge, MA: Belknap. A magisterial attempt to cover the whole field in a systematic way and to present rational choice theory as the only reliable basis for a comprehensive social theory.

Elster, Jon (1989) *The Cement of Society*. Cambridge: Cambridge University Press. An important summary by an advocate of rational choice theory as the basis for a reconstruction of Marxism.

Downs, Anthony (1957) *An Economic Theory of Democracy*. New York: Harper and Brothers. A pioneering study that still has much to offer, especially in relation to the drift towards the centre in competitive political systems.

Becker, Gary (1981) *A Treatise on the Family*. Cambridge, MA: Harvard University Press. A *tour de force* that tries to show, amid much mathematics, that rational economic assumptions have more to offer than any other framework for the study of the family.

Heath, Anthony (1976) *Rational Choice and Social Exchange*. Cambridge: Cambridge University Press. An early critical summary that still has much to offer for a balanced assessment of rational choice theory.

REFERENCES

Barnes, S.B. (1992) 'Status Groups and Collective Action', *Sociology*, **26**: 259–70.
Becker, G.S. (1976) *The Economic Approach to Human Behaviour*. Chicago: University of Chicago Press.
Becker, G.S. (1981) *A Treatise on the Family*. Cambridge, MA: Harvard University Press.
Blau, P.M. (1964) *Exchange and Power in Social Life*. New York: John Wiley.
Coleman, J. (1973) *The Mathematics of Collective Action*. London: Heinemann.
Coleman, J.S. (1990) *Foundations of Social Theory*. Cambridge, MA: Belknap.

Cook, K.S. (1977) 'Exchanges and Power in Networks of Interorganizational Relations', *Sociological Quarterly*, **18**(1).

Cook, K.S. and Emerson, R.M. (1978) 'Power, Equity and Commitment in Exchange Networks', *American Sociological Review*, **43**: 721–39.

Cook, K.S., Emerson, R.M., Gillmore, M.R. and Yamagishi, T. (1983) 'The Distribution of Power in Exchange Networks: Theory and Experimental Results', *American Journal of Sociology*, **89**: 275–305.

Cook, K.S., O'Brien, J. and Kollock, P. (1990) 'Exchange Theory: A Blueprint For Structure and Process', in G. Ritzer (ed.) *Frontiers of Social Theory*. New York: Columbia University Press.

Delanty, G. (1997) *Social Science: Beyond Constructivism and Realism*. Buckingham: Open University Press.

Downs, A. (1957) *An Economic Theory of Democracy*. New York: Harper and Brothers.

Durkheim, E. (1893/1984) *The Division of Labour in Society*. London: Macmillan.

Ekeh, P. (1974) *Social Exchange Theory*. London: Heinemann.

Elster, J. (1983) *Sour Grapes*. Cambridge: Cambridge University Press.

Elster, J. (ed.) (1986) *Rational Choice*. Oxford: Basil Blackwell.

Elster, J. (1989) *The Cement of Society*. Cambridge: Cambridge University Press.

Emerson, R.M. (1962) 'Power – Dependence Relations', *American Sociological Review*, **27**: 692–703.

Emerson, R.M. (1972a) 'Exchange Theory, Part I: A Psychological Basis For Social Exchange', in J. Berger, M. Zelditch and B. Anderson (eds) *Sociological Theories in Progress, Volume Two*. Boston: Houghton Mifflin Company, pp. 38–57.

Emerson, R.M. (1972b) 'Exchange Theory, Part II: Exchange Relations and Network Structures', in J. Berger, M. Zelditch and B. Anderson (eds), *Sociological Theories in Progress, Volume Two*. Boston: Houghton Mifflin Company, pp. 38–57.

Heath, A. (1976) *Rational Choice and Social Exchange*. Cambridge: Cambridge University Press.

Hechter, M. (1987) *Principles of Group Solidarity*. Berkeley, CA: University of California Press.

Hindess, B. (1988) *Choice, Rationality and Social Theory*. London: Unwin Hyman.

Homans, G. (1961) *Social Behaviour: Its Elementary Forms*. London: Routledge and Kegan Paul.

Malinowski, B. (1922) *Argonauts of the Western Pacific*. London: Routledge and Kegan Paul.

Mauss, M. (1925, 1966) *The Gift*. London: Routledge and Kegan Paul.

Olson, M. (1965) *The Logic of Collective Action*. Cambridge, MA: Harvard University Press.

Parsons, T. (1937) *The Structure of Social Action*. New York: McGraw-Hill.

Ridley, M. (1996) *The Origins of Virtue*. London: Viking.

Roemer, J. (1988) *Free To Lose*. London: Radius.

Scott, J. (1991) 'Networks of Corporate Power: A Comparative Assessment', *Annual Review of Sociology*, **17**: 181–203.

Scott, J. (1995) *Sociological Theory: Contemporary Debates*. Cheltenham: Edward Elgar.

Weber, M. (1920) 'Conceptual Exposition', in G. Roth and C. Wittich (eds) *Economy and Society*. New York: Bedminster Press, 1968.

Chapter 10

Complexity theory

Tim Blackman

COMPLEX SYSTEMS

Human knowledge has traditionally been divided between the natural sciences and the social sciences. This division is based on the different types of theory and method that have developed to explain what have been treated as different processes of change in society and nature. Social processes are usually regarded as complex outcomes of interaction between social structure and human agency. Natural processes, on the other hand, are conventionally regarded as determined by laws of nature.

The social Darwinists attempted to explain society in the same terms as Darwin explained the natural world as an outcome of the 'law' of natural selection. These attempts are now seen as at best misinformed and at worst driven by racist ideologies in which some preferred racial characteristics are regarded as superior to others. However, it is clear that there are limits to how far human activities can ignore natural processes because the sustainability of these activities is a major issue. We are realizing that we must organize human activities so that they do not outstrip the recycling capacity of natural systems. This realization has come about through feedback processes between natural systems and human systems, such as the global warming effects of industrialization. Thinking in terms of 'systems' in this way helps us to understand processes which are internally organized and have boundaries that *connect* the system with its environment rather than separate it.

The natural sciences use the concept of 'system' to describe a pattern of relationships between elements that together comprise a whole that is differentiated from its environment, such as the ecosystem of a pond.

Organisms evolve as part of an ecosystem of competing and co-operating populations, species and ways of living. The Darwinian view of this process is that natural selection and successful adaptation to the environment drive evolution. However, biological research is revealing nature as a world not just created by natural selection but consisting of *self-organizing* systems that are *active* in relation to their environments and not purely determined by them. One of the fascinating results of this research is the discovery of behaviour that appears typical of all systems which use information and communication to organize both internally and in relation to the external environment.

The study of change in terms of interactions between systems and their environment is common in the natural sciences but has been controversial in the social sciences. This is mainly because such accounts in the social sciences have tended to be functionalist, portraying society as somehow having 'needs' for particular types of behaviour and institution. For example, crime might be explained as 'needed' by societies in order to define and reinforce what is socially acceptable behaviour. The American sociologist Talcott Parsons (1902–79) developed an elaborate model of systems and subsystems in attempting to explain societies as evolving towards more highly adapted types of social organization, with the USA representing the most 'successful' social and political system in this respect.

Kauffman's (1993) criticism of such accounts of evolutionary change *in nature* as functionalist 'just so' stories applies equally to social systems. These are stories which claim that a given system is a creation of evolution by identifying useful functions that particular features of the system perform. This account of evolution by natural selection cannot alone account for the abundance of variation in the natural or social worlds. As Kauffman (1993: xv) argues, 'we must understand how selection interacts with systems which have their own spontaneously ordered properties.'

Thus, both the natural and social sciences have come to recognize the importance of *self-organization* in explaining change. Systems organize using communication, although they do so in ways that are conditioned by system–environment interactions. These produce non-predictable but ordered patterns of change. A body of new theory has emerged in recent years to explain these processes, which appear common to both natural and social systems. This is known as *complexity theory* and its ideas are increasingly influential in both the natural and social sciences.

The prime aim of this chapter is to explain complexity theory, its origins, its main features and its applications in the social sciences.

EXPLAINING VARIABILITY

The social sciences are concerned with explaining *variability*. What is it that leads to certain predictabilities and similarities, and what is it that leads to non-predictability and dissimilarity? The conventional quantitative approach is to explain the variability in a dependent variable in terms of its statistical association with variability in one or more independent variables. A correlation coefficient of 0.7 is regarded as very high but this still means that a little less than half of the variability is explained in these terms. Often far less than half the variability is explained. This leaves much unaccounted for, but it is this unexplained area that may be able to reveal more about the causal processes at work than the explained linear variation.

The statistical analysis of variability focuses on variability in group properties, such as social class or gender. This variability is of interest when membership of groups is found to influence outcomes (such as health status) or condition action (such as criminal behaviour) differently. While it may be possible on occasions to reduce group properties to individuals, the conditioning and outcome effects of group properties can rarely be reduced in the same way. This is because they are contingent upon combinations of circumstance and cannot be represented by a simple perfect correlation of if A then B. These combinations may or may not mean that the causal powers of a group property such as social class determine the outcome for any one individual (who will have their own causal powers). This has led social theorists to refer to such properties as *emergent*, meaning that they emerge from social combination and have contingent effects, including acting back on the elements from which they emerge. The following example from Archer (1995: 9) helps to explain this point:

> Emergent properties are *relational*, arising out of combination (e.g. the division of labour from which high productivity emerges), where the latter is capable of reacting back on the former (e.g. producing monotonous work), has its own causal powers (e.g. the differential wealth of nations), which are causally irreducible to the powers of its components (individual workers).

Emergence is a process of positive *feedback* between action and its environment. For example, the emergence of an increased proportion of older-person households in the UK living independently rather than with their families arises from a combination of a lifestyle choice for 'intimacy at a distance' and improved housing and economic opportunities enabling older people to live independently. The environment is one of improved housing and economic opportunities. The decision to live independently is an example of positive feedback as the improved opportunities stimulate a change in decisions about living arrangements.

Feedback ideas are common in contemporary work on social theory: Giddens (1984), Archer (1995) and Luhmann (1995) are prime examples. This is because feedback is an essential concept in attempting to understand how the interplay between the individual and society, or agency and structure, either reproduces the *status quo* or produces change. Complexity theory conceives of the world as consisting of self-organizing systems, either reproducing their existing state via negative feedbacks with their environment or moving along trajectories from one state to another as a result of positive feedbacks. Statistical techniques can chart the general properties of a system, its trajectory through time and how it changes within its wider context or parameters, from an individual life or household to a social class or region. This can also be considered in qualitative terms, such as types of welfare state regime or individual biographies.

The emergence of global properties from local interactions is a key idea in complexity theory. Emergent phenomena such as the lone-parent family or the liberal welfare state are described in terms of global properties. This is possible because more-or-less ordered systems have global properties which enable us to distinguish one type of system from another.

While particular global properties are associated with particular outcomes, there is much local interaction which appears to be chaotic (the unexplained variation in a statistical model). Rather than being random noise, this chaotic behaviour can be a source of change in global properties. This is because an important feature of chaotic behaviour is that small changes in initial conditions can produce very large differences in outcome. This is the so-called 'butterfly effect', named after the meteorological possibility that a butterfly flapping its wings in South America could be the ultimate cause of a storm in North America.

Although chaotic, computer models have shown how local interactions give rise to emergent global structures which feed back to influence the local interactions that produced them (Lewin, 1993). These feedbacks either maintain a system in a stable state or generate a trajectory which carries the system on to another state cycle. A state cycle in complexity theory is known as a dynamic *attractor*. The concept of an attractor describes the long-term qualitative behaviour of a system: attractors embody the range of states possible for a system in a given environment. In the social sciences these could be types of household, health status or welfare regime.

BEYOND LINEAR MODELS

Newtonian physics was the model that Comte sought to emulate in the first half of the nineteenth century by defining a role for the new sociology as the scientific solution of social questions. This model was based upon it being enough to know the appropriate 'law' and the initial conditions in order to predict a future state. Such a commitment to establishing 'real facts' of predictive value continues today in various forms of policy-oriented research, although 'facts' are more likely to be expressed as statistical probabilities than certainties. The evidence-based practice movement in health care is a good example (Gray, 1997). This movement is based upon the use of research evidence to make clinical and policy decisions about the most effective and efficient health interventions. For processes that are mono-causal and not affected by feedback, the standard technique of this approach – the randomized controlled trial – is adequate. However, very few pro-cesses in nature or society are monocausal or free from feedback effects: the 'dependent' variables may not be as dependent as expected and may exert an influence back upon the 'independent' variables. For example, an anti-biotic that appears to be effective in a trial can easily lose its effectiveness because of the capacity of pathogenic bacteria to evolve new resistant strains very rapidly. Organisms are not only adapted but adaptable.

The natural sciences – and mathematics – have in general moved beyond the linear clockwork of Newtonian physics when reality demands it, which is surprisingly often. This can be traced back to the pioneering work of the French mathematician Jules Henri Poincaré in the late nineteenth century and resulted from the inability of positivism to solve problems concerning *complex* phenomena by reducing such phenomena to their constituent parts (reductionism). Returning to the antibiotics example, it is only possible to understand the emergent capability of bacteria to overcome potentially lethal environmental change by considering how a bacterium population as a whole *self-organizes* to maintain its adaptability. It achieves this through random genetic change that allows the population to keep exploring genetic solutions in fluctuating environments that include the host's immune system and any antibiotic reinforcements (Brookes, 1998). It is very hard to find a 'magic bullet' antibiotic faced with this complexity.

Non-linear interactive processes are common in society, although social scientists still often represent such processes as linear and regard interaction effects as of secondary importance to the direct effects of particular indepen-dent variables. The relationship between home background and educational achievement is a case in point, where linear graphs show a strong relation-ship between the percentage of pupils receiving free school meals (a proxy measure for poverty) and schools' average performance in examinations. This relationship, though, only holds for aggregate data. For individual pupils the relationship between home background and educational achievement is weak (Fitz-Gibbon, 1996). Both relationships may in fact be misleading.

Using multi-level modelling with individual pupil data, Goddard *et al.* (1996) found that exam results for *all* young people were lower when they lived in deprived areas, while young people from households dependent on benefits fared better than expected when they lived in non-deprived areas. This is evidence of *bifurcation* rather than linear change. Interaction is also likely to be at work because both schools and neighbourhoods with high rates of deprivation tend to worsen as better-off residents move to 'better' neighbourhoods and schools. Similarly, internal measures to improve the performance of individual schools can markedly improve their effective-ness: schools are themselves complex self-organizing systems although they exist in environments very much defined by the general character of their pupil intakes (Byrne and Rogers, 1996; Fitz-Gibbon, 1996).

During the 1970s and 1980s many social scientists were working with concepts of society as structurally determined, but the natural sciences were increasingly conceiving of nature as active and creative. This was based upon a new understanding of natural systems as dissipative systems, with a flux of matter and energy through the system generating emergent structure or order, rather than the system's order being determined solely through natural selection. An example is morphogenesis, the process of cell development in animals and plants. Archer (1995) borrows this term in her version of realist social theory to describe structural and cultural properties as emerging from the socio-cultural relations in which people pursue their projects. Similarly, Archer's (1995: 29–30) rejection of empiricism and its privileging of sense-data in favour of thinking and acting in terms of 'group properties' such as elections, interest rates, theories and beliefs is essentially a systems approach, based on the global properties of systems. It also echoes developments in mathematics that favour describing the general qualitative nature of outcomes rather than precise numerical descriptions which may be inaccurate because of chaotic behaviour.

What appears to be happening is that the natural and social sciences are converging because of a growing understanding of processes that appear to be common to social and natural phenomena due to the prevalence of dissipative systems, chaotic behaviour and emergent properties in both worlds.

INFORMATION AND COMMUNICATION: THE ORIGINS OF COMPLEXITY

Complex systems are self-organizing phenomena, although their behaviour is conditioned and constrained by environmental properties. These exert influences on local interactions, but these interactions may also overcome particular environmental properties and create new, emergent properties. The range of possibilities in this respect are attractors. Complexity, understood in these terms, has been identified extensively in nature and simulated using computer models.

Complex systems persistently dissipate matter and energy. They include cells, single organisms, ecosystems, economies and societies. They maintain themselves in an organized state by processing and accumulating information. Indeed, systems might be thought of as nested bundles of shared information within networks of information exchanges. In human systems, shared information entails shared meaning. This internal communication, together with communication with the environment, enables the system to organize both internally and in relation to its environment. Luhmann (1995) has argued that social systems exist in an environment of other systems from which they are differentiated by being 'self-referential'. He means by this that systems achieve, through the communication of meanings, relations with themselves and a differentiation of these relations from relations with their environment.

All systems, human and non-human, share this ability to maintain an organized state by using information (Stonier, 1992). An organized state is essentially one that enables the system to survive, reproduce and achieve its goals. The better a system is at understanding and using information, the greater is its ability to maintain an organized state by responding with appropriate actions in the face of environmental change.

The rich information environments existing inside human brains and the societies they create enable humans to provide context and meaning to new information inputs. The qualitative ability to perceive and remember patterns and associations is superior to logic alone because logic can be based on erroneous assumptions, take too long to work through or require complete data that often does not exist. Humans' qualitative capacity for understanding means that we can move beyond being controlled by our environment to controlling it and creating environments that are more favourable to human projects. The result is complex social systems with substantial internal integration and co-ordination.

Stonier (1992: 168) has argued that a basic law of nature is that 'simple systems aggregate to form more intricately organised systems'. Evolution appears to select for this increasing complexity because its greater integrating and co-ordinating abilities enhance survivability. If humans are an end result of this process, it is not surprising that the study of society would reveal features typical of complex systems. If these systems are useful to humans as reflective, conscious animals, it would not be surprising to find them reproduced through social action. Indeed, management theory is drawing substantially upon complexity theory in seeking to improve the efficiency and effectiveness of organizations (Stacey, 1993).

Complex systems are a distinctive type of system. They exist in a state that is neither totally ordered nor totally chaotic. This dynamic state is based upon iterative cycles whereby the output from one iterative cycle becomes the input to the next. Positioned between order and chaos in this way, complex systems may exist in a more or less stable state at a particular attractor. The attractor describes the generic properties of the system's state, e.g. a temperate climatic zone, a nuclear family or social democracy. However, environmental change – internally or externally – may cause perturbations within the system which may either be damped down by negative feedback or develop into chaotic behaviour, with positive feedback generating change along a trajectory within the system's 'phase space' (this can be compared with Archer's [1995] morphogenetic approach). The phase space contains the possible alternative attractors towards which a system under perturbation might move. The system moves through its phase space, transforming into a qualitatively different state if it settles on another

145

attractor. In other words, attractors are ways of understanding discontinuous, non-linear change over time. The attractors exert their influence because they are points where the system can re-establish a steady state.

Steady states exist in a variety of forms. Some attractors are stable with regard to small outside perturbations, some are stable with regard to perturbations in one direction but not another, while others are generally unstable. Furthermore, the attractor itself can have different dynamics, with some reproducing uniform conditions in stable cycles while others may be much more chaotic. The latter are known as 'strange attractors' and may generate divergent outcomes in ways that are very sensitive to initial conditions. Thus, the idea of an attractor is very similar to the idea of a *social structure* but it describes a system's long-term behaviour.

Which way a system under perturbation actually moves is usually unpredictable, although it may be possible to identify the possible alternative attractors in a phase space. This idea of trajectories is very important, and appears in much contemporary social science thinking about household, population and economic change. A recent example is John Hills's (1998) account of the work of the Research Centre for Analysis of Social Exclusion at the London School of Economics. He emphasizes the need to understand social exclusion as a process that is dynamic and not static, and the Centre's work includes 'a study of areas which have followed contrasting trajectories in recent years, trying to understand what drives such differences, and a qualitative study which will follow the lives of families living within them' (Hills, 1998: 25).

What is it that causes a system to move towards a new state; what drives change, as Hills (1998) puts it? Mathematical modelling has revealed the importance of certain system parameters passing through critical values which cause the system as a whole to transform. Change in these parameters is caused by perturbations which may arise from the external environment, internal fluctuations or an interaction between both external and internal processes. If a system generates values for this parameter which are below a certain critical value, the system moves towards and maintains a stable state. Cycles of change occur but they remain within the boundaries of the system and its general character. When the critical value is reached, the behaviour of the system changes and it oscillates between two states (a strange attractor). Further increases in the parameter produce oscillations between more states until the system's behaviour becomes chaotic, so that outputs from the system are unpredictable.

Dean (1997) applies this to modelling the prevalence of illicit drug-taking. His model defines x to measure the amount of illicit drug-taking in a community and r to measure the potential within the community for illicit drug-taking. Say that the r value is low due to low knowledge and availability of drugs. A low x value is maintained in a steady state. If r increases over time, however, the prevalence of drug use within the community would change and a new steady state at a higher level of use would emerge. If r rose further, the steady state would break down and levels of use would begin to oscillate over time. As r increases, these oscillations grow until it becomes impossible to predict how much illicit drug use there would be in this community across time. It could oscillate between almost total saturation and very little use. No reductionist social science, which measures certain risk factors such as unemployment or educational underachievement, could predict the likely prevalence of illicit drug use in communities where r is above its critical value.

Failure to predict is not the same as failure to understand or explain. Systems can have properties that are typical or generic and do not depend on the details of how they are constructed. It is possible to theorize about these generic properties because they are the potential attractors within a given phase space of possibilities. A phase space can also be thought of as a 'fitness landscape', with the implication that a landscape may change to create new 'basins of attraction' (Kauffman, 1993). There are parallels here with Marxist social theory and particularly Raymond Williams's account of how modes of production set limits on possible social and cultural arrangements rather than determine them mechanistically (Williams, 1973). The nature of the environment and interrelations between systems create a phase space of attractor sets representing possibilities within limits.

DISCOVERING COMPLEXITY

In the social sciences, this approach involves identifying the controlling parameters of a social system and investigating the effects of change in them (Byrne, 1998). There is therefore a special interest in investigating points of change – in individuals, households, neighbourhoods, regions or countries. As this list suggests, change occurs at different levels which are interlinked in the sense that 'higher' levels emerge from 'lower' ones and feed back to influence them. For example, social inequality is a generic feature which emerges from individual incomes and wealth. It is not only a way of measuring the distribution of income and wealth but has real effects in terms of generating certain societal characteristics and influencing the lives of individuals. Wilkinson (1996), for example, brings together a large number of studies which suggest that when the degree of social inequality moves beyond a certain level it affects the health of individuals independently of the effect of absolute income or wealth levels. This appears to operate through feedbacks between the individual and his or her society which underline the subordinate position of many individuals in unequal societies and create vulnerability to psychological distress and physical illness.

Health is a good example of an emergent property, as the title to Wilkinson's (1996) book, *Unhealthy Societies*, suggests. Health can be a generic property of systems at different levels: for example, an individual, household, social class, neighbourhood or country. As determinants of health, these levels interact so that although genes and biology are individual characteristics that affect health, they interact with medical care, lifestyles, environments and social characteristics, which also influence health (Tarlov, 1996). Historically and internationally, a transition can be observed which involves moving from a fitness landscape in which the major 'unhealthy' attractors are linked to infectious diseases to a landscape in which the main attractors are linked to chronic diseases. This fundamentally influences the health trajectory of individuals, health services and public policies. The transition has occurred as countries have increased their standard of living above basic subsistence levels, and is associated with an overall marked increase in life expectancy. The re-emergence of below-subsistence poverty can, of course, alter the general nature of this fitness landscape for developed countries, with the reappearance of tuberculosis being a prime example.

Byrne (1997) applies the statistical technique of cluster analysis to identify sets of attractors from 1971 and 1991 census data for Teesside in the North East of England. The attractors represent alternative generic properties which a given neighbourhood might have. He demonstrates how different the attractors were in 1971 compared with 1991, a period during which the region experienced major economic, political and demographic change. His interest is in what 'system changes' produced this transformation, which might be conceptualized as a shift from a Fordist to post-Fordist fitness landscape. The key control parameter which changed over this period was the proportion of men of working age not in employment, which increased by a factor of three from 10 per cent to 30 per cent. Work on complex systems by the American physicist Mitchell Feigenbaum in the 1970s found that an increase in a system's control parameter of this magnitude led to a transition from stable to complex behaviour, marked by patterns of bifurcation (Dean, 1997). Byrne's cluster analysis reveals a bifurcation in the socio-economic variables he used to describe the Teesside 'system', with the 1991 geography displaying neighbourhoods divided between relative affluence and relative deprivation.

Complexity theory promises a social science 'that works'. Feedbacks of information about the effects of actions can be used to modify behaviour in complex adaptive systems such as organizations and intervene in trajectories of change. Fitz-Gibbon (1996) uses complexity theory to argue for a 'monitoring-with-feedback' approach to school effectiveness, and calls for more experimental evidence to inform school practices based on local organization. Blackman (1996) suggests the use of local monitoring systems to detect early signs of urban problems that could be responded to with early preventative measures to dampen or prevent positive feedback.

These incremental approaches are not the only option. Byrne (1998) suggests that the huge resource inputs to regional systems during Britain's post-war modernization in the 1960s and 1970s were essentially about re-shaping the fitness landscape so that the attractors of unemployment and physical decay of the 1930s were removed. Blackman's (1987) study of this period shows how the strategy was undermined by change in critical economic parameters beyond the control of the planners' level of intervention. As a strategy contingent upon Fordist capital accumulation, its downfall is explainable if not predictable.

Eve, Horsfall and Lee (1997: xii) comment that complexity theory provides 'concepts to think with' but it also provides concepts to act with. A major challenge for policy and applied social science is to create fitness landscapes that support sustainable systems. One of the findings from investigating biological systems is that successful systems are able to adopt multiple strategies in the face of complex problems, often using 'trial-and-error' methods, and this requires some redundancy in the system (Kauffman, 1995). Similarly, Kauffman's work on networks suggests that systems can become too complex, with so many parts and interactions that the ability to cope with external or internal perturbations becomes compromised.

SUMMARY

Complexity theory is a type of systems theory which approaches explanation in terms of causes and effects but is not deterministic. Its basic principles can be summarized as follows:

- System–environment interaction entails feed-forwards as well as feedbacks.
- Social phenomena have multiple and interacting causes with non-linear trajectories of change occurring within phase spaces of possible attractors.
- Certain parameters govern the general properties of a system and its trajectory in phase space.
- System states are not predictable in the long term but the generic class to which they belong can be described, investigated and perhaps anticipated.

Complexity theory is a realist theory. It allows for purposeful, knowledge-based action which may be capable of changing both causes and effects. Because it focuses on generic emergent properties which are non-reducible it is a theory of the utmost importance to sociology. It expects change rather than stability and, as such, implies a reorientation of the stability-based research techniques of the social sciences which still inform much research practice. There are signs of change in this respect, with an increasing use of longitudinal datasets in quantitative research and approaches such as autobiographical methods in qualitative research. Complexity theory is thus part of a shift of human understanding towards emphasizing the arrow of time and the alternative possibilities for human systems.

FURTHER READING

A good introduction to complexity theory is M. Mitchell Waldrop's *Complexity: The Emerging Science at the Edge of Order and Chaos*. Harmondsworth: Viking (1992).

Stuart Kauffman explains his work in biology and its possible social and economic applications in *At Home in the Universe: The Search for Laws of Self-Organization and Complexity*. Harmondsworth: Viking (1995).

An excellent introduction for social scientists is David Byrne's *Complexity Theory and the Social Sciences*. London: Routledge (1998).

A more detailed read is Raymond A. Eve, Sara Horsfall and Mary E. Lee, *Chaos, Complexity and Sociology*. London: Sage (1997).

The role of complexity theory in bridging the natural and human sciences is discussed in the Gulbenkian Commission's (1996) report, *Open the Social Sciences: Report of the Gulbenkian Commission on the Restructuring of the Social Sciences*. Stanford: Stanford University Press.

REFERENCES

Archer, M. (1995) *Realist Social Theory: The Morphogenetic Approach*. Cambridge: Cambridge University Press.

Blackman, T. (1987) 'Housing Policy and Community Action in County Durham and County Armagh: A Comparative Study', PhD thesis, University of Durham.

Blackman, T. (1996) *Urban Policy in Practice*. London: Routledge.

Brookes, M. (1998) 'Day of the Mutators', *New Scientist*, **2121**: 38–42.

Byrne, D. (1997) 'Chaotic Places or Complex Places: Cities in a Post-industrial Era', in S. Westwood and J. Williams (eds) *Imagining Cities*. London: Routledge.

Byrne, D. (1998) *Complexity Theory and the Social Sciences*. London: Routledge.

Byrne, D. and Rogers, T. (1996) 'Divided Spaces: Divided Schools', *Sociological Research Online*, **1**(2), <http://www.socresonline.org.uk/socresonline/1/2/3.html.

Dean, A. (1997) *Chaos and Intoxication: Complexity and Adaptation in the Structure of Human Nature*. London: Routledge.

Eve, R.A., Horsfall, S. and Lee, M.E. (1997) *Chaos, Complexity and Sociology*. London: Sage.

Fitz-Gibbon, C.T. (1996) *Monitoring Education: Indicators, Quality and Effectiveness*. London: Cassell.

Giddens, A. (1984) *The Constitution of Society*. Cambridge: Polity Press.

Goddard, J.B., Fitz-Gibbon, C., Blackman, T. and Coombes, M. (1996) 'Integrating Administrative and Census-Like Data: Multi-level Models of GCSE Results', ESRC End of Award Report, Ref. No. H514255014.

Gray, J.A.M. (1997) *Evidence-based Healthcare: How to Make Health Policy and Management Decisions*. Edinburgh: Churchill Livingstone.

Hills, J. (1998) 'ESRC Research Centre for Analysis of Social Exclusion', *SPA News*, February–March: 24–6.

Kauffman, S.A. (1993) *The Origins of Order: Self-Organization and Selection in Evolution*. Oxford: Oxford University Press.

Kauffmann, S.A. (1995) *At Home in the Universe: The Search for Laws of Self-Organization and Complexity*. Harmondsworth: Viking.

Lewin, R. (1993) *Complexity: Life on the Edge of Chaos*. London: Phoenix.

Luhmann, N. (1995) *Social Systems*. Stanford: Stanford University Press.

Stacey, R. (1993) 'Strategy as Order Emerging from Chaos', *Long Range Planning*, **26**(1): 10–17.

Stonier, T. (1992) *Beyond Information: The Natural History of Intelligence*. London: Springer-Verlag.

Tarlov, A.R. (1996) 'Social Determinants of Health: The Sociobiological Translation', in D. Blane, E. Brunner and R. Wilkinson (eds) *Health and Social Organization*. London: Routledge.

Wilkinson, R.G. (1996) *Unhealthy Societies: The Afflictions of Inequality*. London: Routledge.

Williams, R. (1973) 'Base and Superstructure in Marxist Cultural Theory', *New Left Review*, **76**: 3–16. Reprinted in R. Williams (1980) *Problems in Materialism and Culture*. London: Verso, pp. 31–49.

Chapter 11

Contemporary liberalism

Gary Browning

INTRODUCTION

Liberalism is a leading if not the leading dominant ideology of the modern world. There is no transhistorical essence of liberalism, however, just as no ideology can be comprehended in essentialist terms that do not allow for debate and development. Theories of liberalism, though, tend to see and value a liberal society as one that is organized by mutual agreement to promote the interests of free and equal individuals. Contemporary liberal theorists, like their predecessors, may disagree over how a liberal society is to be best organized, but they are united in recognizing the worth of a society in which free, equal and rational individuals can flourish. Contemporary liberalism, though, is different at the levels of theory and practice. In practice liberalism is dominant in the Western world, and yet contemporary liberal theory is characteristically circumspect and makes only modest qualified claims on behalf of liberal society.

The fall of communism in Eastern Europe in 1989 was clearly important in emphasizing the practical failure of socialism in Europe. It was taken by Fukuyama as a token of the ultimate triumph of liberalism, signalling the end of history in the sense that liberalism remained the only ideology capable of realizing the social and material demands of individuals (Fukuyama, 1992). Fukuyama's thesis is problematic in that it denies the openness of future historical development. It does, however, register the very severe setback suffered by socialism, the most plausible ideological alternative to liberalism in the Western world after the Second World War, and the countervailing dominance of liberalism in the Western world. The practical success of liberalism is highlighted in its close alignment with capitalism. Capitalism promotes consumerism and engenders calculating individualism on a global scale. These features of capitalism harmonize with core values of liberalism, such as individuality, rationality and freedom, and thereby facilitate the spread of liberalism across the globe.

Liberalism, however, has been subjected to a powerful theoretical critique from a number of sources, notably post-modernism and communitarianism. In response contemporary liberal theorists have tended to become increasingly circumspect about the power and range of application of liberal arguments. Hence liberalism is now seen as being relevant only to a particular type of society and it is justified primarily in terms of its neutrality to rival conceptions of the good. This chapter will develop the argument sketched above. The dominance of liberalism as an ideology will be outlined, communitarian and post-modern critiques of characteristic liberal standpoints will be explored and finally the nature of contemporary liberal arguments, advanced by leading Anglo-American theorists, will be analysed.

THE PRACTICAL DOMINANCE OF LIBERALISM

The history of liberalism is closely related to the shaping of the modern world. It is bound up with the growth of markets, technology, capital, the nation-state and individualism. Its intellectual origins may be traced back to the seventeenth century and are evident in the political theories of Hobbes and Locke, both of whom analysed the logic of political authority in terms of the character and consent of individuals. Subsequent liberal theorists have followed Hobbes and Locke in articulating a conception of a society that maximizes the freedom and the exercise of rationality on the part of individuals in pursuing their goals and in interacting with others. The history of liberalism has allowed for the expansion of the range of individuals considered to be rational actors in society, so that women, for instance, are now taken by liberal theorists to possess the same rational capacities as men.

Classic liberalism is exemplified in the political thought of J.S. Mill who argued for the crucial importance of individual freedom, conceived as the protection of individuals from harmful interference by others, in establishing the welfare of man as a progressive being (Mill, 1989). For Mill, as for Gladstone, the contemporary incarnation of Victorian statesmanship, liberalism was a creed representing the highest achievement of human beings, which was to be justified by the demonstrable merits of cultivating liberal values such as individuality. Mill, though mindful of the problems facing nineteenth-century Europe, took liberalism to be the supreme achievement of humanity as a progressive force. T.H. Green, an exponent of the new liberalism developed in the latter part of the nineteenth century, differed from Mill in espousing the public provision of educational and material resources to promote the freedom of individuals (Green, 1986). Like Mill, though, he was sure that liberalism was an ethical doctrine that positively enables individuals to achieve personal and moral freedom.

The twentieth century has been seen by liberals as endorsing the practical efficacy of liberalism. Von Hayek and Popper are liberal theorists, whose studies encompassed a variety of disciplines and purposes. They developed cogent arguments for the practical superiority of liberalism in the mid-twentieth century when fascism and socialism appeared to offer viable ideological alternatives to liberalism. Popper highlighted the practical effectiveness of maintaining a liberal, open society in which errors can be exposed and he emphasized the lack of a comprehensive, conclusive demonstration of truth that could serve as a blueprint for the collectivist organization of society (Popper, 1966). Von Hayek celebrated a liberal society's capacity to allow for a greater complexity than that developed in a planned society, given the variety that is spontaneously generated by the pursuit of individually chosen pursuits and tasks (von Hayek, 1960). Von Hayek and Popper contrasted a liberal open society with the authoritarian and collectivist control exerted by communist and fascist states. The connections established by von Hayek and Popper between innovation, successful scientific enquiry and liberalism are plausible, and show the harmony between liberalism and the prevalence of scientific, economic and cultural innovation in modern society. This character of liberalism helps to explain its practical success as an ideology.

Liberalism's promotion of individuality and freedom coheres with the logic of modern social practices. Individualism is underpinned by powerful cultural and economic forces such as secularization and consumerism. These forces favour a society in which individuals are free to choose their goals and allegiances and they militate against the promotion of collectivist non-liberal goals. The market, which allows for the freedom of producers and consumers, appears to be the most efficient form of harnessing and allocating resources. Nationalism, unreconstructed socialism, feminism, ecologism and theistic fundamentalism are ideologies which continue to popularize the subordination of self-interest to shared social goals. In the contemporary Western world, however, these ideologies exert significant practical influence only by accommodating dominant liberal values as is exemplified in 'green capitalism', market socialism and liberal forms of nationalism and feminism.

The power of liberalism as an ideology in the Western world is exhibited in its dynamism in the period after the Second World War. In the war's aftermath, a social form of liberalism was embraced that aimed to establish a pattern of welfare provision so that all members of society would have the resources to enable them to exercise autonomy. In Western Europe and the USA, the adoption of Keynesian economics allowed for a deliberate regulation of the economy to secure welfare goals. A powerful and popular theoretical expression of social liberalism maintained in the post-war period was Rawls's *A Theory of Justice*, which combined advocacy of individual freedom with a prescription for regulating resources so as to allow for their socially just distribution (Rawls, 1971). In this work, Rawls maintained that individuals are to be conceived as pursuing their self-chosen conceptions of the good within a fair framework of the distribution of resources whereby differences in material wealth will be allowed only in so far as the worst off benefit.

In the 1970s economic problems including the simultaneous occurrence of unemployment and inflation, combined with unease at the social and economic costs of the bureaucracy required to sustain extensive welfare provision, undermined support for social liberalism. In the context of a disenchantment with interventionist, social liberalism, the classic liberal recipe for a minimal state was revived by libertarian liberalism. Nozick's *Anarchy, State and Utopia* presented a rigorous defence of libertarianism (Nozick, 1974). Nozick argued for a minimal state in which the rights of individuals were seen as ruling out state activity designed to secure any proposed pattern of resource holding. Nozick's defence of the minimal state echoed that of von Hayek. Von Hayek and Nozick were leading ideological advocates of neo-liberalism in defending the robust individualism and minimal state intervention associated with classical liberalism. Neo-liberalism set the political agenda, devised the rhetoric and determined the policies of Western states for most of the 1980s.

LIBERALISM AND ITS CRITICS

Liberalism has been a dynamic and influential political creed in the period after the Second World War in its dual guises of social liberalism and neo-liberalism. None the less it has been subject to powerful theoretical criticism in recent years. Criticism has come from a variety of sources and has been levelled against assumptions entertained in both neo-liberalism and social liberalism. A focus for this critique has been the claims and style of argument exemplified in *A Theory of Justice*, the most famous work of liberal theory in the post-war period. Rawls's *A Theory of Justice*, on its publication in 1971, emboldened political philosophers to resume the practice of traditional political philosophy in developing arguments about substantive political questions, such as how resources are to be distributed justly.

In *A Theory of Justice* Rawls developed an account of justice which resolved justice into the maintenance of two principles, namely the provision of freedoms for individuals to pursue their own conceptions of the good and the distribution of resources so that differences of wealth in society were only to be justified insofar as they benefited the worst off. This form of social liberalism that prescribed the redistribution of resources in society was justified by an imaginative thought experiment in which representative individuals were imagined as deciding upon principles of justice in an 'original position' in which they were assumed to be ignorant of their own particular attributes, status and concrete goals. This ignorance of their own particular qualities relative to others on the part of representative individuals in the original position was taken by Rawls as ensuring that their perspective is fair. If individuals are unsure if they are either advantaged or disadvantaged in relation to others, then Rawls assumed they are likely to adopt a disinterested, just standpoint. Likewise if they do not know what particular notion of the good they support, Rawls envisaged that they will support a framework for society in which all can pursue diverse conceptions of the good. Rawls's advocacy of governmental neutrality between conceptions of the good maintained by individuals was a target for critics of liberalism. The significance of such neutrality for liberalism was emphasized in the central role it assumed in Dworkin's influential essay supporting liberalism of the late 1970s (Dworkin, 1982). Another feature of Rawls's *A Theory of Justice* which was highlighted in critiques of liberalism was the apparent universalism of its argument. This universalism was a feature of Nozick's defence of the minimal state just as much as it informed Rawls's social liberalism. While criticism of *A Theory of Justice* and its paradigmatic argumentation for liberalism has come from many sources, two of the most powerful forms of critique have emanated from post-modernism and communitarianism.

Post-modernism questions the foundations of liberal arguments. The central doctrines of liberalism are depicted by post-modernists as rehearsing questionable 'Enlightenment' assumptions rather than establishing universal truths. Moreover, post-moderns maintain that liberal tolerance of individual standpoints insofar as it rules out the positive promotion of particular conceptions of the good is less neutral than it professes. Lyotard denied the validity of all grand narratives including that of liberalism, and sought to testify to the *differend*, the very impossibility of appraising all standpoints from the perspective of a common, dominant discourse, such as liberalism (Lyotard, 1984). Iris Marion Young criticizes liberal individualism from a post-modern perspective and advocates the deconstruction of hegemonic notions of the public good through the expression of radically distinct group standpoints (Young, 1990). A post-modern critique of the supposed universal foundations of liberalism is supported by radical feminists who identify particular male interests rather than general human needs as shaping dominant liberal perspectives (see Lloyd, 1998).

Communitarians have attacked liberalism from two vantage points. Communitarian philosophers have sought to undermine the methodological individualism they attribute to Rawls and standard liberal theorizing (see MacIntyre, 1981, 1988; Sandel, 1982). Philosophically minded communitarians have observed that individuals are not isolated atoms, but are social agents who develop their particular characters and standpoints by participating in social practices. Politically engaged communitarians have argued for the positive value of 'community', a sense of social solidarity maintained in allegiances or orientations that goes beyond atomistic, egoistic perspectives (Etzioni, 1993).

The critique of *A Theory of Justice* and liberalism undertaken most notably by post-modernists and communitarians has been salutary. Universal arguments for liberalism tend to assume the ubiquity of discrete individual actors only maintained in actual liberal societies. Arguments for a liberal perspective are inherently controversial. While allowing individuals to pursue self-chosen ends appears a plausible response to the propensity for social conflict over ends, it is a contestable response. Liberal neutrality does not guarantee the equal expression of all standpoints. The viewpoints and ways of life of cultural minorities can be overridden by the dominant individualistic perspective of liberalism and liberal neutrality can serve as an alibi or excuse for a lack of direct action to tackle entrenched but unintended forms of racism and sexism. Moreover, the way individuals are reproduced physically and culturally depends upon the character of social practices that cannot be determined by the free choices of merely self-interested individual agents.

The power of this critique of liberalism is reflected in the arguments of liberals advanced in recent years. Liberal theorists can be seen as shaping their formulations of liberalism in response to this critique. Rawls himself now emphasizes the relative rather than universal foundations of liberalism (Rawls, 1993). Raz (1986) defends the key liberal value of autonomy by recognizing its provenance in forms of community. Richard Rorty (1989) undertakes a post-modern defence of liberalism which frankly admits its lack of foundations. The tendency for liberals to see liberalism as a relative rather than absolute good is evident in John Gray's (1995) development of post-liberalism as a pragmatic creed to supersede the bogus universalism of liberalism. The increasingly circumspect style of liberal theorizing is examined in the following section.

CONTEMPORARY LIBERALISM

Contemporary theories of liberalism have tended to respond to its critique by exercising circumspection in the claims they make on behalf of liberalism. Liberalism tends to be justified on the grounds that it minimizes conflict rather than in terms of the positive appeal of a liberal way of life. Contemporary exponents of liberalism are characteristically self-conscious about the lack of absolute foundations for their arguments. Locke's account of a tolerant, free society in which individual rights to life, liberty and property are protected is grounded in the natural and supposedly absolute law of God. Mill's liberalism is defended on the purportedly rationally demonstrable grounds of utilitarianism. These apparently strong foundations are not advanced in contemporary formulations of liberalism. Likewise liberal doctrines are now taken as having a limited range of applicability. Where Mill sees the logic of progressive historical development as promoting liberalism, contemporary liberals are not so sanguine about the course of history. Today liberalism tends to downplay a strong justification of its core values in favour of a defence of liberalism which urges the incompatibility of non-liberal ideologies with the prevalence of value pluralism in contemporary society. The fact of pluralism and the propensity of individuals to conflict irresolvably over ends are characteristic contemporary justifications of liberalism rather than a full-blooded justification of liberal values.

Rawls's work subsequent to *A Theory of Justice* epitomizes the increasing circumspection of liberal theory. The seeming audacity of Rawls's theorizing in *A Theory of Justice* was accompanied, however, by a small print that qualified the apparent universalism of its arguments. Rawls in fact urged that the hypothetical device of the original position constituted a powerful, graphic way of representing the fruit of considered reflection upon the moral intuitions and principles maintained in contemporary liberal society. For Rawls, a theory of justice as fairness was not designed as a piece of universal theorizing which was to be considered as transcending the actual social norms maintained in liberal society. Rawls's subsequent essays, refined in his book *Political Liberalism* (1993), emphasize the dependence of principled liberal argument on actual practice while elaborating a more circumspect account of 'liberal' justice.

In *Political Liberalism* Rawls frames his account of justice as fairness with an historical account of the emergence of the kind of society to which the argument is applicable. Rawls sees the modern liberal democratic society to which his arguments are tailored as being identifiable in terms of its acceptance of its citizens' deep conflict over ends. Rawls cites the religious controversies of the seventeenth century as establishing the paramount importance of devising arrangements for dealing with the prevalence within society of reasonable but conflicting doctrines. Rawls presents his theory of justice as constituting the principles for fair social co-operation, as determined by representatives of society in an 'original position' replicating an ignorance over their own goals and attributes set out in *A Theory of Justice*. Rawls's introductory remarks, however, make clear the socially and historically derived character of the argument. His explicit disavowal of universal foundations for his account of justice in *Political Liberalism* is matched by a circumscription of its application. Rawls maintains that his theory of justice is not to be taken as applying to all aspects of an individual's life but only to political transactions. The most controversial features of this specifically political account of justice, namely the difference principle, is also presented as detachable given its propensity to generate deep controversy. Rawls's interest is in establishing principles of political liberalism which are to regulate the public sphere in a reasonable manner consonant with their generation by constructive argument disconnected from controversial comprehensive doctrines.

Rawls's circumspection is notable for its exaggerated expression of outstanding features of contemporary liberalism. Its concern to be inoffensive, however, while at the same time outlawing non-liberal conceptions of the public good is problematic (see Evans, 1995). The attempt to restrict the kinds of reasoning and doctrines which can be invoked in the public sphere is to divorce the private from the public in a controversial rather than reasonable way. Conservative opponents of abortion who invoke theistic arguments on the sanctity of life and radical ecologists and feminists who demand comprehensive social change highlight the circularity of Rawls's specification of the reasonable. Rawls presents his own 'political' theory of justice as reasonable but this claim is only justified by maintaining the inadmissability of comprehensive theorizing when many would dispute the reasonableness of this inadmissability.

Rawls's latest defence of political liberalism is characteristic of much contemporary liberal theory in that it justifies liberalism primarily in terms of its circumspection in not overstepping the limits within which political theories are taken to be confined. A fundamental feature of Rawlsian liberalism is its concern to argue for public neutrality over the promotion of any particular conception of the good. The public sphere for Rawls is to protect the right of all individuals to pursue their particular conceptions of the good rather than to promote a specific notion of the good. This notion of public neutrality is central to Dworkin's defence of liberalism. Dworkin rehearses the rationale for this position succinctly in a famous piece on liberalism:

> Political decisions must be, so far as is possible, independent of any particular conception of the good life, or of what gives value to life. Since the citizens of a society differ in their conceptions, the government does not treat them as equals if it prefers one conception to another . . . ' (Dworkin, 1982: 84).

Dworkin develops a justification of political neutrality in terms of a comprehensive moral theory rather than in the limited political terms favoured by Rawls. Dworkin urges that the moral goal of equality is best served where all individuals are able to respond to the challenge of pursuing the best life of which they are capable. Central to the pursuit of this best form of life, for Dworkin, is its determination by individuals themselves (Dworkin, 1985). Brian Barry (1995), in his *Justice as Impartiality*, envisages political impartiality in terms of a contract between individuals whereby all have a veto over proposed rules and arrangements which they could not reasonably accept. Impartiality is taken as ruling out constraining an individual's conduct by enforced rules which exemplify other persons' conceptions of the good (see Steiner, 1996).

The defence of liberalism in terms of its political neutrality is inspired by the notion that it fits with the value pluralism of the contemporary social world and the difficulties involved in justifying any distinct conception of the good or positive set of values. This tendency to emphasize liberalism's fit with contemporary society and to make a virtue out of theoretical circumspection is evident in a related trend of justifying liberalism in relative rather than absolute terms. Richard Rorty, for instance, develops a contingent, post-modern, justification of liberalism. Rorty accepts the post-modern notion that truth is not to be conceived in Enlightenment terms as an absolute achievement. In his essays, *Contingency, Irony and Solidarity* (1989), Rorty argues for the contingency of the human world which allows for no absolute, necessary truth. He argues against a representational view of truth whereby language and thought are taken as mirroring an 'external' reality, highlighting instead the metaphorical dimension of all language. For Rorty political beliefs, like scientific beliefs, are not to be conceived as representing an external reality that can be measured in terms of the truth-value of their representation. Consequently, differing political ideas are taken by Rorty to be incommensurable in that they cannot be related to a common standard of measurement. In a revealing essay, 'Postmodernist Bourgeois Liberalism', Rorty (1991) urges that liberalism is not to be defended on universalist grounds, but on relative grounds. Bourgeois liberals, for Rorty, are persuasive to the extent that they convey a sense of the positive qualities of liberal society (Rorty, 1991).

Rorty's justification of liberalism on non-universal grounds reflects a self-conscious adoption of post-modernist scepticism. This scepticism over the earlier universalist justifications of liberalism is reflected in the work of John Gray. In *Post-Liberalism: Studies in Political Thought* (1993) Gray urged that liberalism could no longer be defended on universalist grounds. In contrast he argued for liberalism on the basis that it was the political doctrine most suited to the value pluralism characteristic of contemporary societies. Liberalism, for Gray, was to be justified on historical, pragmatic criteria rather than in the rationalist Enlightenment style adopted by the neo-liberalism of the New Right. In *Enlightenment's Wake* (1995) Gray modifies his position so that liberalism is no longer seen as the only ideology capable of coping with the demands of late modern society. He urges that there can be a variety of ways in which differing traditions in the world can cope with the problems of order, globalism and value pluralism in late modernity.

Raz is relatively isolated in eschewing political neutrality and arguing a perfectionist case for liberalism. In so doing Raz incorporates key aspects of the communitarian philosophical critique of liberalism. He defends liberalism in terms of its articulation of a 'perfect' form of life. He sees the liberal form of life as dependent upon a conception of the good life which is advanced by the political promotion of a conception of the good. Raz argues that the justification for assigning priority of the right over the good entertained in rival liberal theories is as problematic as advancing a case for a particular conception of the good.

Raz argues strongly for autonomy as a key value of the good life, which is to be promoted by public regulation (Raz, 1986). Autonomy is the human capacity to exercise individuality and independence through making choices on how to act. Raz develops a form of argument which leans upon communitarianism in that he recognizes that without the development of a certain sort of community allowing for valuable choices and ways of life then individuals will not be able to exercise autonomy. He argues that individuals have to exercise choice between a set of worthwhile activities. This contextualist justification for liberalism is taken by Raz as justifying public support for certain goods, for instance, the public financing of arts.

Raz's justification of a liberal society in terms of its positive 'perfectionist' promotion of a good, namely autonomy, is at odds with much contemporary liberal theory. Likewise, his recognition of the impact of the social setting upon individual development is largely ignored in rival contemporary theories of liberalism.

Raz's justification of a liberal concern to promote a 'good' form of life is controversial, but argument over values is necessarily controversial and liberal arguments for political neutrality tend to disguise this controversial character. Raz's acceptance of the social context of individual development is insightful, but his recognition of the need to attend to the social conditions for individual development links him to communitarians taken to be critical of liberalism.

CONCLUSION

Liberalism's self-image in the contemporary world is uneven in its theoretical and practical guises. On the one hand, it is the most successful ideology in practice. It is no longer seriously challenged by a radical form of socialism. It is highly compatible with the rapidly changing social and economic forces unleashed by the industrial revolution. Liberalism's key themes of individuality, reason, equality and freedom are well suited to the processes of continuous social and technological change generated by contemporary society. On the other hand, the rhetoric and argumentation of its theorizing is circumspect. It is characteristically defended in negative terms that highlight the dangers of alternative doctrines. The non-liberal pursuit of a common good, for example, is taken to be chimerical and politically oppressive in its subordination of individuality and autonomous choice to a collective goal. Rather than arguing positively in favour of the realization of a liberal ideal of individuality, liberal theorists aim to guard against the unwarranted follies countenanced by other ideologies. Liberalism aims to travel light with a minimum of awkward theoretical baggage. Liberalism now tends to be defended in terms of its consonance with a particular form of modern, democratic society and is not presented as realizing a universal truth about humanity. In reviewing contemporary liberal theory Habermas has remarked perceptively on how 'questions concerning "the impotence of the ought" have again become urgent in the normative discourse' (Habermas, 1996: 57).

Liberalism's renunciation of universal foundations is a recognition of the power of post-modern and communitarian critiques of its standpoint. To recognize liberalism as having a relative rather than a universal justification, however, is not to admit that the positive defence of liberalism should be abandoned in favour of a more pragmatic defence of its fit with contemporary value pluralism. Raz is right to urge that liberal values depend upon the active promotion of the good society in the public sphere and that the controversial character of liberal society is not to be overridden by an argument which urges that the organization of the good society turns upon the maintenance of neutrality between conceptions of the good. Liberal values such as autonomy and individuality reflect the fluid, reflexive social practices encountered in contemporary Western societies. None the less the point and positive worth of these values deserve to be articulated. Autonomy cannot be achieved on auto-pilot; it is a socially learned value that depends upon public recognition of and support for individuals possessing the resources and opportunities to reflect upon and choose between worthwhile options. Liberal values, however, should also be seen as contestable values in that rival commitments, for example, to securing the human species' harmonious relationship with the rest of nature, to establishing relationships of trust and common concern between members of society and to ensuring that a cultural heritage is preserved, represent significant challenges to the current practical dominance of liberalism.

SUMMARY

- Liberalism in practice is the dominant ideology in the contemporary Western world.
- Liberal theory today is characteristically circumspect in style.
- Contemporary liberal theory tends to accept the lack of universal foundations for liberalism.
- Liberal theorists tend to argue for political neutrality which is held to allow individuals to pursue their own conceptions of the good.
- There is a strong case, however, for liberal theorists to argue for the substantive merits of liberal values.

FURTHER READING

Rawls, John (1971) *A Theory of Justice*. Cambridge, MA: Harvard University Press. A classic text of modern liberalism which has spawned countless commentaries and is central to the debate on the character of contemporary liberalism.

Rawls, John (1993) *Political Liberalism.* New York: Columbia University Press. This book collects together Rawls's later thoughts about liberalism. A difficult book to read in that its arguments are intertextual, referring closely to *A Theory of Justice* and to Rawls's critics. It does, however, epitomize the circumspection of contemporary liberal argumentation.

Sandel, Michael (ed.) (1984) *Liberalism and its Critics.* Oxford: Blackwell. A collection of essays which brings together notable liberal theorists as well as communitarian and conservative critics.

Raz, Joseph (1986) *The Morality of Freedom.* Oxford: Oxford University Press. An interesting 'perfectionist' defence of liberalism, which does not maintain a notion of political neutrality.

Beiner, Ronald (1992) *What's The Matter With Liberalism?* Berkeley, CA: University of California Press. A very lively and provocative critique of liberalism. Critical questions are posed about liberal theory and the practices of liberal society.

Mulhall, Stephen and Swift, Adam (1996) *Liberals and Communitarians*, 2nd edition. Oxford: Blackwell. A rigorous analysis of communitarian and liberal theorists. The 2nd edition of this book provides a particularly insightful analysis of Rawls's later work.

REFERENCES

Barry, B. (1995) *Justice as Impartiality.* Oxford: Clarendon Press.
Dworkin, R. (1982) 'Liberalism', in M. Sandel (ed.) *Liberalism and its Critics.* Oxford: Basil Blackwell, p. 64.
Dworkin, R. (1985) *A Matter of Principle.* Oxford: Oxford University Press.
Etzioni, A. (1993) *The Spirit of Community: Rights, Responsibilities and the Communitarian Agenda.* New York: Crown.
Evans, M. (1995) 'Perfectionism and the Liberalism of Inoffensiveness', *Politics* **15**(3), September: 191–6.
Fukuyama, F. (1992) *The End of History and the Last Man.* London: Hamish Hamilton.
Gray, J. (1993) *Post-Liberalism: Studies in Political Thought.* London and New York: Routledge.
Gray, J. (1995) *Enlightenment's Wake.* London: Routledge.
Green, T.H. (1986) *Lectures on The Principles of Political Obligation and Other Writings,* (eds) P. Harris and J. Morrow. Cambridge: Cambridge University Press.
von Hayek, F.A. (1960) *The Constitution of Liberty.* London: Routledge.
Habermas, J. (1996) *Between Facts and Norms.* London: Polity Press.
Lloyd, M. (1998) 'Feminism', in A. Lent (ed.) *New Political Thought.* London: Lawrence and Wishart.

Lyotard, J.F. (1984) *The Postmodern Condition: A Report on Knowledge*. Manchester: Manchester University Press.

MacIntyre, A. (1981) *After Virtue*. London: Duckworth.

MacIntyre, A. (1988) *Whose Justice? Which Rationality?* London: Duckworth.

Mill, J.S. (1989) *On Liberty and Other Writings*, (ed.) Stefan Collini. Cambridge: Cambridge University Press.

Nozick, R. (1974) *Anarchy, State and Utopia*. Oxford: Blackwell.

Popper, K. (1966) *The Open Society and its Enemies*, 5th edition. London: Routledge.

Rawls, J. (1971) *A Theory of Justice*. Cambridge, MA: Harvard University Press.

Rawls, J. (1993) *Political Liberalism*. New York: Columbia University Press.

Raz, J. (1986) *The Morality of Freedom*. Oxford: Oxford University Press.

Rorty, R. (1989) *Contingency, Irony and Solidarity*. Cambridge: Cambridge University Press.

Rorty, R. (1991) 'Postmodernist Bourgeois Liberalism', in R. Rorty (ed.) *Philosophical Papers Vol. 1: Objectivity, Relativism and Truth*. Cambridge: Cambridge University Press.

Sandel, M. (1982) 'Introduction', in *Liberalism and its Critics*. Cambridge: Cambridge University Press.

Steiner, H. (1996) 'Impartiality, Freedom and Natural Rights', *Political Studies*, **44**: 311–13.

Young, I.M. (1990) *Justice and the Politics of Difference*. Princeton, NJ: Princeton University Press.

Chapter 12

Democracy: liberal and direct

Nick Hewlett

In both contemporary practice and current theory, democracy has two strik-ing qualities. First, it is intimately associated with progress, legitimacy, fair-ness and other values which are universally viewed as positive. In most parts of the world even political leaders who are widely viewed as being undemocratic can rarely afford to eschew the label 'democrat' if they wish to retain support. The desirability of 'rule by the people' (the etymology of democracy), rather than by an élite or an autocrat of some kind, is now taken for granted by virtually everyone in the northern hemisphere and probably by the vast majority in the southern hemisphere. Theorists of politics and society also take as read the legitimacy of the quest for democracy, the points for debate lying in what democracy is and whether it is attainable, rather than whether it is desirable. The second striking quality of contem-porary approaches to democracy, and one that helps allow the concept such widespread approval, is that it is an enormously broad notion which cannot be discussed in any depth unless it is qualified with either general terms such as 'liberal', 'representative' or 'direct', or slightly more precise terms such as 'associative', 'social' or 'cosmopolitan'. (The list of qualifying adjec-tives in the literature on democracy is now long.) Indeed it is in part the very vagueness of the term which has allowed debates to rage for over 200 years as to what democracy is and how to achieve it.

Today we are in a period of intense discussion about democracy, par-ticularly in Europe and North America. Since the break up of the Soviet Union beginning in 1989, there are sharply posed questions as to what democracy is, how to maximize it, whether excess emphasis on it is counter-posed to certain individual or business rights, and whether the Western variant of liberal democracy has won definitively. With the decline of the traditional labour movements in West European countries as well, analysts and activists on the left are now going back to first principles to ask what constitutes a just and workable form of political organization.

In this chapter I first place the concept in a historical context by exploring the link between democracy and modernity. Next I examine the fundamental tension between direct democracy and representative, liberal democracy. I then go on to look at some of the burning issues for contemporary theorists, namely: variants of direct democracy; gender; information technology; and globalization. My general argument is that direct democracy would be a fairer form of political organization than liberal democracy and that more research is needed on how to achieve a workable model and a realistic strategy for implementing it.

DEMOCRACY AND MODERNITY

The principle of rule by the people is undoubtedly one of the most successful ideologies of modernity, that is, broadly speaking, the period since the French Revolution of 1789. Indeed, to call democracy an ideology may seem odd, as it is now taken for granted as the best way to organize government of nations, of cities and in some cases international organizations like the European Union. But an ideology it undoubtedly is, in the sense that it is a set of ideas which has appeared legitimate only in certain circumstances and in certain historical periods, rather than being incontrovertibly and for all time a form of political organization to strive for. Indeed the widespread popularity of democracy is relatively recent (Macpherson, 1966: 1), and it is closely associated with some of the core values of the Enlightenment: reason, equal rights as citizens, equality before the law, individual freedom, freedom of expression and political organization, absence of political power due to religion, birth, class or wealth, and by extension order, planning and transparency. Many of these qualities have become buzzwords for good government in many parts of the world, and are seen as the legitimate replacements for such archaic notions as divine right to rule (notably on the part of monarchs), dictatorship, autocracy, oligarchy and excessive mystical or religious influence on politics, all of which are associated with either premodern eras or more recent political systems which are deemed to be politically unjust.

In the nineteenth century, many countries in the West established or moved towards parliamentary and legal systems which took as their guiding principle some form of democracy, although influences of other ideologies such as liberalism and republicanism varied greatly. This was also a time when the individual was becoming more important, but at the same time there were many revolutions, workers' revolts and mass strikes (most famously in 1848 in several European countries) where labour movements attempted to achieve a form of democracy which promoted the group interests of working people and went further than equality before the law and associated measures. In the twentieth century, half the world came to be ruled under the banner of communism which, however distorted a vision of the original intentions of the Bolsheviks in 1917, took as its inspiration Leninism and Lenin's belief that proletarian revolution was in essence the 'extension of democracy'. Those in the Marxist tradition argue for the importance of democracy based on direct participation in decision-making (the original Soviets were established for this function) and on an advanced level of material equality via redistribution of wealth, which makes for reduced power inequalities as well. Then the 1930s and the Second World War saw the two ideologies of fascism and communism fight it out in much of Europe, followed by a defeat for fascism at the hands of a temporary compromise between liberal democracy and communism at the end of the Second World War. Then the Cold War from the late 1940s to the late 1980s was an intense battle *between* these two key political systems (liberal democracy and communism), which were based on very different inter-pretations of democracy.

Finally, from 1989 onwards communism seemed to have permanently lost its fight with liberal democracy, and the USA became the sole world super-power, working within the structures of the North Atlantic Treaty Organiza-tion (NATO) and the Organization for Economic Co-operation and Development (OECD) in particular. Francis Fukuyama (1989: 8–12) has ar-gued that liberal democracy worldwide has triumphed over other ideol-ogies, in particular hereditary monarchy, fascism and most recently communism. More controversially, he has argued that liberal democracy as practised in most OECD countries represents the 'end point of mankind's ideological evolution' (Fukuyama, 1989: 4) and that 'the basic principles of the liberal democratic state could not be improved upon' (Fukuyama, 1989: 5). This final point is particularly controversial, and has been widely criticized (e.g. Anderson 1992: 240–1), but he has made a substantial impact on the debate since 1989 precisely because liberal democracy and capitalism do seem to have triumphed on a global scale, at least for the time being. It is not just the broad notion of democracy that had become the ideology of modernity *par excellence*, but more precisely liberal democracy as practised in the West.

LIBERAL AND DIRECT DEMOCRACY

The above sketch of the relationship between democracy and modernity suggests how successful the idea of democracy has become over the past two centuries. But despite the apparent victory of liberal democracy worldwide, a major fault line in the debate around democracy in the twentieth century has been and still remains the one between liberal, or representative, democracy on the one hand, and direct democracy on the other.

The political system in the city-state of Athens between 450 and 350 BC, generally regarded as the first existing democracy, is frequently referred to as a particularly direct form of democracy (e.g. Held, 1996: 13–35). The Athenian Assembly, whose membership was between 20,000 and 30,000, met regularly, and had total power not only over policy-making, but also over implementation of policy in every detail. Officals who were responsible for executing policy were temporary and selected by lot, so there was no permanent bureaucracy. However, the system was most illiberal, to say the least, by modern standards: only men were allowed to vote, the system approved slavery (the ratio of slaves to other inhabitants was 3:2), foreigners were also excluded, so there was direct democracy for a minority of citizens. The private sphere was, arguably, taken care of by non-enfranchised individuals in order that others could participate in direct democracy; in modern times, by contrast, citizens' private sphere is given greater emphasis and political power is delegated to representatives who are elected by the mass of citizens relatively infrequently. It should also be pointed out that ancient Greek communities were relatively small and were nothing like today's large and complex societies.

Despite these drawbacks and differences, ancient Athenian democracy has remained a reference point for debate for centuries. Discussion of direct and representative democracy is found in the writings of such philosophical giants as John Locke and Benjamin Constant, who both favoured individual rights over the voice of the people, while Jean-Jacques Rousseau and Karl Marx, for example, stressed the importance of popular rule. Marx was particularly critical of representative democracy, arguing that in the 1871 Paris Commune there was for the first time ever the real possibility for the people to be represented fairly, so 'instead of deciding once every three or six years which member of ruling class was going to misrepresent the people in parliament, universal suffrage was to serve the people' (Marx, 1968: 289). Today, direct democracy is still favoured in particular by analysts and activists on the left, who often argue that: (a) material benefits and power in modern societies must be far more evenly distributed before a deeper democracy is possible; and (b) that formal decision-making must take place on a far wider basis than the election of national or local representatives who come from a small élite of semi-professional politicians. Since the early 1970s, feminists and environmental groups and analysts have also often advocated more direct forms of democracy, introducing notions such as diversity, difference and local experience as important areas of consideration.

Proponents of liberal democracy, on the other hand, argue first that there are severe practical constraints on direct democracy. Given the sheer size, complexity and diversity of modern societies individuals simply do not have the time, the inclination or perhaps the ability to become involved in decisions regarding a vast range of issues affecting their lives either directly or indirectly (e.g. Dahl, 1961: 324). This might particularly be the case with increasing internationalization. Second, individual freedoms are at stake as well, which might be compromised by excessive concern with the public sphere or excessive political demands put on people as citizens.

There is no doubt that in terms of practical government, liberal democracy has for the time being at least won the battle against direct democracy. Pure direct democracy, where there was no permanent division of labour between the politically powerful and ordinary citizens, between the elected and electors, is certainly hard to conceive of given the sophistication and complexity of modern societies, however much political, economic and social change took place. So from a practical point of view fully-fledged direct democracy which was a sort of perfected form of Athenian democracy would seem impossible, although it should perhaps remain a model to be striven for. For analysts in the liberal tradition, however, representative democracy is not only more realistic but also more just, because it protects the rights of the individual's private sphere, which are threatened when so many decisions are subject to widespread deliberation.

Today, one of the most developed general defences of representative democracy comes from John Rawls. Rawls (1971: 61) argues that there are certain fundamental liberties that should take precedence over popular rule in order to ensure that individuals are free and equal; these are political liberty (the right to vote and be eligible for public office) together with freedom of speech and assembly; liberty of conscience and freedom of thought; freedom of the person along with the right to hold (personal) property; and freedom, from arbitrary arrest and seizure as defined by the concept of the rule of law. Typical of the liberal democratic approach, Rawls insists first on the inviolability of these basic liberties rather than the importance of popular rule, in part in order to protect the private sphere of individuals against what he sees as often counterposing interests of the public sphere. Liberal analysts establish this hierarchy partly because they believe that the degree of influence of an individual over decisions is small anyway, and needs to be put in perspective by the importance of the private sphere (Berlin, 1969). A major role for the State and the government therefore is to protect the individual against infringement of their freedom in the private sphere, rather than to encourage debate and deliberation to establish norms and strategies in the public sphere.

Critics of liberal democracy often argue that the triumph of a liberal approach has meant that the public sphere is left weak and underdeveloped, with a population that is overly privatized, therefore depoliticized and unwilling or unable to take part in debates about public issues, all of which severely undermines the fundamental principles of democracy. Jürgen Habermas (1989: 52–3) argues that popular sovereignty would need a favourable political culture with 'convictions, mediated by tradition and

socialisation, of a population *in the habit* of exercising political freedom . . . '.
Without this, individuals become passive, depoliticized and less in control of
either public or private spheres. In fact private, individual rights so championed by liberals are impossible without popular sovereignty based on
fuller political participation, debate and education. For how can individuals
properly exercise individual rights if they do not have ongoing and direct
influence over the ways in which their lives are organized via politics?
Constant popular accountability is the essence of direct democracy, a point
made by Jacques Rancière when he comments that,

> democracy does not exist simply because the law declares individuals equal and
> the collectivity master of itself. It still requires the force of the *demos* which is
> neither a sum of social partners nor a gathering together of differences, but quite
> the opposite – the power to undo all partnerships, gatherings and ordinations
> (Rancière, 1995: 32).

While a classic defence of liberal democracy, meanwhile, states that modern
Western societies based on liberalism are less violent and conflictual than
they used to be, Chantal Mouffe (1994: 314) argues that when liberals
suggest that conflict and violence have disappeared they have in fact only
been made invisible.

Another crucial argument by many critics of liberal democracy is that
without greater material equality, rather than mere equality before the law
and formal equal access to elected posts, for example, any deeper form of
political justice is impossible. Liberal democracy notionally allows equal
rights, but without more material equality and more equal potential for
success, these rights are of limited value. Moreover, as Bowles and Gintis
(1986: x) argue, capitalism and liberal democracy allow property rights to
take precedence over democracy:

> the liberal political tradition provides no coherent response to the obvious ques-
> tion: why should the rights of ownership prevail over the rights of democratic
> citizenry in determining who is to manage the affairs of a business enterprise
> whose policies might directly affect as many as half a million employees, and
> whose choice of product, location and technology extends to entire communities
> and beyond?

Large – and probably growing – parts of advanced capitalist societies are
therefore out of the reach of even formal democratic processes, let alone
deeper democracy.

All this raises the question of the role of the State in democratic systems.
Does the State promote or undermine democracy? Does it represent the
people by carrying out their will, or does it give too much importance to
more sectional interests, such as those of big business? Does it defend the
interests of the individual, by protecting them against arbitrary rule, or does
it compromise them by imposing restrictions on individual actions? As these

questions might suggest, there are different attitudes among advocates of both liberal and direct democracy. It seems to me that whereas Marx's suggestion that the State would wither away in a more democratic, post-capitalist society is unrealistic, much of the overall function of the contemporary State works against deeper democracy, and needs changing profoundly.

RETHINKING DEMOCRACY

If we take for granted the legitimacy of the basic principles of democracy, perhaps one of the most important questions we should be asking about contemporary industrialized societies is whether the general trend is for them to become more democratic or less so, and whether the possibilities are emerging for a deeper democracy to be constructed. Liberals might argue that established democracies are becoming more democratic as the extremes of left and right diminish, and an apparent political consensus emerges around the centre, while in former communist countries liberal democracy becomes established. However, although liberal democracy as a political system is vastly preferable to dictatorship of any kind and is a substantial improvement on most other previous forms of government, contemporary capitalism brings with it some important characteristics which undermine the potential for any deeper form of democracy. I will mention three of these.

First, at the most basic level, modern capitalism offers a great deal of freedom to the economic sphere (as mentioned above), which means that huge areas of power and decision-making are beyond the sphere of influence of most voters, and often government itself; the powerful sanction of widespread withdrawal of capital from domestic business in order to invest abroad is, for example, a very real threat to any left-leaning government which oversteps the reforming capitalist mark, and one which is increasingly easy to carry out due to the internationalization of capitalism. (This happened in 1981–82 in France, when after the election of the Socialist President François Mitterrand, he and his government attempted to implement the social democratic programme they were elected on; the flight of capital and plummeting of share prices on the Paris Stock Exchange provoked a government U-turn on economic policy in favour of private enterprise.) Second, the polarization of rich and poor in advanced capitalist societies means that anything up to one-third of the population is living on the margins and feels excluded from the more mainstream developments which government deals with. They are socially, although not politically (in a formal sense, at least) powerless, which undermines their ability to make decisions and influence government, and also undermines their individual liberties, incidentally. Third, neo-liberal, supply-side economic policy which encourages, for example, flexible working practices, and stresses the

171

interests and rights of the consumer and entrepreneur over the collective interests of employees, encourages atomization and political apathy, which no doubt contributes to high levels of abstention at local, national and European elections in well-established liberal democracies. In other words, the realm of the economy in particular is becoming increasingly a law unto itself, with the swing away from social democratic economic intervention on the part of government, widely practised in the post-war period, in favour of neo-liberal economic policies and the increasing internationalization of the economy. (See Chapter 18 on restructuring.)

What, then, are the practical alternatives posed to contemporary forms of liberal democracy which might bring about more participatory, inclusive, direct forms of democracy? Paul Hirst (1994) argues that the political and intellectual climate at the end of the twentieth century offers an unprecedented opportunity to gradually reform and supplement liberal democracy, and he sets out in some detail his ideas for what he describes as 'associative democracy'. Hirst's proposals do not imply a replacement of the present system, but they supplement it with a highly developed network of voluntary organizations based on co-operation and mutuality, which would temper the power of both state bureaucracy and private enterprise. The sheer size and complexity of modern societies, Hirst argues, means that contemporary legislatures are too remote from individuals for them to retain any real control and democracy is thus undermined. The power of large firms would also be tempered in this way. This is in some ways an appealing schema, drawing on nineteenth-century ideas of co-operation and mutuality, and which 'treats self-governing voluntary bodies not as secondary associations, but as the primary means of both democratic governance and organizing social life' (Hirst, 1994: 26). But Hirst's proposals do seem to underestimate the difficulty of reforming the present system and in particular the defence that those with vested interest (and tremendous power) would put up, including not only big business but professional politicians as well. Both these groups would be expected to relinquish considerable power, which they would not do readily. Also, although it envisages far wider participation in decision-making in individuals' immediate spheres, it does not seem to address some of the central flaws of liberal democracy, in particular the feeling of powerlessness of the average citizen as far as overall influence on government is concerned.

Another angle on contemporary political systems and the potential for reform has come from feminist political analysts, who are on the whole critical of liberal democracy, as least as presently practised. Feminists have long argued that domestic, family, sexual and other issues conventionally viewed as falling within the personal sphere are also highly political, and have more generally questioned the strict distinction which liberal democratic theorists make between the private and the public spheres; this (conventional) approach often means in practice a male-dominated public sphere and female-dominated private sphere. In addition to a battle on this front, then, some have argued that local and national representatives should mirror the composition of society as a whole in terms of gender, but also ethnicity, for example. Underrepresentation of women at the various levels of parliamentary fora – local, national, international – also highlights the necessity for adequate child care facilities, career opportunities which fully take account of participation of women in traditional forms of politics, and the sexual division of labour in the home. Carol Pateman (1989: 46–8) has criticized liberal democracy for treating all individuals as if they were equal and neutral, whereas in fact modern societies are still riven with inequalities and differences along the lines of gender, ethnicity and sexual orientation, which are the traditional concerns of neither liberal nor Marxist analysts and activists. Indeed the question of ethnic difference is treated very little in the literature on democracy. Yet such inequalities undermine the preconditions for democratic forms of decision-making. Anne Phillips (1991: 160) sums up the inclusiveness of contemporary feminist approaches to democracy when she comments that 'a fully democratic society would be one in which people held one another in mutual respect and where all relationships, no matter how small or intimate the context, would be permeated by the principle that each person had equal weight'.

Various authors have argued that technological innovation offers unprecedented opportunities for direct democracy. Ian Budge (1996: 1–2) argues powerfully that there are significant impulses towards direct democracy in modern societies, that 'the breakdown of traditional bonds and lines of authority . . . has led to increasing demands for consultation', and that the development of opinion polling since the Second World War, combined with a more critical press and television, makes public opinion on public policies more obvious. Younger people are better educated and more likely to take direct action to defend their points of view. Budge also makes a lively and convincing case for the legitimacy of the principle of direct democracy. But his main point is that electronic networks 'create a physical potential for mass debate and decision-making which has not existed since the evolution of modern states' (Budge, 1996: 33). Certainly, there would have to be moderators to sift, categorize and even prioritize the vast amount of information and opinion being conveyed, and Budge considers carefully the role and accountability of the moderator. But technological innovation has rendered the practical argument against direct democracy invalid. Networked computers and widespread access to information through other media such as television allow not only for votes and opinions to be communicated electronically, but also for interactive debates at many levels. This would be bound to encourage greater interest and participation in politics, he argues.

David Held, meanwhile, argues that given certain developments on an international scale over the past few decades, contemporary forms of democracy have become seriously wanting and he argues for a 'cosmopolitan international democracy' (Held, 1995: 97). The conventional forms of liberal democracy are firmly rooted at the national level, with

173

national government as the most powerful manifestation of democracy today. However, there is an increasing number of issues which escape the control of government based on the nation-state, including economic policy (where one country's policy can directly affect the room for manoeuvre of others, for example), decisions relating to the global environment, such as felling rainforests or building a nuclear plant, and military affairs. The process which is often referred to as globalization (see Chapter 17), then, which means that traditional nation-states find themselves increasingly affected by decisions made outside their borders, has tended to undermine the existing provisions for democracy. Held argues that democratic theory and practice must be redefined, or at least updated, in order to make political, civil and social rights applicable on an international scale. 'Democracy can only be fully sustained in and through the agencies and organisations which form an element of and yet cut across the territorial boundaries of the nation-state. The possibility of democracy must, in short, be linked to an expanding framework of democratic states and agencies'(Held, 1995: 106). One basis for the move towards implementation of such an increased democracy would be a consolidation of the United Nations Charter, which if it had more clout would be more effective in extending best (national) practice on an international level, together with regional parliaments in Africa and Latin America, for example, and an increased role for the European parliament. In the longer term, Held suggests among other measures that there could be a global parliament, a global legal system and an increasing proportion of nations' military capabilities transferred to the international level, with the 'ultimate aim of demilitarization and the transcendence of the war system' (Held, 1995: 111). The strength of Held's argument is that it recognizes the growing threat to present forms of (already limited) nation-based democracy posed by the internationalization and globalization of the economy and other areas, and insists that structures should be set in place to remedy this. It could be criticized, however, for a certain voluntarism, in that it does not address the problem of how to overcome the problem of competing interests. It may be in the interests of all countries to limit the deterioration of the global environment, for example the depletion of the ozone layer. But when it comes to global harmonization of human rights, rights at work and military practices, many groups whose immediate interests were threatened by these measures would surely resist vigorously? It would seem that the social and general power structures of societies would need to be changed alongside the implementation of such international democratic reform.

Returning to the question of whether liberal democracies in the West are becoming more democratic or less so, it seems that no contemporary analyst has adequately dealt at an overall theoretical level with the question of the often low level of participation in voting at elections. Is this a positive development as far as democracy is concerned because citizens are generally content with their governments, an expression of an electorate which condones liberal democracy, or does this reflect a feeling of impotence and apathy, a feeling that the choices and potential for change are too slim within the present system? My own view is that the latter is the case. Surely low levels of turnout at elections reflect a feeling of what Pierre Bourdieu (e.g. 1981) describes as political 'dispossession', rather than satisfaction with the present state of affairs which is so great that no change is deemed necessary. Liberal democracy does seem to limit choice, then, compared with other, more direct types of democracy.

CONCLUSIONS

Contemporary trends with regard to the health of democracy are mixed. Certainly, liberal democracy has never enjoyed greater success and support worldwide, and as many have pointed out, virtually everyone nowadays is a democrat. Also, by contrast with Winston Churchill, who commented famously that (liberal) democracy was a bad form of government but better than all others, liberal democracy now has many supporters among theorists who promote its legitimacy by arguing that it is the best theoretically possible form of government to guarantee individual and other rights (e.g. Fukuyama, 1989; Rawls, 1971). I have suggested that, certainly, liberal democracy represents a substantial improvement on previous forms of government in the West and many of the dictatorial and autocratic regimes in existence at the moment. In this respect as well as historically it is very much an ideology of modernity. However, I have evoked various authors in order to suggest how contemporary liberal democracy as practised in the West is lacking in fundamental ways, notably: in its inability to control the exploitation of the capitalist economy; in the way it fails to recognize individual differences of gender and ethnicity; in the way it depoliticizes large sections of the population (resulting in high rates of abstention in elections, for example); and in the way it fails to control the undemocratic aspects of internationalization and globalization.

Perhaps the key notions for the improvement of contemporary democracy are participation and power. As far as participation is concerned, analysts who promote direct, or more direct, democracy address this question head-on and argue for measures which include more local debate, more education to encourage participation, more recognition of 'difference' among voters, and democratic structures on an international level. But many of the same people seem to avoid the other key issue of the power of those with vested interests in keeping contemporary democracy as weak democracy. How can present structures be transformed in order to reduce the power of big business, professional politicians, the media and patriarchy, forces which resist democratic change precisely by using their tremendous power? There is certainly a place for idealized schema in strategies for change, perhaps along the lines of what Pierre Bourdieu (1998) describes as 'reasoned Utopia'. But there does seem to be a gap in the literature as far as the practical realities and problems with transition is concerned, no doubt partly because of the gap left by the crisis of confidence of Marxism since the late 1980s.

SUMMARY

- Democracy is one of the key ideologies of modernity.
- Liberal democracy is now widely established, both in practice and at the level of ideas.
- Those who champion liberal democracy point both to how it is practical (it works) and how it defends the rights of the individual.
- Defenders of direct democracy call for more debate and popular control, and extension of democracy into more areas.
- Analysts and activists influenced by Marxism stress the importance of greater material equality before political equality is possible.
- Feminists argue that there has been too great a distinction made between public and private spheres, and emphasize the importance of recognizing 'difference' among individual voters.

FURTHER READING

Among the large number of works on democracy David Held's *Models of Democracy* (Cambridge: Polity, 1996, 2nd edition) is probably the best overview.

Anthony Arblaster's *Democracy* (Oxford: Oxford University Press, 1994) is a very readable, short account of debates around democracy, written from within a broadly Marxist framework.

Jürgen Habermas's article 'The Public Sphere', in Steven Seidman (ed.) *Jürgen Habermas on Society and Politics* (Boston: Beacon Press, 1989) contains an influential discussion of the public sphere, which is in danger of disintegration.

Feminist arguments include Carole Pateman *The Disorder of Women* (Cambridge: Polity, 1989) and Anne Phillips *Engendering Democracy* (Cambridge: Polity, 1991).

John Rawls's *A Theory Of Justice* (Cambridge, MA: Harvard University Press, 1971) is an exposition of a now classic defence of the principles of liberalism.

In his book *The New Challenge of Direct Democracy* (Cambridge: Polity, 1996) Ian Budge presents an enthusiastic defence of direct democracy using modern technology.

David Held outlines the threats to democracy from globalization and outlines possible remedies in Daniel Archibugi and David Held (eds) *Cosmopolitan Democracy* (Cambridge: Polity, 1995, pp. 96–120).

REFERENCES

Anderson, Perry (1992) *A Zone of Engagement*. London: Verso.

Berlin, Isaiah (1969) 'Two Concepts of Liberty', in his *Four Essays on Liberty*. Oxford: Oxford University Press, pp. 118–172.

Bourdieu, Pierre (1981) 'La représentation politique. Eléments pour une théorie du champ politique', *Actes de la recherche en sciences sociales*, **38**, février–mars: 3–24.

Bourdieu, Pierre (1998) 'A Reasoned Utopia and Economic Fatalism', *New Left Review*, **227**, January–February: 125–30.

Bowles, Samuel and Gintis, Herbert (1986) *Democracy and Capitalism. Property, Community and the Contradictions of Modern Social Thought*. London: Routledge.

Budge, Ian (1996) *The New Challenge of Direct Democracy*. Cambridge: Polity.

Dahl, R.A. (1961) *Who Governs?* New Haven, CT: Yale University Press.

Fukuyama, Francis (1989) 'The End of History', *The National Interest*, **16**: 3–18.

Habermas, Jürgen (1989) 'La souveraineté populaire comme procédure. Un concept normatif d'espace public', *Lignes*, **7**, September: 49–63.

Held, David (1995) 'Democracy and the New International Order', in Daniele Archibugi and David Held (eds) *Cosmopolitan Democracy*. Cambridge: Polity, pp. 96–120.

Held, David (1996) *Models of Democracy*, 2nd edn. Cambridge: Polity.

Hirst, Paul (1994) *Associative Democracy. New Forms of Economic and Social Governance*. Cambridge: Polity.

Macpherson, C.B. (1966) *The Real World of Democracy*. Oxford: Clarendon Press.

Marx, Karl (1968) *The Civil War in France*, in Friedrich Engels and Karl Marx, *Selected Works*. London: Lawrence and Wishart, pp. 271–309. (First published in 1871.)

Mouffe, Chantal (1994) 'Political Liberalism. Neutrality and the Political', *Ratio Juris*, **7**(3), December: 314–24.

Pateman, Carole (1989) *The Disorder of Women*. Cambridge: Polity.

Phillips, Anne (1991) *Engendering Democracy*. Cambridge: Polity.

Rancière, Jacques (1995) *On the Shores of Politics*. London: Verso. (Translation by Liz Heron of *Au bords du politique*. Paris: Éditions Osiris, 1992.)

Rawls, John (1971) *A Theory of Justice*. Cambridge, MA: Harvard University Press.

Chapter 13

Communitarianism

Elizabeth Frazer

INTRODUCTION: COMMUNITARIANISM IN SOCIAL THEORY AND IN PRACTICAL POLITICS

The theme of community has always had a central and prominent place in social theory. A number of connected problems are at the heart of social theory. How do individuals make a collective whole? Should collective or individual interests have priority? Can the ideal of community be realized in modern social and political conditions? To what extent are individuals 'made' by the social contexts they inhabit? How and by what social bonds should persons be connected with one another? These and related questions are often thought of as variations of the key problem of the relationship between 'the community' and 'the individual'. It might seem anachronistic, then, to focus on the 'emergence' of communitarianism as one of the proliferation of *novel* social and political theories of the last two decades. However, in this period communitarianism has become prominent in a number of distinctive and time-specific ways.

First, in academic political philosophy a coherent theoretical position has crystallized out of a series of criticisms of certain aspects of recent liberal theory (see Chapter 11 of this volume). This communitarianism is related to older theories of community (such as Marxism, pragmatism, romanticism, ethical socialism, and strands of theology from the Jewish, Christian and other religious traditions), but the terms of the debates and the particular set of philosophical controversies that are played out are quite distinctive (and often, for someone who is not very familiar with recent liberalism, quite obscure). Second, a number of government-sponsored social policies have brought the term 'community' to a new prominence in political and social discourses – policies such as community care, community policing and community regeneration. These programmes were controversial at their inception, as during the 1980s in a number of industrial societies they were introduced by right-wing governments who attempted to yoke them together with the freest possible markets in a wide range of goods (including some like education and health care that many people believe should not be commodified), and with a strong sovereign militarily defended state. For many critics, the talk of community in the context of free markets and strong states was self-evidently laughable. Third, since the beginning of the 1990s, and to a large extent in response to these New Right social policies, a novel way of expressing 'communitarian' ideas has made its way into the speeches and developed platforms of a number of politicians and parties, especially in the USA and the UK. On both sides of the Atlantic many pressure groups and campaigns work to promote policies which in turn promote 'strong communities' and 'active citizens'. These ideas have found favour with a significant number of journalists so readers of opinion in the 'quality' press like the *Washington Post*, the *Guardian* and *Observer* will often come across discussions of local people's autonomous fights against crime, or education for citizenship, in which the terms 'community' and 'communitarian' figure prominently. Further, politicians like Bill Clinton, Tony Blair, Gordon Brown, and even traditional socialists like Roy Hattersley, have explicitly stated their commitment to community, citing a variety of sources of inspiration (religion, philosophy, or traditions of political solidarity and organization).[1]

'Communitarianism' is a very good example, then, of a phenomenon which reveals the relationship between academic political and social theory – often of a very abstract and philosophical kind – and practical politics. Political speech often oversimplifies and garbles political and social theory. On the other hand, political and social theory itself arguably is inevitably the development of ideas, values, practices and projects that are in some sense already present in political and social speech and action. Political and social theorists explore and analyse the structure of political and social ideas, values, beliefs and objectives with the aim of seeing whether they are consistent, whether they could be realized in practice, and what they mean for the possibilities of human life and action. Political and social theory is also prescriptive, and when issues are propelled on to the political agenda (as ideas of community have been recently) academics often act as entrepreneurs or parties to the debate – for instance, a number of academic philosophers have presented their ideas in the idiom of journalism, and journalists have made reference to the work of philosophers. So no very clear distinction can be drawn between academic output and political intervention.

KEY TEXTS

Although, as I have argued, in communitarianism as in many other areas of social theory, no very clear distinction can be made between academic and practical political discourses, nevertheless analytic distinctions can of course be drawn. Communitarianism is best thought of as divided into three: philosophical, political and vernacular. However, most 'communitarians', and, indeed, commentators about communitarianism, make contributions that overlap these three.

Philosophical communitarianism consists of a core group of texts, mainly constructed as critique of the most influential liberal text of recent decades, John Rawls's *Theory of Justice* (MacIntyre, 1981, 1988; Sandel, 1982; Taylor, 1985a, 1985b; Walzer, 1983). These core texts themselves make reference back to a wide range of philosophical works in the pragmatist, phenomenological, hermeneutic and idealist traditions (Gadamer, 1960/1975; Hegel, 1821/1967; Heidegger, 1927/1962). The arguments made in them are very much centred on philosophical problems: the question of our knowledge of social processes and of values (epistemology); the question of the nature of the individual and the social world (ontology or metaphysics); the questions of the nature of value and what we should value (meta-ethics and ethics). Political communitarianism, by contrast, consists of a group of books and policy papers written by people taking up the role of political entrepreneurs and attempting to propel communitarian projects on to the practical political agenda. Some of those who contributed to philosophical communitarianism are featured here as well as political actors with background in the social sciences or law (Etzioni, 1993, 1996; Selznick, 1987, 1992), and straightforward politicians (see endnote). The preoccupation of these works is with working out what a communitarian public policy agenda would consist of: what communitarianism would mean for taxation policy, education and welfare, family law, the division between central and local government and so on. Vernacular communitarianism, by contrast, as the label implies, is far less easily gleaned from books and other published works. By vernacular communitarianism I mean the ideas, ideals, understandings and theories of a range of political and social actors who think of themselves as community activists, or think that community is a value, and that community building is an important political project. When such actors compose notices and posters, or write newsletters, or talk to social researchers, they express a range of beliefs and understandings of community: for instance, that community must be 'black and white and everyone together' (Lichterman, 1996: 128) or that people ought to do things themselves, not for themselves but for the community. Together, these propositions (which tend to be strikingly like those set out more formally and explicitly by political communitarians) can be thought of as constituting a discourse – vernacular communitarianism.

In what follows, I will concentrate mainly on political communitarianism. The relationship between this and what I call philosophical communitarianism is not straightforward. In particular, whereas political communitarians have tended to be inspired by the philosophical communitarian critique of liberalism, and have drawn out from it a number of practical political and social implications, for their part the philosophical communitarians have tended to be wary of the resulting political programme. They have tended to assert that they are committed to liberal politics and society (especially to liberal rights and freedoms), but think that liberals are wrong in their philosophical analysis of the foundations of such a society and polity – in particular that the liberal philosophical analysis of the human individual is mistaken in a number of respects, or that liberal accounts of the justifiability of society and government are misleading and based on erroneous premisses. On the other hand, they have also tended to be more sympathetic than libertarian liberals, or capitalists, are about certain communitarian themes such as political education, active citizenship, and the cultural rights of minority cultures in pluralist societies.

THE COMMUNITARIAN CRITICISM OF INDIVIDUALISM

Communitarianism has emerged as gathering together one lot of criticisms of 'liberal individualism'. The philosophical communitarians, in brief, dissent from the implication, which they derive from liberal texts, that there are wholly rational foundations for ethics, politics and knowledge. They argue instead that what counts as justice, say, can only be rooted in human ways of life – in communities. This is also true for social roles and relations, and thus for the 'individual' and the 'rational individual' himself – these terms are social role terms. In response to this criticism, liberal philosophers have tended to concede a number of points, or to argue that communitarians were misreading their meaning in the first place. Liberals agree with communitarians regarding the importance of historically contingent material and social circumstances in shaping moral institutions, and the relevance of culture in sustaining ways of life in which rational choice or autonomy are central (see, for instance, Dworkin, 1986; Rawls, 1993). Liberals do, however, question the extent to which 'the individual' is to be thought of as 'embedded' in a community context, and the moral and political implications of such a theory. Liberals insist that individuals are capable of reflexive scrutiny and revision of their values, characteristics and forms of subjectivity. Any convergence between liberalism and communitarianism at the philosophical level, though, does not settle a number of political questions.

Liberal individualism is the target, because, it is argued, it has something of a dominant position in present society – not just in academic thought, but in the common sense of many social groups, and as the underpinning of a good deal of legal reasoning and of key political institutions like rights, markets, and the rule of law. These themes include the theoretical and practical emphasis on 'the rational individual' as the basic and most valuable unit in society. This individual, according to liberal thought in general, must be protected from state and social power, and the way liberals have done this is by the attribution (or discovery) of individual rights – which protect the individual from the undue interference of others, secure his legitimate property, and guarantee that others will discharge their proper duties and obligations to him.

The communitarian criticism of this scheme has more than one strand. First, communitarians argue that liberal theories of rights are often overly individualistic, and conduce to a picture of the individual as a kind of atom – autonomous, self-sufficient and essentially separate from everyone else. This underemphasizes the extent to which our basic condition is connectedness with other people. We are tied to others by bonds of obligation that are not 'freely chosen' but are nevertheless morally justifiable. Mutuality, reciprocity and cooperation are preconditions for human life, not optional choices. Second, although the acquisition of individual rights and freedoms historically is wholly admirable – it has (at least in theory) ruled out barbaric practices like torture, the withholding of property rights from women, etc. – communitarians believe that 'rights culture' has now gone too far, to the extent that the emphasis on rights has squeezed out any emphasis on duty. This latter point embodies two thoughts which are subtly different. One is that a social and political emphasis on rights itself conduces to a society in which people think of themselves as separate, and are encouraged to live their lives individualistically, disconnected from others. The other is that this is in fact a distortion of a proper understanding of rights – many rights after all do imply duties or obligations on the part of others. If this is the case the individualist's mistake is not the emphasis on rights *per se*, but a misunderstanding of what rights mean and entail.

Third, communitarians point to a wholly undesirable and unintended upshot of a society which emphasizes too much rights and too little duty. In such a society 'communities' cease providing a whole range of goods – notably care, mutual aid, sociability, insurance – which instead are provided either by free markets (leading to deprivation for the poor), or by bureaucracies. The bureaucratic supply and distribution of goods like welfare, education, health or anything else has a number of familiar and deleterious consequences: people feel alienated and distanced, as more value seems to be placed on administrators' convenience than on client needs or satisfaction; and supply is not responsive to need. The unsatisfactory nature of the twin process of bureaucratic supply of some goods, and the commodification and market supply of others, seemed to reach some kind of a crisis point in the 1980s. Conservative governments in a number of countries in that decade set out to shift the supply of many goods from bureaucracy to the market. This, according to communitarian thinking, was out of the frying pan and straight into the fire. According to communitarians the ills that followed on a bureaucratically controlled society – the breakdown of stable family life and sustaining kinship networks, the disappearance of lively and integrated local neighbourhoods where children learned how to behave with respect, the loss of associational life (in clubs, sports teams, etc.) – would certainly not be put right by leaving everything to markets.

So it is in this gap, between government and market, and the widespread perception of their twin failure, that communitarian ideas have become prominent.

COMMUNITARIAN COALITION

One strength of communitarian thought, as far as its promoters are concerned, is that it is 'beyond left and right'. The US-based Communitarian Network considers that one of its great strengths is that both Democrats and Republican politicians support it, that social scientists and theorists from both liberal (in US terms) and conservative standpoints are sympathetic (Etzioni, 1993). The idea and ideal of community resonates in many strands of thought and action. Earlier I mentioned a number of traditions in which the idea of community is prominent. These include many varieties of socialism: Marxism, ethical socialism, and the co-operative movement. Strands of conservatism have also emphasized community – romantic conservatism, 'One-nation Toryism', and the pervasive conservative concern with duty and obligation. Ideals of community recur in all kinds of religious and philosophical traditions: Judaism both secular and religious, dissenting Christianity of all sorts from Puritanism to Shakers and Quakers, and Methodism, Buddhism (which in addition to its continuing influence for many religious and spiritual persons, has seen many of its elements taken up in a good deal of 'New Age' practice), and Confucian thought (widely associated with the success of Asian economies during the last two decades).

In addition, 'community work' and 'community development' have throughout the period of industrialization been the preferred or chosen political strategies for many individuals – whether as professionals, as volunteers, or as active local people who participate or take a lead in community building. The literature on community politics emphasizes the range of reasons why individuals put their efforts there (Lichterman, 1996; Naples, 1998). Some are repelled by national or party politics, or shocked by the failures of corporations or councils, and feel compelled to act locally. Others are simply there: people with particular kinds of personalities and social skills, who are focal points for local interaction ('sociometric stars' as they are sometimes called by network analysts). Others are mobilized by these entrepreneurs and leaders and can be persuaded to put efforts into local work. So community organization and action are part of the political lives of many individuals; and for many of them, the literature and their own accounts also tell us, the ideal of community is prominent in their motivations.

The ubiquity of the ideal and value of community means that communitarians (unlike, seemingly, socialists, or conservatives, or anarchists) can form a great coalition. The communitarian hope is that left and right, liberal and authoritarian, radical and conservative, prominent politicians on the national and international stages and local people working to improve the immediate conditions in which they live, can converge on a certain set of aims, values and principles. Aims include to build strong communities in order to achieve stable and prosperous societies, to build strong communities within which individuals can achieve opportunities and self-fulfilment, to allocate to communities the power and authority to distribute and manage certain goods and resources – for instance to allow communities to decide about leisure facilities in their area, to enable them to discipline unruly vandals and keep common spaces civil. The values include individual responsibility and mutuality, individual rights correlated with duties and obligation to others. And community itself is a value. The principles include the view that communities themselves have rights and responsibilities, and that they therefore ought to be empowered to discharge those responsibilities and defend those rights. Communitarians also insist that individuals need not only material goods but the more spiritual goods that are generated by living in a community that fosters meaningful engagement with others.

One weakness of communitarianism according to many of its critics is that although this coalition might well exist at the point of assenting to these goals, values and principles, it is likely to break down when it comes to enacting them in practice. Conservatives value community because it promises social stability, a self-reliant population who do not drain resources away from the state or the market; by contrast community activists in the socialist tradition see community as the generator of resistance to the state and, especially, resistance to corporate capitalist power – the power of developers, employers, polluters and profit-makers. Many government-sponsored 'community development' projects have foundered just on the contradiction between corporations and councils who want legitimacy for their development schemes, and the attempts of local people to obtain genuine consultation, genuine democracy.

Commentators also observe that projects like 'Neighbourhood Watch' or other community action against drug abuse, vandalism or other disorder, do well precisely where they are least needed – in areas of relatively low crime and relatively high affluence (Crawford, 1998). Other localities would need huge injections of material resources before they could generate the necessary organizational resources – by which time the problems to which these putative organizational resources are addressed would have been ameliorated to a large extent by the material resources. In many areas where poor people nevertheless do find the organizational resources, their ability to effectively tackle deteriorating infrastructure, or provide alternative facilities for young people, or fight vandalism, is severely limited by their lack of ability to command material resources – such as community centres with proper staffing and caretaking, or police or security effort. There is ample evidence that people in situations of so-called 'multiple deprivation' frequently do have organizational resources, and manage to get the institutions and networks together – but without cash they cannot achieve what is necessary.

WHAT IS COMMUNITY?

This all begs a very important question: what is meant by community? In my account so far I have mentioned a number of social institutions (families, kinship networks, clubs, associations, neighbourhoods) and aspects of human life (individuals' connectedness with each other, their duties and obligations towards each other). For a number of communitarians this is all they mean by 'community': it is just the whole range of that sort of group or institution – not the individual, not the family, not the state, not the market, but all the ones in between: churches, neighbourhoods, schools, clubs, kinship networks, associations etc. 'Community' is a collective noun which encompasses all these. We can note that 'families' have an ambiguous position in communitarianism: some communitarians mention them as examples of communities, some think of family and community as disjointed. But this is simply the familiar vagueness of everyday language.

However, it can be objected that there are ambiguities in the concept that are more serious than this. First, it can be argued that there is a true ambiguity in the concept of community – it refers both to a particular class of social entities, and to a particular range of social relations. This ambiguity is genuinely misleading and confusing when people talk about community. Second, it might be argued that the term 'community' has a set of connotations over and above this bare meaning of a particular range of human collectivities, and these connotations are unquestionably brought into play whenever the term 'community' is used, instead of the alternative terms 'locality', 'association', or whatever is actually being discussed. Furthermore, these are connotations that are controversial, and make the use of the term community, in preference to alternatives, overwhelmingly political in itself.

I will explain these points in turn. As we have seen, the most common-sensical understanding of 'community' is that it refers to a kind of entity – a social entity, consisting of human beings organized in a particular way. Most communitarian social theory and philosophy is pretty vague at this point – explaining 'community' by exemplification rather than analysis, proposing a range of examples of communities such as churches, schools, villages, clubs, etc. But something more explicit than this is really meant. To count as a community a collectivity has to be integrated in a way that is distinct from the integration of market relations. Users of the term also usually imply that the collective has some autonomy or separateness from the power of the state. On the other hand, 'community' refers to a range of social entities taken together – this is the use of the term as an umbrella which encompasses churches, schools, villages, etc. According to this usage these are not individually examples of community; rather they are the building blocks of community.

But the implication that an entity has to consist of human individuals integrated or related in a particular way suggests that 'community' more properly refers not to the entity as such, but to the set of relations that constitute it. That 'community' is a relation term is clear: it makes sense to say 'x is in community with y'. But what does this relation, being in community, consist of? Most theorists emphasize a range of relations such as mutuality and solidarity. Other theorists dwell on community as sharing. This meaning is clear in such terms as 'linguistic community', 'ethnic community', 'religious community', 'political community' or 'business community'. Here the implication is that the members of the community in question share some thing, whether that is a language, an ethnic identity and way of life, religious practice, political institutions, or means of livelihood. The same idea is central in such terms as 'communities of adversity' or 'communities of need' which imply a group of people who share risks and hazards (and ways of coping with those hazards), or a group of people who have needs in common. It is notable that 'sharing' has alternative implications: on the one hand, to share something implies that the thing is divided up among the sharers – the more people share a good the less each gets. But in other contexts, sharing can strongly imply augmentation: that although members of a community have very little of some good, the sharing of it seems to make it more; or, in the case of 'bads', that a trouble shared is a trouble halved. That is, in a community sharing is non-competitive (unlike in conventional marketplaces or in other groups).

Even more strongly than this, we may be impressed by the close relationship between 'communion' and 'community': the thought is that in community people are connected not just by mundane exchanges and ordinary social relations like neighbourhood, kinship, citizenship. Instead they experience a connectedness that transcends these mundane and material connections: community literally implies people meeting each other on a whole person to whole person basis, or even 'soul to soul' (Buber 1951/1967). In fact, this idea is extraordinarily frequently suggested by community activists, who value whole rather than partial relations between persons (who would like their colleagues also to be friends, for instance, or who believe that encounters between, for instance, a buyer and a seller should properly be personalized). It is frequently suggested that community is only possible where there is sociability as well as work as well as shared spiritual or religious life as well as shared political and social institutions.

These connotations of the term 'community' can lead us to several thoughts. First, we might think that the idea of community is always more rhetorical than concrete: the ideal of whole person to whole person, or soul to soul relations, after all, is either impossible to achieve, or achievable only in limited ways or in fleeting moments, in a limited range of social groups including, perhaps, religious communities or very special social situations like that of the kibbutz pioneers in Israel. When transported into the realm of locality or neighbourhood development, or the local management of schools, or family policy, the term has a decidedly metaphorical (but of course significant) role. Second, we might think that the ideal of community is actually socially and politically undesirable – that the connotations of whole-person relations, soul meeting soul, are testimony to the inapplicability of community in late modern life. What we need to concentrate on, instead, is concrete social relations: neighbouring, the economy of care, intergenerational and interethnic conflict and co-operation, the density and scope of social networks. It may well be that 'community' in one sense is just a handy shorthand term that covers all of these and more. That is fine in ordinary language. But in social policy and in social science we need to use a more precise analytic vocabulary; and avoid taking 'community' too literally.

Third, though, and in contrast to this sceptical approach we may consider in more detail the value of community. For some theorists and activists community seems to be an instrumental value: the idea is that 'community' is necessary if other values are to be realized: democratic politics, or social stability, or material gains for a disadvantaged locality, or social justice. For others, though, community is a value in itself. Supposing a 'community group' got together and engaged in 'community building' in order to achieve a more just distribution of resources from the authorities; and suppose further that this campaign was in the end unsuccessful. For some communitarians the building of community nevertheless would have been a worthwhile project in itself. The establishment of the relation of community – emphasizing what is shared rather than what divides, personalizing encounters, individuals relating to and valuing the whole as much as they value the individuals who constitute it – would itself be a valued end. Community is a state of affairs in which life can be lived in a more truly human way, on a more truly human scale. For these communitarians community is an ideal always to be striven for.

There is a substantive moral and political disagreement here – between those who value community in itself and those who value it instrumentally if at all. Michael Sandel highlighted these two approaches to 'community' in his philosophical and sociological critique of Rawlsian liberalism (Sandel, 1982: 147–64). At present, as a 'theory of the present', communitarianism is still ambivalent regarding the distinction; the disagreement is far from a purely theoretical one as it often underlies substantial political disagreements.

SUMMARY

- Community has always had a prominent place in social and political thought, but since the early 1980s it has crystallized as a philosophical position, and taken on a novel political salience on both sides of the Atlantic.
- We can distinguish philosophical, political and vernacular communitarianism, although in practice contributions to the various debates overlap.
- Communitarianism's main criticism is towards the ill-effects of what is seen as an overemphasis on rights and individuality, rather than obligations and solidarity
- Because of the ubiquity of concern for community in political and social thought communitarians potentially might construct a broad political coalition.
- However, communitarians differ as to their interpretation of the value of community, and their criteria for the relation of community.

NOTES

1. For this chapter I have drawn on an extensive archive of 'political communitarianism' consisting of pamphlets and books, periodicals, press cuttings and some ephemera (campaign literature, home pages and so on). Articles worth mentioning explicitly are: Tony Blair, 'The Right Way to Find a Left Alternative', *The Observer*, 5 September 1993, p. 20; Gordon Brown, 'Beware the Mask of Tory Social Concern', *The Observer*, 2 December 1990; Roy Hattersley, 'Let's Proclaim our Beliefs', *The Observer*, 29 September 1991, p. 23; Martin Kettle, 'Blair Puts Faith in Community Spirit', *The Guardian*, 13 March 1995, p. 2; Martha Sherrill, 'Hillary Clinton's Inner Politics', *Washington Post*, 6 May 1995, p. D01; Jonathan Steele, 'Clinton Policies Caught in Communitarian Crossfire', *The Guardian*, 12 April 1994.

FURTHER READING

Avineri, Shlomo and de-Shalit, Avner (eds) (1992) *Individualism and Communitarianism*. Oxford: Oxford University Press. A useful collection of the main readings from both sides of the liberal v. communitarian debate.

Buber, Martin (1951/1967) 'Comments on the Idea of Community', in M. Friedman trans., *A Believing Humanism: My Testament*. New York: Simon and

Schuster. Buber is a key inspiration for many contemporary communitarians, both philosophers and activists.

Crawford, Adam (1998) *Crime Prevention and Community Safety: Politics, Policies and Practices.* London: Longman. A study of the contradictions and problems with the ideal of community in contemporary social policy.

Dworkin, Ronald (1986) *Law's Empire.* London: Fontana. A liberal who shares a good deal methodologically and ethically with the communitarians.

Etzioni, Amitai (1993) *The Spirit of Community: Rights, Responsibilities and the Communitarian Agenda.* New York: Crown. This book includes the text of the USA 'Communitarian Agenda'.

Lichterman, Paul (1996) *The Search for Political Community.* Cambridge: Cambridge University Press. A study of community activists and their political dilemmas.

Naples, Nancy (ed.) (1998) *Community Activism and Feminist Politics: Organising across Race, Class and Gender.* New York and London: Routledge. Studies of community activists and their political dilemmas.

REFERENCES

Buber, Martin (1951/1967) 'Comments on the Idea of Community', in M. Friedman trans., *A Believing Humanism: My Testament.* New York: Simon and Schuster.

Crawford, Adam (1998) *Crime Prevention and Community Safety: Politics, Policies and Practices.* London: Longman.

Dworkin, Ronald (1986) *Law's Empire.* London: Fontana.

Etzioni, Amitai (1993) *The Spirit of Community: Rights, Responsibilities and the Communitarian Agenda.* New York: Crown.

Etzioni, Amitai (1996) *The New Golden Rule: Community and Morality in a Democratic Society.* New York: Basic Books.

Gadamer, Hans-Georg (1960/1975) *Truth and Method,* 2nd edn, revised trans. J. Weinsheimer and D.G. Marshall. London: Sheed and Ward.

Hegel, G.W.F. (1821/1967) *Philosophy of Right,* trans. T.M. Knox. Oxford: Oxford University Press.

Heidegger, Martin (1927/1962) *Being and Time,* trans. John MacQuarie and Edward Robinson. London: SCM Press.

Lichterman, Paul (1996) *The Search for Political Community.* Cambridge: Cambridge University Press.

MacIntyre, Alasdair (1981) *After Virtue.* London: Duckworth.

MacIntyre, Alasdair (1988) *Whose Justice? Which Rationality?* London: Duckworth.

Naples, Nancy (ed.) (1998) *Community Activism and Feminist Politics: Organising across Race, Class and Gender.* New York and London: Routledge.

Rawls, John (1993) *Political Liberalism.* New York: Columbia University Press.

Sandel, Michael (1982) *Liberalism and the Limits of Justice*. Cambridge: Cambridge University Press.

Selznick, Philip (1987) 'The Idea of a Communitarian Morality', *California Law Review*, **77**: 445–63;

Selznick, Phillip (1992) *The Moral Commonwealth: Social Theory and the Promise of Community*. Berkeley, CA: University of California Press.

Taylor, Charles (1985a) *Philosophy and the Human Sciences*. Cambridge: Cambridge University Press.

Taylor, Charles (1985b) *Human Agency and Language*. Cambridge: Cambridge University Press.

Walzer, Michael (1983) *Spheres of Justice*. New York: Basic Books.

Walzer, Michael (1990) 'The Communitarian Critique of Liberalism', *Political Theory*, **18**: 6–23.

Chapter 14

New thinking in international relations theory

Kimberly Hutchings

The standard account of international relations (IR) theory identifies two main traditions of thinking and one marginal or subversive tradition. The two main traditions carry a variety of labels but are most commonly known as liberalism (sometimes also referred to generically as idealism or more specifically as liberal internationalism or liberal insititutionalism) and realism (sometimes referred to generically as political realism with its more recent variant usually labelled neo-realism). The marginal/subversive tradition is that of Marxism (recent variants of which are often referred to as structuralism) (see Bayliss and Smith, 1997: 107–63). Like most generalized accounts the reduction of traditional IR theory to three fundamental perspectives is something of a caricature, but it provides a useful way of introducing it. The chapter will begin with a brief account of the three traditions and then go on to examine and evaluate more recent developments in the study of the international.

LIBERALISM

Liberalism as a perspective on IR has its origins in late eighteenth-century European thought about international law and the possibilities of peace between states. In a very famous essay, 'On Perpetual Peace' (1784), the German philosopher Kant envisaged a combination of moral and self-interested factors leading to the setting up of a peaceful international federation of states, in which relations between states would be governed by co-operation and mutually agreed rules and norms (Kant, 1991: 93–130). This ideal gained much broader currency in nineteenth-century Europe, particularly as part of the faith in free trade as undermining the significance of state sovereignty and also as belief in the principle of democratic self-determination spread (Burchill and Linklater, 1996: 35–9). The liberal perspective on the future of international politics was dealt a severe blow by the experience of the collapse of great power politics in the First World War. This did not, however, presage a rejection of the liberal tradition in thinking about world politics. Instead it inspired (in the setting up of the League of Nations) the most systematic attempt yet to bring something like the international federation of states envisaged in Kant's essay to fruition.

In general, as a perspective on international politics, liberalism is characterized by a focus on co-operation between states, by the importance of individual as well as collective rights and by a progressive, evolutionary perspective on history to which economic self-interest as well as moral principle is central (Bayliss and Smith, 1997: 147–63; Burchill and Linklater, 1996: 28–66).

REALISM

The modern state system has its most clear point of origin in the Treaty of Westphalia (1648) which replaced the notion of the overarching identity of Christendom in Europe with the primacy of state sovereignty. In legal and political terms international relations became a matter of the interaction of different independent sources of right over whom no overarching authority existed. Over time, two kinds of theoretical development were encouraged by the Westphalian settlement. First, philosophical work on nationality, culture and history in the late eighteenth century (e.g., Herder, Fichte, Hegel), which emphasized the intrinsic value (and/or destiny) of the nation-state. Second, conceptions of international politics as being a matter of 'raison d'état' and 'Realpolitik' in which states pursued their interests by the best means available, which might be the achievement of a balance of power through diplomacy or through military intervention (Bayliss and Smith: 1997: 110–24; Neumann and Waever, 1997, 7–10). The outbreak of the Second World War heralded the end of liberal optimism about international politics and led to the consolidation of realism as a theoretical perspective on international relations.

In general realism stresses the absence of international norms and therefore the inevitability of competition in international politics. For realists, states pursue their interests in a context of anarchy. This means that history is understood cyclically rather than in terms of a linear model of progress. The best way of preventing war is to ensure a balance of power in the international arena, but such a balance is always precarious and war remains an ever-present possibility in the international system.

MARXISM

The Marxist tradition in thinking about international relations developed in parallel with and in relation to liberal and realist thinking. According to Marxist analysis capitalism would increasingly break down barriers between states. Lenin's analysis of imperialism in the early years of the century underwrote this point by stressing the role of economic imperatives in the imperialism of the European powers (Burchill and Linklater, 1996: 127–30). For Marxists, therefore, the political was to a large extent subordinate to the economic and the State was seen as inevitably decreasing in importance over time. This belief suffered major setbacks during the twentieth century. Two developments in particular discredited Marxist readings of world history and international politics. The first was the fact that the workers identified not with class but with national interest in the First World War. The expected international revolution following the October Revolution in Russia did not happen. The second was that the new Soviet Socialist Republic proved quite as attached to the pursuit of its own interest in the international realm as the former Russian empire. The aftermath of decolonization led to a partial revival of Marxist theory in the study of international relations. The accounts of theorists such as Frank and Wallerstein which offered 'structural' explanation of systemic disadvantage within the world political economy drew to a large extent on Marxist inspiration although they were not classically Marxist as such (Brown, 1997: 186–206).

On the one hand, Marxism challenges liberal optimism about the compatibility of capitalism, democracy and internationalism. On the other hand, Marxism challenges realism's focus on the state as the key explanatory concept in IR as opposed to the economy, and also the realist assumption that there can be no overall progress in history.

BRINGING THE STORY UP TO DATE

Having traced the broad sweep of alternative theoretical approaches to IR it is important to delineate more carefully how they have shaped and influenced work in IR since the Second World War. As an overarching orientation, as already pointed out, realism dominated work in general and particularly during the warmest phases of the Cold War (1950s/1960s, early 1980s). However, the nature of work on IR also suffered a more generic sea change in the post-war period. Whereas prior to the Second World War the study of IR had been largely legal, historical or philosophical in character, after the Second World War it became much more self-consciously social scientific (Brown, 1997: 31–7). One consequence of this development in IR theory was the introduction of a more 'scientific' version of realism (usually known as neo-realism) which emphasized the notion that valid generalizations and predictions were possible in relation to international politics (Brown, 1997: 45–9). Interestingly the increasingly social scientific emphasis of work in IR opened the way for the development of neo-liberal perspectives which drew attention to the significance of non-state actors such as international institutions and the economy in international politics (Brown, 1997: 43–5). These perspectives were not liberal in the classical sense discussed above, but they did make room for recognizing the possibility of co-operation as well as competition in the international order. By the early 1980s it became possible to argue that a convergence between realism and liberalism was under way in which radical differences were giving way to much more nuanced disagreements on emphasis. Critics of mainstream work in the 1980s increasingly emphasized the common ground of the neo-realist and neo-liberals (Neumann and Waever, 1997: 17–21). If we focus on the shared ground, the distinctive assumptions dominant in 1980s IR theory included:

- the assumption of the distinctiveness of international as opposed to domestic politics in terms of the priority of anarchy (weakness of constitutive norms) in the former and order (strength of constitutive norms) in the latter;
- the assumption of the empirical testability of hypotheses about the international order;
- the continuing significance of the State as the central international actor;
- the primacy of perceived self-interest in explaining the behaviour of international actors, whether states or other international actors;
- the essential irrelevance of normative concerns to the study of international politics.

In his address to the International Studies Association in 1988, Robert Keohane distinguished two broadly conceived theoretical approaches within the discipline. He labelled these approaches 'rationalism' and 'reflectivism' respectively (Keohane, 1989: 8). The term 'rationalism' was used to signify those approaches to explanation in international relations which operated on the assumption of the knowability of an independently existing international realm through empirical social scientific work. Under this umbrella heading was grouped work typical of the convergence in mainstream thinking described above (Keohane, 1989: 8). The reflectivist label, by contrast, was used as a generic term for a set of diverse theoretical perspectives which had in common an emphasis on the claim that the object of investigation in international relations was not an externally (and eternally) given phenomenon but was itself constructed historically and theoretically. What differentiated 'rationalist' from 'reflectivist' approaches in general was that the former assumed the possibility of a clear distinction between the social scientific method of the investigator (theoretical, conceptual and technical features of the approach to the object) and the object itself – with the assumption that evidence about the object could and should modify the ways in which it had been conceived and approached. In contrast reflectivism, in a variety of ways, problematized the subject/object distinction foundational to rationalism by focusing on the idea of strong links between the subject and object of knowledge and stressing the historical contingency of both. Keohane's classification bears witness (whether consciously or not) to a shift in the mode of being critical or subversive in the study of international politics. In the 1960s and 1970s, the major opponent of the converging modernist paradigms was another modernist paradigm, Marxism. In a move prefiguring the fall of the Berlin Wall, Keohane marginalizes the relevance of Marxism as an oppositional theoretical approach in post-Cold War IR. Among reflectivist perspectives are included normative theory, critical theory, post-modernism, and feminist IR theory (Bayliss and Smith, 1997: 172–90). In the following section I will go on to look briefly at these four approaches and then assess them in the light of the following questions:

1   How does this theoretical approach change the conception of what is the object of investigation in the study of international politics?
2   How does this theoretical approach change the conception of how international politics is to be understood?
3   How significant is the contribution of this theoretical approach to furthering the possibilities of explanation and judgement in the international realm?

NORMATIVE THEORY

On the face of it, it would seem to be difficult to avoid a normative dimension to international theorizing given the latter's strong relation to the prescriptive question of how international order may best be obtained. However, the disillusionment with liberal hopes for strong international co-operation after the Second World War had the consequence of separating the study of international politics from an explicit focus on issues of justice and right in the international sphere. Essentially the realist approach and the accommodations with realism made in mainstream work in post-war IR operated on the assumption that the international realm was characterized precisely by the absence of principles of justice, right and legitimacy (Bull, 1977). Moreover, one of the assumptions of the post-war realist consensus was that not only had liberal views of world order got things drastically wrong in the interwar period, they had also contributed to the disastrous foreign policy decisions which facilitated the outbreak of war (Brown, 1997: 28–9). This meant that normative concerns were relegated almost entirely to the marginal discourse of just war, the participants in which were much more likely to be moral philosophers, theologians and political theorists than scholars of international relations themselves (Elshtain, 1992).

Since the 1980s, this situation has changed. Normative theory has expanded well beyond 'just war' and more space for the discussion of normative issues has been created within the discipline (Brown, 1992; Groom and Light, 1994: ch. 2). So that, for instance, there will now always be several normative theory panels at national and international IR conferences and far more published work on these themes has appeared (see, e.g., Brown, 1994; Holden, 1996). The kind of work to which I am referring includes work on international human rights (Donnelly, 1989, 1993), global distributive justice (O'Neill, 1991) and cosmopolitan democracy (Held, 1995; Linklater, 1998). All of this work is distinguished by two features which differentiate it from mainstream IR analysis:

1   It presumes a level of international (sometimes global) connection between individuals which transcends or cuts across identification with states. This connection has both an empirical and a normative dimension. First, it relies on empirical claims about the way the actual global order is changing and the significance of globalization of international law in this process (Held, 1995). Second, it relies upon normative claims about human commonality as a basis for rights or obligations which are not constructed by the State (O'Neill, 1991; Donnelly, 1993).
2   It presumes the defensibility of an explicit commitment to certain normative goals and is either implicitly or explicitly prescriptive on the basis of them.

In terms of mainstream thinking in IR these developments are, at best, a return to liberalism in its earliest incarnation in Kant's work or in the post-First World War settlement sponsored by Woodrow Wilson. One interesting recent development which gives some substance to this challenge is the cluster of claims about 'liberal democratic peace' in which scholars claim to find empirical evidence for Kant's claim as to the increased likelihood of liberal states being peaceful in relation to each other (see Brown, Lynn-Jones and Miller, 1996). It is a testimony to the significance of the revival of normative perspectives in IR that the normative basis of state-centric or a nationalistic thinking has also recently become a focus of study (e.g., Miller, 1995).

CRITICAL THEORY

In the context of IR theory, the label 'critical theory' is used to refer to approaches inspired by the work of the Frankfurt School and particularly by Habermas (Burchill and Linklater, 1996: 145–78). Critical theory is reflectivist in the sense used by Keohane above in that it questions the assumptions made about both object and method of study (and the relation between them) in the discipline of IR. Critical theory goes further than this, however. First, it assumes that historical conditions are influential in determining modes of judgement and explanation (Bayliss and Smith, 1997: 175–8). Second, it seeks to demonstrate that different insights into the international realm are yielded when explanation is oriented by emancipatory ideals rather than by an unquestioning acceptance of the current *status quo* (Burchill and Linklater, 1996: 165–8; Groom and Light, 1994: 58–60). Critical theory is critical of the ahistorical way in which mainstream approaches to IR characterize the object of their analysis. According to critical theorists, mainstream theory treats the current nature of the inter-state system as an eternal political verity rather than as a historical construction which came about and is maintained by a complex interaction between states, substate and trans-state forces. In making this critique, critical theorists are drawing attention to the importance of the range of conditions of possibility for international politics, including economic, cultural and ideological factors which are neglected or marginalized by the mainstream. The claim is that if the object of study is not seen to include these conditions of possibility but deals with the international in isolation, then it cannot go beyond work which reproduces and reinforces the common sense of the age.

In relation to the perspectives or methods of study in IR, critical theory identifies modes of social scientific investigation as equally part of the historical development which delivers a particular articulation of the pattern of state power, productive forces and world order. In other words, there is no neutral and guaranteed route to the truth. Methodological approaches themselves always reflect historically conditioned assumptions about politics, power, human nature and knowledge and produce findings which highlight certain features of reality and occlude others. Critical theory's arguments about history and knowledge establish a strong link between the explanatory and the normative in social science. Explanations are seen to derive from the norms embedded in scientific investigation, so that different sorts of insights will be delivered by, for instance, policy-driven research as opposed to research oriented by ideals of emancipation or undertaken from the perspective of the marginalized and oppressed. This directly challenges the line drawn by mainstream international relations theory between normative and explanatory work. In addition, the identification of norms as within history rather than located in the conscience of the historian undermines the assumption common to mainstream IR thinking that the spheres of politics and morality are inherently distinct. Critical theory thus has a prescriptive thrust to it which gives it much in common with the normative approaches to IR discussed above.

POST-MODERNISM

Post-modernism is the 'reflectivist' theory which most clearly matches up to Keohane's classification of such theories as undermining the notion of an independently existing international reality. Post-modernist work focuses less on the specification of what international politics is, than on the ways in which it has been discursively constructed by the discipline of international relations itself. This is largely because post-modernists insist on the impossibility of disentangling questions of what is from discourses about what is (Bayliss and Smith, 1997: 181–3; Burchill and Linklater, 1996: 179–209; Groom and Light, 1994: 60–2). However, the ways in which post-modernists trace and challenge the limits of more orthodox approaches to understanding world politics does echo aspects of critical theory. Like critical theory, post-modernism questions the boundary between the domestic and the international and argues that the conditions of possibility of interstate relations include sub and trans-state forces. Similarly, post-modernists also challenge the epistemological presumptions of mainstream theorizing, the distinction between explanatory and normative work and the conceptual armoury of particular understandings of state, interest and power by which mainstream theory is characterized. When it comes to challenging the morality/politics distinction, however, post-modernists see themselves as being more radical than critical theorists.

As already discussed, critical theorists challenge the distinction mainstream thinking draws between morality and politics both by pointing to the normative agendas implicit in the study of international relations nurtured by strategic (ideology and policy-driven) interests and by arguing for an alternative mode of theorizing oriented by alternative normative values. Critical theorists identify critical theory proper with the possibility of discriminating between emancipatory as opposed to instrumental or strategic theorizing. In contrast, post-modernists are reluctant to suggest that there are any stable criteria by which one version of the international can be judged better than another. They argue that using the notion of emancipation as a ground for criticizing the theoretical and practical *status quo* is itself authoritative and exclusionary. For this reason post-modernists accuse critical theorists of relying on uncritical assumptions about criteria of judgement which collapse critical theory back into Marxist or liberal idealism. Nevertheless, in spite of this rejection of the idea of a substantive vision of emancipation, post-modernists still claim that their theorizing is in a 'register of freedom'. This register of freedom is identified with a Foucauldian notion of an imperative to constantly transgress the boundaries of given limitation (in theory and practice) rather than with any substantive ideal of a world without oppression (Ashley and Walker, 1990).

FEMINISM

The most recent 'new voice' in thinking about international relations is provided by feminism. As with the other perspectives already mentioned feminist IR theory covers a range of different kinds of approaches. One way in which different forms of feminist IR theory could be characterized would be to follow Harding's classification of different approaches in feminist epistemology: feminist standpoint theory and feminist post-modernism (Harding, 1991). In its weakest version, feminist standpoint theory in IR argues that mainstream theory shares an institutionalized myopia when it comes to the recognition of the significance of gendered relations of power in sustaining and reproducing the current world order. It suggests the need for a rethinking of the object of investigation in the study of IR. In particular it draws attention to the consequences for those assumptions of considering gender as one of the crucial conditions of possibility for both contemporary interstate relations and the mainstream world-view (Burchill and Linklater, 1996: 225–36). The work of critics such as Elshtain and Enloe has drawn attention to the ways in which gendered divisions of labour and constructions of femininity and masculinity underlie many of the practices in contexts from diplomacy to the military which are central to the mainstream perception of international politics (Elshtain, 1987; Enloe, 1989).

Feminist standpoint theorists go further in questioning the existing ontological and epistemological assumptions of international relations theory. The work of Tickner and Spike Peterson has challenged the social scientific claim to neutrality by pointing out the gendered assumptions which help to construct the building blocks of mainstream analysis and methodology (Spike Peterson, 1992; Tickner, 1991). Standpoint theorists argue that the assertion of an explanatory/normative split and of a morality/politics distinction collapses in the face of investigation of how that distinction is produced and sustained within theory. Moreover, as with critical theorists, standpoint theorists argue that privileged insights into the contemporary world order are yielded if understanding is premised on the position of the oppressed and excluded as opposed to the powerful with vested interests. With regard to the morality/politics split, one of the most significant strands in feminist thinking about war has been a set of claims about the normative standard inherent in the caring work most commonly carried out by women and its potential both to maintain and to subvert the possibility of war as an acceptable last resort in international politics (Ruddick, 1990).

Feminist post-modernists echo the critique made by post-modernism of critical theory already mentioned. They follow standpoint theorists in their challenge to orthodox understandings of both the object and mode of investigation in IR. However, they are troubled by the assertion of a 'feminist standpoint' as providing privileged insights into international reality. For feminist post-modernists all bases of explanation are open to deconstruction and none can claim to be superior to another in any absolute sense (Burchill and Linklater, 1996: 241–2; Steans, 1998: 177–82).

CONCLUSION: USEFUL OR NOT?

It is clear that there is a very rich body of theoretical work on IR emerging under the four headings given above. It is also clear that there are certain themes that these new voices in IR have in common as well as many differences between them. The question remains as to how useful or illuminating are these new approaches. What do they add to mainstream thinking on IR? What are their strengths and weaknesses? Let us return to the three questions raised above:

1   How does this theoretical approach change the conception of what is the object of investigation in the study of international politics?
2   How does this theoretical approach change the conception of how international politics are to be understood?
3   How significant is the contribution of this theoretical approach to furthering the possibilities of explanation and judgement in the international realm?

In response to the first question it is evident that all of the perspectives alter the conception of the object of investigation in the study of IR. Normative theories bring a whole dimension into the picture which previously had been missing or was only marginally present, that is a concern with normative analysis and prescription. Critical, post-modernist and feminist theories all share the argument that the international cannot be understood in isolation from the domestic and the global, or that the political cannot be understood in isolation from the economic. In the case of feminism, the personal is put on the map as being much more significant as an object of investigation for IR than had previously been allowed. Traditionally IR theory had focused almost wholly on interstate relations with moves to include a limited number of non-state actors as realism accommodated certain neo-liberal insights. The 'reflectivist' perspectives stress the range and complexity of factors relevant to explanation in IR and pose a strong challenge to any taken-for-granted assumptions about the nature of the international. The message of critical theory, post-modernism and feminism goes beyond this, however, since all three approaches also argue that the international is historically constructed and that this affects (or should affect) the ways in which it is understood and judged. For example, if one assumes that anarchy is a necessary, eternal feature of international politics then one is likely to have a different perception of the possibilities of change in international politics than if one doesn't. The failure of mainstream approaches in IR to predict the end of the Cold War has fuelled the reflectivist insistence on the dangers of locking social scientific analysis into a single unquestioned conceptual framework.

In response to the second question, the implications of these new approaches for the issue of how the international is to be understood are radical in the case of all of the theories. For all of them there is an ineliminably normative dimension to theorizing (obvious in the first case but clearly also present in the others). Second, the approaches introduce a whole range of new conceptual tools for the study of IR from justice to emancipation, discourse and gender. Third, in the case of critical theory, post-modernism and feminism, all of these approaches suggest a strong relation between method and object of investigation, to the extent that the object is itself very largely a construction of theory. The upshot is that the international can be studied in diverse ways and with differential effect, but the notion of the achievement of objective truth in the study of IR is put into question. Although mainstream IR theory is by no means insensitive to issues of theory-dependence in explanation the study of IR has remained characterized by greater trust in an externally verifiable and fundamentally constant social reality than is the case in most social sciences. It would be wrong to suggest that the reflectivist theories necessarily reject the notion of an independently existing reality or the possibility of making true claims about it, but they certainly problematize the traditional aims of mainstream IR.

Let us now look at the third and most important question – how useful are these new perspectives? The answer to this is ambivalent. On the one hand, there is no doubt that these new approaches have let a great deal of light on to the limitations of mainstream work in IR. Moreover they have inspired a wide range of new work on subjects ranging from the study of diplomacy and sovereignty to the role of organized prostitution in relation to military bases (Bartelson, 1995; Der Derian, 1987; Enloe, 1989). Some of this new work has done more than challenge hegemonic modes of understanding and has yielded new insights into the nature of the contemporary international order (disorder) and how it is constructed and sustained. Nevertheless, the jury still remains out on whether these new approaches are replacements of or simply supplements to more mainstream work. One of the difficulties implied by the reflexive nature of much new theorizing is that the criteria by which it may be judged superior to other work on a particular topic have become unclear or are stated in terms which are simply incommensurable with more orthodox social scientific criteria. Ironically this tends to keep the orthodoxy in place. However convincing more sophisticated understandings of the work of conceptualization and analysis in IR may be, they are liable to have the effect of rendering their own status questionable along with that of the object of their critique. This is particularly true of post-modernist work which abandons even the security of tying analysis to governing normative ideals. In summary, then, it is clear that these new ways of thinking about the international are interesting and challenging but that they seem unlikely to displace mainstream understanding entirely. What is more likely to happen as IR theory moves into the twenty-first century is a modification of mainstream work in the light of the various theoretical challenges. Whether this will be a radical modification or not remains to be seen, but it is certainly the case that mainstream work is likely to be stronger the more seriously it listens to these new approaches and displays a willingness to rethink taken-for-granted assumptions about how IR is to be understood.

SUMMARY

- Traditional thinking about IR was dominated by two perspectives: liberalism and realism.
- The main oppositional discourse in IR theory until recently was provided by Marxism.
- By the 1980s, the dominant classical traditions in IR theory had converged in a neo-realist/neo-liberal social science. Marxism was becoming an increasingly marginal perspective.
- New ways of thinking which were generically labelled 'reflectivist' began to gain currency in the 1980s and included: normative, critical, post-modernist and feminist theory.
- These new ways of thinking challenged both (a) mainstream understandings of the nature of the international realm as an object of investigation and (b) mainstream assumptions as to the appropriate methods through which the international realm could be studied and explained.
- The new ways of thinking have challenged mainstream complacency and yielded new insights into the international realm. However, the jury is still out on the question of how much mainstream thinking will be transformed by these new approaches in the future.

FURTHER READING

Because the range of work in IR theory is so vast, I have tended to limit my references in this chapter to more general and introductory work. For someone looking for an overall sense of the concerns of contemporary IR, I would recommend Bayliss and Smith (1997). The is an excellent introductory textbook which gives an overview of both theoretical approaches and substantive issues within the overall context of the claim that we are moving from an international to a global world.

A more substantive consideration of the main theoretical approaches (traditional and contemporary) discussed in this chapter is to be found in Burchill and Linklater (1996).

If you want to approach something more challenging then Chris Brown's recent book on international theory (Brown, 1997) provides an excellent and scholarly overview of post-war IR thinking.

A rather different kind of challenge is provided by Neumann and Waever (1997), which is a collection of essays on contemporary IR theorists who exemplify some of the different approaches with which this chapter has been concerned. Both Brown and Neumann and Waever are appropriate for those who already have at least a basic background in IR theory.

Finally, for those looking for something more specialized, I would recommend Enloe (1989) as a very accessible but extremely interesting example of a text in feminist IR theory and Walker (1993) as a less accessible but very interesting and sophisticated post-modernist reading of the state of IR theory today.

REFERENCES

Ashley, R.K. and Walker, R.J.B. (1990) 'Reading Dissidence/Writing the Discipline: Crisis and the Question of Sovereignty in International Studies', *International Studies Quarterly*, **34**(3): 367–416.

Bartelson, J. (1995) *A Genealogy of Sovereignty*. Cambridge: Cambridge University Press.

Bayliss, J. and Smith, S. (eds) (1997) *The Globalization of World Politics*. Oxford: Oxford University Press.

Brown, C. (1992) *International Relations Theory: New Normative Approaches*. New York: Columbia University Press.

Brown, C. (ed.) (1994) *Political Restructuring in Europe: Ethical Perspectives*. London: Routledge.

Brown, C. (1997) *Understanding International Relations*. London: Macmillan.

Brown, M.E., Lynn-Jones, S.M. and Miller, S.E. (eds) (1996) *Debating the Democratic Peace*. Cambridge MA: MIT Press.

Bull, H. (1977) *The Anarchical Society*. London: Macmillan.

Burchill, S. and Linklater, A. (eds) (1996) *Theories of International Relations*. London: Macmillan.

Der Derian, J. (1987) *On Diplomacy*. Oxford: Blackwell.

Donnelly, J. (1989) *Universal Human Rights in Theory and Practice*. Ithaca, NY: Cornell University Press.

Donnelly, J. (1993) *International Human Rights*. Boulder, CO: Westview Press.

Elshtain, J.B. (1987) *Women and War*. New York: Basic Books.

Elshtain, J.B. (ed.) (1992) *Just War Theory*. Oxford: Blackwell.

Enloe, C. (1989) *Bananas, Beaches and Bases: Making Feminist Sense of International Politics*. London: Pandora Press.

Groom, A.J.R. and Light, M. (eds) (1994) *Contemporary International Relations: A Guide to Theory*. London: Pinter.

Harding, S. (1991) *Whose Science? Whose Knowledge? Thinking From Women's Lives.* Milton Keynes: Open University Press.

Held, D. (1995) *Democracy and the Global Order.* Cambridge: Polity.

Holden, B. (1996) *Ethical Dimensions of Global Change.* London: Macmillan.

Kant, I. (1991) *Kant: Political Writings,* (ed.) H. Reiss. Cambridge: Cambridge University Press.

Keohane, R. (1989) *International Institutions and State Power: Essays in International Relations Theory.* Boulder, CO: Westview Press.

Linklater, A. (1998) *The Transformation of Political Community.* Cambridge: Polity.

Miller, D. (1995) *On Nationality.* Oxford: Oxford University Press.

Neumann, I.B. and Waever, O. (eds) (1997) *The Future of International Relations.* London: Routledge.

O'Neill, O. (1991) 'Transnational Justice', in D. Held (ed.) *Political Theory Today.* Cambridge: Polity.

Ruddick, S. (1990) *Maternal Thinking: Towards a Politics of Peace.* London: Women's Press.

Spike Peterson, V. (ed.) (1992) *Gendered States: Feminist (Re) Visions of International Relations Theory.* Boulder CO: Lynne Reiner.

Steans, J. (1998) *Gender and International Relations.* Cambridge: Polity.

Tickner, J.A. (1991) 'Hans Morgenthau's Principles of Political Realism: A Feminist Reformulation', in R. Grant and K. Newland (eds) *Gender and International Relations.* Milton Keynes: Open University Press.

Walker, R.B.J. (1993) *Inside/Outside: International Relations As Political Theory.* Cambridge: Cambridge University Press.

Chapter 15

Utopia and dystopia

Stephen Crook

INTRODUCTION

Students of utopianism frequently raise the prospect of the 'death of utopia' (see Goodwin and Taylor, 1982: 48; Kumar, 1987: 381; Manuel and Manuel, 1979: 801). Recent commentators generally conclude that utopia is not dead but transformed. In Holloway's (1984: 180) formula, for example, it may have 'slipped out of the atlas onto the drawing board or into the government white paper' at some point during the nineteenth century. Those who canvass the possibility of the death of utopia generally maintain that if it came about, some important dimension of our capacity to imagine alternatives to the present social order would be lost. This chapter argues a rather specific version of that case as it bears on the relations between utopianism and academic social theory. In doing so, it excludes from consideration a range of topics that are important in their own right: the development of fictional utopias and dystopias in the twentieth century, or utopian and dystopian strands in ecological and animal rights literatures, for example. The argument has two main elements.

First, Marxist and sociological variants of social theory emerged in the nineteenth century out of a rather specific adaptation of utopian themes. They offered orientations to a future that could be understood as the working-out of principles already present, if hidden, in the existing order. So, for Marxism, the embryo of the socialist future is located in the social resources mobilized by capitalist production and in the organized practice of the working class. The twin legacy of this adaptation of utopianism for contemporary social theory is a reluctance to think of the future as significantly 'open' outside fairly narrow limits and a studied, pervasive abstraction in such reflection as takes place on alternative futures.

Second, to extend Holloway's diagnosis, at the end of the twentieth century utopia has moved off the drawing board and out of the white paper into the fabric of social life itself. In their modern sense, utopian thought and practice require that an alternative order can be conceived as single and unitary, as a whole way of life. In turn, this requires that the present and corrupt order to which utopia is an alternative can also be conceived as a whole. But the present order is one that absorbs into itself critiques, alternatives and escapes: it is heterogeneous rather than homogeneous, multiple rather than singular, incomplete rather than finished and clearly circumscribed. As a result, utopia is simultaneously nowhere – in no total alternative to the total extant order – and everywhere – in computer games, cults, communities and lifestyle magazines.

The chapter is divided into three sections. 'Utopias' explores the dimensions of modern utopianism. 'Utopia, anti-utopia and dystopia in radical social theory' develops the first element of the argument. 'Everywhere and nowhere' explores the second element of the argument, tracing the ways in which utopia is woven into the fabric of contemporary life and experience.

UTOPIAS

Utopias are of interest because they project ways of life that their authors take to be both radically distinct from and ethically superior to those prevalent in their own times and places. As virtually all commentators point out, Sir Thomas More's coinage of 'Utopia' as the title of his 1516 book and the name of the ideal society it describes is a jokingly ambiguous play on Greek words: utopia is both eu-topia, the good or happy place and ou-topia, no place (see Goodwin and Taylor, 1982: 15; Kumar, 1987: 24; Levitas, 1990: 2). Most discussion of More's pun centres on the ambiguity it introduces into the assessment of 'utopianism'. Should we (as social theorists or progressive-minded citizens) take utopias seriously as attempts to reflect on the good life, or be wary of them as fantastic and ungrounded in any reality? Famously, Engels is among those taking the latter course in *Socialism: Utopian and Scientific*. He defers to the 'three great Utopians: St Simon, . . . Fourier; and Owen', placing them in the history of socialist ideas. But he then castigates them, particularly Owen (who should have known better as an Englishman familiar with industrial conditions), for their failure to identify with the cause of the proletariat. 'Like the French philosophers, they do not aim to emancipate a particular class to begin with, but all humanity at once' (Engels, 1892: 5–6).

This rejection of utopianism as unrealistic, ungrounded in the laws of historical change, will be revisited shortly. Immediately, More's pun might be taken to signal what marks out utopianism as a particular way of thinking about alternative societies or ways of life. That is, a double insistence that the good life (however conceived) is to be found only outside the present order (however conceived), and that its power to compel our assent lies only in its goodness. Mannheim's attempt to distinguish 'utopian' from 'ideological' thinking may not succeed, but he catches the first arm of utopianism nicely: utopia is a type of orientation 'which transcends reality and which at the same time breaks the bonds of the existing order' (Mannheim, 1936: 173). One effect of this way of circumscribing utopianism is to make it definitively modern, a point that may be clearer after a brief review of debates about the definition of utopia.

If utopias are defined broadly as projections of an ideal society, we can find them everywhere in the history of Western culture. The rational social and political arrangements proposed in Plato's *Republic* are utopian and so are the mildly scandalous adaptations of Graeco-Roman myth in Ovid's *Metamorphoses*. The celebration of divine grace in St Augustine's *City of God* is utopian, but so is the popular myth of Cockaygne, the land of plenty where food and drink fly into the mouth. Similarly, modern literary satires such as Swift's *Gulliver's Travels* and Butler's *Erewhon* join the earnest socialist projects of St Simon, Fourier and Owen as utopias. The landmark text of recent utopian studies, Manuel and Manuel's (1979) *Utopian Thought in the Western World*, urges just such a broad definition. Others are more restrictive. Davis (1984: 8–9) distinguishes utopia from four other ideal societies: natural abundance (as in Cockaygne), arcadia (natural abundance tempered by a classical restraint), the perfect moral commonwealth (as in Godwin's *Political Justice*) and the millennium (man and nature transformed by an external power). Utopia proper, exemplified by More's *Utopia*, is 'a category of social idealisation dependent upon detailed organisational, legislative, administrative and educational imagination' (Davis, 1984: 10).

Kumar's (1987: 2–32) argument for regarding utopia proper as definitively modern parallels Davis in important respects. Myths of the Golden Age, Cockaygne, Paradise and the Millennium are important elements in the history of utopia but are not themselves utopia. Neither is *The Republic*. Kumar (1987: 21) insists that More's *Utopia* is the 'product of a new age' with 'a rationalism and a realism that we associate typically with the classical revival of the renaissance'. The egalitarianism of *Utopia* and its insistence on the sharing of labour also mark out the modernity of More's vision from Plato's caste-based communalism, with its rigid division of labour, in *The Republic*. Here, Kumar comes close to Mannheim who distinguishes between four modern forms of the 'utopian mentality', arguing that modern utopianism finds its 'turning point' when religious millenarianism 'joined forces with the active demands of the oppressed strata of society' (Mannheim 1936: 190).

The first form is the 'orgiastic chiliasm' ('chiliasm' is the Greek-derived equivalent term to the Latin-derived 'millenarianism') of the Hussites,

Thomas Münzer and the Anabaptists. The ecstatic frenzy of early modern chiliasm had given way by the eighteenth century to a second form that Mannheim (1936: 197) terms the 'liberal-humanist idea' associated with conceptions of economic and political 'progress' and appealing principally to the more idealistic members of the rising bourgeois class. Mannheim's third form of utopianism, 'the conservative idea', is a counter-utopia directed at the manifestations of the second form in the capitalist economy and republican state. Hegel's critique of the 'abstraction' of liberal-humanism and his claim that the rational is present in the real structures of the here and now is taken by Mannheim (1936: 206–15) as his main example of this form. Finally, the fourth form is 'the socialist-communist utopia' which is 'a new creation based upon an inner synthesis of the various forms of utopia that have arisen hitherto' (Mannheim, 1936: 215).

Engels's critique of utopian socialism requires re-examination in the light of the roughly convergent arguments of Davis, Kumar and Mannheim. For Engels, pre-Marxist socialisms are utopian in the positive sense to the degree that they condemn the exploitation and poverty of the present order and project an ideal, egalitarian, society in which these stains are washed away. But they remain utopian in the pejorative sense because they can explain neither 'the essential character' of exploitation in the extraction of surplus value, nor the historical processes that would produce the 'inevitable downfall' of capitalism (Engels, 1892: 42–3). As Engels (1892: 73) puts it later, 'active social forces work exactly like natural forces: blindly, forcibly, destructively, so long as we do not understand, and reckon with them'. But scientific socialism, armed with the materialist conception of history and the theory of surplus value, *does* 'understand and reckon with' social forces. On that basis, 'the social anarchy of production gives place to a social regulation of production upon a definite plan, according to the needs of the community and of each individual' (Engels, 1892: 74).

The question arises, then, of whether Engels's (and Marx's) 'scientific' alternative to utopianism is simply itself another form of utopianism. The emphasis on science and planning meets Davis's requirement and, as he notes (1984: 12), contemporary anarchist critics saw no reason to distinguish between Marxism and utopian socialism in their polemics against the dogmatism, system-building and bureaucratization common to all socialisms. Kumar (1987: 55–65) recognizes the utopianism of Engels's own book and the centrality of utopian themes to Marx's work. Mannheim (1936: 215) quite clearly includes Marxism in the fourth stage of utopianism: Engels's grounding of socialism in real historical processes and economic structures exemplifies the 'synthesis' of liberal-humanist and conservative utopianisms. However, to pose the question in stark and static terms according to which Marxism either 'is' or 'is not' utopian may not be very helpful. Whatever Mannheim's other defects, his view of utopianism as a dynamic and syncretic movement of thought and action may be more useful that Davis's stipulative approach or Kumar's permissiveness. It gives a purchase on the fundamental question of how 'classical' social theories such as Marxism changed ways of thinking about alternative futures, preserving and transforming some features of earlier utopianisms but losing others.

UTOPIA, ANTI-UTOPIA AND DYSTOPIA IN RADICAL SOCIAL THEORY

Engels *believed* that the difference made to his and Marx's version of socialism by its 'scientific' content was a difference of world-historical significance and not simply a minor realignment of established utopian themes. St Simon, Comte and Durkheim similarly believed they had made breakthroughs that generated a uniquely powerful knowledge of how the structures of the present order arose from a transformation of the past that was yet to be completed. In the light of the new knowledge, the process of social transformation could be completed 'consciously'. I wrote about this theme some years ago (Crook, 1991), taking Marx and Durkheim as founding examples of a syndrome in social theory I termed 'modernist radicalism'.

At the heart of that syndrome is a claim to stand at a double 'great divide' between past and present: a divide at the level of social structure marked by the emergence of a new and specifically modern order, and a divide at the level of theory with the discovery of a new form of knowledge uniquely capable of understanding the new order. The 'radicalism' of the syndrome lies in the link between the two, in the claim that the new and privileged knowledge of the social is the key to a new kind of social transformation. The privilege is captured in three themes (Crook, 1991: 10–11). An 'ideology' theme asserts the cognitive overthrow of anachronistic and inadequate knowledges of the social, notably philosophy, 'common sense' and (I would add here) utopianism. A more specific 'end of philosophy' theme announces that the new knowledge can preserve the 'rational kernel' of idealist philosophical (and utopian) speculation. A 'unity of theory and practice' theme warrants the unique capacity of the radical project to bring under cognitive control, and then to complete through informed practice, the process of social transformation.

This model has been enormously influential, shaping the ways social theory orients itself to the future not only directly but also indirectly, through the negations and critiques it has provoked. The most important direct implication flows from what Mannheim sees as the import of a conservative realism into utopianism, a move as typical of Durkheim and the functionalist tradition in Sociology as of Marxism. For modernist radical social theory, the basis for a movement beyond the existing order must already be demonstrably present within it. So, for Engels (1892) the transition to socialism requires both the highly developed productive forces of a mature capitalist economy and an organized working class (both conditions becoming the source of bitter and consequential disputes in the Marxist tradition). Again, for Durkheim (1964) the spontaneous development of the division of labour lays the foundation for a new social order based on mutual interdependence. In the light of his sociological science, that order can be fine-tuned and brought to fruition by a reformist State (through the abolition of 'unnatural' inequalities, the creation of intermediate social institutions and the promotion of 'civic religion').

This 'realistic' adaptation of utopian themes has an important consequence. As reform socialists and functionalist sociologists become ever more realistic, the gap between present and future narrows and those speculative elements that marked earlier utopianisms – dreams of natural abundance, arcadia, the perfect moral commonwealth or the millennium – are ever more rigorously excluded. Modernist radical projects that struggle against this tendency, such as the Leninist and other revolutionary traditions within Marxism, do so by privileging the utopian goal and the disciplined will to achieve it above the limitations imposed by social-theoretic realism. This move amounts to the creation of modern versions of earlier millennial movements, and here too there is a marked aversion to 'speculation' about the future. Lukes (1984: 166) includes the whole Marxist tradition in his charge that 'anti-utopianism' (by which he means the specific adaptation and limitation of utopianism discussed above) has 'systematically inhibited' reflection on goals and the 'institutional and political forms that could embody them'. For Lukes, the practical result of this failure of theoretical imagination is 'the deformed world of "actually existing socialism"'.

Dystopian and anti-utopian themes in social theory can also be linked to the modernist-radical project. Utopianism and dystopianism are very closely linked: Swift's satirical purposes in *Gulliver's Travels* are served equally by the largely utopian depiction of Houyhnhnm society (where patrician horses exercise a benign authority over unruly and uncultivated humans) and the largely dystopian account of Gulliver's third voyage to Laputa and adjacent islands (home to the monumentally futile Academy of Lagado). A critique of the existing order can proceed from a projection of either its worst or its best features on to an imaginary society. The link between the two forms is also conveyed by disjunctions such as 'heaven or hell', or 'socialism or barbarism'. On millennial accounts of the rapid approach of the latter days, whether religious or secular, the impending choice is between utopia or dystopia: if we do not work (spiritually, politically) to create utopia we will end up with dystopia.

There is also a syndrome of anti-utopianism which is to be distinguished from dystopianism by its rejection of all theorizing, optimistic or pessimistic, about imaginary societies. Among the 'founders', Weber is frequently a pessimistic theorist and is sometimes interpreted as a dystopian for his reflections on the 'iron shell' of the modern economic order or the incommensurability of modern 'value spheres' (Weber, 1970, 1976: 181). However, he is more appropriately understood as a forceful anti-utopian critic of modernist radicalism. Weber's arguments are complex (see the account in Crook, 1991: 62–76), but turn on his views that values do not inhere in social reality, that the outcomes of social action frequently confound the intentions of action, and that all knowledge of the social world is partial and relational.

The ironic and relational 'anti-utopianism' of a Weber is quite distinct from the modernist radical adaptation and scientization of utopian themes by an Engels or a Durkheim and equally distinct from speculative dystopianism. It has its own complex philosophical pedigree that draws on Kantian and Nietzschean themes and feeds into the work of social theorists such as Adorno and, more recently, Foucault. One of the marks of this anti-utopianism is an extreme reluctance to make any direct statements about the nature of the good life or the prospects for its future realization. In Adorno's version of critical theory any such 'affirmative' thinking must drift towards an ideological assimilation of radical alternatives by the existing order (see Adorno, 1974, for example). Adorno's insistence on a purely 'negative' criticism is echoed in Foucault's reluctance to specify any goal or normative content for 'resistance' to the dispositions of power-knowledge he outlines (see Gordon, 1990: 255–8). There is a clear contrast here between Adorno's critical theory and the versions developed by his contemporary Marcuse and his pupil Habermas.

Marcuse is often identified as the most 'utopian' of neo-Marxists, with the outlying exception of Bloch's (1986) celebration of the 'anticipatory' force of utopianism. Commentators often note that Marcuse swings between 'optimistic' or utopian and 'pessimistic' or dystopian moments (see Geoghegan, 1981: 37; Levitas, 1990: 133). Marcuse's most obviously optimistic-utopian text, *Eros and Civilization* (1955) helped to shape the sexualized politics and politicized sexuality of the 1960s with its arguments that conventional sexualities were complicit with the 'surplus repression' required by the capitalist order. A re-eroticization of human experience mediated through 'polymorphous perversity' – that is, sexual activities other than genital heterosexuality – could become the vehicle for a transcendence of all forms of repression. By contrast, his *One Dimensional Man* (Marcuse, 1964) emphasized the integrated and bad totality formed by modern technology, Cold War aggression and a consumerism devoted to instant gratification. The key to understanding this oscillation between optimism and pessimism is a recognition that Marcuse's work belongs firmly within the orbit of modernist radicalism.

However it may appear, Marcuse is never a (speculative) utopian or dystopian. That is, he never simply sets out a blueprint for the society of his dreams or nightmares. Throughout his long career, from his early engagements with Heidegger and then Hegel to his last works on aesthetics, Marcuse was searching for the principles or forces hidden inside the present and corrupt social order that would be the basis for its transformation into something better. Sometimes he was more, and sometimes less, optimistic about the prospects for change, but the basic model that links him to the project of Marx and Engels remains constant while its content varies from 'reason' to 'polymorphous perversity' to 'the aesthetic dimension'.

It has been noted that social theory has appropriated utopian themes in ways that narrow the gap between the real and the ideal. A further tendency, which Marcuse struggled against without entirely overcoming, is a drift towards generality and abstraction. A mark of proto-utopias such as Cockaygne or the millennium was their sensuousness, immediacy and detail: one could almost feel and taste them. Even the modern utopia-proper, as defined by Davis, is marked by the detail of the ideal forms of organization it proposes. The clearest contemporary example of that drift is furnished by Habermas's re-working of critical theory. It is notable, first, for its insistence against the unrelieved negativity of his teacher Adorno that a 'positive' moment in critical theory is necessary (see Habermas, 1987). But Habermas develops that moment through the thinnest possible version of the modernist radical project. The principle of transformation lying deep within the structures of the present order is a principle of universalization related to the 'intuition . . . that valid norms must *deserve* recognition by *all* concerned' (Habermas, 1990: 65). In this principle Habermas argues he has located the core of a morality that is presupposed in the reciprocal nature of all human communication. He is residually utopian to the degree that he looks forward to forms of life that openly acknowledge and express such reciprocity, but his is a utopianism that has become entirely formal, as ascetic, mediated and general as possible. Habermas's work surely represents the vanishing point of utopian themes within contemporary social theory.

EVERYWHERE AND NOWHERE

Compared to Habermas, Giddens's approach to utopian themes is direct and robust. He has coined the term 'utopian realism' to capture the future-orientation he thinks appropriate for contemporary social theory. It is 'the characteristic outlook of a critical theory without guarantees' (Giddens, 1994: 249). The 'utopianism' of utopian realism lies in its preparedness to pose the question of 'what alternative sociopolitical forms could potentially exist' in relation to four 'risk environments' (Giddens, 1994: 101). The 'risk environment' of the capitalist economy is presently marked by 'economic polarization', that of industrialism by 'ecological threats', that of the means of violence by the 'threat of large scale war' and that of surveillance by a 'denial of democratic rights'. Against these conditions, utopian realism can conceive (respectively) a 'post scarcity economy', a 'humanized nature', 'negotiated power' and 'dialogic democracy' (Giddens, 1994: 100–1). There are three main planks to the 'realism' of 'utopian realism'. First, its utopian projection of benign alternative sociopolitical forms 'corresponds to observable trends' (Giddens, 1994: 101). Second, it rejects all 'providentialism':

history is not on our side, it will produce no collective agents of world-historical change, it has no direction (Giddens, 1994: 249). Third, and in consequence, there are no privileged agents of change, so that utopian realist themes may as well be carried by 'parties operating within the normal domains of national politics' (to pull an example from the air, the British Labour Party) as by *soi disant* radical social movements (Giddens, 1994: 250).

This is a serious and attractive view of a late-modern politics that acknowledges its own utopian dimension, but it does not escape the tensions of earlier efforts, such as those of the 'modernist radicals' to weave utopian themes into a 'realistic' social theory. For example, there is a tension between the importance accorded to the fact that the utopianism of utopian realism 'corresponds to observable trends' (above) and Giddens's (1994: 249) claim that a recognition of risk and contingency 'opens up space for utopian counterfactual thought'. Cynically, one might imagine this tension becoming the formula of a New Labour hegemony that presents its programmes as the ideal balance between utopianism and realism, so that opponents are either not utopian enough or not realistic enough. More seriously, Giddens struggles at the very end of *Beyond Left and Right* to justify the universalism of utopian realism – its privileging of the four themes noted above – against what he portrays as the Nietzsche-inspired post-modernisms of a 'fragmentation and contextuality' that can produce only 'multiple fundamentalisms' (Giddens, 1994: 252). The main argument is that 'the universal values that are emerging today' have an empirical basis: they 'express and derive from . . . global cosmopolitanism' (Giddens, 1994: 253).

Two difficulties arise here that again mark the limits of social theory's appropriation of utopian themes. First, it becomes clear that the line dividing a utopianism conditioned by a realistic appraisal of 'observable trends' from a utopianism mired in 'providentialism' (a believe that God or history or the working class can guarantee a positive outcome) will be difficult to draw in practice. Engels thought he and Marx fell into the former camp, but with the benefit of hindsight we can place them in the latter. The same fate could easily befall Giddens. Second, there is a problem that can be stated in two ways. Stated theoretically, Giddens has not adequately engaged with the ironic and relational anti-utopianism linked in the previous section with Weber and Adorno. Stated empirically, the 'observable trends' he alludes to do not exhaust the trends one might observe if one chose a slightly different standpoint: a 'dystopian realism' might be as easily grounded empirically as the utopian variety.

For all its merits, Giddens's model of 'utopian realism' does not convincingly break with the figures through which social theory has incorporated and tamed utopian themes since at least the time of Engels and Marx. It could be said to mark their limit-point in mainstream social theory, but no more. If that diagnosis is correct, social theory has developed a very limited repertoire of responses to utopian themes, with an ironic and relational anti-utopianism as the significant alternative to variants of the 'incorporate and tame' move. If Giddens has difficulty in balancing the universalism of utopian realism with the contingency of the future, this is in part because it is difficult to formulate the present as a unified order calling for a unified alternative. Rather, the order of the present is heterogeneous, multiple and incomplete. It contains critiques, alternatives and escapes within itself. Paradoxically, if social theory is to recognize utopian strains in contemporary culture and practice, it requires a stance closer to ironic and relational anti-utopianism than to utopian realism. That is, it needs to pay more attention to the multitude of ways in which individuals and groups imagine, experience and enact alternative realities.

It has never been easier for citizens of the advanced societies to do so. We can take vacations in previously inaccessible regions of the world, moving among people whose culture may seem as remote as that of any utopia. We can luxuriate in a 'tropical paradise' where, for a couple of weeks at least, arcadia or the land of Cockaygne can become a reality (see Rojek and Urry, 1997). We can enter any number of virtual realities with a modest computer and a modem, from the pornotopia of cybersex to imaginary game worlds of dazzling complexity to the virtual relationships and communities of online chat (see Castells, 1996). We can use free-to-air or pay television to lose ourselves for a while in the 'worlds' of sport or popular music or the soaps. In these activities we are 'tourists' in Bauman's (1997: 89) sense, living in a 'continuous present' and freed from the requirement to make an 'identity stand', to be 'fixed'.

To take this argument a step further, we now have unparalleled opportunities to re-imagine and remake our lives. At all but the lowest levels of income and education we face significant choices of 'lifestyle' relating to matters such as body-image, dress and adornment, home décor, food and drink, musical and other cultural tastes, sporting activities or spectatorships, political preferences, sexual orientation and relationship status. To be sure there is a darker side to this circumstance. Post-traditional 'individualization', in Beck's (1994: 14) term, requires inumerable choices that can present themselves as sources of anxiety rather than pleasure: for some of us choosing a shirt, let alone a lifestyle, is not to be relished. Lifestyle choices may become burdensome obligations when linked to the demands of a 'prudentialist' neo-liberalism in public policy that we take more responsibility for ourselves (see O'Malley, 1996). However, the basic point remains: a form of society that makes available lifestyle choices to such large numbers of its citizens is less easy to capture in the image of a single and homogeneous order than one in which lifestyle is determined by socio-economic location. In consequence, it is less easy – or less necessary – to imagine alternatives as entirely outside and opposed to the structures of the present.

Taken to their limits, technically enabled alternative realities and lifestyle choices merge with cults and alternative communities that achieve varying degrees of disconnection from the networks of mainstream society. Such 'communal utopias' have a long history whether in religious or secular form, particularly in America (see Goodwin and Taylor, 1982: ch. 8; Kumar, 1987: ch. 3; Pitzer, 1984), but their significance changes as the shape of the host society changes. One of the more interesting features shared by (say) the Heaven's Gate cult, or the Freemen of Montana is that they are both self-enclosed (as world-views and communal structures) and open to view – indeed, obsessively self-publicizing (if only posthumously in the former case) – through new communications media. They can be known to a degree and in a manner that would have been unheard of for (say) The Harmony Society or Zoar in nineteenth-century Indiana and Ohio (see Goodwin and Taylor, 1982: 186). They are linked to widely circulating millennial-utopian and -dystopian themes: comets, UFOs, higher cosmic intelligences, black helicopters, love-my-country-fear-my-government, survivalism, etc. This tension between connection and disconnection is a symptom of the hetero-geneity, multiplicity and incompleteness of social order in the present. We can zoom in and out of these alternative cognitive and social worlds at will, so that their significance extends far beyond any tiny formal 'membership'.

Putting these three linked phenomena together – alternative realities, life-style choices and what we might term 'neo-communalisms' – yields an image of our experience of the present in which alternatives are part of the package. They are not so much alternative futures as alternative presents that are, literally, 'present'. In significant respects, this definitively contem-porary experience has more in common with pre-modern or early-modern utopias and proto-utopias than with the tidy-minded modernism that aligns the present with reality and assigns alternatives to an increasingly circum-scribed future. When nineteenth-century utopia moves 'off the map' it moves into the future, as well as on to the drawing board. Utopia has now moved back on to the map, becoming respatialized but also dispersed. A further sense in which contemporary alternative presents converge with older utopias and proto-utopias relates to their immediacy and detail. As utopian themes are absorbed into social theory they are progressively etio-lated until they become, at the extreme, something like Habermas's principle of 'universalism'. The alternative realities of the tropical holiday or the com-puter game have more in common on these dimensions with arcadia or the millennium than with the abstractions of social theory. The difference, of course, is that they are widely, if not universally, available.

What stance should social theory take towards these developments and to utopia more generally? Giddens's fear of 'multiple fundamentalisms' has been noted. That critical view is echoed by Boggs (1997) who castigates 'new age utopianism' and would-be radical 'enclave cultures' for their abandon-ment of the public sphere, the real terrain of serious politics. However, to take a more positive view is not to embrace some nihilistic post-Nietszchean doctrine, but to recognize that utopia shares a more general contemporary condition of fragmentation and pluralization. To that degree the modern utopia, conceived as an alternative social totality contrasted to an existing totality, *is* dead. But elements of utopia also live on in many popular and academic forms. Perhaps the most important task of social theory in relation to utopia is the ironic and relational one of tracking these forms, of observing their intersections and divisions and their contribution to the multidimensional reflexivity of contemporary life. If that ironic distance is not quite serious enough, there are avenues remaining for constructive, if partial, utopias. There is surely a utopian spirit at work in Coleman's (1993) model of institutional engineering, in Etzioni's (1993) embrace of communitarianism, or in Hirst's (1994) designs for associative democracy, to take only three examples. The generalities of Giddens's 'utopian realism' can also find their corner of this field, so long as they recognize their perspectival origins and do not claim the privilege of the complete and last word.

SUMMARY

- Utopia, the ideal society, has been an important vehicle for social criticism and social improvement.
- Social theory has appropriated utopia in ways that restrict its speculative dimensions and render it more and more abstract.
- By contrast, in social life more generally, utopian critiques, alternatives and escapes have never been more widely available or more commonly practised.
- Social theory might usefully pay more attention to the ways utopian themes and practices have become integral to the heterogeneous and multidimensional order of the present.

FURTHER READING

Engels, F. (1892) *Socialism, Utopian and Scientific*. London: George Allen and Unwin. This is a classic text that illustrates clearly the way in which social theory, in its Marxist variant, criticizes 'utopianism' while appropriating utopian themes. It is also available in the Lawrence and Wishart edition of Marx and Engels *Selected Works*.

Giddens, A. (1994) *Beyond Left and Right: The Future of Radical Politics*. Cambridge: Polity Press. Giddens locates his 'utopian realism' in the context of his more general model of 'reflexive modernity' and reviews the prospects for radical politics. *The Third Way* (1998) offers a shorter treatment of these themes.

Levitas, R. (1990) *The Concept of Utopia*. Hemel Hempstead: Phillip Allan. Levitas offers a brief but thorough and accessible review of modern utopianism. She is a helpful guide through debates about the definition of utopia.

REFERENCES

Adorno, T.W. (1974) *Minima Moralia*. London: Verso.

Bauman, Z. (1997) *Postmodernity and its Discontents*. Cambridge: Polity Press.

Beck, U. (1994) 'The Reinvention of Politics: Towards a Theory of Reflexive Modernization', in U. Beck, A. Giddens and S. Lash, *Reflexive Modernization*. Cambridge: Polity Press.

Bloch, E. (1986) *The Principle of Hope*. Oxford: Basil Blackwell.

Boggs, C. (1997) 'The Great Retreat: Decline of the Public Sphere in Late Twentieth-Century America', *Theory and Society*, **26**: 741–80.

Castells, M. (1996) *The Rise of the Network Society*. Oxford: Blackwell.

Coleman, J. (1993) 'The Rational Reconstruction of Society' (ASA 1992 Presidential Address), *American Sociological Review*, **58**: 1–15.

Crook, S. (1991) *Modernist Radicalism and its Aftermath: Foundationalism and Anti-Foundationalism in Radical Social Theory*. London: Routledge.

Davis, J.C. (1984) 'The History of Utopia: The Chronology of Nowhere', in P. Alexander and R. Gill (eds) *Utopias*. London: Duckworth, pp. 1–18.

Durkheim, E. (1964) *The Division of Labor in Society*. New York: Free Press.

Engels, F. (1892) *Socialism, Utopian and Scientific*. London: George Allen and Unwin.

Etzioni, A. (1993) *The Spirit of Community: The Reinvention of American Society*. New York: Simon and Schuster.

Geoghegan, V. (1981) *Reason and Eros: The Social Theory of Herbert Marcuse*. London: Pluto Press.

Giddens, A. (1994) *Beyond Left and Right: The Future of Radical Politics*. Cambridge: Polity Press.

Giddens, A. (1998) *The Third Way: The Renewal of Social Democracy*. Cambridge: Polity Press.

Goodwin, B. and Taylor, C. (1982) *The Politics of Utopia: A Study in Theory and Practice*. London: Hutchinson.

Gordon, C. (1990) 'Afterword', in M. Foucault, *Power/Knowledge*. Brighton: Harvester, pp. 229–60.

Habermas, J. (1987) 'The Entwinement of Myth and Enlightenment: Max Horkheimer and Theodor Adorno', in his *The Philosophical Discourse of Modernity*. Cambridge: Polity Press, pp. 106–30.

Habermas, J. (1990) 'Discourse Ethics: Notes on a Program of Philosophical Justification', in his *Moral Consciousness and Communicative Action*. Cambridge MA: MIT Press, pp. 43–115.

Hirst, P. (1994) *Associative Democracy: New Forms of Economic and Social Governance*. Amhurst: University of Massachusetts Press.

Holloway, M. (1984) 'The Necessity of Utopia', in P. Alexander and R. Gill (eds) *Utopias*. London: Duckworth, pp. 179–88.

Kumar, K. (1987) *Utopia and Anti-Utopia in Modern Times*. Oxford: Basil Blackwell.

Levitas, R. (1990) *The Concept of Utopia*. Hemel Hempstead: Phillip Allan.

Lukes, S. (1984) 'Marxism and Utopianism', in P. Alexander and R. Gill (eds) *Utopias*. London: Duckworth, pp. 153–67.

Mannheim, K. (1936) *Ideology and Utopia: An Introduction to the Sociology of Knowledge*. London: Routledge and Kegan Paul.

Manuel, F.E. and Manuel F.P. (1979) *Utopian Thought in the Western World*. Oxford: Basil Blackwell.

Marcuse, H. (1955) *Eros and Civilization*. Boston: Beacon Press.

Marcuse, H. (1964) *One Dimensional Man*. Boston: Beacon Press.

O'Malley, P. (1996) 'Risk and Responsibility', in A. Barry, T. Osborne and N. Rose (eds) *Foucault and Political Reason*. London: UCL Press.

Pitzer, D. (1984) 'Collectivism, Community and Commitment: America's Religious Communal Utopias from the Shakers to Jonestown', in P. Alexander and R. Gill (eds) *Utopias*. London: Duckworth, pp. 119–38.

Rojek, C. and J. Urry (eds) (1997) *Touring Cultures: Transformations of Travel and Theory*. London: Routledge.

Weber, M. (1970) 'Science as a Vocation', in H. Gerth and C.W. Mills (eds) *From Max Weber*. London: Routledge and Kegan Paul.

Weber, M. (1976) *The Protestant Ethic and the Spirit of Modern Capitalism*. London: George Allen and Unwin.

Part II

Themes

Chapter 16

Post-modernity

David Lyon

'Post-modernity' entered quickly, though not uncontroversially, into the lexicon of socially descriptive terms used at the end of the twentieth century. It seemed to connect, in a natural enough fashion, with other concepts, from the European-originating 'fragmentation' and 'différance' to others generated on the Canadian west coast, such as 'cyberspace' and 'Generation X'. These terms each help create a picture of a social world in flux, where unities and uniformities give way to the flexible and the fluid. The first two hint at the disintegration of societies once centred and orderly, and perhaps at the difficulty of describing cultures as homogeneous in their ethnicity or sexuality. The second two, by contrast, evoke a sense of life within a network of global communications in which relationships are mediated electronically, and where consuming and style are more significant to social life than careers and saving. But is there any more to post-modernity than an impressionistic pop-concept?

For a number of sociologists, post-modernity bespeaks social and cultural transformation of a profound kind, which is the theme of what follows. The term tantalizes with the 'post' prefix, begging as it does the question of what is or was the social condition of modernity, and how *post*-modernity is different. Can modernity bear this closer inspection, without doubt being cast on how accurate and helpful a descriptive term it is? Recall that the concept of modernity itself is only a recent creation. And if doubts are entertained about 'modernity', does this also throw in question the validity of the kind of sociology that spawned it? These questions are addressed by looking at, one, the sociological origins of 'post-modernity'; two, the use of the concept to encapsulate present social conditions; three, the counter-argument that, while major changes are occurring, they do not add up to 'post-modernity'; and four, the changing terms of the debate. Under this final heading, one may ask if the cultural turn represented by the debate over post-modernity is complete. Unlike the debate over modernity, this one is surprisngly silent about the religious dimension.

POST-MODERN PREMONITIONS

In the final thirty years of the twentieth century a number of factors prompted analysts, especially in North America and Europe, to suggest that a social-cultural sea change is occurring. The evidence comes mainly from phenomena related to two related sources: on the one hand, technological developments, particularly those associated with microelectronics-based communication and information technologies, and on the other, economic tendencies that seem to shift the emphasis of companies from production to consumption. These changes are related, in turn, to various kinds of explanatory framework that in part echo, and in part are dissonant with, classical sociological concepts such as differentiation, commodification and rationalization.

While some of the analysts examining these phenomena, such as Alain Touraine in France, or Daniel Bell in the USA, are prominent sociologists, it is noteworthy that others, writing after the initial forays of Bell, Touraine and others into the field, made their contributions from disciplinary fields such as literary criticism (Frederic Jameson) architectural theory (Christopher Jencks) or geography (David Harvey). This is because post-modernity is in part about a cultural turn in the social sciences that reflects the rise to social prominence of the factors mentioned above, namely communications media and consumer markets. Indeed, while Touraine and Bell discuss 'post-industrialism', thus indicating their indebtedness to sociological traditions, Harvey, Jencks and Jameson refer to the 'post-modern'.

Daniel Bell's famous 'social forecast' of a post-industrial or 'information' society-in-the-making set the tone – and became the target – for a number of other more and less sympathetic studies from the 1970s onwards. Bell argued that it was time to discard the old labour–capital axis of sociological, and especially Marxist, theory, and replace it with 'theoretical knowledge' as the new 'axial principle'. Just as land-based agrarian societies had once given way to manufacture-based industrial societies, the latter were now giving way to service economies, in which communication and information technologies (CITs) would 'become decisive for the way economic and social exchanges are conducted, the way knowledge is created and retrieved, and the character of work and organizations . . . ' (Bell, 1980: 500).

Though Bell's work would receive a critical battering on all sides, it did so in part just because it neatly pointed up some signficant features of change

occurring in the later part of the twentieth century. The new role of knowledge and of the CITs would feature centrally in theories of post-modernity.
Bell's was a rosily positive account – which was a further catalyst to critique
– but it was based on extensive empirical analysis, that assumed the centrality of the USA in the developments described, and the generally beneficial results of the knowledge-based, service-oriented world he depicted. The
increase of so-called 'information work' relative to manufacturing – dubbed
'Fordist' after the motor magnate, by other theorists – and primary industry
jobs was given particular prominence. Little attention was paid, in Bell's
account, to the possibility of other kinds of trends emerging in the 'information society', of fresh forms of social polarization and geographically distributed inequality, of resistance to the new technologies, or of their uses in
banal and narcotic entertainment, and in new modes of surveillance, social
ordering and control.

But Bell was also sure that the technical and economic changes wrought
by the coming of the information society had no direct connection with the
spheres of cultural change. For him, the knowledge-base of the information
had everything to do with a modern, rational process, and if in an era of
mass consumption questions are raised about the status of this knowledge,
they will not affect the 'axial principle' of technical and economic activity.
For someone like Jean-François Lyotard, however, this dysjunction of realms
simply would not do. The very 'blossoming of techniques and technologies
since the Second World War' (Lyotard, 1979: 37) is draining the power to
legitimate scientific and political projects from supposedly universal truths –
the 'metanarratives' of modernity. Lyotard's own analysis of the situation
parts company decisively with that of Bell, not least in that the archetypical
modern metanarrative of 'progress', writ-large in Bell's 'information
society', is simply absent from Lyotard's 'post-modern condition'. At the
same time, Lyotard also makes more of another contemporary feature of
knowledge than Bell did, namely, its commodification. Whereas Bell's view
of knowledge still relates to Descartes' 'knower', Lyotard insists that as the
exchange-value rather than the use-value of knowledge becomes central, so
'consumers of knowledge' supplant the erstwhile 'knowers'.

Lyotard, like a number of other theorists, argues that a culture of consumerism lies close to the heart of what it is to be post-modern. This represents a distinct shift from the concerns of Bell and his generation of
sociologists for whom, as Mike Featherstone (1991: viii) says, culture and
consumption were 'derivative, peripheral, and feminine'. Having said that,
credit must be given to Bell for at least attempting to produce evidence for
his information society thesis, a practice that is not altogether obvious
among some of those who write of consumer culture as a key to the post-
modern. The empirical referents of the post-modern are easily recognized,
and resonate with the experience of many – zapping across multiple television channels with the remote control and, now, surfing the net; leisure
pursuits centred around Disneyesque shopping malls; tourism channelled

223

towards exotic destinations through architectural lookalike airports; education enhanced by 'hands-on' multimedia attractions and theme-park heritage history – but actual studies of such everyday practices have yet to achieve anything like the sophistication of what Bell produced.

None the less, various indices do give strong clues that consumerism has become much more significant economically, politically and socially than it was in the first half of the twentieth century. For Jean Baudrillard, the economic shift towards consumption, and away from a preoccupation with production, is the decisive marker of the post-modern world. Television symbolizes this, with what Harvey calls its 'production of needs and wants, the mobilization of desire and fantasy, and the politics of distraction' (Harvey, 1989: 61). High culture becomes a thing of the past as musical styles jostle together promiscuously on the radio, and art galleries and artists parade their wares on the World Wide Web. Cultural symbols also become social markers, distinguishing by style one group from another. And through pervasive advertising, commerce and culture entangle as never before – hence, for example, the huge controversies surrounding the sponsorship of sporting and artistic activities by cigarette companies. As Krishan Kumar observes, it is not just that culture has been commodified, but that 'culture has colonized the economy' (Kumar, 1995: 118).

Of course, all this still raises the question of whether interest in culture and consumption reflects some fundamentally changed conditions in the real world, or, alternatively, changes in the ways the 'real world' is understood (or, conceivably, both). If it is the former – the real world is changing – then a further question is, why? Is it a new era of post-industrialism or the information society, as Bell supposes, or a new stage of capitalism, as Frederic Jameson ('late capitalism') or David Harvey maintain? The latter, in particular, resists the technological determinism that sees television, for instance, as a 'cause' of post-modernism. No, 'television is itself a product of late capitalism, and, as such, has to be seen in the context of the promotion of a culture of consumerism' (Harvey, 1989: 61). A third possibility is that the post-modern may not be reduced to a 'stage' of anything, but rather represents either a new social-cultural formation that embraces aspects of older ones, or a new way of looking at what was earlier called modernity.

None of the writers mentioned above will state unequivocally that post-modernity is a social-cultural condition in its own right (though some, despite themselves, come close). Bell allows that the post-modern may be a sort of cultural spin-off of the information society, and Jameson that it is an aspect of late capitalism. They are unready, that is, to abandon the old categories and sociological or Marxist explanations, as theorists like Lyotard or Baudrillard seem more willing to do. This despite the fact that the concept of post-modernity still relies on the concept of modernity for its contrast and, perhaps, for some continuity. One theorist stands out, however, in his attempt to argue for post-modernity as a social-cultural system in its own right. It is not that he throws caution to the winds – his work remains recognizably sociological in some almost surprising respects – but rather, he points to evidence that both presages major transformation, and also questions old categories.

ZYGMUNT BAUMAN'S POST-MODERNITY

If modern sociology tried through its theories to tell a story about the rational ordering of the world, in terms of comprehensible structures and systems, that develop in a particular direction, then something very different is required for the emerging post-modern condition. For many features of the contemporary world defy explanation in conventional sociological terms. It is not merely (though this is important) that the widespread diffusion of CITs have helped to raise questions about reality, in which day-to-day life seems to be 'like' an ongoing soap opera, or that war is conducted remotely, with the most tense engagements occurring between fingers manipulating computer devices and eyes fixed to a screen. Nor is it just that the consumer phase of capitalism throws doubt on many cherished ideas about why people are motivated to work or what maintains the apparent orderliness of local daily life, when neither the State nor large corporations seem to have much say in the matter (though this, too, is far from trivial). The difficulty is more basic: there seems to be a sort of directionless incoherence in what is called post-modernity, such that attempting to capture it in an overarching narrative seems futile.

Now, various features of the post-modern may be listed, in order to give some sense of orientation to the field of study. The best way to do this is to contrast them with those of modernity and, in the first instance at least, to see them as extensions of modernity (see Crook, Pakulski and Waters, 1992). So the highly organized and specialized differentiation characteristic of advanced societies starts to run in reverse, as it were, with both breakdown of boundaries between spheres (de-differentiation) and proliferating small-scale categories (hyperdifferentiation). At the same time, the centralized organization characteristic of modernity begins to give way to forms of disorganization (Lash and Urry, 1987) and polycentric control. These factors affect all the major social spheres, such as politics and the State, work and technology. Modern rationality seems suspect, and uncertainty, rife; the body and the emotions are more significant; and environment and ecology are approached with a new seriousness. At the same time, a new playfulness pervades the arts and entertainment. Governments become more aware of the international and the global, whereas in everyday life, the local is accented.

But none of this adds up to society as a stable, self-regulating system, thrusting forward towards a better future, as imagined by some major theorists of modernity. And this is exactly Zygmunt Bauman's point, to which I now come. As he says, 'Once we remember that incoherence is the most distinctive among the attributes of postmodernity (arguably its defining feature), we need to reconcile ourselves to the prospect that all narratives will be to a varying extent flawed' (Bauman, 1992: xxiv). Of course, only someone who has been immersed in modern social theory, with its often-repeated quest of precisely accurate narratives, following the Enlightenment dream of perfect human knowledge, would realize that such 'reconciling' might be a very reluctant concession! The difficulties presented by 'incoherence' notwithstanding, Bauman offered, from the early 1990s, some 'glimpses', some 'sightings' of the post-modern. True, he views it as a new type of society, but this has more to do with how social relations are seen than about a new era that makes a decisive break with the old.

Bauman notes that other sociologists, observing the same phenomena, interpret them in a number of ways. He identifies two major schools of thought, each of which sees post-modern phenomena as a sign that 'something is wrong'. On the one hand, one finds the 'softening civilization' school that sees a 'comfort principle' gradually supplanting a 'reality principle'. That which previously held things together – perhaps above all the inner-directed, self-controlled Puritan personality – can no longer do so, and so society literally disintegrates. On the other hand, many theorists espouse what might be called a 'contradictions of modernity' position, in which both the motivation to work and the sense that the productive system is legitimate are being eroded. In a society organized around the productive function this is indeed bad news, for what now will provide the means for the mechanism to move smoothly when the differential axle that normally integrates the different gears and actions is broken?

The key to Bauman's alternative view is the word 'normally'. What, he asks, if those symptoms of a diseased society are interpreted rather as signs of a new situation? Not that there is 'nothing wrong' with society – as we shall see, Bauman is still a *critical* theorist with an acute ethical sense – but rather that the ways it 'normally works' are changing. If he is right, then a new model is needed, and that is just what he tried to provide. His own words make the contrast nicely. Today, he proposes,

> consumer conduct (consumer freedom geared to the consumer market) moves steadily into the position of, simultaneously, the cognitive and moral focus of life, the integrative bond of the society, and the focus of systemic management. In other words, it moves into the selfsame position which in the past – during the 'modern' phase of capitalist society – was occupied by work in the form of wage-labour. This means that in our time individuals are engaged (morally by society, functionally by the social system) first and foremost as consumers rather than as producers (Bauman 1992: 49).

Although he has elaborated his position more theoretically, this quotation indicates the essence of Bauman's argument that post-modernity describes a new social condition.

Bauman rightly argues that for the first part of its history, modern capital-ism placed work (or at least paid employment) in a central position. Work held a pivotal role, linking together the individual motivation of the worker, the means whereby a network of social relationships and friendships was developed, and the way that the whole system was kept running efficiently. But work as paid employment has undergone some radical changes over the past quarter-century, and the idea of a secure lifelong job, trade or profes-sion has increasingly become history. Employment has become casualized, part-time, uncertain and insecure (and this affects both women and men), and the multiple career, retraining and early retirement (or layoff) seems more like the norm. This is hardly a basis for personal motivation, let alone the fostering of stable communities and liveable localities. If this is what has been happening with wage-labour, at the level of capital things have also been changing, with much more fluidity in the flows of (especially) finance capital, and the locating of production units in globally dispersed sites, enabled by CITs. Techno-science, rather than struggles over who controls production, or the ongoing rationality of the organization, is seen as the harbinger of social change.

But for Bauman this is not just an absence (of work) but a new presence (of consumer freedom) that has in several significant respects taken over from work as the social linchpin. And in so doing, he suggests, consumer freedom may point the way to a resolution of the antagonism between pleasure and reality principles. Producers may still stick with 'reality' as a guiding principle, but they depend upon consumers *not* doing so. For the consumer, pursuit of pleasure is the point. The consumer system needs credit-card-happy shoppers, and there is also a sense in which consumers feel them-selves bound to shop. They are pressured both by the constant need to keep up with others and to demonstrate their style, up-to-dateness and social fit; and also by merchandizing companies who both define the good life – above all through relentless advertizing – and go to great technological lengths to channel the choices of consumers (see Lyon, 1994: ch. 8). Both symbolic rivalry and social management together form, not a mode of pressure felt as oppression, but a system of (what Pierre Bourdieu [1984] calls) seduction.

The overall effect of this new social type is that the system – of capitalism – is secured. Where once expensive and complex forms of control were required to keep order, now seduction painlessly (indeed, pleasurably) does the same job. At least for those – the large majority in the advanced societies – with the capacity to consume, and who do so most conspicuously in tourism (Bauman, 1997: ch. 6). For those who do not, warns Bauman, the old panoptical methods of control, now technologically enhanced, are brought to bear. Those unintegrated into the system of consumer freedom, for what-ever reason, may not expect their status as 'flawed consumers' (Bauman, 1987) to go unnoticed. Virtually disenfranchised, in the worst instance, flawed consumers find themselves outside the consumerist circus, in an underclass situation where even the bottom rung of the ladder is out of reach. If on one side of the shopping mall are the 'gated communities' of living cocooned within high-tech security systems to protect the spoils of consumption, on the other are the 'grating communities' of homeless, flawed consumers, who huddle in shop doorways for overnight warmth.

Having established this fresh take on the sociology of the present, during the 1990s Bauman devoted himself to consolidating and elaborating his elegant and persuasive argument that post-modernity means a new type of society, at least in the making. He has made extensive comment (in a number of books) on three major implications of his theory – for how sociology is done, for political activity, and for ethics.

As far as sociology is concerned, he argues that the theory of post-modernity abandons the idea that 'society' operates as an organism which, in Parsonian fashion, is cohesive, equilibrated, with a central value system, and a set of elements that perform 'functions' for the system as a whole. Rather, the totality is kaleidoscopic, a 'momentary and contingent outcome of interaction' (Bauman, 1992: 189). Any apparent 'order' is local, transient, and emergent, rather like a river whirlpool that maintains its pattern but is constantly renewed. Rather than use 'society', the term 'sociality' should be adopted to express the processual, the play of randomness and pattern, and the notion of structure as an emergent accomplishment. Human agency (or its habitat) is foregrounded, such that choices made in the agent's life add up to self-constitution or self-assembly. The corresponding item to be dropped is any notion of 'progress'. Mobility and change there may well be, but not in any clear direction. Time is thus unbound, in that ties with the past are weakened, leaving less space for the future to be colonized.

Second, the political realm may no longer be severed analytically (and thus artificially) from the study of social relations. This was encouraged, says Bauman, by modern strategies of both theory (which was construed as 'value-free') and the State (that insisted on the monopoly over policy formation, and on distinct spheres of legitimating policy and theory). Politics in the modern era was dominated by questions of (primarily economic) inequality and redistribution, whereas the contemporary (post-modern) demand is increasingly for the redistribution of human rights, which Bauman takes to be a code for the freedom of choice that constitutes agency in the post-modern habitat (Bauman, 1992: 197). Bauman also discusses newer forms, that go beyond the echo of modern redistributional politics, that he refers to as the 'reallocation of attention: the politics of desire, of fear, and of certainty, along with 'tribal politics'.

Third, and using a similar argument, Bauman insists that ethics may no longer be seen as a separate activity from sociological theory. In this case, modern societies put moral regulation of conduct under the aegis of various formal institutions (from labour unions, to hospitals, churches and schools) or, of course, in what was conceived as the private sphere of the family. Modernity resisted moral self-examination; in post-modern contexts it becomes unavoidable. Ethical concerns remain essentially similar to those of modern times, avers Bauman, but are now augmented by distinctively post-modern questions of pluralism of authority on the one hand, and the centrality of choice on the other. The unavoidability of ethics, and the reduced plausibility of ethics generated by major institutions, also leads Bauman to argue for an approach that focuses on the moral self that *precedes* or perhaps constitutes the social self, or morality prescribed and administered by power-assisted social institutions. 'Being *for* the Other before one can be *with* the Other – is the first reality of the self' says Bauman (1993: 13).

This then is Bauman's sociology of post-modernity, in a nutshell. Note that he does not abandon sociology, but rather argues that sociology should engage with a new object, a different kind of social situation, which is post-modernity. Sociology has itself to alter internally in some respects, and it also has to admit hitherto controversial alliances with politics and ethics. But it still seeks systematic understanding of the social world, now dominated by choice, pluralism and fresh forms of power.

BEYOND THE MODERN, STILL MODERN, NEVER MODERN

Not all sociologists agree with Bauman! While few contemporary social analysts deny that the turn of the twentieth century is witness to large-scale social transformation, there is no consensus that calling it 'post-modernity' is appropriate, correct or helpful. In the three alternative views that are outlined next, we find that some think *all* mention of 'modernity' should be discarded (either because we never were modern, or because though we once were we are no longer) and others urge that 'modernity' still describes well contemporary conditions. The 'post' is in this latter view superfluous and misleading, or at the very least, quite premature.

Taking the last group first, a number of prominent commentators maintain that modernity is still very much with us. Jürgen Habermas speaks for all when he says that the project of modernity is unfinished. The basic motifs of enlightenment and emancipation – seen above all in processes of rationalization – may well be experiencing some profound difficulties, but those difficulties are symptomatic of crises within an ongoing social system, not the death rattle of modernity itself. Jean Baudrillard, for whom the crucial shifts away from modernity occur when the production of consumers rather than goods becomes central, and when the distinction betwen the 'mass' and the 'media' blurs, disagrees, arguing that rationalization is dissolved thereby. But Habermas sees this as unnecessary capitulation to some deep-seated negative aspects of modernity. He persists with the view that the modern project is still worth pursuing theoretically and politically, as a means of giving voice to moral communities and social solidarities within which individuals find an identity and take responsibility.

229

Another high-profile theorist in this debate is Anthony Giddens, whose acknowledgement of profound movements within modernity is seen in the slew of terms he uses to describe it, including late-, high-, reflexive- and radicalized modernity. Anything but 'post-modernity'. For Giddens, modernity is going through some pretty turbulent times, and he sees no clear prospects for their resolution. Indeed, modernity has in some respects become like a 'juggernaut', apparently out of control and with no opportunity left for serious steering. If any means remain of influencing the direction of social change, then they lie in the heightened reflexivity of modern societies, enabled by the increased availability of information. Modernity as the application of techno-science to industrial production meets its nemesis in oil spills, smogs, dustbowls and meltdowns. But widespread awareness of this, individually and institutionally, remakes modernity without rejecting it. Giddens agrees that consumption has become central (not necessarily displacing employment, yet, though), and that the impact of distant happenings on local events, courtesy of the CITs – globalization – is also highly consequential. So some aspects of modernity are becoming more significant, at the expense of others that are of diminishing importance. This is high modernity or, in some contexts, late modernity.

Another analysis of today's turbulence, that focuses especially on the conflicts and fears of everyday life, comes from Ulrich Beck. While discussing some of the same issues as Giddens, he concentrates on the factor that seems to loom largest – risk. Without doubting that ours is a modern condition, Beck argues that the project is in a sense impossible to complete. The idea that the resources of the earth could relentlessly be exploited without penalty has collided painfully with the later twentieth-century realization that there are indeed strict limits to growth, seen everywhere in the risks generated by production. Fear and uncertainty mingle because dangers are often scarcely perceptible, and are also controversial – think of the scientific and policy debates over global warming, for instance. Risk management becomes a vital factor within all spheres of modernity, paradoxically invoking the aid of techno-science (simulation, modelling, the calculation of probabilities) to reduce its own malign influences. In fact, Beck's work underscores Bauman's conclusion that ethics is inevitably involved in the discourses of risk, although it does not persuade Beck that our condition is thus post-modern.

So much for three theorists who doubt that today's conditions are best seen as 'post-modern'. At the other end of the spectrum one can find a few thinkers who, so far from questioning post-modernity as a possibly premature characterization of the present, wish to dispense with any reference at all to the modern. Martin Albrow, for example, in his analysis of 'the global age' (Albrow, 1996) claims that continuing references to modernity – even within the term 'post-modernity' – muddies the conceptual waters. Whereas Giddens sees globalization as a consequence of modernity, Albrow holds that globalization leaves modernity behind. It is a past epoch, supplanted by the global age, that has its own socio-cultural and political-economic logics. To Albrow, the post-modern imagination is 'the hypertrophy of modern innovation rather than the expression of a new age' that 'betrays its modernity by being unable to envisage any other alternative except chaos' (Albrow, 1996: 78). The global age, on the other hand, is a 'shift in recognition that the future does not depend just on humanity's relations to itself, but also on its relations with nature' (Albrow, 1996: 96). One of the difficulties with Albrow's appealing thesis is that it could become, like modernity before it, a totalizing viewpoint, that tries to squeeze everything into a coherent global-age paradigm.

Yet another take on the question of modernity also doubts the post-modernity thesis, but not because modernity is still going strong (as Giddens or Habermas think), or because modernity is over (as Albrow proposes). Bruno Latour (1993) quietly observes that we have never been modern. This certainly throws a monkey wrench into the works! If nothing else, it should remind us that post-modernity is, after all, only a conceptual construction for helping us make sense of our times. Moreover, it has only been in use for a few decades. Although in the social science publishing explosion of the past quarter-century, the debate over modernity has had epic proportions, actual use of this term is of recent provenance (and the verb form, to modernize, is only a little older). But Latour's point is that confusion has arisen because the epochal break between the ancients and the moderns has all too frequently been conflated with the proclamation of a victory of the latter over the former. For Latour, the squabble over post-modernity risks repeating the same error as theorists of modernity have tended to make, namely to assume that modernity ever was a total, evenly distributed, unambiguous situation. In a bid to establish the theory, ideal types are confused with really and fully existing situations. To the contrary, counters Latour, the modern world was only ever 'disenchanted' in a restricted and piecemeal way.

DOES IT MATTER?

When all is said and done, does it matter whether or not contemporary conditions are described as 'post-modern'? Rather than give a direct, unequivocal answer to this question, the final section of this chapter says first, 'no', and then, 'yes'. As far as sociology is concerned, if the point is to understand contemporary conditions, then the debate over post-modernity is a fruitful one. Why? Because it alerts us to broad and sweeping changes currently taking place throughout the world, but especially in the so-called advanced societies. It reminds social theory of its dependence on historical analysis and, increasingly, of the ways that sociological work is increasingly transdisciplinary, and is vitally connected with (at least) politics, ethics and philosophy. As Krishan Kumar says, these theories, both of post- and high- or late- modernity, do capture many aspects of contemporary social change:

> We do live in a world saturated with information and communication. The nature of work and industrial organization is truly changing with unnerving speed. Modern societies have indeed reached a point where, even if they have not given up on modernity, many of its classic attitudes and assumptions have become seriously questionable (Kumar, 1995: 201).

And as Kumar also notes, at a time when the social sciences are expected to be more narrowly technical, expansive, historical theoretical debate is to be welcomed.

However, a good case can also be made for a contemporary social theory that starts with what is arguably the key factor in all theories of post-modernity (and for that matter, of globalization) – information. Although a complex and contested term, it at least has the merit of highlighting a little more precisely one of the most pervasive carriers, or motors, of today's social change. To take the most celebrated recent example, Manuel Castells's trilogy on *The Information Age* (Castells, 1996, 1997, 1998) recognizes the importance of globalization and of the post-modern, without ever assuming that either term can encapsulate completely the transformations of the present. His work has the merit of extensive and careful empirical analysis, but this is also woven into theoretical patterns readily recognizable to those familiar with high-modern, post-modern and globalization theses. He draws attention to the increasingly important 'net-self' axis, and to 'spaces of flows' and 'timeless time', while never losing sight of social inequalities and human suffering, and the need for committed and political approaches to sociology.

If one can argue that post-modernity is a useful working theoretical hypothesis, but perhaps not one that is worth clinging to tenaciously, than one might also argue that the precise answer to the question of the post-modern does not much matter practically, either. Indeed, for many, especially feminist theorists, a marked ambivalence attends the debate. Not that it is seen as trivial or misguided, but rather that, practically, at least as much may be learned from the debate as from some putative settlement of it. If the project of modernity brought in its train – albeit indirectly – the emancipation of women, then some aspects of modernity may be worth struggling to preserve. On the other hand, if that same modern project tended to classify and categorize women and men in particular and perhaps limited ways, then a more post-modern focus on difference and on the possibilities for transcending the boundaries placed around the emancipatory project might be appropriate and desirable. If, for instance, argues Lieteke van Vucht Tijssen (1990: 163), unitary notions of 'female' and 'male' identity gave way to the

> idea of male identities being just as plural and complex as female identities (thus stimulating women to deal in a differentiated way with what was once called 'the

opposite sex'), it could be a major step in breaking down the barriers between the sexes and creating a situation in which equality means the possibility of being.

If the answer to the question 'does it matter?' is, theoretically and practically, 'no', then in what sense might it be 'yes'? It matters because much still hangs upon the debate, and yet the debate may still be missing some important factors. In other words, the terms of the debate could expand to include more than it has hitherto. Despite the fact that the debate over post-modernity represents a cultural turn in social theory, in one crucial respect the debate over post-modernity has generally omitted a factor that was pivotal to the sociological question of the origins and dynamic of modernity – a factor that could variously be headed enchantment, religion or faith.

What, to return to our main example, does Zygmunt Bauman make of this? Well, Bauman's ground-breaking work on post-modernity starts with a discussion of the 're-enchantment of the world'. 'All in all,' writes Bauman, 'post-modernity can be seen as restoring to the world what modernity, presumptuously, had taken away; as a *re-enchantment* of the world that modernity tried hard to *dis-enchant*' (original emphases, Bauman, 1992: x). Setting on one side, for a moment, the fact that for Max Weber, disenchantment was set in train by certain Protestant (and thus Christian) attitudes, it is clear that Bauman intends something fairly broad by his reference to the modern disenchantment of the world, for he regards it also as a 'de-spiritualizing' and a denial of the capacity of the subject. He sees providence and revelation being replaced by modern *techne*, and discusses Dostoevsky's dilemma that if God is dead, all is permitted. However, a theorist like Alain Touraine, working from a position that hopes for modernity finally to fulfil itself, speaks of an earlier 'limited modernity' when 'human beings mistook themselves for gods', but which ended with Weber's iron cage of totalitarian despotism (Touraine, 1995: 366). For Touraine, the current crises of modernity spell not a denial of secularization but a transition to a complete modernity in which Reason and the Subject will at last both be affirmed. So, at least as far as the possibilities for re-enchantment are concerned, much does hang on this debate.

Latterly, Bauman has paid at least passing attention to religion. In *Postmodernity and its Discontents* (Bauman, 1997) he includes a chapter on post-modern religion that discusses, rather clinically, its prospects. He acknowledges that modernity was all about 'doing without God', and that the search for compensations and substitutes does not seem to have slowed. But he makes a point of isolating fundamentalism as a post-modern form of religion, seeing in it the offer of relief from the agonies of choice confronting inhabitants of contemporary consumerist cultures. Like Gilles Kepel, on whose analysis (Kepel, 1994) Bauman leans, he believes that fundamentalism thus reveals the ills of society. But he is clearly unhappy with the certainties offered by fundamentalisms, citing their 'totalitarian genes' as the key problem. As with other theorists of the post-modern – such as Donna Haraway (1997) – it is a critique of the power-assisted aspects of organized religion that dominate the discussion, leading to some hopeful claims about the fresh potential attending the *ending* of the second 'Christian' millennium.

Bauman thus sees only one face of religion (preoccupied as he is with the role of the church in producing legislated morality in earlier times), and has nothing to say about changes in contemporary globalized religious activities and processes, or about alternative, spiritualized forms of religious experience that his initial comments about post-modern re-enchantment might lead one to expect. During the same period in which the post-modern has risen to sociological prominence, many gratuitous aspects of the modern sociological secularization thesis have been thoroughly discredited, and it is clear that numerous forms of what José Casanova calls 'public religion' continue to make their mark, not only as sources of the sacred, but as vital players in the very circumstances that are discussed by others as part of the post-modern experience. One may consider, for instance, the pivotal role of Christian churches in the fall of communism in Eastern Europe (in Poland and Romania especially), or the way in which the Catholic church has shifted its sphere of activity from the State to civil society, contributing to democratizing movements in, for instance, Brazil and the Philippines (Casanova, 1994: 62).

Bauman's dependence on the very narrow and constricting frame within which Kepel works also means that the former fails to note many examples of religiosity and spirituality that appear in a post-modern register. Beyond the continued signficance of organized religion, one cannot also fail to note the widespread contemporary flourishing of numerous spiritualities – such as New Age (Heelas, 1996) – and other forms of deregulated religiosity, which deserve to be theorized as part of today's cultural turn. Although these are directly in line with some classical sociological expectations (such as Weber's), the puzzling persistence of a thoroughgoing secularization model into sociologies of the post-modern seems to have smudged the spectacles of even acute theorists such as Bauman. What Bauman says of politics could equally be said of religion: it 'cannot be kept outside the basic theoretical model as an epiphenomenon, a superstructural reflection or belatedly formed, intellectually processed derivative' (Bauman, 1992: 196).

Whereas Bauman sees in fundamentalism relief from choice provided by fresh forms of authority, he fails to note that many fairly conventional forms of religion as well as the more obvious New Age movements also appropriate and adapt to the cultures of choice and expressive individualism discovered in post-modernity. Indeed, Bryan Turner suggests that it may be religion, not the body or the self, that provides the link between the classical modernism at the end of the nineteenth century, and the post-modern at the end of the twentieth (Turner, 1994: 207). One might add that, in a post-colonial vein, it is only through the understanding of the cultural roots – for which, frequently, read 'religion' – of the different groups that comprise contemporary cosmopolitanism and multiculturalism that any genuine kind of respect and tolerance (for which Bauman does argue) can emerge.

Another curious anomaly is that Bauman's marvellous explorations of post-modern ethics depend on certain philosophers – above all Emmanuel Lévinas – for whom the religious is a clear dimension, not far below the surface. It is impossible to read Bauman on the 'face of the Other' without hearing loud echoes of the Jewish ethical system that first enunciated these ideas (or, for that matter, in a Christian context, of the Samaritan who risked ethnic op-probrium as well as financial loss to care for, and show hospitality to, the brutalized Other). And even if one hesitates to hear specific religious content in these references, it is difficult to deny that there is something of 'faith' in the (Baumanian) claim that the self is first of all moral, confronted with the claims of the Other, whose cry must be heard if any moral act is to be accomplished.

In all these respects, it is clear that there is a gap in present theories of post-modernity. While much signficant ground is covered within the debate over the post-modern, religion, spirituality and faith must also be theorized alongside questions of politics and ethics, both to do justice to palpable social realities and to acknowledge that the ethical and political content of theory relies heavily on commitments that ultimately are rooted in or related to beliefs held in faith.

SUMMARY

- Post-modernity is a concept used to describe contemporary social conditions in which communication and information technologies and consumerism have become predominant.
- Zygmunt Bauman's theory of post-modernity is the most far-reaching, and does not entail abandoning sociological analysis. It does propose that a new social system is in the making.
- Others argue that the real debate is over modernity, which may be seen variously as completed (global age) or incomplete (high modernity).
- Post-modernity helps us to focus on crucial aspects of social change that are long-term and global – as do terms such as global age or information age – but accents the cultural.
- The cultural turn indicated by post-modernity is crucially significant but currently pays insufficient attention to religion or faith.

FURTHER READING

Appignanesi, Richard and Garratt, Chris (1995) *Postmodernism for Beginners*. Cambridge: Icon Books. For those who can't resist cartoons, this is a semi-serious introduction that covers the ground in words and pictures.

Bauman, Zygmunt (1992) *Intimations of Postmodernity*. London: Routledge. The classic text.

Kumar, Krishnan (1995) *From Post-Industrial to Post-Modern Society*. Oxford: Blackwell. An elegant and constructive assessment of social theories of the present.

Lyon, David (1999) *Postmodernity*. Buckingham: Open University Press. Revised and expanded edition of the original (1994) brief, critical and sometimes light-hearted introduction that puts the concept in historical and intellectual context.

Smart, Barry (1996) 'Postmodern Social Theory', in Bryan Turner (ed.) *The Blackwell Companion to Social Theory*. Oxford: Blackwell. A more advanced theoretical perspective that surveys and weighs competing theories.

van Vucht Tijssen, Lieteke (1990) 'Women between Modernity and Postmodernity', in Bryan Turner (ed.) *Theories of Modernity and Postmodernity*. London: Sage. Why women (and others) might have cause to be ambivalent towards the concept and experience of post-modernity.

REFERENCES

Albrow, Martin (1996) *The Global Age*. Cambridge UK: Polity Press
Bauman, Zygmunt (1987) *Freedom*. Buckingham: Open University Press/University of Minnesota Press.
Bauman, Zygmunt (1992) *Intimations of Postmodernity*. London and New York: Routledge.
Bauman, Zygmunt (1993) *Postmodern Ethics*. Oxford, and Cambridge, MA: Blackwell.
Bauman, Zygmunt (1997) *Postmodernity and its Discontents*. New York: New York University Press.
Bell, Daniel (1980) 'The Social Framework of the Information Society', in Tom Forester (ed.) *The Information Technology Revolution*. Oxford: Blackwell, and Cambridge, MA: MIT Press.
Bourdieu, Pierre (1984) *Distinction: A Social Judgement of Taste*. London: Routledge.
Casanova, José (1994) *Public Religions in the Modern World*. Chicago: University of Chicago Press.
Castells, Manuel (1996) *The Rise of the Network Society*. Oxford and New York: Blackwell.
Castells, Manuel (1997) *The Power of Identity*. Oxford and New York: Blackwell.
Castells, Manuel (1998) *The End of Millennium*. Oxford and New York: Blackwell.
Crook, Stephen, Pakulski, Jan and Waters, Malcolm (1992) *Postmodernization: Change in Modern Society*. London: Sage.
Featherstone, Mike (1991) *Consumer Culture and Postmodernism*. London: Sage.
Haraway, Donna (1997) *Modest Witness @ Second Millennium*. London: Routledge.
Harvey, David (1989) *The Condition of Postmodernity*. Oxford, and Cambridge, MA: Blackwell.

Heelas, Paul (1996) *The New Age Movement*. Oxford: Blackwell.

Kepel, Gilles (1994) *The Revenge of God*. Cambridge: Polity Press.

Kumar, Krishan (1995) *From Post-Industrial to Post-Modern Society*. Oxford, and Malden, MA: Blackwell.

Lash, Scott and Urry, John (1987) *The End of Organized Capitalism*. Cambridge: Polity Press.

Latour, Bruno (1993) *We Never Were Modern*. New York: Harvester-Wheatsheaf.

Lyon, David (1994) *The Electronic Eye: The Rise of the Surveillance Society*. Cambridge: Polity Press.

Lyon, David (1996) 'Religion and the Postmodern: Old Problems, New Prospects', in Flanagan, Kieran and Jupp, Peter (eds) *Postmodernity, Religion, and Sociology*. New York: St Martin's Press, and London: Macmillan.

Lyotard, Jean-François (1979) *The Postmodern Condition: A Report on Knowledge*. Minneapolis: University of Minnesota Press.

Touraine, Alain (1995) *Critique of Modernity*. Oxford, and Cambridge, MA: Blackwell.

van Vucht Tijssen, Lieteke (1990) 'Women between Modernity and Postmodernity', in Bryan Turner (ed.) *Theories of Modernity and Postmodernity*. London: Sage.

Turner, Bryan (1994) *Orientalism, Postmodernism, and Globalism*. London: Routledge.

Chapter 17

Globalization

Barrie Axford

INTRODUCTION

As the millennium approaches, globalization retains its allure as a designer concept of choice, despite conflicting claims that we now live in a post-globalized world, that the current frisson is only part of a 'recurrent tendency of world-capitalism since early modern times' (Arrighi, 1997: 1), or that there is no such beast anyway. While these are useful correctives to what one author has described as 'global-degook' (Freeman, 1995), such counter-claims are flawed because they oversimplify the nature, provenance and tenacity of globalization as an historical process which is redrawing the economic, political and cultural geographies of the world.

As part of a critical examination of the concept, I want to offer what might be called a 'strong' version of globalization, albeit one which draws attention to its complex, multidimensional character. While it is obvious that globalization is a fashionable term, it is often used just as a convenient rhetorical device. Debates on globalization show plenty of verve and commitment, but they are often under-theorized and conceptually naïve. Shortcomings include a failure to say what is global about globalization, an inattention to its multidimensional character and a reluctance to recognize the historicity of the process while remaining sensitive to the transformative qualities of particular moments of globalization. In the rest of this chapter I will write in more detail about each of these areas of neglect as a way of substantiating my 'strong ' thesis. I will then discuss some of the fashionable strands of thinking which suggest that globalization is a myth, before concluding with brief remarks on why the study of globalization is important for any attempt to understand the present.

First, let me say a little more about my 'strong' version of globalization. It is strong primarily in the sense that it goes beyond anodyne definitions of globalization as growing interconnectedness. Instead this strong version has it that globalization is the historical process through which the world is being made into one place with systemic properties (Axford, 1995, 1997; Robertson, 1992). This is a fairly robust claim and I will return to it later in the chapter. In contrast to heavily normative positions and teleological accounts (for examples see Gray, 1998) I will argue that globalization is a complex, contradictory and multidimensional historical process. The historicity of the process does not, however, make the outcomes of this, or of any other moment of globalization, entirely predictable. Globalizing processes involve variable, but always significant, shifts in the spatial ordering and reach of networks (for example in trade, communications, finance, technology, migration, cultural goods and ideas) in the stretching of interpersonal and social relationships across time and space, and in organizational forms and functions (including the paradigm political forms of the modern territorial state and the international system of states). It is also a process which triggers important changes in consciousness, as individuals and collective actors embrace, oppose or in some way are 'constrained to identify' with the global condition (Robertson, 1992). The study of globalization requires attention both to material considerations such as the volume of goods traded, or the market penetration of 'global' products like Levi jeans, and to the meanings which attach to these 'transnational connections' (Hannerz, 1996). Only by examining the extent and intensity of global consciousness – in other words by seeing how agents actually experience and respond to globalizing pressures – is it possible to estimate the impact of global processes upon more or less sensitive and vulnerable actors (Keohane and Nye, 1977) and to assess the strength or fragility of global institutions.

My approach is multidimensional in that it does not privilege any one domain as providing the key to or essential dynamics of globalization, but addresses the complex and often contradictory interplay between economic, political and cultural forces, and between local agents and global forces in making the world one place. In this the approach differs from other 'strong' positions which traffic some version of a global entropic field where all differences between local structures are dissolved and individuals become interchangeable at an abstract global level.

GLOBAL SPEAK

At the end of the 1990s globalization is a term found routinely across the social sciences, and one used promiscuously by all manner of folk, from politicians to media moguls. The word has become a paradigm for the allegedly uncertain and labile qualities of the times in which we live, an intimation of epochal changes in train, or a neat encapsulation of millenarian hopes and fears of the apocalypse. More prosaically, it is a convenient shorthand for a number of complex processes which, in David Harvey's felicitous expression, are serving to 'compress the world' in terms of time and space, and to redefine all sorts of borders – to taste and imagination as well as to territory and identities (Harvey, 1990).

Indeed, the burden of much global talk is that boundaries are vanishing, giving way to a world made up of more or less dense networks of communication and exchange and hybridized identities. In global talk it is quite common to hear about the demise of the territorial State, especially in its guise as the manager of economic affairs; about the 'borderless world' (Ohmae, 1989) of financial markets; and about all manner of cultural common denominators, from fast-food to faster entertainment, which pass for signifiers of a global culture. Taking all this on board, it will come as no surprise that global talk is also rife with conflicting interpretations. On the one hand, the processes which are making the world one place are seen as destructive – of localities, of 'real' cultures, of the environment – while on the other, they intimate a future rich in hope for humankind.

SO WHAT IS GLOBALIZATION?

To reiterate: globalization is the historical process whereby the world is being made into a single place with systemic properties. Historically, globalizing forces produced global systems which were of limited extent spatially, and in which the density of social relations across borders and time varied enormously. At the end of this century it is clear that through various media – the burgeoning capacity of electronic communications to compress both time and space, changes in technology which are allowing production and culture to be divorced from place, the pervasiveness of global ideologies on subjects such as the environment and human rights, and recent seismic shifts in the world's geopolitical balance – the world is now thoroughly globalized, a single place. What happens in one place routinely affects perceptions, attitudes and behaviour elsewhere. Indeed, because of technological innovations, this routine impact is almost instantaneous. Because social relations are being stretched across time and space the borders and walls which insulated and isolated individuals and collective actors in the past are being eroded. Gearoid O'Tuathail (1998: 6) says that 'territoriality is being eclipsed by telemetricality', where that refers to forms of electronic communications, and while this may strike us as too glib, even with a proper social scientific caution it deserves to be taken seriously.

Indeed the real charge in the concept of globalization, most poignantly observed in its current phase, is that conventional borders are becoming increasingly irrelevant to the actual patterns of much economic, cultural and even political activity. Translocal and transnational networks – of producers, professionals, exchange students, commodity brokers and human rights activists – populate a truly global cultural economy, and territoriality as the organizational principle of the world polity is everywhere in retreat. The modern 'geopolitical imagination' (O'Tuathail, 1998), used to depicting the world in terms of spatial blocs, territory and the fixed identities usually attached to these, is now in some turmoil. Globalization presages a new geopolitics, and thus requires novel ways of imagining a global space increasingly made up of flows, networks and webs (Appadurai, 1990, 1996; Castells, 1996, 1997).

Of course, in quotidian reality it is all messier. Pretty much everywhere the space of flows of the global subsists with economic, cultural and political architectures characteristic of territorial spaces and the identities tied to them. It is true that global forms are all around us in the shape of transnational business organizations (Nestlé, Nissan), transnational communities (New Age, fundamentalist, diasporic and virtual) and transnational structures (of production, finance, and also governance). But while the rise of transnational interest groups, like Friends of the Earth or Amnesty International, has created a politics which transcends particular boundaries, histories and cultures, and which is outside the remit of any one State, it is too easy to take these as modal phenomena, rather than just as intimations of what Ulrich Beck (1996: 121) has called a 'global sub-politics', one configured by connectivity among non-governmental actors and social movements, and not by space and territorial interests. Despite the claim made by Arjun Appadurai (1996: 46), 'boundaries, structures and regularities' are still very much in evidence. All of which is quite confusing, but does have the merit of focusing attention on what it means to describe the world as a single place.

TREATING THE WORLD AS A SINGLE PLACE: WHAT IS GLOBAL ABOUT GLOBALIZATION?

The idea of globalization creating a world which is a 'single place' should not be taken to imply complete homogeneity, despite the fact that it does produce 'an essential sameness' in the surface appearance of social and political life across the globe (McGrew, 1992). The relationships between situated actors and globalizing forces, or between lived localities and virtual communities, are rarely ones in which globalizing pressures are powerful enough simply to obliterate sub-global identities. Instead we see a global system which has a number of configurations, sometimes overlapping but often confronting each other.

The first, which perhaps comes closest to some notion of global homogeneity, has the globalized world as little more than a map of variable tastes.

'Glocal' consumer products produced and marketed by transnational corporations rely on the skills of designers and marketers to fashion a standard product which is sufficiently flexible to allow for local variation, or else can be packaged to appeal to local idiosyncrasies. This is the global system as McWorld (Barber, 1996), a world made up of MTV, McDonalds and M&Ms. The second configuration depicts a globalized world in which existing identities may be relativized or attenuated by globalizing processes, but where these same processes can be indigenized or used by local actors to meet their own needs (Hannerz, 1996). This sounds more grandiose and certainly more conscious than it is in practice. The point is that cultural commodities (both the material kind and cultural forms like movies which are created for a career as global commodities) are imbued with meaning in particular contexts and by specific agents or populations. In this configuration, the relationships between the local and the global are structured in and through what Zygmunt Bauman (1992: 190) has called 'habitats of meaning' which are produced by individuals as they go about their everyday lives. The local and the global are enmeshed at the intersection of different habitats of meaning – on the Internet, through the availability of fast or exotic foods in supermarkets, or by watching Blockbuster videos. At the same time quite scary brands of politics have been constructed around the claim that local culture has an authentic quality which must be protected, while global cultures are by definition protean and thus inauthentic.

So my third configuration has the globalized world as one which is characteristically, if uneasily, hybridized, and in which whole cultures and identities are being replaced by those which are, to borrow from Salman Rushdie (1991: 46), 'impure and intermingled'. If this sounds relatively benign, it still leaves some locals constrained to identify with the global condition through what they experience as a disabling loss of culture and identity. I am not suggesting that the outcome of hybridity is always, or even often, schizoid cultures and confused or pathological identities, although it can be (Axford, 1995: 167) but that the global 'organization of diversity' is often quite brutal, attesting to great asymmetries of power. Which leads to the last possible configuration, that of opposition to globalizing forces.

Global consciousness may lead actors to support or to oppose aspects of globalization. Local resistance to the homogenizing or hegemonic power of global products and institutions in the form of soft drinks, multimedia technologies or even secular values, often has an anti-American or anti-Western slant. For other actors whose concern is not the preservation of local identities, globalizing trends are to be resisted because they are all part of the 'endless accumulation of capital', the latest iteration of a world-historical process which now includes the entire world within its geography (Wallerstein, 1997). But opposition to globalization can also have a more particularistic slant, especially where borderless worlds and hybrid identities are seen to challenge or to defile more elemental or fundamental beliefs and identities. The emergence of post-national identities and practices in the guise of company cultures and networks of non-governmental organizations, and intimated in the multi-level polity of the European Union, vie with regional realignments and fracturings, nationalist and ethnic separatisms and all manner of fundamentalist credos.

So what sort of a system is this? Clearly it is not a unitary notion of the global. Rather, the process reveals contradictory tendencies towards increasing interconnectedness *and* greater fragmentation. Globalization creates various kinds of linkages, seen in the growing density and reach of networks and flows – of goods between nations, through migration, in business, tourism and knowledge – to create what Ulf Hannerz calls a 'global ecumene', a web of networks consisting of nodes of interaction, rather than centres and peripheries, and which is generally lacking in boundaries. The systemness or unity of the global system is thus a negotiated and contingent condition arising from the articulation of local subjects with global structures.

Today, nowhere is immune from these changes. Global processes affect the reproduction of locals and of localities. As a consequence, economic and probably political and cultural autarky are increasingly hard, if not impossible, to sustain in a globalized world, even taking into account the widespread evidence of resistance to globalization – in other words it is hard to opt out. Pol Pot's Cambodia, Iran under clerical rule, even Red China, have all been constrained to identify with the global system. The more mundane fact is that globalization is making it more difficult for social actors like nation-states, localities and individuals to sustain identity without reference to more encompassing global structures and flows. Interconnections globalize the world in a measurable, perhaps even an 'objective' way, but do so mainly because such forces are redefining the experiences and perceptions of more and more actors. So the global is now the cognitive frame of reference for many actors who are aware of global constraints, although it remains much less so in matters of culture and morality.

MULTIDIMENSIONAL GLOBALIZATION

The dynamic and labile quality of globalization can only be studied by adopting an approach that abjures the conventional distinctions between levels of analysis (personal and global) as well as refusing to privilege the explanatory power of one domain of human activity over others (economics over politics, and both over culture). Yet one-dimensional accounts are legion. For example, many economists and management theorists view globalization as a recent phenomenon driven solely by the ideology and practice of neo-liberalism. Such positions are usually silent on the cultural and technological dimensions of globalization, and treat political questions as secondary. Instead globalization is reduced to a relatively simple affair involving an ever more integrated and unitary global trading and financial system, shaped, as Amin says (1997: 128), by bargaining coalitions among powerful nations, international regulatory institutions and global (or multi-national) private corporations. In Kenichi Ohmae's (1989) anthem to the borderless world, territorial states are seen as irrelevant to what he terms the 'real flows' of the world economy, while for Michael Porter (1990), more of an economic realist than Ohmae, they remain crucial to corporate and sectoral economic success, but only as the providers of the supply-side resources necessary in the global competitiveness stakes.

In each of these accounts of a globalizing world, as well as in others from opposite ideological perspectives, there is a common fault. Nowhere is it understood that the complex and contradictory relations of economy, politics and culture requires the observer to unravel the intertwinings of an economic system admittedly dependent on the principle of commodification and cultural terrains which are both determined by, and yet still manage to elude or even to subvert, that principle. Yet culture is an intriguing domain for the study of globalization because it affects the identity of people and provides them with meaning. The problem is that, apart from the more subtle interventions of cultural anthropologists (Appadurai, 1996; Friedman, 1994; Hannerz, 1996) and some sociologists (Featherstone, 1990; Bauman, 1992; Robertson, 1992), culture is often reified as a kind of social cement, or as an ideological protection for dominant interests. For other writers, the very idea of global culture is an oxymoron (Smith, 1995). What such conceptions lack is any sense of culture being constructed rather than imposed, enacted by individuals in both stable and changing contexts. In other words they omit any developed sense of agency as an active component of globalization. Individuals and whole populations are constrained to identify with the global condition just by being there, through passively consuming global fare in one form or another. While this has to be true for some of the people some of the time, it is at best only part of the story. Users of the Internet are conscious and willing participants in the compression of the globe, as are governments and social movements which buy into globally sanctioned models of behaviour and development in areas such as the environment, gender equality and the treatment of refugees. And, as Ulf Hannerz (1996) says, although conscious and militant anti-globalism is itself part of the dialectic of globalization, at the very least it offers the possibility of alternative imagined worlds.

PRESENT AND PAST GLOBALIZATIONS

Globalization triggers changes in the scale of social organization and changes in consciousness of the world too. Understood in this way the process should not be seen as unique to one moment of world-historical time. As Hannerz (1996: 18) says with typical economy, 'different worlds, different globalizations'. For analysts the trick lies in avoiding the presentism found in those accounts which treat the current *frisson* as *sui generis*, as well as in being able to recognize the transformative potential of particular moments of globalization.

In a recent paper, Giovanni Arrighi (1997) sets down the case for treating current globalization as part of evolutionary changes in world capitalism. Transformations bruited as unique to current globalizing trends – the information revolution, the increased volume of trading in currencies, bonds and equities, the privatizing of key functions of governance – are novel only in terms of their 'scale, scope and complexity' (Arrighi, 1997: 2). Now this looks to me like turning a substantial mountain into a lowly molehill, and is sustainable only by reducing world-historical richness and complexity to an essential systemic identity, that of capitalism.

The notion that the only thing which is distinct about late twentieth-century globalization is its scope and scale is just a throwaway line. Arrighi mentions the evolutionary pattern 'that has enabled world capitalism and the underlying system of sovereign states to become a truly global system', implying a seamless functional transition (Arrighi, 1997: 5). But one of the things which is distinctive about late twentieth-century globalization, certainly when compared with the late nineteenth-century pattern, is that the former is not territorial or imperialistic in the classic sense (Pieterse, 1997: 373). While it might be appropriate to classify late nineteenth- and even mid-twentieth-century globalization as the spread of the territorial state as a global standard, critically, late twentieth-century globalization owes less and less to this form of collective agency, and on some accounts is best characterized through its undoing. To argue that these differences are mere historical detail in a much larger canvas is at best poor social science, and at worst the sort of crude functionalism which has marred Marxist accounts of all large-scale, long-term social change. So that while Arrighi offers a strongly systemic view of world history, he does less than justice to the active version of systemness canvassed earlier, and largely ignores the plea for a multidimensional approach to globalization.

Yet his argument still has the signal virtue of reminding us that globalization is not brand new. Not only that, but that it is a force which ebbs and flows, takes on different appearances in different times, is characteristically uneven and strikes people in wildly different ways. How then to conceptualize and chart this historical variability and still be sensitive to the qualities of particular periods of globalization? I am drawn to the useful schema provided by Held *et al.* (1999). Their position is that globalization can be charted historically as a spatial phenomenon involving more or less extensive networks of economic, political and cultural activity, and one which increases the density of interactions between actors in states and societies. The upshot is a world of multiple interdependencies, which displays hierarchy (because of asymmetries in access to and control of global networks) as well as unevenness (because of the differential vulnerability of actors to global forces). Mapped in this way the contingent and variable nature of globalization can be studied over time. While such an approach presents major difficulties of research design, it is potentially a powerful corrective to one-dimensional and ahistorical accounts of globalization.

THE MYTH OF GLOBALIZATION?

Let me just rehearse the strong position on globalization. Of late the boundaries between societies, cultures, polities and individuals are becoming increasingly fuzzy. Modern conceptions of space and of identity, which relied upon binary notions of the organization of space and time, like traditional/ modern and east/west, are giving way to post-spatial conceptions of the global order. Arjun Appadurai's allusive imagery of a highly contingent global order constructed at the intersection of various 'scapes' – *ethnoscapes* (migration), *finanscapes* (flows of money), *mediascapes* (flows of information and images), *ideoscapes* (the movement of ideas) and *technoscapes* (the realm of technological innovation) – is perhaps the best known example of this sort of thinking. But the starker dichotomy in Benjamin Barber's *Jihad vs McWorld* (1996) also paints a picture in which the world order of national and societal territories is increasingly moribund, and is being replaced by a glocalized networked cultural economy of production and consumption.

These are potent images, yet revisionism is now much in vogue. I want to talk at some length about one line of revisionist argument, the backlash against the 'myth' that globalization is the triumph of borderless capitalism. The revisionist thesis is exemplified most clearly in Paul Hirst and Grahame Thompson's tract *Globalization in Question* (1996). They argue the case against the marked and inevitable erosion of state power, and for new forms of international governance to combat the ideology of neo-liberalism and the practices of an unconstrained free market. For Hirst and Thompson what is often described as an economic system operating on a world scale is in fact little more than the intensification of trade and other sorts of flows within regional groupings which are still largely confined to the so-called 'Triad' economies of Europe, the Americas and parts of South-East Asia. They substantiate this argument by reference to what they see as the continued significance of national governments and economies in the regulation and successes of transnational business corporations (TNCs). At the same time, they admit that the regionalization of economic activity has made life more difficult for national regulatory regimes, thereby increasing the need for more effective forms of international governance. Moreover, Hirst and Thompson are at pains to show that truly global companies (that is, those which have broken free of any sort of national ties), are few and far between. Finally they go to some lengths to show that between 1878 and 1914, the *belle époque* of world capitalism, international flows of goods, investments and people exceeded current levels.

But globalization is not reducible to economic processes and certainly not just to neo-liberalism. Hirst and Thompson offer a detailed and wonderfully knockabout case, but it is based on a reading of globalization which is, to use Ash Amin's phrase, no more than 'a superficial quantitative evaluation of the phenomenon' (Amin, 1997: 128). Because of this a number of problems arise. The first is that because Hirst and Thompson want to cavil at whether there is a 'truly globalized economy', they trivialize the immense amount of transnational economic activity now in train. The phenomenal aspect of this activity consists of the massively extended circuits of production and exchange seen in recent years, largely under the auspices of TNCs. Perhaps more seminal is the spectacular expansion of world financial markets in the last few decades, and the general trend towards 'privatizing' key aspects of the management of economic policy.

But even for businesses this is only one side of the globalizing process. The other is rather more subjective, where this refers to the development of global 'mindsets' among managerial cadres who see the world as an operational whole. It might not be stretching the concept too far to suggest that the taxonomic status of a global company may lie as much in its management style and in how it perceives its market, as it does in more measurable criteria.

Second, Hirst and Thompson have scarcely anything to say about technological changes and how they accelerate globalization, and what they do say underestimates the transformative effects of recent innovations. Manuel Castells (1996), flirting with technological determinism, suggests a new configuration in what he is happy to call the global economy, based upon the role of informational labour, or what others have called knowledge work, in relation to other labour types. These labour types do not correspond to or coincide with particular countries, rather 'they are organised in networks and flows, using the technological infrastructure of the informational economy' (Castells, 1996: 91) to benefit particular companies and sectors. For Castells, the world economic order which is being formed is one in which the 'historically produced architecture' of economic governance, struggles with radically new forces of innovation and competition which do not acknowledge conventional boundaries.

Third, the continued vitality of the sovereign state against globalization is argued empirically and as an article of faith. It is, however, a weak reed upon which to tie a whole thesis. In the first place, as Jan Pieterse (1997: 373) points out, the modern nation-state as a global standard is itself a form of globalization, not a haven from it. While the world is fragmented because of its division into sovereign territorial units, they are themselves part of a constructed and conscious world order, with the policies of individual states often reliant upon prevailing models of national development found in global institutions and practices (Meyer *et al.*, 1997).

Of course, Hirst and Thompson are right to point to the continued vitality of states as players in the world economy and as the guardians of societal values, but in trying to rescue the State from the myth of its powerlessness, they are blind to some key considerations. Except in realist accounts of international relations where the ontology of every state is given, state power is always variable. Once this variability is admitted, it is no great step to acknowledge that globalization must empower some states at the same time as it disempowers others. For example, in East Asia some states have been able to attract and protect mobile capital rather than being supplicants for the largesse of TNCs in the form of direct investments. The whole basis of what has become known as 'Asian capitalism' lies in a much more state-centric model of global financial expansion, one which (up until recently at any rate) seemed to immunize its supporters against the kind of global pressures which have driven others to deregulate their domestic financial structures. At the end of the 1990s the fate of 'Asian capitalism' is still in the balance, but other examples provide evidence of the ubiquity of world-economic and world-polity constraints. The demise of the Soviet Union in 1991 shows how vulnerable even world-class states are to global economic forces, and the limited capacities of various 'quasi-states', most of them former colonial territories, to carry out basic governmental functions makes them especially vulnerable to these same forces. Even among the core states of the capitalist world, some of the most powerful, like Germany and Japan, have been described as only semi-sovereign (Cumings, 1997). Finally, the process of hollowing out state power from below (by regionalist and localist forces, and by various agencies, quangos and task forces) and from above (by various multilateral and supranational institutions) is transforming the architecture of statist governance. The overall message must be that it is not necessary to treat globalization as a myth in order to recognize the vitality of the State, and the more complex reality is that states and state policies have now to subsist in globalized contexts, which are neither illusory nor superficial.

CONCLUSION

As a concept globalization belongs to no single branch of the social sciences. It is not, or not yet, a fully elaborated theory, but its value for the social sciences is that it directs attention to those processes which are making the world into a single place – a global system. The fact that the concept has been popularized through indiscriminate usage, or that it is viewed with suspicion by some strains of social science, should not blind us to its import-ance in this respect. The study of globalization is part of a wider social-scientific recognition that conventional units and levels of analysis – individual, local, societal, national and international – are not separate zones of experience and spheres of social organization, but entwined, and increasingly so. Having said this, my strong version of globalization is perhaps less systemic than proponents of world-systems analysis would find acceptable, in that it views the totality of the global system as a contingent and negotiated order arising from the articulation of economic, political and cultural domains and realized through the routine and dramatic practices of actors in their dealings with globalizing forces. The 'deeper meaning of globalization' spoken of by Alain Benoist (1997) lies in this understanding, and its revelation is possible only by careful attention to both patterns of interconnectedness and the twistings of consciousness.

SUMMARY

- Globalization is the process through which the world is being made into one place with systemic properties.
- This process is both historically variable and multidimensional.
- It involves interconnections across some boundaries and the dissolving of other boundaries.
- It also precipitates changes in consciousness and possibly in identity.
- To treat these profound changes simply as myth relies on a superficial and ahistorical understanding of globalization.
- The study of globalization and of the global system constitutes a potential revolution in the social sciences.

FURTHER READING

Agnew, J. and S. Corbridge (1995) *Mastering Space*. London: Routledge. A comprehensive and materialist theory of modern geopolitics.

Baylis, J. and S. Smith (eds) (1997) *The Globalization of World Politics: An Introduction to International Relations*. Oxford: Oxford University Press. A very useful set of essays written primarily by students of international relations which examines various aspects of the global political economy.

Beck, U. (1998) *What is Globalization?* Frankfurt: Surhkamp. A critical study of the idea and practice of globalization by a leading thinker. Covers issues of global governance, global social movements and the environment as a global problem.

Gray, J. (1998) *False Dawn*. Oxford: Oxford University Press. An interesting if somewhat doom-laden account of the problems facing and general lack of viability of global capitalism.

Kennedy, P. (1993) *Preparing for the Twenty-First Century*. London: Harper-Collins. A historian's view of globalizing tendencies, which deals with how a number of key countries face the challenges of globalization.

REFERENCES

Amin, A. (1997) 'Tracing Globalization', *Theory, Culture and Society*, **14**(2): 123–37.

Appadurai, A. (1990) 'Disjuncture and Difference in the Global Cultural Economy', in M. Featherstone (ed.) *Global Culture: Nationalism, Globalization and Modernity*. London: Sage.

Appadurai, A. (1996) *Modernity at Large: Cultural Dimensions of Globalization*. Minneapolis: University of Minnesota Press.

Arrighi, G. (1997) 'Globalization, State Sovereignty, and the "Endless" Accumulation of Capital.' Paper delivered to the conference on 'States and Sovereignty in the World Economy', University of California, Irvine, 21–23 February.

Axford, B. (1995) *The Global System: Economics, Politics and Culture*. Cambridge: Polity Press.

Axford, B. (1997) 'The Processes of Globalisation', in B. Axford, G.K. Browning, R. Huggins, B. Rosamond and J. Turner, *Politics: An Introduction*. London: Routledge.

Barber, B. (1996) *Jihad vs McWorld*. New York: Ballantine.

Bauman, Z. (1992) *Intimations of Postmodernity*. London: Routledge.

Beck, U. (1996) *The Reinvention of Politics*. Cambridge: Polity.

Benoist, A. (1997) 'Confronting Globalization', *Telos*, **3**, 117–37.

Castells, M. (1996) *The Rise of the Network Society*. Oxford: Blackwell.

Castells, M. (1997) *The Power of Identity*. Oxford: Blackwell.

Cumings, B. (1997) 'Japan and Northeast Asia into the 21st Century', in P.J. Katzenstein and T. Shiraishi (eds) *Network Power: Japan and Asia*. Ithaca, NY: Cornell University Press.

Featherstone, M. (1990) *Global Culture*. London: Sage.

Freeman, M. (1995). 'Global-degook', *Living Marxism*, **80**, June: 1–6.

Friedman, J. (1994) *Cultural Identity and Global Process*. London: Sage.

Gray, J. (1998) 'Global Utopias and Clashing Civilizations: Misunderstanding the Present', *International Affairs*, **74**(1): 149–64.

Hannerz, U. (1996) *Transnational Connections*. London: Routledge

Harvey, D. (1990) *The Postmodern Condition*. Cambridge: Polity.

Held, D., McGrew, A.G., Goldblatt, D. and Perraton, D. (1999) *Global Transformations*. Cambridge: Polity.

Hirst, P. and Thompson, G. (1996) *Globalization in Question*. Cambridge: Polity.

Keohane, R. and Nye, J. (1977) *Power and Interdependence: World Politics in Transition*. Boston: Little Brown.

McGrew, A. (1992) 'Conceptualising Global Politics', in A.G. McGrew and P. Lewis (eds) *Global Politics*. Cambridge: Polity.

Meyer, J.W., Boli, J., Ramirez, F. and Thomas, G. (1997) 'The Structuring of a World Environmental Regime', *International Organisation*, **51**(4), Autumn: 623–51.

Ohmae, K. (1989) *Borderless World: Power and Strategy in the Interlinked Economy*. London: HarperCollins.

O'Tuathail, G. (1998) *Re-Thinking Geopolitics*. London: Routledge.

Pieterse, J.N. (1997) *Going Global: Futures of Capitalism, Development and Change*. **28**: 367–82.

Porter, M. (1990) *The Competitive Advantage of Nations*. London: Macmillan.

Smith, A.D. (1995) *Nations and Nationalism in the Global Era*. Cambridge: Polity.

Robertson, R. (1992) *Globalization: Social Theory and Global Culture*. London: Sage.

Rushdie, S. (1991) *Imaginary Homelands*. London: Granta.

Wallerstein, I. (1997) 'The Rise and Future Demise of World-Systems Analysis.' Paper delivered to the 91st Annual Meeting of the American Sociological Association, New York, August.

Chapter 18

Restructuring

Andrew Kilmister

INTRODUCTION

The concept of 'restructuring' has become widely used in the last two decades by a variety of writers and academic disciplines as a means of characterizing the nature and impact of economic changes. An important expression of this has been its use in Marxist writings, where 'in the last few years, the focus of attention . . . has shifted from the issue of capitalist *crisis* to the question of the *restructuring* of capitalism' (Bonefeld and Holloway, 1991: 1). Restructuring is a central term in Marxist (and post-Marxist) writing on capitalism today. None the less, the notion of restructuring has spread beyond these confines to become a template for a much more varied set of analyses of contemporary developments. Yet while restructuring has been widely invoked in explaining and developing change, there has been relatively little direct discussion of the concept itself. Moreover, the term has come to be used to explain a number of distinct processes with limited examination of the extent to which these are connected.

This chapter will examine the usefulness of the concept of restructuring in accounts of social change. It focuses on two distinct kinds of restructuring, *productive restructuring* and *financial restructuring*. The central argument of the chapter is that there are significant parallels between the development of recent debates in both areas. In each case the introduction of the concept of restructuring, during the 1980s, opened up important areas of analysis, making connections evident which had hitherto been obscured, and advancing bold and interesting hypotheses. In each case, however, those adopting the concept made a number of sweeping claims which were difficult to substantiate. This left them open to a range of detailed empirical criticisms which raised many necessary questions about the use of restructuring as an organizing framework. While these criticisms were to a large extent justified, however, they also had the effect of narrowing the debate over restructuring so that many of the connections originally highlighted became neglected. In particular the 1990s have seen a reassertion of disciplinary boundaries which has come at the expense of some of the broader perspectives opened out in the previous decade. Further progress is likely to depend on recovering some of the vision of the earlier analyses while substantiating them with greater empirical care.

The chapter will look at productive restructuring and financial restructuring in turn; first outlining the arguments of those using the concept and then examining criticisms. The conclusion compares the debates around the two variants of the concept.

PRODUCTIVE RESTRUCTURING

The debate around productive restructuring has its roots in the revival of Marxist economics in the 1970s. Perry Anderson has argued that this revival reached its highest point in three key works which examined 'the laws of motion of the capitalist mode of production as a whole' (Anderson, 1983: 21). These were Harry Braverman's *Labour and Monopoly Capital* (Braverman, 1974), Ernest Mandel's *Late Capitalism* (Mandel, 1975) and Michel Aglietta's *A Theory of Capitalist Regulation: The US Experience* (Aglietta, 1979). In retrospect each of these three works can be seen to have played an important role in the emergence of the concept of restructuring at the turn of the decade.

Braverman's book was crucial in reintroducing the idea of the labour process as central to Marxist thought. Where previous discussions had focused on the theories of value and crisis, Braverman emphasized the lived texture of relations at work, drawing on his own experience of both manual and white-collar jobs. In particular he stressed an in-built tendency for capitalist production to reduce the autonomy of workers and to instigate a process of deskilling. This account encouraged a wealth of historical and contemporary studies of the labour process both agreeing and disagreeing with Braverman's account. From this debate emerged the presupposition that the transformation of work relations should be at the heart of any account of key economic turning points.

Mandel's work was chiefly of importance for the restructuring debate because of his use of the concept of 'long waves' of capitalist development (though this only formed one part of his complete account). This idea can be traced back to the work of the Soviet economist Nikolai Kondratiev in the 1920s. Kondratiev claimed to have identified fifty-year long cycles in a number of variables, particularly prices. Later writers extended this concept to include not just financial variables but also indicators such as production and employment. The idea was that history could be broken up into periods of roughly half a century made up of twenty-five-year long upswings involving economic prosperity, followed by downswings characterized by depressions and slumps.

While Mandel's concept of long waves rejects the deterministic framework of regular cycles adopted by many followers of Kondratiev, it retains the idea of key turning points in capitalist development, occurring every fifty years or so, which provide the basis for periods of sustained accumulation. This growth is seen as leading inexorably to crises which inaugurate lengthy periods of weak growth and periodic recession. Mandel applied this framework to the 'long boom' in the Western economies during the 1950s and 1960s and to the break up of this boom which began with the rise of inflation and trade union agitation in the late 1960s and was accentuated by the oil crisis of 1973.

For Mandel the turning points in long waves were the result of a complex combination of factors including class struggle, technological change and relations between imperialist countries and the rest of the world. However, the concept of long waves was also adopted, at much the same time, by another group of researchers, centred around Christopher Freeman at the University of Sussex Science Policy Research Unit (SPRU). For these writers the role of technological change in generating long waves was crucial, and in their analyses each wave becomes identified with a core cluster of technologies and associated products. For example, the post-war boom is seen as based on the growth of electronics with the accompanying rise of motor vehicle and mass consumer goods production.

Each of these views of long waves fed into the development of the concept of restructuring. Their key contribution was the view that, in addition to conventional accounts of the ten-year business cycle, it is also possible to identify and study major shifts in the organization of capitalist economies, which do not alter fundamental social relations but do have significant effects over a lengthy time period.

The importance of Aglietta's book lay in the concept he developed, following Gramsci, of 'Fordism'. Aglietta saw post-war economic success in the USA as being based on a 'regime of accumulation' in which high levels of production based on the productivity generated by the assembly line were matched with high levels of consumption, in particular of durable consumer goods. This regime of accumulation was backed up by a set of institutional structures which made this matching possible and which were described by Aglietta as a 'mode of regulation'. The mode of regulation included high government spending, especially on welfare; high wages (partly in return for workers ceding control over the labour process) based on a significant role for trade unions and institutionalized wage bargaining; and a financial system willing to extend the credit necessary for sustained accumulation. The combination of this regime of accumulation and mode of regulation was named Fordism by Aglietta. Aglietta also began the process of analysing the limitations and eventual breakdown of the Fordist system in the 1970s.

Aglietta's work inspired a substantial school of 'regulation theorists', first in France and later elsewhere, particularly in Germany. Later analyses of restructuring drew heavily on regulation theory; in particular the connections it drew, first between developments in the areas of production and consumption, and, second, between economic changes and institutional developments elsewhere in society.

The emergence of a concept of productive restructuring in the early 1980s was based in large measure on labour process theory, on long wave theory and on regulation theory. From these diverse sources emerged the idea of profound changes in the productive structure of a society, centred on transformations in the labour process and involving associated developments both in consumption and in the institutional framework governing the economy. Such changes formed the basis of the concept of productive restructuring.

ANALYSES OF PRODUCTIVE RESTRUCTURING

Though productive restructuring has been analysed in a variety of ways, two main approaches to the issue can be isolated: that based on the concept of 'post-Fordism' and that based on the concept of 'flexible specialization'.

The analysis of post-Fordism draws particularly heavily on Aglietta's work and on regulation theory in general, though post-Fordist accounts are not restricted to a regulationist framework and regulation theory is not necessarily committed to an analysis of post-Fordism (Jessop, 1990). The most influential uses of the concept of post-Fordism in Britain in the 1980s were those sponsored by the Communist Party magazine *Marxism Today* (Hall and Jacques, 1989, is a representative collection of articles mainly from this source) and by the Labour-controlled Greater London Council (GLC) in the first half of the decade. The Chief Economic Adviser to the GLC, Robin Murray, was also an important contributor to *Marxism Today*.

The theorists of post-Fordism focused on the break-up of the Fordist framework described above. The causes of this break-up were theorized in various ways but in general were seen as lying in the increasing failure of Fordist production methods to deliver productivity increases, a growing tendency of the financial system and wage bargaining under Fordism to encourage creeping inflation, and the breakdown of the international monetary arrangements that had characterized the post-war boom following the decision of the US government to suspend the convertibility of the dollar into gold in 1971. These changes, and others, were seen as necessitating a fundamental shift from Fordist models of production to post-Fordist approaches.

While Fordism was based on mass production through the assembly line coupled with high wages and collective bargaining through trade unions, post-Fordism was seen as requiring differentiated production to suit more demanding and specialized consumers. This was expected to be coupled with greater individualism in labour relations (for example, profit and performance-related pay, individual contracts and increased flexibility in job descriptions) and a significant weakening in the position of trade unions. The high levels of government spending under Fordism were envisaged as being reduced dramatically, with an emphasis on individual responsibility by citizens rather than reliance on welfare spending. The relatively compliant financial system of Fordism was to be replaced by a more demanding approach with stringent rules for obtaining credit. This was seen as lying behind the rise of 'monetarism' in the late 1970s and early 1980s.

While the post-Fordist structure rested on a number of bases, nearly all analysts in this tradition saw technological change as central to its emergence. It was the rise of Computer-Aided Design and Computer-Aided Manufacturing (CAD-CAM) which was seen as allowing the move away from mass production to greater variety of products (so-called 'batch production') on which the whole system was based. This shift and the move away from the assembly line, in conjunction with the decline of a number of 'traditional' manufacturing industries, in turn were thought to require fundamental changes in the organization of work, both with regard to the range of skills of individual workers and the relations between workers, for example in teams. The emphasis on technology in post-Fordist writings allowed a number of writers to assimilate the Science Policy Research Unit analyses of technological trajectories and long waves mentioned above to the post-Fordist school of analyses (Hirst and Zeitlin, 1992).

There was considerable discussion about the extent to which the emergence of post-Fordism was an inevitable process. However, most writers taking this approach regarded substantial changes along the lines outlined above as extremely likely to occur and saw any attempt to forestall their emergence by holding on to the old Fordist structures as doomed to failure. What was not predetermined was the issue of the social group which would benefit from the shift to post-Fordism. For the majority of writers in the post-Fordist school, whose sympathies were left of centre, the key strategic objective was to ensure that the expected change to post-Fordism would benefit labour rather than capital. This was summed up in Murray and the GLC's concept of 'restructuring for labour' (GLC, 1985: 37).

The concept of flexible specialization has sometimes been regarded as identical to that of post-Fordism. However, as several observers have stressed, they are in fact significantly different. The idea of flexible specialization was originally developed by the American writers Charles Sabel and Michael Piore (Sabel and Piore, 1984). Like post-Fordism, the ideas of flexible specialization were part of the GLC economic strategy; and again their main proponent in this context was an American, Michael Best (Best, 1990).

Ironically, while post-Fordism rested in large part on the analysis of the USA by a Frenchman, Aglietta, flexible specialization was derived from the researches in Europe of US writers, particularly Piore and Sabel's studies of Baden-Württemburg in Germany and the Emilia-Romagna region in Italy.

The central difference between post-Fordism and flexible specialization is that post-Fordism attempts to characterize restructuring in a linear way across a whole society. Post-Fordism is seen as a development affecting a whole society and as following and replacing Fordism as a 'way of life'. Flexible specialization, on the other hand, is a conceptual model of how production is organized, which is counterposed to mass production. The institutional counterpart to flexible specialization is more narrowly defined around specific issues relating to production than is the case with post-Fordism. Further, flexible specialization is not seen as something which *follows* Fordism or mass production, it is rather an alternative model of production which in particular industries may follow, precede or coexist with mass production methods. However, Piore and Sabel do argue that at certain historical points societies are faced with a sharp choice across a wide range of productive activities between the mass production paradigm and the flexible specialization paradigm. In particular they see the crisis of the 1970s as having opened up such a period and the adoption of flexible specialization methods as potentially a way of resolving the crisis.

Flexible specialization has been defined as 'the manufacture of a wide and changing array of customized products using flexible, general-purpose machinery and skilled, adaptable workers' (Hirst and Zeitlin, 1992: 71). As such it is neither superior nor inferior to mass production based on standardized products using assembly-line techniques. The choice between the two rests largely on social, political and cultural factors rather than any inherent economic rationality. However, once a choice between the two approaches has been made by a large number of companies and so built into technological and organizational structures, it will only be reversed at times of considerable economic turmoil. Hence, Piore and Sabel argue, the decision to opt for mass production methods in the early years of the century built up a level of inertia which was only broken down by the period of economic uncertainty in the industrialized economies beginning in the mid-1970s.

While flexible specialization primarily refers to a method of production, the adoption of flexible specialization does have implications for a wider range of social relationships. A key issue here, it is argued, is the creation of an intricate network of relations of trust between companies and between workers and managers. Only on the basis of such trust will companies feel able to invest in the technology, and workers be willing to acquire the skills, which make flexible production possible. Conversely, the control granted to workers in the production process in such a system necessitates a high level of trust on the part of managers. These relations of trust are underpinned by wider social networks enabling the provision of credit, vocational training and other elements of support for production. Regions where such networks function well can become 'industrial districts' where the spread of flexible production methods encourages a high level of prosperity, and such districts are explicitly compared by writers like Sabel to the nineteenth-century regions studied by Alfred Marshall. Industrial districts are based on both the coalescing of innovations arising from networks of small firms and the decentralizing of production and research in large companies.

Both flexible specialization and post-Fordism are analyses of productive restructuring in that they see changes in production methods as key to wider social changes. However, both also link those changes to developments in a wide array of other institutions and processes. Such analyses, though, have been subject to widespread criticism in recent years.

CRITICISMS OF PRODUCTIVE RESTRUCTURING

Initial analyses of productive restructuring rested both on bold theoretical hypotheses and on sweeping empirical claims. They have been criticized on both counts.

On the theoretical side, post-Fordism has been attacked, not least by proponents of flexible specialization, for treating society as a homogeneous whole and neglecting elements of difference both within the area of production and between production and other areas of social life (Hirst and Zeitlin, 1992). Concepts of productive restructuring have been seen as unduly privileging certain areas of analysis at the expense of others; technology in the case of post-Fordism, at least in those versions influenced by the SPRU writers mentioned above, and markets in the case of flexible specialization. Marxist critics of both approaches have argued that they neglect issues of class struggle and of value relations (Gough, 1996a, 1996b), and that they overemphasize the inevitability of the transformations which they analyse in a way which encourages a fatalistic perspective amongst those attempting to resist their effects (Clarke, 1991). Defenders of both approaches have replied to these criticisms and the debate continues. However, the main body of criticism directed at work on productive restructuring has been based on empirical analyses.

Empirically based critiques of both post-Fordism and flexible specialization have followed a number of directions. On the one hand, it is argued that mass production remains much more widespread than analysts of productive restructuring allow. At the same time, it is argued that mass production was never so universal in the past as has been claimed, and that consequently the significance of such departures from it as do exist has been exaggerated (Williams *et al.*, 1987). Another argument is that the elements of continuity between recent innovations in production techniques and previously dominant approaches are much greater than advocates of either flexible specialization or post-Fordism have acknowledged (Garrahan and

Stewart, 1992). Linked to this is the claim that workplace resistance or organizational inertia have been relatively effective in limiting both the spread and effectiveness of new approaches to production. The employment generating potential and scope for innovation arising from networks of small firms has also been questioned (Harrison, 1994).

Over the course of the last decade the analysis of the empirical extent of transformations of production techniques has come to be embodied in a continuing debate around the concept of 'flexibility'. A wealth of material has been presented arising out of detailed organizational studies, much of which has considerably modified the original bold statements by proponents of productive restructuring (Ackers and Smith, 1996). While this work has been extremely valuable it has tended to shift much of the debate about productive restructuring back towards the examination of workplace relations, in relative isolation from the broader issues raised by theorists of both post-Fordism and flexible specialization. The analysis of productive restructuring has largely been conducted in terms of issues of industrial relations and technological change at work with increasingly little discussion of the relationship between production and consumption or the political and social consequences of changes in production. At the same time the rapidly growing body of work being carried out on the sociology of consumption has tended not to analyse links with production in detail.

This tendency to move back towards traditional disciplinary boundaries, with the effect that some of the connections made in the original work on productive restructuring have become obscured, has been strengthened by the focus in the early 1990s on the so-called 'Japanization' or 'lean production' debate. The late 1980s saw an upsurge in Japanese manufacturing investment in both the UK and USA and a consequent interest in the impact of such investment on management techniques and industrial relations. At the same time an influential theorization of Japanese production systems in the motor industry was centred around the concept of lean production (Womack, Jones and Roos, 1990). Lean production (involving teamworking, 'just in time' approaches to inventory management, prioritization of quality as a goal and the elimination of waste from all aspects of the production process) was taken by its advocates to represent a radically new approach to industrial organization, and one which would be generally beneficial. It was argued that foreign investment would lead to the transfer of lean production systems from Japan to other economies (Kenney and Florida, 1993; Oliver and Wilkinson, 1992). Critics of lean production argued that the distinction between it and existing methods had been overdrawn, that its effectiveness had been overrated, and that it involved a dramatic intensification of work based on increased effort from employees (Garrahan and Stewart, 1992; Parker and Slaughter, 1994).

Again, the debate over lean production raised interesting questions. However, lean production differed as an organizing concept in one important way from both post-Fordism and flexible specialization. Unlike the earlier two approaches, it was centred on the analysis of changes internal to a particular workplace or company. The study of external relationships was limited to a restricted range of suppliers and subcontractors. Because of this, the emphasis on lean production shifted discussion of changes in production further towards a framework in which they became separated from wider social issues and developments. In this way the focus on 'Japanization' reinforced the tendencies already instigated by the emerging debate on flexibility. The analysis of productive restructuring has thus led towards a progressive narrowing down of the field of discussion, as compared to the perspective originally opened up by the advocates of post-Fordism and flexible specialization. While many of the claims made by these writers have been shown to be problematical, later advances in conceptual clarity and concrete knowledge have often been made at the expense of losing sight of some of the connections originally drawn and falling back behind rather traditional disciplinary boundaries (though there are exceptions to this; for example, Gough, 1996a, 1996b). In the following section it will be shown that a similar process has occurred in the analysis of financial restructuring.

THE CONCEPT OF FINANCIAL RESTRUCTURING

Concurrent with the debate on productive restructuring discussed above, the concept of restructuring was widely discussed in the USA throughout the 1980s and early 1990s. However, what was referred to in such discussions was very different from the changes analysed by writers like Piore and Sabel. Restructuring in American business came to be associated chiefly with a wide variety of financial transactions. These included changes in organizational form, in particular buying back the shares of public corporations so that they became private non-quoted companies; changes in ownership associated with so-called 'leveraged buy-outs', mergers and acquisitions; changes in structure leading to the divestment of non-core activities and an increased reliance on subcontracting and 'outsourcing'; and the use of new financial instruments and markets, in particular the rapidly growing 'junk bond' market, to effect these transformations. These various developments can be referred to more generally as financial restructuring (for details of financial restructuring in this period see Weston, Chung and Siu, 1997).

Initial developments in financial restructuring remained rather untheorized. However, towards the end of the 1980s an influential analysis of such restructuring emerged against which later discussion of such changes has largely been set. This was set out most clearly by Michael Jensen (1989). Jensen's argument was framed largely in response to observers of the financial markets who were critical of financial restructuring, largely because of the high levels of debt taken on by companies involved in such developments. What was important about his response to such criticisms was that it depended on an explicit theoretical standpoint which had the effect of raising the level of the debate. This standpoint arose from the concept of 'agency costs' previously developed by Jensen with William Meckling (Jensen and Meckling, 1976).

Agency costs arise when a principal hires an agent to do something but is unable costlessly to enforce the behaviour by the agent that they would ideally like to see. For example, shareholders nominally employ managers to run companies for them, but managers in practice have considerable autonomy. Such autonomy arises from monitoring costs (it is expensive for shareholders to find out how effectively managers are performing their function) and enforcement costs (it is expensive for shareholders to act to change the behaviour of managers). Agency costs thus arise from both monitoring and enforcement costs. One important element of such costs is a 'free rider' problem. Each individual shareholder has an incentive to let others carry out monitoring and enforcement and then to reap the benefits of improved managerial behaviour. Yet if all follow this strategy there will be no control of managers and the collectivity of shareholders will lose out.

Agency costs have become a major theme in corporate finance. Jensen's later contribution was to use them to explain and defend financial restructuring. His argument was that the changes associated with such restructuring could be justified through their positive impact on agency costs. Financial restructuring was leading to a new form of corporate organization in the USA in which both managers and workers would be forced to higher levels of efficiency as a result of financial factors. In particular, high levels of debt would require companies to make sustained profits to avoid bankruptcy and would necessitate the distribution of such profits rather than their retention under managerial control. Closely held private shareholdings, largely managed by active investors, would facilitate the monitoring of managers and enforcement of shareholder wishes more effectively than the dispersed shareholdings typical of the public corporation. In many industries then, principally those with high and steady profits but few opportunities for rapid technological change, financial restructuring would dramatically improve productivity and profitability (cf. Yago, 1991).

Just as the analysis of productive restructuring connected areas hitherto seen as distinct and broke down disciplinary boundaries, so too did the accounts given of financial restructuring. In particular, these accounts linked the analysis of the financing of organizations, their organizational structure and questions of workplace relationships. High levels of debt and related takeovers were justified not in purely financial terms but by innovations in company form and the role of active investors and by their impact on the behaviour of workers and managers. However, just as with productive restructuring, the initial accounts of financial restructuring were somewhat sweeping and speculative and were open to criticism on both theoretical and empirical grounds.

CRITICISMS OF FINANCIAL RESTRUCTURING

The defence of financial restructuring by Jensen preceded the collapse of the junk bond market in the USA by only one year. This collapse stimulated considerable criticism of the impact of such restructuring on American companies. It was argued both that the public corporation had continuing advantages overlooked by the supporters of new organizational forms and that the record of borrowers in the junk bond market was not as successful as had been claimed. Increased attention was paid to the agency costs of high levels of debt finance in terms of the encouragement of risky behaviour on the part of company owners and managers who would gain the bulk of profits from speculative projects but would not bear the full costs in the event of bankruptcy, owing to limited liability regulations (Stiglitz and Weiss, 1981). More forcefully, the view was put forward that financial re-structuring had been engaged in, not in order to increase efficiency, but for other motives: to provide the potential for managers and financiers to 'loot' companies by siphoning off funds for their own private use (Akerlof and Romer, 1993) or to lay the basis for the shifting of private corporate costs, such as pension obligations, onto the public purse (Clark, 1993).

Two broader areas of criticism emerged through this debate. One centred on the scope of the notion of agency costs. Jensen and his followers have tended to see these as the basis for a unified theory of organizational forms, and to take the account of financial restructuring as being just one example of the use to which they could be put in this context. Others have argued that, while agency costs may be a fruitful way of analysing the financial decisions of companies, they are less useful in other areas, for example the examination of industrial relations. A second line of criticism argued that the agency cost approach neglects issues of power and control within and between organizations in favour of an individualized model of rational decision-making and contracting. Not only did this apply to attempts to explain worker–employer relationships from the perspective of agency costs; it was also claimed that the agency cost approach neglected the shifting balance of control between, say, banks and industrial companies. Defenders of financial restructuring continued to argue that improved US economic performance in the 1990s rested on the organizational changes of the 1980s and that further restructuring would continue to yield benefits.

The debate over financial restructuring has provided many important insights, in a similar way to the debate over productive restructuring. It has become clear that the impact of financial decisions is more complex than originally hypothesized by Jensen. However, the increased complexity of the discussion has once more been bought at the expense of a certain narrowing of focus. The links between corporate finance, organizational form and workplace relations have been somewhat obscured in favour of a more restricted concentration on the impact of financial structure on company performance. Paradoxically, some of those most critical of financial restructuring have aided this process. They have argued that financial restructuring has been primarily engaged in to secure illicit or undesirable financial benefits for companies or managers and have criticized it on that account. While such developments undoubtedly have occurred, this line of criticism runs the risk of obscuring the links which exist between such restructuring and social relationships within companies. In this way the promise of initial studies of financial restructuring, that the concept of agency costs might link together the study of the financial and productive aspects of organizations, has not been fulfilled and the separate disciplines of corporate finance and industrial relations have reasserted themselves.

CONCLUSION

The progress of the debates on productive and financial restructuring exhibits striking similarities. In both cases bold hypotheses were advanced, resting on forceful interpretations of empirical trends. In both cases these hypotheses have been criticized on theoretical and empirical grounds. In both cases much of this criticism is justified, yet in each case it has resulted in a narrowing of discussion and a reassertion of traditional disciplinary boundaries, when the attraction of the original concept of restructuring lay largely in the potential it showed for overcoming such boundaries. The future development of the concept is likely to lie in the ability of those using it to combine the empirical sensitivity and clarity of recent analyses with some recovery of the audacity of the way in which it was originally used.

SUMMARY

- The concept of restructuring has developed from its origins in Marxist writings to become an important theme in the analysis of contemporary economic change.
- Restructuring has been interpreted in a number of ways – two important variants of the concept are *productive restructuring* and *financial restructuring*.
- Debates over restructuring in both these variants have established important connections which were previously obscured.
- In the case of productive restructuring these connections link changes in production with developments in consumption, industrial relations and politics at regional, national and international levels.
- In the case of financial restructuring these connections link company financial structures and decisions with broader organizational changes and developments in relations between workers and managers.

> • In each of the two cases of restructuring recent debates have tended to lose sight of these connections and to concentrate in a narrower way on analysing developments in production methods and financial strategies in isolation.

FURTHER READING

Amin, A. (1994) *Post-Fordism*. Oxford: Blackwell. This is a very useful collection of some of the major articles on the subject. It looks not only at post-Fordism but also at flexible specialization, and it includes material on social and cultural developments as well as economic issues.

Bonefeld, W. and Holloway, J. (eds) (1991) *Post-Fordism and Social Form: A Marxist Debate on the Post-Fordist State*. Basingstoke: Macmillan. This collection is mainly of articles previously published in the journal *Capital and Class*. It raises some important criticisms of the concept of post-Fordism and spirited replies to these criticisms.

Sabel, C. and Piore, M. (1984) *The Second Industrial Divide: Possibilities for Prosperity*. New York: Basic Books. This is the key account of the ideas behind flexible specialization. It remains a very exciting book to read, though the empirical detail and theoretical structure have been heavily criticized.

Storper, M. and Scott, A. (eds) (1992) *Pathways to Industrialization and Regional Development*. London: Routledge. This is much broader than the title implies. It is a wide-ranging account of post-Fordism, flexible specialization and related approaches, with a special emphasis on their implications for regional issues. The approach is generally favourable to the theories discussed.

Weston, J. Fred, Chung, K.S. and Siu, A. (1997) *Takeovers, Restructuring and Corporate Governance*. Upper Saddle River, NJ : Prentice-Hall. A good up-to-date survey of the ideas behind financial restructuring and the associated empirical evidence.

Yago, G. (1991) *Junk Bonds: How High Yield Securities Restructured Corporate America*. New York/Oxford: Oxford University Press. This is the most detailed defence of the financial restructuring policies adopted by US companies in the 1980s. It draws on Michael Jensen's ideas and adds considerable empirical detail.

REFERENCES

Ackers, P. and Smith, C. (eds) (1996) *The New Workplace and Trade Unionism*. London: Routledge.

Aglietta, M. (1979) *A Theory of Capitalist Regulation: The US Experience*. London: New Left Books.

Akerlof, G. and Romer, P. (1993) 'Looting: The Economic Underworld of Bankruptcy for Profit', *Brookings Papers on Economic Activity*, **2**: 1–73.

Anderson, P. (1983) *In the Tracks of Historical Materialism*. London: Verso.

Best, M. (1990) *The New Competition: Institutions of Industrial Restructuring*. Cambridge: Polity.

Bonefeld, W. and Holloway, J. (eds) (1991) *Post-Fordism and Social Form: A Marxist Debate on the Post-Fordist State*. Basingstoke: Macmillan.

Braverman, H. (1974) *Labour and Monopoly Capital: The Degradation of Work in the Twentieth Century*. New York: Monthly Review Press.

Clark, G. (1993) *Pensions and Corporate Restructuring in American Industry*. Baltimore and London: Johns Hopkins University Press.

Clarke, S. (1991) 'Overaccumulation, Class Struggle and the Regulation Approach', in W. Bonefeld and J. Holloway (eds) *Post-Fordism and Social Form: A Marxist Debate on the Post-Fordist State*. Basingstoke: Macmillan, pp. 103–34.

Garrahan, P. and Stewart, P. (1992) *The Nissan Enigma: Flexibility at Work in a Local Economy*. London: Mansell.

GLC (Greater London Council) (1985) *The London Industrial Strategy*. London: GLC.

Gough, J. (1996a) 'Not Flexible Accumulation – Contradictions of Value in Contemporary Economic Geography: 1 Workplace and Interfirm Relations', *Environment and Planning A*, **28**: 2063–79.

Gough, J. (1996b) 'Not Flexible Accumulation – Contradictions of Value in Contemporary Economic Geography: 2 Regional Regimes, National Regulation and Political Strategy', *Environment and Planning A*, **28**: 2179–200.

Hall, S. and Jacques, M. (1989) *New Times: The Changing Face of Politics in the 1990s*. London: Lawrence and Wishart.

Harrison, B. (1994) *Lean and Mean: The Changing Landscape of Corporate Power in the Age of Flexibility*. New York: Basic Books.

Hirst, P. and Zeitlin, J. (1992) 'Flexible Specialization versus Post-Fordism: Theory, Evidence and Policy Implications', in M. Storper and A. Scott (eds) *Pathways to Industrialization and Regional Development*. London: Routledge, pp. 70–115.

Jensen, M. (1989) 'Eclipse of the Public Corporation', *Harvard Business Review*, September–October: 61–74.

Jensen, M. and Meckling, W. (1976) 'Theory of the Firm: Managerial Behavior, Agency Costs and Ownership Structure', *Journal of Financial Economics*, **3**: 305–60.

Jessop, B. (1990) 'Regulation Theories in Retrospect and Prospect', *Economy and Society*, **19**(2): 153–216.

Kenney, M. and Florida, R. (1993) *Beyond Mass Production: The Japanese System and Its Transfer to the US*. New York: Oxford University Press.

Mandel, E. (1975) *Late Capitalism*. London: New Left Books.

Oliver, N. and Wilkinson, B. (1992) *The Japanization of British Industry: New Developments in the 1990s*, 2nd edn. Oxford: Blackwell.

Parker, M. and Slaughter, J. (1994) *Working Smart: A Union Guide to Participation Programs and Reengineering*. Detroit: Labor Notes.

Sabel, C. and Piore, M. (1984) *The Second Industrial Divide: Possibilities for Prosperity*. New York: Basic Books.

Stiglitz, J. and Weiss, A. (1981) 'Credit Rationing in Markets with Imperfect Information', *American Economic Review*, **71**(3): 393–410.

Weston, J. Fred, Chung, K.S. and Siu, A. (1997) *Takeovers, Restructuring and Corporate Governance*. Upper Saddle River, NJ: Prentice-Hall.

Williams, K., Cutler, T., Williams, J. and Haslam, C. (1987) 'The End of Mass Production?' *Economy and Society*, **16**(3): 404–39.

Womack, J., Jones, D. and Roos, D. (1990) *The Machine that Changed the World*. New York: Rawson Associates.

Yago, G. (1991) *Junk Bonds: How High Yield Securities Restructured Corporate America*. New York and Oxford: Oxford University Press.

Chapter 19

Cities in the global econony

Saskia Sassen

The dispersal capacities emerging with globalization and telecommunication – the offshoring of factories, the expansion of global networks of affiliates and subsidiaries, the move of back offices to suburbs and out of central cities – led many observers to assert that cities would become obsolete in the new economic context. Indeed, many of the once great industrial centres in the highly developed countries did suffer severe decline. But, against all predictions, a significant number of major cities also saw their concentration of economic power rise. Why?

One way of summarizing my answer to this question and the argument I will develop here is to say that place is central to the multiple circuits through which economic globalization is constituted. One strategic type of place for these developments, and the one focused on here, is the city. Other important types of places are export-processing zones or high-tech districts such as Silicon Valley in California and the M4 corridor in England.

The reason that place, or, more precisely, a certain type of place, matters in today's global economy is that the geographic dispersal of economic activities has happened under conditions of continuing concentration in ownership and control in the economy. This has contributed to new or expanded central functions in firms operating across borders: these functions are the top-level management, planning and servicing, often referred to as command functions. These have become more complex because firms now operate in many different countries each with its distinct legal and accounting systems and managerial culture. The complexity of transactions has meant that firms increasingly buy more and more aspects of central functions from highly specialized firms. It is these firms which find in major cities an ideal place for their activities. There are other factors that contribute to explain the new importance of major cities; they will be discussed in this chapter.

In brief, rather than becoming obsolete due to the dispersal made possible by telecommunications and stimulated by globalization, a critical number of cities: (a) concentrate command functions; (b) are post-industrial production sites for the leading industries of our period – finance and specialized services; and (c) are national or transnational marketplaces where firms and governments from all over the world can buy financial instruments and specialized services.

How many such cities there are, what is their shifting hierarchy and how novel a development they represent, are all subjects for debate. But there is growing agreement about the fact of a network of major cities both in the North and in the South that function as centres for the co-ordination, control and servicing of global capital.

Introducing cities in an analysis of economic globalization has the effect of decomposing the nation-state into a variety of subnational components, some profoundly articulated with the global economy and others not. It also signals the declining significance of the national economy as a unitary category in the global economy. Finally, a focus on cities helps us understand processes of economic globalization in terms of concrete economic complexes situated in specific places. It reveals the importance of infrastructure, state of the art office complexes, a variety of labour markets – from professional to manual service workers – for the global economy. Such a focus contrasts sharply with the dominant perspective which emphasizes telecommunications and the hypermobility of capital and posits the neutralization of place.

THE NEW ROLE OF SERVICES IN THE ECONOMY: IMPACT ON CITIES

This new or sharply expanded role of a particular kind of city in the world economy since the early 1980s basically results from the intersection of two major processes. One is the sharp growth in the globalization of economic activity. This has raised the scale and the complexity of economic transactions, thereby feeding the growth of top-level multinational headquarter functions and the growth of services for firms, particularly the growth of advanced corporate services. The second is the growing service intensity in the organization of the economy, by which I mean the sharp trend among firms in all industrial sectors, from mining to finance, to buy an increasing share of service inputs they need for their operation rather than producing these services in-house. This has fed the growth of services for both nationally and internationally oriented firms.

Services for firms are usually referred to as *producer services*. The producer services, and most especially finance and advanced corporate services, can be seen as industries producing the organizational commodities necessary for the implementation and management of global economic systems. Producer services are intermediate outputs, that is, services bought by firms. They cover financial, legal and general management matters, innovation, development, design, administration, personnel, production technology, maintenance, transport, communications, wholesale distribution, advertising, cleaning services for firms, security and storage. Central components of the producer services category are a range of industries with mixed business and consumer markets; they are insurance, banking, financial services, real estate, legal services, accounting and professional associations (for more detailed discussions see Daniels, 1991; Noyelle and Dutka, 1988).

The key process from the perspective of the urban economy is the growing demand for services by firms in all industries and the fact that cities are preferred production sites for such services, whether at the global, national or regional level. The growing service intensity in economic organization generally and the specific conditions of production for advanced corporate services, including the conditions under which information technologies are available, combine to make some cities once again a key 'production' site, a role they had lost when mass manufacturing became the dominant economic sector. They are the world cities or global cities that are the focus of this chapter. While the decline of industrial centres as a consequence of the internationalization of production beginning in the 1960s has been thoroughly documented and explained, until recently the same could not be said about the rise of major service cities in the 1980s. Today we have a rich, growing new scholarship on these cities. (For some of the debates and disagreements in this scholarship see Cohen *et al.*, 1996; *Le Debat*, 1994; *Futur Anterieur*, 1995; King, 1996; Knox and Taylor, 1995; von Petz and Schmals, 1992; Allen *et al.*, 1999.)

There are good reasons why it has been more difficult to understand the role of cities as production sites for producer services than for manufacturing. This is especially the case for one key subsector of the producer services, advanced information industries. These are typically conceptualized in terms of the hypermobility of their outputs and the high levels of expertise of their professionals, rather than in terms of the work process involved and the requisite infrastructure of facilities and non-expert jobs that are also part of these industries. Along with the hypermobility of their outputs there is a vast structure of work that is far less mobile and, indeed, requires the massive concentrations of human and telecommunication resources we find in major cities. The specific forms assumed by globalization over the last decade have created particular organizational requirements. The emergence of global markets for finance and specialized services, the growth of investment as a major type of international transaction, all have contributed to the expansion in command functions and in the demand for specialized services for firms. (See Short and Kim, 1999; Sassen, 2000).

We cannot take the existence of a global economic system as a given, but rather need to examine the particular ways in which the conditions for economic globalization are produced. This requires examining not only communication capacities and the power of multinationals, but also the infrastructure of facilities and work processes necessary for the implementation of global economic systems, including the production of those inputs that constitute the capability for global control and the infrastructure of jobs involved in this production. The emphasis shifts to the *practice* of global control: the work of producing and reproducing the organization and management of a global production system and a global marketplace for finance, both under conditions of economic concentration. The recovery of place and production also implies that global processes can be studied in great empirical detail.

Two observations can be made at this point. One is that to a large extent the global economy materializes in concrete processes situated in specific places, and that this holds for the most advanced information industries as well. We need to distinguish between the capacity for global transmission/communication and the material conditions that make this possible, between the globalization of the financial industry and the array of resources – from buildings to labour inputs – that makes this possible. The second is that the spatial dispersal of economic activity made possible by telematics contributes to an expansion of central functions in so far as this dispersal takes place under the continuing concentration in control, ownership and profit appropriation that characterizes the current economic system. More conceptually, we can ask whether an economic system with strong tendencies towards such concentration can have a space economy that lacks points of physical agglomeration.

A NEW GEOGRAPHY OF CENTRALITY AND MARGINALITY

We can then say that the global economy materializes in a worldwide grid of strategic places, uppermost among which are major international business and financial centres. We can think of this global grid as constituting a new economic geography of centrality, one that cuts across national boundaries and across the old North–South divide. It signals, potentially, the emergence of a parallel political geography. An incipient form of this is the growing intensity in cross-border networks among cities and their political leadership. We can see here the formation, at least incipient, of a transnational urban system.

The most powerful of these new economic geographies of centrality at the interurban level binds the major international financial and business centres: New York, London, Tokyo, Paris, Frankfurt, Zurich, Amsterdam, Los

Angeles, Sydney, Hong Kong, among others. But this geography now also includes cities such as São Paulo, Buenos Aires, Bangkok, Taipei and Mexico City. The intensity of transactions among these cities, particularly through the financial markets, transactions in services and investment, has increased sharply, and so have the orders of magnitude involved. At the same time, there has been a sharpening inequality in the concentration of strategic resources and activities between each of these cities and others in the same country.

The pronounced orientation to the world markets evident in such cities raises questions about their articulation with their nation-states, their regions, and the larger economic and social structure in such cities. Cities have typically been deeply embedded in the economies of their region, indeed often reflecting the characteristics of the latter; and mostly they still do. But cities that are strategic sites in the global economy tend, in part, to disconnect from their region. Or, when the region is a global city region, then it is this region that tends to disconnect from the larger national economy. This conflicts with a key proposition in traditional scholarship about urban systems, namely, that these systems promote the territorial integration of national economies.

Alongside these new global and regional hierarchies of cities, is a vast territory that has become increasingly peripheral, increasingly excluded from the major economic processes that fuel economic growth in the new global economy. A multiplicity of formerly important manufacturing centres and port cities have lost functions and are in decline, not only in the less developed countries, but also in the most advanced economies. This is yet another meaning of economic globalization.

But also inside global cities we see a new geography of centrality and marginality. The downtowns of cities and metropolitan business centres receive massive investments in real estate and telecommunications while low-income city areas are starved of resources. Highly educated workers see their incomes rise to unusually high levels while low- or medium-skilled workers see theirs sink. Financial services produce superprofits while industrial services barely survive. These trends are evident, with different levels of intensity, in a growing number of major cities in the developed world and increasingly in some of the developing countries that have been integrated into the global financial markets (Sassen, 1998: chs 1 and 8).

THE URBAN ECONOMY TODAY

This is not to say that everything in the economy of these global cities has changed. On the contrary there is much continuity and much similarity with cities that are not global nodes. It is rather that the implantation of global processes and markets has meant that the internationalized sector of the economy has expanded sharply and has imposed a new valorization dynamic, often with devastating effects on large sectors of the urban economy. High prices and profit levels in the internationalized sector (for example, finance) and its ancillary activities (for example, restaurants and hotels) made it increasingly difficult in the 1980s for other sectors to compete for space and investments. Many of the latter have experienced considerable downgrading and/or displacement; or lost economic vigour to the point of not being able to retake their economic space when the recession weakened the dominant sectors. Illustrations are neighbourhood shops catering to local needs replaced by up-scale boutiques and restaurants catering to new high-income urban élites.

Though at a different order of magnitude, these trends also became evident towards the late 1980s in a number of major cities in the developing world that have become integrated into various world markets: São Paulo, Buenos Aires, Bangkok, Taipei, Mexico City are but some examples (Knox and Taylor, 1995; Sassen, 2000). Central to the development of this new core in these cities as well were the deregulation of financial markets, ascendance of finance and specialized services, and integration into the world markets, real estate speculation, and high-income commercial and residential gentrification. The opening of stock markets to foreign investors and the privatization of what were once public sector firms have been crucial institutional arenas for this articulation. Given the vast size of some of these cities, the impact of this new economic complex is not always as evident as in central London or Frankfurt, but the transformation has occurred.

Accompanying these sharp growth rates in producer services was an increase in the level of employment specialization in business and financial services in major cities throughout the 1980s. There is today a general trend towards high concentration of finance and certain producer services in the downtowns of major international financial centres around the world: from Toronto and Sydney, to Frankfurt and Zurich, to São Paulo and Mexico City, we are seeing growing specialization in finance and related services in the downtown areas. These cities have emerged as important producers of services for export, with a tendency towards specialization. New York and London are leading producers and exporters in financial services, accounting, advertising, management consulting, international legal services and other business services. For instance, out of a total private sector employment of 2.8 million jobs in New York City in December 1995, almost 1.3 million are export oriented. Cities such as New York and London are among the most important international markets for these services.

There are also tendencies towards specialization among different cities within a country. In the USA, New York leads in banking, securities, manufacturing administration, accounting and advertising. Washington leads in legal services, computing and data processing, management and public relations, research and development, and membership organizations. Some of the legal activity concentrated in Washington serves New York City businesses which have to go through legal and regulatory procedures and engage in lobbying in the national capital.

It is also important to recognize that manufacturing remains a crucial economic sector in all of these economies, even when it may have ceased to be so in some of these cities. This is a subject I return to in a later section.

THE FORMATION OF A NEW PRODUCTION COMPLEX

The rapid growth and disproportionate concentration of producer services in central cities should not have happened according to standard conceptions about information industries. As they are thoroughly embedded in the most advanced information technologies they could be expected to have locational options that bypass the high costs and congestion typical of major cities. But cities offer agglomeration economies – the advantages that come from being located in proximity to a multiplicity of other firms and resources. And they offer highly innovative environments.

The growing complexity, diversity and specialization of service firms makes it more efficient to buy services from specialized providers rather than hiring in-house professionals. The growing demand for these services has made possible the economic viability of a free-standing specialized service sector that benefits, indeed requires, the mix of resources and clients only a city can offer.

There is a production process in these services which benefits from proximity to other specialized services. This is especially the case in the leading and most innovative sectors of these industries. Complexity and innovation often require multiple highly specialized inputs from several industries. One example is that of financial instruments – the variety of legal contracts through which capital passes from one owner to another. The production of a financial instrument requires inputs from accounting, advertising, legal expertise, economic consulting, public relations, designers and printers. Time replaces weight in these sectors as a force for agglomeration. That is to say, if there were no need to hurry, one could conceivably have a widely dispersed array of specialized firms that could still co-operate. And this is often the case in more routine operations. But where time is of the essence, as it is today in many of the leading sectors of these industries, the benefits of agglomeration are still extremely high to the point that it is not simply a cost advantage, but an indispensable arrangement.

It is this combination of constraints that has promoted the formation of a producer services complex in all major cities. This producer services complex is intimately connected to the world of corporate headquarters; they are often thought of as forming a joint headquarters-corporate services complex. But it seems to me that we need to distinguish the two. While it is true that headquarters still tend to be disproportionately concentrated in cities, many have moved out over the last two decades. Headquarters can indeed locate outside cities. But they need a producer services complex somewhere in order to buy or contract for the needed specialized services and financing. Further, headquarters of firms with very high overseas activity or in highly innovative and complex lines of business tend to locate in major cities. In brief, firms in more routinized lines of activity, with predominantly regional or national markets, such as a standardized furniture manufacturer, appear to be increasingly free to move or install their headquarters outside cities. Firms in highly competitive and innovative lines of activity and/or with a strong world-market orientation, for example top-of-the-line financial services firms, appear to benefit from being located at the centre of major international business centres, no matter how high the costs.

But what is clear, in my view, is that both types of headquarters need a corporate services sector complex to be located somewhere. *Where* is probably increasingly unimportant from the perspective of many, though not all, headquarters. From the perspective of producer services firms, such a specialized complex is most likely to be in a city rather than, for instance, a suburban office park. The latter will be the site for producer services firms, but not for a services complex. And it is only such a complex that can handle the most advanced and complicated corporate demands.

THE RESEARCH AND POLICY AGENDA

There are a number of emerging issues for research and policy. I will discuss a few at some length and simply name a few others.

The impact of digitalization on cities

Digitalization (or computerization) is a fundamental force in the reorganization of economic space. This reorganization includes the fact that a growing number of economic activities are being dematerialized through digitalization, for example the computer that replaces the live telephone operator, or the 'production job' that is transformed to a service job through the introduction of computerized manufacturing. These changes have an impact on the geography of the built environment *for* economic activity.

But digitalization has its limits. The vast new economic topography that is being implemented through computers is one moment, one fragment, of an even vaster economic chain that is in good part embedded in non-electronic spaces. There is no fully virtualized firm and no fully digitalized industry. Even the most advanced information industries, such as finance, are installed only partly in electronic space. And so are industries that produce digital products, such as software designers. The growing digitalization of economic activities has not eliminated the need for major international business and financial centres and all the material resources they concentrate, from state-of-the-art telecommunications infrastructure to brain talent.

None the less we are seeing a transformation in the spatial correlates of centrality – centrality being what cities have historically offered the economy. What is centrality today in an economic system where a share of transactions occurs through technologies that neutralize distance and place, and do so on a global scale? Centrality has historically been embodied in certain types of built environment and urban form, such as the central business district. Further, the fact of a new geography of centrality, even if transnational, contains possibilities for regulatory enforcement that are absent in an economic geography lacking strategic points of agglomeration.

The sharpening inequalities in the distribution of the infrastructure for electronic space, whether private computer networks or the Internet, in the conditions for access to electronic space and, within electronic space, in the conditions for access to high-powered segments and features, are all contributing to new geographies of centrality both on the ground and in electronic space. What does this mean for cities?

The place of manufacturing in the new urban service economy

Another subject for research and debate is the relation between manufacturing and producer services in the advanced urban economy. The new service economy benefits from manufacturing because the latter feeds the growth of the producer services sector, but it does so whether located in the particular area, in another region, or overseas. While manufacturing, and mining and agriculture for that matter, feed the growth in the demand for producer services, their actual location is of secondary importance in the case of global-level service firms. Thus whether a manufacturing corporation has its plants offshore or inside a country may be quite irrelevant as long as it buys its services from those top-level firms.

Second, the territorial dispersal of plants, especially if international, actually raises the demand for producer services because of the increased complexity of transactions. This is yet another meaning of globalization: that the growth of producer service firms headquartered in New York or London or Paris can be fed by manufacturing located anywhere in the world as long as it is part of a multinational corporate network. It is worth remembering here that as General Motors was offshoring production jobs and devastating Detroit's employment base, its financial and public relations headquarters office in New York City was as dynamic as ever, indeed busier than ever.

Third, a good part of the producer services sector is fed by financial and business transactions that either have nothing to do with manufacturing, as is the case in many of the global financial markets, or for which manufacturing is incidental, as in much of the merger and acquisition activity which was really centred on buying and selling rather than the buying of manufacturing firms. We need much more research on many particular aspects in this relation between manufacturing and producer services, especially in the context of spatial dispersal and cross-border organization of manufacturing.

New forms of marginality and polarization

The new growth sectors, the new organizational capacities of firms, and the new technologies – all three interrelated – are contributing to produce not only a new geography of centrality, but also a new geography of marginality. The evidence for the USA, Western Europe and Japan suggests that it will take government policy and action to reduce the new forms of spatial and social inequality.

There are misunderstandings that seem to prevail in much general commentary about what matters in an advanced economic system, the information economy and economic globalization. Many types of firms, workers and places, such as industrial services, which look as if they do not belong in an advanced, information-based, globally oriented economic system are actually integral parts of such a system. They need policy recognition and support: they cannot compete in the new environments where leading sectors have bid up prices and standards, even though their products and labour are in demand. For instance, the financial industry in Manhattan, one of the most sophisticated and complex industries, needs truckers to deliver not only software, but also tables and lightbulbs; and it needs blue-collar maintenance workers and cleaners. These activities and workers need to be able to make a decent living if they are to stay in the region.

Yet another dimension not sufficiently recognized is the fact of a new valuation dynamic: the combination of globalization and the new technologies has altered the criteria and mechanisms through which factors, inputs, goods and services are valued/priced. This has had devastating effects on some localities, industries, firms and workers. Thus salaries of financial experts and the profits of financial services firms zoomed up in the 1980s while wages of blue-collar workers and profits of many traditional manufacturing firms sank.

The global city and the national state

Globalization has transformed the meaning of and the sites for the governance of economies (see, e.g., Mittelmann, 1996; Sassen, 1996). One of the key properties of the current phase in the long history of the world economy is the ascendance of information technologies, the associated increase in the mobility and liquidity of capital, and the resulting decline in the regulatory capacities of national states over key sectors of their economies. In order to understand what challenges and opportunities this brings to urban government we need to consider at least two points. First we need to consider the relation between the global economy and subnational units, particularly major cities that are international business and financial centres. This means understanding how global processes are partly embedded in strategic concentrations of resources and infrastructure, such as financial districts, as well as understanding the importance of a whole series of other conditions, for instance, what is often referred to as world-class cultural centres. These are among the crucial aspects making cities more important as a nexus within the global economy.

A second issue is the extent to which deregulation, privatization and generally the declining role of the national state in the economy – all key elements in the current phase of globalization – may contribute to replace the dyad national state/global economy with a triangulation which brings in subnational units, particularly global cities and global city regions. This would clearly have major policy implications. A key aspect of the change and the potential for future change in this relation is the fact that the content of foreign policy has shifted more towards economic issues, so that a greater component of what we call foreign policy is today international economic policy.

The transformation in the composition of the world economy, especially the rise of finance and advanced services as leading industries, is contributing to a new international economic order dominated by financial centres, global markets and transnational firms. Correspondingly we may see a growing significance of other political categories both subnational and supranational. Global cities are sites for direct transactions with world markets. These cities and the globally oriented markets and firms they contain mediate in the relation of the world economy to nation-states and in the relations among nation-states.

Making claims on the city

There are major new actors making claims on these cities, notably foreign firms which have been increasingly entitled to do business through progressive deregulation of national economies and the large increase in international business people over the last decade. These are among the new 'city users'. They have profoundly marked the urban landscape in many major cities. Their claim to the city is not contested, even though the costs and benefits to cities have barely been examined.

City users have often reconstituted strategic spaces of the city in their image: emblematic is the so-called hyperspace of international business, with its airports built by famous architects, world-class office buildings and hotels, state-of-the-art telematic infrastructure, and private security forces.

They contribute to change the social morphology of the city and to constitute what Martinotti (1993) calls the metropolis of second generation, the city of late modernism. The new city of city users is a fragile one, whose survival and successes are centred on an economy of high productivity, advanced technologies and intensified exchanges.

On the one hand, this raises a question of what the city is for international business people, and what their sense of civic responsibility might be. On the other hand, there is the difficult task of establishing whether a city that functions as an international business centre does, in fact, recover the costs involved in being such a centre: the costs involved in maintaining a state-of-the-art business district, and all it requires, from advanced communications facilities to top-level security.

Perhaps at the other extreme are those who use urban political violence to make their claims on the city, claims that lack the *de facto* legitimacy enjoyed by the new 'city users'. These are claims made by actors struggling for recognition, entitlement, claiming their rights to the city (e.g., Body-Gendrot, 1993).

SUMMARY

- Massive trends towards the spatial dispersal of economic activities at the metropolitan, national and global levels are associated with globalization.
- These trends have contributed to a demand for new forms of territorial centralization of top-level management and control operations. National and global markets as well as globally integrated firms need central places where the 'work' of running a global economy gets done.
- Information industries require a vast physical infrastructure containing strategic nodes with hyperconcentration of facilities. Even the most advanced information industries have a work process that is at least partly place-bound because of the combination of resources it requires even when the outputs are hypermobile.
- These conditions have renewed the importance of a certain kind of city, the global city, in the current era dominated by globalization and telecommunications.

FURTHER READING

Castells, Manuel. (1989) *The Informational City*. Oxford: Blackwell. This is an excellent critical introduction to the relation between information technologies and cities, and it discusses much of the literature in these areas.

Cohen, Michael A., Ruble, Blair A., Tulchin, Joseph S. and Garland, Allison M. (eds) (1996) *Preparing for the Urban Future. Global Pressures and Local Forces.* Washington DC: Woodrow Wilson Centre Press. (Distributed by The Johns Hopkins University Press.) An incredible mix of scholars and policy people from a variety of countries are represented in this collection. It grapples with the challenges on the urban agenda around the world.

The Journal of Urban Technology (Fall 1995) 'Special Issue: Information Technologies and Inner-City Communities', **3**(19). This volume shows how poor inner city communities can benefit from information technologies and can gain access to them. It offers a positive look at what is usually discussed in terms of unequal if not impossible access.

Knox, Paul L. and Taylor, Peter J. (eds) (1995) *World Cities in a World-System.* Cambridge: Cambridge University Press. This collection brings together urbanists from all over the world and stands as a state-of-the-art book on the subject.

LeGates, Richard T. and Stout, Frederic (eds) (1996) *The City Reader.* London: Routledge. This is one of the best readers on the city. It includes classic works and some of the most cutting-edge research of today.

Sassen, Saskia (2000, new updated edition) *Cities in a World Economy.* Thousand Oaks, CA: Pine Forge/Sage Press. This book is written explicitly for undergraduate students and is used widely in the classroom. It attempts to bring together the key theories and data sets about the subject.

REFERENCES

Allen, J., Massey, D. and Pryke, M. (eds) (1999) *Unseeing Cities.* London: Routledge.

Body-Gendrot, S. (1993) *Ville et violence.* Paris: Presses Universitaires de France.

Cohen, Michael A., Ruble, Blair A., Tulchin, Joseph S. and Garland, Allison M. (eds) (1996) *Preparing for the Urban Future. Global Pressures and Local Forces.* Washington DC: Woodrow Wilson Centre Press. (Distributed by The Johns Hopkins University Press.)

'Competition and Change' (1995) *The Journal of Global Business and Political Economy,* **1**(1).

Daniels, Peter W. (1991) 'Producer Services and the Development of the Space Economy', in Daniels, Peter W. and Moulaert, Frank (eds) *The Changing Geography of Advanced Producer Services.* London and New York: Belhaven Press.

Le Debat (1994) 'Le Nouveau Paris. Special Issue', Summer. Paris: Gallimard.

Futur Anterieur (1995) 'Special Issue: La ville-monde aujourd'hui: entre virtualité et ancrage', Thierry Pillon and Anne Querrien (eds) vols 30–2. Paris: L'Harmattan.

King, A.D. (ed) (1996) *Representing the City. Ethnicity, Capital and Culture in the 21st Century.* London: Macmillan.

Knox, Paul L. and Taylor, Peter J. (eds) (1995) *World Cities in a World-System.* Cambridge: Cambridge University Press.

LeGates, Richard T. and Stout, Frederic (eds) (1996) *The City Reader.* London: Routledge.

Martinotti, Guido (1993) *Metropoli: La nuova morfologia sociale della cita.* Bologna: Il Mulino.

Mittelman, James (ed.) (1996) 'Globalization: Critical Reflections', *International Political Economy Yearbook 9.* Boulder, CO: Lynne Rienner.

Noyelle, T. and Dutka, A.B. (1988) *International Trade in Business Services: Accounting, Advertising, Law and Management Consulting.* Cambridge, MA: Ballinger.

von Petz, Ursula and Schmals, Klaus M. (eds) (1992) *Metropole, Weltstadt, Global City: Neue Formen der Urbanisierung.* Dortmund: Dortmunder Beitrage zur Raumplanung, Vol. 60, Universitat Dortmund.

Sassen, Saskia (2000) *Cities in a World Economy.* Thousand Oaks, CA: Pine Forge/ Sage Press.

Sassen, Saskia (1996) *Losing Control? Sovereignty in an Age of Globalization.* The 1995 Columbia University Leonard Hastings Schoff Memorial Lectures. New York: Columbia University Press.

Sassen, Saskia (1998) *Globalization and Its Discontents.* New York: New Press.

Short, J.R. and Kim, Yeong-Hyun, (1999) *Globalization and the City.*

Chapter 20

Cultural studies

Richard Maxwell

This chapter is organized into three sections. The introduction discusses the political attitude and characteristic motivations of cultural studies (hereafter CS). The second section traces CS's diversity of origins and innovations. The concluding section confronts the state of CS today.

THE ATTITUDE

Cultural studies does not view culture as simply a fun night at the pictures, a good read or a quiet retreat into a museum. It involves a politics of writing which aims to heighten awareness and understanding of the present conditions and possible purposes of cultural labour. Culture is fraught. People work to make culture. Not only the writers, technicians, artists, carpenters and all those who put together movies, books and such; culture is also made by labour not directly involved in the culture industries. Consider your own daily works of judgement and interpretation about a film plot, your grammar or a classmate's joke. Think of all those whose efforts built the bridges you have crossed, the roads travelled, the means of transport and human relationship . . . your love story, a brief encounter . . . and all the hardship, strikes, solidarity, death, wage negotiations, debt and satisfaction embodied in those structures.

Culture is where you live and, with varying degrees of development and intensity, capitalism shapes political and socio-economic life where you live. As people strive to improve the inherited conditions of life, so do they make their culture. As Marx said, people make history, but not under conditions of their own choosing. That struggle to make history makes culture; it is in the big and little conflicts at the heart of stories we tell ourselves about who we are and want to be as a society.

Cultural studies began in Britain in the 1950s by bringing the culture and sensibilities of industrial workers to the centre of its concerns. Then, awakened in the 1960s and 1970s by anti-imperialist and anti-racist struggles and by feminism, CS broadened its scope and reinforced an expanded critique of capitalism. These struggles have motivated CS writers to become alert to the ways in which culture sustains or undermines empirical forms of oppression, domination and exploitation. There has never been a history of CS written without mention of CS's links to class struggle or emancipatory social movements. Recent criticism of CS, both from without and within CS, has used this standard of radical political commitment to identify its defining ethos.

This is CS's basic set of attitudes: it is anti-capitalist, anti-racist and anti-sexist while being inclusive, pluralizing and pro-democratic. Cultural studies hails from the Left, and it is this politics which gives coherence to the transdisciplinary writings of CS.

ORIGINS AND INNOVATIONS

Britain

Cultural studies emerged in Britain during the 1950s in a context of growing affluence and the attendant changes in the routines of daily life, especially the expansion of consumerism. After the Second World War, the Left's critique of capitalism, which for a while could confidently make reference to the Great Depression as the symbol of capitalism's finality, no longer provided the basis for an adequate analysis of post-war conditions. Capitalism appeared to have leapt to a new and robust level of development, and the Old Left was faced with the warrant to reinvent itself and its vision of politics. Consumer capitalism filled the culture with new gadgets and entertainments and, along with the welfare state, competed with the working-class movement, and in particular with the Labour Party, for the hearts and minds of British society. It was clear to the founders of CS that the Left had to forge a new way of addressing this battle over the direction of social consciousness (Schiller, 1996: 111–15).

Such was the context in which Richard Hoggart (1919–), Edward Thompson (1924–92), Stuart Hall (1932–) and Raymond Williams (1921–88), the catalysts of British cultural studies in the 1950s and 1960s, began to write. They argued that culture *mattered*, and that the Left needed to recognize this phenomenon and organize work around it. All four were teaching outside academia as adult education tutors or secondary school teachers, where they were provoked not only to think and write about culture in terms which were relevant to their mostly working-class students, but also to see social experience as an essential, if imperfect, category of cultural analysis (Turner, 1990: 41–76).

Thompson's cultural studies began with his book *The Making of the English Working Class* (1963) which, along with Hoggart's work, encouraged research into everyday working-class life and popular cultures. This writing may be described as *radical humanist* in that it offered a left-wing analysis which foregrounded the experiences and perceptions of working-class people without privileging abstract theory. Thompson made a lasting influence on CS for his emphasis on writing history from the bottom up, from the perspectives and experiences of the people who daily make and remake working-class culture. Thompson helped to situate the study of culture in the experience of class conflicts that give shape and meaning both to the dominant culture and, more importantly, to popular cultures whose sensibilities, temperaments, entertainments and knowledges are submerged and forgotten in the official histories. In Thompson's hands, a new politics of writing history would emphasize the combined efforts of individuals – the cultural labour – that goes into the making of a class and the 'specific discourses that gave its members' lives their meaning' (Turner, 1990: 70).

Hoggart showed, in his major work *The Uses of Literacy* (1957), that an adequate approach for studying British working-class culture would have to be synthetic and holistic. He borrowed from literary study a way of 'reading' everyday working-class life as if it were a literary text, 'opening up the study of popular culture and applying the interpretive procedures of the humanities to the stuff of social science' (Gray and McGuigan, 1993: viii). Hoggart demonstrated the interconnections between material conditions of life, work and economy, and a range of cultural forms, relationships and lived experiences. Hoggart and Thompson inspired some remarkable writing on youth subcultures, an area that flourished with theoretical advances provoked by the women's movement and feminism and the incorporation of ethnographic methods from sociology and anthropology (CCCS, 1975; Morley, 1992).

Just as Hoggart had pushed beyond literary studies in order to do justice to his subject, Raymond Williams in *The Long Revolution* (1961) and *Culture and Society* (1958) trespassed the disciplinary borders established by his training in literature. Williams wanted to remake the study of culture within a political project which advocated an expansion of the term. The only way to organize against any diminishment of culture was to redefine culture beyond disciplinary limits in the arts, drama and literature, to conceive of culture as a 'whole way of life', and to study complex changes in cultural labour represented in politics, anthropology, history, economics, communication and any and all future sources.

In seeking such a synthesis, Williams opened up the holistic study of culture by resisting economic determinism – that is, the idea that the economy and economic institutions (money, markets, exchange, etc.) occupy a realm independent from politics and culture and have pre-eminent power to determine what happens in those other realms. While rejecting economic determinism, Williams was equally careful to avoid cultural determinism, or the idea that culture was an autonomous arena of activity in its own right with powers to determine outcomes in politics and the economy. Thus the hallmark of Williams's holistic approach was his quest for an integrated understanding of the political economy and culture. As he wrote:

> The pattern of meaning and values through which people conduct their whole lives can be seen for a time as autonomous, and as evolving within its own terms, but it is quite unreal, ultimately, to separate this pattern from a precise political and economic system, which can extend its influence into the most unexpected regions of feeling and behaviour (Williams, 1961: 139).

The identity of British cultural studies probably owes its greatest debt to the institutional base founded at the Centre for Contemporary Cultural Studies at the University of Birmingham by Richard Hoggart in 1964. Hoggart's successor was Stuart Hall, who wrote that the main task of CS was 'to provide ways of thinking, strategies for survival, and resources to all those who are now – in economic, political, and cultural terms – excluded from anything that could be called access to the national culture of the national community' (Hall, 1990: 22).

With Hall as director, the Centre moved British cultural studies in new theoretical and methodological directions. Most significant were critical analyses of race and gender, structuralist procedures for the study of ideology and media, and ethnographic procedures for the study of media audiences. Though influenced by the work of Williams and Hoggart, Hall would come to distinguish his approach by moving, with the 'structuralist turn', away from radical-humanism. Influenced by the writings of Louis Althusser, the French Marxist, Hall wrote that people imagine human actions to be free, or at least self-chosen, when in reality people live life within the limits of cultural frameworks and structured social roles and identities.

Hall was concerned to build a model which also accorded a realm of autonomous development to culture – specified as the historical work of signification, representation and ideology. In doing so, Hall never neglected the polity or economy, but instead he revised their status in relation to culture, to allow for their intermittent interconnection via ideology without any one realm decisively determining the other. These realms could be 'articulated' – i.e., linked *and* expressed in a provisional unity through ideological 'fixes' – with particular historical outcomes. However, they could never influence one another without the intervention of living and breathing people who are bearers of ideology (Hall, 1985).

Like Althusser, Hall incorporated into this model of ideology and subjectivity the work of the Italian Marxist writer, Antonio Gramsci, especially his notion of hegemony. Many CS writers have used this notion to understand the shifting alignments between ruling ideas and popular culture in capitalist democracies, where citizens supposedly give consent freely to ruling ideas as a matter of choice. Here again, the idea of 'articulation' becomes relevant. The aim of doing an analysis of cultural hegemony was to find out how 'common sense', or the moral and political standards of interpretation and judgement common in everyday life, could provide the basis for popular consent and political alignment to the preferences of the dominant culture. The practical political goal for the Left was to understand where to intervene in popular culture in order to take back the words and phrases of common sense, to foster revolutionary thought and break down the popular allegiances with the Right (the technical term for this politics of writing is 'rearticulation'). An exemplary text of CS coming out of this expansive period was *Policing the Crisis: Mugging, the State, and Law and Order,* which Hall and his co-authors said they wrote as an *'intervention* – albeit an intervention in the battleground of ideas' (Hall *et al.*, 1978: x).

Ironically, the structuralist modification of the category of lived experience downgraded human agency; for structuralists, the subject should be 'decentred'. Of course, experience could not be whisked away by a theoretical fiat, and thanks to a number of sources – especially feminist writers, critical analysts of racism, ethnographic fieldworkers and, more recently, queer theory – the structuralist abstraction from lived experience received numerous qualifications (Curran, Morley and Walkerdine, 1996).

Clearly, Hall and the writers who spent time at the Centre during the 1970s and 1980s sought to establish a discernible intellectual identity for CS by way of specifying culture as a separate object of study which was susceptible to a particular set of theoretical and methodological approaches. As Hall commented shortly before leaving the Centre, 'From this point onwards, cultural studies is no longer a dependent intellectual colony. It has a direction, an object of study, a set of themes and issues, a distinctive problematic of its own' (Hall, 1980a: 26).

Africa and Latin America

Beyond Britain, actual revolutions were much more immediate influences, as was the case in the formation of much cultural research in Latin America and Africa where writers linked national liberation struggles of the post-war period to new thinking about culture. Out of the growing resistance to US hegemony in world affairs came some of the early precursors of global CS in which a broad range of media, artistic and lived forms of culture were related to socio-economic conditions. Many of the resulting studies initiated another sort of 'cultural turn' aimed at gaining a better understanding of the cultural dimensions of imperialism.

For example, in his writing on the anti-colonial revolution in Algeria in the 1950s, Frantz Fanon developed a powerful analysis of how national identity and culture formed under colonial domination, revolution and in post-colonial periods (Fanon, 1959; 1963). Likewise, revolution in sub-Saharan Africa served as the catalyst for Amilcar Cabral, who led a successful revolution against the Portuguese in Guinea-Cape Verde, to envision national liberation as an act of culture. Writers such as Ngugi wa Thiong'o and Ngugi wa Mirii of Kenya and those at the Centre for Cultural and Media Studies at the University of Natal in South Africa have carried on this political tradition in African cultural studies, combining studies on the African experience of expropriation, exploitation and revolution with European CS (Miller, 1998: 40, 44–5; Schiller, 1996: 98–102).

The impact of revolutionary struggle is equally evident in the origins of Latin American cultural studies. The socialist ideals that informed the New Latin American Cinema, for example, nurtured a different kind of film-maker and media art and initiated an analysis of regional culture which moved beyond both disciplinary and national boundaries. Critical work in Chile between 1970 and 1973 under the Allende government flourished with many studies that foreshadowed British and US cultural studies. Of note are Michèle Mattelart's studies in the early 1970s on television audiences, popular magazines, pleasure and gender, including research she conducted with Mabel Piccini analysing the ways audiences make sense and derive pleasure from television in different working-class neighbourhoods in Santiago, Chile (Mattelart and Piccini, 1974).

Jesús Martín-Barbero has synthesized ground-breaking work of Latin American writers in combination with British cultural studies and continental theory (see below). Like Williams and Hoggart, Martín-Barbero's major work, *Communication, Culture, and Hegemony: From the Media to Mediations* (1993), attempts to build a holistic theory of culture. Using the idea of hegemony, Martín-Barbero modifies the radical critique of cultural imperialism in order to relate class divisions to processes of 'enculturation' at the national scale while demonstrating how such processes link to transnational processes of modernity and modernization. Martín-Barbero develops a notion of 'mediation', similar to Hall's idea of 'articulation', to explain how a multitude of national and transnational cultural forces intersect and link people's lives. A core concept, which is gaining wider recognition in cultural and communication studies, is Martín-Barbero's use of the process noun *mestizaje*. A *mestizo* is someone of mixed European and indigenous American descent, and *mestizaje* refers to the combination of European, African and indigenous American cultures in the matrix of Latin American memories, music, stories, languages, etc. The idea of *mestizaje* is similar to the postmodern notion of hybridity, about which another important writer in the

Latin American context, Néstor García Canclini, has written. However, both Martín-Barbero and García Canclini think of hybridity and *mestizaje* in terms that are specific to Latin Americans' experience of capitalism, modernity and social identity.

The United States of America

In the USA, CS did not grow directly out of a commitment to class or anti-imperialist struggles, but rather through a latent reaction to diverse influences such as the civil rights movement, the women's movement and feminism, the student movement, radical sociology and historiography, reform within literary studies, and resistance within communication studies and other social sciences to mainstream (cold and hot) war-related research. Also, the work of the 'Old Left' literary movement in the USA, which was animated by the US labour movement and anti-fascist struggles of the 1930s and 1940s, remained part of the reading list and the radical vocabulary of American cultural analysts.

However, CS in the USA was galvanized by the encounter with British cultural studies, which can be traced to the popularity of E.P. Thompson's writing among radicals and to American students who studied with Hoggart, Williams and Paddy Whannel, a co-author with Stuart Hall of an early CS text. Hall lectured in the USA, and his ideas spread in the 1980s through Lawrence Grossberg's work and teaching at the University of Illinois. John Fiske, who had published a high profile text of CS with John Hartley in the late 1970s, moved from Australia (where CS also burgeoned) to the USA to teach at the University of Wisconsin in the 1980s. Cultural studies' influence is also evident in such radical journals as *Jump Cut* and *Social Text*, where concerns with class, culture and power have been central. Cultural studies helped to open up US communication studies and other disciplines to a more materialist cultural analysis and, in those propitious times following the radicalism of the 1960s and 1970s, caused many young researchers to pay greater attention to the way in which class antagonisms and social stratification formed the stuff of culture.

Continental theory

In France and Italy, a different context of intellectual radicalism gave rise to an avant-garde of critics, film-makers and writers whose work CS would adapt and elaborate. In France, a strong current of cultural criticism emerged from the mix of literary studies, linguistics, psychoanalysis and anthropology. The key ingredient was a 'linguistic turn' which asserted that culture was analogous to the language, or languages, through which a nation speaks to itself. French writers, the most important of whom was

Roland Barthes (1915–80), developed in the 1950s and 1960s a systematic means of analysing culture-as-language (or text), borrowing and modifying the structural linguistic tools and terms of semiology. Semiology is the science of signs and of their arrangement into meaningful combinations (like words on this page or the visual elements of a photograph). This work maintained a critical edge throughout the 1960s and 1970s, influenced by the events and residual attitudes flowing from the student and worker rebellions of the 1960s in France and around the world. Semiology was incorporated into the structuralist model of CS with the English translations of Barthes in the late 1960s and eventually offered the set of analytical tools taken up by CS writers who specialized in textual analysis (Turner, 1990: 87).

In Italy, the 1950s were characterized by an extensive de-ruralization followed by internal migrations and sub-urbanization, and film-makers such as Pier Paolo Pasolini (1922–75) and writers such as Umberto Eco (1932–) inspired a radical retelling of Italian life to reflect the shock of Italy's transformation into an industrial power. The beginning of television inaugurated at the same time a new role for national media in the political life of industrial and metropolitan Italy. Worker and student radicalism grew throughout the 1960s, culminating in general strikes, violent student and police confrontations, and a massive demonstration at the visit of the US President, Richard Nixon. Interest in the specific forms and merits of television in the life of the nation grew in parallel to these events (Forgacs and Lumley, 1996). In the mid-1960s the state-run national broadcaster (RAI) commissioned Umberto Eco to write what became hailed as a seminal work of CS. The first English translation of Eco's article, 'Towards a Semiotic Inquiry into the Television Message', appeared in 1972 in the Birmingham Centre's *Working Papers in Cultural Studies*. The essay drew inspiration not only from semiological models in US pragmatism and French structuralism, but also from the national political context in which it was written. Eco showed an extremely high regard for the television audience's ability to rearrange audio and visual signs in a television text in order to create meaning which producers did not intend to be there. This 'aberrant decoding', as he called it, was homologous with the radicalism of Italian students and workers who persisted in decoding national politics and economic developments in ways that deviated from the mainstream.

The linguistic turn and textual analysis

Continental theory was systematically incorporated into work at the Birmingham Centre for Cultural Studies. The Centre produced a series of key textual analyses, starting in the early 1970s with Hall's famous essay on 'encoding/decoding' television discourse (Hall, 1980b). Like Eco, Hall examined how the meaning of a television text may in theory be decoded in ways that diverge from the intended message. Hall's method challenged mainstream communications models which, at the time, mostly thought of a message like a one-way telephone call that travelled from sender to receiver to be heard largely intact whatever static might be on the line. The method also challenged other critical semiotic/structuralist writers who, recognizing the power of codes in film and television texts, saw encoded ideology directly determining the consciousness of spectators.

Rejecting both sender-receiver and dominant ideology models, Hall instead focused on the semiotic elements of television texts that created conditions for a variety of readings (agency) within a limited range of possibilities (the structures) fixed by linguistic codes. The technical term for different reading possibilities in a single text is polysemy. Hall incorporated British sociologist Frank Parkin's work to theorize how these reading possibilities might link up to an audience's divergent social positions to produce particular ideological effects. There were three categories of social positions: the dominant-hegemonic positions, from which readers decoded the text in ways preferred by the dominant culture; the oppositional positions, which provided a reading context that resulted in alternative, even radical, decodings; and middle or 'negotiated' positions, from which readers produced all sorts of contradictory meanings. The latter positions, theorized Hall, were where the meaning of most television discourse ended up.

The ethnographic turn and intertextuality

Many specialists in textual analysis concluded that the encoding/decoding model could not say what an audience was actually thinking and doing in their encounters with media texts. After all, the reading positions were imaginary ones inferred from the television text by semiotic/structuralist logic. Some of these writers felt challenged to break free of text-specific work and began to look outside the text at actual audiences. These writers succeeded in demonstrating that CS needed to take an 'ethnographic turn'. For example, David Morley studied how the polysemy of the television text played out with actual viewers and found that there was no strict equivalence, nor complete randomness, between the textualized audience positions and an audience's readings (Morley, 1980, 1992).

A second group of writers took an opposite turn and dug deeper into polysemy and textuality. These writers explored how polysemy was constituted by intertextual references that left a text's meaning riven with traces of prior interpretive struggles which, in effect, made the text susceptible to divergent readings. Drawing again on the work of Roland Barthes, CS began to explore how polysemy provided the basis for understanding how pleasure could be derived from making meaning, a move which further impelled CS away from and well out of reach of both sender-receiver and dominant ideology models.

Pleasure

The ethnographic turn and the interest in textual pleasure made CS pay greater attention to intersubjective experience of popular culture. Writers such as John Fiske synthesized these insights with the Gramscian approach in order to link anthropological evidence of textual pleasure to political antagonisms within popular culture (Fiske, 1987). Fiske's synthesis, and those of other writers who initiated similar work, produced studies of fandom, shopping and television viewing during the 1980s and 1990s, reinforcing the institutional identity of CS and to a large extent relocating its institutional base to the USA.

The structuralist legacy hereafter made a qualified return to human agency. Nevertheless, events in political, cultural and economic realms were still set apart and thought of as contingent – i.e., always potentially linkable via articulation and intertextuality. Importantly, the common theme of this post-structuralist period involved the critique, not of capitalism *per se*, but of the humanistic perception of people as subjects with identities lying under the surface of national cultural artefacts, styles and traditions.

Power

The structuralist legacy in CS mutated again in work which elaborated on another French writer's theorizations of subjectivity, embodiment and power. Michel Foucault's enormous influence led CS to consider how supposedly autonomous realms of politics, economics and culture were articulated by common discourses. A discourse is a way of thinking, speaking and acting in the world which derives legitimacy and authority from modern social institutions such as the law, asylums, medicine, the prison, the school and the human sciences. Foucault's ideas encouraged CS writers to think about how such institutional discourses form part of everyday life in the modern world, particularly in the way they spread power down to the individual level. Rather than seeing politics organized on a grand scale of struggle against a centralized power, which mainstream social science located within the sovereign state, CS could analyse how a form of micro-politics can be organized around everyday and decentralized, or capillary, effects of power. Cultural studies became interested, for example, in the way in which so-called discursive practices defined people's self-knowledge as subjects who are sexualized, gendered, militarized, criminalized, intellectualized, racialized, professionalized and so on. Any one of these classifications made people's sameness and otherness intelligible while at the same time linking them to microsystems of power. Being raced, gendered and sexualized may help people make sense of who they and others are, but such elaborations of identity and difference are also subject to control within the institutional order of the dominant culture. This paradoxical link between identity and domination has been termed governmentality (govern-mentality). Cultural studies writers such as Toby Miller have studied the problem of governmentality to show how self-government and governing knowledges about the self can be understood as structuring the limits and possibilities of culture, power and experience (Miller, 1998).

Policy

Recently, cultural policy studies has emerged as a field within which CS has attempted to grow practical roots in order to ground its theoretical corpus. Cultural policy studies is represented by such writers as Tony Bennett, a co-founder of the Institute for Cultural Policy Studies at Griffith University in Brisbane, Australia, and now working in Britain at the Open University. Cultural policy studies proposes and formulates cultural programmes which can be implemented by government. This would not only test the value of cultural theory and analysis empirically, but would secure for CS a strategic position where it might have some impact on society. As a further motivation, cultural policy studies attempts to resurrect theoretical notions of human agency by proposing programmes which elevate the role of the citizen in cultural production.

CONCLUSION: MARKET PRESSURES AND PROBLEMS OF DIRECTION

In the forty or so years of their endeavours, CS writers have broadened the consideration of creative, critical and performative dimensions of human labour. They developed a politics of writing with a critical edge opposed to value-free inquiry and aimed at the heart of social conflict in capitalist societies. They sought to ensure that culture mattered within the revolutionary project of the Left while striking down an élitist view of culture as a nation's stock of high art, drama and literature. For CS, culture is made when political and moral constituencies fight to come into being, express themselves, gain recognition, and seek alliances with others. Culture is everywhere that political loyalties can be won or lost, where haves and have-nots compete over the interpretation of life, and where the spoils of victory include the power to define moral and aesthetic value.

Yet as CS became a presence within universities, scholarly organizations and the publishing industry, much of its writing became depoliticized under the pressures and limits of political economic realities in higher education. To begin with, being transdisciplinary has meant running the risk of being unintelligible within the confined and too often parochial world of the academy. In response, CS professors became increasingly professionalized and

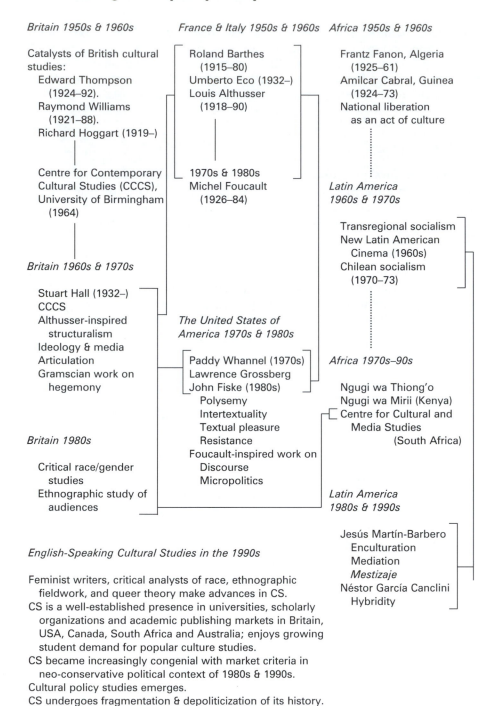

Britain 1950s & 1960s

Catalysts of British cultural
studies:
    Edward Thompson
      (1924–92).
    Raymond Williams
      (1921–88).
    Richard Hoggart (1919–)

Centre for Contemporary
Cultural Studies (CCCS),
University of Birmingham
(1964)

Britain 1960s & 1970s

Stuart Hall (1932–)
CCCS
Althusser-inspired
    structuralism
Ideology & media
Articulation
Gramscian work on
    hegemony

Britain 1980s

Critical race/gender
    studies
Ethnographic study of
    audiences

France & Italy 1950s & 1960s

Roland Barthes
    (1915–80)
Umberto Eco (1932–)
Louis Althusser
    (1918–90)

1970s & 1980s
Michel Foucault
    (1926–84)

*The United States of
America 1970s & 1980s*

Paddy Whannel (1970s)
Lawrence Grossberg
John Fiske (1980s)
    Polysemy
    Intertextuality
    Textual pleasure
    Resistance
Foucault-inspired work on
    Discourse
    Micropolitics

Africa 1950s & 1960s

Frantz Fanon, Algeria
    (1925–61)
Amilcar Cabral, Guinea
    (1924–73)
National liberation
    as an act of culture

*Latin America
1960s & 1970s*

Transregional socialism
New Latin American
    Cinema (1960s)
Chilean socialism
    (1970–73)

Africa 1970s–90s

Ngugi wa Thiong'o
Ngugi wa Mirii (Kenya)
Centre for Cultural and
    Media Studies
      (South Africa)

*Latin America
1980s & 1990s*

Jesús Martín-Barbero
    Enculturation
    Mediation
    Mestizaje
Néstor García Canclini
    Hybridity

English-Speaking Cultural Studies in the 1990s

Feminist writers, critical analysts of race, ethnographic
    fieldwork, and queer theory make advances in CS.
CS is a well-established presence in universities, scholarly
    organizations and academic publishing markets in Britain,
    USA, Canada, South Africa and Australia; enjoys growing
    student demand for popular culture studies.
CS became increasingly congenial with market criteria in
    neo-conservative political context of 1980s & 1990s.
Cultural policy studies emerges.
CS undergoes fragmentation & depoliticization of its history.

Figure 20.1   Cultural studies: origins and innovations

departmentalized, adopting well-defined academic identities. In making such adjustments, CS became fragmented, less politically engaged and increasingly susceptible to conservative politics.

The attempt to make CS intelligible within established departments has diluted CS's radical social theory and critique of capitalism. This trend has been compounded during CS's lifetime by the increasingly dominant influence of the political Right in national and global affairs. Today's neo-conservative political context and the attendant (neo-liberal) contraction of public funding for education, public services and cultural works, along with the crisis of the welfare state and socialism, have compelled CS researchers and writers to find new ways to reform their critique to make it congenial with the perceived demands of culture and education organized by market criteria. At the same time, the growing student demand for popular culture studies, combined with the neo-liberal discourse that thinks of students as retail customers, has turned CS into something of a growth industry within universities and academic publishing, at least in the English-speaking world. Without a doubt, this burgeoning enterprise has led to important advances in the study of popular cultures in each field worked by CS. But the prevailing fragmentation and market orientation have also served to reinforce CS's conservatism and to depoliticize its history by elevating its theoretical advances and diminishing the importance of class struggle and emancipatory social movements.

This turn of events should not discourage newcomers to the field, but instead convince you of the importance of reading more about the radical history of CS and becoming involved in renewing the critique of capitalism that gave CS the basis for its most significant contributions to the study of culture and social change.

SUMMARY

- Cultural studies is a politics of writing which aims to heighten awareness and understanding of the present conditions and possible purposes of cultural labour.
- Cultural studies has many international origins, most of which conceived of CS from within labour, women's, civil rights, national liberation or other emancipatory social movements.
- Cultural studies owes its institutional identity to the work done at the Centre for Contemporary Cultural Studies at the University of Birmingham (now the Department of Cultural Studies and Sociology).
- Cultural studies embraces a number of critical intellectual schools, including Marxism, feminism, critical analysis of race, structuralism and post-structuralism.
- Over the years, CS has yielded to the pressures of market influences and conservative ideologies, blunting its former political motivations.

FURTHER READING

A number of excellent collections introduce readers to theories and examples of CS writing:

Curran, James, Morley, David and Walkerdine, Valerie (eds) (1996) *Cultural Studies and Communications*. London: Edward Arnold.

Dirks, Nicholas, Eley, Geoff and Ortner, Sherry (eds) (1994) *Culture/Power/History: A Reader in Contemporary Social Theory*. Princeton, NJ: Princeton University Press.

During, Simon (1993) *The Cultural Studies Reader*. London: Routledge.

Gray, Ann and McGuigan, Jim (eds) (1993) *Studying Culture: An Introductory Reader*. London: Edward Arnold.

Grossberg, Lawrence, Nelson, Cary, and Treichler, Paula A. (eds) (1992) *Cultural Studies*. London: Routledge

REFERENCES

CCCS (Centre for Contemporary Cultural Studies) (1975) *Resistance through Ritual. Working Papers in Cultural Studies 7/8*. Summer. Birmingham: CCCS/University of Birmingham.

Curran, James, Morley, David and Walkerdine, Valerie (eds) (1996) *Cultural Studies and Communications*. London: Edward Arnold.

Eco, Umberto (1972) 'Towards a Semiotic Inquiry into the Television Message' (first published in 1965), *Working Papers in Cultural Studies*. Birmingham: Centre for Contemporary Cultural Studies.

Fanon, Frantz (1959) *This is the Voice of Algeria*. Paris: F. Maspero. Reprinted (1965) in *A Study in Dying Colonialism*, trans. Haaken Chevalier. New York: Monthly Review Press.

Fanon, Frantz (1963) *Wretched of the Earth*, trans. Constance Farrington. New York: Grove Press.

Forgacs, David and Lumley, Robert (eds) (1996) *Italian Cultural Studies: An Introduction*. Oxford: Oxford University Press.

Fiske, John (1987) *Television Culture*. New York: Routledge.

Gray, Ann and McGuigan, Jim (eds) (1993) *Studying Culture: An Introductory Reader*. London: Edward Arnold.

Hall, Stuart (1980a) 'Cultural Studies and the Centre: Some Problematics and Problems', in Stuart Hall, Dorothy Hobson, Andrew Lowe and Paul Willis (eds) *Culture, Media, Language*. London: Hutchinson, pp. 15–47.

Hall, Stuart (1980b) 'Encoding/Decoding', in Stuart Hall, Dorothy Hobson, Andrew Lowe and Paul Willis (eds) *Culture, Media, Language*. London: Hutchinson, pp. 128–38.

Hall, Stuart (1985) 'Signification, Representation, Ideology: Althusser and the Post-Structuralist Debates', *Critical Studies in Mass Communication*, **2**: 99–114.

Hall, Stuart (1990) 'The Emergence of Cultural Studies and the Crisis of the Humanities', *October*, **53**: 11–23.

Hall, Stuart, Chritcher, Chas, Jefferson, Tony, Clarke, John and Roberts, Brian (1978) *Policing the Crisis: Mugging, the State, and Law and Order*. New York: Holmes and Meier.

Hoggart, Richard (1957) *The Uses of Literacy*. London: Chatto and Windus.

Martín-Barbero, Jesús (1993) *Communication, Culture, and Hegemony: From the Media to Mediations*, trans. Elizabeth Fox. Thousand Oaks, CA: Sage Publications.

Mattelart, Michèle and Mabel Piccini (1974) 'La Televisión y los Sectores Populares', *Comunicación y Cultura* (Buenos Aires) 2 March. Reprinted as 'Chile: Political Formation and the Critical Reading of Television', in Armand Mattelart and Seth Siegelaub (eds) (1983) *Communication and Class Struggle 2: Liberation, Socialism*, trans. David Buxton. New York: International General, pp. 76–83.

Miller, Toby (1998) *Technologies of Truth: Cultural Citizenship and the Popular Media*. Minneapolis: University of Minnesota Press.

Morley, David (1980) *The 'Nationwide' Audience*. London: British Film Institute.

Morley, David (1992) *Television, Audiences, and Cultural Studies*. London: Routledge.

Schiller, Dan (1996) *Theorizing Communication*. New York: Oxford University Press.

Thompson, Edward P. (1963) *The Making of the English Working Class*. New York: Vintage Books.

Turner, Graeme (1990) *British Cultural Studies: An Introduction*. Boston: Unwin Hyman.

Williams, Raymond (1958) *Culture and Society, 1780–1950*. London: Chatto and Windus.

Williams, Raymond (1961) *The Long Revolution*. London: Chatto and Windus.

Chapter 21

Intellectuals

Carl Boggs

One of the main preoccupations of contemporary social theory has been to conceptualize the ever-shifting role of intellectuals within a transformative process that spans pre-modern, modern and 'post-modern' phases of development. As understood here, intellectuals constitute far more than an assemblage of Great Thinkers past and present: defined in the most general sense as mental workers, they have come to occupy distinctly *structural* positions, carrying out a variety of social and political functions that can have important, sometimes decisive historical consequences.

In advanced industrial societies intellectuals enter into many diverse roles, from professionals, scientists, writers and artists, to technical and cultural workers, politicians and leading figures within popular movements. Their functions are performed across broad spheres of work, culture, social life and politics, helping in many ways to either reproduce or challenge the dominant ideologies. Such intellectual functions, however, may turn out to be more highly diffuse in the modern setting in so far as they incorporate the mental activity of the vast majority of human beings who in varying degrees participate in the social world. It is possible to argue, following the dictum of Antonio Gramsci, that each person in modern society is in some sense an intellectual and philosopher since almost everyone upholds a specific view of the world, 'has a conscious line of moral conduct, and therefore contributes to sustain a conception of the world or to modify it, that is, to bring into being new modes of thought.' This viewpoint suggests that 'although one can speak of intellectuals, one cannot speak of non-intellectuals because non-intellectuals do not exist' (Gramsci, 1971: 9). Gramsci adds that not everyone has the capacity to carry out *particular* intellectual functions; not everyone can be a critic or philosopher or political leader, or even a professional. The central argument here is not that all people are intellectuals on equal footing, but that intellectual activities have been so widely dispersed in modern society that the old distinction between learned aristocratic élites and the great uneducated masses has progressively broken down; knowledge and information are today more broadly dispersed than ever – an outgrowth of the rapid expansion of mental labour, the rise of mass education, the spread of informational technology, the enormous influence of mass media and greater accessibility of popular culture.

THE TRANSFORMATION OF INTELLECTUALS

The type of intellectual prevalent in pre-industrial society was the detached, genteel cleric or scholar who was able to monopolize traditional forms of discourse. While generally appearing in some sense to stand 'above' class divisions, this stratum was the bearer of diverse ideologies that served to justify aristocratic power, the monarchy and the Church. With the onset of revolutionary turbulence in late eighteenth and nineteenth-century Europe, however, traditional intellectuals often gave way, at certain historical junctures, to what might be called the 'Jacobin' mode of intellectual whose political debut came with the French Revolution and whose leadership role in countries like Italy and Russia was later also decisive. Jacobinism became part of both the liberal and Marxist traditions despite a profound hostility toward élitist and statist approaches common to both ideologies, and it shaped fascist and Stalinist experiences of the twentieth century. As might have been expected, the revolt against Jacobinism moved in a variety of theoretical and political directions, including anarchism, syndicalism, council communism and Western Marxism – all of which reaffirmed the primacy of popular self-activity and mass spontaneity (and thereby also sharply devalued the role of critical intellectuals). One of the most sophisticated responses to the authoritarian impact of Jacobinism was Gramsci's now famous theory of 'organic' intellectuals, which turned out to be rather consistent with Marx's own (less-developed) approach to the role of intellectuals in historical development. Writing in the years after the First World War, Gramsci began to theorize the role of an intellectual grouping that could transcend the extremes of both Jacobinism and spontaneism, that could be transformative yet grounded in everyday working-class experience.

The predominant intellectual type of the modern period, however, belongs to a *technocratic* stratum that typically accompanies high levels of industrialization and the rationalization of social life. This stratum has become the locus of an Enlightenment rationality rooted in the centrality of science and technology as the historical basis of human progress, the repository of such universal values as freedom, democracy, community and justice. Situated primarily within the state system, big business, universities, the military, mass media and culture industry, technocratic intellectuals carry forward basic features of the *status quo*: hierarchy, commodity production, efficiency, a commitment to economic growth, and so forth (Boggs, 1993: ch. 5). Frequently emerging out of and against this grouping is a *critical* intelligentsia located in higher education, the mass media and the arts but confined mainly to local spheres of influence. It is the mounting conflict between technocratic and critical intellectuals that shapes the cultural terrain of post-Fordist society – a conflict shaped by the endemic stresses and dysfunctions of the industrial order (Gouldner, 1976). Taking this epochal transformation into account, one can no longer argue, in the tracks of the Frankfurt School, that rationalization always and everywhere implies a system of total domination in which oppositional ideologies (and critical intellectual activity) are totally absorbed. The reality is that the crisis of modernity, or what might be called the shift towards conditions of post-modernity, opens up new fissures in the power structure that technocratic élites have been unable to seal. If the great complexity of post-Fordist social and political structures undermines any potential role for Jacobin (not to mention traditional) intellectuals, the likelihood of increasing *critical* tendencies has to be taken more seriously, especially in the wake of strong globalizing pressures.

A series of challenges to modernity has disrupted prospects for a totally administered system, while at the same time the historic linkage between universal belief-systems (communism, socialism, liberalism, nationalism) and political action has increasingly deteriorated since the 1960s. If power remains concentrated in the State, corporations and the military, ideological discourses and forms of knowledge have become more dispersed, localized and fragmented. In this post-modern milieu universities, the media and popular culture emerge as contested social and ideological arenas even as they become more vulnerable to various rationalizing and professionalizing influences. Conflict between the technocracy and local sites of resistance has generated the nucleus of a critical intellectual subculture; modernity is punctured by the very reality of fragmented discourses in which critical intellectual work thrives even in the midst of globalization. In part this results from the unravelling of Fordist-Keynesian strategies that prevailed throughout the post-war years, in part from the impact of corporate colonization, generalized bureaucratic power, and the expanded culture industry which, taken together, have completely transformed social life.

Theorists as diverse as Gramsci, George Lukacs and Max Weber agreed that modernity would eventually give rise to a new ideological paradigm – technological rationality – that would reshape the contours of education, culture, social life and politics. As Gramsci put it: 'In the modern world, technological education, closely bound to industrial labor even at the most primitive and unqualified level, must form the basis of a new type of intellectual' (Gramsci, 1971: 35). Contemporary Europe, of course, far transcends anything Gramsci could have observed in Italy during the 1930s.

Still, the consequences he projected from his understanding of the celebrated 'American' model, inspired by Taylorist scientific management in the USA, turned out to be valid enough. As he anticipated, the emergence of large-scale corporations, expansion of governmental power, growth of a massive technological labour force and wide diffusion of technological values all contributed to the development of a 'new type of intellectual'. Modernity has thus brought into being conditions favouring the increased assimilation of intellectual roles and functions, involving the spread of specialized knowledge and skills, the growing importance of mental work and the dissemination of ideological and cultural values, within the institutional framework of industrialized society. As Edward Shils was probably the first to observe, this absorption process can be viewed as the natural outgrowth of industrialization (Shils, 1972: 13). The reliance of modern structures on science and technology, on the entire knowledge industry and informational system, suggests that the technocratic intellectual *qua* worker will increasingly take up a dominant position not only in the apparatus of production but in most other areas of public life. Yet if modernity serves to empower this new stratum of intellectuals as technicians and experts, as conveyors of professionalized knowledge, the very process of rationalization tends to restrict their creative and political autonomy.

THE RISE OF ACADEMIC PROFESSIONALISM

Modernity has undeniably given rise to an expanded stratum of rationalizing intellectuals attached to Enlightenment values of reason, secularism, technological progress and mastery of nature; this stratum has been at the centre of industrialization. From a distinctly *political* standpoint, however, the great influence of this stratum has been bought at a rather steep price in so far as modern intellectuals have lost their global capacity to reshape society, to transform the world in accordance with time-honoured Platonic notions of an ideal society. The Jacobin type of intellectual was freed from the limits of church authority, inherited beliefs and traditions, even social or material obstacles, capable of acting upon some kind of evangelical mission. But modernity, as we have seen, imposes a whole new set of restraints on intellectual autonomy in the form of technology, large-scale organization, norms of professionalism, and so forth.

A major locus of such restraints is the university which, in an era of technocratic mass education, has absorbed more and more intellectual functions into its domain. Nowhere has the impact of modernization been more deeply felt than in the realm of higher education, where the traditional intellectuals (classical scholars, philosophers, clerics, literary figures, etc.) have been increasingly replaced by a technocratic intelligentsia organically tied to the knowledge industry, the corporate economy and the State. While conventional (liberal, conservative) wisdom views the university as an autonomous sphere where truth and knowledge can be dispassionately sought, in modern society higher education has become fully integrated into a matrix of institutionalized power relations. The ideal of a self-enclosed community of scholars subordinated only to higher values of reason and justice – the sort celebrated by Alan Bloom in his *Closing of the American Mind* – today stands as a relic of pre-industrial or early industrial systems (Bloom, 1987). In material terms, the university facilitates capital accumulation by generating necessary forms of labour power, carrying out tax-supported research and development, and helping absorb surplus labour. Ideologically, academic institutions are a vital source of legitimation: they socialize large sectors of the population (teachers, students, administrators, professionals, etc.) into system-reproducing values such as competitive individualism, deference to expertise and social discipline. Scholarly work, classroom social relations and professionalism within the university are all integral to economic and bureaucratic interests that daily replicate the division of labour existing beneath the liberal, pluralistic veneer of modernity.

Like the scientific rationality that underpins it, modern professionalism flows from an Enlightenment optimism which upholds a dynamic role and elevated status for intellectuals. First inspired by the French *Philosophes*, the concept of a professional intellectual offered hope for an accumulated reservoir of knowledge that would, in stops and starts, eventually propel humanity towards social progress. By the twentieth century, in a world characterized by omnipresent change and conflict, by widespread fear of social or political breakdown, the growth of a professional stratum was often seen (at least by élites) as a source of institutional strength and continuity – a strong counterweight to crisis tendencies inherent in capitalism. Over time, the professional intellectuals won privileged status within the division of labour – a position from which they could advance their own interests on the basis of their monopoly of knowledge and expertise, social standing and bureaucratic leverage. Professions evolved into vast empires of institutional and economic control in virtually every sphere: medicine, law, academia, mass media, business and of course science. As Thomas Haskell wrote, 'as a remedy to the problem of self-interest in the market society, professionalism was very much a matter of fighting fire with fire, competition in one dimension with competition in another, self-interest of one kind with self-interest of another kind' (Haskell, 1984: 219).

The process of rationalization that gave birth to a technocratic intelligentsia simultaneously reinforced state-corporate domination over civil society. Capital accumulation, bureaucratization and growth of a professional stratum were all part of the same historical dynamic, one that was shaped and controlled by 'corporate rationalizers' who had the power to set broad agendas. While specialized expertise was naturally essential to economic development, the autonomy of mental work was severely restricted because such expertise was mobilized around larger interests, part of what Charles Derber calls 'integrative professionalism' (much along the lines of Clark Kerr's famous vision of the 'multiversity') (Derber, 1982: 201; Kerr, 1965: 38–59). The professional norms of universality, openness and creativity were easily undermined by a power structure that was always suspicious of such norms, but loss of autonomy never really compromised the intellectuals' privileged status within the professional-managerial stratum. In fact the technocratic intellectuals' rise to prominence came precisely at the historic moment when liberal ideology was disintegrating as a popular belief-system (Larson, 1984: 30–2).

The technocratic, yet fragmented world of academic life militates against development of a common public discourse within which intellectuals could address the larger philosophical and social concerns which have preoccupied human beings throughout history. The esoteric codes of specialists, while perhaps appropriate to the technical requirements of modernization, seem ill-suited to the task of grasping complex social problems that demand creative political intervention (Winner, 1986: pt 1). For one thing, the refusal to entertain broader, holistic frames of reference contradicts efforts to establish linkages across fields (and subfields) of research and study. The territorial impulse and obscure language of hyperspecialization favour insular, provincial, sometimes fiercely competitive styles of work often detached from everyday social life. Out of belief that the road to enlightenment lies in a patient, unbiased accumulation of facts, academic culture strives for ever-greater rigour, objectivity, even predictability, aided by sophisticated technology that seemingly renders the troublesome detours of philosophical or historical reflection superfluous. The intelligentsia was, historically, a stratum immersed in forms of discourse that addressed the *meaning* of social existence, that explored the deep questions of history, politics, religion and aesthetics even if such discourses rarely extended into the popular realm. Modernity ultimately served to transform all this by paving the way towards an institutional setting where, as Michael Ghiselin notes, the enterprise of philosophy became a profession and logic itself 'has become a jargon, a means of obfuscation, a language of pedantry, not scholarship . . .' (Ghiselin, 1989: 189). Thus the technological underpinnings of higher education not only instrumentalize theoretical discourse but work to depoliticize intellectual activity in general. In the modern university empirical and formal work dwells upon a range of phenomena that is most readily measurable – elections, opinion surveys, growth rates, productivity levels, etc. – while excluding a wide range of 'ideological' or 'normative' discourses that do not fit mainstream technocratic assumptions.

For conservative writers like Bloom this conundrum results from a general malaise of intellectual and cultural life, from the absence of discourses related to human values, which typifies scholarly work in the modern university. The destruction of academic community comes less from the incessant pressures of technological rationality than from various contaminating influences *outside* that structure. In Bloom's view, the New Left and counterculture opened the university to turbulent manifestations of public opinion, with the passions of immediate political action substituting for calm and reasoned intellectual discourse. Because 'the sixties were the period of dogmatic answers and trivial tracts', the longstanding distinction between educated and lay public broke down; obsession with social 'relevance' and political ideologies gave rise to a simplistic and vulgar intellectual discourse (Bloom, 1987: 322). Bloom's critique reflects the nostalgia for a past when traditional intellectual work could be carried out in a relatively self-contained, autonomous setting, where contemplative life could flourish without bothersome intrusions of social and political demands. This turns out to be a hopelessly utopian vision in so far as it is thoroughly abstracted from the context of modernity that so fully shapes academic life. The conservative stance is turned upside-down by Russell Jacoby, whose similarly pessimistic conclusions are more more solidly grounded in the actual technocratic predicament of higher education in post-Fordist society. Inspired by a Marcusean emphasis on technological rationality, Jacoby argues that the growing impoverishment of intellectual life results from a profoundly *declining* public sphere in the academy, where prevailing styles of mental work have been incorporated into the professional structure. Public intellectuals who once took up significant issues before a general audience – and who wrote in literate, intelligible prose – have vanished from the scene, giving way to the more esoteric specialists. With smaller and more insular audiences confined to small enclaves of academic initiates, the range of debate inevitably shrinks, destroying conditions needed to sustain a critical public intelligentsia (Jacoby, 1987). Whereas Bloom laments the disappearance of an autonomous, contemplative *traditional* intellectual stratum, Jacoby sees just the opposite: the waning of committed, modern *critical* intellectuals who could bring their talents and insights to bear on urgent social problems.

With only a few exceptions, the modern university stands far removed from the chaotic, politicized, menacing world that Bloom observes and fears: the dominant pattern is in fact more one of privatized competition, intense professionalism, depoliticization – all hallmarks of a technocratic intelligentsia. Most academic fields of study have less to say about the world even as their 'methodologies', texts and narratives become ever more technologically sophisticated and rigorous. At the same time, Jacoby's implicit alternative model of élite individual thinkers immersed in their own independent sphere of discourse – something akin to the Great Thinkers – seems likewise nostalgic, for it downplays both the obstacles and the new possibilities already present in the transformed situation of post-Fordism. For Bloom, vague historical forces undermine the detached, comfortable life of the intellectual typical of pre-industrial, gentlemanly scholars at Oxford and Cambridge; ferment in the real world intrudes upon their peaceful search for knowledge and meaning. For Jacoby, the academicization of intellectual work (including the work of Marxists and others on the Left) has created a stratum of bureaucratic professionals and technicians cut off from the flow of social forces outside the university. If both embrace romanticized versions of an independent intellectual, they also agree – quite correctly, but for entirely different reasons – that authentic rational inquiry has been under assault within the public sphere.

The modern university has become more interwoven with corporate, state and military structures, partly in response to the demands for new sources of knowledge and legitimation. Since the 1950s it has been *de rigueur* for planners in higher education to link their agendas to a variety of systemic objectives: corporate marketing and advertising, military research and development, techniques for assisting in administrative efficiency and control, foreign intelligence, and so forth. Universities have been in the forefront of developing new technologies that could help displace human labour-power. Indeed, the bulk of research that is sponsored within academia has been funded by either the government or corporations, which suggests that élite interests ultimately play an enormous role in shaping the course of supposedly neutral modes of scholarly inquiry. Further, such funding rarely flows in the direction of projects that might be viewed as too critical or nonconformist; more often, the money goes to support research around established priorities, including above all those oriented towards technology and the most sophisticated informational tools (Zelewski, 1997). In this milieu the overpowering influence of economic interest, of moneyed research – working in tandem with the specialized modes of discourse – functions to obscure any intellectual commitment to distinctly public concerns or goals; the university becomes a locus of both technocratic and commodified paradigms of institutional activity.

CRITICAL VERSUS TECHNOCRATIC INTELLECTUALS

Although the technocratic intelligentsia occupies an indispensable position in the high-tech global economy and informational revolution, its hegemonic role is by no means unassailable, especially in view of certain authoritarian and destructive consequences of technology itself. Moreover, if intellectual functions have been increasingly appropriated by the university, mass media and government, these arenas are hardly monolithic – nor can they possibly colonize every realm of mental work. Post-Fordist society is permeated with ferment and struggle, involving sustained (and most often *local*) efforts to carve out social as well as intellectual modes of autonomy. Today critical intellectual activity is no longer the domain of élite strata, whether among the traditional learned groupings or some type of Jacobin or quasi-Jacobin vanguard. While rationalization serves to resolve or at least stave off crisis tendencies within capitalism, the process itself ultimately generates new sources of social cleavage and conflict. On the one hand, an expanded modern intelligentsia carries out functions designed to reproduce existing class relations and culture; it seeks to maintain a privileged status by means of its ability to monopolize intellectual capital. In many ways it has become an integral part of the structure of domination. Thus, as André Gorz notes, 'the subcultures of science and technology remain narrow, fragmented, and divorced from general life and culture because their subject matter, the means and processes of production, are themselves separated and alienated from the people' (Gorz, 1976: 166). At the same time, as Gouldner insists, the new intellectuals are not merely the repository of technocratic ideology; their education, skills and social awareness all instil the desire for open, emancipatory forms of discourse that bring them into conflict with hierarchical authority. Never fully assimilated into the main centres of power and often denied genuine creativity, these intellectuals have a vested interest in critical dialogue and democratic participation that, however, is often compromised by their privileged role and élitist world-view (Gouldner, 1979). From this standpoint, modern intellectuals can best be understood as the locus of many conflicting pressures and identities rather than as a single cohesive social formation.

In advanced industrial society, as Alain Touraine suggests, there is perpetual conflict between the imperatives of organizational domination and the struggle for personal or social autonomy, between the opposing thrusts of bureaucratic control and democratization, and this epochal conflict enters into and deeply influences every realm of life (Touraine, 1971). Touraine's view of social change converges in many ways with that of Michel Foucault. In Foucault's perspective, modern society is structured around particular 'discursive formations' and rules of communication that shape a wide range of intellectual practices. In so far as most discourses are tightly bound up with both the attainment of knowledge and the exercise of power, they are necessarily interwoven with the requirements of social control. In a rationalized milieu the far-reaching autonomy of intellectual life is profoundly restricted since discourses, being extensively immersed in power relations, function to sustain institutional order and popular consensus. Professional and managerial intellectuals are entrusted with vital tasks such as providing expertise, making key decisions and mobilizing public opinion.

None the less, intellectual life is permeated with deep tensions as the rules of hegemonic discourse run up against demands for open, critical forms of communication: the result is that intellectuals are frequently caught in an explosive vortex of conflicting pressures and interests. The tensions and contradictions of modernity – and the subsequent rise of post-modernity – produce a diffusion of critical intellectual functions that conflict dramatically with all other types – traditional, Jacobin and technocratic. In the course of history critical intellectuals have adopted an oppositional stance towards established authority, traditions and values, but they were usually marginalized either as Great Thinkers or as representatives of scattered ideological tendencies (sceptics, nonconformists, radicals, free spirits, prophets and iconoclasts of varying types). The critical impulse in recent times has involved questioning codes of discourse rooted in hegemonic ideologies. Such critical intellectual activity, however, has rarely forged any durable stratum or movement that might leave its own distinct political legacy. In the twentieth century there has been a series of independent, critical legacies which have left their historical imprint – anarchism, neo-Marxism, critical theory, feminism, ecology and surrealism, for example – all of which entered, in one form or another, the orbit of new social movements during the 1970s and 1980s. The critical intellectual vocation in modern society has been celebrated by such theorists as Gramsci, Luxemburg, Sartre, Marcuse, Gouldner, Freire, Chomsky and Said.

In Edward Said's view, the critical intellectual is one who works assiduously to break down stereotypes and myths, who dismantles all forms of reductivist, abstract, categorical thought which so harshly restricts genuine human freedom and creativity. Critical thinking fights against the power of gods, all-encompassing narratives and 'sacred texts'; it goes 'beyond the easy certainties provided us by our background' (Said, 1996: xiv). From this standpoint the critical intellectual appears as an outsider, a nonconformist, a troublemaker who resists the inducements of ego, status and worldly power in favour of the 'engaged self' who interrogates all traditions and forms of received wisdom. Said laments the decline of such intellectual life in a technocratic world that invests little value in the vocation of critics. Thus: 'the space for individual and subjective representation, for asking questions and challenging the wisdom of a war or an immense social program . . . has shrunk dramatically from what it was a hundred years ago . . .' (Said, 1996: 82). Yet the need for such critical intervention is probably greater than ever, for which Said turns towards the ideal of 'amateurism' – risky ventures into the public sphere. In a similar vein, Noam Chomsky looks to critical intellectuals as uncompromising seekers of truth and knowledge, who stand up to power and 'speak the truth and expose lies' (Chomsky, 1967: 325). This obligation is especially pressing in the modern world, where a greater number of intellectuals than ever before are materially privileged, have more access to information, can take advantage of relatively free speech, and often have a ready public forum for their views (the university, mass media, cultural arena, etc.). Thus:

> Intellectuals are in a position to expose the lies of governments, to analyze actions according to their causes and motives and often hidden intentions . . . For a privileged minority, Western democracy provides the leisure, the facilities, and the training to seek the truth lying hidden beneath the veil of distortion and misrepresentation, ideology, and class interest through which events of current history are presented to us (Chomsky, 1967: 324).

The appearance of a critical intelligentsia is made possible by a number of historical conditions: mass education and the enlarged role of the university, increased demand for mental and technical labour, the intensification of social contradictions (class, bureaucratic, ecological, etc.) and the growth of popular movements. But this intelligentsia does not emerge from, and cannot be reduced to, any single or particular class location; it often evolves from the ranks of the professional élite (Gouldner), technical workers or the 'new working class' (Gorz, 1967), marginals and 'outsiders' (Marcuse, 1964; Sartre, 1963), or simply dispersed individual thinkers (as in the representations of Chomsky and Said). In some cases they might be 'organically' connected to broad popular movements (as Gramsci had earlier theorized), where the 'critical' element presumably would take on new meaning. In any event, a critical intellectual stratum has indeed flourished in post-Fordist conditions, generally in the form of influential cultural, literary or political figures immersed in the work of journals, projects, institutes, grassroots campaigns and movements. But such intellectuals never constitute a distinct class or social bloc in so far as their interests, culture, lifestyles and interests vary and sometimes conflict enormously; they do not exercise their own unique impact on historical change, but can emerge as a transformative force only within the complex interplay of larger social forces. In the final analysis, further expansion of a critical intelligentsia (however defined) depends upon an enlarged public sphere where open dialogue, free speech, and popular access to the networks of information and communication are possible – conditions that are hardly facilitated by post-Fordist structures of domination.

THE POST-MODERN SHIFT

The deepening crisis of modernity – reflected in the growth of bureaucracy, the commodification of social life, the destructive impact of industrialization and pervasive feelings of alienation and disempowerment – has given rise to multiple and dispersed centres of resistance (see Laclau and Mouffe, 1985: ch. 2). Critical intellectuals have assumed a key role in the historical process, embracing a different set of agendas in the universities, mass media, popular culture, grassroots projects and social movements. So too have organic intellectuals, though surely in different ways and in different locales than what Gramsci has in mind when he upheld the potential of a distinctly *proletarian* intelligentsia ready to assist the working class in its struggle for ideological hegemony. Of course, modern circumstances depart fundamentally from what Gramsci and other Marxists confronted seventy years and more ago in a Europe where capitalism had yet to mature. If the theme of organic intellectuals retains any currency today, the idea of a unified proletariat mobilized around a global theory as the essence of such a formation has become obsolete given a class structure that is far more complex and diversified along with social and ideological conditions typically understood as 'post-modern'. The very subversion of modernity suggests that social change will most likely pass through a series of local or micro encounters where sites of resistance become increasingly decentred (Castells, 1984; Laclau and Mouffe, 1985). Since the late 1960s feminism has given expression to multiple discourses and struggles that clearly fit this new pattern and help define the contours of a new (non-technocratic, critical, possibly organic) intellectual stratum.

With its emphasis on pluralism, local knowledge, autonomy and identity, post-modernism naturally lends itself to a celebration of free-flowing, open, critical dialogue. By definition, the post-modern outlook indulges an intellectual probing of entrenched power structures and their legitimating ideologies (including liberalism and nationalism no less than Marxism or socialism). However, because of the shifting, ambiguous, and always provisional character of post-modern motifs, the *political* significance of critical intellectuals in the post-Fordist setting turns out to be extremely problematic. Clearly this is one of the great dilemmas of the famous post-modern shift: turbulence, conflict and change do not logically point towards any specific mode of historical transformation or type of political outcome. While post-modernism might correspond to the emergence of a broadened public sphere, the idea that critical interrogations or oppositional insurgencies will cohere within a viable social bloc is much harder to sustain (Heskin, 1991).

Whatever the immediate fate of critical (and organic) intellectuals in post-Fordist society, transformed historical conditions have pierced the hegemonic armour not only of technocratic intellectuals but also of Jacobin intellectuals in their multiple ideological guises. Further, the legacy of intellectual élites as the repository of humane, rational and progressive values rooted in the Enlightenment, with its facile equation of power, knowledge and social progress, seems to have been fatally undermined by the onset of ecological crisis (Ophuls, 1997). Under these circumstances, as Gramsci anticipated, the powerful effects of both modernity and post-modernity sooner or later blur efforts to differentiate between intellectuals and non-intellectuals to an extent scarcely appreciated in the literature.

The post-modern turn reflects a milieu in which intellectuals can fall back upon fewer established points of reference: social and intellectual identities, now less uniform and secure, are the product of a perpetually changing and fragmented universe of experiences, interests and loyalties. While this phenomenon opens up new space for critical discourse and even local movements, it also militates against the formation of political community at the general societal level (Best and Kellner, 1991: 196–214). If social boundaries have in certain ways evaporated, this does not automatically rule out *any* connection between structural factors and subjective political responses (Eagleton, 1996). Even within a post-modern frame of reference one can argue that a multiplicity of discourses is not arbitrary but can be made intelligible as part of historically grounded social and material conditions.

The limits of an eclectic irrationalism, however 'critical' its thrust, seem rather obvious: clearly, a recognition of the fact that identities are complex, ever-changing and discursively constituted does not in itself mean that such identities unfold independently of particular social or historical contexts.

Since it entered intellectual life in the late 1970s, post-modernism has given rise to a theoretical milieu in which a variety of academic fashions have thrived: semiotics, difference feminism, identity politics, diverse expressions of 'post-Marxism', etc. While this shift has been a healthy one in many respects, for a growing stratum of scholars (located mainly in élite universities) it has become a focus of more ambitious if often more obscure professional discourses that generally wind up skirting the political terrain even as they uphold some form of radical faith. A good deal of post-modern theorizing has degenerated into modes of research and analysis befitting intellectual cults with their own insular social circles, highly esoteric jargon, and strictly academic venues. Grounded thoroughly in academic culture, post-modernism seems more and more afflicted with a kind of scholastic irrelevance; its rather overt contempt for the public sphere can be traced to such pioneering theorists as Baudrillard, Derrida and even Foucault. In Barbara Epstein's words:

> The implicit values of poststructuralism, its celebration of difference and its hostility to unity, make it particularly inappropriate as an intellectual framework for movements that need to make positive assertions about how society could be better organized and that need to incorporate difference within a collective unity for social change (Epstein, 1995: 85).

A close scrutiny of the literature reveals that post-modern academics seem to have little interest in pursuing the 'critical' task of confronting the *status quo*, preferring to couch their critiques within the safe framework of relatively obscure texts and narratives. As Russell Jacoby adds:

> At the end of the radical theorizing project is a surprise: a celebration of academic hierarchy, professions, and success. Never has so much criticism yielded so much affirmation. From Foucault the professor learned that power and institutions saturate everything. Power is universal; complicity with power is universal, and this means university practices and malpractices are no better or worse than anything else (Jacoby, 1994: 182).

Despite its commonly oppositional and critical language, therefore, post-modernism has frequently turned into a system-reproducing body of ideas. Its celebration of fragmented, localized and (often) privatized frames of reference is perfectly compatible with the overriding imperatives of corporate colonization. Further, it easily coexists with trends towards disintegration of social and public life and with the pervasive ethos of despair and nihilism. The collapse of optimism and hope, so central to the legacy of Enlightenment rationality, can only serve to reduce the scope and vitality of citizen participation – not to mention the efficacy of a radical intelligentsia. From this standpoint, the general decline of collective subjectivity and the atrophy of political language reflects the historical thrust of both post-modernism and civic decay.

If an enduring mood of futility, pessimism and powerlessness defines the culture of late modernity, the discourse and participation within the public sphere will likely be increasingly depoliticized; the connection between in-tellectual work and politics will disintegrate even further. The assault on modernity, which gained momentum through the legacies of Baudelaire and Nietszche and then existentialism, surrealism, ecological radicalism and contemporary post-modernism, has gathered intellectual strength over time and today appears to converge with the tide of strong historical forces. One result of this development is the familiar erosion of global narratives, or universalistic *ideologies*. At the same time, technocratic intellectuals may en-counter new obstacles in their pursuit of ideological hegemony in so far as their *own* form of global rationality will be highly compromised (Kellner, 1989: 144). Élite attempts through the mass media, culture industry and advertising to impose social conformity on mass publics can be expected to face a series of detours and blockages. In either their technocratic or critical incarnation, post-modern intellectuals will be hard put to penetrate the dense fortresses of media control and manipulation in a social order that dwells so much upon surface appearances, images and commodified fashions, that so routinely depoliticizes public life.

The time-honoured purpose of critical intellectual activity is to challenge, probe, question, confront and possibly disrupt – that is, to represent an ideological alternative to the deceits and mystifications of the *status quo*. The issue in the context of post-modernity, however, is whether such critical interrogations can be heard, and given force, at least within the dominant public sphere (Debray, 1981). Further, the very conditions that subvert ideological universality of the sort associated with traditional, Jacobin and technocratic intellectuals – conditions that seem to bolster Foucault's idea of a 'specific intelligentsia' – call into question the concept of any decisive historical role for intellectuals in the contemporary period. More than any-thing else, perhaps, this post-modern impasse epitomizes the great social and political dilemmas of present-day intellectual life.

SUMMARY

- Industrial society transforms the role of intellectuals, replacing tradi-tional and Jacobin-élitist types with modern technocratic and critical types.

- Within modernity, intellectual life increasingly falls within the domain of a highly professionalized academic stratum.
- As industrial society matures, giving rise to new fissures and conflicts, antagonisms between technocratic and critical (or oppositional) intellectuals begins to sharpen.
- Against modernity, with its focus on the technocratic or professionalized intelligentsia, the post-modern shift generates conditions of fragmentation, diversity, critical opposition and the rise of localized 'specific' intellectuals.

FURTHER READING

Boggs, Carl (1993) *Intellectuals and the Crisis of Modernity*. Albany, NY: SUNY. Boggs analyses the social and intellectual role of intellectuals within the unfolding crisis of modernity, with a focus on the growing conflict between critical and intellectual functions in academic life and elsewhere.

Best, Steven and Kellner, Douglas (1991) *Postmodern Theory*. New York: Guilford. Best and Kellner explore the complex ramifications of intellectual work that unfolds within a fragmented, dispersed and localized discourse of post-modernity.

Gouldner, Alvin (1979) *The Future of Intellectuals and the Rise of the New Class*. London: Macmillan. Gouldner outlines the case for an emergent stratum of oppositional intellectuals in advanced industrial society which gives rise to a distinct 'culture of critical discourse'.

Jacoby, Russell (1994) *Dogmatic Wisdom*. New York: Doubleday. Jacoby shows how modern academic life has professionalized and narrowed intellectual discourse to such an extent that it has been largely detached from its larger environment.

Said, Edward (1966) *Representations of the Intellectual*. New York: Vintage. Said's book involves a collection of brief lectures, delivered over BBC radio in 1993, which seek to uphold the virtue of intellectuals as critics and outsiders within a conformist order.

Winner, Langdon (1977) *Autonomous Technology* (Cambridge, MA: MIT Press. Winner presents a seminal argument that stresses the intrinsically social and political dimensions of technology when presented as an autonomous, frequently destructive, force in modern society.

REFERENCES

Best, Steven and Kellner, Douglas (1991) *Postmodern Theory.* New York: Guilford.

Bloom, Allan (1987) *The Closing of the American Mind.* New York: Simon and Schuster.

Boggs, Carl (1993) *Intellectuals and the Crisis of Modernity.* Albany, NY: State University of New York Press.

Castells, Manuel (1984) *The City and the Grassroots.* Berkeley, CA: University of California Press.

Chomsky, Noam (1967) *American Power and the New Mandarins.* Harmondsworth: Penguin.

Debray, Regis (1981) *Teachers, Writers, Celebrities.* London: Verso.

Derber, Charles (1982) *Professionals as Workers.* Boston: G.K. Hall.

Eagleton, Terry (1996) *The Illusions of Postmodernism.* Cambridge, MA: Blackwell.

Epstein, Barbara (1995) 'Why Poststructuralism is a Dead End for Progressive Thought', *Socialist Review*, **25**(2).

Ghiselin, Michael (1989) *Intellectual Compromise.* New York: Paragon House.

Gorz, André (1967) *Strategy for Labor.* Boston: Beacon Press.

Gorz, André (1976) 'Technology, Technicians, and Class Struggle', in A. Gorz (ed.) *The Division of Labor.* Atlantic Highlands, NJ: Humanities Press.

Gouldner, Alvin (1976) *The Dialectic of Technology and Ideology.* New York: Seabury.

Gouldner, Alvin (1979) *The Future of Intellectuals and the Rise of the New Class.* London: Macmillan.

Gramsci, Antonio (1971) *Selections from the Prison Notebooks*, eds Quintin Hoare and Geoffrey Nowell Smith. New York: International Publishers.

Haskell, Thomas (1984) 'Professionalism vs. Capitalism', in T. Haskell (ed.) *The Authority of Experts.* Bloomington, IN: University of Indiana Press.

Heskin, Allan (1991) *The Struggle for Community.* Boulder, CO: Westview Press.

Jacoby, Russell (1987) *The Last Intellectuals.* New York: Basic Books.

Jacoby, Russell (1994) *Dogmatic Wisdom.* New York: Doubeday.

Kellner, Douglas (1989) *Critical Theory, Marxism, and Modernity.* Baltimore: Johns Hopkins University Press.

Kerr, Clark (1965) 'Selections from *The Uses of the University*', in S.M. Lipset, S.M. and Sheldon Wolin (eds) *The Berkeley Student Revolt.* Garden City, NJ: Anchor Books.

Laclau, Ernesto and Mouffe, Chantal (1985) *Hegemony and Socialist Strategy.* London: Verso.

Larson, Magali Sarfatti (1984) 'The Production of Expertise and the Constitution of Expert Power', in T. Haskell (ed.) *The Authority of Experts.* Bloomington, IN: University of Indiana Press.

Marcuse, Herbert (1964) *One Dimensional Man.* London: Routledge and Kegan Paul.

Ophuls, William (1997) *Requiem for Modern Politics.* Boulder, CO: Westview Press.

Said, Edward (1996) *Representations of the Intellectual.* New York: Vintage.

Sartre, Jean Paul (1963) *Search for a Method.* New York: Vintage.

Shils, Edward (1972) *The Intellectuals and the Powers.* Chicago: University of Chicago Press.

Touraine, Alain (1971) *The Post-Industrial Society.* New York: Random House.

Winner, Langdon (1986) *The Whale and the Reactor.* Chicago: University of Chicago Press.

Zelewski, David (1997) 'Ties that Bind', *Lingua Franca*, June–July.

Chapter 22

Higher education

Frank Webster

Higher education today is distinguished chiefly by two criteria: one the age after which most students participate, the other academic level. Thus it is something which takes place after compulsory schooling and it is at a level above that pursued either in schools or in further education colleges. Typically higher education involves study for an undergraduate degree or postgraduate qualification, and it is usually undertaken by students between 18 and 24 years of age. Higher education is concentrated in institutions known as universities and, while there are exceptions to this, all are authorised to award diploma and degree certificates. In addition, it is usual for universities to undertake research, the major reason for which is to underpin high-level teaching.

British higher education has recently undergone rapid change, the most visible aspect of which has been the increase in participation rates of young people. For most of the twentieth century the UK had an *élite* system of higher education, in which only between 2 and 10 per cent of the age group attended university. Since the 1970s, and especially since the late 1980s, many universities have been created, and all have expanded, to increase that participation rate to over 30 per cent. Britain has developed a system of *mass* higher education, thereby coming into line with other advanced nations such as the USA, Canada, Germany and France (Trow, 1970).

The concern of this chapter is with two related questions: *why* has mass higher education come into being in the late twentieth century, and with *what consequence*? When one asks why, there is widespread agreement that the major and most immediate transformative factor has been a cluster of socio-economic changes, collectively termed *post-Fordism*, with which higher education is intimately tied. Here globalization, new forms of organ-ization, heightened competition and an emphasis on information work, are all said to contribute to an irresistible pressure to produce more highly educated employees, who are capable of succeeding in a fast-changing and knowledge-intensive environment.

Post-Fordist thinking also has much to say about the consequences of these factors for the university, but there are two additional assessments of these changes. The first of these is *modernist* in orientation. While it acknowl-edges the adaptation of the university to changing circumstances, a modern-ist interpretation insists that *established* features of universities remain. The second account of what changes in higher education signify evokes the notion of *post-modernism* to suggest the doubt, uncertainty and fluidity of the new epoch, a notion which has invaded the university to challenge, and indeed to turn upside down, many of its traditional practices and assump-tions, so much so that any defining idea of the university is lost.

POST-FORDISM AND HIGHER EDUCATION

In recent years it has become orthodox to argue that shifting socio-economic circumstances are transforming the university. Crucially, post-Fordist press-ures (Brown and Lauder, 1995) are more closely integrating the university and the economy. 'Higher education should serve the economy more effec-tively' demanded government (DES, 1987) a decade ago, and this insistence has been unrelenting.

Several elements of post-Fordism are highlighted. These include the suggestions that:

- *Globalization* has massively accelerated change and increased competi-tive challenges, thereby heightening uncertainty and raising the stakes in economic affairs. It has also developed a worldwide and largely auton-omous market system which imposes massive constraints on nations while being largely out of the control of governments (Soros, 1998).
- Universities must respond to these new times by ensuring that em-ployees are equipped with up-to-the-minute *skills and knowledge* that may match changing circumstances.
- A crucial quality of employees is possession of the *flexibility* allowing adaptation to constantly changing conditions, and the ability to train – and routinely re-train – throughout working life.
- Since universities must produce graduates with the requisite flexibility to make their way in this unsettled world, so it follows that the *university must enhance its own flexibility*.
- Increased proportions of occupations, and the most appealing, are *sym-bolic or knowledge-intensive*.

These factors hoist the university to centre stage of economic policy since it is charged with equipping workforces (and responsible for continuing to prepare them), and because these are increasingly information dependent. Moreover, since governments are impelled to abandon national economic policy by the forces of globalization, then they must promote those things over which they do have leverage – hence the prioritization given to higher education systems that are charged with making sure that the country's young have the qualities that will allow them to capture the best jobs going.

This analysis and policy outcome may be called 'Reichian', after the influential account offered by Robert Reich (1991). In his *The Work of Nations: Preparing Ourselves for 21st Century Capitalism*, Reich affirms that the central concern of government must be with its higher education system's capacity to produce sufficiently appealing products so as to win a disproportionate share of the world economy's top jobs. Reich's focus is on the USA where the President may best act in the national interest by prioritizing policies that will ensure many people find employment as 'symbolic analysts'. These are the experts who are 'continuously engaged in managing ideas' and who 'solve, identify, and broker problems by manipulating symbols' (Reich, 1991: 85, 178). They are highly educated, thereby in command of, and comfortable with, the key skills of abstraction, system thinking, experimentation and collaboration. They are at home in the fast-paced world of global capitalism, a world where very large numbers of 'knowledge workers' will be found inside the nation which can maintain a university system capable of producing the high-level qualities of its symbolic analysts. Appropriately educated in top-flight universities, symbolic analysts hold together and operationalize the global market system, and any nation which can locate large numbers of them within its boundaries is ensured prosperity and contentment. This analysis also undergirds Tony Blair's insistence that New Labour's main policies are 'education, education, education'.

More and more, higher education is understood as a site of 'human capital'. For instance, Manuel Castells's (1996–97) category 'informational labour' identifies those jobs which generate change, bind together economic activities, and generally involve the thinking, conceiving, planning and operationalizing required by 'informational capitalism'. These occupations 'embody knowledge and information' (Castells, 1997b, ch. 6), something nurtured by the university.

Informational labour's major quality is what Castells terms *self-programmability*. That is, informational labour possesses a range of general and specific skills, but none is more important than the capacity to re-train, an axial skill of 'learning how to learn' that is the requisite of the adaptability and opportunism demanded of the post-Fordist world. It is this requirement that lies behind efforts to inculcate an ethos of 'lifelong learning'.

It is in this context of profoundly altered socio-economic circumstances that we need to situate the transition in Britain, at breakneck speed, from élite to mass higher education, as well as the cognate restructuring of universities in other advanced societies (Slaughter and Leslie, 1997). The extra-ordinary expansion of universities owes much to the widespread conviction that informational capitalism's occupational structure means that the most desirable jobs are those of the 20 to 30 per cent of the workforce engaged in information/knowledge work. If a nation hopes to prosper, then it must seize a good number of these for its citizens. Dearing (1997) saw this and accordingly concluded that 'the UK must plan to match the participation rates of other advanced nations: not to do so would weaken the basis of national competitiveness' (Dearing, 1997: para. 27).

PORTFOLIO CAREERS

It is often observed that we are witnessing a *de*bureaucratization of organizations. This finds expression in 'delayering' and 're-engineering', a process that has led to significant redundancies among sections of white-collar work (Hammer and Champy, 1993). A result of organizational changes is that bureaucratic career pathways are often blocked, and with this come serious consequences for much educated labour. The option of entry to a large organization with which the employee might stay for years, and in which he or she will rise steadily up the hierarchy, is being closed off.

The argument has it that the rigours of market competition combine with the necessary rapidity of response to constant turmoil to make bureaucratic structures both expensive and unwieldy. Furthermore, bureaucratic hierarchies lose much of their purpose where information networks facilitate decision-making and implementation (and where speed of reply is more imperative than ever). A consequence is what Castells (1996: ch. 2) describes as the decline of the 'vertical', and its replacement by the 'horizontal', organization, by which he means that, as institutions have cut out levels of their bureaucracies, so have they empowered those who remain behind. In these new organizations, where 'flat management' prevails, those who remain are the crucial ingredient of success, and to act in a timely and efficacious manner they must be free of hindrance from above.

However, while those remaining are essential, they cannot anticipate promotion through bureaucratic ranks. It is suggested that such a prospect is not missed by such workers who do not perform effectively when constrained by hierarchies. Rather, in an increasingly networked society where fax, email and computer simplify information analysis and transfer, these workers value the (horizontal) links they make when working on a particular project. Their allegiance is thus more to the project and the 'global web' (Reich, 1991) of relationships they maintain rather than to a particular corporation. Their primary reference group thus becomes the peer group which is found in similar domains to themselves (for example, the realm of software engineers, or of advertising copywriters) and their first priority is to the success of the particular project on which they happen to be working rather than to the company which has contracted for it. It follows that they experience little concern about loss of security in their careers which are marked by movement from one contract to the next, developing reputations among a reference group that cuts across corporations. They want to be acknowledged more as fine designers or journalists than as employees on a certain point of the organization's pay scale. By the same token employers cannot command much loyalty from these transitory workers, and for precisely this reason they cannot readily control them. These are autonomous workers who are pivotal to corporate success, and for that reason must be given their heads.

It is striking how much the university system has colluded with 'portfolio career' enthusiasts to facilitate the development of these sort of employees. Here the primary concern has been to develop flexibility among students as a means of appearing attractive to potential employers and surviving in uncertain and unstable circumstances. The commitment to flexibility is at the heart of most of the concern among university students about developing *transferable skills*. Of course, in so far as a skill is transferable it is inherently flexible, but often the association is a good deal more explicit. For instance, 'skills' such as 'adaptability', 'enterprise', 'self-starting' and 'self-reliance' directly respond to the new world of employment. And 'transferable skills' like 'time management', 'problem-solving' and 'working in teams' fit neatly with the needs of the flexible economy.

THE MODERNIST CRITIQUE

Employers identify possession of transferable skills as essential qualities in those whom they recruit. Not surprisingly, when universities, especially those more recently established institutions, which have been pioneers in this regard, determine to incorporate transferable skills into their curricula, then this has been received warmly by many of their students. Graduates are well aware that their credential is no longer the passport to a 'good job': accordingly very many students are content to spend time developing transferable skills as an integral element of studying for a degree.

Time and again employers of graduates stress that they want recruits to have transferable skills, but time and again they appear to find these manifest, not in those students from the new universities who have most often undergone programmes that have consciously nurtured them, but in the products of the more élite – and preferably ancient – universities, where the language of transferable skills has penetrated least. Indeed, employers regard those graduates from the newest universities, who have undergone explicit training in transferable skills, as deficient for that very reason: had they been any good in the first place such students would not have required this compensatory education.

Brown and Scase (1994) account for this paradox by arguing that transferable skills are but a code word for 'middle-class cultural capital'. Employers do want transferable skills, but these turn out to be highly subjective characteristics chiefly found in graduates who have attended the most prestigious institutions and who have come disproportionately from professional and managerial homes. Employers select staff on the basis of a *reputational* model of universities, in which graduates from the top-ranked places are presumed to have the core transferable skills so much sought after. In this respect the lower ranked universities, and their students who come from less advantaged social backgrounds, face massive hurdles – even if they have assiduously developed their transferable skills, and even if they have had them tabulated and scored, because such 'skills' are imprecise and perverted by employers' subjective perceptions.

Moreover, what we appear to be witnessing is the permeation throughout hiring practices of what has long been the situation as regards recruitment for the higher corporate levels. The 'high flyers' among graduates were always scrutinized for appropriate qualities that singled them out as 'executive material'; and 'leadership', 'independence of thought' and 'enterprise' have always been the sort of thing found most often at the ancient universities. The difference is that today's recruiters seem to be applying this approach to the selection of *all* their graduates. Above and beyond possession of a degree, employers now want the 'charismatic character', someone with a 'personality package' bursting with 'commercial acumen', 'self-starting capacities', 'confidence', 'oralcy' and 'entrepreneurial' zeal. And they discover these traits in students by recruiting people like themselves, while those least mirroring their self-reflection (concentrated in the less prestigious universities) are the last to be looked at (Purcell and Pitcher, 1996).

What this draws attention to are inequalities that are deeply entrenched, and with which universities, the curriculum and employers' preferences are closely intertwined. Such inequalities alert us to the possibility that the expansion of higher education may result in there being markedly differing employment opportunities for graduates dependent on their social origins and the standing of the institution they have attended.

Furthermore, and integrally related to these inequalities, one may cast doubt on the presupposition that our post-Fordist economy really does require as much as 30 per cent of the labour force to be graduates (Keep and Mayhew, 1996). There is, for instance, evidence that many are now doing jobs previously performed by those with A levels. This may also be related to doubt about the claimed maintenance of academic standards through time and the alleged equality of institutions awarding degrees. Though in principle a degree from Derby is equivalent to one from Durham, and though it is asserted that standards throughout the system have been maintained despite the rush to mass higher education, few employers are so convinced. It has to be conceded, moreover, that it is not just employers who express concern that the quality of graduates may either have declined and/or be differentiated by institution (Halsey, 1992; HEQC, 1996a). Research from the Policy Studies Institute (Callender and Kempson, 1996) which found that 30 per cent of all students were in paid employment during their undergraduate days (and not just in vacations when the proportion soars), and thus unavailable for academic study for that period of time, provides support for a great deal of anecdotal evidence inside universities about declining standards. Yet increased attainment in degree classifications would seem to counter this interpretation. Today about half of all students graduate with an upper second or first class honours degree, though this stood at less than one in three twenty years ago. But sceptics reason that this is a consequence, not of harder working students or even of improved teaching, but of a general easing of assessment criteria. They contrast the modest entry requirements of many students with their final achievements – all against the trend towards overcrowded universities, poorer library facilities, and less access to teachers – and explain the discrepancy in terms of a shift towards coursework assessment and as indicative of variable standards between universities (HEQC, 1996b).

A serious consequence of this weakening of confidence in the quality of degree standards is reinforcement of the reputational model which employers use when recruiting graduates. After all, if one cannot be sure that an upper second from Guildhall (a new university in London) is the same as one from Glasgow, then recourse to the perceived hierarchy is understandable, though it may be a rough and ready composite of personal experience, research excellence, publicity, age and ancestry. None the less, such recourse is remarkably socially selective, confirming a high degree of recruitment to the premier employment positions of those from socially advantaged backgrounds. The predilection of employers for prestigious residential universities when seeking recruits means that graduates from the new universities are especially handicapped. In turn this is a disadvantage of class, since the more élite the university, then the more exclusive are the origins of its students.

Moreover, it has to be emphasized that this is not a reflection of prejudice on the part of those in charge of admissions policies. Quite the contrary, in recent years higher education in Britain has come to be markedly meritocratic, in so far as selection is on the basis of attainment in the anonymous and public A level examinations. But the fact is that, over the same period, there has been a remarkable increase in the capacity, especially of private schools, to achieve extremely high scores at A level. More generally, it is the children of the professional and managerial groups who have shown an astounding capacity to do well at A level, whatever school they happen to attend, and it is due to this rather than to bias that they disproportionately gain access to top universities, and then in turn occupy a front place when employers look for recruits. In such ways we see the reproduction of social inequalities (cf. Bourdieu, 1996).

THE POST-MODERN UNIVERSITY

There is a broad range of opinion which regards higher education as being driven by economic circumstances that have resulted in rapid expansion of student numbers while closer ties have been developed with industry. The imperatives of the post-Fordist, flexible, economy are widely perceived to have diminished the quality of higher education, reduced the autonomy of universities, and set back questions of social justice by throwing judgements on to reputational hierarchies.

However, there has been another sort of response which is noteworthy. On the whole it does not dissent from the empirical description of what is occurring in higher education, but supporters of the notion that we are witnessing the spread of the *post-modern university* are quick to reject the 'narratives of decline' which abound in much writing. It may be agreed that new vocational pressures have had an enormous effect inside the university, but proponents of the post-modern university refuse to interpret these changes as symptomatic of a fall from grace.

The post-modern university has a number of distinguishing features, though the primary one is the *differences* which abound in higher education. These differences – of courses, students, purposes, academics and disciplines – subvert any 'idea' of the university which conceives it in unitary terms. Instead heterogeneity is a key word: the transformations of higher education over recent decades, from the push of additional numbers and new constituencies, to globalization itself, means that what we now have is an extraordinary diversity of universities which are, moreover, themselves in a constant state of flux. This is consonant with the arrival of post-Fordism since the latter's stimulation of flexibility in employment (and in lifestyles more generally) also encourages the development of the flexible, post-modern university which never stands still. Peter Scott (1995) even envisages a correspondence between the post-Fordist economy and post-modern times in which no certainties are accepted and life is lived without fixed reference points. Necessarily, he continues, the post-modern university absorbs and incorporates the 'pluralism', 'fluidity' and 'fuzziness' that both post-Fordism and post-modernism engender.

Higher education institutions are nowadays so internally and externally differentiated that the title 'university' evokes little if anything by way of common traits. For instance, there can be no common inner life to the university when fragmentation has extended so far that not only is it colleagues across departments who cannot understand one another, but even those within departments share next to no concerns (Bauman, 1997). Today's university is no more than a haphazard collection of different concerns and voices. Extending this, Bill Readings (1996) argued that it is this multiplicity of differences which lies behind university proclamations that they are 'excellent' – equally so in anything and everything, from sports facilities, research outputs, overseas connections, equal opportunities, entertainments, to catering services. It is the absence of underlying purposes which allows universities to endorse this wild relativism where absolutely anything may be claimed to be 'excellent'.

Moreover, when the Internet is just the most obvious source of information available from outside, then the university's role as the authoritative source of knowledge is subverted, and it becomes just one voice among many others now available. Zygmunt Bauman has drawn attention to the corresponding decline in the standing of university academics: they are now but one of many conflicting contributors to knowledge, and they are themselves internally divided as well as routinely challenged from without. This signals a shift from intellectuals as *legislators* to *interpreters* (Bauman, 1987): since we can no longer conceive of a university dedicated to providing authoritative knowledge then we must view it as no more than a diverse collection of commentators.

This accords with Jean-François Lyotard's (1984) well-known argument that a *principle of performativity* (use) predominates today, thereby undermining the former Enlightenment justification that it pursued 'truth'. If science is no longer discovery-led, but is rather guided by the search for patents and inventions, and if use-led subjects like management and engineering have fully entered universities, then we must acknowledge that the demands of performativity are the new definers of knowledge, as are new performativity-led subjects such as Women's Studies, Popular Culture and Biotechnology.

But if the former defences of what might be included in the university are breached by utility criteria, then the boundaries of exclusion from the university also collapse, and with them the former hierarchies at the top of which were subjects such as Classics, Natural Science and Philosophy. If performativity alone is what matters, then why not degrees in Tourism, Golf Course Studies, Environmental Change, or even Leisure Studies? And if this is so, then what characterizes the university today other than its being a diversity of activities pursued – and routinely abandoned – only because there is some performativity justification for their adoption?

This has been conceived as the transformation from a Mode 1 type of knowledge that is homogeneous, rooted in strong academic disciplines which are hierarchically organized, and transmitted to novitiates in an apprentice–master relationship, towards Mode 2 knowledges which are non-hierarchical, pluralistic, transdisciplinary, fast-changing and responsive to diverse needs such as students' experiences, industrial priorities and social problems. This plurality of knowledges must announce an end to common purposes of the university, there being no possibility of agreement on goals or even on methods of work (Gibbons *et al.*, 1994). By extension, we must forego thinking about how to define what a university might be, instead simply accepting that there are an enormous number of very different institutions with radically different purposes and practices that might be called universities (for want of a better term).

The university is also being undermined because of the increasing difficulty of distinguishing it from growing sectors of industry. Knowledge-rich corporations such as Microsoft and Zeneca 'already possess many of the features of a university' (*Economist*, 1997). These are brimming with highly educated employees who are working on cutting-edge projects such as in software production, advanced electronics, biotechnology or social investigation. Moreover, such companies have many connections with universities that blur previous distinctions, frequently in the form of joint deals, shared staff and even facilities. Thus the university can no longer be identified by virtue of its separation from the 'outside world', while simultaneously 'big companies . . . are becoming more conscious of their role as creators, disseminators, and users of knowledge – a definition not altogether different from that of a university' (ibid.).

Relatedly, questioning the once privileged role of the university as regards research weakens its former distinctiveness. Serious questions are now asked about the supposed indivisibility of teaching and research that, in the view of many, characterizes a genuine university. As more and more students take up places on degree programmes, then it may be asked whether it is really essential that all of their teachers are research active. Though it is unpalatable to many university personnel, the evidence just does not support the assertion that research and teaching are mutually supportive (Astin, 1993).

Correspondingly, voices have been raised to observe that there is no compelling reason to locate research inside universities. As the *Economist* (1997) puts it, 'an intelligent Martian might wonder why a university – autonomous, chaotic, distracted by all those students – should be an efficient place in which to sponsor economically worthwhile research'. Perhaps then the best place for it is in dedicated research institutes.

Finally, what of the educational potential of technology? In the minds of some academics is fixed the idea of the university as a residential experience, but new technologies promise distance learning from one's own home, at one's convenience, accessing the best available informational sources, all at a fraction of the cost of attendance at a traditional university. The 'virtual university', already available in embryonic form, promises to undermine yet another foundation stone of the traditional university, leaving it unclear as to its justification or even to its location, as customized network facilities allow students to study how, when and what they judge appropriate.

THE END OF THE UNIVERSITY? A MODERNIST RETORT

It is not unusual for commentators to become excited by the 'flexibility, synergy and volatility' (Scott, 1995: 70) of the post-modern university. But it is these very characteristics which, if unchallenged, would announce the end of the university as a meaningful term. If instead of an academic community we have mutual incomprehension, if research may be pursued perfectly satisfactorily outside academe, if utility is the only criterion for inclusion in the curriculum, if effective teaching does not require the support of research, if courses can be studied without attendance . . . if all we encounter is a plurality of differences, then, to say the least, the concept of the university is problematic (Delanty, 1998).

However, many would challenge the protestations of pluralism that lie at the heart of these claims that we now have a post-modern university. The rhetoric of 'difference', captured in the shift towards performativity, evokes a notion of infinite pluralities of knowledges being generated as universities internally fragment simultaneous with heterogeneous external forces making increased headroads into (as well as alternative routes outside) universities. But quite to the contrary of this argument, the reality appears to be that universities across nations (Slaughter and Leslie, 1997) have been shaped decisively in *a limited direction*, namely one which makes universities most responsive to contemporary capitalism's needs and strictures. The neo-liberal consensus, which today is hegemonic around the globe, demands that marketization principles and practices permeate the entire social domain. This has meant that the relatively autonomous space that universities have long occupied has markedly diminished, *not* as universities have become more plural, but rather as market forces have told more decisively on universities themselves to develop in directions favourable to commercial life.

Aspects of this include:

1 The by now routine insistence from research councils that projects to be funded will be driven, not by intellectual curiosity, but by their contribution to improvements in competitiveness. In this way the State has thrown its weight strongly behind capitalist interests (cf. DTI, 1998; Monbiot, 1998).
2 State policy, bolstered by industrial advice, that universities should strive to produce the 'human capital' that equips graduates to function effectively in the global commercial world.

These two factors certainly express a force which represents the interest of capitalism as a whole rather than that of specific segments of capital, and to this degree there remains a distance of the university from front-line commercial operations. None the less, there is today a much greater degree of representation of business interest both on university governing boards and in the development of courses that have specific connections (for example, in partnership deals involving research programmes and in contracts entered into to deliver training courses for identified companies). Such measures ensure that universities are shaped to service capitalism, since anything not in the mainstream will find survival and sourcing problematic.

3   The by now routine practice of regarding students as 'customers' who must be satisfied that their 'investment' in education gains a satisfactory return. Of course, responding to students' needs is not in itself a negative thing to do. Yet it can be – as it is more and more nowadays – when the university's 'customers' are perceived to be demanding that they are made more employable, or that their courses are demonstrably of practical use. Such demands easily come into conflict with alternative educational ideals, such as introducing students – regarded as novitiates in learning who are not always right – to alternative philosophies to those which are approved by the wider society.

4   Perhaps the most striking dimension of the consequences of commercial practices has been evident in the ways in which they have engendered change inside universities, privileging certain subject areas (e.g. business studies, biotechnology) and demoting others (e.g. music, aesthetics). This has gone so far that Sheila Slaughter and Larry Leslie (1997), in a comparative study of four advanced nations, adopt the concept 'academic capitalism' to describe a situation where faculty increasingly find themselves in hybrid public sector and market contexts. That is, they are paid from public revenues for the most part, but called upon largely to service the commercial elements of the wider society. The effects have been remarkable, resulting in academics becoming much more competitive one with another, and becoming increasingly entrepreneurial as they seek out funding opportunities. In addition, the spread of what Slaughter and Leslie term 'entrepreneurial knowledge' is striking – *vide* the continuous expansion of business schools, contract research and computer science courses over the last generation.

'Academic capitalism' does have some paradoxical consequences, not all of which work in favour of the commercial realm. For instance, the market, when allowed to determine student choice of courses, may well stimulate the expansion of some arts and humanities programmes. However, we should not let this blind us to the fact that most recent developments have impelled the university to move closer than ever to the practical world of the market system. To regard such developments as the spread of post-modern pluralism is to confuse rapid and radical transformation of the university in favour of capitalist interests with an explosion of pluralism.

Moreover, modernist critics believe that defining features of the university remain. We may appreciate these better when we raise doubts about the post-modern emphasis on differences by drawing attention to the empirical fact that there are *hierarchies of difference* within and between universities, hierarchies which are underlain by criteria of judgement which, at root, define the university. It is superficially appealing to contend that throughout the hundred or so institutions in Britain boasting the title university there runs rampant diversity and differentiation. It is also a radically democratic outlook since it denies the option either to compare institutions and then arrange them hierarchically or to exclude aspirants from membership of the university club. But while the post-modern position highlights the complexities of locating universities on matrices of difference, it is an absurdity to suggest that differences are such as to subvert hierarchy or negate judgement. Post-modernists may resist it, but employers, students, academics, and indeed the public as a whole do not. The upshot is that, while judgement has its gradations and grey areas, universities as a whole, and in turn departments and subject areas, are accorded a place. Of course, such judgements are nuanced, but acknowledgement of the difficulties of weighting differences does not negate the fact of their hierarchical character.

It is not blind snobbery to recognize these hierarchies. Nor is it the prejudice of subject panels which assess and position research outputs and the quality of teaching provision at periodic intervals. The most telling judgements of universities concern research, the calibre of students and staff, and teaching quality. And research activities, students' qualifications at entry, and staff attainments are indisputably at higher levels in some institutions than in others. Arguably, too, assessment standards are less rigorous in some institutions than elsewhere. To pretend that all universities are equal – equal in some way due to their exhibiting a plurality of differences – is to turn a blind eye especially to the inequalities that abound in higher education. If these are to be addressed, then the relativism of post-modernism must be refused.

If university hierarchies are judged largely, if not exclusively, on the quality of their research, their students and staff and their teaching, then, logically, some institutions will be excluded from the category university on the grounds that some or all of their research, members and teaching are in some ways lacking. There is, however, another feature, connected to these but reducible to none of them, which defines the university. This involves the right to bestow, and have acknowledged, *credentials* on students upon satisfying the requirements of the university. It is revealing that universities have maintained the monopoly of awarding degrees and that these are recognized as the sole legitimate form of accreditation. To be sure, degrees from different universities are not seen as of equal value, but there remains in the accrediting function a defining feature of the university.

Acknowledgement that a university has a right to bestow academic qualifications, in a way not granted to private corporations however knowledge-centred they may be, highlights the fact that university work cannot be reduced to the merely performative if credibility is to be retained. The legitimacy of university qualifications hinges on public confidence that the teaching that takes place there, and the research that accompanies it, are guided by ideals, and maintained by standards, higher than those of the merely performative. These ideals – disinterestedness, critical inquiry, open debate, rigorous examination of evidence and the like – are a crucial element of university life which, if under some strain, remain defining features.

SUMMARY

- Britain has shifted rapidly from mass to élite higher education, thereby coming into line with other advanced societies.
- The most common explanation for this change is that it is a result of socio-economic shifts towards post-Fordism which require closer integration of higher education and the economy. The move to post-Fordism prioritizes flexibility and induces a parallel change in the university which finds expression in things such as modularization, the development of transferable skills, and new subject areas.
- Modernist critics acknowledge changed socio-economic circumstances, but point to continuities of university hierarchies and employers' recruitment practices.
- Post-modern commentators argue that we are witnessing the emergence of a new phenomenon, the post-modern university, which is characterized by differences (of students, courses, institutions . . .), and is consonant with the post-Fordist economy and post-modern culture.
- Modernist critics retort that the post-modern university is an untenable concept, since its emphasis on differences denies the possibility that there may be any distinguishing features of the university.

FURTHER READING

Scott, Peter (1995) *The Meanings of Mass Higher Education*. Buckingham: Society for Research into Higher Education/Open University Press. This is an an intellectual *tour de force*, offering an historical account of the growth of mass higher education in Britain, and suggesting a connection between post-Fordism, post-modernism and mass higher education.

Barnett, Ronald (1994) *The Limits of Competence: Knowledge, Higher Education and Society*. Buckingham: Society for Research into Higher Education/Open University Press. Barnett is a long-term opponent of instrumentalism in higher education, but one who refuses the nostalgia of a lost 'golden age'. Informed by the critical theory of Habermas, Barnett is an incisive and accessible analyst of the contemporary university.

Brown, Phillip and Scase, Richard (1994) *Higher Education and Corporate Realities: Class, Culture and the Decline of Graduate Careers.* London: UCL Press. An empirically informed and sceptical analysis of employers' recruitment practices in British universities. An essential counter to excessive theorizing about, as well as naïve enthusiasm for, the post-modern university.

Smith, Anthony and Webster, Frank (eds) (1997) *The Postmodern University? Contested Visions of Higher Education in Society.* Buckingham: Society for Research into Higher Education/Open University Press. Articles which debate the condition of the university today, contrasting those who argue for the post-modern university (Bauman, Scott) and those of a more modernist persuasion (Kumar, Filmer, Jacoby).

Readings, Bill (1996) *The University in Ruins.* Cambridge, MA: Harvard University Press. Study of the undermining of the role of the university by forces of globalization that have denuded its former contribution which was chiefly to promote national culture. The book is difficult, but worth persevering with for its account of the transformation of the university into a consumer-oriented corporation.

REFERENCES

Astin, Alexander W. (1993) *What Matters in College: Four Critical Years Revisited.* San Fransisco: Jossey-Bass.

Bauman, Zygmunt (1987) *Legislators and Interpreters: On Modernity, Postmodernity, and the Intellectual.* Cambridge: Polity.

Bauman, Zygmunt (1997) 'Universities: Old, New and Different', in Anthony Smith and Frank Webster (eds) *The Postmodern University? Contested Visions of Higher Education in Society.* Buckingham: Society for Research into Higher Education/ Open University Press, ch. 2, pp. 17–26.

Bourdieu, Pierre (1996) *The State Nobility: Élite Schools in the Field of Power*, trans. Lauretta Clough. Cambridge: Polity.

Brown, Phillip and Lauder, Hugh (1995) 'Post-Fordist Possibilities: Education, Training and National Development', in Leslie Bash and Andy Green (eds) *World Yearbook of Education 1995: Youth, Education and Work.* London: Kogan Page, ch. 2, pp. 19–51.

Brown, Phillip and Scase, Richard (1994) *Higher Education and Corporate Realities: Class, Culture and the Decline of Graduate Careers.* London: UCL Press.

Callender, C. and Kempson, E. (1996) *Student Finances: A Survey of Student Income and Expenditure.* London: Policy Studies Institute.

Castells, Manuel (1996–97) *The Information Age: Economy, Society and Culture.* Oxford: Blackwell; published in three parts: (1996) Vol. 1, *The Rise of the Network Society*; (1997a) Vol. 2, *The Power of Identity*; (1997b) Vol. 3, *End of Millennium.*

Dearing (1997) (Report of National Committee of Inquiry into Higher Education), *Higher Education in the Learning Society*, July. London: HMSO.

Delanty, Gerard (1998) 'The Idea of the University in the Global Era: From Knowledge as an End to the End of Knowledge?' *Social Epistemology*, **12**(1): 3–25.

DES (Department of Education and Science) (1987) *Higher Education: Meeting the Challenge*, Cmnd 114. London: HMSO.

DTI (Department of Trade and Industry) (1998) *Our Competitive Future: Building the Knowledge-Driven Economy*, December. London: HMSO.

Economist (1997) 'Survey: Universities', 4 October.

Gibbons, Michael, Limoges, Camille, Nowotny, Helga, Schwartzman, Simon, Scott, Peter and Trow, Martin (1994) *The New Production of Knowledge: The Dynamics of Science and Research in Contemporary Societies*. London: Sage.

Halsey, A.H. (1992) *Decline of Donnish Dominion: The British Academic Professions in the Twentieth Century*. Oxford: Clarendon Press.

Hammer, Michael and Champy, James (1993) *Re-Engineering the Corporation: A Manifesto for Business Revolution*. London: Brealey.

HEQC (Higher Education Quality Council) (1996a) *Academic Standards in the Approval, Review and Classification of Degrees*. London: HEQC.

HEQC (Higher Education Quality Council) (1996b) *Inter-Institutional Variability of Degree Results: An Analysis in Selected Areas*. London: HEQC.

Keep, Ewart and Mayhew, Ken (1996) 'Economic Demand for Higher Education – A Sound Foundation for Further Expansion?' *Higher Education Quarterly*, **50**(2), April: 89–109.

Lyotard, Jean-François (1984) *The Postmodern Condition: A Report on Knowledge*, trans. Geoff Bennington and Brian Massumi. Manchester: Manchester University Press.

Monbiot, George (1998) 'Integrity for Sale', *Guardian*, 17 December.

Purcell, Kate and Pitcher, Jane (1996) *Great Expectations: The New Diversity of Graduate Skills and Aspirations*. Manchester: Careers Services Unit.

Readings, Bill (1996) *The University in Ruins*. Cambridge, MA: Harvard University Press.

Reich, Robert B. (1991) *The Work of Nations: Preparing Ourselves for 21st Century Capitalism*. New York: Vintage.

Scott, Peter (1995) *The Meanings of Mass Higher Education*. Buckingham: Society for Research into Higher Education/Open University Press.

Slaughter, Sheila and Leslie, Larry L. (1997) *Academic Capitalism: Politics, Policies and the Entrepreneurial University*. Baltimore, MD: Johns Hopkins University Press.

Soros, George (1998) *The Crisis of Global Capitalism*. London: Little, Brown.

Trow, Martin (1970) 'Reflections on the Transition from Élite to Mass Higher Education', *Daedalus: Journal of the American Academy of Arts and Sciences*, **90**(1): 1–42.

Chapter 23

Mass communication

Kaarle Nordenstreng

Mass media occupy today such a central place both in people's everyday lives and in society's political and economic life that they cannot be ignored in any effort to understand the present. The point is not whether they should be included in a repertoire of vital themes which determine the theory of society in the contemporary Western world. The key point is, rather, how they relate to other social factors – are they just technical carriers of political, cultural and economic forces (literally media), or do they possess independent and substantive qualities which make them a social factor in their own right (a fourth branch of government, cultural industry, etc.)?

In this chapter, I will first outline the emergence of mass communication during the past four centuries, and then review its significance in the contemporary world. Third, I shall observe the concentration of media power; and finally, I shall address the recurrent questions of the study of mass communication, notably the nature of its power and influence in society.

HISTORICAL GROWTH

Mass communication is typically understood to have been born with the printing press in the late fifteenth century. Therefore, its German inventor Johann Gutenberg became the Christopher Columbus of the new media world, and the mass media became 'the Gutenberg galaxy', as the Canadian Marshall McLuhan (1962) expressed it in one of his works on the history and nature of the media. The first medium of mass communication was the book, which exploded the technical capacity of the written word to reach a great number of people – something that worked particularly in the interest of the Reformation with its need for a personal Bible and a larger number of interpreters to challenge the Catholic church. In the seventeenth century, books were followed by the periodical press, which came to serve especially the growing sphere of bourgeois politics and the capitalist economy of the time (Boyce, Curran and Wingate, 1978).

In brief, mass communication in the form of the written word became part and parcel of the big shift from feudalism to capitalism, later also to (state) socialism in Russia and elsewhere (by now collapsed in Eastern Europe). Books and papers, followed by film, radio and television, were essential for the Age of Enlightenment, the development of democratic order, and for the parallel Industrial Revolution with its growth of commerce and industry – for the whole historical stage known as the 'modern project'. We may say that mass communication is an essential component of modernity, where independent thinking and literate individuals have constituted a civil society and its public sphere (Habermas, 1989; Thompson, 1995).

This overall view of history needs to be complemented, first, by the fact that printing was invented in northern Asia long before Gutenberg, and second, that throughout history there have been news media based on other forms of distribution than the printed paper, notably the handwritten news-letters known in Rome as *acta diurna* and in China as *tipao*. Moreover, de-bates about trivial and sensational news date back to ancient times (Stephens, 1988). In general, mass communication as a social phenomenon can be seen to have existed centuries before the invention of the print media – just think how Jesus spread his messianic message and how the masses reacted with a powerful public opinion that influenced political leaders such as Pontius Pilatus. On the other hand, journalism as a specific type of mass communication emerged only in the second half of the nineteenth century (Chalaby, 1998). Papers which since the seventeenth century were predomi-nantly religious or political – straightforward extensions of belief systems – gave way during the past hundred years to more independent ways of reporting reality, known as professional journalism.

Accordingly, the history of mass communication cannot be understood in simplistic terms. Yet one thing is clear regardless of which perspective we use to approach history: mass communication has always served some social, political or economic purpose; it has played a role in society, one way or another. It has never been a luxury item in the course of history; instead, it has reflected and supported more fundamental forces in social develop-ment. The same can be said about communication in general: interpersonal communication based on speech was one of the basic elements through which people evolved and created human civilization. Likewise, the art of writing was a vital instrument in the formation of permanent societies and economies based on land and taxes. The printing press and, later, the elec-tronic media were crucial in facilitating the Industrial Revolution. Currently,

329

we live amidst a new transformation into a post-industrial or information society – communication again playing a pivotal role, now largely based on computer and other digital technologies.

It is not surprising, then, that communication in general and mass communication in particular has been recognized as an element in theories of society. Already in the late nineteenth century and early twentieth century, when (mass) communication was rapidly developing, the classics of European and American sociology and political science were theorizing about the press as 'nerves of society', 'a mirror of society' and 'the conscience of society' (Hardt, 1979). Typical of these early theories was a notion of society as an organism in which (mass) communication flows across the networks of this social organism (Mattelart and Mattelart, 1998). Later theories, while no longer viewing society as a kind of collective body but emphasizing instead subjective individuals and their social interactions, still needed and used communication to serve as 'cement' or 'mediation' in society.

MEASURES OF SIGNIFICANCE

Today there is no doubt about the importance of mass communication in society. Both laymen and social scientists typically document this by three forms of measurement: (1) the media as setters of public opinion and political agendas, (2) the place of media in everyday life, (3) the share of mass and telecommunication in the national economies. Each of these offers impressive data, and taken together they show how central a role mass communication indeed plays in society today.

Actually, this holds first and foremost in what is known as the 'Western world' – the industrialized countries of Europe, North America and parts of Asia (Australia, Japan . . .). However, it should be recalled that the majority of humankind lives in the so-called developing countries of Africa, Asia and Latin America, where mass communication remains, for the most part, where it used to be in the pre-industrial Europe. On the other hand, notable parts of the developing world (South Africa, China, Brazil) are actively involved in the modernization process, and even many less developed countries do have significant media systems – not the least television which, particularly in Latin America, reaches millions of people with television sets in slums and has huge regional programme industries such as Globo Televisa. As noted in Unesco's *World Communication Report*:

> In the vast Southern hemisphere, numerous countries have emerged from an almost uniformly poor Third World to make up a more differentiated South . . . These new growth opportunities cannot mask significant economic inequalities, however, both between the industrialized countries and the developing world, and within the group now benefiting from increased growth (Maherzi, 1997: 10).

If we focus on the Western world today and look at the first form of measurement listed above, the graphic evidence reveals how central a role mass media play in generating popular consciousness on public affairs – no matter whether these affairs are significant (such as the World Bank's policies) or insignificant (such as gossip around local celebrities). It is also increasingly obvious that politics is being waged through and by the media; whereas political parties originally used newspapers as their weapons, the media today (predominantly electronic and instant) have gained independent power, making politicians function more and more as servants of those modern agenda-setters. Textbook examples of 'media events' of the 1990s are the Persian Gulf War, Princess Diana's death and President Clinton's sex trial.

The second type of measurement emphasizes the significance of mass communication today. Statistics reveal how far media have penetrated into people's everyday lives. Take television in Britain and the USA: 97–98 per cent of households have at least one television set (over half have two sets and some 70 per cent have a videorecorder); people spend on average from five to seven hours per household, and from three to four hours per individual watching television each day (Abercrombie, 1996: 2–3). The viewing time is less in most other countries; for instance, in Scandinavia between two and three hours per average individual (Carlsson and Harrie, 1997).

Television, together with radio, and counting more or less concentrated exposure, occupies up to seven hours of the average person's daily time in a typical Western country. Nowadays this time seems to have reached a saturation point; the total no longer increases despite additional channels at the disposal of the viewer and listener. What time was earlier occupied by few national broadcasters is now divided between a number of outlets, including the videorecorder and the record/CD player, assisted by the remote control. Moreover, the new computer-based media connected to the Internet compete for these hours as well.

Besides using the electronic media, an overwhelming majority of people in all industrialized countries read daily newspapers and magazines, which take up over an hour of their average daily time. Adding books, records and cinema (the latter two particularly significant among young people), we arrive at over eight hours of average mass media 'consumption' a day. Even if we concede that some half of that is just background exposure to radio and television, we still must conclude that, statistically speaking, the mass media occupy more of our so-called free time than any other type of activity (hobbies, sports, pubs, etc.). As a matter of fact, in people's daily lives, it comes third only after sleep and work. Taking into account advertising as well – not only mixed with media messages but widely distributed in public places – we can infer that life in a modern society is impossible without constant exposure to mass communication.

The third measure of significance is the economy: the amount of money circulating in the business of mass communication. A single figure usually given to indicate the size of a sector in the national economy is the percentage of the gross national product (GNP). This GNP share for all mass media in industrialized countries has gradually increased and is nowadays typically around 3 per cent. This is no small portion; it compares with major sectors of industry, and it includes a notable investment by households in electronic receivers and players/recorders. Moreover, mass communication is closely connected to telecommunication (from telephone to new digital media transmission) which occupies an equally large and, today, even faster growing share of the GNP.

The GNP share of mass communication is today made up of roughly equal divisions of the print and electronic media, although in countries with strong press traditions the print media still dominate. For instance, in one such country, Finland, the print media constitute over two-thirds of the whole media economy, the newspaper industry alone making 30 per cent. We should also note that about one-third of the media economy in Western countries is based on advertising, while the rest comes from customers as subscription fees and individual purchases. In addition, some countries provide state subsidies to newspapers, books and film production and distribution – including public libraries – but these subsidies remain relatively small in the total picture of the media economy, which belongs predominantly to the private sector dominated by market forces.

MEDIA POWER

The story of mass communication begins, then, with a historical period of growth which leads into a phenomenon recognized as a highly significant factor in society. The story continues as one theme rises above all others: power, both political and economic, and variations such as media concentration, globalization and commercialization. A typical way of telling this story is through newspaper history: first several papers existed in a town, reflecting various interests, but despite economic growth, they began to die until just one so-called independent paper was left. Thus, freedom of the press, and free enterprise, have not led to a multiplicity of outlets but rather to a paradoxical scarcity within a flourishing industry, whereby, for example, of the 1,500 daily newspapers in the USA, 99 per cent are the only daily in their cities.

Stories like this have given rise to critical voices which see democracy being threatened by this concentration of media power. A contemporary classic example of this approach is Ben Bagdikian, dean emeritus of the Graduate School of Journalism from the University of California at Berkeley, whose *The Media Monopoly* (1997), now in its fifth edition, was first published in 1983 as a warning about the chilling effects of corporate ownership. He documents the media concentration, which ever since the first edition of the book has increased so much that the number of corporations controlling most of the US daily newspapers, magazines, radio, television, books and movies has dropped from fifty to ten. He suggests that Americans are in fact living under a 'Private Ministry of Information'. Bagdikian's Preface to the fifth edition is entitled 'The New Communication Cartel', and it begins with a pathetic note: 'In the last five years, a small number of the country's largest industrial corporations has acquired more public communications power – including ownership of the news – than any private business has ever before possessed in world history' (Bagdikian, 1997: ix).

The same line was pursued earlier by Herbert Schiller whose classic *Mass Communications and American Empire* (1969) was followed by a number of critical examinations (e.g. Schiller, 1981). Media mergers – nationally and internationally, both within and across media boundaries – and media barons such as Rupert Murdoch, inspired a whole line of literature with a more or less critical approach (e.g. Altschull, 1995; Herman and McChesney, 1997; Smith, 1991; Tunstall, 1977). This exposure of the emerging global media power can be seen as a variant of a much earlier critical approach to culture and communication adopted by the *Frankfurt School* led by Theodore Adorno and Max Horkheimer. They introduced, for example, the concept of 'culture industry' already in the 1940s (see Golding and Murdock, 1997, vol. I: 533–40).

However robust the evidence of media concentration, we should not miss a point made by Jeremy Tunstall. He suggests that while the number of dominant media companies may be small, the range and diversity of different media outlets can still be considerably bigger, suggesting a pluralist argument against a Marxist concern about concentrated capitalist control: 'Genuine monopoly may co-exist with equally genuine competition' (Tunstall, 1983: 175) where several titles compete against one another, even if grouped under the same organizational umbrella. Moreover, we should note the fact that even 'the largest media conglomerates are small- and mid-sized compared with major manufacturing and retailing companies' (Picard, 1998: 195). Robert Picard also points out that the electronic and entertainment industries, at least in the USA, 'are far more competitive and less concentrated today than they were twenty-five years ago' (Picard, 1998: 200). This development follows changes in technology, which have facilitated more channels and new media which in turn have reduced the average audience size (in the USA): 'prime-time network shows could count on one-quarter to one-third of the audience three decades ago, but today are lucky to pull 10 to 12 per cent because audiences are watching scores of other channels and networks' (Picard, 1998: 198).

Picard does not suggest that media power is not a problem:

> Just as state-owned media convey the interests of the state, privately owned media disseminate the interests of their owners and of the media themselves. The content of privately owned media nearly universally and continually convey

> pro-business, antiregulatory biases . . . Among the main problems associated with
> concentration and commercialization are the use of media for the political pur-
> poses of their corporate owners, the homogenization of news and emphasis
> placed on mainstream voices, cross promotion of communication products and
> services, and the increasing reliance on celebrity even in news and public affairs
> (Picard, 1998: 208).

Indeed, the problem is not so much concentration as such, but rather the
commercialization and the so-called market forces behind it. Actually, it is
off the point to romantically long for the early twentieth-century city with
several independent papers. As Picard reminds us:

> Although the existence of multiple media outlets makes theoretically possible for
> more views and opinions to be communicated, the mere existence of media plu-
> rality does not ensure message pluralism – that is, diversity of viewpoints. Most
> studies of media content have shown that different units of a medium and dif-
> ferent media tend to provide relatively similar content, programming, and views
> because of commercial concerns, the adoption of standard industry norms and
> business practices, and dependence on a few similar sources of news and opinion
> (Picard, 1998: 213).

This kind of critical approach to commercial pressures on mass communication is shared in Europe, although a lot of sentiment against media concentration as such flourishes as well, with media 'empires' and 'moguls'
seen as threats to democracy. Actually, the European Commission has
issued a *Green Paper on Pluralism and Media Concentration in the Internal
Market* and the European Parliament has repeatedly expressed its concern
over media concentration, including 'the negative consequences of having
an information society which is subject solely to market forces, and the need
to take account of the cultural, ethical, social and political implications' (see
Nordenstreng, 1997: 16).

In general, pluralism and diversity are the catchwords most used in public
media policy debates concerning structures of mass communication. But
there is no consensus about what to do in practice to ensure pluralism and
diversity; few if any effective measures have emerged at the European level
to regulate media industries. The dominant doctrine is, both nationally and
regionally, that strong media conglomerates are after all acceptable and even
desirable, because they seem to serve as safeguards against foreign – for
Europeans mostly American – competition. The problem is, however, that
media enterprises are increasingly international and global in character; they
are part and parcel of global capital markets.

Consequently, the real question is whether mass communication should
follow the logic of commercial capitalism or should rather be understood as
belonging to the socio-cultural sector of society next to institutions of education, science, art, etc. (as suggested by the above quoted European Parliament position). Public service broadcasting represents the latter approach,

but it has lost a virtual monopoly under increasing pressure from market-driven private radio and television enterprises. On the other hand, public service broadcasting was granted a kind of life insurance policy by the European Union in 1997, when its summit in Amsterdam adopted a protocol to the original Treaty of Rome allowing this form of enterprise to depart from the rules of free internal market (Nordenstreng, 1998: 425).

Media power, then, leads us to the fundamental distinction between commercial-industrial and socio-cultural values. At the same time, it focuses attention also on the distinction between national-local culture and transnational-global culture. In fact, the critical school referred to above has opened up not only chilling visions of media monopolies and empires but also perspectives of media imperialism or 'transnational corporate cultural imperialism' (Herman and McChesney, 1997: 49). While these perspectives have been criticized for presenting too simplistic views (Tomlinson, 1991, 1998), everybody seems to agree that mass communication today cannot be understood without relating it to the ongoing processes in the world arena, which undermine sovereignty and highlight globalization (Golding and Harris, 1997; Nordenstreng and Schiller, 1993).

RECURRENT QUESTIONS

Media power is one of the permanent topics which have galvanized media experts as well as ordinary people to ask hard questions about the nature of mass communication in society. Other long-standing questions in the field relate to the effects of mass communication and the freedom of the media. I shall briefly review these questions which, while they are not easily answered, do serve as opportunities to consider further challenges in the study of mass communication.

Question 1: Who has the power over the media?

To begin with, four categories of power-holders can be listed: owners, producers, advertisers and audiences.

Media owners have central power since they define the policy and they hire and fire the personnel. But even a private owner is no longer a simple concept; media moguls notwithstanding, ownership is typically divided between several parties with more or less distant participation in the actual decision-making of the media enterprise. As in other areas of economic life, managers often play a more important day-to-day role than the real owners. Also, a State as an owner is far from a simple case; we cannot take the State as a fixed entity, but must ask what are the socio-political interests pursued by the State in question. Likewise, corporations of public service broadcasting such as the

British Broadcasting Corporation (BBC) pose a third category of problematic ownership, leading us to consider how the political representation of the population at large affects the management of media institutions.

Journalists and other media producers are often seen as powerful gatekeepers of the media machinery in front of the general public. True, they do exercise power in the media, but few of them possess independent power in the final instance. Most of them are just paid labour in an industry. On the other hand, this is a peculiar industry which needs not only mechanical workers but also creative labourers to ensure permanent innovation. For example, the film and music branches function as extensions of the creative arts, just as literature has for centuries – the media workers facilitate a constant search for new content and form, which ensures a degree of autonomy.

Advertisers have a strategic role in the power constellation around the media, at least in the newspaper and commercial radio-television industries, which typically rely on advertising for over 50 per cent of their finances. Their exercise of power is seldom immediate and direct; it is structural, defining which message production lines are kept open and which are closed. This power is quite pervasive – often even greater than the power of the owners and producers. Naturally, it has little or no role in non-commercial media, including public service broadcasting – unless the latter is financially dependent on advertising and chooses to be integrated in the commercial market.

The audience finally has a role to play in determining who has power over the media. After all, media are meant to be received or consumed by the public; no media can disregard the audience behaviour and reaction for a long time. Spokespersons of commercial interests, including Right-leaning media scholars, tend to stress this component of media power, claiming that the public gets what it wants – that the reader/listener/viewer is 'the king'. On the other hand, spokespersons of public service broadcasting and other socially oriented observers tend to emphasize the role and responsibility of the owners, producers and advertisers.

A central argument in this clash of perspectives is the concept of an *active audience* – an audience which does not passively consume the flow of messages fed by the media, but instead actively works itself into the communication process by decoding the messages according to its own interests. Reception studies have shown that readers, viewers and listeners independently interpret and use media messages – from hard news to soft soap operas (see, e.g., Corner, 1996). This has given ammunition to both commercial spokespersons and post-modernists, both stressing the cultural role of the media and 'consumer sovereignty'. Against this, those who stress media power argue that even the most active audience reacts to the messages provided by the media and that the general terms of the game are set by the media structure rather than the meanings recipients bring to the communication process.

336

In brief, the complexity of the question concerning power in the media is expressed in the concluding words by the Glasgow Media Group after re-thinking media influence and power in modern Britain: 'The media do not operate as a single force in a hermetically sealed ideological conspiracy. It is all much more messy and contradictory . . . ' (Eldridge, Kitzinger and Williams, 1997: 180).

Question 2: What are the media effects?

This leads us to the origins of mass communication research in the 1920s, inspired by a socio-political concern about the popular media in a mass society. A common belief at the time was that the media – not least the new medium of cinema – have a direct and big impact on people and society. This 'hypodermic needle' concept was countered by psychological and so-ciological research, which showed that instead of a simple stimulus-response (S-R) model, a much more complicated model with a socially con-ditioned organism in the middle (S-O-R) exists. For example, political cam-paigns were seen to follow a two-step flow model, whereby the message proceeds first from media to a core of influentials who then distribute it through social networks in their natural surroundings.

Consequently, media effects were no longer understood in terms of a direct cause and effect but always seen as mediated by social or cultural factors. In general, since the 1960s, this has been accepted by all research on media effects (see, e.g., Livingstone, 1996). While thinking about and debat-ing media effects has continued to evolve and change, not least in relation to television violence and children, Grossberg, Wartella and Whitney articulate today's conventional wisdom:

> Our review should suggest that the media may have many different impacts on public behavior. At the same time, several generations of research on the impact of the media suggest that it is quite difficult to be specific about the effect of any content, indeed any *class* of content on its audience. The same content, indeed, may have different effects on different segments of the audience. Moreover, by its very nature, most social science research must be highly qualified about its find-ings: It is very difficult to speak definitely about media impact (Grossberg, War-tella and Whitney, 1998: 314).

Critical scholars like Schiller and Bagdikian would not be this careful, giving rather a more straightforward reply: the media do have an impact – why would advertisers otherwise spend their money! While such a perspective does not deny an active audience, it emphasizes that in a commercial system people are just consumers and that the ownership and financing structures of the media determine ultimate rules of the game. Accordingly, this school of thought answers the media influence question by looking mainly at the media structures and related contents, while others pay most attention to the receiving side, with reservations such as those quoted above.

These perspectives lead us to consider also those empirical facts which show that knowledge and information is distributed quite unevenly in contemporary societies – media abundance notwithstanding. There are information-rich and information-poor people, and there is cultural exclusion in the so-called information society. Few would accuse mass communication alone for these evils, but few would deny that media do play a role in these processes – particularly at a time when media turn more and more 'tabloid', when information turns 'infotainment', and education turns 'edutainment'.

Question 3: How free are the media?

This question follows logically from the previous two: freedom depends on potential power and impact. Seen in this light, media freedom is conditioned at various levels. Indeed, we may say that mass communication in society is determined by so many economic, social, political and cultural factors that the whole concept of freedom becomes highly problematic, almost empty.

Yet it remains one of the most used concepts in speaking about the media, and it is particularly dear to those employed by the media. Journalists and other creative media workers are characteristically sensitive about their perceived freedom, but largely fail to see the structural limits of freedom – not least the limits set by their own profession. The sharpest criticism of the media today leads us to challenge the role of professionalism in the media.

In general, media are less free than we are accustomed to think. Media freedom should not be taken at face value but should be problematicized and related to civic liberties in society. From this perspective, media freedom can be seen even as the opposite of a citizen's freedom of speech (Nordenstreng, 1997). Moreover, by asking how free are the media, we cannot help also introducing the other side of the concept of freedom: responsibility. This, again, leads us to issues of media ethics and media regulation – by law, market or self-regulation – which in turn invites us to question the place of media in democracy (Curran, 1996).

The central question, combining the three discussed here, remains: to what extent is mass communication an independent force and to what extent does it reflect other factors in society? The present story suggests a contradictory answer to this question: on the one hand, the media have grown to occupy a significant place in society, but on the other hand, whatever the angle from which we view the media, they are highly conditioned and determined. Discovering the answer requires a balanced approach – something that Golding and Murdock (1996) call a 'critical political economy of communications'.

SUMMARY

- Mass communication is an integral part of modernization over the past few centuries.
- Mass media occupy today a significant place in the political, economic as well as everyday life of Western industrialized societies.
- Media pluralism and diversity is limited by commercialization rather than concentration.
- Media power does not operate as a single force and media exercise multiple influences.
- Media freedom is conditioned by several factors and media independence is largely an illusion.

FURTHER READING

Boyd-Barrett, Oliver and Newbold, Chris (eds) (1995) *Approaches to Media: A Reader*. London: Arnold. A compilation of seventy-one texts by classics and contemporary scholars introducing the field. The 550 pages offer a fairly comprehensive overview of the research traditions relating to mass communication, under the labels of mass society, media effects, political economy, the public sphere, media professions, cultural hegemony, moving image, feminism, and the new audience research.

Curran, James and Gurevitch, Michael (eds) (1996) *Mass Media and Society*, 2nd edn. London: Arnold. A collection of seventeen essays by leading contemporary scholars mainly from the UK and USA, discussing the state of research on media and society in general and on media production and reception in particular. This is a revised edition of a volume originally published in 1977 as readings for the Open University course on mass communication and society – a volume that became a standard textbook on the topic in the UK and abroad.

Eldridge, John, Kitzinger, Jenny and Williams, Kevin (1997) *The Mass Media and Power in Modern Britain*. Oxford: Oxford University Press. An introduction to the role and importance of the mass media in contemporary British society by the founder of the Glasgow Media Group and his associates. Beginning with the historical development of the mass media, the book examines their ownership and power in the public and political sphere focusing on topics such as moral panics, the royal family, advertising and public relations – also from the viewpoint of media audiences and reception.

Golding, Peter and Murdock, Graham (eds) (1997) *The Political Economy of the Media*. Cheltenham: Edward Elgar. A 'library' of readings in two volumes, nearly 700 pages each. The thirty-three texts in Volume I reproduce excerpts by contemporary classics from Herbert Schiller and Dallas Smythe to Jeremy Tunstall and the editors themselves, but also selected old classics from Karl Marx to Theodore Adorno. Volume II includes twenty-eight texts under titles 'Private Interests to Common Goods' (with Jürgen Habermas among others), 'Public Broadcasting and the Public Interest' (from Reith to Pilkington and Peacock), 'Policing the Public Interest', 'Institutionalizing Diversity'.

Grossberg, Lawrence, Wartella, Ellen and Whitney, Charles (1998) *Media-Making: Mass Media in a Popular Culture*. London: Sage. A synthesis of current knowledge about the media in the context of culture and society. The authors, belonging to the post-war television or rock and roll generation, do not follow the customary approach of introductory textbooks by looking at each medium separately (newspapers, magazines, books, radio, television, film). Instead, they look at mass communication as a whole, inviting the reader to study the media in relation to reality, ideology, power, public, etc.

Servaes, Jan and Lie, Rico (eds) (1997) *Media and Politics in Transition: Cultural Identity in the Age of Globalization*. Leuven: Acco. An overview of contemporary thinking in the field mainly from a political science viewpoint. The sixteen chapters by notable authors from around the world provide both global and regional perspectives as well as theoretical excursions on the media in relation to topics such as public opinion, civil society, identity and global/local. While the book does not offer a synthetic view, it highlights the questions dominating the field towards the end of the century.

REFERENCES

Abercrombie, Nicholas (1996) *Television and Society*. Cambridge: Polity Press.
Altschull, Herbert (1995) *Agents of Power: The Media and Public Policy*, 2nd edn. New York: Longman.
Bagdikian, Ben (1997) *The Media Monopoly*, 5th edn. Boston: Beacon Press.
Boyce, George, Curran, James and Wingate, Pauline (1978) *Newspaper History: From the 17th Century to the Present Day*. London: Constable.
Carlsson, Ulla and Harrie, Eva (1997) *Media Trends 1997 in Denmark, Finland, Iceland, Norway and Sweden: Descriptive Analyses and Statistics*. Göteborg: Nordicom.
Chalaby, Jean K. (1998) *The Invention of Journalism*. London: Macmillan.
Corner, John (1996) 'Reappraising Reception: Aims, Concepts and Methods', in James Curran and Michael Gurevitch (eds) *Mass Media and Society*, 2nd edn. London: Arnold, pp. 280–304.
Curran, James (1996) 'Mass Media and Democracy Revisited', in James Curran and Michael Gurevitch (eds) *Mass Media and Society*, 2nd edn. London: Arnold, pp. 81–119.

Eldridge, John, Kitzinger, Jenny and Williams, Kevin (1997) *The Mass Media and Power in Modern Britain*. Oxford: Oxford University Press.

Golding, Peter and Harris, Phil (eds) (1997) *Beyond Cultural Imperialism: Globalization, Communication and the New International Order*. London: Sage.

Golding, Peter and Murdock, Graham (1996) 'Culture, Communications, and Political Economy', in James Curran and Michael Gurevitch (eds) *Mass Communication and Society*, 2nd edn. London: Arnold, pp. 11–30.

Golding, Peter and Murdock, Graham (eds) (1997) *The Poltical Economy of the Media*. Cheltenham: Edward Elgar.

Grossberg, Lawrence, Wartella, Ellen and Whitney, Charles (1998) *MediaMaking: Mass Media in a Popular Culture*. London: Sage.

Habermas, Jürgen (1989) *The Structural Transformation of the Public Sphere*. Cambridge: Polity Press.

Hardt, Hanno (1979) *Social Theories of the Press: Early German and American Perspectives*. Beverly Hills, CA, and London: Sage.

Herman, Edward and McChesney, Robert (1997) *The Global Media: The New Missionaries on Corporate Capitalism*. London: Cassell.

Livingstone, Sonia (1996) 'On the Continuing Problem of Media Effects', in James Curran and Michael Gurevitch (eds) *Mass Media and Society*, 2nd edn. London: Arnold, pp. 305–24.

Maherzi, Lotfi (1997) *World Communication Report: The Media and the Challenge of the New Technologies*. Paris: Unesco Publishing.

Mattelart, Armand and Mattelart, Michelle (1998) *Theories of Communication: A Short Introduction*. London: Sage.

McLuhan, Marshall (1962) *The Gutenberg Galaxy*. Toronto: University of Toronto Press.

Nordenstreng, Kaarle (1997) 'The Citizen Moves from the Audience to the Arena', *Nordicom Review*, **18**(2): 13–20.

Nordenstreng, Kaarle (1998) 'Hutchins Goes Global', *Communication Law and Policy*, **3**(3): 419–38.

Nordenstreng, Kaarle and Schiller, Herbert (eds) (1993) *Beyond Sovereignty: International Communication in the 1990s*. Norwood, NJ: Ablex.

Picard, Robert (1998) 'Media Concentration, Economics, and Regulation', in Doris Graber, Denis McQuail and Pippa Norris (eds) *The Politics of News, the News of Politics*. Washington, DC: Congressional Quarterly Press, pp. 193–217.

Schiller, Herbert (1969) *Mass Communications and American Empire*. New York: Augustus M. Kelley. (2nd edn, 1996, Boulder, CO: Westview Press.)

Schiller, Herbert (1981) *Who Knows: Information in the Age of the Fortune 500*. Norwood, NJ: Ablex.

Smith, Anthony (1991) *The Age of Behemoths: The Globalization of Mass Media Firms*. New York: Priority Press.

Stephens, Mitchell (1988) *A History of News: From the Drum to the Satellite*. London: Penguin Books.

Thompson, John B. (1995) *The Media and Modernity: A Social Theory of the Media*. Cambridge: Polity Press.

Tomlinson, John (1991) *Cultural Imperialism*. Baltimore, MD: Johns Hopkins University Press.

Tomlinson, John (1998) 'Review Essay: Unfinished Business. Varieties of

Retrospection in the Analysis of Global Communications', *European Journal of Communication*, **13**(2): 235–44.

Tunstall, Jeremy (1977) *The Media are American: Anglo-American Media in the World.* London: Constable.

Tunstall, Jeremy (1983) *The Media in Britain.* London: Constable.

Chapter 24

The Web

Vincent Mosco

> We stand at the brink of another revolution. This one will involve unpreceden-
> tedly inexpensive communication; all the computers will join together to com-
> municate with us and for us. Interconnected globally, they will form a network,
> which is being called the information highway. A direct precursor is the pres-
> ent Internet, which is a group of computers joined and exchanging information
> using current technology (Gates, 1995: 3–4).

These words from Bill Gates, the enormously successful President of the
Microsoft Corporation, give us more than just a definition of the World
Wide Web. They announce a vision of a world transformed by computer
communication. This chapter takes up the vision that Gates and others have
promised and evaluates it against what we know about the World Wide
Web in all of its technical, social, political and economic dimensions. In order
to do this effectively we need to start with what the Web means and with
how it has developed. Where did the Web originate and what can we learn
from the stories of similar technologies?

WHAT IS THE WEB? WHERE DID IT COME FROM?

As Gates tells us, the World Wide Web describes a network of computers
that are connected to one another through different means of communication. When we log on, we are, in effect, dialling a phone number that puts
our computer in touch with a more powerful one, typically called a server.

343

Our personal computer (PC) and the server are connected by a phone line, although other forms of connection are increasingly used. These include coaxial cables that also bring us cable television services and ethernet cables. Each of the latter are faster and can carry more information than a typical telephone line, but most of us will use the phone line for some time to come because it is most readily available to most people with personal computers. A few people also connect without wires making links in the same way we connect with a mobile telephone.

Once linked to a server, we can use that link to connect to computers around the world enabling us to send and receive messages by electronic mail (email), look for information, find software, such as games, and download it to our computer, enter a 'chat room' and talk to a group of people who are online at the same time, buy anything from a new coat to airline tickets, or express our opinion about an issue or a political candidate. Typically, we pay for the service in the telephone charge (almost always a local call to a server in our town or city) and a monthly fee to a service provider who owns the server and makes sure that we can connect to it without busy signals and provides us with room on the server to store our own material such as email or a home page. Schools and universities manage their own computers and often provide students and faculty with free or low-cost access.

The World Wide Web is more than just a network of computer communication technologies. The specific characteristics of the Web result from the particular way it has developed. That is why it is important to learn about the history of the Web, its relationship to the history of similar technologies, and how the Web is influenced by trends in business, government, and in society and culture.

The Web grows out of the convergence of computer and communication technologies which began at the end of the Second World War. In fact, the computer developed during the war to enhance the effectiveness of automatic weapons. In the 1950s almost all of the funding for computer research came from the US military which gave large contracts to commercial firms like IBM and AT&T. In turn, these companies sold the first computer systems, including the first networks that linked them to telephone lines, to the US Defense Department. Between 1958 and 1974 the US military bought 35 to 50 per cent of all computer circuits. By providing a major market for these products, the US military was able to influence the development of computers and to provide the industry with the funding that kept it alive. So dependent was the electronics industry on military contracts that in 1957 the prominent American business magazine *Fortune* worried about the future of the computer if the Cold War were to end: 'Peace, if it came suddenly, would hit the industry very hard' (Harris, 1957: 216). In 1958 the military agency responsible for developing computing technology created the very first example of the World Wide Web, Arpanet (for Advanced Research Projects Network) which was made up of computers that connected military researchers and their commercial contractors by phone lines. The Web there-fore did not originate, as popular myths describe, in the work of amateur tinkerers toying with new technologies in their home workshops. Rather, it began out of the need to bring together military researchers and their indus-trial partners who were responsible for the major arms build-up in the West from the 1960s to the 1980s. True, the personal computer arose in part from the work of a few brilliant young amateurs. But by the time Steve Jobs was creating the first Apple computer and Bill Gates sold his first operating system software to run the IBM PC, computer networks were an established tool in Western military and business operations.

This early history is important for understanding the contemporary Web because it helped to establish the intense interest in putting business and military security interests first. This meant networks were under tight cor-porate or government security control, run on the authoritarian principle of centralized management of the network, with little opportunity for people to freely use these networks for anything more than established rules permit-ted. One commercial example of this principle was the Dialog network which was set up by major military contractors General Electric and Lock-heed. Dialog permitted subscribers to dial up a database to search for infor-mation for which they would pay a subscription fee and a charge for the amount of time spent on the system. Subscribers could not send information nor communicate with one another. They paid to search available stores of information.

Nevertheless, even as the military and business were perfecting forerun-ners of the Internet, individual engineers, university researchers and people interested in exploring the democratic uses of technology, were trying out the potential for connecting the new stand-alone personal computers through telephone lines. By the mid-1980s, the first of what we would today call electronic bulletin boards sprang up to use computers for unrestricted communication, ranging from just chatting and playing games to mobilizing citizen groups for political action. The WELL, a network of California com-puter enthusiasts, was one of the first, and on a much larger scale, Peacenet was established in the mid-1980s as a non-profit network that by 1987 con-nected 2,500 subscribers and 300 organizations in seventy countries to ad-vance communication among citizen activists. It provided some of the first public email, bulletin board, computer conferencing and data research ser-vices for activists around the world including the earliest links between people working for democratic social change across what was then the great divide between the Soviet Union and the USA and its allies. It also helped to establish the first computer networks among environmentalists including Greennet in the UK (Roach, 1993).

By the time of the Web's arrival, the pattern was set between a dominant centralized set of networks which were based on the model of ability to pay with careful security controls that limited communication and another set of networks that were more open, democratic and committed to the widest possible flows of communication. This pattern continues today. The dominant model includes large corporations, such as America Online, Microsoft and the major telephone companies, providing Internet services for a monthly or hourly fee. It also features software providers like Microsoft and Netscape using their browser programs to direct, or in the more popular terminology, 'push' users to selections offered by other large businesses, including other media conglomerates like Time-Warner, which rely on extensive advertising and have financial deals with these software providers. Another variation on the dominant model is a handful of data service providers, such as the oldest of them all, Lexis-Nexis, a subsidiary of the giant publishing firm Reed-Elsevier, which, for a very high per usage fee, provides mainly businesses with immediate access to an archived database of the world's newspapers, business publications, government reports and a variety of other material. The alternative pattern lives on in community networks, mainly called Freenets, which rely on community support to provide free access to the Web through terminals located in public schools, libraries and post offices, in addition to free home access. It also lives on in the tens of thousands of individual and community 'publishers' who develop home pages and special interest bulletin boards and chat rooms that encourage a freer and more broadly based exchange of information.

LESSONS FROM THE HISTORY OF TECHNOLOGY

The immediate history of the Web teaches us that how the network operates, who controls it, and who benefits from it, are not determined by the technology itself. The pattern of convergence between computers and telephone lines could have taken many different forms. But the particular dominant and alternative patterns in place today were set by the differences in power among a wide range of interests who defined the Web in many different ways, including as a way to make money, to maintain centralized control over information flows, to bring about social change and to extend democracy.

There are also lessons to be learned from the wider history of technology that are especially important for understanding the significance of the Web. Those who speak about the Web as a revolutionary technology are just the latest in a history of people who felt that the newest technology would transform the entire world for the better. For example, it is an increasingly popular myth that computer communication ends geography by completing a revolution in the process of transcending the spatial constraints that historically limited the movement of information. *The Death of Distance* (Cairncross, 1997) is just the latest in a series of books announcing the triumph of technology over place or the annihilation of space with time. The argument is simple. The convergence of computer and communication technologies permits people to meet anywhere at any time, thereby enabling the ubiquitous exchange of information from the simplest two-person exchange to the operation of a multinational conglomerate with its vast requirements for moving information and ideas rapidly, efficiently and with close to complete security. In the nineteenth century, spatial barriers meant that news took weeks by packet boat to get from New York to New Orleans. Now, distance is by and large insignificant and, particularly with the arrival of global mobile satellite systems which will permit seamless wireless communication between any points on the globe, soon to be completely irrelevant. According to this myth, all space is becoming cyberspace, because communication is migrating there. And, the myth continues, cyberspace is fundamentally different from geography as we know it because this space is almost fully transparent with respect to communication.

Notwithstanding the occasional nuance in the 'death of distance' research, it is typically a breathlessly overstated argument. In this respect, it follows in a long tradition of writing about technological change, particularly electronic technology, which has been announcing the death of distance for over a century. In the nineteenth century, people felt that the railroad would unite Europe as no conqueror ever did, that the telegraph would overcome class and racial divisions in America, and that electricity would bounce messages off the clouds to isolated villages, which would nevertheless need to cope with the minor irritant of what was charmingly called 'celestial advertising'. In the twentieth century, the telephone and broadcasting would do what these earlier technologies could not. The historian David Nye (1990) refers to these as visions of the 'technological sublime', a literal eruption of feeling that overwhelms reason with enthusiasm. Partly because they are so seduced by the technology, the death of distance advocates have missed significant characteristics of communication that call for a modification of its meaning.

Assuming that overcoming distance improves communication, supporters miss the equal tendency of more communication to increase dissonance and intensify conflict. The railway, telegraph and broadcasting brought Europe closer together in war as well as in peace. Moreover, proponents of the end of geography idea underestimate the importance of face-to-face contact and of informal networks whose connections are based partly on and certainly facilitated by physical proximity. Finally, they miss the tendency of large monopolies to take control over new technologies and use them for their own purposes. For example, in the USA, the telegraph, which received the same hope and praise that the Web receives today, was rapidly controlled by the monopoly Western Union Telegraph Company which marketed it for business rather than consumer use because that is how they would make the most money from it. As one historian of technology puts it:

> Virtually all subsequent developments in telecommunications, can be seen, in latent form, in the conversion of telegraph technology into a commodity bought

and sold for profit and saved from the 'wastes of competition' by the collective actions that preserved monopoly prerogatives within the industry and shielded their beneficiaries from public accountability (DuBoff, 1984: 53–4).

To recap, there are three important points to draw from the general history of communication technology. First, every communication technology is mythologized as the source of an overwhelmingly beneficial worldwide revolution. Yes, there has also been a tendency to demonize communication technology, as readers of Orwell's *1984* would attest, but these compare weakly to the general and understandable enthusiasm of those who would invest their hopes and money in it. Second, in spite of democratic visions for communication technology, control and profit are rapidly being concentrated in a handful of companies that understandably focus on how to use it to further their control and profit. Finally, this has historically led to resistance from citizens who grow impatient with the failure to make good on promises of widespread benefit. One result of this is the growth of public control or regulation of communication services to provide universal access at low cost and to ensure that the technology is used in education, political participation and other applications that are unlikely to appeal to profit-conscious businesses. Public education, public libraries, public postal, telegraph, telephone and broadcasting services are one result of this opposition, as are the establishment of government regulatory authorities that monitor pricing, access and use.

TODAY'S WEB: COMMUNICATION, INFORMATION AND ENTERTAINMENT

One of the most striking things about today's World Wide Web is its remarkable diversity. First, it is a way to communicate in a variety of forms primarily through electronic mail which enables two or more people to exchange messages without being online at the same time. Messages can range from the briefest line to a long text, audio or video file. Communication also takes place among entire groups of people who join a bulletin board service so that they can post messages to a large number of people with (presumably) a shared interest and receive messages from them. For those interested in exchanging messages with people at the same time, there are 'chat rooms' which people 'enter' to communicate online about a common interest. Rules for these vary but tend to be more rigorous than for bulletin boards because online communication can be more personally intense.

The value of the Web for many people lies more clearly in the links it provides to information and entertainment. With more information stored in the digital form required to be accessed on the Web, people increasingly turn to it for everything from simple inquiries to extensive library and document research. They also use the Web to post information about themselves, for example on personal or institutional home pages. For example, my home page (http://www.carleton.ca/~vmosco/vm.html) contains information on my professional background, describes my recent book, lists other published work and contains articles that I have decided to post for interested readers. You can turn to the Web for information relevant to this chapter by logging on to the site containing the Blair Government's White Paper outlining its plans to provide Web services to schools and communities: http://www.ukoln.ac.uk/services/lic/newlibrary/dcms-15oct97.html. Or, for the criticism offered by a leading historian of technology, David Noble, who worries about the creation of 'Digital Diploma Mills': http://www.journet.com/twu/diplomamills.html.

Of course, the Web has also become a major entertainment medium, a place for people to turn to in order to learn about films, music, television, etc. and to post and download games, images, audio and video material. Given the power of the Web to distribute material from any computer to any other, many people foresee a time when it will either replace or merge with television as the major mass entertainment and news medium.

The costs of building and expanding the Web have become an increasingly important issue because until now governments have paid for much of this either directly through budget allocations to research and development or indirectly through funding universities or subsidizing Web-related companies. But this is declining now because governments have cut budgets and because many believe that the private marketplace should sustain the Web. Although governments are still providing help to construct the Web, support research to improve it, and help those who cannot afford access, even these activities are coming under considerable criticism from those who believe that government should not intervene in what are believed to be private marketplace decisions and from those who wonder about the wisdom of building computer networks when governments are cutting back on providing essentials like food and health care to the poor. As a result, alternative means of funding the Web have grown and these will likely have a significant impact on its development.

COMMERCIALIZATION OF THE WEB

We take for granted the commercial nature of much of the mass media. Television and radio broadcasters make money by selling advertising. Some so-called pay-television channels earn revenue by selling a subscription to the channel that provides a service if the viewer pays by the month for the entire channel or by the programme selected. Newspapers sell individual copies and subscriptions, but they make most of their income from selling space to advertisers. The means of funding media was not always obvious to investors and, when chosen, was not always approved by audiences. For example, when radio broadcasting came along, many people felt that a device that could bring news and entertainment directly into the home was too powerful to permit private developers to control and so many countries, Britain for example, maintained complete government authority over radio. Others, like the USA, with a weaker tradition of government control, experimented with various forms of funding until a few private broadcasters hit on commercial advertising as the best means of making money. But many Americans reacted angrily against commercial messages because it was considered inappropriate to sell products directly in people's living rooms at all hours of the day. The government was forced to step in and regulate the hours of advertising (mainly to daytime hours during the week) until by the 1930s, after commercial radio had been on the air for over ten years, regulations were relaxed.

We have become so used to advertising in the mass media that there is nothing like the resistance to radio advertising when companies turn to Internet advertising as a way to make money. Nevertheless, with the Web still in its early years, there is a lot of experimentation with alternative ways to use the Web for profit. Many companies, including some of the largest like Microsoft, invested heavily in developing Web newspapers, magazines, games and other entertainment, that they hoped to sell directly to subscribers. The view was that if people pay for the daily newspaper, wouldn't they pay for a regular paper or magazine delivered to their homes electronically? As it turns out, people are very reluctant to pay for information on the Web, particularly if there are print alternatives. Almost every venture in this area has failed and most companies provide news and information on the Web without a charge and make money by selling advertising and by using their Web-based media as a good advertisement for their print editions. Time-Warner, the global media conglomerate, uses its Pathfinder website to sell advertising and to promote its magazines, films, cable television channels and other media products. Web-based games and entertainment have met a similar fate. Although it is premature to conclude that people will not pay for Web information and entertainment, a mass market is not likely to develop in this area for some time.

The other major alternative for commercializing the Web is through the sale of products or e-commerce as it is widely known. Today supporters of turning the Web into an electronic shopping mall like to say that you can buy just about anything on the Web. Anyone who has surfed the Web would have to agree that it is possible to use a credit card or telephone to buy anything from the standard products you would find in a department store, shop or printed catalogue to less legitimate products and services including pornography, prostitution and gambling. Nevertheless, because people are reluctant to trust Web companies with sensitive information like a credit card number or because they would rather go to a shop to look at a product before making a purchase, the Web has not become a site for mass consumption. Although e-commerce is growing, it remains an infinitesimal proportion of retail sales. Nevertheless, many of the major Web companies are investing heavily in e-commerce in the hope of taking a large chunk of the market from traditional retailers. Microsoft, for example, is joining up with companies knowledgeable in specific markets to provide travel, ticket purchasing, music CDs, videos and other retail goods. New companies like Amazon.com hope to become major booksellers simply by taking Web orders for a list of several million titles. Governments are providing help by holding off on enforcing sales tax statutes for Web purchases. In the meantime, advertising increasingly fills the Web pages of companies large and small, as well as those of individual home pages. Commercialization is perhaps the most important trend on the Web and many of the new Web start-up companies based in high-tech districts like Manhattan's 'Silicon Alley' have found they cannot remain in business unless they fundamentally shift their work to produce new and innovative forms of electronic advertising (Mosco, 1997).

CONTROL AND THE WEB

Businesses are increasingly interested in using the Web to sell more than products and services. They see enormous opportunities for profit in selling information about the people who purchase or even just come into a shop or browse. This is very much the case on the Internet as information about visits to a site, measured in clicks or actual purchases, is sought after by companies that would use this information to advertise more efficiently to people with specific interests. Although this is a major motivation to gather detailed information on how people are using the Web, it is not the only one. Governments, particularly the police and other security authorities, are interested in using Web data to develop background information on citizens to determine their possible connection to criminal activities, to further intelligence investigations, and to make connections among people and their activities. There is nothing fundamentally different between this activity and more traditional forms of phone-tapping and surveillance, except that the Web provides a more powerful form of surveillance than any previous technologies.

There are enormous economic and governmental incentives to intrude on and violate people's basic right to privacy on the Web. Nevertheless, this interest in using the Web to learn about and control people's behaviour does clash with the business need to provide people with privacy guarantees in order to convince them to feel comfortable enough to shop on the Web. As long as it is impossible for companies to guarantee security, including security from intruding hackers, people will be reluctant to shop at the electronic mall. Efforts to provide a software solution have failed because of the technical difficulties of guaranteeing against hacking and because of the clash of basic interests. Governments, particularly the US, do not want to approve of highly sophisticated security or encryption software because they want to retain the right to tap into the Web for what they believe are legitimate police activities.

THE INFORMATION HAVES AND HAVE-NOTS

Although the resolution of the privacy issue will have an important bearing on future Web use, it is likely that more and more of our daily routine will require a growing amount of Web activity. But this is a significant problem because the vast majority of the world's people, including a majority of people in the industrialized world, do not have access to the Web. For people in the less developed world even the telephone remains a luxury, so the likelihood that Web access will be made available to anyone other than the richest people in major cities is remote. Although access is more widespread in the developed world, it remains concentrated among the wealthiest in society (as does access to all other electronic media) and among university populations whose access is subsidized. For most people, the cost of hardware, software, and access fees are priced well beyond their budgets. Although this was a problem with earlier technologies like the telephone and broadcasting, access bottlenecks were eased because government commitments to public service balanced the tendencies of the market to concentrate access among the rich. This is no longer the case so that, except for a handful of government programmes that provide little more than media publicity, people have to pay their own way to ride the Web.

The absence of government involvement has consequences beyond the ability to afford Web access. The lack of educational programmes to teach people how to use the Web effectively and the dearth of access sites in public places like post offices, community centres or government facilities make it more difficult for people to develop their Web capabilities. Consequently, even if governments changed policies and expanded the subsidized distribution of hardware and software, or provided support for low-cost access freenets or community nets, the lack of training would leave a major access bottleneck. This means that as more and more information is transferred to the Web, including everything from consumer, school and community information, those who cannot afford access or lack access skills will be at a distinct disadvantage.

352

COMMUNITY AND CITIZENSHIP

In the early days of the Web, commentators felt that with its ease of electronic mail connections and opportunities for people to offer their views on politics and the issues of the day, the Web would enrich our sense of community and of citizenship. The growth of community-based freenets certainly added to the talk about virtual electronic communities. However, the expanding commercialization of the Web, the packaging of content to look like television programming, and the expansion of pay services over freenets, have raised the concern that the Web is turning out to be just another medium whose major providers are primarily interested in expanded markets rather than in building communities, and more focused on building a base of consumers than in producing better citizens. There remain strong groups of people for whom the idea of building local and global communities through the Web remains a major goal. One can certainly find a wide variety of such communities based largely on interest in a spectrum of political issues from the rights of women and labour to the advocacy of religious fundamentalism. These groups may very well be defining a new form of citizenship, one that is either too large for the nation-state because it encompasses people worldwide, or too narrow for the nation-state because its aim is to enrich a local community. It may be that we are observing elements of an effort to replace what appears to be a declining identification with the nation-state with genuine alternatives that are facilitated by electronic connections. The global electronic links forged by the Zapatista rebels in the Mexican province of Chiapas beginning in 1996 provided a remarkable window into this new possibility. Nevertheless, it remains questionable whether groups will use the Web for exercising new forms of citizenship and building new forms of community when the pressures mount to make the Web a global shopping mall.

SUMMARY

- Communication technologies have always carried with them enormous promise to change the world. The World Wide Web is no exception with its promise of an electronic superhighway to connect the world's people in a single global village or of a network of interconnected electronic communities where genuine citizen participation in democratic life will flourish.
- The history of communication technologies demonstrates that there is certainly nothing automatic about this and that, in fact, the pressures to create markets for products have tended to overpower the efforts to

build communities. The specific history of the Web, particularly its origins in efforts to expand military control and to provide corporations with information and entertainment products to sell, has marked it with both a control and a commercial drive that are powerful forces shaping the contemporary Web.

- Nevertheless, there also remains from the history of the Web the drive to use it to connect people in many different places in an effort to construct genuine new communities and build forms of civic participation that transcend the drive to turn the Web into a global shopping mall. This is an enormous challenge today because government budget cutbacks and the near eradication of the public service model of electronic media leave people with few resources to use the Web as a genuine community alternative. Yet such resources are needed more than ever because the growing gap between the information rich and poor and the threats to our basic rights to privacy and to personal control over information about ourselves require immediate and forceful attention.

FURTHER READING

Doheny-Farina, Stephen (1996) *The Wired Neighborhood*. New Haven, CT: Yale University Press. Computers promise to make communities better places in which to live by helping neighbours communicate and by giving them access to more local information. Is this happening? Can 'virtual' communities be communities?

Hakken, David with Andrews, Barbara (1996) *Computing Myths, Class Realities: An Ethnography of Technology and Working People in Sheffield, England*. Boulder, CO: Westview Press. What happens when computers come to working-class communities? This detailed study of computers in the day-to-day lives of people in Sheffield has a lot to say about the strengths and weaknesses of the new technologies.

Rheingold, Howard (1993) *The Virtual Community: Homesteading on the Electronic Frontier*. Reading, MA: Addison-Wesley. Rheingold is one of the leading supporters of the Web and of online communities. He describes the potential and some of the pitfalls of cyberspace.

Stoll, Clifford (1995) *Silicon Snake Oil: Second Thoughts on the Information Highway*. New York: Doubleday. A computer expert and former hacker describes the perils of surfing the Net. Stoll is worried that cyberspace harms our ability to learn, diminishes social life and substitutes the rich variety of real experience with an increasingly commercial-driven corporate culture.

Sussman, Gerald (1997) *Communication, Technology and Politics in the Information Age*. Thousand Oaks, CA: Sage. A critical look at the impact of computers and the Web on politics and the economy. Who are the information rich and poor? What can be done to diminish information inequalities?

Turkel, Sherry (1995) *Life on the Screen: Identity in the Age of the Internet*. New York: Simon and Schuster. Turkel studies the lives of computer users who log long hours in 'chat rooms' adopting multiple identities and personalities. What is life like 'on the screen' and what does it mean for us when we log off?

REFERENCES

Cairncross, F. (1997) *The Death of Distance*. London: Orion Business Books.

DuBoff, R. (1984) 'The Rise of Communication Regulation: The Telegraph Industry, 1844–1880', *Journal of Communication*, **34**(3) Summer: 52–66.

Gates, B. (1995) *The Road Ahead*. New York: Viking.

Harris, W.B. (1957) 'The Electronic Business', *Fortune*, April: 137–226.

Mosco, V. (1997) 'Citizenship and the Technopoles', *The Public*, **4**: 35–45.

Nye, D. (1990) *Electrifying America: Social Meanings of a New Technology, 1880–1914*. Cambridge, MA: MIT Press.

Roach, C. (ed.) (1993) *Communication and Culture in War and Peace*. Newbury Park, CA: Sage.

Chapter 25

Nationalism

Murray Low

Nationalism is an ideology which legitimates the existence and activities of territorial states on the basis of characteristics ('ethnic', cultural, linguistic, historical, etc.) supposedly shared by, and specific to, their inhabitants. It is a primary medium through which culture and politics are related in the modern world. It has some influence on virtually every sort of political conflict. This is easily seen in contemporary cases like the conflicts over Bosnia or Kosovo, the reshaping of nationalisms in Russian and Indian politics, the relationships of Britain and other member states with the European Union, and controversies over immigration and citizenship rights. Nationalism is, however, perhaps most pervasive where it permeates other political ideologies and animates controversies which are less obviously 'nationalist' in content. Class conflicts are often underwritten by alternative visions of the nation, and theorists are keen to point out that no revolution has been successful without clothing itself in the paraphernalia of national identity. Participation in environmental movements is often strongly influenced by views of nature in which certain landscapes take on heightened significance as symbols of national heritage. The use of the imagery of nationhood by contemporary identity-based movements (such as Queer Nation, Aryan Nation or the Nation of Islam) testifies to its ongoing centrality in struggles for political recognition.

For all its pervasiveness, nationalism is still not well understood. Part of the difficulty lies in a common tendency to isolate it from other more 'intellectually challenging' political ideologies and, consequently, to spare it the kinds of debate and elaboration accorded to culturally more 'neutral' bodies of ideas such as liberalism, socialism or communitarianism. For example, the recent proliferation of nationalist conflicts is sometimes described as an unfortunate reversion to an obsolete, or even irrational political ideology. Nationalism, it is implied, is currently filling the vacuum left by disillusionment with the more respectable ideologies of socialism and liberalism. Yet these other modern ideologies have never been free of nationalism as a travelling companion that has helped define them. Nationalism itself has generally been, and usually still is, influenced by one or other of these in turn (Freeden, 1998). This 'vacuum theory' of contemporary nationalism, then, seems inadequate. In reality, nationalism has, in some form or another, not only been subscribed to by far more people than most ideological systems but also shaped liberal and socialist doctrines far more than most of their adherents would like to admit.

Nationalism is notoriously difficult to explain. This is partly due to a lack of agreement over what it is. This in turn is due to the entanglements with other social conflicts, movements and ideologies just noted, and also to its changing character in different historical and cultural contexts. It is, like many social science concepts, something of a moving target. It can be plausibly viewed as originating in medieval concepts of community and ethnicity (Cobban, 1945; Reynolds, 1984). Key studies have emphasized the mid-to-late eighteenth century (Colley, 1992), and there is a common (but perhaps too convenient) view that it, like so many other modern political phenomena, *really* took off during the French Revolution (Hobsbawm, 1990). The early nineteenth century has proved the happiest hunting-ground for intellectual historians (Berlin, 1979; Thom, 1995). Others, linking the 'real' origins of political nationalism with the consolidation of systems of territorial states, cautiously emphasize the end of the nineteenth century or later (e.g. Mann, 1995). In the context of a 'post-colonial' turn in the humanities and social sciences, there have been extensive debates about whether nationalism is properly 'Western' at all (Anderson, 1991; Chatterjee, 1986).

To be fair, it is hardly any easier to track the emergence of liberalism or socialism, let alone 'individualism', 'capitalism', 'class' or the 'modern state'. Yet these concepts have been the bread and butter of the social sciences since their inception. Until recently, nationalism has occupied a decidedly marginal role in their conceptual world, and it is perhaps not surprising that, as a result, the critical faculties of many seem to fail when questions about national identity arise. Breuilly (1996: 154), for example, notes that nationalism is commonly explained by pointing to a 'need for identity', usually triggered by some or other breakdown in, or external disruption to, the social environment. Many current discussions of globalization invoke this kind of mechanism. But, as he suggests, this functional explanation raises far more questions than it purports to answer. In other far from distant research fields, explanations of social movements or industrial unrest in terms of disrupted psyches and the 'stresses' of social change have been considered unhelpful, even patronizing, by most scholars for some time (see Chapter 32). Nevertheless, in many accounts, while liberalism or environmentalism, for example, are things that people adhere to through reasoning, national-ism just seems to happen to them. While the former call for a history of thought, the latter calls for a history of collective psychology.

Recent writings on nationalism strongly suggest a focus on its relations with and dependence on both other ideologies and other forms of collective identity. In this chapter, I begin by considering some prominent work on nationalism arranged around the two poles, politics and culture, between which it is located, emphasizing the importance of concepts of legitimacy and history in clarifying some problems which emerge in the literature. I then contrast attempts to define and understand nationalism in terms of its origins with a more recent emphasis on how its basic terms, such as 'nation', derive meaning from their relationships with other concepts informing other identities. In conclusion, I emphasize the difficulties faced by attempts to find substitutes for nationalism in communitarianisms or in the splitting of identities between different geographical scales. These solutions, however appealing, do not address some difficult problems of legitimacy *inherent in* modern democracy, a political ideology with which nationalism is less closely affiliated than is sometimes suggested and which cannot provide answers to some questions which, for better or worse, nationalism handles with ease.

NATIONS AND STATES: POLITICAL THEORIES OF NATIONALISM

Nationalist movements are typically associated with a desire for their nation to control its own territorial state. Modern territorial states are, indeed, often called 'nation-states', a name which presupposes the necessary connection between nations and states crucial in nationalist arguments. After 1945, this connection became central to social-scientific analyses of 'nation-building' which studied the formation of integrated national societies with shared lan-guages, cultures and values. This idea was particularly important in Western discussions of Third World 'political development', where political stability seemed to Western eyes to depend on the promotion of homogeneous politi-cal cultures. But because the nation-building framework tended to merge questions about the formation of nations and states, rather than keeping ques-tions about their possible relations open, it was ill-equipped to cope with myriad post-colonial conflicts within political boundaries which often bore little or no relation to the cultural affinities of the peoples they enclosed.

Recent theories of modern states have avoided the nation-building con-cept, recognizing the risk of circularity involved in assuming simple re-lationships between the development of 'nations' and the formation of territorial states. The fact that there are at any given time far more aspirant nations than there are states, suggests the need for definitions and analyses of 'national-states' which do not presume national homogeneity, or imply that nations normally produce states. Giddens (1985), for example, has defined the 'nation-state' entirely without reference to its cultural or 'national' characteristics. Tilly (1990) has stressed the importance of a dual process, involving the concentration of capital in cities and the concentration of coercive power in centralized state organizations, in explaining variations in the development and character of European 'national states'. National states took shape, according to his appealing formulation (Tilly, 1985), as highly effective 'protection rackets' providing political roofs for increasingly bounded and mutually exclusive populations and their economic activities.

The detachment of theories of state formation from the framework of nation-building has proved, paradoxically, to be very productive in terms of the analysis of nationalism. Breuilly (1982) and Mann (1995) are perhaps the most prominent current proponents of 'political' theories of nationalism. Breuilly has developed a typology of nationalisms in relation to different forms of modern state. He views nationalism in the light of attempts to find an ideological solution to the problems posed by the separation of state and civil society characteristic of political modernity. Mann examines the development of nationalism in terms of changing state–citizen interactions, arguing that it has at different times formed a means of popular contestation of different phases of state intervention. Mobilization for war, in terms of taxation and recruitment, and the development of modern administration are central to this process. Nationalism, on this account, was inseparably linked with the 'drive towards democracy' (Mann, 1995: 44). Brubaker (1996) has recently examined the 'resurgence' of nationalism in the former Soviet bloc within an institutional framework in which nationalist activity, when it occurs, is viewed as an event rather than an underlying force capable of explaining political change.

Simply put, this literature has tended to view nationalism primarily as a response to, rather than cause or prerequisite of, modern state institutions. We might generalize by noting that the formation of territorial states helped make the notion of 'the nation' possible, initially as the aggregate of people sharing the protection of a given state organization (Keane, 1995: 182–3). Once nationalism became a pervasive political ideology, such 'nations', increasingly defined in terms of ethnic or cultural homogeneity, could be regarded as the populations of possible territorial states which could be engineered into existence. Under certain circumstances, nationalism could become a prime cause of the creation of new 'nation-states', but this has been by no means usual. The boundaries of most territorial states have come into being as a product of violent interstate conflict, territorial seizure and colonialism. In this context, nationalism has formed a crucial means of mobilization, recruitment, control and indeed of resistance, but it has rarely been the primary determinant of geopolitical outcomes.

Beliefs in the political salience of nations and national sentiment have been more important in reproducing already existing territorial states than they have in creating new ones. These have as a result achieved a kind of geographical fixity unknown in earlier times. The most plausible way to view the relationships between the development of modern states and the rise of nationalism is therefore to examine transformations in the *legitimation* of state activities, that is, changes in the principles by which state activities are generally justified. The most significant transformation from a Western perspective is the geographically uneven shift in the balance between primarily theological or hereditary-dynastic justifications of state activity and justifications based largely on popular sovereignty. As a result, the American and French revolutions of the late eighteenth century have taken on great importance, not only in the literature on 'enlightenment' ideas about power deriving from 'the people', but in analyses of nationalism. From the moment states were supposed to derive their power from their 'people', the question of who 'their' people as opposed to other 'peoples' were, became highly salient, along with disturbing questions about the circumstances under which individuals or categories of individuals could join this newly sovereign body. Questions about circumstances of birth, acculturation, language and blood took on a vastly heightened political importance (Brubaker, 1992).

I will return to the question of legitimacy, in the context of concerns about nationalism's possible obsolescence and its relationship to modern democracy. For now, it is enough to say that if nationalism is best viewed through the lens of legitimacy, it is easy to appreciate why accounts plausibly stressing the dependence of nationalism on the development of the modern state seem incomplete, and why the best known theories of nationalism, those of Gellner (1983) and Anderson (1991), address it more directly as a cultural matter. For, although the development of the modern state system was a necessary condition for nationalism's emergence, this cannot by itself account for the form or content of nationalist ideology.

THE POSSIBILITY OF NATIONALISM: 'CULTURAL' THEORIES

In the twentieth century, most theories of nationalism have been 'constructivist' (Stargardt, 1995): they refuse to see nationalism in its own terms as a primordial, even natural, phenomenon deriving from the existence of real sociological entities called nations. Most theories of nationalism taking culture as their starting point emphasize the constructed, 'fictive' or 'imagined' quality of nations, are much more inclined to grant reality to nationalist movements and ideology, and tend to be suspicious of nationalist claims that their nations have primordial, rather than modern, roots (Smith, 1998). Gellner and Anderson develop theories of nationalism which overlap at many points, particularly in their concern to establish how it became possible to imagine a cultural basis for modern politics.

In Gellner's model, agrarian societies and industrial societies sit on either side of a fundamental historical divide. In agrarian civilizations, distant élites are rigidly separated from virtually everyone else, who in turn are segmented into immobile communities experiencing little interdependency. In industrial societies, as the result of a complex division of labour, social mobility becomes a central mechanism of development. Learning specific skills 'by doing' becomes vastly less important than possessing generic communication skills, such as literacy, required to move between different tasks. As a result, states become concerned with generating homogeneous cultures through education, within which their subjects can move fluidly from position to position.

These homogeneous industrial cultures are 'high cultures', the elements of which can be understood independently of local contexts, that is, of particular traditions, repertoires of gesture and dialect. Particular vernacular (spoken) languages, generally those of traditionally dominant regions or social strata, are selected as general languages of state and commerce within increasingly clearly demarcated cultural boundaries. The emerging landscape of nation-states becomes like a series of mutually exclusive fish tanks within which 'nationals' all swim around effortlessly thanks to the obstacle-free medium of a shared culture.

A series of shared high cultures suggests some imperative to cultural homogeneity within political units. It does not in itself create 'nationalism'. Accordingly, Gellner focuses on 'blockages' within (generally highly mobile) industrial stratification systems. Certain groups, particularly during early industrialization, find that their linguistic or other cultural traits act as barriers to employment or promotion because a majority group, defined by its facility with the dominant high culture, dominates firms and bureaucracies. Encounters with these 'barriers' lead minority intelligentsias to align themselves with similarly disadvantaged middle- and lower-class groups. The latter have often recently migrated to urban settings. Movements appear, developing counter-cultures based on usually elaborately fictionalized versions of their rural origins. Their aim is to secure new 'political roofs' under which to construct administrative and economic divisions of labour open to the talents of minorities, which have now been given political shape by their development of all the trappings of 'nations'.

Gellner's account is clear but rather abstract. It relies on models of society constructed at a very high level of generality, and on ideal typical case studies which allow for miniature demonstrations of the connections he posits between culture, industrialism and politics. Nevertheless, a worrying lack of evidence results at key points. For example, his argument that state education in shared high cultures is necessary for the operations of mobile industrial societies, and indeed necessitates the building of nation-states, is interesting, but it is not shown that the drive to national education was the major force constructing the modern geopolitical landscape. War, and the mobilization for war, central in more 'political' accounts, are strangely absent from his model.

Moreover, the binary division between agricultural and industrial societies encourages an overly categorical view of nationalism's history, in which it emerges as a defence mechanism for the victims of the transition to the era of generalized high cultures. Gellner (1996) outlines a more concrete analysis of the history of nationalism where the agricultural-to-industrial trajectory is filled out with stages. But he continues to view it as characteristic of early industrialism and has some difficulties accounting for why, in terms of his model, it just might not eventually go away. Gellner's view that the fictive quality of 'national' cultures shows nations to have a purely subjective reality reinforces his inclination to see nationalism as a weak, rather than powerful political force. He invokes in this connection the sheer number of such minority 'national' groups globally in relation to the small number which have succeeded in forming new states. His account reads like that of a liberal rationalist who takes for granted that nationalism can be isolated from other phenomena and ideologies, shown to be nonsensical, even feeble, and thereby exorcised through clear-thinking and societal development.

To scholars who think nationalism draws its force from the reproduction of ethnic sentiment over long spans of human history, Gellner's lack of sympathy with nationalism gets in the way of understanding its pervasiveness, durability and power. Yet nationalism does not make much sense outside the context of the modern territorial state. It thus seems difficult to infer its pre-modernity from the existence of ethnic ideologies of however long duration. Anderson (1991), like Gellner, sees nations as constructed or imagined entities. He also uses a set of binary oppositions between prenationalist and nationalist worlds to develop his arguments. But he cleverly portrays nationalism as a phenomenon which is modern yet depends on a set of deeply held images of historical time and community. These give the 'invented' histories of nationalism a tremendous power over social attitudes and behaviour and make them the 'common sense' way modern people think about history. The difference between Gellner's and Anderson's constructivist theories of the nation is that, while Gellner views nationalism as illustrating the fictional nature of something which many take to be powerful, Anderson is concerned to account for the power of an important fiction.

He sketches a pre-nationalist Europe in which written sacred languages were divorced from everyday speech; a political landscape of dynastic states was conceived in terms of centres rather than mutually exclusive territories; and time was conceptualized in such a way that historical development and cultural differences could not become central to cultural or political identities. National sentiment became possible through three transformations. Overseas expansion and culture contact fostered the *relativization* of European religious practices. They could now be viewed as one set among many simultaneously adhered to across the Earth. Sacred authority was undermined in the long run, and the special authority of Latin as a written language underpinned by such authority was an early casualty. The development of a 'print-capitalism', allied with the Reformation, which increasingly generated texts in *vernacular* (spoken) languages for readers within territorially confined markets, made new popular identities possible. Second, the *legitimation* of dynastic monarchies became more problematic as they intervened more systematically in the lives of their subjects. Third, history began to be conceived as occurring in a linear, measurable, 'clock-able' time in which events could be ordered, changes could be seen as irreversible, and 'through' which societies could be imagined as moving up and down history, progressing and regressing but at any given moment coexisting with each other in the same present. Men and women came to believe confidently in their membership in 'imagined communities', the vast majority of whose members they would never see or meet, as a result of being able to think about society as something where many interconnected things went on simultaneously.

Anderson's explanation of why the compartmentalizing of people into vernacular language communities should have generated political senti-ments and movements focused on 'the nation', like Gellner's, hinges on blocked mobility. First, creole (colonial-born European) administrators in North and South America, then middle-class intelligentsias in Europe, then small educated strata in nineteenth- and twentieth-century European col-onies found themselves 'cornered' into limited career paths as a result of the geographical, ethnic and linguistic circumstances of their birth. Like Gellner's unassimilable city migrants, these groups turned to nationalism to make sense of their restricted mobility, to shape a positive identity for them-selves based on their own imagined communities, of which their confine-ment had sharpened their awareness.

Anderson stresses nationalism's 'modular' nature, which makes it poss-ible to distinguish different forms of nationalism across time and space. In the era defined by creole liberation struggles in the Americas and the French Revolution, nationalism emerged as an almost accidental combination of several tendencies. Once formed, however, it became a model which could be 'pirated', taken up by a variety of social groups in other locales and reshaped according to circumstances, as a powerful political weapon in the service of very different aims. In the early nineteenth century, nationalism became a model for 'popular' resistance, not only to colonialism or French expansionism but to dynastic rule in general. Threatened rulers quickly discovered that the model could furnish a means of reclothing their regimes in nationalist colours and that the imagined community, whose contours states either had or could develop the means of shaping, could serve as a strong source of legitimacy. The colonial export of this 'official' nationalism in turn encouraged the development of imagined communities in colonial space, which informed the great wave of anti-colonial nationalisms cresting in the twentieth century.

Because nationalism's character can alter radically within the same gen-eral outlines, politically less-appealing 'official' versions can be separated from those used in popular liberation struggles. National sentiment is rooted in very general conceptions of time and community, answering people's basic questions of collective origins and belonging. Its hold derives, he suggests, from its operating at a level of political life deeper than that at which 'choices' can be meaningfully made. National identity is not something we can decide on: it has the character of an unavoidable background against which all our other choices are made. In stressing this, Anderson reconciles the deeply embedded nature of nationalist sentiment which has fascinated proponents of its 'primordiality', with its 'constructed' or 'invented' character. Our critical ability to recognize, crudely put, 'good' and 'bad' forms of nationalism is important because, on this account, a non-nationalist politics is hard to imagine. Nationalism is the product of a style of imagining which is distinctively modern, but which operates at such a basic level that an equally thoroughgoing set of transformations to those that brought it about would be necessary to bring it to an end.

Both these theories of nationalism are better at examining key transformations which make nationalist discourse and mobilization possible than at accounting for why emergent homogeneous cultures should produce political ideologies and *movements* which are nationalist in content and aim. The recourse to arguments about restricted social mobility is surely the weakest element in both theories, and reminds us that the study of nationalism has remained oddly disconnected from that of social movements, parties and related phenomena. There is, moreover, much to be said for synthesizing some elements from theories such as Gellner's and Anderson's with insights from those focusing on states and politics considered above, as the contents of politicized discourses about the nation have obviously been shaped by changing conceptions and practices of states and statehood.

All of this has encouraged the development of more 'modest' or focused accounts (see, e.g., Brubaker, 1996), and indeed in many ways Gellner's and Anderson's remain the last of the 'grand' theories of nationalism. Similarly, in recent years, critical scholars have tended to follow Anderson's cue, and developed his concept of constructed or imagined communities in more specific contexts. However, by drawing on post-structuralist and other varieties of critical theory, they have questioned the fascination with explaining origins built into the general theories considered thus far, and worked to show the ways in which nationalism depends on a series of shifting relationships with other forms of ideology and identity.

ORIGINS AND DESTINATIONS

Origins and destinations are central to nationalist ideology. It works by linking the imagined pasts of specific national communities to equally imagined futures. The cultural content focusing particular nationalist ideologies is heterogeneous: flags and symbols; songs; languages, dialects and accents; 'traditions' of various kinds; religions; particular landscapes and commemorative monuments. Students of nationalism have frequently been bemused by the question of what makes nationalism coherent, given that different nations are focused on different combinations of these elements. Nationalist ideology is, however, given a kind of unity by the centrality in it of narratives of origin and 'destiny'. Much work has taken issue with the ways in which nationalism settles blurry questions of identity by reducing historical complexities to invented traditions (Hobsbawm and Ranger, 1987). Searching for answers about nationalism in its own origins appears to suffer from some of the same problems, as does endless speculation about its future. Partly as a result, grand theories of nationalism have been superseded by more partial attempts to show how nationalism relates to other forms of identity and to undermine its constructions of history.

Defining nationalism has often taken an etymological form, with scholars tracing the derivation and early uses of the words 'nation', 'nationalism' and 'nation-state'. In this way, the problem merges with the equally unsettled question of nationalism's historical origins. The often invoked debate between those advocating 'primordial' and 'modern' roots for nationalism may be a little unreal: most see national as opposed to ethnic identity as modern (Brubaker, 1996; Smith, 1998). Yet this recognition hardly solves the problem of origins as typically posed. If pre-modern ethnicity is conceded to be relevant to, if not identical with, nationality, part of an explanation will involve contextualizing the 'ethnic origins of nations' (Smith, 1986) in the obscure (and in many ways unresearchable) historical origins of ethnic communities. If pre-modern ethnicity is disconnected from nationality, theories can emphasize the modernity of nationalism through binary comparisons between agrarian and industrial, traditional and modern or pre-capitalist and capitalist societies. But the moment these schema come into contact with more detailed historical narratives, as they inevitably do in this literature, their oversimplifications are highlighted.

Perhaps 'knowing roughly' when nationalism originated is all that matters for most purposes, and in this context 'modernity' will do. Yet there is much at stake in being more precise. If it originated in the French Revolution, for example, nationalist politics is given a strongly popular-democratic colouration underlining its uses in later revolutionary movements. If it originated in anti-Enlightenment thinking in the early nineteenth century, its later associations with racist authoritarianism are correspondingly highlighted. Post-colonial perspectives on nationalism have opened up new avenues for research and theorization. They also point to the ongoing importance of origins in framing nationalism: concern over Eurocentrism can readily become deflected into a contest over the status of 'origin' for nationalist politics, as if subscribing to the common assumption that nationalism originated in Europe was tantamount to denying the imaginative abilities of peoples elsewhere (see Chatterjee, 1996).

In short, just as narratives of origin, development and destiny are central to nationalist ideology, they have become central to the way in which it has typically been theorized and researched. These narratives have also strongly affected the sorts of conclusions writers have drawn. Most theories of nationalism treat its origin as a phenomenon needing its own peculiar set of explanations. Nationalism is looked at in its own terms, very much those of the nineteenth-century philologists and language scholars so prominent in its histories in Europe and elsewhere. Recent 'anti-essentialist' approaches to nationalism and ethnicity (see Tonkin, McDonald and Chapman, 1989) are suspicious of treating nationalism in ways which might reinforce its view that nations are autonomous, self-sufficient bearers of homogeneous traditions. These approaches share the constructivism informing many other theories but refuse to view nationalism and national identity as matters which should be theorized by themselves. Much current writing takes its inspiration from literary criticism and cultural studies, often focusing less on large-scale historical-political processes and more on nationalist discourses.

How we think about other forms of identity strongly informs how we think about nations. At one level, this is unavoidable even in writings seeing nationalism as something requiring its own theory: think of the comparisons implied by the labels 'imagined communities', 'ethno-nationalism' or 'civic nationalism'. Feminist scholars are currently emphasizing the way in which concepts of the nation are informed by assumptions about the family and 'home' (see Antheas and Yuval-Davis, 1989; McClintock, 1996). Furthermore, the conceptual walls which have periodically been erected between nationalism and ethnicity and race have undergone renewed questioning. All but the most sympathetic scholars recognize that particular nationalisms take shape through often unflattering series of contrasts with other nations. Colley (1992), for example, has shown in some detail how the eighteenth-century imagining of a 'British' nation was dependent on a set of cultural, religious and political contrasts with the French. Yet this sort of process does not only involve the comparison of nations. Gilroy (1988) has criticized Anderson for insisting that nationalism and racism are basically separate phenomena, noting how concepts of British or English nationality have been given definition in relation to, and by excluding, Afro-Caribbean and Asian communities long present in the UK. Much innovative work has been carried out by theorists like Balibar (1991) on the interrelations of race and nationality in the context of changing immigration and citizenship regulations, and political mobilization against the presence of racially different immigrants and residents, in Europe and North America.

The reluctance to theorize nationalism *per se* has been viewed as an unfortunate development (Smith, 1998: xi, 219). However, the different aims of this recent work have fostered more positive accounts of the piecing together of identities involved in nationalism, while opening established identities, national and otherwise, to new elements. Particularly in the context of globalization, insisting on the non-homogeneous and non-self-sufficient nature of nations allows us to imagine more complex, hybrid forms of identity that combine a number of different geohistorical origins and open up broader sets of possible national destinations (Hall, 1992). Thinking about diasporic communities and experiences of migration has led some to rethink identity as developing 'in between', rather than 'in', bounded geographical contexts such as territorial states (Bhabha, 1993). Finally, questions of history and memory, far from being ignored as a consequence of setting nationalism within more relational contexts, have been revisited in highly inventive ways, with attention being focused on how the study of national narratives can be informed by the analysis of literary texts (Bhabha, 1990) and through study of the ways in which popular memory is embodied in a range of conflicting selections from and recollections of remarkably plural national pasts (Samuel, 1995).

NATIONALISM AND THE PRESENT

Nationalism has often been disconnected too quickly from other forms of identity politics. It is at its most unsettling when we consider how far it derives its force from its relationships with other ideologies and concepts. Some of these are apparently more benign than others. In academic writing the implications of specific comparisons, contrasts and distinctions used to define nationalism are, like different viewpoints on its origins, rarely value-free. Nationalism can be made to appear positive in relation to 'narrower' local attachments or feudal loyalties, but negative in relation to ideologies of 'civic' community in early modern city-states (Thom, 1995; Viroli, 1995). It can seem positive in the context of combating imperialisms yet negative in relation to other supranational phenomena such as 'humanity' or international class solidarity (Hobsbawm, 1990). Much of the slipperiness of nationalism can be explained because at different times and places different contrasts or relations seem most relevant to the situation at hand.

It is often suggested that nationalism is becoming obsolete as a result, for example, of globalization. This seems doubtful (Mann, 1993) and those occasions usually touted as moments when a global imagined community comes into view (the Gulf War, Princess Diana's funeral, the millennium) are but blips on our mainly nationally confined attention spans. Moreover, nationalism's characteristically simplifying ways of answering questions about origins, destinations, identity and history are easily transferred to its apparently less-threatening conceptual neighbours such as 'community', or 'humanity.' It therefore needs a lot of continuing critical attention within the kind of relational frameworks for understanding political identities I have discussed.

Yet, although these more relational perspectives have entailed anything but an uncritical revaluing of the importance of national identity, nationalism still has an unusual power to provoke speculation about the *specific* risks it might entail. A valid reason for concern with nationalism's peculiarity is its special relation to the State generated by the link to popular sovereignty mentioned earlier. It is *the* particular form of identity centred on the major instrument of violence in modern society. Even if most nationalist movements are basically well intentioned and armed with little but their often justified grievances, the riskiness which is thus built into nationalism deserves all the critical scrutiny it receives. Racism is arguably more crucial to explaining many of the negative examples (German National Socialism, Pol Pot's Cambodia) dogging contemporary nationalists. But it is unusual for a 'race', as such, to control a state. It usually takes nationalism, nationalist justifications, and articulations of 'the national interest' to enable the expulsion of 'non-nationals', the firing of the gun or the pushing of the button. Can we make it more benign? Can we displace it by recentring identity around substitute collective affiliations such as community? Can we dilute it by decentring political identity to a series of loyalties at different geographical scales, such as attachments to cities, regions and international institutions like the European Union (EU) (Keane, 1995)?

We are surely up against the limits of social science here. Let us leave aside the problem of whether changes in identity can be consciously engineered. As I indicated at the outset, the fundamental issue posed by nationalism concerns not only identity, but the way in which states and their actions are legitimated. Modern states have come to *need* nationalism in the sense that, dictatorships or democracies, they all generally claim to act on behalf of 'their' people. Nationalism has become the indispensable means of connecting general ideas about popular sovereignty to particular state institutions. Nationalism, then, reminds us that even if the people are said to be the source of authority in a state, this idea of popular sovereignty is not equivalent to democracy, which is embodied in a set of modern institutions and procedures centred on individual choices and responsibility (Rosanvallon, 1990).

A major challenge nationalism poses is the degree to which it is indispensable to democracy. Democracy's characteristic ideas about political responsibility relate to choices in the present. In contrast, recall Anderson's suggestion that nationalism exercises its power at a level beneath that at which choices are made. It does this by placing individuals in an imagined history, or time-scheme, in which they are vastly outnumbered by past and future national generations. Nationalism works as much or more on their behalf than it does for present citizens. It does not, in other words, merely act as a friendly support to democracy by identifying who 'the people' of a particular state are or should be. It redefines democracy by relating it to a long-term structure defined by its imagined origins and destinations. Thanks to nationalism, modern states are not only legitimated by the moment-by-moment decisions of their present citizens, but in a very real sense by a political majority which does not exist.

In doing this it helps democracies imagine solutions to problems involving their heritage and responsibilities to future generations. These questions are unavoidable aspects of virtually every decision which democracy faces. What is unsettling is that it is consequently not clear that democratic legitimation can operate without an imagined history of a nationalist type which operates at cross-purposes with any vision of a society built on autonomous popular decision in the present. We have yet to come up with a politically viable form of 'community' which would justify state power through different constructions of historical time. Moreover, to work to 'decentre' political identities to multiple geographical scales without seriously thinking through the consequences which this might have for political accountability and legitimacy seems ill-advised, as the example of the EU suggests. It is exceptionally difficult to imagine any liberation from nationalism, or something like it, resulting from globalization or similar processes, because it has become vital to our sense of what popular sovereignty means. The paradox of nationalism is similar to that raised by many forms of identity politics: in letting us know who we are, its construction of past and future complicates our capacity to live in the present.

SUMMARY

- Nationalism legitimates, or justifies, the existence and activities of modern territorial states on the basis of a range of characteristics which are conventionally shared by, and specific to, their inhabitants.
- Theorists of nationalism have focused both on the relationships of nationalism to modern states and on the historical transformations which have made national identity possible.
- Grand historical theories of the origins of nationalism have been less important in recent years than more partial accounts of the relationships of nationalism with other identities and ideologies in particular situations.
- Nationalism is strongly connected with the legitimation of violence. This makes continued critical analysis imperative, especially in a context where it is often misleadingly suggested to be obsolete.
- The relationship between nationalism and democracy is ambiguous. Nationalism's persistence is connected with the difficulties democracy encounters when it has to cope with unavoidable questions about history and the future.

FURTHER READING

Anderson, Benedict (1991) *Imagined Communities* (revised edn). London: Verso. Originally published in 1983, this is full of stimulating argument and contains probably *the* most discussed theory of nationalism in recent years.

Balakrishnan, Gopal (ed.) (1996) *Mapping the Nation*. London: Verso. A series of excellent, contrasting essays by many of the major theorists of nationalism discussed in this chapter.

Eley, Geoff and Suny, Ronald Grigor (eds) (1996) *Becoming National: a Reader*. Oxford: Oxford University Press. An imaginatively edited collection, covering more material on post-colonial issues, race and gender than Hutchinson and Smith (below).

Hutchinson, John and Smith, Anthony D. (eds) (1994) *Nationalism*. Oxford: Oxford University Press. A very useful reader which, because it is built from a very large number of short extracts, effectively conveys the outlines of an enormous literature.

Smith, Anthony (1998) *Nationalism and Modernism: a Critical Survey of Recent Theories of Nations and Nationalism*. London: Routledge. A perceptive overview of the theoretical literature, taking issue with the dominant view that nationalism is a modern phenomenon and also with the 'post-modern' challenge represented by recent unease with grand theories of nationalism among scholars of gender, race and identity.

REFERENCES

Anderson, Benedict (1991) *Imagined Communities* (revised edn). London, Verso.

Antheas, Floya and Yuval-Davis, Nira (1989) (eds) *Woman–Nation–State*. London: Macmillan.

Balibar, Etienne (1991) 'The Nation Form: History and Ideology', in Etienne Balibar and Immanuel Wallerstein, *Race, Nation, Class: Ambiguous Identities*. London: Verso, pp. 86–106.

Berlin, Isaiah (1979) 'The Counter-Enlightenment', in his *Against the Current: Essays in the History of Ideas*. London: Hogarth Press, pp. 1–24.

Bhabha, Homi (ed.) (1990) *Nation and Narration*. London: Routledge.

Bhabha, Homi (1993) *The Location of Culture*. London: Routledge.

Breuilly, John (1982) *Nationalism and the State*. Manchester: Manchester University Press.

Breuilly, John (1996) 'Theories of Nationalism', in Gopal Balakrishnan (ed.) *Mapping the Nation*. London: Verso, pp. 146–74

Brubaker, Rogers (1992) *Citizenship and Nationhood in France and Germany*. Cambridge, MA: Harvard University Press.

Brubaker, Rogers (1996) *Nationalism Reframed*. Cambridge: Cambridge University Press.

Chatterjee, Partha (1986) *Nationalist Thought and the Colonial World: a Derivative Discourse*. London: Zed Books.

Chatterjee, Partha (1996) 'Whose Imagined Community?' in Gopal Balakrishnan, (ed.) *Mapping the Nation*. London: Verso, pp. 214–225

Cobban, Alfred (1945) *Nationalism and After*. London: Macmillan.

Colley, Linda (1992) *Britons: Forging the Nation 1707–1837*. London: Pimlico.
Freeden, Michael (1998) 'Is Nationalism a Distinct Ideology?' *Political Studies*, **46**(4): 748–65.
Gellner, Ernest (1983) *Nations and Nationalism*. Ithaca, NY: Cornell University Press.
Gellner (1996) 'The Coming of Nationalism and its Interpretation: The Myths of Nation and Class', in Gopal Balakrishnan (ed.) *Mapping the Nation*. London: Verso, pp. 98–145.
Giddens, Anthony (1985) *The Nation-State and Violence*. Cambridge: Polity.
Gilroy, Paul (1988) *There Ain't No Black in the Union Jack*. London: Routledge.
Hall, Stuart (1992) 'The New Ethnicities', in J. Donald and A. Rattansi (eds) *Race, Culture and Difference*. London: Sage, pp. 252–60.
Hobsbawm, Eric (1990) *Nations and Nationalism since 1780*. Cambridge: Cambridge University Press.
Hobsbawm, Eric and Ranger, Terence (1987) (eds) *The Invention of Tradition*. Cambridge: Cambridge University Press.
Keane, John (1995) 'Nations, Nationalism and European Citizens', in Sukumar Periwal (ed.) *Notions of Nationalism*. London: Routledge, pp. 182–207.
Mann, Michael (1993) 'Nation-states in Europe and Other Continents: Diversifying, Developing, Not Dying', *Daedelus*, **122**(3): 115–40.
Mann, Michael (1995) 'A Political Theory of Nationalism and its Excesses', in Sukumar Periwal (ed.) *Notions of Nationalism*. London: Routledge, pp. 44–64.
McClintock, Anne (1996) ''No Longer in a Future Heaven'': Nationalism, Gender and Race', in Geoff Eley and Ronald Grigor Suny (eds) *Becoming National*. Oxford: Oxford University Press, pp. 260–84.
Reynolds, Susan (1984) *Kingdoms and Communities in Western Europe (900–1300)*. Oxford: Oxford University Press.
Rosanvallon, Pierre (1990) *Le sacre du citoyen*. Paris: Gallimard.
Samuel, Raphael (1995) *Theatres of Memory*. London: Verso.
Smith, Anthony (1986) *The Ethnic Origins of Nations*. Oxford: Blackwell.
Smith, Anthony (1998) *Nationalism and Modernism: A Critical Survey of Recent Theories of Nations and Nationalism*. London: Routledge.
Stargardt, Nicholas (1995) 'Origins of the Constructivist Theory of the Nation', in Sukumar Periwal (ed.) *Notions of Nationalism*. London: Routledge, pp. 83–105.
Thom, Martin (1995) *Republics, Nations and Tribes*. London: Verso.
Tilly, Charles (1985) 'War-Making and State-Making as Organized Crime', in Peter B. Evans, Dietrich Reuschemeyer and Theda Skocpol (eds) *Bringing the State Back In*. Cambridge: Cambridge University Press, pp. 169–91.
Tilly, Charles (1990) *Coercion, Capital and European States*. Cambridge: Cambridge University Press.
Tonkin, Elisabeth, McDonald, Maryon and Chapman, Malcolm (1989) *History and Ethnicity*. London: Routledge.
Viroli, Maurizio (1995) *For Love of Country: an Essay on Patriotism and Nationalism*. Oxford: Oxford University Press.

Chapter 26

Islam

Sarah Ansari

To many people living in the West, Islam is something which still remains firmly 'outside' their immediate reality. As a collection of ideas mapping out a way of life, it appears to be spiritually as well as culturally alien to the beliefs which they cherish or hold dear. The gulf which separates them from Islam as a concept, let alone a religious system, is apparently profound and insurmountable. Yet, for the last 1,500 years, ever since its emergence in seventh-century Arabia, growing numbers of people across the world have become followers of Islam, and today's one billion Muslims now constitute a fifth of current humanity, 'a global presence which cannot be ignored' (Robinson, 1996: x). In particular, the development of what often looks like a homogeneous Islamic 'fundamentalism', operating both outside and within Western societies, has reinforced popular perceptions in the West of what appears to be 'wrong' with Islam. In the choice between 'Mecca or mechanisation', the common impression is that 'religion' rather than 'progress' seems to be winning the argument for many of today's Muslims (Lerner, 1964: 508).

Islam, of course, is first and foremost a religion, but understanding what 'Islam' means today involves recognizing the extent to which it has also come to represent in many minds a very specific and undifferentiated combination of cultural and political values, which in turn stand for a particular form of religio-political organization. The accentuated sense of the 'Other' which has been attached to Islam, on the one hand, emphasizes the distinctions which do exist between developments in many Muslim societies and trends towards secularization in the West. On the other hand, however, it disguises the breadth of diversity and opinion which can be found wherever there are Muslims (Geertz, 1971).

A GLOBAL RELIGION?

Islam emerged relatively late in relation to other worldwide religions. The last of the great monotheisms, it distinguished itself from its predecessors, Judaism and Christianity, by its belief in the Qur'ān or Holy Book as the direct speech of God or Allah and, hence, we can appreciate why subsequent generations of Muslims have taken great pains to preserve this text in its original Arabic form. Muslims believe that the contents of the Qur'ān were revealed over a period of time to the Prophet Muhammad, a Meccan trader living in the Arabian peninsula in the seventh century. Muhammad's uncompromising insistence on one supreme God eventually clashed with prevailing Meccan belief in a range of deities and threatened to disrupt the *status quo* of the city. He and his followers were forced to flee to Medina where the revelations continued. It was here that, alongside the Qur'ān, the other main source of Islamic authority developed in the form of the Hadiths or traditions, that is Islam's 'collective memory of the Prophet and his companions' who were the first interpreters of Allah's message (Waines, 1995: 11).

By the time of Muhammad's death in AD 632, Muslims had demonstrated moral and military superiority over their local rivals and occupied Mecca. Within a hundred years, Islam had extended its influence westwards towards Spain and as far as the borders of China in the east, growing 'swiftly from a tiny central Arabian commonwealth to an empire of international compass' (Waines, 1995: 36). Although divided between Sunnis and Shias and other smaller 'sects', the number of Muslims multiplied through conquest and conversion during the Umayyad and Abbasid periods. In the long term, however, what was left of the initial political unity of Islam splintered, albeit into a number of highly successful imperial ventures such as the Ottoman, the Mughal and the Safavid empires which had reached the heights of their power by the seventeenth and eighteenth centuries AD. The expansion of these empires helped to consolidate the presence of Islam into regions of the world such as South Asia where Muslims remained a numerical minority but came to play an enormously important role in influencing the character of local society. Meanwhile, Muslim merchants and spiritual leaders plied their respective trades, helping to spread the message of Islam to new, sometimes even more distant, lands. In some parts of Africa, the entry of Islam more or less overlapped with the arrival of the West, and so here the loss of local political independence coincided with the continued expansion of Islam's adherents. Colonial ties in time drew Muslims to the West itself, either as colonial subjects of one sort or another, or in pursuit of the various opportunities which the West could offer.

Thus, today, the majority of the world's Muslims clearly do not live in the place usually associated with Islam, that is the Middle East where the religion developed but where now only about one in four are to be found.

It is clear why the Middle East retains its dominance over popular Western perceptions for it was here that the West first encountered Islam while Arabic, the language of the region, is Islam's sacred liturgical expression. Yet, it is Indonesia in South East Asia, for instance, which has become the proud possessor of the world's largest Muslim population, and similarly more Muslims live in South Asia than in the Arabic-speaking countries of Islam's traditional 'heartland'. Of growing significance, too, it could be argued, are the twenty million or so Muslims who form essential strands in the fabric of the Western societies in which they now live.

From this overview of the spread of Muslims around the globe, it is clear that, down through the centuries, Islam has become progressively 'decentred', to the extent that there is a greater need than ever to acknowledge the diversity that exists within the framework of Islam. While the Arabian peninsula remains at the heart of Islamic religious life, with the timing of the annual *haj* or pilgrimage to Mecca still constituting a vital pulse felt by Muslims everywhere, today's reality is one in which a range of social, economic, political and cultural forces intervene to shape the lives of individual followers of Islam, just as they often did in the past. Thus, alongside the religious beliefs and rituals which act as ties, both visible and invisible to outsiders, binding Muslims into a common rhythm of life, considerable differences can be found between urban and rural Muslims, between the rich and the poor, and along sectarian or doctrinal lines.

Far too frequently, however, Islam has been 'essentialized', to the extent that outsiders, as well as many Muslims themselves, have failed either to notice or to acknowledge the variations and intense debates which have existed and continue to exist within it (Eickelman and Piscatori, 1996: 162). There is still a tendency to assume that Muslims represent one reality and all speak with one voice, even though historical events have never really supported this conclusion. The central importance of the Qur'ān and the Hadith, together with the emphasis on the 'Five Pillars of Islam' (comprising the *shahadah* or witnessing that 'There is no god but Allah and Muhammad is the Messenger of Allah', the ritual observances of prayer or *salat*, fasting during the month of Ramadan, alms giving or *zakat*, and the performance of pilgrimage to Mecca or *haj*), constitute a shared structure of beliefs which continues to underpin the Muslim *umma* or community. But difference, both religious and political, has repeatedly hindered attempts by Muslims to create greater unison among themselves and, despite the vitality of contemporary debates on the subject, the prospects of a universal Islamic state, for instance, are arguably as distant as they ever have been. At the same time, it is possible to chart the emergence of a new kind of political geography for Islam, involving transnational 'horizontal' linkages across political borders which blur boundaries between communities and states, and influence the concerns and activities of both individual and groups of Muslims. The globalization of Islamic issues has become a fact of contemporary life, with developments such as the recent crises in Bosnia and Kosovo generating a sense of enhanced solidarity among Muslims in many different and far-flung countries (Eickelman and Piscatori, 1996: 136–64).

Today's Muslims are divided religiously speaking into a variety of groupings. The two main camps are the Sunni and the Shi'i. Distanced by rival visions of salvation dating from the period immediately following Muhammad's death, Sunni Islam today comprises some 90 per cent of the total Muslim community worldwide. Four main schools of jurisprudence, however, developed within the Sunni framework, each with its own geographical power base: hence, the Hanafi school remains very influential among South Asian Muslims and in the territories of the former Ottoman Empire; the Maliki school dominates much of northern and sub-Saharan Africa (as it did Spain prior to the Christian reconquest of the Iberian peninsula); the Shafi'i stronghold, formally in Egypt, Arabia and East Africa, is now to be found in South East Asia; and the Hanbali school has its main centre in Arabia where its teachings underpinned the Wahhabi movement and the rise of the present Saudi state. While these schools have more in common with each other than with other sects within Islam, there are important differences between them in terms of particular interpretations of the Sunna which are of significance to their adherents.

The minority faction in the struggle for authority within the early Muslim community became known as the Shi'i, differentiated, in particular, from their opponents by their special devotion and loyalty to Muhammad's cousin and son-in-law, Ali, whom they regard as the only legitimate and rightly guided leader, *caliph* or *imam* after the Prophet. But Shi'is, like Sunnis, subsequently split into several groups. The most important are the Twelvers or Imamiyah Shi'is who constitute a majority in Iran and parts of Iraq and the Lebanon. Sensitivity in relation to sectarian differences makes it difficult to obtain accurate figures regarding the number of Shi'is living in Sunni-dominated states, and so estimates of their numbers in somewhere like Pakistan, which has a majority of Sunnis, can range from 10 to 25 per cent. Other well-known, if not necessarily very sizeable, Shi'i factions include the Ismailiyyah of South Asia and East Africa and the Zaydiyyah found mainly in the Yemen.

On top of, or perhaps alongside, these main divisions, is the Sufi tradition of mystical contemplation which has permeated Islam from its earliest times and which continues to play a part in the religious consciousness of large quantities of Muslims. Often regarded by the more orthodox mainstream as suspect and superfluous, with practices and traditions which can appear alien to the bare essentials of Islam, the reality is that Sufism has always been intrinsic to the way that many Muslims have practised their faith, providing through its networks of spiritual leaders, brotherhoods and shrines complementary as well as alternative loci of worship for both men and women in many corners of the Muslim world.

MYTHS AND IMAGES?

Of course, myths and partial images taken at face value have for long affected and often distorted understandings about Islam and the so-called Muslim world when viewed from the West. Stereotyping and conflict between Islam and the largely Christian West have repeatedly fostered levels of ignorance, with the 1979 Iranian revolution, the *Satanic Verses* controversy and the 1991 Gulf War representing some of the more recent 'culprits' in this process (Akhtar, 1989; Esposito, 1990). The irony of the present situation is increased when, as already pointed out, we recognize that the West itself now, geographically at any rate, forms part of that world: the two, not so separate, worlds, whose boundaries in fact have always been blurred, now overlap more than they have ever done so before.

A main stumbling block, however, which inhibits Western understanding of Islam and the realities of contemporary Muslim life, is the extent to which the West requires a certain kind of Islam and a certain kind of Muslim in order to reinforce its own sense of itself. This highly selective 'imaging' of Islam and Muslims is nothing new. Daniel (1958) and Southern (1962) both highlighted more than thirty years ago ways in which the West has made Islam the subject of attention, paving the way for Edward Said's more controversial 1978 analysis of Western attitudes to Islam in his discussion of Orientalism and the various forms which it has taken. Yet despite the recognition that stereotypes of Islam and Muslims have dubious roots, there has been a growing tendency among some Western commentators to substitute Islam for communism as the new 'threat', based on the proposition of an essential clash of civilizations. In the new simplified map of the post-Cold War world, the colour for the West to beware is not the red of communism but the green of Islam, which writers, such as Lewis (1993) and Huntingdon (1993), have assumed represents the greatest contemporary threat to Western agency. A sickle-shaped moon, rather than the sickle of the working classes, has become the paramount symbol of danger.

Politicized Islam, a feature of contemporary Muslim politics around the globe, epitomizes this danger to Western norms and beliefs. Western responses to the idea of *jihad*, or Islamic holy war, similarly highlight current fears. For the Christian West, its own experience of 'holy war' has come to be associated firmly with the distant past in contrast to the apparently enduring significance of 'holy war' for Muslims, discussion of which periodically reverberates through the Western media helping to reinforce perceptions of the latter as less advanced and less rational than their Western counterparts. Indeed, the fact that *jihad* has a much more complex set of meanings attached to it than simply 'warfare' is rarely recognized by those who operate in a Western context. Within the Islamic framework, the idea of war for religion 'is associated with continuous striving in the path of faith' with *jihad* itself the Arabic word for 'striving'. 'Striving by the sword' represents the lesser *jihad* while the greater *jihads* are those which take place at a more personal level within the heart, the tongue and the hands (Turner Johnson, 1997: vii).

All the same, these concepts of *jihad* do reflect deeply rooted under-standings and impressions of the very close relationship between religion and politics which exists within Islam. Unlike modern Western culture, in which church and state have become increasingly separate, religion re-mains much more integral to concepts of political community and the conduct of community affairs for perhaps the majority of Muslims. However, as Eickelman and Piscatori point out, it can be unhelpful to presuppose an automatic union of religion and politics among all Muslims. Not only does this presumption support the largely erroneous impression that church and state in the West have always been separate, it also re-inforces misperceptions about the degree to which Islam can or cannot cope with change. Hence, both Muslims and non-Muslims have tended 'to take at face value the ideological claim by some Muslims that the key elements of Islamic tradition are fixed' (Eickelman and Piscatori, 1996: 28). Premising their arguments on the basis of religion and politics being insep-arably intertwined within Islam, commentators have frequently regarded modernity and tradition to be diametrically opposed to each other in Mus-lim societies. Observers, therefore, have been pessimistic about the chances of the peoples living in these societies ever crossing the great divide which separates the developed from the non-developed world. Thus, Muslim societies to many outside them seem be moving in the wrong direction, away from the rules of political engagement as laid down in the post-Enlightenment West and back towards an intrinsically and comparatively less developed past.

However, oversimplifying the dichotomy between Islam and moderni-zation has underestimated very greatly the complex process of interac-tion which has characterized the relationship in many Muslim contexts. Indeed, with greater awareness of how far 'tradition' has been re-invented in the West in pursuit of change, more credence is now being given to the role of tradition as a profound vehicle for evolutionary and revolutionary change among Muslims who have often invoked a frame-work of tradition in order to make valid and facilitate innovation. Changes to the *Sharia* or Islamic law, commonly held by Muslims and non-Muslims alike to be inviolate, have frequently taken place in the form of reinterpretations with religious and legal experts using the legiti-mate power of *ijtihad*, or personal reasoning, to bring about reform, de-spite the 'pious fictions' which have helped to play down the extent of this re-visioning. Religion, which many in the West expected to wither away as Muslim societies inevitably became more 'modern', has fre-quently done just the opposite, in the process not just surviving but also asserting its ability to manipulate and reconfigure the meaning of that modernity in ways which have helped to keep change within the essence of Islam (Eickelman and Piscatori, 1996: 24–5).

STATIC AND UNCHANGING?

Thus, all too often, the established Western view of non-Western societies has been that of static, monolithic entities steeped in unchanging traditions and practices. This has certainly been the case as far as Western understandings of societies influenced and shaped by Islam have been concerned. In contrast, the last 200 years have been a period of intense activity and re-thinking for Muslims, triggered off in large part by the expansion of the West but also generated by processes taking place internally within Islam. These processes created and consolidated a breadth of diversity in terms of both religious and political belief and practice, something which is rarely appreciated as fully as it could be in the West.

From a Muslim point of view, the Islamic world system which had evolved by the nineteenth century was largely 'overwhelmed by forces from the West, driven by capitalism, powered by the industrial revolution, and civilised, after a fashion, by the Enlightenment' (Robinson, 1996: x). While some Muslims accepted their political misfortune quietly as 'the judgement of God', others set about finding ways of remedying the evils which beset them. Consequently, there was an upsurge in movements of religious reform and revival concerned to revitalize Islam and with it Muslim society. Muslim thinkers increasingly contrasted the attributes of Western dominance with the elements of decline and apathy which they had identified in their own cultures, and reworked existing ideas about the relationship between individual Muslims, their religion and the modern world.

The result was a range of responses, connected by their common desire to strengthen Islam in relation to the challenges which it faced. With political power diminished if not completely lost, the task of safeguarding Islam was deemed to lie more than ever before with individual Muslims who increasingly needed to take personal responsibility for their religion, excising from their practices anything which was presumed to be suspect or damaging to its integrity. Muslims increasingly saw themselves as responsible for their own futures – it was up to them to use the strengths on offer in the West such as its rationalism and efficiency to build up their intellectual stamina and reassert their independence, moral or otherwise.

Islamic modernism, spearheaded by nineteenth-century activists and thinkers such as Jamal al-Din al-Afghani, Muhammad Abduh and Sayyid Ahmad Khan, stressed individual interpretation based on *ijtihad*, and enjoined Muslims to explore freely what was best here and now within the framework of the moral norms of Islam. The shift to a this-worldly Islam with its new sense of responsibility increased the importance of self-instrumentality, self-affirmation, the affirmation of ordinary life, and self-consciousness among Muslims to the extent that 'the fashioning of a new human self was the central activity of the reformist project' (Robinson, 1997: 13). It helped to create conditions in which rulers in a range of Muslim countries metaphorically bit the bullet and began over the course of the nineteenth century to introduce reforms designed, with varying degrees of success and failure, to keep the West at bay.

The combined impact of increased Western political control and the concomitant drive for a kind of Muslim-style modernization produced mixed results, among which was the scenario for the emergence of Muslim nation-states. Indeed, most Muslim societies by the middle of the twentieth century had accommodated themselves to Western secular visions of progress, as epitomized by the nation-state, and most still retain, if not necessarily uncontested, the state structures which they acquired as a result. By and large, the governments of these Muslim societies, such as Turkey, Egypt and Iran, rejected religion in favour of secular alternatives with which to bind their new nation-states together and, while accommodations may subsequently have been made in response to changing religio-political climates, most still adhere to them. Even somewhere such as Pakistan, which in 1947 emerged out of British India as a home for the subcontinent's Muslims, was envisaged by its early rulers as a modern and largely secular state, with a fairly superficial role allocated to Islam. In 1971, the breakaway of East Pakistan to form Bangladesh exposed the fact that, in this South Asian context at any rate, a shared religion could not resolve adequately differences based on ethnicity, culture, language and the imbalance of political and economic power.

A major area of concern to the waves of reformers, who emerged from the mid-nineteenth century onwards, was how to 'rationalize' and in effect bring up to date the religiously inspired personal laws which in theory guided and governed Muslim lives. At the same time, a key element of the nationalist agenda in these Muslim states was the defence of Islamic culture. By the twentieth century, reformist ideas on changes to these religious laws had influenced the climate of opinion sufficiently to permit governments in many Muslim societies to introduce reforms relating to the family, personal relationships and issues such as marriage, divorce and inheritance. These were precisely those areas of *Sharia* law which had been left largely untouched by the introduction of European-style law codes as a result of colonial control. They were also very sensitive areas, for they dealt with the institution of the family, which for many Muslims symbolized the one area of life in which they had been able to retain a degree of autonomy in the face of growing Western interference, and whose retention had been used by some early nationalists to symbolize the rejection of an alien culture (Esposito, 1982).

But just as most of the nineteenth-century reformers were united in their belief that the future well-being of their Muslim community lay in re-creating a strong moral base within the family and the home, so their more politicized successors later advocated state-sponsored legal reforms, designed in particular to raise the status and profile of their womenfolk, as a way of asserting their claims to be taken seriously as modern nations, able to stand proudly alongside their Western counterparts. Women and the laws associated with them in effect became the litmus test of modernity, symbolic of the community and its values, and, while the context surrounding these issues has continued to evolve, the concern with women's rights and their proper conduct remains central to debates on religious and legal reform in all of today's Muslim societies (Yamani, 1997).

THE APPEAL OF ISLAMISM?

Thus, for a range of reasons and in different ways, the last 150 years have seen Muslims make enormous accommodations to Western secular visions of progress. This degree of compromise and adjustment, however, has come to be overshadowed by the growth over the second half of the twentieth century of more radical responses to the challenges arising from the Muslim encounter with the West and the crisis between Islam and modernity. Organizations, such as the Muslim Brotherhood, which has spread out from Egypt to other parts of the Middle East, and the Jamaat-i Islami, active across South Asia, epitomize this radical face of Islam, even though they have been outflanked more recently by less accommodationist and more uncompromising groups. These trends within Islam have often been grouped together and labelled rather derogatorily as 'Muslim fundamentalism' but have now earned their own, technically more correct, description of 'Islamism' (Mitchell, 1969; Nasr, 1994).

Muslim governments have been dealing with the ramifications of these religio-political movements since the Second World War, but it took the 1979 Iranian revolution to wake up Western observers to the dangers which these trends are perceived to pose to the *status quo*. Western observers have tended to see Islamism's opposition to things Western as being its most distinctive feature, and by implication have assumed that what they are witnessing is a call for a return to seventh-century Arabia, out of tune with the modern world. Hence, Ayatollah Khomeini, the axis around which the Islamic revolution in Iran appeared to revolve, has frequently been presented as 'an anti-modern character', involved in 'turning back the clock of history' (Sayyid, 1997: 89). In fact, while Islamist movements do argue for a return, it is back to the principles embeddied in the Qur'ān and Sunna which they regard as 'the only authentic expression of the Islamic experience' (Waines, 1995: 240). Against what is usually a backdrop of enormous economic and social change and pressure, they have demanded the establishment of an Islamic order or *nizam*, in which religion and politics are properly integrated. The deficiencies of the materialistic Western-style nation-state, they feel, can best be remedied by a 'theo-democracy', administered not by the kind of Islamic government which existed in the past to create the right conditions for Islam to flourish, but by a new-style government, with the enhanced power of the modernized state at its command, to take responsibility for the Islamic renewal.

Interestingly, this idea of an Islamic state, based on a social contract between the ruler and the ruled, does not depend on 'traditional' religious experts or *ulama* for leadership and direction, even though images of 'Islamic fundamentalism' are dominated by the Iranian case where Shi'i clerics or *ayatollahs* have obviously had a major influence over events. Instead, for most Islamists, ordinary men are expected to fill a central role in this new kind of polity in which the State is supposed to exercise much greater responsibility for the people than has ever before been the case within the Islamic world, intervening in and shaping their lives, and this crucial difference, it is argued, gives a distinctly modern aspect to the relationship between Islam and the State.

Secular critics of Islamist claims often dismiss them as utopian: 'the hope, or conviction, that rulers can be kept out of mischief by adhering to a certain set of doctrines, or leading an ascetic way of life, is as old as the notion of Utopia in human history . . . one which has so far rarely worked in practice' (Enayat, 1982: 104). But with the strains of rapid modernization, translated into stressful living conditions for expanding numbers of Muslims in many parts of the developing world, Islamist movements have not had too much difficulty in generating support for what they assert to be the authentic Islam. Indeed, the appeal of Islamism in particular, and perhaps Islam more generally, is closely linked to aspects of modern life which facilitate its spread. Mass education and mass communication, which are fairly recent arrivals in many Muslim societies, play an important part in heightening mass awareness and disseminating ideas more widely, hence intensifying debate. Greater self-consciousness means that '"being Muslim" acquires more political significance in the modern world . . . because of the self-conscious identification of believers with their religious tradition'. This systemization of Islam, combined with more direct and broader access to sources of religious authority via the printed word, has produced Islamists 'committed to implementing their vision of Islam as a corrective to current "un-Islamic" practices' (Eickelman and Piscatori, 1996: 39–44). Of undoubted interest to the West are the significant numbers of Muslim women who have been drawn to Islamist movements, either as activists or 'on the fringes, variously adopting degrees of "Islamic" dress, supporting the moral values, or voicing anti-imperialist themes' (Bodman and Tohidi, 1998: 16). The veil, whose rejection symbolized to such a great extent the apparent modernizing of Muslim societies in the early part of the twentieth century, has reasserted its centrality as an indicator of change, with new groups of Muslim women adopting different kinds of ways of covering their heads in order to signal and in the process reinforce their religious and political identities, as well as to facilitate new roles for themselves (MacLeod, 1993).

While Islamism looks set to dominate the Muslim political agenda for the foreseeable future, its claim to have grasped the essence of Islam does not go unchallenged from within the ranks of Muslim thinkers. Alternative voices still operating from within an Islamic framework have rejected European universalism as destructive to the Muslim world, marginalizing Islamic traditions, but have condemned those Muslims 'who by virtue of superior knowledge claim to distinguish the "true" Islam from the false, the "true Muslim" from one who simply calls himself or herself a Muslim'. Hence, they reject the argument of contemporary Islamists that reason must be subordinate to faith, as for them 'a tyranny of faith is no more acceptable than the tyranny of reason' (Arkoun, 1994: ix–x). Similarly, assertions that 'there are as many Islams as there are situations that sustain it' (Al-Azmeh, 1993: 1) suggest that within Islam there is a readiness among some commentators to engage constructively with the realities of the so-called postmodern world even when their arguments go unnoticed by the vast majority of Muslims and non-Muslims alike.

Indeed, if contemporary debates on post-modernity succeed in decentring both the West and Islamism, then, in addition to the assertion that it was 'the deconstruction of the relation between modernity and the West which produced a space into which Islamism could locate itself' (Sayyid, 1997: 120), alternative space might well be opened up for more wide-ranging debate among Muslims about 'Islam' in the next millennium. Of course, the millennium itself and the celebrations which have been organized to accompany it reflect the Eurocentric reality with which Muslims have to live. Islam still has several centuries to go before it enters its next millennium. The fact that the West takes its involvement in an 'alien' calendar more or less for granted demonstrates how far the non-Muslim world still has to travel in order to understand the religio-political impulses which are flowing though late twentieth-century Islam.

SUMMARY

- For the West, Islam in the late twentieth century represents more than just a religious alternative to Christian or secular values – to many Westerners, rightly or wrongly, it symbolizes the major contemporary threat to their beliefs and ways of life.
- Islam has become a truly global religion with patterns of conversion and migration making it into a worldwide force with growing numbers of adherents in the West itself.
- Muslims have had to grapple in dynamic fashion with the challenges of modernity over the last 200 years, and this has produced a range of responses within Islam, designed to strengthen and reinforce Muslim religion and culture.
- Islam, therefore, has never been a monolithic force – sectarian and political differences have repeatedly fractured its unity, and, while the emphasis today is on the phenomenon of Islamism, it is important to understand this in the context of its time as well to appreciate the presence of other strands of religio-political thinking among Muslims.

FURTHER READING

John O. Voll's (1982) *Islam: Continuity and Change in the Modern World*, Boulder, CO: Westview Press, still provides an excellent overview of the Islamic world from early times through to recent developments, as does Ira M. Lapidus (1988) *A History of Islamic Societies*, Cambridge: Cambridge University Press.

Studies which examine the rise of the West and the variety of Muslim reactions to the challenge posed to Islam by new frameworks of power such as the modern state and Western knowledge, include Fazlur Rahman (1974) *Islam and Modernity: Transformation of an Intellectual Tradition*, Chicago: University of Chicago Press, and James P. Piscatori (1986), *Islam in a World of Nation States*, Cambridge: Cambridge University Press.

An introduction to Islamism is provided in Richard M. Burrell (ed.) (1989) *Islamic Fundamentalism*, London: Royal Asiatic Society, while John L. Esposito (1992) *The Islamic Threat: Myth or Reality*, New York: Oxford University Press, argues that the dangers of the 'green peril' have been overexaggerated.

For interesting insights into the spread of Islam in the West, see Larry Poston (1991) *Islamic Da'wah in the West: Muslim Missionary Activity and the Dynamics of Conversion to Islam*, Edmonton: University of Alberta Press.

REFERENCES

Akhtar, Shabbir (1989) *Be Careful with Muhammad: The Salman Rushdie Affair*. London: Bellew.

Al-Azmeh, Aziz (1993) *Islams and Modernities*. London: Verso.

Arkhoun, Mohammed (1994) *Rethinking Islam: Common Questions, Uncommon Answers*, trans. and ed. Robert D. Lee. Oxford: Westview Press.

Bodman, Herbert L. and Tohidi, Nayereh (eds) (1998) *Women in Muslim Societies: Diversity within Unity*. Boulder, CO: Lynne Reinner.

Daniel, Norman (1958) *Islam and the West: the Making of an Image*. Edinburgh: Edinburgh University Press.

Eickelman, Dale F. and Piscatori, James (eds) (1996) *Muslim Politics*. Princeton, NJ: Princeton University Press.

Enayat, Hamid (1982) *Modern Islamic Political Thought*. London: Macmillan.

Esposito, John L. (1982) *Women in Muslim Family Law*. New York: Syracuse University Press.

Esposito, John L. (1990) *The Iranian Revolution: Its Global Impact*. Miami: Florida International University Press.

Geertz, Clifford (1971) *Islam Observed*. Chicago: Chicago University Press.

Huntingdon, Samuel (1993) 'The Clash of Civilisations?' *Foreign Affairs*, **72**(3): 22–49.

Lerner, Daniel (1964) *The Passing of Traditional Society: Modernising the Middle East.* New York: Free Press.

Lewis, Bernard (1993) 'Islam and Liberal Democracy', *Atlantic,* **271**, February: 89–94.

MacLeod, Arlene E. (1993) *Accommodating Protest: Working Women, the New Veiling and Change in Cairo.* New York: Columbia University Press.

Mitchell, Richard P. (1969) *The Society of the Muslim Brothers.* London: Oxford University Press.

Nasr, Seyyed Vali Reza (1994) *The Vanguard of the Islamic Revolution: The Jamaat-i Islami of Pakistan.* Berkeley and Los Angeles, CA: University of California Press.

Robinson, Francis (ed.) (1996) *Cambridge Illustrated History of the Islamic World.* Cambridge: Cambridge University Press.

Robinson, Francis (1997) 'Religious Change and the Self in Muslim South Asia since 1800', *South Asia,* **20**(1): 1–15.

Said, Edward (1978) *Orientalism.* London: Routledge and Kegan Paul.

Sayyid, Bobby S. (1997) *A Fundamental Fear: Eurocentrism and the Emergence of Islamism.* London: Zed Books.

Southern, R.W. (1962) *Western Views of Islam in the Middle Ages.* Cambridge, MA: Harvard University Press.

Turner Johnson, James (1997) *The Holy War Idea in Western and Islamic Traditions.* Pennsylvania: Pennsylvania State University Press.

Waines, David (1995) *An Introduction to Islam.* Cambridge: Cambridge University Press.

Yamani, Mai (ed.) (1997) *Feminism and Islam: Legal and Literary Perspectives.* Reading: Ithaca Press.

Chapter 27

Cultural pluralism today

Avigail Eisenberg

Most societies exhibit cultural pluralism – that is, their citizens belong to different cultural or linguistic communities. What to make of this fact has been the subject of serious academic debate. The following essay provides a map of the analyses and debates about cultural pluralism in contemporary Western liberal democracies. It begins by examining some lessons that political and social theories of pluralism might helpfully contribute to the study of cultural pluralism. It then guides the reader through two projects in which theorists who write about cultural pluralism today are engaged. The first project is to determine the different spheres of social and political life in which cultures might be empowered or disadvantaged. What counts for a cultural group as a resource which can be drawn upon to improve its cultural security, or what are the circumstances that disempower a cultural group? In this regard, one of the most common concerns today is that seemingly neutral policies, practices, institutions and ways of thinking maintain the dominance of one cultural group over others. The second project is to determine whether or under what circumstances the balance of power between cultures within the same state ought to be altered. This second project can be subdivided into two distinct, though related inquiries, one in moral theory and the other in social science. Moral theorists want to know what justice requires in terms of distributing power between different cultures. For example, in what senses is it unjust, illiberal or intolerant to deny minorities special protections for their culture? Social scientists attempt to determine the sort of distribution of power required to protect or enhance societal stability. The question for them is whether multicultural policies result in social fragmentation and backlash or whether they provide a better means to integrate minority groups.

PLURALISM: DEFINITIONS AND RESOURCES

Within political analysis, cultural pluralism is not merely a synonym for ethnic diversity. Theories of cultural pluralism, which here include multi-culturalism, identity politics, the politics of difference and the 'new' pluralism, involve questions about how the distribution of power and resources is or ought to be affected by cultural membership. In other words, just as the study of class asks that we view laws and policies in terms of their differential impact on classes, and just as feminist theory focuses upon how gender makes a difference to one's opportunities and well-being, the study of cultural pluralism looks at how power and resources are distributed to cultural groups. In some societies the cultural division of power is plain: for example, the Ottomans governed their empire, from 1456 until the First World War, by a millet system whereby the three non-Muslim minorities were accorded official recognition as self-governing communities. But in liberal societies, such as Britain, Canada and the USA, the cultural division of power is often far from plain and, if power was found to be distributed to particular cultures and not others, this would seem to violate the liberal aims of guaranteeing to all individuals equal rights and establishing undifferentiated citizenship. However, since all societies contain more than one cultural group, the question is not whether power is distributed to cultural groups, but rather to which culture(s) it is distributed and in what proportions. Issues as disparate as affirmative action, ethnic conflict and secession fall under the umbrella of inquiries about cultural pluralism because all essentially involve debates about how power and resources ought to be distributed among people of different cultural identities.

Striking similarities exist between the new theories of multiculturalism, identity and difference and theories of pluralism dating back to the beginning of the twentieth century. Several theorists who have recently turned their attention to the history of pluralist theories have argued that these theories, though not designed to address *cultural* pluralism *per se*, none the less contain a wealth of resources upon which current theories of cultural pluralism can draw, but which these theories often ignore (Eisenberg, 1995; Goulbourne, 1991; McClure, 1992; McLennan, 1995; Sartori, 1997). Three lessons can be derived from pluralist theories, which I will label the lesson of tolerance, the lesson of social equality, and the lesson of state sovereignty.

The lesson of tolerance

In the liberal tradition, pluralism is often linked to tolerance. Its original meaning is located in the sixteenth and seventeenth centuries 'with the gradual acceptance of toleration in the aftermath of the wars of religion' in Europe (Sartori, 1997: 58). Sartori argues that most theories of pluralism since that time have impoverished the concept to the point where the new pluralists – those who advocate multiculturalism and 'cultural separation' – are, in Sartori's estimation, 'anti-pluralists' (Sartori, 1997: 62; see Wolin, 1993). While one might disagree with Sartori's conclusions, he correctly identifies one of the most complex problems for theories of cultural pluralism, namely how to promote the toleration of difference at a group level while protecting the right of individuals to dissent from the group. For example, the Ottoman millet system mentioned above may have successfully promoted the toleration of religious diversity between the four groups of the empire. But religious dissent was not tolerated within any of these communities (see Kymlicka, 1992). The system protected individual identity only in so far as individuals conformed to group norms. The millet system was not designed to protect *individual* identity and well-being. Rather, its aim was to secure stable relations between large minority groups and the Muslim majority so that the Ottomans could continue to rule their empire unimpeded by dissension from these communities. All political systems that recognize the rights of groups to govern themselves potentially give rise to the problem of tolerating diversity for groups but not for individuals – or at least not for individuals who want to dissent from the community in which they have membership.

This problem provides good grounds to be sceptical of group rights and instead to seek means of addressing cultural diversity that simultaneously protect groups and empower individuals to escape the dictates of the group and/or to mobilize resources to change the group. Theorists of pluralism have argued that individuals ought to be able to use the resources of one group in which they have membership to change the policies and practices of another. As long as groups are not insular, pluralism offers a form of political self-defence (Eisenberg, 1995; Rosenblum, 1989) and can provide a safeguard to individual liberty.

The lessons of social equality

The lessons of social equality require that we retain a healthy scepticism about the prospect that pluralism can improve democratic governance and social equality. Some advocates of cultural pluralism may uncritically celebrate pluralism, plural society, plural community and pluralist democracy. They assume that pluralism or multiculturalism is a means of addressing social inequality (Goulbourne, 1991: 24). Yet, more often than not social and cultural pluralism has coexisted and reinforced social inequality. J.S. Furnivall, who distinguished between plural societies, such as Indonesia, and societies with 'plural features' such as Canada and the USA (Furnivall, 1948: 305), observed that plural societies often contain a division of labour along cultural lines with some cultures dominating others. Within a truly plural society, individuals of different backgrounds live 'side by side, but separately, within the same political unit' (Furnivall, 1948: 304). Both Furnivall and M.G. Smith (1975), who wrote thirty years later, concluded not only that cultural membership helped to determine one's economic and social status in plural societies, but more disturbingly that the cultural domination of one group was an essential means to holding plural societies together (see Kuper, 1969:13).

Clearly, the differentiation of people on the basis of culture is no guarantee that social equality will be enhanced. Apartheid in South Africa, Indian reservations in Canada and the USA, and racial segregation in the American South are all ways in which majorities protect their advantages by distinguishing between people on the basis of culture or race. In order to succeed at improving social equality, arguments for cultural recognition must be explicitly tied to this aim (Rex, 1987: 219-20; Samad, 1997: 243).

But even when aimed at enhancing social equality, some critics worry that when policies reinforce multiculturalism, they undermine the power of a community to advance social justice. Multiculturalism may fragment communities along cultural lines. It may divide and weaken their ability to engage in the sort of collective action necessary to advance just causes (see Miller, 1995: 97–8, 135–40). At the heart of this concern, is another central problem for cultural pluralism to address, namely that policies which reinforce cultural pluralism might end up fragmenting communities and undermining social cohesion. Without social cohesion, communities are unable to address the causes of cultural oppression. The problem of fragmentation and responses to it will be further discussed below.

The lesson of state sovereignty

The new cultural and identity-based pluralism is also distinct from two types of political pluralism: British pluralism developed in the 1910s and 1920s, and post-war American pluralism (Goulbourne, 1991). The aim of British pluralists, such as Harold Laski, was to discredit the idea that the state had a *prima facie* claim to restrict the power of groups – in particular the power of trade unions – or to restrict the freedom of individuals to associate in groups. Only by recognizing the right of associations to advance the interests of their members could liberty be preserved. In order to recognize this right, sovereign power must be seen as distributed pluralistically to many groups in society.

Contrary to Laski's understanding of pluralism, today's advocates of cultural pluralism require that the State have more rather than less power in defining and brokering the interests of cultural groups. They place the onus on the State to abandon assimilationist policies and adopt policies that recognize cultural difference. For instance, Britain's Swann Report on educational reform (1985) addresses the concerns of parents from cultural minorities about the underachievement of their children by recommending that the State become more rather than less involved in using the educational system to construct a specific vision of British society – namely, a multicultural vision. Advocates of multiculturalism want their cultural experiences and contributions to be recognized in the public sphere through sensitizing public institutions to their cultural and linguistic differences.

Charles Taylor has written extensively about the importance of *recognition* to the health of identity (Taylor, 1992). But again the problem with putting a high premium on official, public and constitutional recognition, as Taylor does, is that doing so places in the State's hands the power to determine which identity-based groups are significant and what aspects of their identities will receive public recognition. In the case of the Swann Report, for example, it may be far easier for a government to require that culturally sensitive materials be included in the curricula than to address the social inequalities that are probably more to blame for the underachievement of children within some ethnic communities (see Goulbourne, 1991: 221). The more the State becomes involved in the recognition and regulation of ethnic minorities, the more groups must craft their interests and even their identities in terms of categories to which the State is likely to respond.

Three lessons have been identified as relevant to today's theories of cultural pluralism. First, the relation between pluralism and tolerance raises the question of how any system of government that ensures tolerance of group differences by according to groups limited forms of autonomy can ensure that tolerance is extended to individuals who dissent from the group. Second, cultural pluralism provides no guarantee of social equality, especially in societies that are 'plural' in the sense that anthropologists identify. In societies with 'plural features', such as Canada, the USA and Britain, the concern is that policies that promote cultural distinctions may fragment society. A fragmented society lacks the social cohesion necessary to engage in the sort of co-operative projects that advance social justice. In other words, some forms of multiculturalism may imperil the welfare state. Third, the point of pluralism, according to Laski, is to protect liberty by decreasing the authority of the State over groups. Today, many measures designed to address cultural disadvantage aim to increase the State's power.

Two theories of pluralism have been identified so far: the anthropological theories developed by Furnivall, and the British political pluralism developed by Laski, Figgis and Cole. Perhaps the best known theory of pluralism has yet to be mentioned – the post-war American pluralism. The lessons it contained are directly relevant to the first of two projects of cultural pluralism, namely the issue of what is to count as cultural power, which is discussed in the next section.

CULTURAL PLURALISM AND POWER

As described above, cultural pluralists are usually engaged in one of two projects: (1) to identify the different spheres in which power is exerted on a cultural basis, and (2) to determine how power ought to be distributed and to what end. Put in terms of a question, those engaged in the first project ask 'what are the sources of cultural power and disadvantage?'

Individual and group rights

Individual and group rights are the first and most obvious source of power for cultural groups. Freedom of religion, assembly and speech, while guaranteed to individuals, have historically been used to protect minority groups. In the liberal tradition, these rights developed out of a need to devise ways in which different groups, mainly religious groups, could peacefully coexist.

Group rights for cultural minorities, including language rights, special rights to representation, special land use rights and limited forms of self-determination, are other means of according power to groups. They are often thought to be inconsistent with the liberal tradition because they are 'special' and therefore not universally applicable to all individuals. Liberalism has been championed by thinkers who have sought to eliminate differences between individuals by arguing that all individuals are worthy of the same treatment. For example, both Hobbes and Locke devised theories that purposely circumvented associations in order to forge an unmitigated bond between the individual and the State. Rousseau argued that the general will requires that there be no subsidiary groups within the State. The social contract required that feudal loyalties and factions be eliminated, that individuals express only their own opinions and act only on their own interests. Even John Stuart Mill, for whom diversity was the life pulse of a healthy democracy, argued only for individual rights.

A tendency to recognize individual and not group rights deepened in twentieth-century liberal thought largely due to the political circumstances of liberalism's leading interpreters, Britain and the USA (see Kymlicka, 1995: 56–61). Post-war Britain withdrew from the political circumstances – such as its colonies and nationalist conflicts in continental Europe – that would otherwise have forced it to think more carefully about what policies and principles ought to regulate relations between cultural minorities and majorities. The USA acquired a vested interest in ignoring national and ethnic minorities. Post-war America viewed itself as the defender of universal and individual rights and became committed to eliminating legal barriers erected on the basis of race and gender within its jurisdiction. The lessons of *Brown vs the Board of Education*, which required that schools be desegregated in the American South, and of the Civil Rights campaigns, was that cultural, ethnic and racial divides ought not to make any difference to one's opportunities.

Despite this history, both liberal and non-liberal regimes have used group rights to stabilize relations between groups. In addition to the Ottomans' millet system, in The Netherlands 'pillarization' allowed Calvinist, Catholic and secular groups to lead relatively isolated and self-contained existences. A similar model for cultural accommodation, called consociational democracy, is found in Switzerland and Belgium. In Canada, federalism has been used to protect the French and English languages and cultures. Moreover, both Canada and the USA employ special constitutional procedures and rights to govern the relation between the State and indigenous peoples. For instance, some American Indian tribes have a legally recognized right to self-government which means that their governments are not subject to the American Bill of Rights.

Interest-group power

A second source of power for cultural groups is the political influence that interest groups have over governments. The pluralist theory developed in the USA in the post-war period focused on this type of power. Robert Dahl, in developing what is often called interest-group pluralism, held that individuals form groups in order to advance their shared interests. These groups compete with each other and form coalitions in order to obtain the most resources possible – such as money, public support and votes – which are then used to influence governing decisions. Dahl insisted that, in a healthy pluralist democracy, no single resource dominated and no group is able to dominate the system (or not for very long, given the unstable nature of interest-based coalitions). The direction of public policy depends on the coalition of groups that dominate the policy-making scene at any given time. So in a pluralist democracy, neither a ruling élite nor a majority rules. Rather, government is run by continuously shifting coalitions of minorities (Dahl, 1967: 133).

Although cultural groups are not the same as interest groups, the need to protect cultural identity has led most cultural minorities to form interest groups and advance their identity-related interests in the political arena by fund-raising, undertaking anti-racism campaigns, lobbying government and forwarding candidates for election. However, the outcome of this sort of political activity, when it involves cultural minorities, often discredits rather than confirms the vision of democracy advanced by interest-group pluralism. Competition between cultural groups for decision-making power in the democratic State reveals significant cultural biases inherent in democratic governing systems which make it impossible for all identity-based interest groups to compete on an equitable basis for the State's resources.

Systemic advantages and disadvantages

The disadvantages conferred on minorities because of systemic discrimination have been part of the critique of pluralism since the 1960s. Critics of post-war pluralism argued that pluralists such as Dahl were blind to the biases inherent in different systems because of their strict focus on quantifiable behaviour and concrete instances of decision-making (Bachrach and Baratz, 1962). One leading theorist of the politics of difference has recently argued that theories that focus solely on the distribution of resources will fail to provide adequate accounts of the oppression that occurs in society. Young identifies five sources of oppression: exploitation, marginalization, powerlessness, cultural imperialism and violence (Young, 1990: 48–65). She argues that the biases of institutional structures are often ignored in distributive theories yet have a profound effect by ensuring systemic advantages for some groups and disadvantages for others: 'a distributive understanding of power which treats power as some kind of stuff that can be traded, exchanged, and distributed, misses the structural phenomena of domination' (Young, 1990: 31).

Most democratic and liberal theories fail to account for systemic biases and instead presume that institutions are, or at least can be, neutral between different interests, including different cultural interests. For example, interest-group pluralists assumed that power is available equally to whichever group is best organized and best able to mobilize public support. Yet, with respect to cultural politics, this assumption is implausible. All nation-states favour particular cultural values if only by choosing a national language with which to conduct life in the public arena. Moreover, many liberal states recognize a state religion, adopt religious symbolism and structure public life according to the values and traditions of one particular religion. The institutions of all liberal states, while purportedly serving citizens of different cultural backgrounds equally, promote particular interpretations of history, particular myths and values, including some which demean the values of other cultures. For example, in Canada, parliamentary institutions and rituals reflect the country's history from a British point of view and unapologetically relay the story of colonial occupation. Members of Parliament, including aboriginal peoples, who as a group were colonized and coercively assimilated by Britain and Canada, are expected to participate in rituals which symbolize acts of submission such as bowing to the Speaker and the mace (White, 1991: 506). While these rituals may not be central to the current decision-making practices employed in government, they are clearly relevant to the atmosphere in the legislature and thus to the values projected by the institution onto those who are elected to participate in it. As one might expect, aboriginal peoples are underrepresented in Canada's legislatures relative to their population in the country. The same problem and conclusion also apply to other cultural minorities and women.

Cultural texts

Compelling arguments within cultural theory require that we cast the net in search of power and sources of domination further than postwar conventions required to include a fourth source, namely, the biases written into cultures through their literary and philosophical texts and traditions. For instance, Edward Said argues that imperialism was written into Western culture through the novel (Said, 1994). Because culture develops in relational terms, literary works that explore the cultural character of one group do so by juxtaposing it to the character of another. Western culture (particularly Western imperialism) is largely built upon the construction of others or 'the other' with whom Westerners have had cultural contact. The self-image of Westerners as colonizers and civilizers of the 'unexplored' and 'savage' world relied upon the construction of non-Western cultures – 'Orientals', Africans, Asians and indigenous peoples – as the other: savage and childlike, in need of 'our' governing hand and civilization (Said, 1994: xi).

Politically, at least two concerns stem from these cultural constructions. First, the imperialist and racist world view written into Western cultures persist today in the way in which social and political thought distinguishes between members and non-members, immigrants and citizens, European and non-European peoples. Second, many of the students who are made to read the 'great works' without a critical eye towards these cultural constructions, find reflected, at least in the Western canon, distorting and disempowering images of their cultural group as the conquered, the childlike, and the savage. This second problem has given rise to a wealth of debates within education about teaching the 'canon' and developing culturally sensitive curricula. It has also impelled many political theorists and literary scholars to reread the history of political thought and literature in terms of the cultural relations conveyed there (see, e.g., Arneil, 1996; Goldberg, 1994; Mills, 1997).

In sum, at least four sources of power are viewed as crucial to protecting and empowering cultural identity. First, individual and group rights are used within liberal democracies to enhance cultural security. Even those liberal democracies that are the most ideologically committed to individualism, such as the USA, none the less accord special legal protections to some groups. Second, cultural minorities purportedly have access to decision-making power if they organize themselves as interest groups and compete with other groups for resources. Their success in this forum largely depends on their access to a third source of power, namely the cultural biases inherent in society's structures and institutions. Fourth, systemic biases are reinforced by the cultural messages conveyed through literature and ideas.

Both the third and fourth types of power (or disempowerment) are especially difficult to 'redistribute' because they are built into the cultural, legal and political structures. This may partly vindicate Young's argument that distribution-based theories are unable to secure justice for oppressed groups. However, abandoning the idea of redistribution might exacerbate the already difficult task of eliminating oppression. Part of the critique that Bachrach and Baratz offered in the 1960s was that, had post-war pluralists viewed institutional biases as resources, they would have been less complacent about their conclusion that power is distributed pluralistically. Similarly, theorists today ought not to conclude that power is distributed equitably if institutions, legal and political conventions, education curricula, and public life esteem one culture while neglecting or demeaning others. If theories fail to count these biases as resources which make a difference to the power that groups wield in society, then they ought to be found deficient, not because of a mysterious and novel accounting system, but rather because they do not adequately grasp the nature of equality and justice.

DISTRIBUTION AND CULTURAL POWER

Stability-based arguments

This leaves one last issue, namely, when and how to redistribute culturally relevant resources. There are two reasons that special powers ought to be distributed to (some) cultural minorities. First, the stability of a region might be improved by recognizing the special rights of groups, and second, justice might require that cultural groups receive special protection. In any given case, these two reasons overlap. But they are importantly distinct and rest upon distinct types of arguments. Arguments concerned with stability are largely empirical and predictive: violence will occur, secessionist movements will succeed, or nationalist aspirations will turn militant unless special protections for cultural minorities are recognized. Stability-based arguments, while important and compelling, are fairly ubiquitous in political analysis. Stability is assessed and weighed in all political circumstances and can serve many different political regimes, including those that fail to live up to ethically acceptable standards. In relation to cultural pluralism, stability is a relevant consideration for both those who advocate special protections for groups and those who reject special protections for fear that they will fragment society.

Justice-based arguments: promise-keeping

The justice-based arguments for cultural protection rest on two possible bases – promise-keeping and equality. First, many groups have historical claims to special protection by the State based on treaties or agreements that have been signed in the past. In many cases, these agreements have been abrogated or rescinded by the more powerful group. For example, although language rights were guaranteed to Chicanos in south-western USA under the 1848 Treaty of Guadeloupe Hidalgo, the treaty was abrogated soon after it was passed, once anglophone settlers formed a majority in the region (see Kymlicka, 1995: 116). In some cases, these treaties have successfully become present-day components of national constitutions and jurisprudence. The Treaty of Waitangi was signed between New Zealand and the Maori in 1840, rescinded by New Zealand in 1877, and is now part of the country's constitution. In Canada, the Royal Proclamation of 1763, in which Britain set out its obligations to aboriginal peoples, is also considered part of the Canadian Constitution. Because these documents are recognized as having constitutional status, they are often used in present-day court cases to establish or expand the rights and protections offered to aboriginal peoples by the State.

Even in the absence of such tangible agreements, various cultural minorities have attempted to expand the protection they receive from the State on the basis of implicit understandings they claim to have with the State or other cultural groups. An interesting illustration of this is in *Wisconsin vs Yoder*, a case in which the Amish in the USA argued, on the basis of freedom of religion, to be exempted from the provision that required children to attend school until the age of 16. While no written agreement exists between the Amish and the USA giving the group special constitutional status, a legal brief submitted on behalf of the group sought to establish the existence of an unwritten understanding. It discussed the history of Amish persecution, dating back to the sixteenth century, and their understanding, upon migrating to the USA, that the religious liberty guaranteed there allowed them to live 'as a separated community of peaceableness and mutual aid'. In other words, the Amish came to the USA because they thought that freedom of religion there meant they could live their lives free from the dictates of an intrusive state. Historical understandings in the absence of explicit agreements also feature frequently in establishing the cultural rights of aboriginal peoples. In Canada, for example, many Indian bands have successfully argued for special fishing or land use rights based on evidence that their tribe or clan has fished or hunted in a particular spot for centuries predating colonization.

Justice-based arguments: equality

In addition to promise-keeping, justice requires that the individual's right to equality be respected and this might require that groups are protected as well. Special provisions to protect cultural minorities might be required in order to compensate minorities for the disadvantages they suffer because they are a minority living within a foreign cultural context. Will Kymlicka argues that understanding our culture, its history, traditions and conventions 'is a precondition of making intelligent judgements about how to lead our lives' (Kymlicka, 1995: 83). Cultural minorities, especially ones that speak a different language from the majority, are disadvantaged because, as a minority group, their cultural narrative does not define public life, is not taught in the schools and does not inform the practices, conventions and traditions of public institutions. The cultural cues written into the literature, political and philosophical texts they learn in school are the cues for some other culture with a different history. Cultural minorities have a very limited access to their own cultural structure. They have less cultural resources than the majority has on which to draw in making meaningful choices about their lives.

One way to ensure that each culture has access to a rich cultural context of its own is to institute a system of group rights, such as in the Ottomans' millet system or the 'pillars' of the Dutch system. To do so in liberal democracies today would require a radical form of multiculturalism in which each cultural minority is encouraged (and possibly subsidized) to develop its own educational curriculum, national history and literary canon. Educational systems, social services and some governing bodies could be semi-autonomous for each cultural community that is large enough. Institutions that are unavoidably public, such as central government agencies, could institute strict affirmative action programmes to ensure that all managerial and decision-making power is distributed equitably to all cultural groups.

Two criticisms of this solution have already been identified as 'lessons of pluralism'. First, group rights to autonomy might fragment society and undermine its ability to engage in co-operative projects, especially those that could advance social justice. Examples of such programmes include public health care and public pension plans, both of which redistribute wealth in society and thus require a high degree of social cohesion and co-operation in order to work. Notwithstanding this problem, for oppressed cultural minorities, even a fragmented society might be better than a society united by imperialistic institutions and marginalizing social practices.

A second criticism of group rights is that they create additional categories of oppression. The substance of any culture's identity is a hotly debated issue. '[T]he very concept of culture disintegrates at first touch into multiple positionings, according to gender, age, class, ethnicity, and so forth' (Werbner, 1997: 3). Members of any culture disagree about what are the key features of a group's identity, who gets to define this identity and who will be chosen to protect it. This disagreement is partly why cultural groups are fluid and ever changing: at different times, different understandings of the group's membership and core characteristics will predominate. Legally recognized group rights artificially freeze the parameters of the group's identity by protecting that group from outside influences. While the purpose of group rights is to protect groups from external influences, group rights also protect groups from changes brought about by their own members. Specifically, those who exist at the margins of a group, e.g. religious dissenters, feminists and cultural hybrids, will attempt to change their cultural group's values. Dissenters often use legal and political instruments outside their communities to change its internal practices. When practices are protected by legally sanctioned group rights, they are far more resistant to change than when they are not.

Kymlicka defends a less radical form of multiculturalism. He argues that group-differentiated rights (such as territorial autonomy, veto powers, guaranteed representation in central institutions, land claims and language rights) might be appropriate for colonized groups, particularly those, such as aboriginal peoples in Western societies, who have suffered from profound cultural insecurity due to continuous attempts by European peoples to coercively assimilate them. However, immigrants who voluntarily uproot themselves to gain the advantages prospectively found in new countries 'relinquish the rights that go along with their original national membership' (Kymlicka, 1995: 96), and forego the benefit of enjoying the cultural security of being a majority or protected minority. These groups primarily require the means to integrate successfully into the mainstream culture. They need social services and educational programmes that will help them to learn the language and culture of their new country. They also need policies and programmes that fight prejudice and discrimination against them. Affirmative action is also a required part of 'multicultural citizenship' because of the need to compensate minority groups for disadvantages that affect them in living their lives within partially foreign cultural contexts.

In sum, the best distribution of cultural power depends on the requirements of stability and justice. Justice-based arguments require that historical agreements are honoured and that the principle of equality is respected. The principle of equality serves individual well-being by equalizing the resources individuals have available to them to lead good lives. Group rights might be required because some types of resources are only available to individuals through the groups to which they belong. Some minority groups cannot enjoy the security required to build a meaningful and rich cultural context without the additional protection of rights. However, the benefits to individual well-being of any system based on group rights must be weighed against the costs of potentially undermining social cohesion and essentializing group identity.

Finally, the distinction between cultural groups that are minorities against their will and those who voluntarily immigrate to a foreign country is useful in addressing at least one of the recurring concerns about cultural pluralism, namely, that it undermines social cohesion. Multiculturalism is a means of rethinking post-war policies towards cultural minorities and thus 'renegotiating the terms of integration' (Kymlicka, 1998). Most arguments for multiculturalism and the recognition of difference aim to improve, not undermine, social cohesion by providing minority groups with the cultural security they require in order to integrate successfully into the societies of which they are a part.

CONCLUSION

The study of cultural pluralism – of how power is distributed on a cultural basis – has advanced some of the most difficult challenges to contemporary liberal democracies and liberal-democratic theory. For this reason, cultural pluralism is one of the most dynamic fields of study in political and social theory.

Cultural pluralists today argue that liberal regimes do not tolerate all cultural groups and, indeed, demean the values and traditions of some groups. Pluralists have pointed to a variety of arguments for redistributing cultural power through rights and interest-group influence or for compensating cultural minorities for the systemic and cultural biases that are written into the majority's institutions, literature and ideas. These arguments, some of which are discussed above, give rise to several concerns that here have been identified as three lessons of pluralism. First, the need to tolerate and protect difference must not essentialize group identity or impose onerous obstacles to individual dissent from their communities' traditions and values. Second, recognizing cultural differences does not automatically enhance social equality and may undermine it. Projects that advance social justice may be weakened in a society that lacks social cohesion. Third, many of the means advocated to protect cultural minorities do so by expanding the State's power. As cultural pluralists have clearly shown, the State is not neutral about the worth of different cultural values and therefore may prove to be an inadequate adjudicator and regulator of cultural power in the multicultural state.

SUMMARY

- Cultural pluralism studies how power is distributed on a cultural basis in contemporary societies
- Sources of cultural power include: individual and group rights, interest-group influence, systemic biases and the biases written into cultural texts
- Arguments to redistribute cultural power rest on considerations of stability, promise-keeping and individual equality
- Advocates of cultural pluralism must bear in mind three lessons drawn from the pluralist tradition: (1) individual dissent is easily sacrificed in the course of protecting group rights; (2) recognizing cultural difference is no guarantee of social equality; and (3) multicultural policies may expand the State's role in adjudicating and regulating the values of cultural minorities.

FURTHER READING

Goldberg, David Theo (ed.) (1994) *Multiculturalism: A Critical Reader*. Oxford: Basil Blackwell. This anthology examines multiculturalism from an interdisciplinary perspective that includes mainly sociologists and anthropologists in the USA. Approximately half of the essays engage in cultural critique and half focus on the particular situations of minority groups in the USA.

Hirst, Paul (1993) *Associative Democracy: New Forms of Economic and Social Governance*. Cambridge: Polity Press. Hirst resurrects pluralist ideas of association and group life in arguing that the primacy of group identity ought to shape the democratic polity and that associations, working under the umbrella of the central state institutions, ought to orchestrate social, political and economic life.

Kymlicka, Will (1995) *Multicultural Citizenship: A Liberal Theory of Minority Rights*. Oxford: Clarendon Press. Kymlicka assesses various means of protecting the rights and interests of cultural minorities using the resources of liberal theory. The book offers a thorough and thoughtful analysis of the relation between cultural pluralism and liberal-democratic theory.

McLennon, Gregor (1995) *Pluralism*. Minneapolis: University of Minnesota Press. McLennon offers an interesting account of the history of pluralism which includes addressing the radical critics of post-war pluralism The book assesses the relation between pluralism and post-modern thought specifically with respect to cultural pluralism and a politics of difference.

Werbner, Pnina and Modood, Tariq (eds) (1997) *Debating Cultural Hybridity: Multi-cultural Identities and the Politics of Anti-racism*. London and New York: Zed Books. This anthology juxtaposes the post-modern notions of identity with the politics of multiculturalism, cosmopolitanism and globalization. The essays focus on emerging concerns about identity politics in the New Europe.

Young, Iris Marion (1990) *Justice and the Politics of Difference*. Princeton, NJ: Princeton University Press. Young argues that distributive theories of justice fail to translate into justice for many groups including those based on culture, race, sex and class. She proposes a new theory of justice in which identity-related differences shape the way in which societal institutions function.

REFERENCES

Arneil, Barbara (1996) *John Locke and America: The Defence of English Colonialism*. Oxford: Clarendon Press.

Bachrach, Peter and Baratz, Morton S. (1962) 'Two Faces of Power', *American Political Science Review*, **56**(4): 947–52.

Dahl, Robert (1967) *Pluralist Democracy in the United States: Conflict and Consensus*. New Haven, CT: Yale University Press.

Eisenberg, Avigail (1995) *Reconstructing Political Pluralism*. Albany, NY: State University of New York Press.

Furnivall, J.S. (1948) *Colonial Policy and Practice*. New York: New York University Press.

Goldberg, David Theo (ed.) (1994) *Multiculturalism: A Critical Reader*. Oxford: Basil Blackwell.

Goulbourne, Harry (1991) 'Varieties of Pluralism: The Notion of a Pluralist Post-imperial Britain', *New Community*, **17**(2): 211–27.

Kuper, Leo (1969) 'Plural Societies: Perspectives and Problems', in Leo Kuper and M.G. Smith (eds) *Pluralism in Africa*. Berkeley and Los Angeles, CA: University of California Press, pp. 7–26.

Kymlicka, Will (1992) 'Two Models of Pluralism and Tolerance', *Analyse & Kritik*, **14**(1): 33–56.

Kymlicka, Will (1995) *Multicultural Citizenship: A Liberal Theory of Minority Rights*. Oxford: Clarendon Press.

Kymlicka, Will (1998) *Finding our Way: Rethinking Ethnocultural Relations in Canada*. Toronto, Oxford and New York: Oxford University Press.

McClure, Kirstie (1992) 'On the Subject of Rights: Pluralism, Plurality and Political Identity', in Chantal Mouffe (ed.) *Dimensions of Radical Democracy: Pluralism, Citizenship, Community*. London: Verso, pp. 108–27.

McLennan, Gregor (1995) *Pluralism*. Minneapolis: University of Minnesota Press.

Miller, David (1995) *On Nationality*. Oxford: Oxford University Press.

Mills, Charles (1997) *The Racial Contract*. Ithaca, NY: Cornell University Press.

Rex, John (1987) 'The Concept of a Multi-Cultural Society', *New Community*, **14**(1–2), pp. 218–229.

Rosenblum, Nancy (1989) *Liberalism and the Moral Life*. Cambridge, MA: Harvard University Press.

Said, Edward (1994) *Culture and Imperialism*. New York: Vintage.

Samad, Yunas (1997) 'The Plural Guises of Multiculturalism: Conceptualising a Fragmented Paradigm', in Tariq Modood and Pnina Werbner (eds) *The Politics of Multiculturalism in the New Europe: Racism, Identity and Community*. London and New York: Zed Books, pp. 240–60.

Sartori, Giovanni (1997) 'Understanding Pluralism', *Journal of Democracy*, **8**(4): 58–69.

Smith, M.G. (1975) *The Plural Society in the British West Indies*. Berkeley and Los Angeles, CA: University of California Press.

Swann, Lord (1985) *Education for All: The Report of the Committee of Inquiry into the Education of Children from Ethnic Minority Groups*. London: HMSO.

Taylor, Charles (1992) 'The Politics of Recognition', in Amy Gutman (ed.) Multiculturalism and the 'Politics of Recognition'. Princeton, NJ: Princeton University Press.

Werbner, Pnina (1997) 'Introduction: The Dialectics of Cultural Hybridity', in Pnina Werbner and Tariq Modood (eds) *Debating Cultural Hybridity: Multi-cultural Identities and the Politics of Anti-racism*. London and New York: Zed Books, pp. 1–28.

White, Graham (1991) 'Westminster in the Arctic: The Adaptation of British Parliamentarism in the Northwest Territories', *Canadian Journal of Political Science*, **24**(3): 466–524.

Wolin, Sheldon (1993) 'Democracy, Difference, and Re-Cognition', *Political Theory*, **21**(3): 464–483.

Young, Iris Marion (1990) *Justice and the Politics of Difference*. Princeton, NJ: Princeton University Press.

Chapter 28

Families and households

Mary Maynard

INTRODUCTION

The changing nature of the family in Western societies has come under much critical scrutiny. Moralists, the media and politicians profess anxiety about family breakdown, incompetent lone mothers, feckless fathers and the wayward children they are likely to produce. Academics and researchers have attempted to adapt their definitions and theoretical frameworks in order more accurately to account for and understand the transformations in family forms and relationships which are taking place. Although little agreement on these issues seems to be emerging, it is possible to chart the trends and kinds of analyses which are at the forefront of discussion and debate.

This chapter presents an overview of work on the family/household which has taken place during the second half of the twentieth century. It begins by examining some of the changes which have occurred during the period, offering some explanations for these. It also considers some difficulties in conceptualization, how these have been resolved and some of the debates concerning how to theorize the family. The chapter concludes by briefly examining three issues of importance which have been less well covered in mainstream family literature. These concern relationships in later life, the nature of obligations, and the significance of love and emotional needs.

THE CHANGING NATURE OF FAMILY HOUSEHOLDS

Social scientists are agreed that British and US forms of family/household have changed significantly during the second half of the twentieth century

(Acock and Demo, 1994; Robertson Elliot, 1996; Zimmerman, 1995). During the 1950s, for instance, there was much emphasis on the nuclear family, which was regarded as the form specific to modern times. The main characteristics of the nuclear family were its privatized nature, assumptions about the close emotional ties between a husband and wife and parents and their children, together with increased independence from relatives and other family members (Robertson Elliot, 1996). It was assumed that marriage was for a lifetime and, at the most ideal, that the man would be the breadwinner, while the woman stayed at home to undertake the mothering, child-rearing and domestic responsibilities. Despite the prevalence of this picture, however, there is much evidence to suggest that only some groups organized their lives in this way, especially those who were white and middle class, and that the model is distorted by class and race bias. Overall, though, it was the nuclear family which was lauded as the most progressive and regarded as being in the best interests of all its members, as well as of society more generally.

The view that the nuclear family is no longer an integral part of British and US ways of life is not, in fact, borne out by the statistical evidence. Zimmerman (1995) indicates, for the USA, that married couple households represented 69 per cent of all households at the beginning of the 1990s, although, admittedly, the trends show this to be continually decreasing. Similarly, for Britain, research suggests that four out of five families are headed by a married couple (Family Policy Studies Centre, 1997). In both studies it is estimated that the numbers of children under the age of 16 who are living with two adults is around three-quarters. Nevertheless, there is also evidence that some dramatic changes have taken place. For example, there has been a rapid rise in the level of divorce, with three in five new marriages in the USA and two in five in Britain likely to fail (Family Policy Studies Centre, 1997; Robertson Elliot, 1996). In both countries there has also been a big increase in the numbers of births occurring outside of marriage, with the UK having a teenage fertility rate which is significantly higher than elsewhere in Europe. Another aspect of the changing nature of the family/household is the growth of single-parent families, the majority of whom tend to be lone mothers. Also important are increased numbers of step-families and reconstituted families, the rise of dual-earner families and of never-married single persons, together with a rise in the average ages at which women and men enter partnerships, get married and have children (Acock and Demo, 1994; Family Policy Studies Centre, 1997; Robertson Elliot, 1996; Zimmerman, 1995). Such trends, however, are not distributed evenly across the population and appear to be particularly affected by ethnicity. For instance, African-American and Afro-Caribbean groups place less emphasis on formal marriage than their white counterparts, whereas South Asians in Britain are more likely to marry and to do so earlier than their white equivalents. Care must be taken, though, in interpreting such differences. In particular, it is important to avoid moral judgements and negative racist stereotypes of what are simply diverse cultural practices.

Various explanations have been put forward as to why so many transformations in the family/household might have taken place. One interpretation is that they are the result of increased sexual freedom associated, in particular, with more widely available and reliable contraception, especially the Pill. This is also related to an increased emphasis on self-realization and individual autonomy which has freed women, especially, from having to conform to previous moral norms which condemned sexual intercourse outside of marriage. Another factor is the reconstruction of marriage from being a lifelong institution to one that can be ended. The liberalization of divorce laws in Western societies has been of particular importance, giving couples the ability to decide for themselves when their marriage has ended, rather than some 'fault' (for example, adultery) on the part of one partner having to be publically established. This has led, in both the USA and Britain, to the increase in the divorce rate and to a tendency to divorce at earlier stages in a marriage (Robertson Elliot, 1996). A significant number of women and men who divorce, however, also go on to remarry, indicating a trend towards having a series of partners, if only one at a time.

Together, increased sexual freedom and the reconstruction of marriage, along with serial monogamy, have led to the separation of parenthood from marriage. It has been estimated that, by the end of the century, approximately 50 per cent of British and American children will not experience or not continually experience living with two parents who remain married until the child reaches adulthood (Robertson Elliot, 1996). While the majority of such children will live with their mothers, most remain in some kind of contact with their absent fathers (Family Policy Studies Centre, 1997). However, a child's family structure and relationships may change significantly during the period of growing up. A child who starts out in life living with a lone parent may experience the cohabitation and later marriage of that parent, a partnership breakdown, followed by remarriage. It is clear also that family conflict before, during and after separation is stressful to children, who may become anxious, aggressive and withdrawn. Yet, only a minority of children experience long-term adverse effects, with most having short-term distress at the time of the separation (Rodgers and Pryor, 1998).

A final reason as to why family/households are changing relates to women's increased labour market participation, which has been growing since the 1960s. Married women's involvement with paid work has grown particularly, with that of married women with children rising dramatically, so that over two-thirds of that group on both sides of the Atlantic are employed (Witz, 1997; Zimmerman, 1995). The resulting financial independence has given women greater opportunity to leave an unsatisfactory relationship than was the case in the past. However, inequalities in the labour market mean that women's earnings are generally less than those of their male counterparts. As a consequence, divorced and separated women are frequently unable to compensate for the loss of a partner's income and, despite policy initiatives to enlarge and enforce men's obligations of financial support, such households tend to have lower incomes, poorer housing and greater financial hardship. In fact, children from separated families are twice as likely as those from intact ones to suffer such adverse economic circumstances (Rodgers and Pryor, 1998).

Some commentators suggest that a radical restructuring in the family/household has been taking place, this being judged negatively by conservatives and positively by those who view the nuclear family as stultifying and restrictive. Others insist that, although change has occurred, there are still major continuities in family life, with high rates of marriage and remarriage indicating the value with which the institution is still regarded. However, it is clear that the old norms of exclusivity and permanence which were fundamental aspects of the nuclear family unit have been transformed (Scanzoni *et al.*, 1989). These have been replaced by non-binding commitments and the serialization of relationships. The diverse array of family types has been characterized by some as the 'post-modern family' (Acock and Demo, 1994). They certainly have implications for the ways in which the family/household has been conceptualized, theorized and analysed.

CONCEPTUALIZING THE FAMILY/HOUSEHOLD

Changes in family formation have led to crucial debates as to how it should be defined and described. These have been of two major kinds. The first has been concerned with how far it is necessary to distinguish between the concepts of 'family' and 'household'. It has been argued that to focus on 'the family' overemphasizes the nuclear family form (Jackson, 1997). It also implies relations of kinship and social ties and obligations which are established through blood or marriage. But who belongs to families is not necessarily straightforward in this way. For instance, it excludes the possibility of a cohabitee being treated as a family member and suggests that gay and lesbian couples should not be regarded as families at all. In other words, people's living arrangements do not necessarily follow conventional kinship ties. It is, therefore, becoming increasingly accepted to retain the idea of family for the conventional kinship links and to use household when referring to social groupings who share a range of domestic activities, such as the same accommodation and meals (Morgan, 1996). This emphasizes the sharing of a domestic economy where work, housework and other activities take place rather than just the affective side of living. A concern for households suggests a different focus for analysis than that implied by the term family.

A second debate concerning the conceptualization of changes in family/households has involved moving from a life-cycle to a life-course perspective (Harris, 1987; Pilcher, 1995). The life-cycle approach was quite commonly used until the 1980s. It was based on the assumption that people typically move through a series of relatively fixed and routine stages of family forms. They are born into a nuclear family of parents and siblings. Eventually they leave home, marry, have their own children, who also subsequently leave home, with the parents remaining together until one of them dies. Although this was a rather simplistic model even before the changes of the last thirty years, the latter have highlighted the universal, deterministic, asocial, ahistorical and culturally specific weaknesses of such a formulation. A crucial aspect of life-course analysis is the focus on transitions, rather than stages. These signify particular turning points in family living when crucial decisions are likely to influence future outcomes. They indicate that individuals may move back and forth between a variety of family forms and circumstances, situating an understanding of each within an entire life continuum. Morgan (1996: 143) explains that 'these transitions entail some realignment, additions and subtractions within the set of relationships described in family terms'. The nature of early transitions is likely to have implications for the ways in which later ones are experienced. Thus, unlike the life cycle, the idea of the life course is sensitive to both flexibility and variation in family forms and to their timing and sequencing (Pilcher, 1995).

THEORIES OF THE FAMILY/HOUSEHOLD

Systems, community and Marxist approaches

The 1950s and early 1960s analyses of the family tended to be rooted in functionalist or systems theory perspectives (Morgan, 1996; Rodger, 1996). These tended to stress: the separate, but interdependent, roles of family members; the importance of maintaining boundaries around families; the need for stability and equilibrium within them; and their task performing functions, especially those of socialization and 'tension' or emotional management more generally (Morgan, 1985; Rodger, 1996). Overall, such an approach sees the family as undertaking tasks which are beneficial to both the individuals concerned and the social organization of life more generally. Stability and equilibrium are presumed to be disturbed by any behaviour which threatens the interdependence of roles and duties within the family, for example an absent father or a woman who does not adequately mother (Rodger, 1996). Although this way of looking at the family/household has long been superseded in sociological analyses, it still plays a significant part in family therapy and family medicine work.

Other perspectives have also been influential. In Britain, where family studies have always been less developed than in the USA, consideration of family relationships in the 1950s was linked into an understanding of communities as a whole (Morgan, 1996). Such an emphasis, however, gradually fell into disrepute with the recognition that a lot of this work tended to dwell on the nostalgic re-creation of a way of, largely working-class, life which was being lost as a result of the post-war reconstruction. It is interesting to note, though, that some aspects of the community studies approach have been re-created more recently via the communitarian movement. Communitarians focus on the importance of the way in which individuals' social behaviour is influenced by the quality of their social and community relationships, especially the family and neighbourhood (Friedman, 1996). At the heart of this analysis is the idea of a moral reciprocity between self, family and community. Alongside people's expectations concerning their rights and social entitlements, they also have a duty to contribute to community life. However, whether it is possible to establish such ethical principles in contemporary society is questionable, especially when, as feminists have pointed out, some of the assumptions upon which they are based are highly oppressive of women (Friedman, 1996).

Another important influence on theorizing the family came from Marxism (Morgan, 1996). The privatized nuclear family type was regarded as necessary to capitalism, both as a unit of consumption of the goods which were produced and as an insitutional means through which workers might be rendered docile. The family was seen as a form of social control. It socialized groups, especially the working class, into ideological acceptance of limited roles and opportunities. It encouraged them to accept family intimacy and privacy as compensation for alienation in the public sphere of work, leaving the latter to operate unchallenged. Resulting similarities with the systems approach meant that the term 'Marxist-functionalism' was often used to label this kind of analysis.

Feminist theory

In the last two decades feminist theory has had a considerable impact on analysing the family/household. This has largely concentrated on the inequalities and power struggles which exist within family relationships (Jackson, 1997). Attention has been paid to the unequal sexual division of labour, with women still undertaking more domestic chores and responsibilities than men, even when they are in full-time employment. The control and distribution of resources has also been highlighted. Access to money, food and space, for instance, has been shown to be unequally distributed along gender lines.

During the late 1970s and early 1980s, some feminists argued that this unpaid domestic work was of central importance to capitalism. It provided free goods and services for consumption within the family, which otherwise would have had to be bought on the open market, resulting in demands for increased rates of pay. Not only this, but women's domestic work maintains their husband's continued ability to undertake paid work and prepares the next generation of workers (their children) for this task. Because it is assumed that women are dependent on a male partner's wage, it is possible to justify paying them less than men when they do take up paid employment.

One limitation of this approach is that it underplayed the extent to which men might benefit. Some writers have argued that housework takes place within a patriarchal, as well as a capitalist, mode of production. For example, Delphy and Leonard (1992) develop a materialist analysis of marriage, characterizing it in terms of a 'class-like' relationship between men and women wherein husbands exploit women's household labour. They argue that these relationships are also ones of dependency and that the obligation upon women to complete household tasks is lifelong. Women's entrapment within marriage or a cohabiting relationship lies at the heart of their more general subordination. Delphy and Leonard recognize that men's power within the family is not unlimited, that they, too, have responsibilities and that women (and children) may resist. However, although men may have to struggle to maintain their position, this does not mean that 'a patriarchal hierarchy does not exist and is not being continued' (Delphy and Leonard, 1992: 100).

Another aspect of feminist work on the family aimed to open up the private and intimate aspects of personal relations for analysis on the grounds that they are arenas of authority and control. One emphasis was on the compulsory nature of heterosexuality, that is the assumption that a normal person will engage in heterosexual partnership, marriage and the procreation of children. It was pointed out that this marginalized same-sex couples and households, also rendering people who are celebate, bisexual or transexual invisible. The assumptions about sexuality rooted in analyses of the family are, therefore, heterosexist, serving to pathologize other kinds of sexual relationships (Jackson, 1997). A further emphasis involves the potentially violent nature of family life. Much previous analysis of the family had emhasized, either implicitly or explicitly, its benign and stabilizing characteristics. By contrast, feminist research has highlighted the extent of male domestic violence towards women and of child sexual abuse by men (Maynard and Winn, 1997). Such violence contributes, it is argued, to the maintenance of patriarchal power. It is a mechanism whereby men as a group, as well as individual men, control women and children and continue the latters' subordination, thereby also reinforcing the institution of heterosexuality.

Many white Western feminists have tended to regard the family/household as a major factor in men's oppression of women and the existence of patriarchal power, since there are several levels at which systematic control over the routines of family living lie in the hands of men. However, black feminists and those from other ethnic groups have strongly criticized arguments that the family comprises *the* overriding instrument of women's subordination (Hill Collins, 1990). They point out that for non-white women, although they may also experience oppression within it, the family can be a place of protection from, and resistance to, everyday racism. Their work highlights the significant dangers of overgeneralizations and lack of cultural specificness when analysing family matters.

Post-structuralism

Post-structuralism, which raises important issues concerning the conceptualization of power and control, has also influenced recent analyses of the family/household (Rodger, 1996). Foucault, for instance, sees power as being inherently tied into forms of knowledge. Rather than power being located in particular groups or with particular collectivities (men, the ruling class, governments), he regards it as existing everywhere, being constructed through discourses which make social phenomena become visible in certain kinds of ways (Foucault, 1974). For example, it was not until the idea of madness began to be labelled as such, through discourse, in the eighteenth century that the old system of incarceration, in which the mad were housed along with criminals and vagrants, was dismantled and a new form of confinement, the asylum, was put in its place (Foucault, 1977). In other words, the development of new kinds of knowledge led to different kinds of institutionalization and containment. The generation of knowledge, and the rise of the professional with expertise, was closely linked with powerful forms of regimentation and social control. Analysts of the family have attempted to draw on these kinds of insights in varying ways. One area which has received significant attention is that of mothering. Researchers have focused on health professionals' 'policing' of the family by analysing how their language and training is used to create ideas of good and bad mothering (Abbott and Sapsford, 1990; Symonds, 1991). This involves applying expert knowledge in order to regulate family living (rationalization), inculcate good domestic practice through instruction and advice (normalization) and observe closely the family/household (panopticism) (Rodger, 1996). Similarly, utilizing an historical approach, Smart (1996) deconstructs the meanings of motherhood, showing how the dominant character of the discourses and policies surrounding them change over time.

Together, feminist and post-structuralist theory have contributed to some shifts of emphasis which have taken place in the analysis of family/households. More stress is now placed on the nature, fluidity and meaning of relationships and less on a static unit. Attention has also been drawn to the importance of agency as well as structure. This implies that family members are actors constructing and making decisions about family life, although they are also constrained by social and material factors. The significance of gender in how families are experienced has also been highlighted, along with their conflictual and, for some, violent nature. It is somewhat ironic that at the end of the twentieth century, when families are more diffuse and fluctuating than ever before, they are also prone to regulation, surveillance and outside interference.

CURRENT ISSUES FOR THE FAMILY/HOUSEHOLD

Currently, work on the family seems to be moving in two particular directions. One is concerned to explore the reasons for family breakdown and disintegration. Proponents of an 'underclass' identify a clustering of those who, without proper parenting, have developed an anti-work culture of welfare dependency and are now threatening the organization and security of wider society (Murray, 1994). By contrast, other writers explore the ways in which patterns of social and economic disadvantage might be alleviated and reversed through policies of intervention and regeneration (MacDonald, 1997).

A second focus on families is concerned further to explore the diversities which exist. For instance, research has been undertaken on black families' survival strategies, the role of fathers and fatherhood, families with parents or children who have disabilities, step-parenting, teenage parenting and the effect of a violent home on children (Elliot Robinson, 1996). This, along with other work, examines the possibilities and difficulties faced by families during a period of rapid socio-economic change and development.

Three other interrelated areas are also of importance, since they are less well covered in the literature. The first relates to the increasing significance of families and households in later life. In most countries of the Western world the number and proportion of older people in the population is increasing significantly, with particular growth in the 80+ age group. Furthermore, the ageing process is gendered; the older a person gets, the more likely she is to be female (Arber and Ginn, 1991). Most older married men continue living with their wives until they die, whereas many older women become widows and live on their own This, therefore, has implications for our understanding of later stages of the life course and the impact of these on family life.

Second, most people keep in some kind of contact with their parents and other family members. Families remain more important as sources of social support than friends (Family Policy Studies Centre, 1997). Social policy analysts, writing from a political economy perspective, suggest that an obligation to provide family care exists quite widely (Qureshi and Walker, 1989). This, it is claimed, is reinforced through poor welfare provision and an ideology that portrays it as women's responsibility. Feminist researchers, however, have indicated a more complex and ambiguous picture (Finch, 1989). Although women are overwhelmingly the carers, there are some situations, for instance a disabled wife, where men do undertake the care. The range of relatives expected to provide assistance is quite circumscribed, with spouses, daughters, daughters-in-law and sons located in a hierarchy of responsibility. Further, older people are vigorous defenders of their rights to independence and any care provided is underpinned by an often un-spoken norm of reciprocity, that is the obligation to give as well as to receive (Elliot Robinson, 1996). It is also the case that caring is not only perceived in terms of some kind of moral duty. Feelings of love, emotional ties, degrees of closeness and repayment for support in the past all feature in the equation of what, and how much, is to be provided. Thus, the will to care is still an important component of people's relation with relatives. That this is a 'la-bour of love', as well as a moral obligation, is an underplayed aspect of much of the literature.

Third, attention has recently been drawn to the lack of consideration given to love and emotional feelings in material on the family/household (Dun-combe and Marsden, 1993; Jackson, 1993). In academic writing, interest in the instrumental side of family life has obscured the expressive aspect and feelings of love and intimacy which, it is said, people regard as the key element in their personal relationships (Duncombe and Marsden, 1993). Yet, it is clear from the divorce statistics that marriage based on romantic love does not always deliver what was expected. There are certainly no logical or empirical grounds for claiming that marriages formed in this way offer any greater guarantees of happiness than marriages which are arranged (Jack-son, 1997). In the context of the changes taking place in modern societies, Giddens (1992) has written about 'confluent love', a form in which commit-ment is premised entirely on the satisfactions and pleasures which the re-lationship intrinsically bestows. This is not embedded in marriage vows about the future, nor is it structurally located within the broad institutional framework of the family. Once the relationship no longer meets the needs or desires of the incumbents, this in itself is sufficient justification for its end-ing. This is the new form of emotional attachment, it is suggested, that will characterize the next millennium. If so, it has implications for the whole spectrum of family forms, family obligations and members' general commit-ments to them.

CONCLUSION

It is clear that, despite its apparently enduring nature, the family in Western society is in something of a state of flux. Variety of forms and diversity of meanings indicate a patchwork of phenomena concerning which there are no absolutes or certitudes, in the way in which some were able to claim in the past. In addition, further changes confront those involved in family studies in the new century. Commentators are already grappling with no-tions of social exclusion and underclass and the need for increased research on the meanings and implications of some of the current changes in family relations. The chapter has suggested that a concern for the ageing population and households in later life, a keener focus on the meaning of obligation, and an analysis of the role in families of love and emotion should also be put on the agenda for further work.

SUMMARY

- Western families have changed significantly in structure and meaning.
- There is a distinction between family and household.
- Emphasis is now placed on the life course rather than the life cycle.
- Theories of the family have moved from an emphasis on stability and harmony to a focus on gender inequalities and conflict and issues relating to power and control.
- Current concern about families relates to social exclusion and the formation of an underclass.
- A concern for later life, the nature of obligations and love and emotional feelings, in relation to the family, should be on the agenda for the future.

FURTHER READING

Arber, Sara and Ginn, Jay (eds) (1991) *Gender and Later Life*. London: Sage. This book examines gender differences among older people and the circumstances influencing their dependence and independence. It is particularly concerned with those factors which help to promote independent living and the autonomy of older person households.

Duncan, Simon and Edwards, Rosalind (eds) (1997) *Single Mothers in an International Context*. London: UCL Press. This collection examines the relationship between single mothers and paid work in a range of countries, including Britain, the USA, France, Germany, Japan and Australia. It challenges the negative stereotyping which is often applied to this group and examines the discourses and structures which facilitate or obstruct labour market participation.

Gittens, Diana (1993) *The Family in Question*, 2nd edn. London: Macmillan. This is a readable introductory overview of debates and research on family life, from a feminist perspective. It has a strong historical emphasis and addresses many of the major issues concerning women's family situation.

Jackson, Stevi and Moores, Shaun (eds) (1995) *The Politics of Domestic Consumption: Critical Readings*. Hemel Hempstead: Prentice-Hall/Harvester Wheatsheaf. This reader explores the everyday practices of domestic consumption, emphasizing the inequalities and power relations which influence the distribution of resources in family/households. It focuses on economic inequality, food and clothing, leisure and media, domestic technologies and the cultural construction of home.

Morgan, David (1996) *Family Connections. An Introduction to Family Studies.* Cambridge: Polity. This book provides a comprehensive overview of debates in the field, while also developing a distinct perspective involving such themes as the body, time, space, food and the home.

Robinson Elliot, Faith (1996) *Gender, Family and Society.* Basingstoke: Macmillan. This book offers a succinct account of recent changes in family life, focusing, particularly, on the relationship between sexual, gender and family structures. It also includes chapters on some of the major concerns of contemporary Western societies: ethnic differentiation; unemployment; ageing; sexual violence; and AIDS.

REFERENCES

Abbott, Pamela and Sapsford, Roger (1990) 'Health Visiting: Policing the Family?' in P. Abbott and C. Wallace (eds) *The Sociology of Caring Professions.* Basingstoke: Falmer.

Acock, Alan C. and Demo, David, H. (1994) *Family Diversity and Well-Being.* London: Sage.

Arber, Sara and Ginn, Jay (1991) *Gender and Later Life.* London: Sage.

Delphy, Christine and Leonard, Diana (1992) *Familiar Exploitation.* Cambridge: Polity.

Duncombe, Jean and Marsden, Dennis (1993) 'Love and Intimacy: The Gender Division of Emotion and Emotion Work', *Sociology*, **27**(2): 221–41.

Family Policy Studies Centre (1997) *A Guide to Family Issues. Family Briefing Paper 2.* London: Family Policy Studies Centre.

Finch, Janet (1989) *Family Obligations and Social Change.* Cambridge: Polity.

Foucault, Michel (1974) *The Order of Things.* London: Tavistock.

Foucault, Michel (1977) *Madness and Civilization: A History of Insanity in the Age of Reason.* London: Tavistock.

Friedman, Marilyn (1996) 'Feminism and Modern Friendship: Dislocating the Community', in S. Avineri and A. de-Shalit (eds) *Communitarianism and Individualism.* Oxford: Oxford University Press.

Giddens, Anthony (1992) *The Transformation of Intimacy: Sexuality, Love and Eroticism in Modern Societies.* Cambridge: Polity.

Hill Collins, Patricia (1990) *Black Feminist Thought: Knowledge, Consciousness and the Politics of Empowerment.* London: HarperCollins.

Harris, C. (1987) 'The Individual and Society: A Processional Approach', in A. Bryaman *et al.*, *Rethinking the Life Cycle.* Basingstoke: Macmillan.

Jackson, Stevi (1993) 'Even Sociologists Fall in Love: An Exploration in the Sociology of Emotions', *Sociology*, **27**(2): 210–20.

Jackson, Stevi (1997) 'Women, Marriage and Family Relationships', in D. Richardson and V. Robinson (eds) *Introducing Women's Studies.* Basingstoke: Macmillan.

MacDonald, Robert (ed) (1997) *Youth, the 'Underclass' and Social Exclusion*. London: Routledge.

Maynard, Mary and Winn, Jan (1997) 'Women, Violence and Male Power', in D. Richardson and V. Robinson (eds) *Introducing Women's Studies*. Basingstoke: Macmillan.

Morgan, D. (1985) *The Family, Politics and Social Theory*. London: Routledge and Kegan Paul.

Morgan, David (1996) *Family Connections: An Introduction to Family Studies*. Cambridge: Polity Press.

Murray, Charles (1994) *Underclass: The Crisis Deepens*. London: Institute of Economic Affairs.

Pilcher, Jane (1995) *Age and Generation in Modern Britain*. Oxford: Oxford University Press.

Qureshi, Hazel and Walker, Alan (1989) *The Caring Relationship: Elderly People and their Families*. Basingstoke: Macmillan.

Robinson Elliot, Faith (1996) *Gender, Family and Society*. London: Macmillan.

Rodger, John, J. (1996) *Family Life and Social Control: A Sociological Perspective*. Basingstoke: Macmillan.

Rodgers, Bryan and Pryor, Jan (1998) *Divorce and Separation: The Outcomes for Children*. York: Joseph Rowntree Foundation.

Scanzoni, John, Polonko, Karen, Teachman, Jay and Thompson, Linda (1989) *The Sexual Bond: Rethinking Families and Close Relationships*. Newbury Park: Sage.

Smart, Carol (1996) 'Deconstructing Motherhood', in E. Bortolaia Silver (ed) *Good Enough Mothering*. London: Routledge.

Symonds, Ann (1991) 'Angels and Interfering Busybodies: The Social Construction of Two Occupations', *Sociology of Health and Illness*, **13**(2): 249–64.

Witz, Anne (1997) 'Women and Work', in D. Richardson and V. Robinson (eds) *Introducing Women's Studies*. London: Macmillan.

Zimmerman, Shirley L. (1995) *Understanding Family Policy*. London: Sage.

Chapter 29

The body

Chris Shilling

INTRODUCTION

In this chapter I chart the rise of the body in social theory and contemporary culture before focusing on the 'naturalistic' and 'social constructionist' traditions of thought that have forged the background for recent debates in this area. I then examine various attempts to move beyond this conceptual opposition by outlining the work of a number of theorists who have analysed how human embodiment has its own properties which both shape and are shaped by the constitution of social interaction and social systems. The subjects analysed by these writers include the formation and re-formation of gendered bodies, of sensual bodies and of knowledgeable bodies. The chapter concludes by identifying future trends in what has become one of the most rapidly growing and analytically productive areas of modern thought.

The body is at the height of cultural and academic fashion. Unprecedented numbers of books and magazines interrogate the shape, size, experience and appearance of our physical selves, while issues concerning our flesh, blood and bones are central to science fiction and sport, social theory and history, art and theology. Doctors, health educators and social workers make increasingly interventionist attempts to shape how we see, touch and treat our own, and other people's, bodies, while the businesses of keep-fit, beauty and dieting continue to flourish. While interest in the social significance of bodies has intensified in the last decade, it is not new. Puritanism has, since the sixteenth century, sought to promote a 'moderate' diet and lifestyle that would avoid inflaming the 'sinful passions of the flesh', while nineteenth- and twentieth-century social policy reforms were often associated with concerns about health, racial 'degeneration' and economic efficiency. Academically, anthropology, archaeology and art have long examined representations of bodies, while Park and Burgess's (1969) *Introduction to the Science of Sociology* (a collection that has been described as the most influential in the discipline's history), includes a section on the senses.

Social science has not ignored the body, then, and there is much of value to be found on the relationship between sensual activity and alienation, repression and the construction of society, in classical writings. Important contributions have been made by Schopenhauer, Comte, Marx and Engels, Nietzsche, Durkheim, Weber, Freud, Elias and, more recently and from a feminist perspective, de Beauvoir. Nevertheless, while society's impact on human physicality, and the embodied nature of agency, meant that aspects of embodiment could not be overlooked entirely, the body has rarely been interrogated systematically and has remained something of a 'ghost in the machine' of much modern Western thought.

THE GROWTH OF THE BODY

There is nothing 'secret' about the importance of the body within *contemporary* social theory. Turner's (1984, 1996) text represents an early theorization of the body in society, but studies (e.g. Freund, 1982; Hirst and Woolley, 1982; Johnson, 1983; Martin, 1989; O'Neill, 1985), reviews (e.g. Frank, 1988), collections (e.g. Featherstone, Hepworth and Turner, 1991; Scott and Morgan, 1993), histories of the body (Feher, Naddaff and Tazi, 1989), distinctive theoretical approaches to the body (e.g. Falk, 1994; Grosz, 1994; Mellor and Shilling, 1997; Shilling, 1993), and the establishment of the journal *Body & Society* have together made embodiment a thriving object of study. Four major factors contributed to this development.

First, academics focused on the diverse ways people related to their bodies. In analyses which draw critically on Giddens's (1991) notion of the 'reflexive self', and Tönnies (1957) *Gemeinschaft/Gesellschaft* distinction, it has been suggested that the increased malleability of the body after the Second World War stimulated a tendency in the affluent West to perceive the body as a 'project' (Shilling, 1993). This means the body is treated as something to be shaped as part of an individual's self-identity. Body-building and dieting are two body projects: they also illustrate how these projects are gendered, yet can be used to construct identities that challenge stereotypes of femininity and masculinity. This contrasts with the tendency for medieval communities to promote *body regimes*. Here, the body was decorated and altered through inherited norms manifest in rituals and collective ceremonies such as those characteristic of early Christian baptism. Body projects also contrast with the unprecedented range of (partly futuristic) *body options* associated with cybertechnologies, transplant surgery and genetic engineering, and virtual reality. While body projects help us explore the possibilities of living in *one* body, body options promise us the potential of exploring bodies which differ substantially according to time and place (Mellor and Shilling, 1997).

The second reason for the body's popularity involves 1960s 'second wave' feminism, and distinctive feminist academic analyses of the gendered body. Politically, feminism highlighted issues concerning abortion and health rights. Academically, feminist writers examined how patriarchy reduced women's control over their bodies (e.g. Oakley, 1984), and emphasized through their critical interrogation of the sex/gender divide that there was *nothing natural* about women's corporeality which justified their public subordination. Certain feminisms were highly ambivalent about theorizing further about the body. This was partly because de Beauvoir (1949) had problematized the subject by suggesting there was a tendency for women's bodies to be a source of alienation and frailty, and partly because 'malestream' philosophers associated men with freedom and the mind, and femininity with 'the unreason associated with the body' (Grosz, 1994: 4). Resisting such negative judgements, however, other feminisms sought to re-evaluate women's physicality. This was reinforced *in part* by the growth of 'men's studies', by a growing sociological interest in sexuality, and by concern over the categorization of 'pure' and 'polluted' bodies accentuated by social responses to HIV and AIDS.

Third, the ageing populations of many industrial societies posed serious questions about welfare (Turner, 1984). People are living longer, placing increased demands on social services, while the financing of health care has come under scrutiny in an era of fiscal retrenchment. Issues concerning the prioritization and distribution of particular treatments and medicines inevitably raise questions concerning whose bodies should/should not be treated, while euthanasia and the 'right to die' movement have sparked a number of debates in Europe and North America.

The fourth major factor behind the body's 'rise' concerns a shift in the structure of advanced capitalism. From the work, save and invest mentality characteristic of early capitalism and manifest in Weber's analysis of the Protestant ethic, economic reorganization, the growth of consumption and leisure industries have made 'consuming bodies' as important as 'producing bodies'. The body is no longer exhorted to control in order to *dampen* its sensual emotions, but is encouraged to consume in order to *experience* excitement in the shopping mall, health club and bedroom; experience that is a *duty* as much as a right (Featherstone, 1982).

If the body is fashionable in social theory, what are the most influential traditions of thought it has drawn on, and reacted against, that form the background for contemporary debates?

NATURALISTIC BODIES

'Common-sense' views of the body as a pre-social, biological entity which determines self-identity and social institutions, dominate much popular thought. Such naturalistic approaches are particularly apparent in the view that gender inequalities result from women's 'unstable' bodies, and have been reinforced by the socio-biological argument that genetic and physical differences between men and women are responsible for these inequalities (Wilson, 1978). Culture does not *create* differences, it merely 'replicates' them within the social sphere or, at most, 'amplifies' them.

This view has long helped limit women's participation in the public sphere, yet is scientifically flawed, and insensitive to historical change. Scientifically, the socio-biological assumption that 'male' and 'female' refer to absolute opposites has been complicated by such considerations as testicular feminizing syndrome (where individuals are genetically male but appear to be female even though they cannot reproduce); the existence of oestrogen (a 'female' sex hormone) and testosterone (the 'male' sex hormone) in men and women; and the enormous difficulties involved in demonstrating *any* correspondence between even average biological differences and social inequalities (Kaplan and Rogers, 1990). Such difficulties become greater when we consider how social interactions and biological processes have intertwined and shaped each other for thousands of years of human evolution (Benton, 1991).

Historically, the view of women and men as corporeal opposites did not even originate until the eighteenth century. Previously, human physicality was perceived as ungendered and generic: the male body was 'the norm', but the female had the parts of the male; they were simply rearranged in an inferior pattern. The vagina was an interior penis, the labia a foreskin, and the ovaries interior testes. It was also believed women emitted sperm (Laqueur, 1990). This 'one-sex/one flesh' model dominated from classical antiquity until the end of the seventeenth century. Women were considered inferior to men, but this inferiority did not inhere specifically within their bodies.

Naturalistic views also justified racial inequalities. 'Race' is a social and cultural concept without basis in science, but Western colonial powers sought 'proof' of African and Asian inferiority to justify slavery. Broca, an influential figure in nineteenth-century craniometry (concerned with skull size and intelligence), argued that the 'intellectual and social inferiority' of black races was marked on their bodies (Gould, 1981). Fanon (1970) demonstrated how myths about animalistic sexuality were fabricated by white slave owners to justify brutality, while Doy (1996) has looked at images of black women in French art of the mid-nineteenth century. Sinha's (1987) research into the nineteenth-century British ideology of moral imperialism in Bengal reveals a Victorian gender ideology which framed the 'effeminate Bengali' as unfit for self-rule.

Naturalistic approaches reduce complex social phenomena to apparent biological mechanisms, and frame their research within highly problematic assumptions about social reality. As Kemper (1990) concludes, when sexist and racist ideologies employ science to justify inequalities, the science is usually false.

SOCIALLY CONSTRUCTED BODIES

Naturalistic views contrast with the sociological focus on how the body is shaped by such institutions as the family, school and labour market. Minimally, all sociological approaches to the body are constructionist in so far as they recognize that society exerts *some* influence in shaping bodies. Social constructionism, then, represents a *continuum* rather than a single perspective; the theoretical sources it draws on are extremely diverse. In this section, however, I reserve the term 'social constructionism' for theories which have been most influential and have asserted most strongly that human physicality can be derived from or explained by social phenomena, and focus on two of the most important sources for this approach.

Foucault's post-structuralist analyses of discipline, punishment, madness and sexuality seek to demonstrate the ubiquity of power within the 'discursive formations' that construct human embodiment. The importance of the body to Foucault is such that he described his work as constituting a '"history of bodies" and the manner in which what is most material and vital in them has been invested' (Foucault, 1981: 152). Central to this history is a mapping of 'the body and the effects of power on it' (Foucault, 1980: 58). This includes examining how the 'micro-physics' of power operates in institutional formations 'through progressively finer channels, gaining access to individuals themselves, to their bodies, their gestures and all their daily actions' (Foucault, 1980: 151–2). For an example of this we could cite the battery of tests and evaluations which dominate children's education: tests which measure every aspect of a pupil's performance and are used to grade, classify and shape the individual and their future.

Foucault's work has proved productive for feminist theories of gender identities (e.g. Diamond and Quinby, 1988; Sawicki, 1991), and is a provocative source for social analyses of the body. It is, however, problematic. Foucault's theory of knowledge suggests the body is 'always already' constructed by discourse; a view which means the body virtually *disappears* as a material phenomenon. Human physicality can never be fully grasped as our understanding of it is blocked by the 'grids of meaning' placed over it by discourse. Foucault's view of the mind/body relationship, for example, suggests that once the body is contained within modern disciplinary systems, the *mind* becomes the location for discursive power. Foucault's position changes somewhat in his last two volumes on the history of sexuality. Prior to those, however, the body in modernity becomes an inert mass controlled by discourses centred on the mind. This ignores the potential for disciplinary systems to become 'lived experiences' which do not simply affect thoughts, but shape people's senses.[1]

This problem of *discursive reductionism* is reflected in the most influential appropriations of Foucault's work. Butler's (1990) *Gender Trouble* treats the body, sex and gender as discursive constructions, and rejects the idea of a pre-discursive body even partially outside the determining cultural 'laws' of society. This perspective is not fundamentally changed in Butler's (1993) *Bodies that Matter* when she emphasizes that the body's materiality is discursively and institutionally *constructed* by regulatory norms. Butler's work is by no means restricted to or uncritical of Foucault's analyses, but shares with them the problem of being unable to conceptualize the body outside of *extant* power relations. This not only ignores the thousands of years of 'socionatural' (Burkitt, 1999) evolutionary history that have equipped humans with particular capacities, but makes it impossible to evaluate cultural practices in relation to people's bodily well-being. If we do not have some idea of our body's *own* needs and abilities at a particular time, how can we judge whether an institution or a society is good or bad for our well-being? As Soper (1995: 138) argues, if we refuse to recognize that human embodiment is associated with extra-discursive needs, we lose grounds 'for challenging the authority of custom and convention, and must accept that it is only on the basis of personal preference (or prejudice) that we can contest the "necessity" of a practice such as clitoridectomy or foot binding, challenge the oppression of sexual minorities, or justify the condemnation of any form of sexual abuse or torture.'

To analyse whether a social system is oppressive or beneficial for a particular gender, 'race' or class, then, we need recourse to theories of the body which recognize that people's embodiment is *irreducible* to the contemporary exercise of discourse, culture or law.

If Foucault's writings constitute one of the most influential sources for social constructionist views of the body, Talcott Parsons's theories are also enormously important. It is rare for Parsons to be explicitly associated with theories of the body, but his work informs many sociological assumptions concerning the ability of bodies to be socialized and the social system's importance in determining the content of this socialization. As such, I want to suggest he is one of *the* major forces behind social theories of embodiment.

Parsons is best known for his 'structural functionalism' which suggests social systems are marked by a structure which confronts them with a set of 'core problems' that have to be overcome if they are to survive. This approach is also central to Turner's (1984 [1996]) structuralist theory of 'bodily order'. Turner examines the structural problems posed by the body for the government of social systems by combining Parsons's 'core problems' perspective with Hobbes's concern with the 'geometry of bodies'. For Turner, all social systems must solve 'the problem of the body' which has four dimensions: the reproduction of populations through time; the restraint of desire; the regulation of populations in space; and the representation of bodies. Having established this typology of the problem of the body in society, Turner emphasizes the critical intent to his work and examines the control of sexuality by men exercising patriarchal power.

The scope of Turner's analysis is highly impressive, examining a *mode of control* by which society has sought to manage each dimension of the government of the body, a *dominant theorist* of each dimension, and a *paradigmatic disease* liable to 'break down' bodies as a result of society's imposition of these tasks (Turner, 1984, 1996). Having learnt what gets 'done to' the 'body', though, we get little sense of the body as integral to human agency or of the 'lived experience' of what it is like to be an embodied subject at a particular time. Turner's 'core problems' approach might enable us to 'work down' from the problems confronting social systems to the choices confronting individuals but, like Parsons's 'voluntaristic theory of action', this would be vulnerable to the criticism that these 'choices' only exist in relation to the norms of the social system.

Constructionist approaches have instituted a valuable 'epistemological break' from common-sense thinking about the relationship between the body, self-identity and society, but ultimately produce unsatisfactory views of the body. Indeed, theorists such as Turner (1992) have supplemented their work with foundationalist views which distinguish between how the body is *classified*, what the body *is*, and how it is *experienced*. This accepts that the experience of ageing, for example, can be shaped by gender and ethnicity, but also insists that '[t]he human body has definite and distinctive biological and physiological characteristics' (Turner, 1984, 1996: 30). In highlighting people's *experiences* of their bodies, Turner also points us in the direction of phenomenological approaches developed by such theorists as Merleau-Ponty (Crossley, 1995). For theorists who refuse any significant notion of the materiality of the body, in contrast, and remain entirely within the parameters of (post-) structuralism, 'the lived body drops from view as the text', or discourse, or the structural 'interpellation' of subjects 'becomes the all-pervasive topic of discourse' (Turner, 1984, 1996: 28).

EMBODYING SOCIAL RESEARCH

Naturalistic perspectives collapse the realm of culture to the 'really valid' realm of nature, while social constructionism minimizes the material body's power to *shape* as well as be shaped by society. In contrast, social theorists who have drawn selectively from philosophical anthropology and pragmatism in order to examine the interrelationship between social and physical processes suggest these ontological oppositions are unnecessary (Honneth and Joas, 1988; Joas, 1996). The body has been evolving for thousands of years and forms a basis for human societies: those species capacities we have at birth (e.g. the potential for walking, speech and tool use) allow us to forge particular types of social and cultural structures. Society and technology constantly change our bodily abilities, but social systems still have a corporeal basis (e.g. cybertechnologies remain limited by the human need for food and drink, and by the difficulties people have in adapting to these environments; Heim, 1995).

In opposition to naturalistic and constructionist perspectives, then, an increasing collection of work can be interpreted as both recognizing human physicality as a socio-natural entity, and demonstrating the analytical importance of distinguishing between an existing stage in the development of human bodies and the transformative effects that culture *subsequently* exerts on them. Bodies may be partially formed even before their birth into this society, and provide a basis for social institutions, but their openness to social factors also means they are *re-formed* over their lifetime (Mellor and Shilling, 1997). Re-formations of gender, emotions and knowledge illustrate these changes and suggest that overcoming the naturalistic/constructionist divide is a vital prerequisite for the exploration of further issues and other distinctions concerning our knowledge and experience of bodies as objects and subjects.

Re-forming gender

Connell's (1983, 1987, 1995) analyses of gendered power show how social practices shape bodies. Connell first examines how socially constructed gendered *categories* inaccurately reflect people's biological constitution. For example, numerous studies have shown that people label, play with and dress babies differently according to whether they are dealing with a girl or a boy. While babies are usually capable of feeding, defecating, vomiting and keeping their parents awake, however, they are not capable of significant sex specific social tasks. Nevertheless, unjustifiable categorizations continue into education and beyond, and have helped exclude women from sectors of work and sports.

Connell next examines how social practices actually *transform* people's physicality. The 'cults of physicality' teenage boys are encouraged to engage in, for example, involve exercise which can affect muscular growth, skeletal development and stature. Mauss's (1973) analysis of 'techniques of the body' is pertinent here, focusing on how even walking and talking involve complex processes of education, imitation, practice and power, and suggesting that socially differentiated body techniques can lead to broader inequalities.

Finally, Connell examines how *categorizations* and *transformations* interrelate; bodies can be moulded in ways which support social stereotypes. As Hargreaves (1985: 44) notes, the lifestyles encouraged among middle-class Victorian women meant they "did" swoon, "were" unable to eat, [and] suffered continual maladies . . . The acceptance by women of their "incapacitation" gave a . . . moral weighting to the established so-called "facts". More generally, this interaction between categorization and transformation means that gendered ideologies are not simply *beliefs* but become *imprinted* on people's bodies 'into muscle tensions, postures, the feel and texture of the body. This is one of the main ways in which the power of men becomes "naturalized"' (Connell, 1987: 85).

Connell (1995) has also explored the emotionally and physically damaging consequences for men, and their relationships, of the pressures exerted by forms of masculinity. Military training, for example, may discourage men from verbally articulating their feelings, and encourage them to release emotions through acts of aggression. Similarly, analyses of socially approved forms of femininity suggest that the pressures placed on women's appearance are related to eating disorders, and that even small changes to the face or body can affect women's self-confidence (Davis, 1995).

Re-forming sensuality

This mention of emotions introduces a growing collection of work on the sensory and sensual capacities of humans; on how our experiences of health, illness, pain, ageing and emotion form a basis for and are shaped by social relations of domination and subordination (e.g. Bendelow and Williams, 1997; Featherstone and Hepworth, 1991; Frank, 1995; James and Gabe, 1996).

Freund (1990), for example, suggests that stressful situations which contradict our sense of who we are can have neuro-hormonal consequences that adversely affect blood pressure and immune systems, and that these situations are related to the levels of power we exercise. Such analysis becomes increasingly important with the growth in *emotion work* expected from employees. As Hochschild (1983) argues, service sector jobs increasingly require employee willingness to *present* a particular emotional state (e.g. of confidence in their firm); to *subdue* emotions which conflict with this 'public face' (e.g. irritability at clients); and to *induce* emotional responses from customers (e.g. flight attendants seek to reassure passengers). The costs of emotion work may, however, be high. Constantly subduing one's anger, for example, may detrimentally affect one's health (Freund, 1990).

Overload and underload in any form of waged work, as well as being unemployed, can also increase 'stress related' and other illnesses (Hardey, 1998). Assembly-line workers illustrate this as, in a different way, do office workers at risk from repetitive strain injury. As Freund (1982: 101) argues, the body 'becomes a machine but cannot tolerate what a machine can'.

These writings provide further examples of how social practices and categories build on material bodies but also *produce* differences between people. Social expectations may push women towards caring, 'flight attendant' type emotion work while directing men to aggressive, 'debt collector' type work, and make it more difficult for individuals to work in non-stereotypical forms of emotion work. In such jobs, emotional responses may be produced which reinforce stereotypical views of masculinity and femininity.

Re-forming knowledge

In examining what I refer to as the 'embodied bases of knowing', theories of the body have challenged the dominant tradition in, and applications of, Western philosophy: the tradition which associates the mind with what makes us distinctively human, and rational thought with our ability to acquire knowledge, truth and control. In the seventeenth century, for example, Descartes constructed a complex model of mind–body interaction, but doubted the evidence provided by the senses and affirmed his principle *cogito ergo sum* – 'I think therefore I am' – as the foundation for knowledge. In the eighteenth century, Kant emphasized the importance of duty over bodily desire and located the 'good' in compliance with moral laws which are both unconditional and freely constructed by individuals.

Of most interest to sociologists, however, are the *practical* uses to which such perspectives have been put. Turner (1984, 1996: 9) argues that an adapted Cartesian 'world view' became one part of early modern individualism, 'scientific rationalism and [a] Protestant spirit which sought to dominate external nature' through instrumental rationality. This became one factor in the realm of thought which helped to deny the magical; in the disciplining of the body to regulate sexuality; and in the growth of colonialism whereby 'other cultures were subordinated to the instrumental control of Western technology and civilization' (Turner, 1984, 1996: 10).

Post-modern thought has sought to relativize the foundations of 'knowledge' and 'truth' in deconstructing the objectivist view of the world behind Western modes of control and oppression, and by promoting 'standpoint epistemologies' which tie knowledge to experience (though it is worth remembering that those 'arch modernists' Marx and Engels [1970: 51] constructed a sophisticated theory of knowledge on the basis that 'Consciousness is . . . from the very beginning a social product'). Those concerned with explicating the bodily bases of knowledge, however, allow us to move beyond relativism to a *corporeally situated* theory of knowledge in which communication is possible because of what unites us as human beings, as much as what divides us into social groups.

Elias's (1991) theory of 'symbol emancipation', for example, emphasizes the links which exist between knowledge and our shared embodiment. Symbol emancipation results from evolutionary processes which provided humans with the physical means of communicating, thinking and orienting themselves to reality via symbols. This produced a unique ability to learn and synthesize symbols, to develop these into language, and to transmit knowledge between generations (Elias, 1991: 31–2, 43, 131). Symbol use remains dependent on individuals learning language, however, and other social contingencies. In their study of a divided community, for example, Elias and Scotson (1965) show how spatial separation and contact based on limited sensory information can lead to the stigmatization of social groups and the proliferation of 'fantasy knowledge' about others.

424

The 'experiential realism' of Johnson (1987) and Lakoff (1987) reinforces this view of the embodied bases of knowledge by emphasizing that any explanation of meaning and rationality should account for the sensory structures through which we grasp our world. Johnson focuses on 'imagination' (how we abstract from certain bodily experiences and contexts to others in order to make sense of new situations) and 'categorization' (how the classificatory schemes we work with depend on our perceptual capacities and motor skills).

These perspectives suggest that far from discourse determining the body in a Foucaultian sense, the body is integrally involved in the *construction* of discourse. This is central to Mellor and Shilling's (1997) theory that distinctive forms of knowing are integral to those shifting forms of embodiment that have formed bases for, and are subsequently transformed by, successive historical epochs. Theories of the body, in short, suggest that knowledge is not abstract and disembodied, but is tied to distinctive organizations and hierarchies of the senses (especially to the Western dominance of the eye) (Jencks, 1995). Post-modern analyses and modernist theories of communicative rationality which ignore such factors are likely to remain problematic.

FUTURE DIRECTIONS

Featherstone and Turner (1995) have noted that in contrast to the breadth of theoretical writings on the body, substantive research has been concentrated into relatively few areas such as images and signs; health and illness; sport and technology; gender, sex and sexuality; and organizations. These areas could usefully be expanded, especially in relation to the development of appropriate methodologies, but there remain crucial theoretical issues to be addressed. Turner (1984, 1996: 33–4) identifies four: we need a more comprehensive understanding of the philosophical understanding of embodiment; a view of how the body functions in social space; an understanding of the communal nature of embodiment; and a greater historical sense of the body's cultural formation. This warrants particular interrogation of:

1 *What the body is*. This can help us avoid reductionism, examine the body's interplay with (beneficial or detrimental) cultural and social structures over time (Sayer, 1997), theorize adequately the body/sex/gender distinctions which are frequently conflated in contemporary feminist writings (Hughes and Witz, 1997), and examine the phenomenological questions associated with the 'lived experience' of embodiment.
2 The 'interaction order' of bodily co-presence among individuals (Goffman, 1983; Shilling, 1999), of the moral issues raised by the embodied character of interaction, and the impact the widespread promotion of what Falk (1994) refers to as 'consuming bodies' has on these issues.

3   The relationship between particular forms of embodiment and forms of
    sociality at *collective* levels, and the forms of emotional effervescence
    central to maintaining and transforming these phenomena (Durkheim,
    1995; Mellor and Shilling, 1997; Scheff, 1994).
4   The resources provided by existing theories of historical and contempor-
    ary development. Particularly important here is Elias's (1939a; 1939b)
    theory of civilizing processes which has at its centre analyses of historical
    transformations in monopolies of violence, the social division of labour,
    behavioural codes and forms of affect control, and the significance of the
    body as a bearer of value in European court societies (see also Bourdieu,
    1984).

The success of these investigations is likely to determine whether issues
concerning embodiment will be central to the reconstruction of twenty-first-
century social theory.

SUMMARY

This chapter has argued that:

- The body is at the height of intellectual and cultural fashion and has also
  become one of the fastest growing and most productive areas of modern thought. While there is much of value to be found on the relationship
  between sensual activity, alienation and the construction of social systems in the work of classical writers, the body has more frequently
  remained something of a 'ghost in the machine' of modern Western
  thought: it is only relatively recently that social theory has systematically
  made embodiment central to its considerations.
- Four of the major reasons for this 'rise' of the body are: the importance
  of the body as personal project and a cultural object; the rise of 'second
  wave' feminism and academic feminism's (ambivalent) interest in the
  body; the ageing populations of many advanced industrial societies;
  and a shift in capitalism from a work and invest mentality to a work
  hard/consume hard disposition.
- Naturalistic and social constructionist approaches to the body have
  been enormously important in shaping contemporary popular and academic approaches towards issues related to human embodiment. The
  overcoming of this division is, however, simply a vital prerequisite to the
  development of more sophisticated theoretical analyses concerned with
  such issues as the phenomenology of the 'lived' body, the relationship
  between forms of embodiment and forms of sociality, and how each of
  these are subject to being re-formed through time and space.

> - Examples of this 'going beyond' of the naturalistic/social constructionist divide can be seen, for example, in the areas of (the re-formation of) gender inequalities, emotions, and the embodied basis of human knowledge.
> - Despite the explosion of work on bodies since the 1980s, there is much substantive work to be done on the subject, and there are a number of theoretical issues which still need to be resolved (see Turner, 1996). While post-modern theorists have sought to appropriate the body in order to disrupt existing theory, it is time to move beyond this fracture and use embodiment as a way of reconstructing social theory in order to deal with the serious issues of poverty, environmental decay, violence and community which confront humanity in the twenty-first century.

NOTES

1. Accompanying Foucault's discursive reductionism, however, are occasional intimations of a primeval, ahistorical body that has always existed, ready to be 'written on' or reconstructed by discourse. This creates a tension in his work that remains unresolved (see Butler, 1998: 129–30; Shilling, 1993: 79–80).

FURTHER READING:

Turner, B.S. (1984, 1996) *The Body & Society*, 2nd edn. London: Sage. The first edition of this text, published in 1984, did much to launch the current interest in matters of embodiment, and this 1996 edition includes a new introduction analysing developments since that time, the rise of 'somatic society' and suggested lines of future investigation. Turner's analysis of such issues as desire, patriarchy and disease provides a powerful structuralist theory of bodily order.

Shilling, C. (1993) *The Body and Social Theory*. London: Sage. Written to provide an accessible overview and analysis of the rise of the body in social theory and sociology, a critical examination of the major traditions informing contemporary writings on embodiment, and an original approach to future body analysis which builds critically on the writings of such authors as Elias, Bourdieu and Giddens.

Butler, J. (1993) *Bodies That Matter. On the Discursive Limits of Sex*. London: Routledge. One of the most influential feminist books on the body which follows on from the theory of gender performativity Butler established in her 1990 book *Gender Trouble*. Here, Butler is concerned with the materiality of sex and with examining how this materiality is itself constructed by regulatory norms. Althusser is added to Butler's use of Foucaultian and psychoanalytic perspectives, but there is a substantial theoretical continuity between her two books.

Synnott, A. (1993) *The Body Social. Symbolism, Self and Society*. London: Routledge. Synnott surveys the history of thinking about the body and the senses and then focuses on the specific themes of gender, beauty, the face, hair, touch, sight and smell. The book contains a wealth of historical and empirical detail about human bodies and concludes with a consideration of some of the various theoretical approaches which have been adopted to the body.

Falk, P. (1994) *The Consuming Body*. London: Sage. Falk brings together sociological, anthropological and critical theory in this complex theory of the consuming body. By examining such issues as the anthropology of taste, orality and desire; body, self and culture; and how representations mediate people's relationships with culture, this book provides us with a sophisticated theory of the historical transformation from the open body/closed self of traditional societies to the closed body/open self of contemporary society.

Featherstone, M. and Burrows, R. (eds) (1995) *Cyberspace, Cyberbodies, Cyberpunk. Cultures of Technological Embodiment*. London: Sage. An innovative collection of articles exploring the fast shifting boundaries between bodies, minds and machines, and critically examining the potentialities of virtual reality and the possibilities of a post-human species liberated from the time-space constraints of the modern body. Especially useful in its analyses of how a 'post-modern world' might change and transform the actual materiality of human embodiment.

Mellor, P.A. and Shilling, C. (1997) *Re-forming the Body: Religion, Community and Modernity*. London: Sage. This book seeks to bridge the gap between social theories and empirical sociologies of the body, and between the sociology of the body and the sociology of emotions. It examines how bodies and their senses and sensualities are re-formed through time as a result of their participation in shifting forms of community and association, and as a result of their varying experiences of the sacred, and argues that contemporary society is characterized by a growing tension between the formal institutions and informal relationships and sensory knowledges characteristic of embodied life.

REFERENCES

de Beauvoir, S. (1949) *The Second Sex*. London: Everyman.

Bendelow, G. and Williams, S. (1997) *Emotions and Social Life: Social Theory and Contemporary Issues*. London: Routledge.

Benton, T. (1991) 'Biology and Social Science: Why the Return of the Repressed Should be Given a (Cautious) Welcome', *Sociology*, **25**(1): 1–29.

Bourdieu, P. (1984) *Distinction. A Social Critique of the Judgement of Taste*. London: Routledge.

Burkitt, I. (1999) *Bodies of Thought*. London: Sage.

Butler, J. (1990) *Gender Trouble*. London: Routledge.

Butler, J. (1993) *Bodies that Matter*. London: Routledge.

Connell, R. (1983) *Which Way Is Up?* Sydney: George Allen and Unwin.

Connell, R. (1987) *Gender and Power*. Cambridge: Polity Press.

Connell, R. (1995) *Masculinities*. Cambridge: Polity Press.

Crossley, N. (1995) 'Merleau-Ponty, the Elusive Body and Carnal Sociology', *Body & Society*, **1**(1): 43–63.

Davis, K. (1995) *Reshaping the Female Body. The Dilemmas of Cosmetic Surgery*. London: Routledge.

Diamond, I. and Quinby, L. (eds) (1988) *Feminism and Foucault*. Boston, MA: Northeastern University Press.

Doy, G. (1996) 'Out of Africa: Orientalism, ''Race'' and the Female Body', *Body & Society*. **2**(4): 17–44.

Durkheim, E. (1912 [1995) *The Elementary Forms of Religious Life*. New York: The Free Press.

Elias, N. (1939a) *The Civilizing Process, Volume 1: The History of Manners*. New York: Pantheon Books.

Elias, N. (1939b) *The Civilizing Process, Volume 2: State Formation and Civilization*. Oxford: Basil Blackwell.

Elias, N. (1991) *The Symbol Theory*. London: Sage.

Elias, N. and Scotson, J. (1965) *The Established and the Outsiders*. London: Sage.

Falk, P. (1994) *The Consuming Body*. London: Sage.

Fanon, F. (1970) *Black Skin, White Masks*. London: Paladin.

Featherstone, M. (1982) 'The Body in Consumer Culture', *Theory, Culture and Society*, **1**: 18–33.

Featherstone, M. and Hepworth, M. (1991) 'The Mask of Ageing and the Postmodern Lifecourse', in M. Featherstone, M. Hepworth and B.S. Turner (eds) *The Body. Social Process and Cultural Theory*. London: Sage.

Featherstone, M., Hepworth, M. and Turner, B.S. (eds) (1991) *The Body. Social Process and Cultural Theory*. London: Sage.

Featherstone, M. and Turner, B.S. (1995) 'Body and Society: An Introduction', *Body & Society*, **1**(1): 1–12.

Feher, M., Naddaff, R. and Tazi, N. (1989) *Fragments for a History of the Human Body*, 3 vols. New York: Zone.

Foucault, M. (1980) 'Body/Power', in C. Gordon (ed.) *Michel Foucault: Power/Knowledge*. Brighton: Harvester.

Foucault, M. (1981) *The History of Sexuality, Vol. 1. An Introduction*. Harmondsworth: Penguin.

Frank, A. (1988) 'Bringing Bodies Back In: A Decade Review', *Theory, Culture and Society*, **7**: 131–62.

Frank, A. (1995) *The Wounded Storyteller. Body, Illness and Ethics*. Chicago: University of Chicago Press.

Freund, P. (1982) *The Civilized Body: Social Domination, Control and Health*. Philadelphia, PA: Temple University Press.

Freund, P. (1990) 'The Expressive Body: A Common Ground for the Sociology of Emotions and Health and Illness', *Sociology of Health and Illness*. **12**(4): 454–77.

Giddens, A. (1991) *Modernity and Self Identity*. Cambridge: Polity Press.

Goffman, E. (1983) 'Presidential Address: The Interaction Order', *American Sociological Review*, **48**:1–17.

Gould, S.J. (1981) *The Mismeasure of Man*. Harmondsworth: Penguin.

Grosz, E. (1994) *Volatile Bodies. Toward a Corporeal Feminism*. Bloomington, IN: Indiana University Press.

Hardey, M. (1998) *Social Dimensions of Health*. Oxford: Open University Press.

Hargreaves, J.A. (1985) 'Playing Like a Gentleman while Behaving Like Ladies: Contradictory Features of the Formative Years of Women's Sport', *British Journal of Sports History*. **2**(1): 40–52.

Heim, M. (1995) 'The Design of Virtual Reality', *Body & Society*, **1**(3–4): 65–77.

Hirst, P. and Woolley, P. (1982) *Social Relations and Human Attributes*. London: Tavistock.

Hochschild, A. (1983) *The Managed Heart*. Berkeley, CA: University of California Press.

Honneth, A. and Joas, H. (1988) *Social Action and Human Nature*. Cambridge: Cambridge University Press.

Hughes, A. and Witz, A. (1997) 'Feminism and the Matter of Bodies: From de Beauvoir to Butler', *Body & Society*, **3**(1): 47–60.

James, V. and Gabe, J. (1996) *Health and the Sociology of Emotions*. Oxford: Blackwell.

Jencks, C. (1995) 'The Centrality of the Eye in Western Culture: An Introduction', in C. Jencks (ed.) *Visual Culture*. London: Routledge.

Joas, H. (1996) *The Creativity of Action*. Cambridge: Polity.

Johnson, D. (1983) *Body*. Boston: Beacon Press.

Johnson, M. (1987) *The Body in the Mind: The Bodily Basis of Meaning, Imagination and Reason*. Chicago: University of Chicago Press.

Kaplan, G. and Rogers, L. (1990) 'The Definition of Male and Female. Biological Reductionism and the Sanctions of Normality', in S. Gunew (ed.) *Feminist Knowledge, Critique and Construct*. London: Routledge.

Kemper, T. (1990) *Social Structure and Testosterone*. New Brunswick, NJ: Rutgers University Press.

Lakoff, G. (1987) *Women, Fire and Dangerous Things*. Chicago: University of Chicago Press.

Laqueur, T. (1990) *Making Sex: Body and Gender from the Greeks to Freud*. Cambridge, MA: Harvard University Press.

Martin, E. (1989) *The Woman in the Body: A Cultural Analysis of Reproduction*. Milton Keynes: Open University Press.

Marx, K. and Engels, F. (1970) *The German Ideology*, edited and introduced by C. Arthur. London: Lawrence and Wishart.

Mauss, M. (1973) 'Techniques of the Body', *Economy and Society*, **2**: 70–88.

Mellor, P.A. and Shilling, C. (1997) *Re-forming the Body: Religion, Community and Modernity*. London: Sage.

O'Neill, J. (1985) *Five Bodies: The Human Shape of Modern Society*. Ithaca, NY: Cornell University Press.

Oakley, A. (1984) *The Captured Womb*. Oxford: Basil Blackwell.

Park, R.E. and Burgess, E.W. (1969) *Introduction to the Science of Sociology*. Chicago: University of Chicago Press.

Sawicki, J. (1991) *Disciplining Foucault. Feminism, Power and the Body*. New York: Routledge.

Sayer, A. (1997) 'Essentialism, Social Constructionism and Beyond', *Sociological Review*, **45**(3): 453–487.

Scheff, T. (1994) *Bloody Revenge. Emotions, Nationalism and War.* Boulder, CO: Westview Press

Scott, S. and Morgan, D. (eds) (1993) *Body Matters.* London: Falmer Press.

Shilling, C. (1993) *The Body and Social Theory.* London: Sage.

Shilling, C. (1999) 'Towards an Embodied Understanding of the Structure-Agency Relationship'. *British Journal of Sociology.*

Sinha, M (1987) 'Gender and Imperialism: Colonial Policy and the Ideology of Moral Imperialism in Late Nineteenth Century Bengal', in M. Kimmel (ed.) *Changing Men.* Newbury Park, CA: Sage.

Soper, K. (1995) *What is Nature?* Oxford; Blackwell.

Tönnies, F. (1957) *Community and Association.* Michigan: Michigan State University Press.

Turner, B.S. (1984, 1996) *The Body and Society.* Oxford: Blackwell.

Turner, B.S. (1992) *Regulating Bodies.* London: Routledge.

Turner, B.S. (1996) *The Body and Society*, 2nd edn. Oxford: Blackwell.

Wilson, E.O. (1978) *Sociobiology. The New Synthesis.* Cambridge, MA: Harvard University Press.

Chapter 30

Intimate choices

Ken Plummer

I wish my life and decisions to depend on myself, not on external forces of whatever kind. I wish to be the instrument of my own, not of other men's [*sic*] acts of will. I wish to be a subject, not an object; to be moved by reasons, by conscious purposes, which are my own, not by causes which affect me, as it were from outside . . . I wish, above all, to be conscious of myself as a thinking, willing, active being, bearing responsibility for my choices and able to explain them by reference to my own ideas and purposes (Berlin, 1969: 131).

Isaiah Berlin's notable remark captures the views of many people living in the West as they think about their intimate lives at the turn of the century. Despite the critical onslaught on 'humanism' from many directions, the idea that we are autonomous human beings who can choose the kind of personal life we wish to live has become a deeply entrenched one. We surely must be allowed to choose, for example, who (and if) to marry, as well as when to divorce; how many children we can have and indeed what kind of erotic life we are to lead and with whom (be it bisexual, homosexual, heterosexual or monosexual). To suggest the opposite – that others can tell us who to marry, or when we can have children or what kind of sex we should have – is to suggest a world that some see as rapidly in decline. Intimacy in the late modern, globalizing Western world has been shaped massively by the rise of an individualist ideology which seems to proliferate with personal choices. For many – the poor, the unemployed, the old – these choices may be frustratingly limited; but for others, they may be wide and growing.

To get the issue clear at the outset: who would have thought at the start of the twentieth century that by its very end we would be seriously discussing such matters as:

- *new families*: divorce, 'single mothers', out of wedlock conception, cohabitation, remarriage, single parenting, gay partnerships, living alone;
- *new reproductive technologies*: surrogate mothers, test-tube babies, in vitro fertilization (IVF), egg donation, artificial insemination by donor (AID), gamete and intra-fallopian transfer (GIFT), widespread contraception, the decline of male fertility and fertility boosting;
- *new body technologies*: silicon implants, heart pacemaking implants, genetic engineering, 'cyborgs';
- *new sexualities*: non-procreative, non-penetrative, non-reproductive, 'recreational', same sex, 'safer' sex, telephone sex, cybersex, sex work, sadomasochism and the fetish scene;
- *sexual abuses*: rape, sexual harassment, domestic violence, marital rape, date/acquaintance rape, child sexual abuse;
- *new genders*: new men, post-feminist women, bisexualities, gender benders, queers, transgender warriors, lesbian daddies, dyke boys and drag kings.
- *new kinds of people and problems* – found ubiquitously in counselling, talk shows and the self-help industry: sex addicts, people with AIDS, 'women who love too much', the 'fat movement', 'Iron Johns', 'post-traumatic stress disorders', 'false memory syndromes', and the like.

The list could go on. It simply flags new choices and debates around intimacies that have been appearing during the last decades of the twentieth century. Not everyone is engaged with them, but a lot of people are. And each one of these issue compounds the questions: *How do we live and how are we to live in an emerging late/post-modern world?* From a great many sources, there are signs – at century's end, at the end of the millennium – that *some* personal lives are changing in very significant ways. We could see them as instances of increasing regulation, control and discipline; but we could also see them as instances where some are gaining a greater control over their lives.

POST-MODERN INTIMACIES?

This entire book is concerned with a characterization of change and the present. Just what kind of society are we living in, and what are the worlds of intimacies we find there? A leading North American sociologist of sexuality, William Simon, has recently argued that we may now increasingly be living our lives in ways that are different from any that humanity has previously known (Simon, 1996: 3). For him, this is the post-modern, or post-paradigmatic, age, characterized by an intense *pluralization, individuation and a multiplicity of choices*, unknown in any other era. Rapid social change has become our normal condition. The modern world has seen change speeding up and impacting more and more lives. Consensual meanings have dissolved into pluralism, authority has been weakened, 'choices' have proliferated, time and space have become reordered, and what we take for 'the natural' has been deconstructed and denaturalized. Processes have been put into play which increasingly recognize differences, relativities, changes: potential chaos yet enormous possibility. With this comes the radical options for new intimacies divorced from traditional religions, traditional family structures, traditional communities, traditional politics and traditional restricted communication channels.

Yet these changes should not be overstated. While Simon's account captures rapid social change in our sexual lives, most of the empirical research done on sexuality in recent years suggests just how conservative most of our sexual behaviours remains (cf. Laumann *et al.*, 1994; Wellings *et al.*, 1994). We are, I think, living *simultaneously* in traditional, modern and post-modernizing worlds.

Traditional intimacies are still to be found embedded in intense communities, surrounded by families, neighbours, and strong bonding rituals. For many people, traditional worlds remain their core. For many elderly in the West and most families outside the West, for example, the prevalence of new forms of intimacy is minimal (Fukuyama, 1995). What Simon describes is not a rupture with the past so much as an acceleration of changes already found in the modern world.

Modern intimacies have emerged over the past 200 years or so and have become enmeshed in all the features of modernity discussed profusely by social scientists: urbanism, anomie, bureaucratization, commodification, surveillance and individualization. As societies become more and more 'modern', so all these features rapidly multiply. There is a downside and an upside to all this – a series of traps. On the one hand, intimate relations in modernity become a form of life engaged in a search for authenticity, meaning, freedom. On the other, intimate relations become a form of life increasingly trapped within wider bureaucratizing and commercializing forces: relations become McDonaldized and Disneyfied. They are lodged in contradictory tendencies.

Late-modern (or post-modern) intimacies incorporate the latter stages of the above with newer possibilities grafted on to the old in a high-tech and global world. We are just on the edge of all this, but some of the most telling examples of these newly arriving forms of intimacy might be:

1 *Individuation and self-reflexivity*. Late-modern intimacies reflect the death of the 'Grand Narrative of the Personal Life', of the 'one true family', of

what it really means to be a man or a woman, of the truth of our sexuality, of what the body really is, of the search for identity. Increasingly individuals are cast adrift to decide what kind of men or women they will become, what kind of relationship they will live in, what kind of sexual encounters they will have, what kind of identity they can assume. In part this may be seen as 'the reflexive project of the self' (Giddens, 1991: 5). Although an increase in 'self-consciousness' is common to both modernity and post-modernity, the newer order sees a rapid spiral in such concerns. Both Beck and Giddens have highlighted this fact: for 'the more tradition loses its hold . . . the more individuals are forced to negotiate life style choices among a diversity of options' (Giddens, 1991: 5). Indeed, 'for the sake of individual survival, individuals are compelled to make themselves the centre of their own life plans and projects' (Beck, 1992: 92). As people are released from the traditional (especially gender) roles prescribed by industrial society and are encouraged more and more 'to build up a life of their own', so all manner of relationships must now be 'worked out, negotiated, arranged and justified in all the details of how, what, why or why not' (Beck and Beck-Gernsheim, 1995: 5, 6). Thus a growing characteristic of new style relationships and intimacies is the desire to reflect upon them, and indeed to talk about them with partners. This is a trend towards disclosing intimacies – 'a process of two or more people mutually sustaining deep knowing and understanding. . . through talking and listening, sharing thoughts, showing feelings' – which is starting to permeate more and more relationships (Jamieson, 1998: 158). Not only are couples expected to talk more to each other about their innermost desires, but if they do not then this may be taken as a sign that the relationship is not working. A whole panoply of experts – counsellors, psychiatrists, social workers – may then be called in to assist.

2   *The democratization of personhood and the ethos of pluralization.* Closely allied to the above is the arrival of an 'ethos of pluralization' (Connolly, 1995) in which a wider range of possibilities become available. The past was sensed as a singular world, while the post-modern world is one of plurals. Thus whereas the past spoke of men and women, the post-modern speaks of *masculinities, femininities* and, indeed, *genders*. Whereas the past spoke of sexuality, now there is a recognition of *sexualities*. And *post-modern families* are ones of 'pluralism and flexibility (representing) a democratic opportunity in which individuals' shared capacities, desires, and convictions could govern the character of their gender, sexual and family relationships' (Stacey, 1996: 37). Perhaps over-optimistically, Manuel Castells in his epic account of late-twentieth-century social change, *The Information Age*, suggests we are moving into a 'post-patriarchal world', one where marriage, family, heterosexuality and sexual desire – always treated as a unity in the past – are now becoming increasingly de-linked and separated from each other (Castells, 1997:

235). They are indeed becoming their own autonomous spheres. 'Sex', for example, no longer works its prime task of procreation: it now serves a multiplicity of purposes, including both recreational goals and the defining of relationships. It incorporates a much wider range of potential sexual practices. 'Sex' becomes autonomous (or in Giddens's less felicitous term, 'plastic'). Under pluralization, people's very characters become more open and democratized.

3 *The mediazation of intimacies.* A third feature of the late or post-modern landscape is the ways in which patterns of intimacy are increasingly embedded in media relations. This is true not just in the simple sense that most media forms provide endless stories, images and debates over questions of intimacy – from the soap opera tales of sex and family found in *Friends, Eastenders* or *Home and Away*, to the talk shows of *Jerry Spinger* or *Oprah* which flaunt the endless possibilities of the tragic personal life (cf. Gamson, 1998). It is also true in the wider sense that much of our daily talk and conversation is both about and informed by these media. Watching television and talking about it, for instance, may now be a prime activity for families, lovers and friends. The death of a Princess Diana, the sexual antics of a Madonna or Michael Jackson, the seeing of the film *Titanic* or the Clinton/Lewinsky 'cigar capers' disseminated throughout the world on the Web may start to infuse our most intimate talk and relationships in telling ways. I am not suggesting any straightforward or direct impact of the media on our lives – the crude suggestions, for instance, that pornography leads us to commit pornographic acts. Rather, I am suggesting that the very air we breathe in a postmodern world is saturated with simulations from media. Many – and especially new generations – live their intimacies through media.

4 *The globalization of intimacies.* A fourth feature concerns the processes by which local cultures pick up, and usually transform, global elements of intimacies. There are numerous instances: major new markets in holiday travels, including but not limited to sex tourism; 'intimate images' sent around the world through films, television programmes, videos and pop culture; worldwide social movements which debate intimacies – the Women's Movement and the Lesbian and Gay Movement; and new diseases such as AIDS which involve major international organizations. Not least important are the growing numbers of people who now conduct their actual personal relationships on a global scale. Many partners, for instance, no longer live together in the same country let alone under the same roof.

5 *The emergence of post-identity possibilities.* Much of the above can also be seen as a radical shift in the ways in which some people now come to see themselves. Kenneth Gergen, for example, depicts a journey from the romantic self via the modern self to the post-modern. For him, the postmodern means 'the very concept of personal essences is thrown in doubt' (Gergen, 1991: 7). He argues that the new 'technologies of social

saturation' (from phones and television to computers and virtual realties) lead to a 'multiphrenic condition' whereby new patterns of post-identity relationships ('fractional', 'microwave', etc.) start to appear. Thus he talks of 'fractional relationships' – in families, in sexualities, in daily life – which are more limited in scope, less totalizing than in the past. Nowhere is this clearer than in the emerging new etiquette and relationships which surround electronic mail and web sites (Turkle, 1995).

6   *The McDonaldization of intimacy.* In stark contrast to many of the images of increasing choice, this feature suggests a major counter-trend. For here our intimacies – far from bringing choice and individuality – become very standardized. It is the image of efficiency, calculability, rationality and predictability applied to the world of relationships (Ritzer, 1996). Thus, sex may become safely commodified into telephone sex, computer dating lines, and masturbatory porno videos; relationships become subject to counsellors and standardized self-help books which suggest twelve steps to the perfect relationship; and families become Disneyfied through consumer goods (babies need their special clothes, chairs, foods, alarms, medications and toiletries from baby-care chain stores, and this sanitized world then continues throughout every stage of life).

GENDERS AND THE SHIFTS IN INTIMACIES

There are many crucial dimensions to these changing characteristics of late-modern intimacies which I have started to depict above, but gender is usually singled out as central. The distinction between modern and post-modern genders may be most salient here. The former inhabit a world where the differences between men and women organized around heterosexuality and the family are clear and striking. A gender war infuses such relationships. The latter inhabit a world where the bipolar dualism of men and women starts to break down, and genders themselves are seen as unstable categories, socially constructed and performed.

Gender wars?

Modern intimacy debates have been lodged in the 'gender war' where the worlds of men and women are seen as being distinctively at odds with each other. Classically, problems centre around what Norbert Elias talks of as a 'lust economy' (1994: 456–519). Here, the so-called 'lust balance' may be seen as an 'attempt to find a satisfying balance between the longing for sex and the longing for love' (Wouters, 1998: 229); between the pursuit of transient, passionate, lusty, sexual excitement and the search for a more enduring 'love' and care. In the modern world, the common perception is that women search for a more emotional, bonding, caring, 'loving' world while men search for a more erotic, sexual, even physical world. This is common sense backed, indeed, by detailed arguments from socio-biology.

This divide is at the heart of much radical feminist criticism of contemporary intimacies which obviously has a much less sanguine view of the changes I have located above. For here sex itself is defined as being male: male sexual power (phallocentrism), orchestrated through the institution of heterosexuality and buttressed by marriage and the family, works to define women's lives. The dark side of intimacies are here foregrounded: domestic violence, pornography, sexual harassment, rape and sexual violence, marital rape, date rape/acquaintance rape, child sexual abuse, stalking, sexual murder (Kelly, 1988; MacKinnon, 1987). The radical response to this power has been to avoid intercourse altogether (Dworkin, 1987) and/or to enter radical lesbianism. It leads to scathing attacks on heterosexual intercourse because this is seen as incapable of offering egalitarian relationships, a view which poses serious problems for heterosexual feminists.

This view is, in turn, also challenged from within feminism by those who argue it sides too easily with the neglect of women's eroticism and desires (Segal, 1994). Throughout much of the second wave of feminism, a recurring divide has been between 'pleasure' and 'danger' feminists, between those who see the desires of women as a key focus for development and those who see such desires as merely perpetuating the dangers derived from male sexualities. Ironically, some more recent arguments, including those of some post-modern and third wave feminists, have suggested a straining towards a greater equality – with some women becoming more and more erotic (what some writers have called the 'feminization of sex') (Ehrenreich, Hess and Jacobs, 1986) and some men becoming 'new men': more sensitive, caring, loving. Indeed, the sexualities of women and men do seem to have been changing since the arrival of the women's movement, and 'third wave' feminists have provided confident assertions of women's sexualities and detailed accounts of their own sexualities, as well as their own disagreements with past feminist orthodoxies around such issues as relationship rape (Stan, 1995). At the same time, both masculinity and heterosexuality have been made more and more problematic.

Changing relations?

There may, then, be a shift taking place in the so-called 'lust balance', which is generally experienced as one befitting post-modern times: a time of profound ambiguity, confusion, disarray, uncertainty. Manuel Castells sees these recent changes in intimacy as being closely connected to 'a mass insurrection of women against their oppression throughout the world' (Castells, 1997: 135), and suggests they have been caused by four key changes: in the economy and labour market; in shifts in technology over child bearing; in globalization and the hearing of women's voices all over the world; and in the growth of new social movements. Others see a blurring of the traditional divides between men and women: a 'sexualization of love' along with an 'eroticization of sex' (Seidman, 1992); a move towards 'androgynous love' (Cancian, 1987) ; and a 'pure relationship' (Giddens, 1991). Here 'a sexual relation is entered into for its own sake, for what can be derived from a sustained association with another; and which is continued only so far as it is thought by both parties to deliver enough satisfactions for each individual to stay within it' (Giddens, 1991: 58). Ironically, the model for this may well be derived from gay relations where procreation and sexuality have long been divorced from each other. Again, choice and individualism are the key themes and the sense of following traditional blueprints has gone.

There is a clear downside to all this. Intimacy may be in the process of becoming more democratic for some, creating a democracy in the personal sphere to mirror that of the public sphere. But for others it is becoming increasingly antagonistic, with men and women's relationships becoming polarized and separate. Women have started to 'need' men less and less, while men have become more and more absent, distant, irresponsible or coercive. In an increasingly post-modern world where boundaries are less clear and strong narratives of how to live an intimate life have weakened, problems with gender relations may well multiply (Beck and Beck-Gernshiem, 1995).

CULTURE WARS AND INTIMATE CITIZENSHIP: THE DEBATE OVER LIFE POLITICS

The late/post-modernization of intimacies leads to an ongoing moral and political struggle over the kinds of lives people should be leading. While there is little that is new about this debate, these end-of-century, end-of-millennium times may serve as critical moments where moral anxieties run even higher than usual. Showalter's elegant study of *Sexual Anarchy* suggests direct parallels between late-nineteenth-century *fin-de-siècle* crises and those of today: from concerns over sexual disease and new women to fears over homosexuality and the crisis of the body. But she is not gloomy about it: 'If we can learn something from the fears and myths of the past, it is that they are so often exaggerated and unreal, that what looks like sexual anarchy in the context of *fin-de-siècle* anxieties may be the embryonic stirrings of a new order' (Showalter, 1991: 18).

In recent years few could have missed these struggles – and they are global – demanding a return to 'family values' and suggesting we get 'back to basics'. The moral, intimate and personal life has become a truly publicly contested domain. For some we are witnessing 'the de-moralisation of society' (Himmelfarb, 1995). This is the time of the 'culture wars' where realignments are taking place in politics over morality and lifestyles, cutting across old divides of religion, class and political party. Briefly, I think several main positions of argument can be detected.

Traditionalizing claims

Much public debate lies in the hands of *traditionalists, tribalists, fundamentalists and demodernizers*. With varying emphases, these all see chaos around and seek a return to an old order with a clear authority and firm moral structure. The buzzwords include a return to 'family values', to 'community', and to well-disciplined families, schools and streets. Enemies are created such that the world becomes divided into a virtuous, righteous, well-intentioned group of citizens (my tribe) and a vicious, dangerous, immoral corrupting group (often the underclass).

I suggest two key problems with these arguments. First, they usually assert a return to a past world where all was better. But these are worlds we never had, and ways we never ever were. The ravages, short lives, dangers and brutalities of much of history are overlooked for a presumed more idyllic past. But there can indeed be no return to a simple happy past because that past is itself a fiction. Second, even if the past was more rosy than today, we cannot set the clocks back. All the contemporary developments, ranging from urbanization and shifts in media communications to new technologies and the growth of individualistic ideologies, cannot simply be removed. And the post-modernization of intimacies is contingent upon them. The moral changes we are experiencing are all bound up with these wider social and cultural changes, and they cannot be easily separated. As a noted, yet rather conservative, sociologist Peter Berger once put it while discussing the modernization of consciousness:

> once established, modern consciousness is rather hard to get rid of. Its definitions of reality and its psychological consequences are dragged along even into the rebellions against it, providing the ironic spectacle of an assault on modernity by people whose consciousness presupposes the same modernity. [There are thus] intrinsic limits to any de-modernising enterprise (Berger, Berger and Kellner, 1973: 192).

Since Berger was writing some twenty-five years ago, the changes of the modern world have accelerated greatly. Moral debates hence should in fact focus on how we can live with these changes and not simply decry them by seeking a return to a simple, mythical past. The traditionalists and the tribalists refuse to recognize the changing nature of the social worlds in which we are living. In a world that is radically different from the past, the old solutions cannot simply be drawn upon. Though this is not to say we cannot learn from past ways and mistakes.

The relativist-individualist response

A second position is equally untenable: the radical individualist response. Here, the rapidity of change is accepted, along with an extreme moral relativism and a sense that anything goes. This position accepts the changes, and then prostrates itself before them. It harbours an anti-sociological view that a society without rules or ethics is indeed possible. It is an anarchist's utopia of a society-less society and I believe it can be dismissed quickly because it so radically flies in the face of how society works. It is a kind of throwback from the late 1960s 'do your own thingism'.

Dialogues, discourses and democratic visions

A third position is the one I favour, and I explore it more fully elsewhere (Plummer, 1995). Drawing from many recent developments in political and post-modern theory, it suggests the need for a new kind of politics (which I call 'Intimate Citizenship') that can accept the move into a new kind of world. Here many voices have to be heard, even voices that oppose each other. Dialogues have to be invented between voices that are radically oppositional to each other: anti-abortionist or 'right to lifers', for instance, need to make limited common ground with pro-abortionists and those favouring 'the right to choose'. The oppositional tensions need to be lived with 'before the shooting begins' (Hunter, 1994). This may be seen as part of both a 'politics of life style' (Giddens, 1991) and the search for a 'post-modern ethics' (Bauman, 1993). These seek – against a backdrop of recognizing ambivalence, contradiction and the 'incurably aporetic' nature of morality (Bauman, 1993: 11) – to develop ethical and moral positions around the question 'how should we live in a post-traditional order?' (Giddens, 1991: 214–15, 231). Both within and outside academic circles, then, the new and changing forms of intimacies have generated heated debates and little consensus. Sometimes these conflicts are mapped on huge stages; at other times only small groups are involved. But everywhere the meanings of intimacies are contested.

There is obviously a strong evaluative element to most of these debates, and there are no easy solutions. What seems required is a position which recognizes the dangers and crises of our changing climate, seeks an open debate about 'values', 'morals' and 'ethics', abandons the search for absolute foundations, aims to provide clarifications of the principles which do inform our choices, acknowledges differences in positions and yet continues to search for areas of common agreement.

The struggle for such a position is increasingly widespread among contemporary theorists of intimacy. Jeffrey Weeks's position is 'radical democratic humanism', and he seeks a common concern with the values of 'care, responsibility, respect and love' (Weeks, 1995: ix). For the Becks, love is likely to become the new religion giving meaning to individual lives while also providing a sense of togetherness. '[F]ree will and mutual consent are its guiding stars' and it 'becomes a radical form of personal responsibility'. Yet 'the actual content of the love package is a subjective mutual invention, and all around it are pitfalls and potential disaster' (Beck and Beck-Gernsheim, 1995: 194). Likewise, Steven Seidman disavows any 'universal moral imperative that can guide sexual practice', but at the same time does agree that simple sexual libertarianism will not do. Instead he seeks pragmatic guidelines for a sexual ethic allowing that 'different groups evolve their own sexual culture around which they elaborate coherent lives' (Seidman, 1992: 190-2). Like Weeks, he wants a sexual ethics bound to meanings, contexts, recognition of diversities, respect, the importance of consent, responsibility and the consequences of acts. But there can be no prejudging – he even takes the case of paedophilia to show just how tricky this moral debate must be. Seidman is looking for what he calls a 'pragmatic culture of knowledge' which 'leaves permanently unsettled or unresolved an ongoing social world of interpretative social dispute' (Seidman, 1997: 257–8). This is a world which respects differences. It depends on a culture of deep reflexivity and demands living with 'a level of ambiguity, uncertainty, contingency, and social fluidity that many of us may find psychologically and sociologically challenging' (Seidman, 1997: 258).

The challenge for the next century is whether we can live in such a world.

SUMMARY

- The contemporary world is simultaneously traditional, modern and late/post-modern, and is characterized by a growing flow of choices for many people around families, bodies, sexualities, identities and reproduction.
- Late-modern intimacies may be linked to individuation, the ethos of pluralization, mediazation, globalization, post-identity possibilities and McDonaldization.
- They bring with them simultaneously potentials for both gender conflicts and a new harmony in gender relations
- Modern politics is increasingly concerned with these debates, with some making claims for a return to traditional cultures, others seeking a relativist 'do your own thing' and others seeking a 'dialogic, democratic discourse'.
- This latter is the best but the hardest route as it involves talking through differences and seeking out commonalties; of recognizing there is no longer one authority while trying to establish limited sets of authoritative agreements that enable people to move forward in making their choices.

FURTHER READING

A useful overview of the whole field is: Jamieson, Lynn (1998) *Intimacy: Personal Relationships in Modern Societies*. Cambridge: Polity Press.

Two major studies which establish this debate are:

Beck, Ulrich and Beck-Gernsheim, Elisabeth (1995) *The Normal Chaos of Love*. Cambridge: Polity Press.

Giddens, Anthony (1992) *The Transformation of Intimacy: Sexuality, Love and Eroticism in Modern Societies*. Cambridge: Polity Press.

On the moral and political conflicts, see:

Chancer, Lynn S. (1998) *Reconcilable Differences: Confronting Beauty, Pornography and the Future of Feminism*. Berkeley, CA: University of California Press.

Weeks, Jeffrey (1995*) Invented Moralities: Sexual Values in an Age of Uncertainty*. Oxford: Polity Press.

REFERENCES

Bauman, Zygmunt (1993) *Postmodern Ethics*. Oxford: Blackwell.
Beck, Ulrich and Beck-Gernsheim, Elisabeth (1995) *The Normal Chaos of Love*. Cambridge: Polity Press.
Berger, Peter, Berger, Brigette and Kellner, Hansfried (1973) *The Homeless Mind*. Harmondsworth: Penguin.
Berlin, Isaiah (1969) *Four Essays on Liberty*. Oxford: Oxford University Press.
Cancian, Francesca M. (1987) *Love in America: Gender and Self-development*. Cambridge: Cambridge University Press.
Castells, Manuel (1997) *The Power of Identity* (vol. 2 of *The Information Age*). Oxford: Blackwell.
Connolly, William E. (1995) *The Ethos of Pluralization*. Minneapolis: University of Minnesota Press.
Dworkin, Andrea (1987) *Intercourse*. London: Secker and Warburg.
Ehrenreich, Barbara, Hess, Elizabeth and Jacobs, Gloria (1986) *Remaking Love: The Feminization of Sex*. New York: Anchor Press.
Elias, Norbert (1994) *The Civilizing Process*. Oxford: Blackwell.
Fukuyama, Francis (1995) *Trust: The Social Virtues and the Creation of Prosperity*. Harmondsworth: Penguin Books.
Gamson, Joshua (1998) *Freaks Talk Back: Tabloid Talk Shows and Sexual Non-Conformity*. Chicago: University of Chicago Press.
Gergen, Kenneth J. (1991) *The Saturated Self: Dilemmas of Identity in Contemporary Life*. New York: Basic Books.

Giddens, Anthony (1991) *Modernity and Self Identity: Self and Society in the Late Modern Age*. Oxford: Polity Press.

Himmelfarb, Gertrude (1995) *The De-moralization of Society: From Victorian Virtues to Modern Values*. London: IEA Health and Welfare Unit.

Hunter, James Davison (1994) *When the Shooting Begins: Searching for Democracy in America's Culture War*. New York: Free Press.

Kelly, Liz (1988) *Surviving Sexual Violence*. Cambridge: Polity Press.

Jamieson, Lynn (1998*) Intimacy: Personal Relationships in Modern Societies*. Cambridge: Polity Press.

Laumann, Edward O., Gaynon, John H., Michael, Robert T. and Michaels, Stuart (1994) *The Social Organisation of Sexuality*. Chicago: University of Chicago Press.

MacKinnon, Catherine (1987) *Feminism Unmodified*. Cambridge, MA: Harvard University Press.

Plummer, Ken (1995) *Telling Sexual Stories*. London: Routledge.

Ritzer, George (1996) *The McDonaldization of Society*, 2nd edn. London: Pine Forge Press.

Segal, Lynne (1994) *Straight Sex: The Politics of Pleasure*. London: Virago.

Seidman, Steven (1992) *Embattled Eros: Sexual Politics and Ethics in Contemporary America.* London: Routledge.

Seidman, Steven (1997) *Difference Troubles: Queering Social Theory and Sexual Politics*. Cambridge: Cambridge University Press.

Showalter, Elaine (1991) *Sexual Anarchy*. London: Bloomsbury.

Simon, William (1996) *Postmodern Sexualities*. London: Routledge.

Stan, Adele M. (ed.) (1995) *Debating Sexual Correctness*. New York: Delta.

Stacey, Judith (1996) *In the Name of the Family: Rethinking Family Values in the Postmodern Age*. Boston: Beacon Press.

Turkle, Sherry (1995) *Life on the Screen*. London: Weidenfeld and Nicolson.

Weeks, Jeffrey (1995) *Invented Moralities: Sexual Values in an Age of Uncertainty*. Cambridge: Polity Press.

Wellings, Kaye, Field, Julia, Johason, Anne M. and Wadsworth, Jane (1994) *Sexual Behaviour in Britain: The National Survey of Sexual Attitudes and Lifestyles*. Harmondsworth: Penguin.

Wouters, Cas (1998) 'Changes in the "Lust Balance" of Sex and Love since the Sexual Revolution: The Example of The Netherlands', in Gillian Bendelow and Simon J. Williams (eds) *Emotions in Social Life*. London: Routledge.

Chapter 31

Environmentalism

David Pepper

INTRODUCTION: ENVIRONMENTALISM AND ANTI-ENVIRONMENTALISM

An 'environmentalist', says the *Oxford English Dictionary*, is 'one who is concerned with protection of the environment'. Nowadays most of us in the West are 'environmentalists' by this simple definition. We are uneasy about living in what Ulrich Beck (1995) calls 'a risk society', i.e. one subjected to risks seemingly beyond our control and potentially far-reaching in magnitude and spatial extent. Many of these risks are environmental, ranging from global warming, post-Chernobyl contamination, harmful food additives, to polluted city air.

Many people will also have heard that technological and economic growth, i.e. 'development', which has long been thought desirable and even the measure of 'progress', are somehow the culprits producing environmental degradation. Even more unsettling. However, we might have been reassured after 1992's United Nations Conference on Environment and Development, held at Rio de Janeiro. There, world leaders decided that development, economic growth and environmental protection *can be* compatible – by following a model of development called 'ecological modernization' we can have our cake and eat it. So the environmental doomsters of the 1960s and 1970s were perhaps wrong after all.

Although I say that 'most' of us today are environmentalists, not everyone falls into this category. A recent wave of anti-environmentalism has emerged (Rowell, 1996). Anti-environmentalists include some on the political Right (e.g. the Global Climate Coalition, supported by multinational oil companies), and some on the Left (e.g. the Revolutionary Communist Party in the UK). They both accuse environmentalists of being against *any* development, so undermining the prospects of the world's poor. Other commentators have branded environmentalism as romantic rather than rational, or as anti-humanist – preferring the welfare of animals and plants over humans and pedalling, in a new guise, the doctrine of humanity's inherent, 'original sin' and fall from a state of grace with nature (Bramwell, 1989).

What these attacks have in common is that they tend to paint all environmentalists with the same brush. In so doing they oversimplify and misrepresent what is a wide-ranging, eclectic and hugely diverse movement. Indeed, since it embraces most of us in the West, and a growing number in the Second and Third Worlds, environmentalism is less a coherent movement, and more of a turn in late-twentieth-century thought. As such it defies succinct categorization and description. Hence I cannot map it adequately in the space of this chapter, and readers wanting a systematic review should look elsewhere (Dobson 1995; Martell, 1994; Pepper, 1996). What I will attempt is to demonstrate this diversity in environmentalism and to comment on its possible significance. I will suggest that in an intellectual sense (and as a practical movement) different branches of environmentalism, and differing attitudes within the same branches of environmentalism, face in different directions. I will also speculate that this Janus-like stance might echo the seeming position of Western thought at the end of the millennium, caught between continuing faith in modernism and a largely negative reaction to it, known as a condition of 'post-modernity'.

DIFFERENT ENVIRONMENTALISMS

Figure 31.1 shows different forms of environmentalism when considered from the standpoint of political and economic ideology. It differentiates between *radical* and *reformist* environmentalism. The latter embraces mainstream culture's ideologies of liberalism and 'democratic' (as practised by labour and social democrat parties) 'socialism'. It would reform capitalism to a greater or lesser degree, essentially reacting to environmental problems, and adopting a perspective which some call 'technocentric' (O'Riordan, 1989). Technocentrism manifests faith in science, technology and rational management of ecosystems and society, to solve environmental problems. The arguments within it are largely about *how much* to intervene in the market economy. While free-market liberals consider that unmitigated market forces coupled with maximum private ownership of the environment will secure environmental objectives (Anderson and Leal, 1991), social reformists would impose wide-ranging environmental taxes, incentives and regulations on firms and individuals (Pearce, Markandya and Barbier, 1989). Elements of conservative thinking also may mingle with this reformist

RADICAL, COUNTER-CULTURAL
(mainly anti-capitalism, tends to be
proactive)

REFORMIST, MAINSTREAM CULTURAL
(pro-capitalism, tends to be
reactive)

[4] **Deep Ecology:** based on ecocentrism,
intrinsic value in nature.

[3] **Conservatism:** Preservationism,
NIMBY-ism, stewardship
of nature.

[4] **Social Ecology:** looks to both humanism
and ecocentrism, based
on anarchist and feminist
principles.

[1] **Free Market
Liberalism:** Market mechanisms and
privatization of the
commons.

[4] **Eco-socialism:** humanistic and socialist
politics (libertarian,
decentralist, utopian
socialism).

[2/3] **Social
Reformism:** Market intervention, e.g.
environmental taxes,
tradeable pollution rights
plus voluntary agreements
plus regulation.

[2/3] **MAINSTREAM:**
(ambiguous about capitalism, but demanding
considerable reform)
– Incorporates and reflects both sides.
Some radical long-term aims, but reformist
methods – pragmatic Green parties, pressure
groups and lobbies – Friends of the Earth,
Greenpeace, World Wide Fund for Nature, New
Economics Foundation, non-governmental
organizations.

Note: Figures in brackets refer to The 'Ladder of
Sustainable Development' (see Table 31.1):

4. Ideal model
3. Strong sustainability
2. Weak sustainability
1. Very weak sustainability (treadmill)

Figure 31.1 Environmentalisms, and their political ideologies and approaches

approach of the cultural mainstream. This would protect and steward nature – for instance in preservationism, and in the EU-adopted 'precautionary principle', which presumes against development where environmental outcomes are unknown and uncertain. Traditional conservative attitudes also manifest in the 'Not In My Back Yard' (NIMBY) syndrome, which tries to displace pollution and environmentally damaging development to communities and countries relatively willing to have them, or simply unable to resist them for political or economic reasons.

By contrast, *radical environmentalism* is inclined to be proactive, seeking to eliminate environmental problems at their root rather than simply reacting to the damage caused by the normal operations of global capitalism. This entails fundamental social change by either eliminating or completely reconstructing capitalism, so the debate about the environment is shifted out of the cultural/economic mainstream and becomes counter-cultural – often drawing on older counter-cultural traditions such as romanticism, anarchism or utopian socialism. It includes:

- *social ecology*, based largely on anarchist principles as interpreted particularly in the work of Murray Bookchin (e.g. 1990);
- *eco-socialism*, which is libertarian, decentralist and communalist in principle and a brand of socialism ultimately opposed to the State; and
- *deep ecology*, which focuses on fundamental changes in attitudes and values towards nature (Devall and Sessions, 1985), bringing societies everywhere to conform to ecological principles (for instance the principle of 'carrying capacity', which implies limits to population and economic growth).

Deep ecology's approach is 'eco-' or 'bio-'centric: that is, focused on non-human nature and the whole biosphere, which is said to have its own, intrinsic, value rather than the value conferred simply by humans. Eco-socialism, by contrast, shares with reformist environmentalism an anthropocentric stance. This regards humans as the ultimate source of all value and is prepared, if it comes to a crunch, to elevate human interest above that of animals and plants. Social ecology claims to transcend both anthropocentrism and biocentrism.

For years, many environmentalists (e.g. Eckersley, 1992; Milbrath 1989; Porritt, 1984) have dismissed socialism as being equally culpable with capitalism in creating environmental crisis. They have regarded it as part of mainstream culture because of its unashamed anthropocentrism and would baulk at seeing it categorized in Figure 31.1 as engendering a form of radical *environmentalism*. But their objections should be overruled, for socialism itself is more complex that they seem to believe. And eco-socialism derives from particular socialist traditions that in fact have nothing to do with the kind of gung-ho materialism and disregard for nature traditionally associated with the state-centralist, self-styled 'socialist' regimes behind the old

Iron Curtain. Eco-socialism's roots lie in utopian socialism and the Marxism of William Morris, not of Stalin. As such it is clearly counter-cultural, radical and opposed to mainstream values. Though eco-socialists and social ecologists criticize each other, they also have much in common (Pepper, 1993).

Mainstream environmentalism, as represented by the examples in Figure 31.1, is a hybrid – a melange of both radical and reformist approaches. As Dobson (1995) suggests, its proponents and actors often hold radical views (including ecocentrism and opposition to capitalism), but they are also politically pragmatic, recognizing that to make some environmental headway by reform is better than none at all. Hence they may both collude with *and* denounce mainstream politics, business and industry. They will lobby and protest, sometimes undertaking non-violent direct action, but may also become Green Members of Parliament. This ambiguity has underlain much publicized splits between 'realists' and 'fundamentalists' within European Green Parties and virtually every other environmental grouping: indeed Friends of the Earth formed as a radical splinter group from the American Sierra Club. The works of some of mainstream environmentalism's most influential figures (e.g. McKibben, 1990; Porritt, 1984; Schumacher, 1973) particularly reflect influences from both deep ecology and social reformism.

Recent opposition to major road developments in the UK, such as at Twyford Down and Newbury in the south of England, well illustrate these diverse and sometimes contradictory elements in mainstream environmentalism. Tree-dwelling and ecological sabotage were undertaken by radical, counter-cultural groups, but their actions were sometimes augmented by strident middle-class NIMBY activists. Additionally, pressure groups and lobbies were mobilized, enlisting the aid of some Members of Parliament and local politicians from the traditional parties. Such pressure has influenced mainstream political parties into reviewing approaches to road transport, producing reformist measures like road taxes and tolls.

SUSTAINABLE DEVELOPMENT

Sustainable development (SD) is development which does not damage, now, the environmental foundations on which the welfare of future generations might depend. *All* the environmentalisms described above now enthusiastically embrace some version of SD. Since the highly influential Brundtland Report (United Nations, 1987), so does the World Bank, the EU, the World Trade Organization and the US President. Sadly, this does not mean that environmental problems and risks are about to be vanquished, since what different actors imply when they use the term 'sustainable development' varies hugely: SD has almost become a meaningless slogan in the hands of politicians, who rarely define this term which they use so enthusiastically.

Table 31.1 *The ladder of sustainable development*

	Approach to sustainable development	Approach to nature	Geographical focus	Technology	Economic policy instruments	Equity/social justice	Civil society
Ideal model of SD	Radical social change. Production for need not profit. Local self-reliance in a global framework. Development in quality of life.	Promoting/protecting biodiversity, for material and non-material good of all community and for nature's own sake.	Decentralization. Local/regional focus, with federation up from communities, eventually to global networks.	Appropriate/intermediate, democratic. Soft, renewable, energy.	Markets subordinate, community ownership of means of production, economic/social/environmental policy fused by community-led political decisions.	Strong emphasis on inter- and intra-generational equity.	Bottom-up community structures and control. Direct democracy. Confederalism.
Strong SD	Market-based incentives + regulation, to attain environmental standards. Environment in mainstream of policy, whose goal is economic growth ('ecological modernization').	To be managed for market exploitation and social purposes: productive capacity to be maintained/enhanced.	Global markets + concern for local/regional sustainability.	Encouraging 'clean' technologies (e.g. catalytic converters).	Demand, supply and price mechanisms + taxes, fines and incentives. Legal and planning policies. Public spending.	'Trickle down' plus some redistribution. Discounting for inter-generational equity. Local community consultation in policy-making.	Bottom-up initiatives within top-down economic/political framework. Dialogue.
Weak SD	Including environmental impacts in costing development. Economic growth the objective.	A capital asset, valued in money terms and maintained by 'efficient' costing and use.	Global economy, some regulation via international agencies and agreements.	Mainly end-of-pipe solutions.	Demand, supply and price mechanisms, incorporating some environmental indicators. Cost-benefit + environmental impact analyses.	'Trickle-down' + discounting techniques for incorporating inter-generational equity.	Top-down initiatives, within parliamentary democracies.
Very weak SD ('treadmill')	Free-market + privatization + unrestrained technological development, in search of economic growth, will solve environmental problems.	Unlimited exploitation unless obvious environmental risk. Presumption in favour of economic welfare.	Global capitalist economy.	High tech, capital intensive.	Demand, supply and price mechanisms. Conventional accounting.	Limited amount, via 'trickle down' processes.	Limited democracy, dominated by economic power.

Source: Freely adapted from Baker *et al.*, 1997: 8–18.

There are in fact many different forms and degrees of SD, just as there are diverse environmentalisms. These may be represented as a spectrum, or 'ladder', ranging from 'very weak' to the 'ideal model' (ideal, that is, from the viewpoint of radical environmentalism) – see Table 31.1 (and Figure 31.1, which maps these categories on to the different environmentalisms discussed above).

Very weak SD is little more than 'sustainable' capitalism, that is, capitalism which is not so blatantly harmful to the resource base and environment on which it ultimately depends that it destroys itself, at least in the short run. It is the 'treadmill' of economic growth, capital accumulation and reinvestment for more growth which is now turning the world into a global marketplace. Its advocates (e.g. Simon, 1981) maintain that as they get materially wealthier people are more disposed to limit their family size ('overpopulation' thus recedes). They also acquire 'post-materialist' values, which include concern for the environment, and this translates into green and ethical consumerism. Furthermore the operation of laws of demand, supply and price ensures that as resources became scarce they are more valued, and are therefore conserved or replaced by satisfactory substitutes. And maximum privatization of the commons would ensure that people look after them – on grounds that what is unowned is unvalued.

However, intra- and inter-generational *social justice* is increasingly recognized as a vital constituent of SD, and since social justice is not a feature of unmoderated capitalism, most environmentalisms except the free-market variety explicitly reject very weak SD.

By contrast, the ideal model of SD really amounts to a new sort of society, based on self-sustainable, decentralized and directly democratic communities. The social ecology version of this is called 'confederal municipalism' (Fotopoulos, 1997). Both deep ecology (Callenbach, 1978) and eco-socialism (Coleman and O'Sullivan, 1990) share similar ideal, 'utopian' visions of SD – albeit based on different principles. While deep ecology is ecocentric, eco-socialism is anthopocentric and humanist. The ideal model is the only one to abandon the global market economy, in favour of localism with systems of networking to achieve global objectives. It also rejects conventional economic growth in favour of 'adequate' (community-defined) material standards coupled with growth in general welfare for all (including provision of pleasing environments that contribute to social and spiritual satisfaction).

Between these two models are 'weak' and 'strong' versions of SD, both still embracing degrees of material economic growth and market economics. They would, however, intervene in the market at varying levels, with financial incentives and penalties coupled with regulations, to induce sustainable behaviour. Strong SD is enshrined in the European Union's Fifth Environmental Action Programme, which embraces an 'ecological modernization' approach. This seeks to encourage clean technologies as a way to business profitability, to legislate for internalizing pollution costs via the 'polluter pays principle', and to curb overexuberant risk-taking via the conservative precautionary principle.

A major distinguishing feature between different types of SD is the extent to which they would allow trade-offs between human and natural 'capital'. Some economists, like Wilfred Beckerman (1994), consider it justifiable and feasible to sacrifice any amount of 'natural' environment to development, provided that there is a substantial gain in human welfare. This is very weak SD (indeed Beckerman believes that the whole concept of SD is invalid). With their 'Earth First' principles, however, deep ecologists would allow little trade-off, in the ideal model of SD.

It is therefore clear that the recent rise of the concept of SD has done nothing to clarify and focus environmentalism into a discrete and unambiguous set of nostrums.

MODERNITY AND POST-MODERNITY

The above account, generalized as it is, none the less indicates the political-economic diversity – some would say incoherence – of mainstream environmentalism today. Enough has been said to suggest that environmentalism contains many cross-currents and potentially contradictory factions. However, this state may be no more nor less than a reflection of the society of which environmentalism is born, caught between the mood of modernity which has apparently served it well for some centuries and the condition of post-modernity which some say we are now entering.

Table 31.2 is an attempt to summarize and compare some features of modernity and post-modernity. This table should be treated with caution, as it is a convenience; illustrative of tendencies but masking complexities of the academic and cultural debates about these 'conditions' in Western society. Indeed the very process of tabulation in itself suggests a clear break between them when the reality is more blurred. None the less it may be instructive to try to situate aspects of environmentalism, as represented in Figure 31.1, in the context of Table 31.2, to see where environmentalism stands in relation to the post-modern turn in thought.

Given that environmentalism feeds from, and on, both counter-culturalism and elements of mainstream politics and economics (Figure 31.1), it is likely that it will show affinities with both modernity and post-modernity. The political-economic mainstream in Western society (right-hand side of Figure 31.1) is underwritten by a conventional wisdom, a set of values, that still could be described as modernist in outlook: counter-culturalism (left-hand side), however, by definition challenges many assumptions and suppositions of the mainstream culture. However, the taxonomy of Figure 31.1 does not lend itself to a simple dichotomy between modernity on the right-hand side and post-modernity on the left.

Table 31.2 *A comparative summary of some characteristics of modernity and post-modernity.*

Modernity	Post-modernity
1) Support for universal principles which should apply to everyone. Judgemental about absence of principles.	1) Rejection of universal principles. Relativism, diversity, difference, plurality are celebrated. Reality is a variety of 'discourses', none of which should be judged. Hence moral relativism and respect for 'otherness'. For some, hedonism, randomness and freedom are sufficient 'principles' for living.
2) Search for overarching explanations (of society) and reasons for social change. This based on identifying underlying social/political/economic explanatory structures in society (e.g. in Marxism, economic reductionism, or revealing social relationships behind capitalism's commodity fetishism) or psychological characteristics in the make-up of people. Hence essentialism: getting below the surface to what's really going on.	2) Critical questioning of overarching explanations of society: need to relate explanations to context within which they are formulated. Search for objective truths and theories seen as a prelude for planning and arranging other people's lives. This produces tyranny, war and obliteration of cultures. There is no essential, universal, natural condition, and all truths are context-bound and complex. 'The other' is impenetrable, so there can be no search for underlying 'reality'. Surface and style, superficiality, ephemera and consumerism are celebrated.
3) Faith in continuous material 'progress', based on notions of transcendent causes and history with meaning and continuity. Hence defence of rational forms of social organization (organized capitalism, or socialism, and industrialism and planning). Conscious construction of 'better' social futures (utopianism).	3) Scepticism about possibility (and benefits) of continuous material 'progress'. History seen as discontinuous (reflected in the eclectic plundering of history in post-modern architecture). Questioning of '-isms', and any attempts at rational organization of society. Capitalism today seen as decentralized, 'flexible' and disorganized and seeking to externalize risks associated with it to wider society. Utopias criticized for their totalizing tendencies.
4) Recognizing and discovering natural laws (e.g. carrying capacity, natural limits). Manipulating them via technology and scientific management of nature is the route to such progress, avoiding environmental disaster (e.g. ecological modernization).	4) Rejects idea of objective (externally existing) natural limits and laws. High technology has produced negative results.
5) Faith and trust in science and scientific, rational, valuation of nature.	5) Cynicism/mistrust about scientific, rational valuation of nature.
6) Is an objective nature. Society and nature objectively knowable. Determinacy in science. Science (including rationality, dualistic thinking) atop a hierarchy of knowledge.	6) Focus not on search for a 'true', authentic nature but on ways of talking about the world. Nature is culturally and individually constructed: a 'text' to be infinitely interpreted in different discourses. Subjectivism (no subject-object distinction), indeterminacy in science (e.g. chaos theory). Questioning of hierarchies of knowledge: non-scientific, non-rational valuations of nature can be as valid as other valuations. Desire to recapture pre-modern ways of relating to nature (holism, organicism, spiritual) and a deep sense of unity with it.
7) Faith in traditional universalist politics, and traditional groupings and alliances as agencies of social change.	7) Rejects traditional class politics in favour of identity politics. Questions traditional authority (e.g. the State). Embraces cultural relativism and localized struggles. (Localities are 'interpretive communities'). Hence social conflict is in the cultural, not political domain: 'political' problems are different for different political groups.

Sources: Atkinson, 1991; Cosgrove, 1990; Eagleton, 1996; Harvey, 1990.

The inclusion of eco-socialism in the proactive, radical, counter-cultural stream immediately complicates matters, for socialism traditionally embraces modernity's search for overarching explanations of social phenomena and places faith in the 'Enlightenment project'. This project represents the aspirations of the modern period, and is based on the idea that it is legitimate to manipulate nature, through science, for the universal material benefit of humankind.

Eco-socialism, then, inclines towards modernity. This, even though its proponents wish to reconstruct Marxism by moderating and downplaying its anthropocentric element, which saw liberation for humankind through taming nature; and even though they wish to emphasize neglected parts of Marx's writings that spoke of a more subtle, interactive relationship between society and nature that did not imply exploitation and destruction of the latter (see, for instance, Dickens 1992). So eco-socialism has little affinity with the condition of post-modernity, regarding it, in fact, as merely a manifestation of late capitalism rather than any new mood of real opposition to the cultural values of the prevailing economic system. As social ecology's principal spokesman, Murray Bookchin (1995) also vigorously repudiates post-modern 'nihilism' and anti-humanism in the environmental movement (though he also attacks any totalitarian tendencies in eco-Marxism).

Universalism and utopianizing

Eco-socialist and social ecology influences apart, there are other apparently modernist currents detectable in mainstream environmentalism. Prominent among them is support for a form of universalism resting on a perceived need for *all* economies, societies and individuals, *all* multinational companies and trading blocs, to observe and live by ecological principles. These principles include observing limits to growth and other sustainability constraints, such as the need for inter- and intra-generational justice or the precautionary principle. They would form the basis of any ecological utopia, and there is indeed a strong tradition of utopianizing in radical environmentalism. It appears not only in eco-socialism – Morris's *News from Nowhere* (1890) is generally recognized as a partly ecological vision – but also in deep ecology (Callenbach's *Ecotopia*) and social ecology, in the 'confederal municipalism' of Bookchin and Fotopoulos. (Ironically, though, some environmentalists – such as Garret Hardin or the Ehrlichs – maintain that the scale and imminence of environmental crises are such that for us to survive we must all sacrifice some other widely held principles, like freedom to choose family size. They still universalize, but in a dystopian way.)

However, all this sits uneasily with another, equally strong, mood in environmentalism; one that vigorously defends local cultural traditions and inclinations, and by implication, *many*, diverse utopias. This mood resembles the post-modernist advocacy of cultural (and perhaps moral) relativism, of the desirability of economic and social diversity, and of respect for 'otherness' – an advocacy which, as Table 31.2 points out, would be suspicious of the total solutions implied by ecotopianizing, because they smack of totalitarianism. Enviromentalism's post-modern style emphasis on difference and discourse feeds into the cynicism about 'traditional' doctrinaire politics and '-isms', that is so typical of green politics. It is expressed, too, in the localism of green political economy. Indeed some environmentalists (e.g. Atkinson, 1991) consider that post-modernity is the proper condition of green politics and that if any principle is required for green living, that 'principle' should be hedonism alone.

Again it should be stressed that any ambiguities here do not simply reflect a mainstream environmentalism feeding from two different but internally coherent strands that incline towards modernity on the one hand and post-modernity on the other. Ambiguities occur within subcategories in Figure 31.1, that is *within* the same branches of environmentalism. So, for instance, deep ecology fiercely proselytizes notions of limits to growth as globally applicable – as universals. But equally, in bioregionalism (a form of localized socio-political organization based on natural boundaries), it defends the idea that local and regional communities should be free to go their own way economically, socially and politically. Consequently deep ecologists may find it difficult to answer awkward questions about, for example, what to do should a particular 'ecotopian' local community, following its own democratic will, decide to flout some universally desirable sustainability principle. What if they decided that rampant consumerism, for instance, was acceptable in their bioregion?

Of course this is an old problem for any radical movement advocating universal principles (for instance human rights) but also championing self-determination. Eco-socialists claim to resolve it by welcoming all differences 'except where they threaten the equal rights of others to liberty of expression and self-respect', so that equally imposed political rights, respect and access to resources are seen as prerequisites for diversity to flourish (Red-Green Study Group, 1995). This still begs the uncomfortable question of who might judge and police any breaches of equal rights, and whether that policing amounts to an imposition of the values of one culture/group on to another.

Objectivism and subjectivism

These questions spill over into other areas of environmentalism where modernist and post-modernist tendencies might be seen to coexist in tension. For instance, there is a strong claim in both mainstream and radical environmentalism (such as social ecology) that the science on which claims of impending environmental crisis are based, the science of ecology, presents objectively true 'facts' about the state of the world, and about 'natural laws' (the principles by which all should live). The modernist implication here (see Table 31.2) is that science (ecology) offers us an objective, rational evaluation of our relationship to nature, and we should rationally act in accordance with it.

Counterpoised to this, however, is widespread mistrust within environmentalism of any rational management approach, based on 'objective' scientific appraisal. For this lends itself to technocentrism and therefore faith in scientific and technical fixes alone.

Indeed environmentalists, radical and mainstream, often align themselves with elements of post-modernity when they contemplate concepts like rationalism and objectivity. For instance, in Capra's interpretation of the science of the Enlightenment period this science stands accused of setting up a false dichotomy; one between humans as 'subjects', and nature as an object. Like others (Merchant, 1982), Capra insists that this rationalist Enlightenment way of thinking about humans and nature opened up a false separation between them, whereby it became easy for the former to manipulate, exploit and dominate the latter. Herein, they say, lie the seeds of our present environmental predicament: failure to identify with nature, because we see it as external to us, encourages our destructive attitudes and actions.

A common mainstream environmentalist and deep ecology reaction to this supposed Enlightenment mindset evokes post-modernity. It embraces subjectivism (see Table 31.2), in the form of mysticism, romanticism, and the controversial interpretations by Capra and others of twentieth-century scientific inquiry – dealing with quantum theory, relativity, chaos, indeterminacy, Gaia theory, co-evolution and the like. Environmentalists often read off from all these the message that our true relation to nature is intimate. It is *part* of us, the subject, and we and it are a unity. To harm it is to harm ourselves. Cosgrove (1990) considers that this post-modern conception of nature resurrects certain pre-modern ideas – for instance, of the Earth as an organism and of ourselves as a mirror of the larger cosmos.

The Capra-style interpretations of the findings of twentieth-century science, like the teachings of Eastern mysticism, essentially make nature's qualities a function of human perceptions of, and intentions towards, it. Nature is not to be objectively regarded and defined; its nature is contextual (Table 31.1). Capra (1982) and Zukav (1980) argue, for instance, that light cannot be objectively defined. According to the way that we decide to observe and measure it, it consists of particles, or it consists of waves. Similarly all properties of nature are observer-dependent: indeed without us nature would *have* no properties, it would not exist – and without nature we would not exist.

This is a deeply subjectivist position, which, however, creates further tensions in environmentalist thinking, since it sits uneasily alongside another cornerstone of ecocentrism. This is the idea of nature's *intrinsic* value: that is, value residing in nature of itself, whether humans are there to value it or not. The intrinsic value philosophy underwrites deep ecology's ethical position, and also the mainstream environmentalist approach to SD. It is the reason why, in the ideal model of SD, it is not permissible to substitute human welfare for natural capital. However, intrinsic value is clearly objectively existing value. And as we have just discussed, such a concept is valid in modernist perspectives but questionable in post-modernity, with its penchant for subjectivism. Again, environmentalism seems to face both ways.

Progress and technological ambiguities

Radical and mainstream environmentalism also reflect the post-modern turn when they are sceptical about the fruits of Enlightenment 'progress', and the high science and high technology by which this progress has been attained. Environmentalists often attack large-scale modern industrialism, technological complexity and materialism in the form of consumerism, as the causes of, rather than the solution to, impending environmental crisis. So much is this deep ecology's position that Merchant (1992) and Bookchin (1995) have characterized the movement as 'primitivist', i.e. romanticizing the past and rural Arcadian images of simple but innocent lifestyles in subjugation to nature. 'Traditional societies' and 'indigenous' aboriginal communities are idealized (for instance by Goldsmith, 1992). They are championed commercially by the Body Shop, itself perhaps a living environmentalist contradiction, since it is part of consumer society.

Environmentalism also takes other apparently contradictory stances. There are those who maintain that they want 'progress', marked by unlimited growth in human 'wealth'. Here, they seem to accept a fundamental Enlightenment principle. But they do question the way that it has been interpreted. For they challenge the idea that a technologically complex, industrially dominated centralized and large-scale society, led by a technocracy, does actually constitute 'progress'. E.F. Schumacher (1973) considered that such a society is *regressive* and he argued for a different version of 'progress'. He inspired much contemporary green economics, which call for a reappraisal of what constitutes 'wealth'. If wealth is construed generally as *welfare* there are theoretically no limits to growth, because welfare includes many non-material things. These contribute to *quality of life* (a key concept), and they range from satisfying work to good and just human relationships, and spiritual fulfilment in the presence of nature.

So, in this way environmentalists might simultaneously embrace both modernist and post-modernist perspectives, as they also do when they challenge notions of technology as progress. Deep scepticism towards high technology is manifest in long-standing opposition to nuclear power, green revolution agriculture, and genetic engineering. However, coexisting with this is a very upbeat appraisal of the potential of 'alternative', 'intermediate', 'soft' and 'radical' technologies, for instance for conserving and generating

457

energy. Some of these technologies are quite complex. Although most are amenable to grassroots democratic control, they can also be commandeered by the much vilified multinational corporations. Much the same can be said of different aspects of information technology, and it seems true to say that mainstream and radical environmentalism is uncertain as to whether information technology, or even technology in general, constitutes friend or foe.

It would be possible to find more examples of apparently ambiguous strands within environmentalisms. However, enough has been said to demonstrate that mainstream environmentalism as well as deep, and possibly social, ecology, all display affinities and correspondences with *both* modernity and post-modernity. Does this mean that environmentalism is uncomfortably at odds with itself, or is it perhaps effecting some kind of a satisfactory compromise or reconciliation between the two? And are these inconsistencies and ambiguities themselves symptomatic of a post-modern condition?

CONCLUSION

Environmental campaigners are often positive about their eclecticism, regarding diversity, and rejection of many of the firm values and perspectives of modernity, as a strength. Diversity makes for wide appeal, and to reject modernity is not, arguably, to be totally negative but to embrace a 'new' paradigm, more appropriate for the twenty-first century. This paradigm could appeal to many who do not believe that traditional political struggles are still relevant. And the fact that there are so many environmentalisms might seem to testify to the success of environmentalism's central ideas. As Figure 31.1 suggests, environmentalism has permeated mainstream political-economic culture, and the counter-culture, as well as staking out some ground which can be claimed as mainstream environmentalism's own.

For those whose traditional political values still reside in modernity, however, any post-modern affinities carry worrying implications. Not least among these is that ideological incoherence or indeterminacy could constitute a fatal strategic weakness, since it would probably be a source of internal disputes, and make for ambiguous and confusing messages to the wider public.

From a modernist, Marxist, perspective, Eagleton (1996) presents a very negative view of the roots of post-modernity. He says they lie in the defeat of those who do not like capitalism, but no longer see any realistic prospects of its removal – they are too young to remember a mass radical politics. This leads them, says Eagleton, to an interest in anything marginal and minority, seen as good in itself, to the demonization of the very ideas of system, consensus and organization and to commitment to tolerant relativism. Hence an initially radical impulse is shifted from the goal of transforming mainstream society and becomes merely a desire to subvert it. A fresh style of Left ideology arises: that of 'libertarian pessimism', which dreams of liberation but scorns the notion that it can ever be achieved, and does not demand rigorous, determinate knowledge but is satisfied to take refuge in subjectivism and pseudo-mystification. Given, says Eagleton, the short supply of purposive political action nowadays; given a uniformly oppressive regime where everything is regulated; given lack of real freedom and political influence over our own lives, we would expect political radicalism to be transmuted into a loss of faith in social progress, a desire for pleasure, randomness and freedom, and an inward focus on psychoanalysis, inner being and the body (the only realms where we still seem to have considerable control).

It may be tempting also to interpret environmental movements largely in this dismissive light, and the post-modern characterizations (or caricatures?) offered by Eagleton do indeed resonate with many publically prominent environmentalist sentiments and attitudes. However, as emphasized above, environmentalism is complex: it may be in part a negative reaction to modernity, but it also has its own very positive and universalist agenda, which, in stronger versions of SD, by no means forsakes key aspects of the Enlightenment project. As Peter Christoff (1996) says, the ecological critique as a whole is not necessarily anti-modern, since it clearly accepts and uses the tools of the modern period (think of the success with which Greenpeace has manipulated the media for its ends). But it challenges the almost universal process of 'modernization', which increasingly distances people from local culture and traditions, and from locality, place and their ties to the land, making them instead global citizens participating in a global market – a process which sociologist Anthony Giddens calls 'disembedding'. While there are some benfits to this, radical environmentalists also see disadvantages and they may seek at least partially to 're-embed' societies in local places and communities, and in nature. This does not, says Christoff, mean that they seek post-modernism: rather, they propose a range of 'alternative ecological modernities'. As such, radical environmentalism could still represent a most potent force for necessary change in Western society; a passage towards continuing 'progress', but in a post-material sense.

SUMMARY

- Environmentalism is a wide-ranging, eclectic and diverse movement, influenced by both social reformist and radical political traditions.
- Reformist influences come mainly from liberal and social democratic traditions: radicalism comes from romanticism, anarchism and utopian socialism.

- 'Sustainable development' is a wide-ranging concept: 'weaker' versions correspond to reformist environmentalism, while 'stronger' versions are radical and reject the global market.
- Because of these diverse roots and positions, environmentalism shows affinities with elements of both modernity and post-modernity.
- There are particular tensions between localism and universalism, objectivism and subjectivism, and in attitudes to technology and the concept of progress.
- We may be tempted to interpret much environmentalism as a negative reaction against the worst features of modernity, but it could equally be seen as a search for more positive 'alternative modernities'.

FURTHER READING

Coates, P. (1998) *Nature: Western Attitudes Since Ancient Times*. Cambridge: Polity Press. A very readable introductory volume reviewing the developments in thinking about nature and environment in Western society since Greek and Roman times. It also reviews contemporary radical environmentalism.

Doyle, T. and McEachern, D. (1998) *Environment and Politics*. London: Routledge. A comprehensive and basic book which clearly and concisely introduces environmental thinking in political theory, environmental movements, political parties, business and institutions.

Martell, L. (1994) *Ecology and Society: An Introduction*. Cambridge: Polity Press. A most accessible text reviewing environmentalism's implications for social issues and social organization, also covering philosophical issues, political ideologies and social theory.

Pepper, D. (1996) *Modern Environmentalism: An Introduction*. London: Routledge. A comprehensive review of the basic issues in environmentalism, together with some discussion of the history of environmental thought since medieval times and the roles of modern and post-modern science.

REFERENCES

Anderson, T. and Leal, D. (1991) *Free Market Environmentalism*. San Francisco: Pacific Research Institute for Public Policy.

Atkinson, A. (1991) *Principles of Political Ecology*. London: Belhaven.

Baker, S., Kousis, M., Richardson, D. and Young, S. (1997) 'Introduction: The Theory and Practice of Sustainable Development in EU Perspective', introduction to *The*

Politics of Sustainable Development: Theory, Policy and Practice within the European Union. London: Routledge, pp. 1–42.

Beck, U. (1995) *Ecological Politics in an Age of Risk*. Cambridge: Polity Press.

Beckerman, W. (1994) 'Sustainable Development: Is It a Useful Concept?' *Environmental Values*, **3**(3): 191–209.

Bookchin, M. (1990) *Remaking Society*. Montreal: Black Rose Books.

Bookchin, M. (1995) *Re-enchanting Humanity: A Defense of the Human Spirit against Anti-humanism, Misanthropy, Mysticism and Primitivism*. London: Cassell.

Bramwell, A. (1989) *Ecology in the Twentieth Century: a History*. London: Yale University Press.

Callenbach, E. (1978) *Ecotopia*. London: Pluto Press.

Capra, F. (1982) *The Turning Point*. London: Wildwood House.

Christoff, P. (1996) 'Ecological Modernisation: Ecological Modernities', *Environmental Politics*, **5**(3): 476–500.

Coleman, S. and O'Sullivan, P. (1990) *William Morris and News from Nowhere: a Vision for Our Time*. Bideford: Green Books.

Cosgrove, D. (1990) 'Environmental Thought and Action: Pre-modern and Postmodern', *Transactions of the Institute of British Geographers*, **15**(3): 344–58.

Devall, W. and Sessions, G. (1985) *Deep Ecology: Living as if Nature Mattered*. Salt Lake City: Gibbs M Smith.

Dickens, P. (1992) *Society and Nature: Towards a Green Social Theory*. Hemel Hempstead: Harvester Wheatsheaf.

Dobson, A. (1995) *Green Political Thought*. London: Unwin Hyman.

Eagleton, T. (1996) *The Illusions of Postmodernism*. Oxford: Blackwell.

Eckersley, R. (1992) *Environmentalism and Political Theory: Towards an Ecocentric Approach*. London: University College London Press.

Fotopoulos, T. (1997) *Towards an Inclusive Democracy: The Crisis of the Growth Economy and the Need for a New Liberatory Project*. London: Cassell.

Goldsmith, E. (1992) *The Way: An Ecological World View*. London: Rider.

Harvey, D. (1990) *The Condition of Postmodernity*. Cambridge: Polity Press.

Martell, L. (1994) *Ecology and Society: An Introduction*. Cambridge: Polity Press.

McKibben, W. (1990) *The End of Nature*. Harmondsworth: Penguin.

Merchant, C. (1982) *The Death of Nature: Women, Ecology and the Scientific Revolution*. London: Wildwood House.

Merchant, C. (1992) *Radical Ecology: The Search for a Livable World*. New York: Routledge.

Milbrath, L. (1989) *Envisioning a Sustainable Society*. New York: SUNY Press.

Morris, William (1890) *News From Nowhere*. London: Routledge.

O'Riordan, T. (1989) 'The Challenge for Environmentalism', in R. Peet and N. Thrift (eds) *New Models in Geography*. London: Unwin Hyman, pp. 77–102.

Pearce, D., Markandya, A. and Barbier, E. (1989) *Blueprint for a Green Economy*. London: Earthscan.

Pepper, D. (1993) *Eco-socialism: From Deep Ecology to Social Justice*. London: Routledge.

Pepper, D. (1996) *Modern Environmentalism: An Introduction*. London: Routledge.

Porritt, J. (1984) *Seeing Green*. Oxford: Blackwell.

Red-Green Study Group (1995) *What on Earth is to Be Done? A Red-Green Dialogue*. Manchester: The Red-Green Study Group.

Rowell, A. (1996) *Green Backlash: Global Subversion of the Environment Movement*. London: Routledge.

Schumacher, E.F. (1973) *Small is Beautiful: Economics as if People Really Mattered*. London: Abacus.

Simon, J. (1981) *The Ultimate Resource*. Oxford: Martin Robertson.

United Nations (1987) World Commission on Environment and Development, *Our Common Future* (The Brundtland Report). Oxford: Oxford University Press.

Zukav, G. (1980) *The Dancing Wu Li Masters: An Overview of the New Physics*. London: Fontana.

Chapter 32

Social movements

Abigail Halcli

INTRODUCTION

Social movements are a distinct form of collective action in contemporary societies. Movements such as organized labour, women's liberation and Islamic fundamentalism have inspired participants, challenged authorities and sometimes changed societies in dramatic ways. At least since the mid-nineteenth century, social scientists have been interested in explaining the conditions that give rise to and the consequences of transitory phenomena such as crowds, panics, mobs and revolutions. It is only more recently that analysts turned their attention to the study of collective action that is enduring, organized and involves an effort to promote or resist social change. In particular, the surge of movement activity across Western Europe and North America in the 1960s, brought on by the civil rights movement, student mobilizations and anti-war protests, led to a flourishing of social movement theory. As observers, and sometimes as participants in these movements, new generations of social analysts changed the ways that movement participants and activities were understood. Social movements, therefore, are a good example of how theory can effectively respond to social development.

A wide range of social and political activities can be considered under the banner 'social movements'. A great deal of scholarly attention has been paid to progressive and international movements such as the environmental, women's and peace movements. Others have looked at conservative or reactionary mobilizations such as the New Christian Right and militia movements in the USA, and neo-Fascist and anti-immigration movements in Europe. Still others have examined the activities of locally based citizen initiatives that mobilize around a single issue such as opposition to the construction of a nuclear power plant or efforts to prevent shops from selling pornographic materials. These movements differ widely in terms of goals and ideological positions, but what links them is that they represent a style of political engagement distinct from that typical of the institutionalized realm of political parties and other formalized systems of representation.

While recognizing the unique features of contemporary social movements, it is also important to point out that the line between conventional politics and movements is in fact quite blurred. Many social movements do remain resolutely independent from the political establishment, and use confrontational and disruptive activities, such as demonstrations, civil disobedience, encampments and 'street theatre' to promote their goals. Nevertheless, social movements may also participate in a range of 'conventional' behaviours such as lobbying, letter-writing and fund-raising in their efforts to institutionalize particular policies or practices. In fact, over the last two decades some European nations have even seen the formation of movement parties, including regional, tax-revolt, and ecology or Green parties, that operate within the realm of conventional party politics while maintaining strong organizational links to movement groups.

In this chapter I trace the development of social movement theory over the last several decades. The three major approaches to social movement theorizing – classical social movement theory, resource mobilization theory, and new social movement theory – are discussed in terms of their historical development, theoretical assumptions and research agendas. Finally, I discuss the current trend towards synthesis in social movement theory, in which cultural, historical and political economic approaches are combined.

CLASSICAL SOCIAL MOVEMENT THEORY

Early efforts to theorize social movements (roughly 1920 to 1970) can be grouped under the heading of classical social movement theory. Before discussing some of the approaches typical of this school of thought, it is useful to situate classical social movement theory in light of some of the wider intellectual and historical trends which shaped its development. For one, a turn towards micro social theorizing was under way in which the individual became the focal point of analysis. Many had turned against grand narratives of social change in terms of rationalization or changes in the mode of production. As a result, research during this period tended to focus on the social psychological determinants of individual participation in social movements. In addition, the dramatic geopolitical conflicts characterizing the Second World War and the post-war period were reflected in the theorizing of the time. Nazism and Stalinism, as well as McCarthyism, race riots and lynchings in the USA, led many analysts to be deeply concerned about mobilizations of individuals pursuing what were seen as anti-democratic goals. These conditions contributed to a negative perception of movement behaviour in general and a view of activists as irrational (Garner and Tenuto, 1997: 8–9).

The *collective behaviour approach* represents an early effort to explain the origins of collective action such as crowds, panics and mass movements. Collective behaviour was thought to be distinct from 'normal' social behaviour in that it was spontaneous, unorganized and occurred outside institutionalized channels. Some viewed collective behaviour as resulting primarily from aroused and extreme emotional states, such as those likely to emerge at political rallies or religious revivals, which distorted people's abilities to think critically and increased their 'suggestibility' (Blumer, 1946; Park and Burgess, 1921). Other proponents of this approach conceived of collective behaviour more as an adaptive response to unstructured and undefined situations (Lang and Lang, 1961; Turner and Killian, 1957). From this perspective, collective behaviour was likely to emerge in the event of some form of cultural or structural breakdown as people collectively engaged in problem-solving behaviours as they struggled to make sense of ambiguous situations.

Still other classical social movement theorists attempted to link movement participation to large-scale structural changes occurring in modern societies. The *mass society approach*, for example, focused attention on how rapid modernization and the accompanying changes in social organization, norms, and traditional forms of social control led to anomic urban environments in which individuals experienced anxiety, frustration and social dislocation (Kornhauser, 1959). Such conditions were thought to make individuals more susceptible to participation in social movements, which were viewed as irrational and extremist responses to changing social conditions. Like mass society theory, the *relative deprivation approach* highlighted the negative outcomes of rapid social change on individuals. A variety of factors, including socio-economic changes, urbanization, political modernization and increased exposure to education and mass media, were put forward as explanations for changes in people's expectations. Rising expectations could lead individuals to perceive that they were deprived in relation to other social groups. This in turn might lead to feelings of anger and frustration, which could find an outlet in participation in social movements (see, for example, Gurr, 1970; Huntington, 1968). As with the collective behaviour approach, these theories ultimately viewed movement participation as an emotional and often irrational response to some type of social strain. As a result, their explanations focused primarily on the emergent phases of collective behaviour and did little to account for the organizational bases of movements or their potential links to larger political movements.

A number of later approaches in this tradition provided a bridge between these early efforts to theorize collective behaviour and social movements and the structural models which were to come (see, for example, Smelser, 1962). For instance, proponents of the *status politics/symbolic politics* approach viewed extreme-right wing, backlash and moral reform movements as attempts by declining groups to preserve their social status and privileges against a variety of real or imagined threats (Bell, 1964). Gusfield (1963), for example, linked the rise of the American temperance movement (the movement to discourage alcohol consumption) to a number of macro level changes that challenged the way of life of certain groups. In particular, he claimed that in the early part of this century temperance had became symbolic of a small-town, Protestant and middle-class lifestyle that was being threatened by urbanization, immigration and Catholicism. He argued that participants in moral reform movements that organized around temperance and other issues such as gambling and birth control, were more concerned with gaining public affirmation of the superiority of their norms and values, and not so much with putting an end to the actual 'deviant' behaviours. Gusfield's focus on the 'strain' caused by status threats links him to classical social movement theory, but at the same time this work pointed to important issues for future research on social movements – particularly the significance of cultural conflicts for the emergence of collective action and the symbolic potential of numerous social issues.

In general, classical social movement theory has been criticized for its emphasis on the transitory nature of collective action and for the underlying assumption that participation in movements is irrational behaviour. As we will see in the following sections, new generations of social movement theorists challenged this perspective by focusing attention on collective action which occurs in organized movements with specific goals and strategies for social influence.

THE RESOURCE MOBILIZATION APPROACH

By the 1970s resource mobilization theory had become the dominant approach to the study of social movements in the USA. In part, its development was a reflection of a wider shift in the social sciences from a focus on individual level explanations to a focus on social structures (Garner and Tenuto, 1997: 20). In addition, political events such as the rise of the civil rights, peace and decolonization movements around the world led to a view of movement participation as a legitimate and rational form of political expression with the goal of reforming or transforming institutions.

In an effort to overcome the normative components of the collective behaviour approach, resource mobilization theorists started with the assumption that social movements should be viewed as an extension of institutionalized political behaviour. The focus of research became the *social movement organization* and the efforts of organizational leaders to mobilize a variety of tangible and intangible resources, including participants, funds, media attention, favourable public opinion and élite support. Organization leaders were seen as strategically and rationally planning their actions in order to achieve their goals. This focus on the rationality of movement behaviour was an important corrective to the classical social movement theory assumption that strain or grievances led to collective action. Rather, grievances were viewed as a relatively constant feature of society, deriving from institutionalized power relations. The key determinants of collective action were therefore the availability of resources, the effectiveness of organizational structures, and the constraints and opportunities provided by the larger environment.

However, some early efforts to integrate the notion of rational actors into social movement theory were criticized for their emphasis on self-interest as the motivating factor for movement participation. It was thought that individuals, engaging in cost-benefit analysis, would choose to participate in collective action to achieve goals that could not be achieved as efficiently by other means. Other formulations have provided a more complicated understanding of participation by arguing that 'self-interest' is itself a collective process, and that values, solidarity and feelings of responsibility to the group also motivate individual participation (Fireman and Gamson, 1979; Klandermans, 1984).

In a variant of the resource mobilization approach, proponents of the *organizational-entrepreneurial model* argued that professional social movement organizations were the key form of collective action in the US context (McCarthy and Zald, 1973, 1977). Professional movement organizations, such as the National Association for the Advancement of Colored People and the National Abortion Rights Action League, have a full-time paid leadership cadre that runs the movement organization, defines grievances for its 'beneficiary constituents', and engages in largely institutionalized social change activities on their behalf. They attain their support and resources from 'conscience constituents' who do not benefit directly from the achievement of organizational goals. Other social movement theorists, however, have questioned the strategic usefulness of formal organizations for movement maintenance and success. In their study of poor people's movements, Piven and Cloward (1977) argued that the bureaucratic organizations that emerged to advance these movements actually served to weaken them by demobilizing mass defiance and channelling activists into electoral politics. By discouraging more disruptive and confrontational actions, movement organizations were thought to deny activists their main source of political influence. Still other researchers have found that formal organizations can actually be useful in mobilizing mass defiance (Gamson, 1975; Jenkins, 1984).

Another variant of the resource mobilization approach, *the political process model*, was developed by movement researchers who wanted to move beyond a narrow focus on the internal life of movement organizations and to examine how political environments condition collective action. In contrast to the pluralist understanding of politics, the proponents of the political process model claimed that not all social groups have the same type of low-cost access to political institutions; in fact, they could be divided between polity members and challengers (Tilly, 1978). Researchers using this approach highlighted how political opportunity structures, including political system variables, dynamics between movements and counter-movements, relationships with élites, political cultures and crises can create both opportunities and constraints for challengers (see, for example, Jenkins and Perrow, 1977; Kitschelt, 1986).

Resource mobilization theory has been utilized in the study of the women's movement (Freeman, 1975), the civil rights movement (McAdam, 1982; Morris, 1984), the farm workers' movements (Jenkins and Perrow, 1977) as well as many others. For instance, in his study of the civil rights movement Aldon Morris identified the central mobilizing role played by the African-American churches and colleges in supplying indigenous resources including leadership, money, meeting spaces and participants. Also, these pre-existing organizations provided a space where collective attribution could take place, that is, where members could come to define their situations as unjust and subject to change. In addition to these indigenous organizational resources, McAdam (1982) drew attention to the decline of the plantation economy, urbanization of African-Americans, and their emergence as a significant voting bloc in creating the social and political conditions in which black insurgency arose.

Resource mobilization reminds us that much of the work of social movements is done in organizations that must plan and strategize, and that larger social and political environments condition movement origins and success. However, this approach has been criticized for overemphasizing the role of organizations and politics while neglecting the cultural and ideological components of social movements. In addition, by assuming that grievances are ubiquitous in society, resource mobilization theorists have not paid adequate attention to the role of movement organizations and leaders in shaping collective beliefs and translating them into collective action. As we will see in the following sections, other researchers were to put these questions at the centre of their analyses of movements.

THE NEW SOCIAL MOVEMENTS APPROACH

During the 1970s a number of critical theorists in Western Europe turned their attention to the 'new social movements', including the feminist, peace, environmental, gay and lesbian, and student movements, which had emerged since the late 1960s. These analysts came from a very different theoretical tradition from that of American social movement theorists. While resource mobilization theorists were interested in the nuts and bolts of mobilization, the new social movements theorists were concerned with examining movements in terms of broader theories of social change. They argued that the rise of new movements was indicative of people's dissatisfaction with the social and political institutions of advanced capitalist societies. Unlike workers' movements, which were organized along class lines and sought to effect changes through the institutions of the State and political parties, new movements embraced different values, organizational structures, and tactics in their efforts to bring about cultural and political change.

The transformation from industrial to post-industrial society was central to the rise of these new movements. Inglehart and his colleagues for example, argued that economic expansion and the redistributive policies of the welfare state had secured a level of prosperity capable of satisfying basic human needs for most citizens. As a result 'the quest for economic gains has less urgency and in the long run may give way to an emphasis on other types of goals' (Inglehart, 1990; Inglehart and Rabier, 1986: 461–2). Living in a period of relative affluence, people born in the post-war period appear to be less concerned with the materialist issues that were of central importance to earlier generations, such as economic and military security. Rather, post-war cohorts exhibit post-materialist values, and place greater importance on quality of life issues such as environmental protection, increased citizen participation, and individual freedom and self-expression. Generational replacement means that the proportion of post-materialists in the population has steadily increased over the last few decades and therefore their impact on politics has grown.

The rise of new social movements has also been explained as a reaction against the processes of modernization. The continual push for economic expansion and the intrusion of the State into economic, social and family life has led to the 'colonization of the life world' in that more areas of life are subject to state and market regulation (Habermas, 1981). New social movement participants recognize that further state intervention will not alleviate the problems of modern societies because the State has a 'structural incapacity' to control the vast power and resources it has created (Offe, 1985). Rather, new movements attempt to politicize the institutions of civil society, and thus create a new arena for political engagement where they can pursue their goals of autonomy, direct democracy and self-expression free from state regulation.

While new movements are thought to operate under a 'new paradigm' of politics that mixes post-materialist values and libertarian themes, they are also characterized by a self-limiting radicalism (Offe, 1985) in that new movements lack a revolutionary rhetoric typical of older leftist movements. Rather, participants in new movements want to change and reform existing institutions so that they operate more democratically. Still, their anti-institutional orientation means they do not look to the workers' movement for models of organization, but instead seek non-hierarchical, decentralized organizational forms. New movements are also noted for using new methods of political action and unconventional protest tactics that fall outside the traditional structures of politics, such as civil disobedience, direct actions and cultural innovation.

New social movements draw from a new social base, recruiting most of their participants from the 'new middle class' of educated professionals, often employed in the public sector, and who exhibit high levels of support for issues promoted by new movements. Participants are not recruited based on their class position, but rather on the basis of characteristics such as race, ethnicity, sex and sexual orientation, thus placing the construction and politicization of identities at centre stage for new movements. In fact, some argue that social movements should be viewed largely as cultural rather than political phenomena, as much of the work of movements occurs not in organizations but in 'submerged networks' that generally are not visible to the public (Melucci, 1989). It is within these networks that individuals continually construct new meanings and identities that challenge dominant representations of social relations.

New social movement theory is an important addition to our understanding of movements in that it highlights the ideological and socio-cultural aspects of their activities. However, its focus on the emergent phases of movements neglects the internal life of movement organizations and how they maintain themselves over time. In addition, this approach has been criticized for exaggerating the extent to which efforts at cultural change can be separated from more conventional political issues such as legal and distributive equality (Plotke, 1990). 'Cultural' issues such as identity and autonomy have clear political implications as well, and even cultural movements must often engage with the political system to institutionalize their goals. Finally, others argue that conceptualizing new movements as a novel product of advanced capitalist societies detracts from our ability to see linkages between movements over time. Other researchers have identified how a wide variety of movements in the nineteenth to mid-twentieth centuries also displayed many of the characteristics thought to be unique to new social movements, including decentralized and consensual organizational forms and an emphasis on quality of life and identity issues (Calhoun, 1993; D'Anieri, Ernst and Kier, 1990). As we will see in the final section, current research on social movements attempts to address some of these deficiencies.

CURRENT TRENDS IN SOCIAL MOVEMENT THEORY

The upsurge in social movement research in recent decades has spawned a great deal of critical analysis of how we should conceptualize and study contemporary movements. Current theorizing in this area may be seen as an effort to synthesize some of the major themes of the various approaches. As Garner and Tenuto (1997: 46) state: 'Micro and macro approaches, social psychology and organizational studies, and discourse analysis and structural theories all can find room in this emerging synthesis.' In this concluding section I highlight just a few of these trends.

Social movements should be viewed as vehicles for personal, cultural and political change, and movement theories need to account for their dynamics on all these levels. For instance, in my study of the radical AIDS activist organization ACT UP (AIDS Coalition to Unleash Power) I explored the ways in which activists engaged in both unconventional protest actions and more conventional political campaigning in their efforts to influence social and political responses to the AIDS epidemic (Halcli, 1999). ACT UP is perhaps best known for its dramatic and confrontational direct actions that challenged the cultural perceptions of AIDS and the stigmatization of people with AIDS. For example, during demonstrations activists would use 'street theatre' as a tactic, which might include staging a 'die-in' where participants 'die' while others drew chalk outlines around their bodies. Fake blood, coffins and 'red tape' were also used as props to illustrate the effects of the AIDS crisis in a shocking and dramatic manner. In addition, ACT UP served important functions for participants by providing a positive identity around which activists could mobilize. By joining with others who were concerned with the devastating impact of the epidemic, or were themselves living with HIV, ACT UP members also created what they felt was a constructive outlet for their anger about the inadequacy of the response to AIDS. At the same time, ACT UP took a more instrumental approach to fighting the epidemic by trying to affect AIDS funding and legislation through more conventional channels. Some ACT UP participants, for instance, focused on working to influence policy-making and create dialogues with the medical and social institutions managing this epidemic. Research on other social movements, including the women's, gay, lesbian and bisexual, and environmental movements, has highlighted the centrality of identity and cultural issues to movements while also documenting their efforts to institutionalize their goals.

Social movement researchers should continue to develop linkages between the structural determinants of collective action and explanations which focus on individual participation and identity formation. On the latter topic, recent research has made strides in developing a more nuanced account of the mobilization and recruitment of participants. These approaches move beyond a simplistic account of rational actors who weigh the costs and rewards of participation in collective action. By examining *micromobilization contexts*, current analyses provide a more complex portrait of individuals as socially embedded actors engaging in the collective processes of constructing meanings and identities, and interpreting grievances, opportunities and events. The concept of *collective identity*, for example, is useful in helping us to understand how movements recruit and maintain commitment among participants over time. As Taylor and Whittier (1992) have noted, politicized collective identities derive from a group's common interests and solidarity between members. Their research on lesbian feminist communities shows how movements may create and reinforce identities by constructing cultural boundaries between themselves and the larger society, developing an oppositional consciousness that challenges dominant understandings of the group, and politicizing everyday life so as to valorize their differences from the male heterosexual 'norm'.

Frame analysis is another tool for conceptualizing how movements organize the experiences of participants and guide their actions. Developed by Snow and his associates (Snow *et al.*, 1986; Snow and Benford, 1988, 1992), framing provides an approach for understanding how meanings and grievances are communicated and comprehended in a social context. Movements are conceptualized as 'signifying agents', that along with the media, governments and others engage in the struggle over how issues will be framed and understood by different groups. In order to attract participants and maintain commitment, movements define grievances and identities in ways that resonate with, and modify, elements of the dominant culture. Framing also helps movements to define particular conditions as unjust, to identify causes and to develop solutions.

Tarrow's (1998) work provides a very useful synthesis of many of these topics while also connecting them to the historical and structural dimensions of social movements. He advances a theory of collective action which is broad enough to encompass social movements, cycles of contention, and revolutions. In this framework he links the rise and decline of movements to a number of factors. On the one hand, movements must be able to sustain solidarity and the collective identities of their members. On the other hand, movement leaders and organizations must confront a range of political opportunities and constraints which shape their fortunes as well as those of other movements in larger cycles of contention. This type of research has tremendous potential to connect recent interest in identity politics with large-scale historical questions.

As they continue to develop new strategies and action forms, and to challenge and sometimes infuriate authorities and bystanders, social movements will continue to provoke researchers into developing new ways of conceptualizing and explaining their activities. Phenomena such as transnational mobilizations and the use of new technologies such as the Internet and globalized media preoccupy many activists and observers alike. Whether we are sympathetic to their goals or find them reprehensible, movements represent a dynamic and pervasive force which continues to generate some of the most exciting theory and research in the contemporary social sciences.

SUMMARY

- Social movements are collective efforts to promote or resist political and/or cultural change.
- Classical social movement theorists tended to regard collective behaviour as an emotional and often irrational response to some form of structural or cultural change.
- Resource mobilization theorists view social movement participation as an extension of institutionalized political behaviour. Movements are analysed in terms of factors such as organizational structure and effectiveness and the constraints and opportunities of the broader environment.
- New social movement theorists see contemporary movements as a response to the perceived inadequacies of the political and economic structures of post-industrial societies. New movements are distinguishable from 'old' movements in terms of their decentralized organizational structures, their use of unconventional tactics and the focus on cultural and identity issues.
- Current social movement theorizing represents an ongoing synthesis of earlier approaches, and focuses attention on movements as vehicles of personal, cultural and political change.

FURTHER READING

Dalton, Russell J. and Kuechler, Manfred (eds) (1990) *Challenging the Political Order: New Social and Political Movements in Western Democracies*. New York: Oxford University Press. An interdisciplinary anthology which explores political action across a range of Western democracies. An important focus of this volume is the relations between social movements and the State and their impact on partisan politics.

McAdam, Doug and Snow, David A. (eds) (1997) *Social Movements: Readings on Their Emergence, Mobilization, and Dynamics*. Los Angeles, CA: Roxbury Press. This reader compiles some of the most significant research on social movements over the last few decades, and serves as an excellent introduction to the field. It covers a broad range of social movements in several national contexts.

Morris, Aldon and Mueller, Carol McClurg (eds) (1992) *Frontiers in Social Movement Theory*. New Haven, CT: Yale University Press. Topics covered in this collection include the social psychology of movements, political cultures, frame analysis, cycles of protest, and the relationship between movements and the State. The significance of factors such as race, gender, sexuality and class to the formation of collective identities and political consciousness is also explored.

Tarrow, Sidney (1998) *Power In Movement: Social Movements and Contentious Politics*, 2nd edn. Cambridge: Cambridge University Press. This book provides an important synthesis of many current strands in social movement theorizing. Tarrow explores the relationships between different forms of mobilization, identity formation, organization and opportunity structures, and their impact on the rise of social movements and cycles of contention.

REFERENCES

Bell, Daniel (ed.) (1964) *The Radical Right*. Garden City, NY: Anchor Books.

Blumer, Herbert (1946) 'Collective Behavior', in Alfred McClug Lee (ed.) *New Outline of the Principles of Sociology*. New York: Barnes and Noble, pp. 170–222.

Calhoun, Craig (1993) ' "New Social Movements" of the Early Nineteenth Century', *Social Science History*, **17**(3): 385–427.

D'Anieri, Paul, Ernst, Claire and Kier, Elizabeth (1990) 'New Social Movements in Historical Perspective', *Comparative Politics*, **22:** 445–58.

Fireman, Bruce and William Gamson (1979) 'Utilitarian Logic in the Resource Mobilization Perspective', in Mayer N. Zald and John D. McCarthy (eds) *The Dynamics of Social Movements*. Cambridge, MA: Winthrop, pp. 8–44

Freeman, Jo (1975) *The Politics of Women's Liberation*. New York: David McKay.

Gamson, William (1975) *The Strategy of Social Protest*. Homewood, IL: Dorsey.

Garner, Roberta and Tenuto, John (1997) *Social Movement Theory and Research: An Annotated Bibliographical Guide*. Lanham, MD: Scarecrow Press.

Gurr, Ted (1970) *Why Men Rebel*. Princeton, NJ: Princeton University Press.

Gusfield, Joseph (1963) *Symbolic Crusade*. Urbana: University of Illinois Press.

Habermas, Jürgen (1981) 'New Social Movements', *Telos*, **49**: 33–7.

Halcli, Abigail (1999) 'AIDS, Anger and Activism: ACT UP as a Social Movement Organization', in Jo Freeman and Victoria Johnson (eds) *Waves of Protest: Social Movement Since the Sixties*. New York: Rowman and Littlefield.

Huntington, Samuel (1968) *Political Order in Changing Societies*. New Haven, CT: Yale University Press.

Inglehart, Ronald (1990) *Culture Shift in Advanced Industrial Societies*. Princeton, NJ: Princeton University Press.

Inglehart, Ronald and Jacques-Rene Rabier (1986) 'Political Realignment in Advanced Industrial Society: From Class-Based Politics to Quality-of-Life Politics', *Government and Opposition*, **21**: 456–79.

Jenkins, J. Craig (1984) *The Politics of Insurgency*. New York: Columbia University Press.

Jenkins, J. Craig and Charles Perrow (1977) 'Insurgency of the Powerless: Farm Workers and Movements (1946–1972)', *American Sociological Review*, **42**: 249–68.

Kitshcelt, Herbert (1986) 'Political Opportunity Structures and Political Protest: Anti-Nuclear Movements in Four Democracies', *British Journal of Political Science* **16**: 57–85.

Klandermans, Bert (1984) 'Mobilization and Participation: Social Psychological Expansions of Resource Mobilization Theory', *American Sociological Review*, **49**: 770–83.

Kornhauser, William (1959) *The Politics of Mass Society*. New York: Free Press.

Lang, Kurt and Lang, Gladys (1961) *Collective Dynamics*. New York: Crowell.

McAdam, Doug (1982) *Political Process and the Development of Black Insurgency, 1930–1970*. Chicago: University of Chicago Press.

McCarthy, John D. and Zald, Mayer N. (1973) *The Trend of Social Movements in America: Professionalization and Resource Mobilization*. Morristown, NJ: General Learning Press.

McCarthy, John D. and Zald, Mayer N. (1977) 'Resource Mobilization and Social Movements: A Partial Theory', *American Journal of Sociology*, **82**: 1212–41.

Melucci, Alberto (1989) *Nomads of the Present: Social Movements and Individual Needs in Contemporary Society*. Philadelphia: Temple University Press.

Morris, Aldon (1984) *The Origins of the Civil Rights Movement: Black Communities Organizing for Change*. New York: Free Press.

Offe, Claus (1985) 'New Social Movements: Challenging the Boundaries of Institutional Politics', *Social Research*, **52**: 817–68.

Park, Robert and Burgess, Ernest (1921) *Introduction to the Science of Society*. Chicago: University of Chicago Press.

Piven, Frances Fox and Cloward, Richard A. (1977) *Poor People's Movements: Why They Succeed, How They Fail*. New York: Vintage Books.

Plotke, David (1990) 'What's So New About New Social Movements?', *Socialist Review*, **20**: 81–102.

Smelser, Neil (1962) *Theory of Collective Behavior*. New York: Free Press.

Snow, David A., Rochford, E. Burke Jr., Worden, Steven K. and Benford, Robert D. (1986) 'Frame Alignment, Micromobilization, and Movement Participation', *American Sociological Review*, **51**: 464–81.

Snow, David A. and Benford, Robert D. (1988) 'Ideology, Frame Resonance, and Participant Mobilization', *International Social Movement Research*, **1**: 197–217.

Snow, David A. and Benford, Robert D. (1992) 'Master Frames and Cycles of Protest', in Aldon D. Morris and Carol McClurg Mueller (eds) *Frontiers in Social Movement Theory*. New Haven, CT: Yale University Press, pp. 133–55.

Tarrow, Sidney (1998) *Power In Movement: Social Movements and Contentious Politics*, 2nd edn. Cambridge: Cambridge University Press.

Taylor, Verta and Whittier, Nancy (1992) 'Collective Identity in Social Movement Communities: Lesbian Feminist Mobilization', in Aldon D. Morris and Carol McClurg Mueller (eds) *Frontiers in Social Movement Theory*. New Haven, CT: Yale University Press, pp. 104–29.

Tilly, Charles (1978) *From Mobilization to Revolution*. Reading, MA: Addison-Wesley.

Turner, Ralph and Killian, Lewis (1957) *Collective Behavior*. Englewood Cliffs, NJ: Prentice-Hall.

Chapter 33

Social inequalities: coming to terms with complexity

Harriet Bradley

There is a strange paradox about the current practice of social science. On the one hand, statistical evidence collected by social scientists and government agencies shows that inequalities between social groups have been increasing during the past decades; inequalities, for example, between rich and poor families in Britain and America or between the more developed countries and those of the 'Third World'. At the same time interest in material inequalities as a topic for social scientific analysis has been steadily diminishing, especially those forms of inequality such as those mentioned above which were formerly explained in terms of relationships of class and capitalism.

This is particularly marked within sociology, a discipline formerly notorious for its preoccupation with class divisions. In the decades following the Second World War, class was probably the central conceptual device within British sociology; concern with class was also heightened by the radical challenge of Marxism to mainstream sociology during the 1960s and 1970s. What has subsequently happened to class can be illustrated by looking at the 1997 catalogue of the publishing company Routledge, a leading publisher of social science texts. Seven pages are devoted to the sociology of culture, seven to gender and four to 'race' and ethnicity. Class does not merit its own category and there are only two pages given to the sociology of work and industry. Indeed, there are only two books specifically on class, and the word also appears as a part of the title of two books on 'race'. Particularly indicative is the title of a book in a rather new area of sociology: 'Death, Gender and Ethnicity'. Class, it seems, is not particularly significant in the experience of dying and bereavement.

476

This development reflects what has been called the 'cultural turn' in social science, with cultural studies replacing sociology at the leading edge of critical analysis. More broadly this is shown within the political sphere where class-based movements and institutions, such as Old Labour and the trade unions, have seen their fortunes wane in comparison with those of the 'new social movements' such as the nationalist groupings which have risen across Europe, the gay and lesbian movement or the campaigns against sexism and racism. The last decades have witnessed a switch from the politics of class and inequality to a politics of identity and 'difference', or, in the influential phraseology of Charles Taylor (1992) and Nancy Fraser (1995), from a concern for 'redistribution' (of material wealth) to a demand for 'recognition' (of cultural expression). Fraser (1995: 68) summarizes the current political trend succinctly: 'In these "post-socialist" conflicts, group identity supplants class interests as the chief medium of political mobilization. Cultural domination supplants exploitation as the fundamental injustice. And cultural recognition displaces socioeconomic redistribution as the remedy for injustice and the goal of political struggle.'

In this chapter I review briefly the causes and consequences of such a shift in focus. What factors have contributed to the decline of interest in class? What forms of social division are currently dominant? How can we analyse inequalities after the cultural turn? Is a politics of cultural recognition the solution?

TOWARDS A NEW PARADIGM

Without doubt the fall of the Berlin Wall in 1989 and the collapse of the communist bloc made a major impact upon social theorizing in the capitalist world. Marx's critique of capitalism as an inherently unstable socioeconomic system and his analysis of the developments which should lead to socialism now appeared fatally flawed. As a result neo-Marxism lost its hold as the chief radical mode within British sociology; former influential Marxists, such as Stuart Hall and Michèle Barrett, turned to the works of Foucault to develop an alternative critical account of power and domination.

This was not the only reason, however, for the decentring of class within sociology. During the 1980s a critique of the dominance of class in stratification theory had been building up, led by those concerned with exploration of gender, racial and ethnic divisions. Within Marxist theory these other forms of social difference had characteristically been seen either as secondary to class or as explicable within the terms of class analysis. Consequently Marxists argued that with the coming of socialism other aspects of inequality such as gender would automatically 'wither away'; but feminists pointed out that patriarchy as a system of male domination over women both preceded capitalism and persisted after its eclipse in the post-capitalist

477

Soviet states (Bradley, 1996). Thus theorists of gender, 'race' and ethnicity were asserting that these other dimensions of inequality could not be reduced to class: they existed as autonomous forms of social relationship and must be analysed separately in their own terms even though they were habitually found in interaction with each other (see, for example, Anthias and Yuval-Davis, 1993; Gilroy, 1987; Walby, 1990).

The recognition that social inequalities and divisions could not be subsumed under one monolithic theory, that of class, led to a growing appreciation of the complexities of social differentiation in multicultural, post-colonial societies, where many sources of difference – class, gender, ethnicity, 'race', age, region, dis/ability, sexual orientation – intertwined to produce multifaceted and intricate forms of social hierarchy. This appreciation fed into another crucial development in social theory, the rise of the post-modern perspective which has been discussed more fully in other chapters in this book. One important aspect of post-modern theory and politics was its endorsement of social complexity and radical pluralism. Post-modernists saw society in terms of a multitude of social groupings which formed round different potential sources of identity and had their own distinctive cultures, lifestyles and consumption patterns. Some such groups might be transient and relatively short-lived (the fans of particular television shows or popular musicians, Star Trekkies and Spice Girl wannabes, for example); others, such as those developing on the basis of struggles over gender or ethnicity, would be more long-lasting (Crook, Pakulski and Waters, 1992; Lyon, 1994). Such post-modern accounts also suggested that 'new social movements' (some long established, such as environmental groups or the peace movement, some based on specific single issues, such as the demonstrations against the rearing of calves for veal, the anti-Poll Tax movement or the campaign to legalize cannabis) were the characteristic political formations of post-modern societies; that class was fading as a base for collective organization and identification; and that consumption issues were generally of more significance in people's lives and political activities than the old issues of production so central to Marxist theory.

All these developments, then, suggested that social relations of differentiation were more complex than past theorization had suggested and that it was quite unlikely that any type of single or 'unified' theory could be developed to explain them all. Such a theory would anyway be suspect in the eyes of hardline post-modernists who would regard it as a kind of 'grand narrative', a fictive account imposed on a social reality too complex and irregular to be analysed in terms of causality. This suggests that social analysis must take a more modest form, looking at social relationships in particular times, places and contexts and not trying to generalize too much from such particularities. Post-modernists endorse a switch away from concerns with origins, causes and stable structures to looking at social processes and shifting linguistic practices, or discourses, as a way of understanding social interaction. This entails a different way of thinking about how societies work, as summarized in this account by Ali Rattansi of 'a postmodern frame': 'Social formations are no longer regarded as tightly knit complexes of institutions with necessary, predetermined forms of connection or logics of development – there are no final determining instances or levels such as the economy, and no laws of motion as posited in most versions of Marxism' (Rattansi, 1992: 251).

FRAGMENTATION AND DIVERSITY

One of the most important facets, then, of this 'paradigm shift' is the appreciation of the complexity of social differentiation. This complexity is commonly conceptualized in terms of 'fragmentation', 'diversity' and 'difference'. While earlier theories tried to develop general categories such as 'class' and 'gender' to explain social relations, the new trend is to 'deconstruct' such categories and to explore the differences which they tend to cover up. For example, there has been a major change in the exploration of ethnicity. Where earlier analysis of race relations commonly spoke in terms of 'black' and 'white' people in Britain, recent work highlights the complexities of ethnic belonging; Africans, African-Caribbeans, Chinese and the various South Asian groups (Pakistanis, Bangladeshis, Indians, African Indians) occupy very different places in the occupational hierarchy and have distinct communities and cultures. Recent studies have emphasized the complexity of patterns of ethnic and racial inequalities in Britain, Europe and America (e.g. Anthias and Yuval-Davis, 1993; Fenton, 1999; Modood *et al.*, 1997). Similarly, feminist works of the 1970s were criticized by black feminists for assuming that all women shared common experiences and for generalizing from the position of white middle-class women. Post-structuralists like Donna Haraway (1990) and Denise Riley (1988) suggested that the use of the category 'women' served to perpetuate simplistic binary views of gender and to cover up the complexities of changing gendered experience.

It should be noted that fragmentation is not a new concept in the analysis of inequality. There has long been a recognition that classes are internally divided and this goes right back to the classic theories of Marx and Weber. A very influential example was Goldthorpe and Lockwood's typology of three different segments within the working classes in Britain (Goldthorpe *et al.*, 1969; Lockwood, 1975). They distinguished deferential workers, such as farm labourers and shop assistants who had close relations with their employers and accepted inequalities as legitimate; traditional workers, such as miners and shipbuilders who had a strong 'them and us' mentality and were prone to industrial conflict; and privatized or affluent workers who cared particularly about money and consumption, aspiring to share the lifestyles and incomes of the middle classes. However, there is now a more intense interest in exploring the nature of fragmentation which is seen to take many forms.

Elsewhere (Bradley, 1996) I have discussed four sources of fragmentation:

1 Internal fragmentation, such as the divisions within classes sketched out above.
2 External fragmentation which arises from the interaction of different dynamics of difference, so that the experience of gender varies for women and men according to age, ethnicity and class.
3 Fragmentation that arises from processes of social change, as for example that caused by the feminization of contemporary employment relations; polarization is occurring between young women who can take advantage of opening opportunities for careers and older women, especially those of working-class origin, who remain trapped in low-paid, dead-end jobs.
4 Fragmentation arising from increased individualism as people become more detached from the old collectivities and communities, with more people experiencing upward mobility, moving away from the places in which they were born and developing work trajectories and lifestyles very different from those of their parents.

The combined effects of all these processes contribute to the sense of 'fractured identities' in contemporary social life. There are currently three aspects of fragmentation which seem particularly significant in understanding contemporary relations of inequality.

Interacting dynamics

A crucial feature *both* of our new understanding of inequality *and* of people's current experience of inequality is the way that different axes of inequality and differentiation interact together. Thus as individuals we are placed at particular points of intersection between the social dynamics of class, gender, ethnicity, age, religion, region, sexuality and other factors of social differentiation, what we might describe as *multiple positioning*. No wonder we are currently so concerned with exploring and understanding processes of social identification, since our multiple positioning opens up to us a wealth of possible identities – at the same time as debarring us from others (see Bradley, 1996, conclusion). Walby (1992) in a critique of postmodernism has argued that a deficit of previous theories of inequality is that they typically failed to deal with more than one or two of these interacting dynamics. I take this further by suggesting that it is impossible to develop a general abstract theory of inequality which can deal with multiple positioning.

Thus one key task for contemporary study of inequality is to look at particular contexts or aspects of social life (schools, workplaces, health, leisure) and explore the specific forms which inequality and difference take within them as a result of multiple positioning. For example, in my own research I studied the way gender, class and age came together to produce a particular pattern of disadvantage for women working in a pharmaceuticals factory in the North East of England (Bradley, 1999). Their working-class position meant that they all left school without qualifications and faced limited opportunities in a restricted local labour market; moreover, many of their husbands and sons were victims of the widespread male unemployment which has devastated lives in northern cities, so that many women were forced to become major breadwinners for their families. Within the factory, their gender position confined them to the less skilled jobs, which they found monotonous and tiring, and debarred them from promotion chances; outside the factory, they continued to bear the major responsibility for housework and childcare which further restricted their labour market opportunities. Finally the older women felt constrained in various ways by their age. Because of their domestic responsibilities, they felt unable to take up chances offered by the expanding higher education system, such as taking access courses leading to degrees in the local northern universities (going to a university in another part of the country was of course quite out of the question!). Also some of the women found themselves victims of age discrimination if they tried to seek more interesting jobs in the white-collar sector; while others were in the ironic position of having to train young graduate men to act as their own line managers.

These women, then, experienced social inequality in a very specific way. Such an example alerts us to the need to dig beneath generalizations to understand how inequalities work today. As Malcolm Waters, one of the post-modern critics of class analysis, argues: 'The most instructive recent sociological studies are those that emphasise the intersection of multiple status cleavages within a single local context' (Waters, 1997: 37). At the same time such studies can be the basis for careful formulations of sociological generalizations. The experience of the factory women, for example, provides support for Walby's (1997) recent claim that an age polarization is developing among women: older women lack the educational backgrounds to compete in the evolving labour market and grew up in a different 'gender regime' in which they were steered more firmly towards domesticity. But we should emphasize more clearly than Walby does that this is also a polarization of class.

Shifting identifications

More unsettling to the understanding of inequality, however, is the claim that fragmentation occurs not just through the interaction of different forms of differentiation but as a result of instabilities within social categories. This relates to the position of post-structuralists and deconstructionists who see forms of difference such as gender or ethnicity as social constructs. Thus, for example, Judith Butler (1990, 1993), in her highly influential feminist work, argues that gender must not be seen as a fixed and stable attribute that we are born with, but as something that is perpetually created and recreated through performance; we persistently act out gender in our daily lives and interactions. The illusion of stability is gained because we tend to repeat the same performance over and over again as a result of habituation; but we ourselves can challenge conventional norms and attributes of gender by transgressive forms of performance such as drag or cross-dressing. Lesbians and bisexuals are particularly well-placed for this process of subverting the binary categories of female/male and woman/man.

While this approach does not deny disparities of power or the existence of inequalities, it does throw into doubt established ways of conceptualizing the relation between inequality and consciousness, such as Marx's contention that social being (by which he meant material factors such as class) determines social consciousness. The post-structuralist approach allows no necessary connection between social positioning and identification. Identities are seen as fluid, contingent and chosen. Riley, for example, in her classic text *Am I That Name?* (1988) discusses the fragility of the identity of 'woman' both as a base for collective social organization (such as feminism) and as a source of personal identity. We do not go about persistently thinking of ourselves as women and men; most of the time we see ourselves as people, as individuals. It is only in specific circumstances which may be adverse (sexual harassment or pestering for women, the demand to be tough for men) or celebratory (stag and hen nights, single-sex friendship groups, sexual encounters) that we acknowledge our genderedness and think of ourselves in gendered terms. Similarly, it has been noted that ethnic identification is not necessarily constant throughout an individual's lifetime, but may come to the fore, for example, at moments of crisis or as a result of the experience of racism and stigmatization (Allen, 1994; Modood, 1992).

Hybridity

These considerations have contributed to our current preoccupation with 'identities' and attempts to explore more adequately the processes of identity formation. Another conceptual development which has been particularly useful here has been the concept of 'hyphenated' or 'hybrid' identities. Thus theorists of ethnicity and post-colonialism (Bhabha, 1990; Modood, 1992) point out that to be Chinese-American or British-Pakistani is something different from being on the one hand American or British and on the other Chinese or Pakistani. Such identities draw on elements of different experiences and cultures to construct something that is quite new and distinct. And this in its turn feeds back into the cultures and lifestyles of both countries of origin and countries of settlement: America is different for having within it significant Chinese communities and Britain for having many

Pakistani citizens. Haraway (1990) makes a similar point about gender when she uses the metaphor of the cyborg: the cyborg, a creature half-human, half-mechanical disrupts the nature/culture binary and presents us with a utopian image of the possible transcendence of gendered boundaries. Bhabha and Haraway imply that such impure, mongrel identities are typical for those of us living in complex post-colonial societies; and both suggest that the experience of hybridity is important as providing a space for dispassionate critique of the established power relations in which we live.

The concept of social hybridity may be fruitfully applied in the study of class. It throws a challenge to the dominant orthodoxies of class analysis which seek to place individuals in the class structure through the use of occupational categories. Mainstream class theory has become increasingly internalist, bogged down in debates about which occupations fit in which classes and where the class boundaries should be drawn (see Crompton, 1993). Such debates have decreasing relevance as few of us now experience totally 'pure' class identities. Changes in the nature of the economy, the rise of mass unemployment and the spread of mass education systems have brought high degrees of upward – and downward – social mobility to many modern societies. People often experience movement between different class locations. Many people will end up in a different class position from that of their parents and grandparents; and a reasonable proportion of people grow up in families in which their mother and father come from differing class backgrounds. All these situations can be seen as forms of class hybridity – and they are quite widespread. In my study of North East organizations 27 per cent of the employees I interviewed came from hybrid class backgrounds (for example, mother a teacher and father a miner, father a manager and mother a shop assistant); while 32 per cent could be described as upwardly mobile in terms of their family background. This augments the complexity of current experiences of class and helps explain the weakening of class identities in contrast to the early twentieth century when classes were more stable.

BEYOND THE CULTURAL TURN

Notions such as these begin the task of grappling with the complexities of contemporary relations of inequality and their effects on individual lives and consciousnesses. But how can we combine our new awareness of cultural diversity and fractured identities with an understanding of inequalities and their obstinate persistence? For statistical evidence within and across societies still point to astonishing regularities in disparities of wealth, power and opportunities. The gap between the richest and poorest households in Britain and America steadily increased throughout the 1980s and early 1990s. Five million people in Britain live in workless homes, while merchant bankers, corporate executives and barristers earn annual incomes of £500,000 and upwards. In 1994 one-quarter of children under three in America were said by the Carnegie Trust to be living in poverty. Even more stark is the gap between rich and poor nations: the $8 billion that Americans spend each year on pornography could liberate twenty of the poorest nations from their burden of debt (Sharkey, 1997); meanwhile a billion people survive on less than a dollar a day.

Such examples suggest that if anything the world is becoming more rather than less unequal. While many young researchers have recently been drawn to the study of what may appear more interesting and dynamic aspects of social life (the body, sexuality, popular culture, media representations, New Age protests), we must not lose touch with the sociological inheritance of concern with the study of injustice and inequality. Poverty, hardship and deprivation are still the lot of millions of people. In our enthusiasm for exploring the intricacies of gender and ethnic identification, we must not allow ourselves to forget the hard realities of class inequalities.

It is crucial, therefore, to realize that all social relationships have both material *and* cultural aspects. Cultural phenomena do not evolve in a vacuum but in very specific economic and political contexts. They reflect and are structured by prevailing relationships of wealth and power. Similarly economic phenomena are embedded in cultural contexts and have meaningful aspects. Thus any social event or situation can be 'read' in a material or a cultural way; and a thorough understanding of any social phenomena will involve analysis of both economic and cultural aspects.

We may take as an example the gender division of labour in employment. This may be analysed as a remarkably persistent structure of material inequalities between men and women: women and men are typically found segregated in 'women's jobs' and 'men's jobs'; men hold top posts and women are concentrated in the lower ranks; men are commonly found in positions of authority over women; men earn more than women. Such inequalities have been shown to be stable over time and space. Yet the *particular* form of the sexual division of labour in any given period and country is strongly shaped by prevailing cultural values concerning femininity and masculinity; and it is upheld by gendered work cultures, by images and representations of male and female workers and by the sexualization of work relations (sexual harassment, heterosexual flirting and bonding). For example, recent studies of women workers by Halford, Savage and Witz (1997) and McDowell (1997) explore both continuing inequalities between men and women in pay and promotion chances and the embodiment of gender in organizational arrangements. McDowell shows how the female body is out of place in the world of corporate finance, so that women have to tread a fine line between what is seen as an appropriate display of their femininity (smart but not too sexy suits, high heels and skirts) and fitting into a male world in which their sexuality marks them as deviant. At the same time, such studies show how the experience of gender at work for particular groups of women (women in the finance sector, clerical workers, nurses) is influenced by their age and class so that the specific pattern of inequality to which they are subjected is different, for example, from that of the factory women discussed earlier in the chapter.

RECOGNITION AND REDISTRIBUTION

We can begin to see, then, how the study of inequality might fruitfully proceed. We need to consider both material and cultural aspects of social difference; we need to look at the way diverse forms of inequality intersect in different settings; we need to explore the complexities of consciousness and identification in a world of increasing social hybridity. We must continue to develop our understanding of gender, ethnicity, age, disability and all other forms of social distinction, but we must also try to get to grips with the changing dynamics of class.

Where, then, does this leave us in terms of contemporary political outcomes? We may return here to the issue of recognition and redistribution. Fraser (1995) suggests that gender and ethnicity involve demands for both recognition and redistribution, which she suggests may be in tension with each other. Claims for cultural justice (recognition) are based on the celebration of difference and the granting of particularistic privileges; while claims for economic justice rest on the removal of difference and the notion of universal rights. Class, by contrast, she sees as a more purely economic form of difference, which promotes claims only for redistribution. But the common perception is that currently political activity hinges more on recognition than redistribution, which is why class has fallen from view.

By contrast I would argue that class injustice, too, has both economic and cultural aspects. For example, the North Eastern factory workers experienced both gender injustice and class injustice and made claims for both recognition *and* redistribution. The women in the factory wanted better pay and equal access to opportunities with men; but they also called for their distinctive contributions and skills to be revalued, and to be freed from sexual stereotyping and harassment. Both men and women, as wage labourers, wished for better wages and conditions and resented having workloads increased without extra pay; but also they wanted their dignity as working people to be upheld and demanded to be treated with respect. This relates to a long-standing denigration of working-class people as 'thick', uneducated and uncultivated (see Skeggs, 1996).

Thus cultural and economic injustices might both be the basis for contemporary collective organization. While in the current context we can clearly see the tensions between the demands generated by different forms of inequality and the claims of competing interest groups, we need not resign ourselves to particularistic political fragmentation. The struggles for cultural recognition by the various marginalized groups in our societies may be the first steps to a more culturally democratic social climate, in which claims for redistribution and economic equality are harder to resist, since difference is so often used as the justification for inequality.

SUMMARY

- The analysis of inequality after the post-modern and cultural turn must involve coming to terms with complexity.
- We need to explore how class, gender, ethnicity, age and other factors interact in particular contexts.
- However, such a preoccupation with difference must not lead to neglect of material inequalities of wealth and power and the constraints they impose.
- We need to grasp that all social phenomena have both material and cultural aspects.
- Class is still important in the way it shapes people's lives but we need to rethink our approach to class, for example in terms of *class hybridity*.
- Individual identities reflect the complexity of *multiple positioning*, but the fight against inequality must include both demands for cultural recognition and for economic redistribution.

FURTHER READING

Bradley, Harriet (1996) *Fractured Identities*. Cambridge: Polity Press. An introduction to theories of social divisions of class, gender, ethnicity and age which also discusses the interaction between them.

Anthias, Floya and Yuval-Davis, Nira (1993) *Racialized Boundaries*. London: Routledge. A very useful contribution to the reconceptualization of ethnicity and 'race' which also considers them in relation to gender and class

Phizacklea, Annie (1990) *Unpacking the Fashion Industry*. London: Routledge. An exemplary case study showing the coming together of disadvantages of 'race', class and gender in a particular context, the Midlands textile industry.

Fenton, Steve (1999) *Ethnicity*. London: Macmillan. An introduction to ethnicity which pulls together material and cultural aspects of racial and ethnic difference and inequality.

Owen, David (ed.) (1997) *Sociology After Postmodernism*. London: Sage. A slightly more difficult book, which explores the consequences of the post-modern turn for sociological analysis and includes discussion of class, gender and ethnicity.

Skeggs, Beverley (1996) *Formations of Class and Gender*. London: Sage. An important attempt to rethink the notion of class using Bourdieu's notions of different forms of capital to explore its cultural and symbolic dimensions.

REFERENCES

Allen, S. (1994) 'Race, Ethnicity and Nationality: Some Questions of Identity', in H. Afshar and M. Maynard (eds) *The Dynamics of 'Race' and Gender*. London: Taylor and Francis.

Anthias, F. and Yuval-Davis, N. (1993) *Racialized Boundaries*. London: Routledge.

Bhabha, H. (1990) 'The Third Space', in J. Rutherford (ed.) *Identity*. London: Lawrence and Wishart.

Bradley, H. (1996) *Fractured Identities*, Cambridge: Polity Press.

Bradley, H. (1999) *Gender and Power in the Workplace*. London: Macmillan.

Butler, J. (1990) *Gender Trouble*. London: Routledge.

Butler, J. (1993) *Bodies that Matter*. London: Routledge.

Crompton, R. (1993) *Class and Stratification*. Cambridge: Polity Press.

Crook, S., Pakulski, J. and Waters, M. (1992) *Postmodernization*. London: Sage.

Fenton, S. (1999) *Ethnicity*. London: Macmillan.

Fraser, N. (1995) 'From Redistribution to Recognition? Dilemmas of Justice in a "Post-socialist Age"', *New Left Review*, **212**: 68–93.

Gilroy, P. (1987) *There Ain't no Black in the Union Jack*. London: Routledge.

Goldthorpe, J., Lockwood, D., Bechhofer, F. and Platt, J. (1969) *The Affluent Worker in the Class Structure*. Cambridge: Cambridge University Press.

Halford, S., Savage, M. and Witz, A. (1997) *Gender, Careers and Organization*. London: Macmillan.

Haraway, D. (1990) 'A Manifesto for Cyborgs: Science, Technology and Socialist Feminism in the 1980s', in L. Nicholson (ed.) *Feminism/Postmodernism*. London: Routledge.

Lockwood, D. (1975) 'Sources of Variation in Working-class Images of Society', in M. Bulmer (ed.) *Working Class Images of Society*. London: Routledge.

Lyon, D. (1994) *Postmodernity*. Milton Keynes: Open University Press.

McDowell, L. (1997) *Capital Culture*. Oxford: Blackwell.

Modood, T. (1992) *Not Easy Being British*. Stoke-on-Trent: Trentham Books.

Modood, T., Berthoud, R., Lakey, J., Nazroo, J., Smith, P., Virdee, S. and Beishon, S. (1997) *Ethnic Minorities in Britain*. London: PSI.

Rattansi, A. (1992) 'Just Framing: Ethnicities and Racisms in a Postmodern Framework', in L. Nicholson and S. Seidman (eds) *Social Postmodernism*. Cambridge: Cambridge University Press.

Riley, D. (1988) *Am I That Name?* London: Macmillan.

Sharkey, A. (1997) 'Land of the Free', *Guardian*, 22 November.

Skeggs, B. (1996) *Formations of Class and Gender*. London: Sage.

Taylor, C. (1992) *Multiculturalism and 'the Politics of Recognition'*. Princeton, NJ: Princeton University Press.

Walby, S. (1990) *Theorizing Patriarchy*. Oxford: Blackwell.

Walby, S. (1992) 'Post-postmodernism? Theorizing Social Complexity', in M. Barrett and A. Phillips (eds) *Destabilizing Theory*. Cambridge: Polity Press.

Walby, S. (1997) *Gender Transformations*. London: Macmillan.

Waters, M. (1997) 'Class', in D. Owen (ed.) *Sociology After Postmodernism*. London: Sage.

Author and Subject Index

Main entries are given in bold.